Contemporary Authors

Autobiography Series

ISSN 0748-0636

Contemporary Authors

Autobiography Series

Joyce Nakamura
Editor

volume **16**

 Gale Research Inc. · DETROIT · LONDON

EDITORIAL STAFF

Joyce Nakamura, *Editor*

Shelly Andrews, Laura Standley Berger, and Motoko Fujishiro Huthwaite, *Associate Editors*
Michael J. Tyrkus, *Assistant Editor*
Marilyn O'Connell Allen, *Editorial Associate*

Victoria B. Cariappa, *Research Manager*
Mary Rose Bonk, *Research Supervisor, Biography Division*
Reginald A. Carlton, Clare Collins, Andrew Guy Malonis, and Norma Sawaya, *Editorial Associates*
Mike Avolio, Patricia Bowen, Rachel A. Dixon, Shirley Gates, Sharon McGilvray,
and Devra M. Sladics, *Editorial Assistants*

Peter M. Gareffa, *Senior Editor*

Mary Beth Trimper, *Production Director*
Shanna Philpott Heilveil, *Production Assistant*

Art Chartow, *Art Director*
C. J. Jonik, *Keyliner*
Willie Mathis, *Camera Operator*

Donald G. Dillaman, *Index Program Designer*
David Jay Trotter, *Index Programmer*

The paper used in this publication meets the minimum requirements of American National Standard for Information Sciences—Permanence Paper for Printed Library Materials, ANSI Z39.48–1984. ∞™

Library of Congress Catalog Card Number 86–641293
ISBN 0–8103–5349–0
ISSN 0748–0636

Printed in the United States of America

Published simultaneously in the United Kingdom
by Gale Research International Limited
(An affiliated company of Gale Research Inc.)

Contents

Preface

Each volume in the *Contemporary Authors Autobiography Series (CAAS)* presents an original collection of autobiographical essays written especially for the series by noted writers. *CAAS* has grown out of Gale's long-standing interest in author biography, bibliography, and criticism, as well as its successful publications in those areas, like the *Dictionary of Literary Biography, Contemporary Literary Criticism, Something about the Author,* and particularly the bio-bibliographical series *Contemporary Authors (CA),* to which this Autobiography Series is a companion.

As a result of their ongoing communication with authors in compiling *CA* and other books, Gale editors recognized that these writers frequently had more to say than the format of existing Gale publications could accommodate. Inviting authors to write about themselves at essay-length was an inevitable next step. Added to that was the fact that the collected autobiographies of current writers were virtually nonexistent. *CAAS* serves to fill this significant information gap.

Purpose

CA Autobiography Series is designed to be a meeting place for writers and readers--a place where writers can present themselves, on their own terms, to their audience; and a place where general readers, students of contemporary literature, teachers and librarians, even aspiring writers can become better acquainted with familiar authors and make the first acquaintance of others. Here is an opportunity for writers who may never write a full-length autobiography to let their readers know how they see themselves and their work, what carefully laid plans or turns of luck brought them to this time and place. Even for those authors who have already published full-length autobiographies there is the opportunity in *CAAS* to bring their readers "up to date" or perhaps to take a different approach in the essay format. Singly, the essays in this series can illuminate the reader's understanding of a writer's work; collectively, they are lessons in the creative process and in the discovery of its roots.

CAAS makes no attempt to give a comprehensive overview of authors and their works. That outlook is already well represented in biographies, reviews, and critiques published in a wide variety of sources. Instead, *CAAS* complements that perspective and presents what no other ongoing reference source does: the view of contemporary writers that is shaped by their own choice of materials and their own manner of storytelling.

Scope

Like its parent series, *Contemporary Authors,* the *CA Autobiography Series* sets out to meet the needs and interests of a wide range of readers. Each volume provides about twenty essays by writers in all genres whose work is being read today. We consider it extraordinary that twenty busy authors from throughout the world are able to interrupt their existing writing, teaching, speaking, traveling, and other schedules to converge on a given deadline for any one volume. So it is not always possible that all genres can be equally and uniformly represented from volume to volume, although we strive to include writers working in a variety of categories, including fiction, nonfiction, and poetry. As only a few writers specialize in a single area, the breadth of writings by authors in this volume also encompasses drama, translation, and criticism as well as work for movies, television, radio, newspapers, and journals.

Format

Authors who contribute to *CAAS* are invited to write a "mini-autobiography" of approximately 10,000 words. In order to give the writer's imagination free rein, we suggest no guidelines or pattern for the essay. We only ask that each writer tell his or her story in the manner and to the extent that feels most natural and appropriate. In addition, writers are asked to supply a selection of personal photographs showing themselves at various ages, as well as important people and special moments in their lives. Barring unfortunate circumstances like the loss or destruction of early photographs, our contributors have responded generously, sharing with us some of their most treasured mementoes. The result is a special blend of text and photographs that will intrigue even browsers.

A bibliography appears at the end of each essay, listing the author's book-length works in chronological order of publication. Each entry in the bibliography includes the publication information for the book's first printing in the United States, and if an earlier printing has occurred elsewhere, that information is provided as well. The bibliographies in this volume were compiled by members of the *CAAS* editorial staff from their research and the lists of writings that were provided by many of the authors. Each of the bibliographies was submitted to the author for review.

A cumulative index appears in each volume and cites all the essayists in the series as well as the subjects presented in the essays: personal names, titles of works, geographical names, schools of writing, etc. The index format is designed to make these cumulating references as helpful and easy to use as possible. For every reference that appears *in more than one essay*, the name of the essayist is given before the volume and page number(s). For example, W. H. Auden is mentioned by a number of essayists in the series. The entry in the index allows the user to identify the essay writers by name:

> Auden, W.H.
> Allen **6:**18, 24
> Ashby **6:**36, 39
> Bowles **1:**86
> Burroway **6:**90
> Fuller **10:**120, 123
> Hall **7:**58, 61
> Hazo **11:**148, 150
> Howes **3:**143
> Jennings **5:**110
> etc.

For references that appear *in only one essay*, the volume and page number(s) are given but the name of the essayist is omitted. For example:

> Stieglitz, Alfred **1:**104, 109, 110

CAAS is something more than the sum of its individual essays. At many points the essays touch common ground, and from these intersections emerge new patterns of information and impressions. The index, despite its pedestrian appearance, is an important guide to these interconnections.

Looking Ahead

Each essay in the series has a special character and point of view that sets it apart from its companions. A small sampler of anecdotes and musings from the essays in this volume hint at the unique perspective of these life stories.

George Bowering, on overcoming his aversion to umbrellas: "Umbrellas are not for men and boys to carry, I thought, so for my first two years in Vancouver I walked around city and campus in my old air force trench coat, my hair plastered to my skull. In semi-desert Oliver it rained about seven times a year, usually just in time to split the ripe cherries on the trees, for instance. If it started raining chances were that the sun was still out in part of the sky, and in half an hour you could go out on your bicycle or picking ladder again. When I came to the coast and it started to rain I would step into a downtown doorway to wait it out. I could have starved to death. I saw male students holding big black umbrellas over them, but big city ways are the slope to dissipation, I reasoned. In Oliver I had never seen a man carry an umbrella. I had never seen a man push a shopping cart, either. After a couple of years of plastered hair I acquired an umbrella and an ability to be patronizing toward small semi-desert towns. Here is the way you acquired an umbrella: you went to the university lost and found; you maintained that you had misplaced an umbrella; when asked to describe it you mentioned that it was black with a brown wooden handle. Yes, that's the one, you said."

Nicole Brossard, ruminating on the inevitability of autobiography in her writing: "Sooner or later, whatever past lives on in me will, probably in spite of myself, find its way into the coming books, novels, or poems, will astonish me, amaze me, will dawn on the horizon of thinking like a discovery. It will propel me toward further enigmas to unravel, to unfold, it will come forth like a story to invent, it will stretch itself out inside me like a dreamed memory, it will lead me toward other norths, a thousand souths, it will come back to the present to seduce me in the suggestive guise of the word fiction. Whatever of the past still lives in me will resemble Montréal and Montréal will change once more in midsentence. What lives on will come back to inscribe its yes, a proud yes amid energy and anguish, at the heart of that which never changes inside of us for, as we know, the body never forgets that other very ancient body which obliges us to sign our very brief story in history."

Austin C. Clarke, remembering a faux pas before his writer friends: "Once, on the way to Princeton with LeRoi, or as he was called by his close friends, Roi; in the company of Larry Neal the poet, and accompanied by my agent—my black agent—agent to H. Rap Brown and all of us, we decided to have breakfast in Grand Central Station before setting out to Princeton. I was fully acculturated by appetite to the South. Larry ordered juice and toast. My agent, thin as if perpetually on a diet, ordered nothing. Roi ordered orange juice. And I, tea, toast, bacon, fried eggs, hash browns, and grits. I had covered every vicissitude and nuance of ethnic dietary eccentricity. And as I cut the first morsel of egg and bacon, ready to lift it to a hungry mouth, Roi said, as if he was talking to someone sitting at the other table, 'Brother, do you eat the *piiiig?*' For five years the *piiiig* never crossed my lips. And it was not only because he had taken from his briefcase a pamphlet put out by the Muslims, showing in graphic words and compelling illustrations the depravity of slaughter evisceration and devouring of this animal so precious and essential and fundamental to the diets of millions of peoples of the Southern Hemisphere. I remember Malcolm X castigating Martin Luther King and lumping his civil rights philosophy to the things he and his ilk ate. 'Pork-chop-eating Baptist ministers.' Roi said, after I had left my breakfast untouched, as if it had been afflicted by a plague, 'You are *what* you eat.'"

Wilson Harris, warning of the consequences of environmental neglect: "We are now coming abreast of the pollution of environments in the late twentieth century. But apart from this the object lesson of the conservancy for me was the mirror it held up to the life of great rivers—such as the Demerara, the Essequebo, the Berbice in the Guyanas—which have their rushing headwaters in untamed and peculiar regions. A frame of settlement and reservoir on the Atlantic coast—however remote it appears from such headwaters, however fortressed to serve its own ends—may become a trigger of environmental crisis within a system of intricate forces and dimensions extending into the body of a continent. That continent may be despoiled. The dangers as our century draws to a close are manifest in Brazil and elsewhere. The consequences would be dire for humanity. Then the tyranny of immediate gratification or parochial blindness to the mysterious book of landscapes would have triumphed. It has not yet happened. There is still a chance."

Jeanne Wakatsuki Houston, on discovering the pleasures of reading while detained at Manzanar (internment camp for Japanese-Americans): "In the first months at Manzanar, there were no schools or libraries. And so, it seems, some charitable organizations, apprised of this, had sent truckloads of books to stock a library. Unfortunately, there were no available buildings to shelter them, so they were dumped in the middle of the spaces between barrack blocks—bleak, sandy acres left open in case of fire. The pile was a jagged mountain range as huge as a two-story building. I had never seen anything like it and scrambled up the peak with other kids, sliding over slick pages, jamming legs between crevices. We played mountain climbing and war, throwing books at each other and hiding in foxholes dug into the sides. It didn't occur to us to read the material which provided us with such a wondrous playground. But after a week or so of diligent mountaineering, a few thunderstorms and dust storms dampened our enthusiasm. The book heap, now worn down to a hill, was abandoned. One sunny afternoon, as I walked across the firebreak, a glint caught my eye. The book graveyard was still except for pages fluttering in the wind like earthbound kites. I soon discovered the source of light. Framed in shiny gold gilt, a scene of Rapunzel letting down her long hair from a tower's window shone from a book of fairy tales. I was entranced. Who was this beautiful lady with long yellow hair? I leafed through the book and found I could read the print. That afternoon I sat down amidst the torn and water-stained wreckage and read every story in Hans Christian Andersen's *Fairy Tales.*"

These brief examples only suggest what lies ahead in this volume. The essays will speak differently to different readers; but they are certain to speak best, and most eloquently, for themselves.

Authors Forthcoming in *CAAS*

Bella Akhmadulina
Russian poet, translator, and short-story writer

Mulk Raj Anand
Indian novelist, nonfiction writer, and critic

Philip Appleman
American poet, novelist, and nonfiction writer

Cyprian Ekwensi
Nigerian novelist and short-story writer

Loren D. Estleman
American author of mystery and Western novels

Philip José Farmer
American science-fiction writer

Charles Gordone
American playwright, actor, and director

Daniel Halpern
American poet and editor

Michael S. Harper
American poet

John Hollander
American poet

Josephine Jacobsen
American poet and short-story writer

John Jakes
American author of historical novels

Hugh Kenner
Canadian literary critic of major modern authors

Walter Laqueur
German-born historian, journalist, and novelist

William Manchester
American biographer and novelist

Seymour Mayne
Canadian poet

James Alan McPherson
American short-story writer and editor

Jessica Mitford
English essayist and journalist

Bharati Mukherjee
Canadian novelist and short-story writer

John Frederick Nims
American poet, translator, and editor

Harry Mark Petrakis
American novelist and screenwriter

Alastair Reid
Scottish poet, essayist, and translator

Sonia Sanchez
American poet

James Still
American poet, novelist, and short-story writer

Anne Waldman
American poet

Acknowledgments

We wish to acknowledge our special gratitude to each of the authors in this volume. They all have been most kind and cooperative in contributing not only their talents but their enthusiasm and encouragement to this project.

Grateful acknowledgment is also made to those publishers, photographers, and artists whose works appear with these authors' essays.

Photographs/Art

Russell Atkins: p. 8, Cole.

George Bowering: p. 21, Paul Little; p. 34, © 1990 Robert Blake; p. 36, Roy Miki.

Nicole Brossard: p. 50, Germaine Beaulieu; p. 51, Kèro.

Ed Bullins: p. 64, © 1988 Randall White.

Hal Clement: Photos by Jay Kay Klein. p. 89, © 1982; p. 96, © 1966; p. 99, © 1969; p. 100, © 1990.

Calvin Forbes: p. 115, Mary Ann Lynch.

Rolando Hinojosa-Smith: p. 140, H. J. Sieg/ p. 146, Cover of *Mi querido Rafa*, by Rolando Hinojosa. Copyright © 1981 by Arte Público Press. Arte Público Press, 1981. Reprinted with permission of Arte Público Press./ p. 147, Cover of *Dear Rafe*, written and translated by Rolando Hinojosa. Copyright © 1985 by Arte Público Press. Photo by Francisco Blasco. Arte Público Press, 1985. Reprinted with permission of Arte Público Press./ p. 150, © Cynthia Farah.

James Houston: p. 155, Barbara Hall.

Jeanne Wakatsuki Houston: p. 171, © 1984 Susan Gilbert Photography.

Joanne Kyger: p. 187, Susanna Acevdeo; p. 188, Josepho Shick; pp. 190, 191, Helen Adams; p. 193, Jim Hatch; p. 198, Dr. John Doss; p. 202, Steve Lovi.

William F. Nolan: p. 205, sketch by Donn Albright.

Jay Parini: p. 227, photo © Miriam Berkley; pp. 238, 239, Jay Parini.

Antonis Samarakis: p. 245, Ludwig Schirmer.

Nathaniel Tarn: p. 275, Marion-Valentine; p. 281, AP/Wide World Photos, Inc.; pp. 283, 285, Janet Rodney.

Text

Contemporary Authors
Autobiography Series

Russell Atkins

1926-

Part I

Now that my mother and aunt are deceased—Mama in 1983 and A'Mae in 1987—the rest of my life is beginning to seem like a "coda" after the main body of the music.

A'Mae (a contraction of Aunt Mae, A' [short *a* as in hat] followed by Mae) and Mama (as I called them) stand as my whole life's configuration. In some way they account for practically everything I've done and how I've done it. Strangely enough, I realize now how little they told me about themselves.

Mama was secretive to the point of aberration. Any question put to her was countered by her reply, "Who wants to know?" or "That's for *me* to know," uttered with a forbidding tone. My aunt, A'Mae, was much more considerate by nature. She would say, "Well, we'll just let that rest where it is," when she did not want to discuss something. This left the feeling that wherever it was, it wasn't open to question. As they fade into my past, they seem like two wonderfully fateful spirits that organized my existence for sixty years.

A'Mae was the older, dominant force in spite of her gentle tolerant way. She had a permanence about her, an unchanging, absolutely dependable feeling that was irresistible. You felt that she knew the right answers to everything even though she seldom made any opinionated statements. Her comforting feeling tended to make her seem motherly to everybody and, ultimately, I grew dependent on it.

Mama, however, was as different from A'Mae as night from day. Tolerance was not her guiding principle. You agreed with her or you were dismissed as being frivolous or irretrievably wrong . . . hers was the only way.

A'Mae cared nothing for the arts, but she was not a person to try to convince you to be one thing or the other. She was careful of offending you unless she was provoked. She thought of Mama's piano playing and singing as amusing, especially when Mama would recite poems. But A'Mae's chief characteristic was her feeling of fierce protectiveness for her relatives and her support for anyone she trusted, admired, or loved.

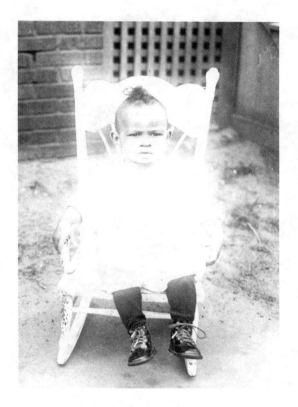

Russell Atkins at two years of age

Born in Tennessee, and eventually moving to Atlanta, Georgia, A'Mae and Mama were the daughters of John D. Atkins and Carrie Louise Howard. John Atkins was mixed racially someway and was accepted as a bricklayer, which I gathered was a favored "profession" among some nonwhites in the South. At any rate, they lived well, had a horse and buggy, which my aunt never forgot to mention because she loved the horse, Dan, and remembered how soft his nose was! They went to school which I assume had some effect on their speech because they never had a so-called Southern accent, especially Mama, who was always very particular about her speech. She corrected me during my growing up with "Don't say ain't!"

1

"A'Mae (my aunt Willie-Mae) on left and Mama (Mamie Belle Atkins)"

Finally, all of them were of light complexion (which seemed to have made some difference in the South), all except their mother, my grandmother, or "Gramma" as I called her. The most bizarre memories from my childhood are those of Gramma. From what I understood (when A'Mae consented to tell anything), Gramma's half sisters were indistinguishable from whites in color while Gramma had derived of a darker lineage. This led to her difficulties as the years progressed. She saw herself as the "little light-skinned lady" (which was untrue) so that she became a victim of the "hant," which seemed to have been a folklike idea of the devil. This "hant" pursued Gramma constantly and made her life miserable; its main thrust, seemingly, was to make her black. This she would not tolerate, and it led to a kind of phobia that took this form: wherever she lived that house was inevitably invaded by the "hant." Since this "hant" communicated only with her, she became the sole source of "protection" against what it was doing. She

extended this "protection" to me when I was a child by noting regularly that I was getting too "dark."

I remember her constant murmuring to herself all day (talking with the "hant") and then suddenly leaping up and demanding that it leave the house and be quick about it! She turned race into such a ghost story of goblins and devils and religious quotations that it was impossible to take her seriously.

Mama had come to Cleveland from Atlanta, Georgia, for reasons I was never told. A'Mae's ex-husband, Charles Welbourne, had come to Cleveland and opened a shoe repair shop. A'Mae arrived to take care of Mama as she had done all through their childhood. Gramma followed them. I was born on February 25, 1926. My father had deserted us and was never seen by me. This left me, Mama, A'Mae, and Gramma living together on Seventy-sixth Street. A'Mae—who was four years older than Mama—was the most practical. Mama lacked a certain amount of common sense and was dependent on A'Mae when it came to serious matters or a crisis.

I have only a few brief images of those days on Seventy-sixth Street: a room kept with the shades down to protect my eyes when I was sick with diphtheria; a toy automobile which I pedaled violently up and down the sidewalk in front of our house; a woman—a friend of the family—with a camera trying to take my picture from across the street and calling to me just as a car turned the corner; my mother and aunt rushing out to pick me up and I remember nothing much else except that the woman—the family friend—was never kindly spoken of again.

A'Mae and Mama did occasional housework for a living, although A'Mae had help from "Uncle Charlie," as they called Mr. Welbourne. I don't remember who Mama worked for but they were rich, benevolently sending us gifts, especially toys and clothes for me—some very expensive.

I was the center of A'Mae and Mama's lives. When they had to leave the house simultaneously, Gramma was left to take care of me. The lady upstairs in the two-story house also watched out for things since Gramma was inclined to pursue the "hant" outside of the house and down the street since she also extended her "protection" to the neighbors.

When Mama was home her chief pastime was singing and "thumping" (her term) on the piano. Occasionally, she would recite poems she liked but with no real attention to the meaning of the words as I later discovered. How Mama came to love and play classical music is still a mystery. Such music made A'Mae nervous and she would say, "Opera sounds like somebody pleading for help." Most of the phonograph records that A'Mae brought from the South were blues, spirituals, and gospel, along with some Al Jolson and Morton Downey. Uncle Charlie had given A'Mae a Victrola to play them on. Mama seldom played it, and when she did it was a recording of Caruso and Frances Alda singing the "Miserére" from *Il Trovatore,* or Caruso and Schumann-Heink singing "Ai nostri monti," or a Columbia record about a quarter of an inch thick with Martinelli and either Rosa Ponselle (or Galli-Curci) singing the "Miserére" again! According to A'Mae, I had at age two a stunning way of finding any record you wanted. But Mama, very deliberately, would turn off the blues and jazz ones saying, "Bad, naughty." I know now that she couldn't be blamed for that assessment because that was the general critical feeling about jazz for so long.

But her love of classical music was genuine. She bought a player-piano—rolls and all. It had a bench of which the top opened. She filled the hollow bench with lots of sheet music that fascinated me to no end. I would open the seat and have all the music spread on the floor! Sometimes this would anger her and

"With A'Mae (left) and Mama," 1928

then at other times she would sit me on the bench while she "thumped" out some of her favorites. Let me assure anyone that she did not profess to be a connoisseur in taste. She liked what we think of now as the warhorses of music (besides, they were still somewhat fresh back in the '20s). I recall her playfully mouthing the "Figaro, Figaro" part of *Il Barbiere di Siviglia*'s "Largo al factotum" aria and the "Toreador Song" from *Carmen.* Much of the music she could not really play but she "thumped" recognizable versions of Schubert's "Serenade," the "Barcarolle" from *Les Contes d'Hoffmann,* Rimsky-Korsakov's "Song of India," Beethoven's "Moonlight" Sonata (first movement), etc.

Gramma's struggle with the "hant" seemed to grow worse. "Get away from this child," she'd say in a deep voice. Evidently the "hant" was making headway with my complexion, and its invasion of the house called for strong measures. According to A'Mae and Mama, they came home one day and found us gone—Gramma and me. After some desperate inquiries, the police were brought in. We were found in a broken-down set of rooms that Gramma had rented.

It was clear from this that the "little lightskinned lady" could not be trusted to take care of me. This led to many new adjustments in the long run. When both Mama and A'Mae had to leave home at the same time, they left me with various friends, or with Uncle Charlie at whose shoe repair shop I spent the day climbing up on the old chairs watching shoes get shined and wondering about the whirring machines that were used.

Then came a curious turn of fate, so to speak: I was occasionally left with Bessie Allen and her husband, Palmer Leroy. Bessie had been a longtime friend of A'Mae's from days in the South. Bessie has remained a phantomlike figure, extremely kind, who washed my face so tenderly when A'Mae and Mama would come to take me home.

Bessie died. Her funeral was a traumatic occurrence in my life, for I never forgot the dark, awesome-looking hole of her grave and the creaking of the pulleys as she went deeper into the gloom. I was about four years old.

Mr. Allen was lost without a wife and somehow fixed his sight on A'Mae. Though he had a slightly stoic approach to life and tended to drink, he had a totally honest, undeceitful character. Wholly dependable about his job, he had held it for years and managed to make money during the depression as a delivery truck driver for the Packard Company.

Mama was furious that he wanted to take A'Mae away from us, and I can vaguely remember a kind of tension in the air whenever he stopped by on a run for the company to talk with A'Mae. She was not too enthusiastic and Mama was outspokenly harsh. But A'Mae was practical: the depression was deepening, Mama had decided to go to Poro School (something to do with being a hairdresser), and A'Mae's dressmaking was not in any large demand. Gramma had— while continuing to fight the "hant"—become "Queen of the churches" (by her own definition). According to A'Mae she had become a "religious fanatic," preaching and ranting in storefront churches so that she would disappear for months at a time.

Then Uncle Charlie died.

Whether it was for good or bad, I can't say, but an "agreement" or "arrangement" was made with Mr. Allen: if he would consent to help A'Mae (and Mama) with me, she would consider marrying him.

From that time on, my childhood was, in the physical sense, an ideal one. I was given everything that a youngster in a poor social or economic stratum could have: enormous Christmases, vacations, good clothes, and Uncle Roy (as I called Mr. Allen) acting as father started an expensive model railroad in the basement. He would read me bedtime stories each night. My favorite was *Hansel and Gretel* until it was superseded by *Snow White and the Seven Dwarfs.* Sometimes my cousin Winifred would stay with us and it was like having a sister. And though all of this was, in a way, A'Mae's weaving—like a Norn—she had also put together a web of resentments which little-by-little configured my life.

Mama, living alone now, had moved to Seventy-first Street and was in the business of hairdressing. A'Mae and Uncle Roy lived on Seventy-third Street, which was really right around the corner. I stayed, alternately, with them and then with Mama. Finally, A'Mae and Roy moved to a nearby set of apartments called the Emrose or "horseshoe" terrace. It was a beautiful group of suites, each amounting to seven rooms. It was from here that I started Giddings Elementary School. Resentments began here also, for Mama, doing daywork along with her hairdressing, found me difficult to accommodate. A'Mae, who was already the "sage" to whom all listened, suggested that I stay with her and Uncle Roy while going to school. I remember that Mama, who had always called A'Mae "Willie-Mae" from childhood, now suddenly referred to her as "Allen." She said it with a tone that implied that she did not approve of the way things were going. From those days onward she spoke of A'Mae as just "Allen."

Under the watchful protective eye of A'Mae, I entered elementary school. It became clear that I was a paradox: "stupidly brilliant." Brilliant because I had the ability to read anything required and this made teachers happy. The second-grade teacher made a point of having me read to the class quite often. The other "brilliance" was my capacity for drawing pictures, which proved to be astonishing. Unfortunately, these were balanced (or unbalanced) by a complete disinterest in anything else. In fact, I could say that this began the basis of my philosophy of life: *Do only what you want to do and try never to do what you don't want to do!*

So it went.

My work in other studies was passable, but it was progressively clear that I was at my best when it came to the arts. I entered the upper grades—the fourth, fifth, and sixth grades—and remained at the head of Reading Table No. 1, one of three tables to which good, medium, and poor readers were assigned.

The sixth-grade art teacher sent a note to A'Mae suggesting that I be enrolled in the children's art classes held at the Cleveland Museum of Art on Wednesdays and Saturdays.

Mama was somewhat indifferent to this because she was trying to interest me in taking piano lessons with her while she continued her lessons with a family friend, "Professor" Murray Adams. Finally, she insisted that I learn the keyboard and scales. Consequently, when I would stay with her I was taught the piano and listened to the Metropolitan Opera broadcast on Saturdays. Mama's choices were mainly Verdi and Rossini, Verdi and Rossini. I liked them but it was years before I made any attempt to find out anything about Verdi and Rossini. It was just the music that Mama liked.

When I returned to A'Mae's and Uncle Roy's house, I attended the art classes at the museum.

Things were different at the museum. Even though Gramma's "hant" had finally decided on my color (far removed from what Gramma wanted), I encountered no race problems. In fact, I cannot recall a single incident even though the classes were all made up of white kids. Part of this was due to the teacher, Milton S. Fox, who was one of the liveliest, more spellbinding teachers that I can remember. I've never forgotten some of the things he said.

We were out in the Fine Arts Gardens, which abutted the museum, sketching. The sun was widely diffused over much of the foliage. We began to shadow accordingly. Suddenly the sun disappeared and a cloud took over. One of the kids complained, "Now I can't finish. I don't know where to put the shadows." Mr. Fox said loudly, "You're an artist, aren't you? You can *imagine* where they should be!'' For some reason this struck me forcefully. From that time on I seldom drew or painted exactly what was in view but altered it to suit my taste.

Another day we were being led through galleries while Mr. Fox analyzed paintings. We stopped before Thomas Hart Benton. I don't recall the painting's title. He asked us if we liked it. "Oh, yes," we answered. Then he stunned us a little by saying that everything was painted without reference to specific textures. We still liked it, but it did give me a sudden awareness of "style" as against photographic reality.

On another occasion we stood looking at Rembrandt's "Anatomy Lesson," which I tried over and over to copy. I was hypnotized by the way the light fell on the corpse. I don't recollect what Mr. Fox said here—something about the old masters.

Before I left elementary school I became totally enamored of the puppets my sixth-grade teacher could make. Her name was Miss Emma Martin, a pioneer African-American teacher in Cleveland. She was one of the few black teachers of the day and had a bizarre combination of informality and strictness. I could not take my eyes off of those puppets which she made when the school was preparing for a marionette show.

I went home and fell wildly into puppet making. A'Mae, being a dressmaker at the time, had all kinds of cloth scraps, silk, satin which she would give me. All I wanted to do was to make puppets and more puppets. I began to write the words based on books I found, Greek myths, a book on the opera, *Dick Whittington and His Cat,* etc.

My paintings were disappointing me—for pretty obvious reasons since I was making copies of "Virgin of the Rocks" by Leonardo da Vinci, and doing my best to capture Rembrandt's shadows, and, finally, El Greco's elongations and Delacroix's dash. My stuff looked awful, I thought. Actually, in my mind I had started to put painting aside while everyone, not knowing this, kept encouraging me toward it. A'Mae and Mama continued to supply money for paint and canvas, but I felt trapped in a fading interest. My attention had turned to writing.

I had taken to memorizing poems and writing little sketches for the marionettes. I began "composing" on Mama's piano which she (in her abrupt way) told me to stop doing.

"You're just fooling around. Why don't you learn the piece I started you on?"

I did finally learn Schubert's "Serenade," a few bars of "Song of India," and the first movement of Beethoven's "Moonlight" Sonata.

Mother, Mamie Belle Atkins

But I insisted that I was going to *write* music.

A'Mae's "agreement" or "arrangement" had begun to unravel somewhat. My uncle began to show little resentments; after all, I was not his child. Mama's hairdressing yielded next to nothing financially. The house she'd rented as a beauty parlor became more crummy and discouraging since the owners did nothing to improve it. Finally, the thought of marrying again had resurfaced even though I had never been told when she'd applied for a divorce from my father and I certainly wouldn't have asked. "Who wants to know?" would probably have been the answer. In fact, Mama was getting to the point where she would never answer any question, no matter how trivial.

For some reason I began crying at the slightest thing. A'Mae seemed worried and spoke to my uncle about "getting help." He was not enthusiastic and expressed the idea that I was not normal-acting anyway, which, I assume, had reference to all this making of puppets and messy painting, and now I'd taken to overt reciting and acting out what I'd written.

My uncle may have been accurate: I did show signs of becoming unruly as I grew bent on my course of "doing only what I wanted to do" (and admittedly, I have never really seen any reason to change). It seemed to be the only course in life, but somehow inspired a violent reaction in others.

I was now eleven years old. I could recite sizable passages from Shelley, Bryant, Shakespeare's plays, Byron, and so on. I had wearied of painting, even though I was enrolled in the Special Classes at the museum. Again, it was Mr. Fox who made a suggestion. We were in watercolor class upstairs in what seemed like the museum's attic. Mr. Fox told us that we were to use the paints as we listened to Schubert's "Unfinished" Symphony. I hesitated, even though I knew that Mama and I "thumped" out his "Serenade."

"Do you like symphonies?" Mr. Fox asked me when he came to my side of the table.

I said, "No, I like operas," clearly thinking of Mama and her Saturdays with the Metropolitan broadcasts.

"Why not try symphonies?" he asked.

I did try them by listening to them in the record room of the museum.

A'Mae seldom allowed me to go alone anywhere except down the street to the Cedar Show, a movie house. And when I enrolled at the museum she took me there until I felt I could make it back and forth alone. It was clear that A'Mae felt more like my mother. This was all right with Mama when we lived together on Seventy-sixth, but Mama resented it when A'Mae became "Allen."

About this time, A'Mae took me downtown to the Hippodrome theater to see the newly released *Snow White and the Seven Dwarfs*. Until this day, I cannot adequately explain why that movie stunned and mesmerized me to the point of trauma. Was it that it was all done with drawings that made the unreal so graphically alive (especially a story that my uncle had read to me nightly at bedtime), or the startling way that Disney imbued a cartoon with a level of horror unmatched up to that day?

Snow White—so to speak—finished off my childhood. I dropped everything else to concentrate on seeing it wherever it was shown by running all over town for the first time. I drew pictures of it, memorized it, recited it.

I entered Central Junior High School where my grades fell to nothing. I forgot about Delacroix, El Greco, and all the rest. My almost obsessive pursuit was *Snow White and the Seven Dwarfs*. When I completed my sketches from memory, I had seven hundred

Palmer Leroy Allen, or Uncle Roy

manila sheets of drawings which I took to school, before which my homeroom teacher stood bewildered.

But the teachers were kind to me. I was allowed to go from classroom to classroom performing *Snow White*, using all the voices: I was Doc, Sneezy, Grumpy, and so on, including the Wicked Queen!

I can only contrast the schools of today with those of that day, for the kids in the class were delighted. I can't imagine anybody today (especially a male) saying before a seventh or eighth grade class, "I'm Snow White," when Doc asked, "Who, or what are you, my dear?"

After *Snow White* I resolved to do nothing but practice the arts. I became a teenager vowing to recite, write, and compose music for the rest of my life. It was obvious by now that I would never make a "student" as such because I was taken over by obsessions which would put me completely out of control. My grades went up and down with a seesaw-like motion that made it impossible for the teachers. My history teacher thought I was the most duncelike pupil she'd ever encountered, until she found out that I had rewritten several chapters of the textbook as poetry. My English teacher, Miss Hilda Foster, on the other hand, made me her pet. She saw me as a last vestige of better days in the school. (Actually, I was the opposite: I represented what was to come.) I had a slight disdain for the subjects because they seemed wholly unequal to my capacities. You might say this: when I became interested in a study (or "motivated" as they say now), my "IQ" jumped.

Miss Foster and her brother invited me to their house for tea and on one occasion she visited us and met A'Mae. She gave me several valuable poetry editions: Wordsworth's complete works and Thomas Moore's work (plus a copy of Dante's *Inferno*—the infamous Carey translation!). She was a major influence on the traditional side; she constantly touted Sir Walter Scott, Shelley, Dickens, and others. She did not admire Byron. He had had an "affair" with his half sister, Augusta, and therefore could not be a great poet. "He was insincere," she said. Fortunately, I had begun to make a few judgments on my own and felt that there was something wrong with making such a statement.

It was now clearly perceived by others that I was somewhat "erratic" in behavior, although some teachers referred to me as being "eccentric." My resistance centered around letting others know what I knew. What I was doing and what I knew (or didn't know) became my own private concern, I felt. I would not share that. I refused to take tests. Finally, I stopped going to classes altogether. I had to find the time to do the things I *wanted* to do. I had no time for things I did *not* want to do. I did not want to be "well-rounded."

This brought in the truant officer and the school psychologist. He asked questions like this: Did I think the world was out of step with me? I don't remember my answer, but I must have had a protective aunt and mother and grandmother and a reasonable uncle flash through my mind.

Another mentor of these school days was my dramatics teacher, Mr. Benjamin Sachs. It was he who led the way out of the traditional milieu into the "modern" in art, which headed me toward the avant-garde.

It was at that time, age fourteen, that I decided to write my "philosophy of life." Mr. Sachs felt that I should stick to one thing or the other. Nevertheless, I plunged into philosophy and what did I choose? Kant's *Critique of Pure Reason.* Mr. Sachs laughed outright but said, "Try it."

He probably thought it would teach me a lesson about what I didn't know. However, I seldom got anything but my own messages from things. I found a translation of Kant's work, and, making no sense at all

of this, I found an explanation of the translation and then a criticism of the explanation (which reminds me of Byron's comment on Coleridge, "I wish he would explain his explanation.") I finally managed a decent, simplified semblance of Kant's *Critique* and went on to others: Descartes, Leibnitz, Schopenhauer, Bergson, heavens knows how many others as I became obsessed again. Nothing mattered now except philosophy and music.

In those days, the music department in junior and senior high schools was important. Due to Mama's influence I took music appreciation and elementary theory and harmony. Once again, a new obsessional attack took over from philosophy: the band director had a cupboard full of classical records. He generously allowed me to make full use of that cupboard and the school's up-to-date record player. I stayed long after school listening to records until the building closed. To me the cupboard was a treasure house of recorded works. I could hardly wait until the end of the theory class to get to it. Even now I have several records that he allowed me to "borrow": Toccata and Fugue in D Minor (Stokowski's transcription) and the "Dance of the Apprentices" from Wagner's *Die Meistersinger.*

About this time, I decided to give up piano study with Mama's music teacher, "Professor" Adams, and decided to take lessons at the Cleveland Music School Settlement. It was here that I studied piano with Rebecca Schandler, who became a lifelong friend from my teens to her death a few years ago. Again, I took harmony lessons, but they required more concentration than I was willing to give at this point.

Central Junior High students were to take classes in Latin and French. My Latin teacher was none other than Miss Helen Chesnutt, daughter of the renowned author Charles Waddell Chesnutt.

We didn't hit it off too well. My handling of Latin was too flamboyant for her. "This is not the dramatics class, Russell. Sit down," she'd say.

I didn't try Latin again after that year. Instead, Mr. Sachs, hoping to help me "find myself," suggested French class. This was more on target. Ms. Excel—yes, that was her name—found me as interesting as Miss Chesnutt had found me irritating.

When I did complete the course, at least I could say "dans la maison" and "sur la table."

Mr. Sachs, long-suffering, said something had to be done. The school would not permit me to go on this way, doing exactly as I pleased.

I don't know how common this was, but a trial program was arranged in which I was to be free to

"Mama (second row from back, third from left) with her Poro Class," 1932

take or study anything I chose without attending classes since I had become a sort of *enfant terrible*, disruptive and whatever. There was one condition: I had to report to Mr. Sach's office as my homeroom with some written evidence of what I had done during the semester. Many objected to this as "special treatment" which encouraged me in what was regarded as potentially "sick" behavior. In fact, a staff meeting was held to determine the feasibility of this trial program. It was sanctioned and the principal of the school told me that I could accept this plan but that it would not lead to a diploma.

"A diploma?" It sounded almost trivial.

Our discussions on my reports in Mr. Sach's office homeroom were much more challenging than the regular classes (which had been duck-soup whenever I did choose to pay attention). I was introduced to Untermeyer's *British and American Poetry* including Pound, Eliot, Marianne Moore. We talked about music, Shostakovich, Stravinsky, Prokofiev, who, at that time, were still the "new" composers who sounded dissonant. I was hurtled out of the past into the modern and finally into the avant-garde.

I remember several other encounters that clinched my determination to go experimental. One was an exhibition at the Art Museum, around 1940, of the work of Salvador Dali. I moved around the galleries in amazement. Not since *Snow White* had I been so shocked. The double-image in the painting, the symbolism, and, most astonishing of all, the photographic technique used for the unreal. The other exhibit, circa the early '40s, was Picasso's. In one of the back galleries across the entire wall was *Guernica!* Were you free to paint like this? And finally Van Gogh!

However, I knew by then that I would never return to painting. But how could all of this be made to function in poetry and music? I wanted to find a way to use all three.

While I pursued these things with an energy that might have been reprehensible, what many people refer to as "reality" was intruding on the family. In quick succession: Uncle Roy lost his job as the company folded; Mama found it necessary to give up her place and move in with us (causing considerable strain on my aunt's "arrangement"); Gramma appeared and reappeared, much more deranged, making inspections as to how much damage the "hant" had done, and found that it had wreaked havoc on my complexion. "This child is almost black," she declared.

Nevertheless, the advantage to me was that Mama's piano was now available. That meant that I could "compose" without stinting all day. Poor A'Mae! Mama didn't like Uncle Roy and he didn't like her; Mama resented A'Mae's control over me and that we depended on A'Mae's regulations about the house. A'Mae balanced all of this plus my plans to "compose" all day.

During these years, the '40s, a number of things happened in quick succession: Miss Foster, my English teacher, introduced me to two people, Rowena and Russell Jellife. The Jellifes had opened a settlement house, Karamu House, down on Thirty-eighth and Central Avenue. Miss Foster praised me to the skies as being very creative. For a short time, I became a member of a small dramatics club there at Karamu. Karamu had only recently had a bad fire and things were getting going again. I adapted a short story by Tolstoi called "Too Dear," and we presented it. I went on to read *Anna Karenina* with an ambitious idea of presenting *that.* The club folded. I also met a new addition to the staff, Walter Anderson, whose composing further kindled my drive for plunging even more into composition.

While I continued as "dissident" at school, Karamu and the Art Museum started a joint scholarship at the Cleveland School of Art headed by a Mr. Ege. I could not tell anybody that my desire to paint was practically gone! I was now writing poetry and composing music. But I met with Louise Dunn and Dr. Thomas Munro, Curator of Education at the museum, and received the scholarship.

My last days in high school were sheer mayhem. The principal informed me that I had not fulfilled my part of the bargain of reports and that I would have to return to attending classes for the remaining twelfth grade.

I said, "Never!" I had too much that *I* wanted to do. They tried transferring me to another high school, John Addams. The principal met me at the door and hurried me into his office where he explained that he would have none of my "nonsense" at his school, and that it was his personal opinion that I was a "misfit."

I was surprised. Nobody'd talked to me like that. (A'Mae and Mama would have been furious.) Ultimately, I completed the missing grades at John Hay night school.

I was never able to explain to people that *I* was in charge of myself and listened only to *me.* This caused me to be thought of as someone without gratitude for "opportunities" which I had not had a chance to examine. My teacher at the art school, Mr. Travis, despaired of me. I doodled mostly, thinking of the "Klingsor of Bayreuth" whose music had become another emerging "obsession." Mama did not like Wagner and had hardly made any mention of him. I think he was too chromatic and dissonant for her taste. I have a faint recollection of her "thumping" the "Pilgrims' Chorus" from some sheet music. But I recall her giving me money for phonograph records with which I purchased the "Tannhauser Overture" under Stokowski. I have that record even now sitting on my cabinet.

True enough, Wagner became my next obsession. Listening to the Met entirely on my own, I became wild about *Die Walküre.* I still have the old 78s: I bought the entire opera—that inimitable performance with Lotte Lehmann and the tenor of tenors, Lauritz Melchior! Mama was furious that I had spent my little allowance savings on that and threatened to cut the allowance off. On Saturdays, when it was time for the Metropolitan, A'Mae would throw up her hands in desperation and almost cry, "Is VAHGnah on today?" as if it were the last straw. Finding out that the worst was true, she'd add, "I'll go downtown and shop," and she did just that.

Uncle Roy was not home, of course. He was usually working overtime because of World War II. He'd been hired by a select small-parts delivery department at Thompson Products and began to make what was, for that day, a good income under the Atomic Energy Commission.

My aunt bought lots of clothes, put in a telephone, refurbished the apartment, and things recovered from a downturn. Again, I felt free to write, "compose," and attend Severance Hall concerts where Eric Leinsdorf had become the conductor of the Cleveland Orchestra.

Halfheartedly, Mama had married again to a man who had some property. She moved now to one of the houses on Ninety-third Street, and—horrors!—the piano went with her. I was devastated, for who would tolerate my "composing," the sharpening harmonies, my increasingly theoretical approach to "music"?

Sure enough, I'd only been to visit her but a few times at her new home and had only casually touched the keyboard when her husband began to wonder why I didn't "work," assuming a kind of parental authority to ask this. That ill-defined word "work" had hardly ever been mentioned. Mama didn't like his presumption either, and, as was customary with her, gave him no answer. Even though she had her doubts, she would defend me against "outsiders" just as A'Mae did. As for the piano, actually it was hopelessly out of tune by now, though I was not paying that much attention to sounds but, rather, making the notes *do* things that *used* sounds.

Talk of "work" became threatening. It seemed that nobody understood that I had devoted myself to art and that I definitely intended to do nothing else. The answer to that from others was, "What will you use for money?"

Money, money, I thought, they always brought *that* up.

In spite of my resolutions, I took a job at a disgusting restaurant downtown. Here I was, picking up dishes.

"Get those dishes right there!" the manager yelled at us.

"I can *see,*" I replied.

After a full hour of torment, I had to quit!

I told A'Mae that I could never again do anything like that! Hours away from my thoughts, art, self-fulfillment!!

"Maybe you can try part-time," she replied. "Don't worry."

From then on, A'Mae stood between me and an increasingly difficult world totally unsympathetic to anyone finding the time for art *only*. With A'Mae behind me and Mama less enthusiastic but supportive, with Uncle Roy resentful but cooperative, I took on those who thought that art was something you did as a child and put aside when you were an adult. I talked of my talent in glowing terms without believing it myself. I had only a handful of poems and scattered pieces for the piano. But I had no other way of defending my determination to do what I wanted to do which was to be wholly wrapped up in poetry, music, and the pursuit of the unusual.

Through recommendations, I can't recall whose, I finally got into the Cleveland Institute of Music as a special student with the option of becoming accredited if things developed. I took a few classes with Ward Lewis to test my ear, then was turned over to a Clement Miller.

I went along for a while until I received, in 1944, a 1-A army classification. Another battle!

The idea that I could be whisked off to war served to blunt my plans. World War II ended but the draft continued. I was 1-A then 4-F. This limbo went on almost up to the Korean War. Because of a bronchial infection, I was rejected.

A friend, Raoul Abdul, started a Coffee Concert series. I was on one of the programs and played a Suite for Piano, wrongly listed as a "sonata." Also, a local funeral home provided a place for concerts. I performed at a number of "teas" with a room full of corpses below. I went about playing this out-of-tune "music" which I began to refer to as "composition" and sound applied. I'm sure that this was due to having written most of it on Mama's out-of-tune piano.

During this interim I couldn't quite decide on a focus for artistic practice. Everything seemed uncertain. Finally I concluded that I would emphasize sounds in my poems, and (since I could no longer use Mama's piano) I would "sketch" music to hold it in thought until I could notate it. Also, having become avant-garde (by others' definition), what was to prevent me from writing these poems as shapes? Thus a dichotomy was put in my mind in which I would "compose" like a painter and write poems like a composer. By then poetry was under the spell of Pound's ideogrammic devices.

It may be hard for many today to comprehend a person's behavior over forty years ago. There were differences that might cause one to reason differently. *Cultural bias in the arts was pretty solid.* A certain amount of individualism was indispensable. Also, judged from today, things were harder and slower: such things as telephones were not yet accepted as household necessities; radio broadcasting wasn't much older than I was, and television was just beginning; computerization was still futuristic. As for education, it hadn't become hysterical as part of the industrial complex. You could learn things because you wanted to know them without being hung-up on who'd make the most money and thereby purchase approval.

Part II

Cleveland's Phillis Wheatley Association, an African-American social agency, began to hold a Folk Festival (I believe it was called that) each year. Langston Hughes was the speaker at one of them. I was introduced to him by a good friend, Helen Johnson Collins, who had attended Central High School when Langston was there. Helen had already started the Free Lance Poetry and Prose Workshop around 1942. We wanted Langston's interest since she knew him well. (Later on he did write the introduction for the first issue of *Free Lance* magazine.)

I'm somewhat vague on the exact sequence, but I mentioned that I had heard from Carl Van Vechten who had suggested that I contact Langston.

At any rate, I sent him a batch of poems which I referred to as "savagely experimental" or something like that. I had, in effect, pulled out all the poetic stops. In the meantime, I had sent work to *View* magazine through Van Vechten's recommendation and through *Experiment* magazine's editor, Carol Ely Harper. Quite suddenly I had acceptances from everywhere, it seemed. *View*'s Parker Tyler and Charles Henri Ford took "The Fall of Year," "Nightly Subterfuge," and "Christophe." Then came a letter from Doubleday concerning a Hughes and Bontemps anthology. Then Carol Ely Harper in her warm, kindly letters of advice, informed me that Alan Swallow would publish several of my poems in *Experiment.* Later editors, John Gross, Roland Ryder-Smith also published my stuff and seemed to catch the thrust of the work. All very exhilarating! However, it was appearing in *View* that thrilled me the most—to find myself at age twenty listed across the page from drawings by Picasso and Dali and Duchamp, Tchelitchew and work to come by Sartre, Edith Sitwell, and Rilke!

Cleveland was a somewhat desolate place for anything "way-out" in those days. The Ohio Poetry Society dominated the city's poetic values. The Society was, to some extent, a gathering of kind, smiling, and probably quite well-to-do ladies. The president of the group was Loring Eugene Williams who had married Hart Crane's aunt. Williams was also a friend of Helen Collins. Though he was pretty conservative (even to the point of considering Crane the black sheep of the family), Williams had a generous streak for helping those far less conservative than he was. Helen, who was a librarian at Cleveland Public Library, found Williams helpful at *Free Lance's* inception. Being the publisher of the leading poetry magazine in Cleveland, *American Weave,* he had available printing facilities.

Free Lance Workshop's beginning (around 1942) reflected the general taste in the immediate community: Alfred Tennyson, Paul Lawrence Dunbar, Elizabeth Barrett Browning, James Weldon Johnson, and Joyce Kilmer. Before I got published I'm sure some of the members thought that I was joking when I read my stuff—an early version of "Night and a Distant Church" and this:

> and yet it frames the average on a more contingent
> and interdependent basis that the reciprocal
> refragable material denotes thereby
> amorphous selective superiority
> called athanasia

"Mama at a friend's house," 1965

I suppose it was wicked of me, but I began to wonder what could be done to change the values. Fate stepped in, you might say; the membership declined, some died, and finally Helen said we'd had it with the workshop and asked Williams if he could print a small booklet of our poems by which the club could be remembered.

I spotted a chance here to direct things toward a new milieu. Since I had begun publishing in "little magazines," and now had a correspondence going with Marianne Moore, and was scheduled to appear in *Voices* and elsewhere, I brought up the idea that the few of us left—Helen, myself, and Casper L. Jordan—should convert the booklet to a "little magazine" with a board like *Experiment*'s. Helen managed to put one together: Florence Barnard, Marie Corrigan, and others from the Cleveland Public Library. Finley Nix, one of the members, was asked to be the editor, but for almost a year nothing happened. Finally, it was delegated to me and in 1950 I launched *Free Lance, a Magazine of Poetry and Prose,* with all kinds of plans for things avant-garde in mind.

The late '40s consolidated and brought into perspective most of my friends, all important to me in my artistic efforts: Annetta Gomez, who never doubted that I had talent and who, herself, has become a consummate director of plays at Wooster College; Casper L. Jordan, without whom *Free Lance* would never have lasted thirty years; Gladys Tiff, excellent singer, of whom Mama was very fond; Rebecca Schandler, my music teacher, and her husband, Hyman Schandler, who had founded the Cleveland Women's Symphony; and, finally, Hale Smith, Jean Jackson, et al.

The day of the condominium was arriving and a real estate agency purchased our apartment as part of a plan to turn the building into a condominium-type residence. My uncle and A'Mae did not wish to buy our suite. They wanted a house free and clear. They bought the present house and we moved in by 1950. Once settled in, I returned to reorganizing *Free Lance*'s editorial policy with Helen Collins, who referred to herself as the "bread lady" since she often paid some of the bills.

Ever since seeing Dali's double-image device, I had been trying to do something like it in poetry. I began to see it as a device for cataclysm: train wrecks, earthquakes, shipwrecks, and nightmares. *View* magazine rejected my "disaster" poems, but I continued by putting pictures directly into the poems—wind, stars, fire, shadows—and "concretizing" many of them with typewriter-key volume. Carol Ely Harper, in a letter dated August 12, 1950, stated that "our editors may think there's a little too much use of the typewriter on the same keys. . . ." In October 1950, Arna Bontemps wrote, "Something tells me you will have to reconcile yourself to being considered an experimental poet. . . ." He followed that with a letter, dated November 9, 1950, that said, "We'll just have to wait and see what the future holds for this type of expression, but I'm pretty sure that most of the publishers we know are not ready for it."

At any rate, when Marianne Moore recommended me to the *Beloit Poetry Journal,* I sent them "Nocturne and Prelude," my most ambitious "concretized" double-image poem which they published. *Free Lance* followed with "Lisbon" around 1951, which was followed by *Four Winds* printing "Trainyard by Night." It astonishes me that some of these poems have been reprinted somewhere every few years even though they are now about forty years old. Much experimental work would go into *Free Lance,* but by 1951 a comment by Parker Tyler brought my "concretism" to an abrupt termination: "It's too much like drawing pictures with the typewriter," he

wrote. He was right, because if I'd wanted to "sketch," why not use pen-and-ink or charcoal?

Temporarily derailed, so to speak, I turned to drama for some new technique for poetry devices that could extend into poem-plays or "poems in play-form," or "drama form." Then it occurred to me to try "music-form," that is, a short poem in play-form that would parallel a sonata or rondo, *not* as defined in prosody, but as defined in music. The idea followed that, just as contemporary composers had challenged western diatonicism with chromatic dissonance, I could distort grammar to a similar purpose by shifting parts of speech and exaggerating the distortion. This would make the poetry "conspicuous" and make the poetry drama *dependent* on it. I then brought the "refrain" idea from poetic devices and used it for the dialogue as leitmotif. With this amalgam, I hoped to bring a new dimension into both my poems and the plays.

On the Demolition

of abject, listen full'd, full'd up
somber'd into illusion'd mystery
as in expectation of some unearthly'd appear!
a bleak consternation, perhaps,
at Judgment after'd by skeleton'd rouse!
abrupt dark'd out at my approach
footfall'n through the hush fellingly yew
along'd by shadowy lamps: about null, dole of outcast
the erst of which, blown,
no dawn's, vast'd through
    monstrous'd fled
(as of leaves that roar away in horroring astound)
left its ceased
    (for a moment,
as in a thenced, I saw
its late illumned;
diagram'd into diagram;
sag's lax Euclid'd
and the Eratosthenesian measured anew)
—notwithstanding, towers up
vain endurance under the confectioning sun,
that, little in immeasurable,
lessens down the sky

About the sidestreets more:
filth'd hush nigh or gutter,
seldom open silences of doors,
or around train rails further;
warehouses lone flung,
cryptic bridge over
which a car went on'd!
(but even decay passes:
    if but a death *could* permanently kill!)
shorn houses? shadows in veer
toward progeny next year

tonight, re-visiting, feel
    furious'd air!
everyplace a vacant exclaim

in this, a momentary illusion of end,
while keptsakes of yesterness
wild terribly hither and fro
under the medusa'd over
—clad of shrub shreds to rush
and for the exodus'd
difficult will snow

(From *Free Lance*, 1960)

About this time I began to think of reentering the Cleveland Institute of Music, although I don't know why, since my ideas about composing were set. However, the late J. Harold Brown took the job as music director at Karamu House. I'll admit that J. Harold had a convincing way of talking you out of things. I told him that I had studied music since childhood and quite clearly had decided that if you *really* had talent (and weren't worried about "acceptance"), you were not dependent on some of the absurdities of the western harmonic system. He was determined to prove me wrong. He had won several awards in composition and his teacher had been Virgil Thomson. He touted the superiority of Percy Goetschius's *Theory of Tone Relations*. I began, wearily enough, to take harmony for the third time, complaining that there was no need for this since I intended to use any old sound I wanted in any way I chose (based on Mama's out-of-tune piano) and that I was developing my own system which seemed to be much more effective.

At any rate, we began in 1950. J. Harold was a brilliant musician. He could take some of the most complex music and transpose it at sight. I was impressed, of course, but this had nothing to do with using tones as though you were putting paint on a canvas where the "composition" had already been fixed.

It was in this frame of thought that I knocked at the door of Hale Smith, who was known then as an arranger in jazz. He was studying at the Cleveland Institute of Music as a student of composer Marcel Dick. Hale and his wife, Juanita, probably stood behind the door and whispered together, "He's here again! Don't answer!"

I had, for some reason, become associated in the minds of many with social nonconformity—a person who had been offered "opportunities" but had ungratefully rejected them. As I mentioned before, this was nonsense. I simply did not like "opportunities" that I had not had a chance to examine beforehand. They might have been out of synch with my own aims and purposes.

As my friendship with Smith developed, we argued violently about Schönberg's twelve-tone tech-

nique, which was at its zenith in the early 1950s. I argued that it contained devices that did not fulfill psychological functions for "mind." Smith preferred to think of me as a fanciful poet rather than deal with the concept of composition as visual and sound applied. Angrily leaving his house at 1:00 A.M., I sat in Woodland Cemetery (a shortcut between my street and Quincy Avenue). Cooling off there, I conceived of my next poem-in-play-form, *The Corpse*. I considered writing some music for it in the twelve-tone idiom.

Instead of writing a twelve-tone anything, I was "commissioned" to write something for a dance concert to be given at Severance Hall by a local arts group. It turned out to be a rather banal piece called "Incidental Music to Riders to the Sea," the play by Synge.

I returned to music for *The Corpse* and did a few pages when I received a hurried request from Marianne Moore for a copy of "Trainyard at Night" for her appearance on WEVD radio's "The World in Books." Suddenly, I got another letter from Langston Hughes saying that he would be reading "Upstood upstaff'd," my poem on Henri Christophe, at the University of Chicago and in Atlanta. Momentarily, I put composing aside, just as J. Harold had begun counterpoint exercises. He canceled the lessons in 1954 after I reminded him that I would have very little use for counterpoint since it wasn't the way I *saw* "music."

At any rate, I sensed why musicians were always referring to each other as "bad musicians" (Ravel on Berlioz): the trouble was the word "music"—it was, basically, meaningless.

Things had begun to fall apart at home. Gramma, who could often be seen wandering all over the city talking to herself—actually talking to the "hant"—came to find us in the new house. Suddenly, she got very quiet, then collapsed. She'd had a stroke. A'Mae could not bear the thought of a nursing home for Gramma, so she and I assumed the task of caring for Gramma. My time for art was in jeopardy!

However, Mama, who had halfheartedly married in the first place, had become almost deranged about housecleaning on Ninety-third Street. Rugs on the floor were white and not to be walked on; the furniture was painted white, the walls were white. She made trying to get a drink of water a thing of fear.

"I'll get it for you. Just sit still," she'd say.

To visit her was to sit in utter silence almost without moving for fear of doing something wrong.

"What are you doing?" she'd ask if you looked out of a window.

There was a terrible blow-up with her husband. She decided that they should part. None of us understood what happened.

"Besides, *my* mother needs me," she told A'Mae, as if Gramma weren't A'Mae's mother as well.

She moved back with us. A'Mae did not object because Gramma had become a major nursing job.

However, with Mama back I was needed only at night to sit up with Gramma.

As you might guess, Mama's now broken and out-of-tune piano had been abandoned.

Through Mama's long-time friend, Gladys Tiff, I now worked on my compositions at the Phillis Wheatley Music School directed by Nell S. Guinn. Where else could my "applied tones" have been tolerated? I composed "The Burial" (1953) and began work on a piece for violin and piano in which I struggled to do the hardest thing possible, namely, to get rid of "melody"—that lingering concept of a single line of tones. I struck on the device, object-form.

This was the early '50s. Continuing to work on my "poems-in-play-form" and "music-form," I attended a playwriting class at a settlement. There I met Adelaide Simon, who was to become a dear friend. Her husband, Martin Simon, cellist, had just joined the Cleveland Orchestra. They had two daughters, Cecily and Celeste. When Adelaide and I found out that we both were deeply interested in poetry, her affiliation with *Free Lance* magazine was inevitable. She was delighted that there was a "little magazine" coming out of Cleveland. I explained that Langston Hughes, Van Vechten, Moore, and Bontemps had been corresponding with us and that my two poetry dramas in "music-form," *The Abortionist* and *The Corpse,* were in the works from *Free Lance* and the University of Iowa's *Western Review.*

Regarding the *Western Review,* I had sent a voluminous manuscript to the editors Paul Engle, Ray West, Donald Justice, William Dickey, and W. D. Snodgrass. They accepted "Elegy to Hurt Bird" and *The Corpse,* both of which Marianne Moore had "corrected." In the meantime, a friendly couple—the Delmar Jacksons—had come from the Iowa Workshop to live in Cleveland. Delmar (or "Stoney," as we called him) had just published a novel with Harcourt, Brace and Company, *Cut of the Axe,* and when well-wishers came to Cleveland from Iowa, the Jacksons held a small party. When my poetry came out in the *Western Review,* there, coincidentally, was the publicity for Delmar's book. It made for a small touch of Iowa in Cleveland. Some of the *Review's* editors visited here and suggested that I contact Marguerite Caetani—who had married an Italian prince—and

send her my work for *Botteghe Oscure* in Italy. She accepted "Love Night" and sent me a check for nearly a hundred dollars. This was heady stuff for me in 1954.

It was easy now to put composing on the shelf for a while since my poems were appearing in many places and *Free Lance* was beginning to distribute widely.

I now devoted every minute to literary pursuits. The two poetry dramas delineated my thrust for forms to fit the grammatical distortions. After "Love Night" was accepted, I experimented with the short narrative poem, compressed and depending heavily on the force of the diction. I wrote "Four of a Fall," on the subjects of drugs and sexual deviation; *Accent* (the magazine) rejected this in 1954 with one of the editors, Walter Edens, writing that it had a "restless, perpetual ingenuity that acts to overwhelm rather than reveal." My "conspicuous technique" approach was working! I followed this with "The Prelude," about the world's birth (using the old Laplace, Chamberlin-Moulton theories); next, "The Infanticide," and finally "Of Angela," which my coeditor, Adelaide Simon, called "a saga of lust." These were all done in the Grand Guignol style.

Free Lance, with Casper Jordan, Adelaide Simon, Helen Collins, and myself, was now in full avant-garde swing, even though *The Abortionist* had cost us some subscriptions. Casper was now Chief Librarian at Wilberforce University and was able to handle necessities like flyers, rejection slips, and stationery. Adelaide and Martin had moved to Shaker Heights and we began to hold the *Free Lance* soireés at what was now the magazine's new address. Because letterpress printing was cheaper abroad, *Free Lance* was printed by Villiers, London, England, with James Boyer May, the editor of *Trace* magazine, as liaison here in America.

Suddenly, in 1953, I was visiting Hale and we were in our usual state of disagreement on composing when it struck me: composing was but an extension of how we think, comprehension-as-composition, attention spans, closures, object-forms.

"It's *psychovisual,*" I told Smith. "We see comprehension machinery at work by which the tones attach themselves although we fail to notice much of it because of the force of sound stimuli." Composing is a *deconstruction* method that is fixed for the "mind's eye."

Let me clarify something here: *the word "deconstruction" was not in current use during 1954 to 1958. In fact, according to the* Oxford Dictionary, *it had not been used since 1882 for specification of any group. I resurrected the word and redefined it for my theory.*

One of those old obsessions seized me; my composing had fallen off, my lessons with J. Harold were over, and my visits to the music school were casual, so why not write *about* "composing" and why I had concluded that much musical pedagogy was superfluous to the problems of the "composer," or "deconstructor."

It had been observed before that when motivated my capacity to absorb stretched. At any rate, philosophy had entered my thoughts again, compounded by my *own* theories. I began to write *A Psychovisual Perspective for "Musical" Composition.*

With everything working smoothly at home, I spent almost the next four years disappearing into the Cleveland Public Library's Philosophy and Religion Division. This wonderful room—now a sad little room of photographs and newspaper clippings—had everything. I picked up where I left off with Kant, but this time I had, at my disposal, forty years of the *Journal of Experimental Psychology* dating from the 1920s into the 1950s. How could I substantiate that "mind" through inertia worked in such a way as to "compose" the small fragments of tones (dot numbers) that we hear? I slipped over into science and ran afoul of Newton, Dirac, Einstein, Max Planck, and Erwin Schrödinger. Totally at sea for a while (since I

had never been a whiz in math), I made full use of my flair for *concepts*. Schrödinger's wave theory served as a base, plus Heisenberg, et al. (I put these notes together later in "The Hypothetical Arbitrary Constant of Inhibition.")

Fortunately, I was surrounded by friends who knew German: Martin Simon, Becky Schandler's next-door neighbors, Casper's German Department at Wilberforce University, and others. Things were different then: there were no photocopying machines. My notes were longhand copies of foreign languages out of obscure journals. But I was obsessed, though I promised myself that I would never again wander into the field of subatomic physics—especially when thirty "basic" particles got involved with "disembodied spin," neutrinos, etc.

During the writing of the theory, I had jotted down thoughts, references, hypotheses, etc., on little scraps of paper, book margins, cards, you name it. Becky Schandler, now a member of the editorial board, suggested that I put these in *Free Lance* since Casper promised to have his secretary type them. However, his obligations at the university prevented this and as a result the notes appeared without much editing in *Free Lance,* 1955–56. The issue also included Irving Layton, Robert Creeley, Robert Sward, Alan Donavan, Hollis Frampton, and others. In some circles, the theory's notes made *Free Lance* seem like the ultimate in avant-garde incomprehensibility. Nonetheless, I received a letter from a composer, the late Stefan Wolpe, who asked permission to introduce the work during the Festival of Avantgarde Music at Darmstadt, Germany, 1956. I had sent the late Geoffrey Sharp, editor of the *Music Review* in England, a letter concerning the theory. After Wolpe at Darmstadt, Sharp consented to read the whole work with a view to publishing an "abstract" of its main tenets.

Before I could reply to Sharp, Gramma grew steadily worse and died, leaving a sad, discordant mood in our household. A'Mae and Mama were getting on each other's nerves; my uncle was thoroughly resentful and was showing signs of illness; and here I was hopelessly entangled in a theory almost without purpose.

Suddenly I knew that it was time to return to poetry for the sake of objectivity. I compiled my manuscript and sent it to the Bread Loaf Writers Conference. I felt I might get away somewhere. I was accepted only to discover that the little money that Gramma had left us would have to go for her funeral expenses and tombstone.

Several other things happened: Smith decided to move to New York, and Helen Collins left to take a

"My cousin Winifred (left)
and A'Mae on a cruise in the Caribbean," 1969

A'Mae in 1969

job in California's public library system. Thus, Adelaide Simon and I were left to handle the magazine here in Cleveland.

When the theory was completed, the somewhat dreamlike feeling of compulsion faded. What could I do with something like this? It wasn't poetry in the ordinary sense, nor was it "music." I subsequently decided that it was to become the artistic basis for my ideas of art and "scientific aestheticism."

Casper dispatched the work, an "Anniversary Issue" of *Free Lance*, to Villiers in London, though I don't believe we had even fifty dollars in the treasury. Sankey, the managing head of Villiers, kindly agreed to try to print it, though, as he explained, Villiers was not set up for printing investigative papers.

Every month or so we would receive an ultimatum: "We can't print any more of this without a small payment. We'll have to cut ———. This is worse than *Finnegan's Wake*."

Rather than have it cut, I suggested that the paragraphs be compressed; to do this, I hastily reworded some of them by phone to Casper. Now, looking back, I wonder that it came out as well as it did. At least we got it all in!

Immersed as I was in theorizing and in handling *Free Lance*'s widening distribution, I had failed to notice the changes that had started up in poetry. Something called "Beat" was emerging which was

clearly a hybrid out of the ghetto world of jazz. The real delineation of a "new" movement came in 1957 when the Russians sent up *Sputnik* and the suffix "nik" was added to everything including "Beat"— thus "Beatnik!"

It irritated me that people did not recognize art as "work," and that I was hard at it was taken lightly; that I was right in this matter and that the world was wrong got to be unequivocally clear! I needed something to consolidate my efforts, to objectify them. The theory was certainly a consolidation of my views on some things, but I needed something conveniently presentable. Of course! I needed a book of my poems—I began to put *Phenomena* together as my first book. This, however, was interrupted by my being offered a job at a music school, the Sutphen Music School, directed by Nell S. Guinn. The school moved into a newly constructed annex attached to the main building of the Phillis Wheatley Association. My friend Gladys Tiff thought I would be the perfect office manager (since there was very little to do and thus not posing a threat to time needed for art). Also, as a writer, I could act as publicity manager as well.

I took the job. A'Mae was delighted, Mama was pleased but thought that it wasn't "work." I told her that "work" had yet to be clearly defined. Uncle Roy was now suffering from phlebitis and had to go into the hospital so that the news of my employment did not have much effect on him.

Frankly, I, too, was pleased because I was surrounded by pianos: Steinways, Baldwins, Acrosonics! Think of the psychovisual composing in which there would not be any more out-of-tune harmony, but actual *dissonance!*

Nineteen fifty-eight found me finishing my "objects" for cello, but I allowed "melody" to dominate shape. I continued to put bits of music to *The Corpse*—the title of which amused those who took a cavalier attitude toward my compositions; I considered changing the name to "The Widow."

I heard again from the former editor of the *Minnesota Quarterly*, E. V. Griffith, who had held a number of poems for a while, "Four of a Fall" among them. Griffith published it in *Hearse* magazine in 1957–58.

That things were changing couldn't be doubted: Uncle Roy took seriously ill—"suspicions of lung cancer" seemed to be the diagnosis; Mama was becoming a different person, more resentful about life, with all traces of her love of classical music degenerating into increasing talk of "God's help" and "salvation" through Jesus (all totally foreign concepts to me) leading to a kind of estrangement. She took to listening to hymns all day. She would tell others that she had "nobody in the world." This was done almost deliberately because she knew that it distressed A'Mae who prided herself on protecting her loved ones.

"Mamie, why do you say that?" A'Mae would cry. "You've got me and Russell."

"Oh, him—he's going to get it!"

Sometimes she'd laugh at this herself, but it was becoming less of a joke.

The decade closed with an odd occurrence: A'Mae and Mama had a brother—my uncle Earl—who'd left home in the South and was never heard from. Strangely enough, Gramma, before she died, told A'Mae that he was being held in a room against his will. A'Mae assured her that it was more likely that he was dead. Out of the blue, after Gramma's death, a letter came from the State Hospital in New York saying that Earl Atkins wished to be released in the *custody* of his relatives whom he described as living in Cleveland. He had been missing—and boozing—for almost forty years.

Earl's papers were finally ready and A'Mae and Mama went to Poughkeepsie, New York, to bring him to Cleveland. A'Mae, sweet as she was, did not like her brother. But she would never have slighted him. Mama, on the other hand, declared that now *she* had "somebody in the world" and seemed wildly happy. She rented an apartment and she and Uncle Earl moved out, leaving A'Mae and me alone and sad—especially me as I realized that they were all getting old and could die. As far as I know, we were the last of the Atkins family: my uncle Earl with Mama, and I with A'Mae. This "arrangement" was final.

The music school was doing so well, with its affiliation with the National Guild of Community Music Schools, that it required full-time hours from its part-time staff. Full-time, of course, was anathema to me. There must be nothing to interrupt the bringing-into-existence of things (eating, sleeping, clothes-buying, eroticism, status symbols, etc.), all of this had to take a secondary place or no place at all in some instances). It was necessary for me to resign. Needless to say, A'Mae and Mama made such single-mindedness possible because they were still around. However, I was depressed for a while and felt lost without the Steinways and Baldwins. Perhaps it was just as well because Uncle Roy came home from the hospital. He was not in the best shape; in fact, he was dying—at the most, the doctors hadn't told him he was "cured," so we drew our own conclusions. Heart failure returned him to the clinic where he died in December 1962.

My grief for my uncle's passing was violently mixed, but he had—however resentfully—stood firmly behind A'Mae's "arrangement." I was now convinced that the "real" is a kind of natural programming *against* which one creates by resistance. Unfortunately, in order to maintain a nonrepresentational freedom from the world, one needs money. However, "fate" had granted my youthful wish: *to spend my life doing very little other than practicing the arts.*

I had returned to putting *Phenomena* together. The works had all been written in the middle '50s. When the book was published in '61, it went (as expected) unnoticed by the establishment. I had combined many devices with a sense of horror plus straightforward narrative using a kind of systematic connotation behind the "exaggerated" grammatical distortion. In short, *Phenomena* represented certain technical ideas as *I* saw them. My only criticism of the book is that my excitement in experimenting led to haste. The poetry-dramas do not have as compact a diction as the later ones. *Free Lance* and Wilberforce University, by publishing the work at the start of '61, unintentionally made it a precursor of subjects and events to come in the '60s: nudity, four-letter words, police brutality, sexual aberration.

About this time another member of the Iowa workshop had arrived in town and was teaching at Fenn College. Lewis Turco had founded the Fenn College Poetry Forum in 1962–63. He asked me to read at Fenn's Ohio Writers Conference which he directed with Loring Williams. While it was not my first reading, it was the first for which I received any money. It came at a fortunate time by giving me a push toward poetry lecture-readings.

Under a friend's Poets and Lecturers Alliance I made several appearances. From '63 to '78 I visited a number of colleges and universities as a paid speaker (namely, Findlay College, State University of Oswego, Howard University [under Woodie King Associates, see *Forerunners* anthology], Lake Erie College, Defiance College, Western Reserve University's Services Program, and others). Then with the Ohio Poets Association (under the Ohio Arts Council funded by the National Endowment for the Arts), I joined the writers-in-the-schools program. (That experience left me glad that I had not chosen teaching as a "career.")

As the late '60s developed, I was consultant for a public television series edited and produced by my close friend, Annetta Gomez (Jefferson). During the turbulent years of rioting and burning, I was involved in establishing writers' workshops for "ghetto" writers.

The author

Then, quite suddenly, *Free Lance* lost two of its most important supporters: Langston Hughes died, May 22, 1967, and Adelaide Simon passed away on September 30, 1967. We published two memorial issues; friends sent in their condolences with short written remembrances. Among them were Barriss Mills, Sara Ruth Watson, Jim Lowell, Owen Dodson, John Ciardi, John Oliver Killens, Julian Bond, Marianne Moore, et al.

I had a brief experience with Hollywood. Paramount Pictures came to town to make the movie, *Uptight.* Through a friend, Norman Jordan, I signed on as an extra largely for the experience. Being on a movie set, it was exciting to watch Jules Dassin at work (accompanied by his wife, Melina Mercouri) and the crew getting camera angles and planning shots. One scene involved Roscoe Lee Browne, Ruby Dee, Julian Mayfield (and myself). But the waiting around between takes dampened enthusiasm somewhat—standing from 7:00 in the evening until 5:00 in the morning. The final *coup de grace* was when the fire department dumped gallons of water on us for rain.

However, this encounter with moviemaking brought on another bout with those obsessions of earlier years. I was suddenly inflicted with the urge to write movie scripts. I wrote two such scripts and managed to get a New York agent to handle them, but my artistic habits placed me entirely out of my depths. The agent insisted that I stop using so much dialogue, although it wasn't badly written. She forced me to cut my 250-page screenplay to 150 at most. I did so feeling that I was betraying myself as a poet by agreeing with necessities that reduced the function of words. When I was told that you could spend ten years before ever selling a single script, I measured that time against my being in my forties. I abandoned script writing forthwith!

In 1971, friends, who admired my experimental approach to the arts and my stylistic developments, decided that I had been subjected to a "conspiracy of silence" because of downright foolish critical assessments of my work. They banded together at Karamu Theater and presented a sampling of what I had done.

If one can imagine "fate" taking sides, it certainly seemed so here: the woman writing the publicity committed suicide; the director of the play entered a mental hospital (due to marital problems) and emerged to direct the cast as part of her therapy; and a musician's car was stolen after a rehearsal. However, the evening's "Tribute" to my work went off successfully with some of Cleveland's best musicians: Frieda Schumacher, Martin Simon, Gino Raffaelli, Dolores White, and Alsbrooks Smith.

In 1972 I was hired as Instructor of Creative Writing at Karamu House, where I remained for fourteen years.

Further recognition followed: the Ohio Arts Council Board and Panel members were appointed by Governor Gilligan in 1974; I was put on the Literary Advisory Panel. Later, I received an Individual Artists Fellowship from the Council.

In 1976 I received an honorary doctorate from Cleveland State University. The citation read in part:

. . . composer and poet, generous teacher of an example to aspiring writers, promoter of racial understanding through the arts, a lifelong Cleveland resident, you have written of its social foibles, and its graces, its natural beauty and the hopes of its people.

BIBLIOGRAPHY

Poetry:

Phenomena, Free Lance Poets and Prose Workshop, Wilberforce University Press, 1961.

Objects, Hearse Press, 1963.

Objects 2, Renegade Press, 1963.

Heretofore, Paul Breman [London], 1968.

Presentations, Podium Press, 1969.

Here in The, Cleveland State University Poetry Center, 1976.

Whichever, Free Lance Press, 1978.

Musical compositions:

(With Langston Hughes and Hale Smith) *Elegy* (poetry set to music), Highgate Press, 1968.

Objects (for piano), Free Lance Press, 1969.

Also composer of unpublished musical works.

Contributor to anthologies:

Paul Breman, editor, *Sixes and Sevens,* Paul Breman (London), 1962.

Adelaide Simon, editor, *Silver Cesspool,* Renegade Press, 1964.

D. A. Levy, editor, *Four, Five, Six,* Seven Flowers Press, 1966.

Richard E. Peck, editor, *Sounds and Silences: Poetry for Now,* Delacorte, 1969.

Anthologies in Braille, Bell Telephone Laboratories, 1970.

June Jordan, editor, *Soulscript: Afro-American Poetry,* Doubleday, 1970.

Alberta Turner, editor, *Poetry: Cleveland,* Cleveland State University Poetry Center, 1971.

Langston Hughes and Arna Bontemps, editors, *Poetry of the Negro, 1949–1970,* Doubleday, 1970.

Raoul Abdul, editor, *Magic of Black Poetry,* Dodd, 1972.

Lewis Turco, editor, *Poetry: An Introduction through Writing,* Prentice-Hall, 1972.

Willemien Vroom, editor, *Penguin Book of Verse,* Penguin (England), 1973.

Arnold Adoff, editor, *The Poetry of Black America,* Harper and Row, 1973.

Robert McGovern and Richard Snyder, editors, *The Strong Voice,* II, Ashland Poetry, 1973.

Paul Breman, editor, *You Better Believe It,* Penguin, 1973.

Robert McGovern, editor, *Poetry Ritual for Grammar School,* Ashland Poetry Press, 1974.

Geoffrey Singer and C. A. Smith, editors, *Cleveland Anthology,* Pranayama Publications, Cleveland Area Arts Council, 1975.

Woodie King, Jr., editor, *The Forerunners,* Howard University Press, 1975.

Eugene Redmond, editor, *Drumvoices,* Doubleday, 1976.

Arnold Adoff, editor, *Celebrations,* Follett, 1977.

Peter Hargitai and Lolette Kuby, editors, *Forum,* Mentor Press, 1978.

Citino, Turner, and Bennett, editors, *Seventy-three Ohio Poets,* Ohio State University, 1978.

Robert Fox, editor, *Poems, 1978–1983,* Ohio Arts Council, 1984.

Robert McGovern and Joan Baranow, editors, *80 on the 80s: A Decade's History in Verse,* Ashland Poetry Press, 1990.

Marie Harris and Kathleen Aguero, editors, *An Ear to the Ground: An Anthology of Contemporary American Poetry,* University of Georgia Press, 1991.

Beyond the Reef (children's reader), Houghton, 1991.

Other:

A Psychovisual Perspective for "Musical" Composition (chapbook; musical theory), Free Lance Press, 1958.

Two by Atkins: The Abortionist [and] *The Corpse* (two poetic dramas to be set to music), Free Lance Press, 1963.

"The Hypothetical Arbitrary Constant of Inhibition," *Free Lance Magazine,* vol. 8, 1964.

The Nail (opera libretto adapted from the short story by the same name by Pedro Antonio de Alarcon), Free Lance Press, 1970.

Maleficium (short stories), Free Lance Press, 1971.

"By Yearning and by Beautiful" (poem set to music by Hale Smith), first performed at Lincoln Center for the Performing Arts, New York, N.Y., 1986.

Contributor of poems and articles to *New York Times Book Review, Beloit Poetry Journal, Western Review, Counter-Measures, Hearse, Poetry Now, Works, Gamut,* and numerous other journals.

George Bowering

1935-

ALPHABIOGRAPHY

George Bowering—in his study, Vancouver, British Columbia, 1980

ANGELA Luoma and I got married at Vancouver city hall on December 14, 1962. We were living in a very old apartment building on Yew Street with a hill outside that was steep enough to park my 1954 Austin on, so that it would start if you got it rolling. On this day it would not start for several blocks in the light rain, and Angela Luoma was waiting at the hairdresser's, speaking of me with impolite language. The hairdresser was necessary. He was trying to get her hair all one colour of blonde because the hairdressing student had made it three colours the day before.

We were fifteen minutes late at city hall, but Angela was used to this, because it is her way, and now more than half a life later, though I see that it seems to work for her, I am still not used to it. I would have liked to have been at city hall a half hour early, in my black hopsack jacket and narrow bebop tie, and now when Angela is not with me I always get there early. When we are together we get there after something has started. I hope she gets to my funeral before it's over. That's a jest.

She was beautiful with her blonde hair and green eyes and we were married before my first book was published, when I had published a few poems in the magazines. I was a graduate student at University of British Columbia, where I was helping to publish an international poetry newsletter called *Tish,* with Frank Davey and Fred Wah and some other young poets. Robert Duncan encouraged us to start the mag, and gave it its title. First Fred got married to Pauline Butling, then I got married to Angela, and then Frank got married to Helen. Their ship never came in.

Angela Luoma is half Finnish and half Anglo-Scottish, as we say. She has read everything that I have not read, Plato and Tolstoy and Jung.

She is interested in gardens and psychology and mortgages and genealogy. She is not a poet, and she does not often write anything beyond her stacks of personal journals, but she has published a book on Sheila Watson's wonderful novel *The Double Hook.* She is an expert on Sheila Watson. That is the part of her that I like best.

Angela Bowering has a short fuse, and I do not play with matches around her. I like her large green eyes, but I would never strike a match to make the pupils dilate.

BIRTH was something I have been trying to get over all my life. My mother, Pearl, gave birth to me, her first child, in Penticton, B.C., at 11:30 P.M. on December 1, 1935. She was nineteen years old, it was the middle of the Depression, and her school-teacher husband received ninety dollars a month, or nothing at all if the school district could not manage it.

It took more than two days for her to manage it, November slipping away, her husband Ewart trudging up the hill to the Penticton hospital whenever they would let him. I came into the world, such as it was, sideways. My enormous head was black and all mushy, they say, and my mother tried to resolve herself to the likelihood that after they took the baby away somewhere she might not see it again, or that it would have no appreciable brain. Still, she and her husband gave it a name. The name had been Richard for six months, but now they did not want to run the risk of wasting that name. They called me George Harry Bowering, after my father, Ewart Harry Bowering, and his English immigrant father, Jabez Harry Bowering. If this baby were to live, Penticton hospital said, the damage to its head would likely demand your patience in the coming years.

They worked all through the day, Dr. McGregor, Miss Riley, Miss Miller, Miss Dawson. The sideways thing with the bleeding head was only seven pounds and fourteen ounces. Average. In the baby book, under remarks: "?"

A question mark. Looking at that page all these years later, I bless the hand that wrote it. My father,

according to the family joke, was playing bridge with their friends down the hill when the awkward flesh began its journey to death or maybe life in the Okanagan Valley. But then there he was and there I was and maybe he could see me soon. Pearl was a year and a half out of school where they lived in Peachland.

When they let us leave she was back in her polka dot dress and a coat to cover her bare arms, at the end of the year in the very centre of the Depression. She was full of milk and looking forward to the summer when she could get back on the ball field. When his head was better someone else could hold him for a little.

CHILDHOOD is thought, by people better read than I am, to be a powerful determinant of one's later life. It could be. A lot of people look back on their childhood as an Edenic time, filled with innocence and clean air. I grew up in the Okanagan Valley. It was gouged out in the ice age, became a semi-desert and a string of lakes. When I was a child it was a couple hundred miles of orchard, blossoms in the spring, heavy fruit all summer, from the cherries in June to the apples of September.

The hills were dry and looked just like the landscape in Western movies. Children hiked around those hills all year round, looking out in summer for cactuses and rattlesnakes, in winter for a frozen pond to stomp on. In elementary school they instructed us on what to do in case of a rattlesnake bite. We sometimes heard about tourists getting bitten, but I never knew anyone who got bitten by a rattler. We would acquire their rattles and then sneak up behind someone and shake them. I have jumped a mile.

When we lived in Oliver, where my father was a science teacher, we had Bowering relatives up the valley, in Summerland and Penticton and Naramata, and Brinson relatives over in the Kootenay Valleys. We were always visiting the Bowering relatives, and I loved it. In the Okanagan Valley I had only one cousin older than I, Russell Bowering the jazz saxophone player, and he died when I was a kid. So I managed to develop that solitariness the oldest kid learns about. It leads you to such things as books and California radio stations, and the peculiarities of the Okanagan geology.

For most of my childhood I had a dog, and this was back when there was open space right in town. A dog could crap wherever he wanted to, except on Mrs. Wilkins's lawn. First I had Caesar, and I dont remember what happened to him. Then I had Caesar the Second, a wire-haired terrier. He always fought ferociously with my uncle Red's wire-haired terrier

"What am I? Eight?"

named Beans. We left him tied in the orchard when I was in grade three, and when we came back he was gone. Then there was the cocker spaniel Monty. When we moved into town we sent him to the orchard where my uncle Gerry lived, and Monty got run over by a tractor. Then there was Dinky, an English rat terrier with a big letter S scar on her back. I inherited her when my grandmother Brinson died. Dinky was my favourite. She took twenty million steps in the hills over Oliver.

DEATH always bothered me more than birth did. When I was four I thought I could get older till I was very old and then get younger a year at a time. You would have to pick your friends carefully, in case they might be coming down when you were going up. When I was five I thought I might be the first person in modern times to live forever. When I was six I thought I could start as someone else after I died, with no memory.

When I was sixteen I thought I would die before I was thirty. When I was twenty-nine I had been married for two years. I lived with my widow in Calgary. My unlucky number has been fifty-two ever since I was a child. Several of my books go directly from chapter fifty-one to chapter fifty-three. I wondered whether I would end in my fifty-second year or when I was fifty-two. I was living with my wife and orphaned daughter in Vancouver. Years ago people used to wonder what political life would be like in 1984. We found out that books are just books.

Death is one of the very biggest subjects of poetry. I have been writing about it all my life. I usually try to show a humorous side to the subject. My 1992 book *Urban Snow* includes a funny poem called "Death." The publisher demurred when I told him I wanted to call the book *Death and Other Poems*. It seems to me that as I have grown older we have enjoyed more nice machines in our houses while watching our particular world dying. In the Okanagan Valley there are more and more stumps where there used to be peach trees, and new houses with paved driveways where there used to be sagebrush hills that looked like Western movies.

After my cousin Russell died my grandmother Bowering died. The only time I ever saw my father weep was at her funeral in the Baptist church in Summerland. I was fascinated by the beauty of a young woman in the choir, and I felt that I was an awful human being because I did not cry at all. When I was in elementary school the news came that Tom Moojalski's father had been killed by a log falling off a truck. When I was in junior high school my classmate Tibor Palley died in the Oliver hospital while telling Jesus that he loved him.

On my twenty-ninth birthday I got the news by telephone and telegram that my best friend Red Lane had died in Vancouver. He was just starting to be a poet.

EWART Bowering was just my father, and he died on March 12, 1975. His funeral was held at the United Church in Oliver, on the Ides of March. I held my mother's hand and my sister's hand, hard. We were in the front row, privileged and vulnerable. I thought I heard his voice saying "It's all right."

He was just my father, but now I have come to know and to admit that he is a kind of hero to me, a standard against which I measure my behaviour. When I was younger I maintained this story—that he was a very smart and promising man who settled for less because it was the Depression. He was smarter than all his brothers and sisters but he always got along with them well, playing bridge, working summers in the orchard.

He was a preacher's son and an athlete. I have his small town newspaper clippings in which he is usually the best player in the basketball game, or he got two singles in the baseball game. I have his first school inspector's reports, in which he is praised for his dedication and chided for his shortcomings as a disciplinarian. He had blue eyes and a straight nose. He was just about six feet tall and handsome. My mother was a schoolgirl athlete from a hillbilly family and she snagged him.

He was a quiet man who paid a lot of attention to his community. He coached young people's basketball teams and softball teams. He was secretary-treasurer of the Elks Club but he seldom had a drink; he organized their Save the Children fund. He worked on the committee to get the new hospital in Oliver. He started the fire every morning. He never drove over the speed limit. He wrote sports reports for the small town newspapers when he got to be too old to be in them. He took off his shirt and in his undershirt built our house. He didnt like it when people said "nucular" or made plurals out of apostrophes.

He was the chemistry teacher at Southern Okanagan High School. I had to take a senior science course to graduate, so I took chemistry. I got 56 percent in chemistry. At school I called him Sir and

George, his parents Pearl and Ewart Bowering, sister, Sally, and (in front) brothers Roger and Jim, 1952

he called me Bowering. After his funeral we went to the desert cemetery up Fairview Road in Oliver, and I broke away from the cluster of family and put my lips to his casket. I was surprised at myself.

FIRST times at things are supposed to be memorable, and some are, though they will be fictionalized or made lyric by the memory. At the time they are part of a continuum, confused with everything else that is happening that day in that body and mind. Is this the first time I have written autobiography? Well, yes and well, no.

We do a hundred thousand things for the first time, and really one can argue that everything we do we are doing for the first time. The game of baseball is so damned beautiful because so familiar. We know that Devon White will lead off and reach base, and then Roberto Alomar will hit in the second spot, for instance, just as Billy Herman followed Peewee Reese. The first time I ever came to bat in organized junior baseball I hit a single with the bases loaded. Shortly after that I had to move out of town, to work in the orchard in Naramata.

Three important firsts are in baseball, sex, and writing. My first honest-to-god all-the-way sexual initiation occurred one afternoon in Portage la Prairie, Manitoba. My guide, though I still like to think she didnt know, was a farmer's daughter named Eileen, who was a wonderful one year older than I. In all probability I was finished awfully early, and because I was in the air force my dog tags clinked on her teeth. I didnt know whether it was all right to think things were funny while you were doing it. Thank you, Eileen.

There are a lot of little writing firsts, arent there? Poems in school magazines, a letter published in *Baseball Digest,* a story in an anthology in Toronto. My first real book, *Points on the Grid* (1964), made me happy in a sense. I was in my late twenties, and full of myself, a big fan of Charles Olson, and now I had a book or poems published by Contact Press, the best small press for the new poetry in Canada. Of course we were living in Calgary, where no one, including the people who taught poetry at the university, knew anything about the world I had taken my first step into.

A few years ago a copy of that book was sold for $1,500. The poetry in it isnt very good. But this isnt the first time one has perceived the relationship between art and commodity.

GEORGE was not supposed to be my name, but at the last minute that is what they gave me. I've never been satisfied with it. When I have to tell an

Poet Red Lane, George Bowering, and his roommate Fred Bing

answering machine who it is that's calling, I'm a little embarrassed to say the word. My mother once told me how neat it is that all the letters of my first name also show up in my last name. The same can be said for my kid brother Roger. And when I see my name on the cover of a book, for instance, I like the way that only the capitals stick up above the rest, and the g's stick down. I'm glad my name isnt Elroy Holmquist.

But when I was a boy I thought I'd like the name Ted. Theodore. My aunt Dorothy died shortly after I was born. She was a nurse in a meningitis hospital, and died of the same thing Thomas Wolfe died of, in the same year. They were both fatally sick in British Columbia. The next year Theodore Samuel Williams arrived in the American League. He was to become my favourite ball player.

Maybe if I had been born Richard or Theodore I wouldnt have tried to make a name for myself.

The only other George in my family is my mother's uncle George, who was some kind of gambler and later crank religion pamphleteer in Louisiana. He and his siblings all came up to Canada

from the Ozarks to be hillbillies on the prairies. He married his brother Emmett's wife's sister, and headed back south. The last I heard of him he was in Georgia. I've never been there.

But the Bowerings got here when my other grandfather Jabez Harry came as an orphaned boy to be an indentured farm labourer. He got smart or religion and became a circuit rider on the prairies. By the time I knew him he shuffled with a crutch and a cane, and was the postmaster at Summerland. Once he showed me a thousand dollar bill. When he got old and moved from Summerland to Penticton he took his furnace with him. After his wife Clara died he moved in with us in Oliver. My father being the way he was, naturally it was to our house that Grandpa came. My father built some more of our house.

I guess the name George is all right for writers as long as they are writers. I have always liked the work of George Oppen, George Stanley, George Economou and Georgia Savage. People who have read more than I have tell me that Lord Byron is pretty good.

HOME is very important to me, I have found out to my surprise in various self-examination exercises. I have been living in the same house now for eighteen years, which is a bit shocking, because when I was younger I thought that I would keep on moving every year from house to house, every couple years to another town. But when you live in Vancouver at last, do you want to live in another town?

I have lived in thirty houses and apartments, not counting temporary shelters like tents, bunkhouses, borrowed houses, barracks, dormitories, and hotels. Before I left my parents' home at age seventeen, I lived in Summerland, Greenwood, and Oliver. Then I went for a year of college in Victoria. I was in the Royal Canadian Air Force as a photographer for three years, living in Ontario, Quebec, and Manitoba except for temporary duty elsewhere. After that I became a student again, at University of British Columbia, and I strung that out as long as I could, living in a basement here, a loft there.

So we got married, Angela Luoma and I, in December of 1962, and in 1963 I got a teaching job in Calgary, where we lived in three apartments, going to Mexico for a while in the summers. One of our addresses in Mexico was on Calle Béisbol. In 1966, after my first summer in Europe, we went to London, Ontario, for a year, where I did course work for my Ph.D. and Angela worked in a psychology laboratory where they put pigeon brains in other pigeons. Then we went to Montreal where I could be a writer-in-residence at Sir George Williams University, and we stayed for almost four years. They expected me back in Calgary. They expected me back in London.

Instead I quit my job again and we headed for the west coast. I wrote some books and we had a baby, Thea Bowering, in 1971, and a year later I landed a job at Simon Fraser University. Every time I get a job it is by the skin of my teeth.

When our daughter was born we were living in a commune on York Avenue. A little later we finally bought a little house on Balaclava Street, so there was one of my rules, broken. Then eighteen years ago we bought a big old house on Thirty-seventh Avenue, and that is where the three of us have been ever since, except for the year I was writer-in-residence in Rome and Berlin.

I dont hang my hat. I put it on a shelf.

INDIANS and baseball, that's what W. P. Kinsella writes about, and come to think of it, that's what I write about. Come to think of it, the last time I saw W. P. Kinsella we were in Cleveland Stadium, watching the Indians play baseball quite well against the White Sox.

With Angela, London, Ontario, 1966

When I was a kid in Western-movie Oliver, the Wenatchee Chiefs professional baseball team held their spring training at our park. Manuel Louie, the chief of the local band, would let the fake Chiefs use his sweat house in exchange for letting him take batting practice. He was always old, Manuel Louie, and everyone loved him, who wore a big round Stetson hat with an eagle feather in it, and placed his powerful belly over the rail of the snooker table back of the Orchard Cafe. He was old and fit, and I thought of him and the pictures of Honus Wagner in my baseball magazines. They were both bowlegged and old and perfectly qualified to be legends.

My novel *Caprice* (1987) is dedicated to Manuel Louie and Windy Bone. *Caprice* is about Indians and baseball. Windy Bone told me "The Indian Way To Catch A Deer," and it is funny as hell. I sat in the Desert Arms pub, which used to be the Reopel Hotel beer parlour, and had a beer while Windy had a Coke. I said there are white professors who say Native, or Indigene, or First Nation instead of Indian. Windy thought that was funny as hell.

The difference between the west and the east is that if you're a white guy growing up in the west, you work with Indian guys, and if you shoot pool you lose snooker games to Indian guys. In the east if you're a white guy you hardly ever see Indian guys, or Indian people at all, except on the television news.

So poetry and fiction. In Canada, poetry and fiction in the east dont have Indians in them anymore. But look at western Canadian fiction. It's like growing up in western Canada. Indians fill up books by Robert Kroetsch, Sheila Watson, Rudy Wiebe, Susan Musgrave, W. P. Kinsella, and me. Now look around some more. Jeanette Armstrong, the Okanagan Indian writer, is from Penticton. The first novel written by an Indian woman, Mourning Dove, also came from the Okanagan. Keep an eye out for Lee Maracle and J. B. Joe. All women, all Indian, Native women, if you like. I dont think any of them play baseball, though.

J OURNEYING is not the opposite of home; it is the partner—my friend bp Nichol's first book of poetry was called *Journeying and the Returns.* That means coming home is part of the journey, and it suggests that travel is always going on, while getting home is plural. I wrote a novel about that, *Harry's Fragments* (1990).

When I was a kid in the Okanagan Valley I did not live in a family that travelled. My father never got off this continent, and only once in his life went as far east as Montreal. I took him to see a game between the Expos and the St. Louis Cardinals. When I was a kid in the Okanagan, I sometimes went to other towns up the Valley. Kelowna, for instance, was sixty miles away. It was pretty romantic: you had to take a ferry across the lake to get to Kelowna, until they built the bridge.

By her twentieth birthday my daughter had been to Europe four times. I first got to Europe in the summer of 1966, when I was thirty. My friend Tony Bellette went to Germany to buy a Volkswagen, and I went with him. We rode from England to Turkey and back in the Bug, and my budget was six dollars a day. I took my portable typewriter and wrote a book about the trip, 1500 words a day for six weeks. I also kept my diary, and wrote home every day.

Since then I have been to Europe fairly often. It's my favourite foreign destination, as they say. I go to all the cathedrals and all the art museums. I have never been to a nightclub. People who like to know favourites will hear that my favourite cathedral is the white Romanesque marble one in Pisa, and my favourite art museum . . . well, I keep changing my mind. Lately it's been the Prado.

I have been to the Antipodes five or six times, and I have been to some art museums there, but I dont often go into churches in Australia or New Zealand. I went to the humble clay-like cathedral in Papeete once. I felt like Paul Gauguin.

My favourite city in the world is Trieste. When I was ready to write my novel *Burning Water* (1980) I had the excitement and luxury of choosing a place to write it. Having been through Trieste with Tony Bellette in 1966, I chose that old James Joyce Hapsburg spy city of white mountains, red roofs, and blue sea. Since then I have found a way to work Trieste into most of my other books and the autobiography of one of my pen names.

K EROUAC had to be a watermark for me. For some reason I have always been fond of books by writers whose names start with K. Often I am connected with them. When I was a new poet down out of the mountains and looking around for my kith and kin at University of British Columbia, the first guy I hooked up with was Lionel Kearns, who had come down out of the mountains just east of mine, i.e. the Kootenays. We learned and stole a lot from each

Montreal, 1969

other. My first book, *Sticks & Stones* (1964), is dedicated to Lionel Kearns.

Lionel introduced me to the writing of Jack Kerouac, who made my blood sing and my sentences zip. I gobbled his books up. I'm still playing tapes of Kerouac in my Volvo.

My second book, *The Man in Yellow Boots* (1965), was published bilingually in Mexico, the year in which Lionel Kearns stayed at our house on Calle Béisbol. It contains collages by Roy Kiyooka. It also contains, in both languages, a poem by Roy. I've long been glad of my association with Kiyooka, and I've written several essays about his painting, sculpture, and poetry.

I have never read a book by Franz Kafka. But I have quoted, translated, and plagiarized John Keats for years. Joy Kogawa and W. P. Kinsella were born the year I was born, though earlier, I always remind myself, in the year. I get along with both of them. But I am a little more likely to read Milan Kundera or Ivan Klima.

But I always say that the best writer in Canada is Robert Kroetsch. I suppose that I ought not to say the best this and my favourite that. But when I first read Kroetsch's fiction it was with that rare coupling of feelings—the prose was a delight to read, and its formal ideas spoke their importance confidently. You can get that double whammo from Italo Calvino, or William H. Gass.

Kroetsch has, for two decades, also written wonderful eccentric essays, reaching postmodern European discourse theory, and standing on western Canadian tricksterism. Usually the best novelists and essayists are busts when they dare to write poetry. But Kroetsch set his hand and wonky head to poetry and changed the world for some of Canada's best poets.

He also married a young Greek woman who was to become a major avant garde critic and more recently a fiction writer. Her name is, of course, Kamboureli.

LITERATURE got me when my guard was lowered by books. Since I was fourteen years old, or was it twelve?, I have been writing in scribblers the titles and authors and publishers of all the books I read, and keeping track of the number of books I have read by each author. I have read seventeen books by Fielding Dawson. I have read thirty-two books by Robert Creeley.

In the first scribbler the books are often by Max Brand and Robert Heinlein. In the second scribbler they are often by James M. Cain and James T. Farrell. You see how it was going. In the most recent scribbler they are by Nathalie Sarraute and Adolfo Bioy

Casares. First I read books, and as I got older I read literature.

I have often said that growing up with some loneliness and intelligence in a semi-desert village led to my being a writer. What can you do after reading a lot of books other than to write some? In Oliver there was really no painting, no sculpture, no ballet, no symphony. There was amateur drama, especially at school, so I acted in a lot of plays. There was *Life* magazine, and my pal Bill Lyttle and I had a darkroom under his basement stairs. And there was the bus depot candy store across from the movie theatre. It had baseball magazines and mass-market paperbacks.

I wanted, mainly, to be a baseball writer, so I wrote baseball for the weekly Oliver *Chronicle* and the daily Penticton *Herald*. I got paid ten cents a column inch. And I guess I wanted to write mass-market paperbacks. Years later I wrote a swashbuckling sea story called *Burning Water*, a western called *Caprice*, and an international spy novel called *Harry's Fragments*. But by then literature had got hold of me. *Burning Water* is a reflexive fiction about a novelist's voyages, *Caprice* is an anti-western, or what the postmodern critic Linda Hutcheon calls a "historiographic metafiction," and *Harry's Fragments* is a narrative translation of Heraclitus. I have also written an unpublished novel of teenage science fiction. Genre precedes literature, and is its victim.

My mother, Pearl, still lives in Oliver. She reads books to relax, to pass the afternoon, to get ready for sleep. I travel around a lot and all I bring home is literature.

MONTREAL, for writers of my generation, was mysterious, glamorous, foreign, big, old, and reputed to be terrific for jazz and vice and other nightlife. I was first there as a teenage air force recruit on weekend leave, and I got drunk because of Montreal's unpuritanical streets, and saluted the epauletted doorman in front of the Ritz Carlton Hotel.

For young Canadian writers Montreal had a reputation as the place where new poetry movements started, in French or English. For me the origins of Contact Press, for instance, had been in the 1940s and 1950s literary magazines and manifestos of Irving Layton and Louis Dudek and Torontonian Raymond Souster. The English-language poetry scene in Montreal 1940–1965 has left us a record of great squabbles and momentous inventions. I became aware of all that ferment when Lionel Kearns showed me the small press magazines and books he had brought home to UBC from his summer in Montreal. This must have been about 1959.

In 1967 Angela Bowering and I moved to Montreal. It was the year of Canada's centenary and Expo '67 in Montreal. The city was full of USAmericans and others. There were two apartments available on what the locals call the west side of Montreal. One was over a Greek cafe on Greene Avenue. The other was on Grosvenor, just off the main drag of Sherbrooke Street. We lived in that long narrow flat for nearly four years, the longest we had lived anywhere by a long shot.

Pretty Exciting. I was thirty-one years old and a writer-in-residence. I met all the Montreal poets, who stood around and talked about the old days when the young Marxists and the young aesthetes clashed. There was a new subway. The buildings were made of stone, long ago. I started to buy inexpensive velvet clothes. Friends from the rest of Canada and the U.S. slept all over our apartment. It was the big city. In a couple of years the Montreal Expos and the National League arrived. You could get to New York on the train. Really young poets came to see me and I told them about Jack Spicer and Frank O'Hara, and in some cases it stuck.

But I didnt write much about Montreal. One very short story got finished. A thin volume of poems occurred a few years later, nothing to write home about. It was while we lived in Montreal that I got into the habit of writing long poems instead of lyrics about my surroundings. I have been writing long poems longer and longer ever since.

NORTH is supposed to be an important concept for Canadians, maybe the way West was for USAmericans. North is supposed to be mystical, national, psychological. During the heyday of thematic criticism in the post-centenary 1970s we often heard of the Northern Experience, something we Canadians were supposed to share with Scandinavians, I think.

But I grew up in a desert valley, where the temperature often went over a hundred, back when we used impressive Fahrenheit degrees. I went on to live in Alberta and Manitoba, in Ontario and Quebec, but I never learned to have fun in the snow. Nowadays I live in the southwest corner of the country and make flying visits to snow country, to do a reading in Montreal, say, or Edmonton. I revel in the experience of a "Canadian winter" for a few days, pull my toque down off the shelf and over my moussed hair, knowing I'll be back out of the blizzard next week.

With daughter, Thea, 1971

The Australians have a similar myth. Where we have the north they have the outback, and its apotheosis, Ayre's Rock, is in the middle of the country, of that continent. But most Australians have never been to the outback; most of them travel by air from city to city on the coast. So it is in Canada, with our great myth. Most Canadians have never been to the north.

For one thing it is very expensive to get up north. It helps to be a civil servant or petrochemical expert, so someone else will pay your way. It helps to be a Canadian writer. As a Canadian writer I have been to Yukon twice, during the annual spring Book Festival. The first time I was there an outdoor-loving schoolteacher named Joyce Sward fed us some moose meat she had been keeping in the freezer. I thought nothing could be better. Then next time I was there she fed us some caribou. Maybe I'll never have caribou again, but I'm glad I had it once. It was just the best meat I've ever eaten.

One August I did a reading tour that started right at the top of continental Canada, in Inuvik, and wended southward to Fort Smith, Northwest Territories. I did not do what a lot of Canadian poets would do—I did not write poems about the journey. But I will say something about it now: I cannot give you words about the north. I just wish I could go back, in the winter.

OLSONITES, we jokingly called ourselves. Olsonite was the brand name for a toilet seat, but we were confident enough about where we stood. We

Bowering with writer Robert Kroetsch, Geelong, Victoria, Australia, 1986

were a crew of young poets around 1961, who created what Canadian literature professors would call the Tish Movement. As far as we could see, Charles Olson was the main USAmerican poet, as Pound and Williams had been before him.

Olson told us to dig exhaustively into our local concerns. We began to do so, and the geography, history, and economics of Vancouver became the grid of our poetry. In the late 1960s and the 1970s xenophobic critics and professors in Ontario accused us of selling out the "Canadian Tradition" to USAmerican interests. The latter would include Charles Olson and the anti-Vietnamese war machine. They started calling us Black Mountain poets. I dont know any Canadian poets who ever went to North Carolina. Once a typically poorly informed eastern professor asked me where in Vancouver Black Mountain might be. I was quizzical and tired, I said Black Mountain was just a few kilometers north of the city. To my surprise I found out years later that there is a ski hill called Black Mountain right there.

This is true: Charles Olson, Robert Duncan, Denise Levertov, and Robert Creeley were important

to us. They were the previous generation. We were amazed to learn that while these poets constituted USAmerican poetry as far as we were concerned, they were still being marginalized in the U.S. Some visiting professor would start talking about Anthony Hecht or John Berryman, and we would be amazed.

> but under these petals
> in the emptiness
> regard the light, contemplate
> the flower
>
> whence it arose

—said Olson. He told us, with that demonstrative, what Heraclitus told us around the same time, to attend our own particulars, and if you will listen, to attend sometimes with simple beautiful song. That is, speak those words aloud. When Pound said that form is the test of a poet's sincerity, he was, demonstrably, right.

Some of us went to Buffalo, say, to study with Olson. I studied with Creeley in Vancouver. We are older than they were in 1961, but they are the history of the New World for us.

PROSE or poetry, photography, plays? Probably more than any others, Canadian writers work in more than one category. The more restive, such as Daphne Marlatt and Michael Ondaatje, like to transgress the apparent boundaries between fiction and poetry, say, or autobiography and novel. Others such as Margaret Atwood and Robert Kroetsch keep parallel careers (poet, novelist) going.

First I wanted to be a sports reporter. I wanted to be a baseball writer for the St. Louis *Post-Dispatch*, like Bob Broeg. Reporters are reputed to keep their secret and unsuccessful novels in their desk drawers, along with the flask of whiskey. I've always been a closet sports journalist (and jazz writer). In Montreal I wrote sports for a short-lived community arts and politics magazine called *5¢ Review*. Back in Vancouver I covered the Kosmik League anti-baseball league for the *Georgia Straight*, in the 1970s, the most famous underground newspaper in Canada. The daily Vancouver *Province*'s sports editor was Eric Whitehead, so I wrote under the name Erich Blackhead. That's how we did things in those days, but I wrote my jazz reviews under my own name.

Once I got really lucky. The Canadian Broadcasting Corporation fitted me with a sound man, and we went to Santa Barbara to do a profile on Diane Jones, who was training to represent Canada in the pentathlon at the 1976 Olympics. This was in early spring. I got a sunburn along the part in my hair.

But you have to grow older in your trade, and you have to drop most of your occupations. I dropped sportswriting, photography, acting, jazz—criticism, playwriting, cartooning, songwriting, badminton, and beer.

Still, when people introduce me at a panel discussion or a reading they say poet, novelist, short-story writer, critic, and radio person. I like it that way. In the U.S. I would probably be thought a dilettante, but in Canada we cross boundaries often. People suspect us of being smugglers. Michael Ondaatje smuggled himself into his book "by" Billy the Kid, and he smuggled Billy the Kid into his book about Buddy Bolden in turn-of-the-century New Orleans.

bp Nichol said that I write essays like stories and stories like essays. I like that, too. Writing an essay, unless it is the kind of essay I used to find to my dismay in the *Kenyan Review*, can be as much fun as writing a story. Writing a poem is a duty.

QUICKNESS has always been my favourite quality. My father in heaven is probably thinking about how slow I was mixing concrete when we were building our house in Oliver. I dont like the quickness of our cat with the goldfinches, but I like the quickness of Clyde the Glide Drexler going around Vlady Divac for a lay-up in the fourth quarter.

It usually takes me seven years to get a novel written, but when I am sitting in some foreign town writing it I like to go quickly. Quick is not the same as fast. Lots of baseball players are fast but you have to be quick to become a great base stealer. I like the prose of Jerome Charyn because though he writes pretty long novels his sentences are quick. Quick means alive rather than monumental.

Some people's novels are fast food, and that is no more interesting than a McDonald's shake.

Even with my bad back, I go along sidewalks quick. I slip between slowpokes. They might be listening to some white boys' bam bam on their Walkmans. I'm skipping by. I'm trying to walk like Charlie Parker on "Happy Bird Blues."

My pulse is fast. My hands, people have always told me, are warm. I wanted to be a drummer but I gave it up. The snare brushes I bought in Winnipeg on a winter's day in 1956 are now hanging on the fireplace in my study. Jack Kerouac ran down the Matterhorn in California, like writing. In Oliver I liked to run down a fan of shale slide. You had to take another giant step before you knew where you were going to put your foot. I used to tell people that before I read William Carlos Williams that was the most important influence on my poetry.

Whenever I get into a radio station and on the air I start talking and thinking very quickly. My first book, *Points on the Grid*, didnt come out till I was twenty-eight, but the poems go quick—not very good but quick. I know I'm reading well when my voice is quick. When I'm reading someone else's book silently I am one of the slowest readers in bookland, but when I'm reading one of my books out loud I zip.

If I do a crossword—zip. If I give a lecture—zip. One night in a hotel room in Melbourne I spoke my confessional autobiography full of fiction, quick as a wink for four hours to a bunch of sleepy-heads—zip. But this piece you are reading? I've been on it for two weeks, a zip at a time.

READING is what I do with my life. This is an answer to the schoolboys who saw me always with a book and said why dont you live life instead of reading about it. What could I do? I somehow caught on how to read before I went to grade one in Greenwood. Parents told their kids that the war would end sometime and that the Allies would win it. I greeted that idea with mixed feelings. I thought that once the war was over there would be no more newspapers.

I read while I'm eating, of course. I actually did read under the covers with a flashlight on school nights. I read on the stationary bike at my gym; I wear industrial ear-protectors against the loud teenager music they play there. I read popular magazines while watching ball games on television. I read literary magazines between books. I'm a year behind on *Paideuma* and *Japan Quarterly*. I used to have a pile of books I had to read immediately. Then I had a big bookcase of them. When Thea got old enough I took over her playroom across from my study, and now I have a room full of books I must read immediately. I read slowly, so if I dont add any books to the room I should finish it around A.D. 2040. But over the past couple of decades I've averaged $11 a day on books. I used to read three newspapers a day, but now read only one or two, unless I'm travelling.

I'm always remembering how lovely and magical reading a novel used to be, and feel sorry for myself that the gleam has gone while I've grown more knowledgeable. But I think that if I'm lucky enough to be reading in A.D. 2010, I'll look back on the Thomas Hardy novel I've just read and remember fondly the excitement.

On the Toronto subway and in Air Canada 767s I notice a lot of people reading books. But it saddens me to see that almost all of them are reading thick bestsellers by some USAmerican whose name I vaguely recognize—Ken Follet, say. When I see someone reading a book of literature I want to hug her. I'd probably find out that she has to read it for a course she's taking. But one time Smaro Kamboureli paid me a great compliment: while flying to Venezuela to attend her brother's wedding, she read two books, my book of poems *Kerrisdale Elegies* (1984) and the latest translation of Jacques Derrida.

SCHOOL was always something I liked, and perversely, admitted to liking. Work, with very few exceptions, was not. Eventually I figured it out—that the reason I liked school was that it kept me away from work. When I left home at the age of seventeen to go to college in Victoria, it was with the comfort that it would keep me away from full-time work till spring. Spring used to depress me.

After I got my B.A. in history from University of British Columbia, where I had gone after three years

With my bibliographer Roy Miki, National Library of Canada, Ottawa, 1990

of work and goofing off in the air force, I faced a crisis. A B.A. in history did not prepare one for anything but work, or a graduate program in history. Things were going too fast. I was twenty-four years old. I registered as an "unclassified" student, neither grad nor undergrad, and took a heavy program of literature courses, Chaucer, Shakespeare, Eighteenth Century, Japanese literature, and the Twentieth Century. It was the neatest year I ever spent in school.

Then I had the opportunity to avoid a full-time job for another couple years, while pursuing an M.A. in English. A professor said that while doing so I should be a teaching assistant for two hundred dollars a month. I said no, I'd be too scared, I'd just be a marker. Teaching assistant, he said. So I taught and marked first-year English students. In my second year of grad school I also taught literature to third-year engineers and foresters, and got an additional hundred dollars a month.

While doing this I also wrote a 550-page novel and hundreds of poems, acted in a few plays, helped edit *Tish,* wrote book reviews, put stickers on windshields in a parking lot, wrote a weekly column for the *Ubyssey,* UBC's campus paper, wrote another weekly column for the Oliver *Chronicle,* and worked on my papers and thesis. I was in school because I didnt want to have to find and keep a full-time job.

But then I graduated, and before I could figure out what they were doing to me, I had a full-time job teaching at University of Alberta in Calgary, for $5200 a year. A hundred times my unlucky number. Angela and I had a furnished apartment with the lawn at eye level, and I became the superintendent to cut down on the rent payments. I shovelled a lot of snow.

Now, when I cant wangle a grant, I teach at Simon Fraser University. Teaching is not as good as writing, but it is better than working.

T HEA Bowering is a name that has begun to show up in local student-driven literary magazines. Of course the author writes both poems and stories.

When Angela Luoma and I got married we were both students, and very soon I was a teacher. We made a deal that we would not have an offspring for the first five years of our marriage. This way we were able to go to Mexico in the summer, after I taught at summer school for some more money. We drove the ten-year-old Chevrolet I bought from my father, and then next year we flew down in a DC8. We spent a lot of wonderful time with our dear friends Margaret Randall and Sergio Mondragón, who kept having

children and editing *El corno emplumado.* My second book, *The Man in Yellow Boots,* was published in Mexico.

When the five years were up we had just moved to Montreal. I said what about having an offspring, and Angela said not this year. A year or two later she said what about a little Bowering, so we did but we didnt have an offspring that year.

During our last year in Montreal we went to New York City after Christmas, and came home on New Year's Eve. We were supposed to go to a big party across Grosvenor Avenue, but after New York City we said let's just go to bed instead. We bowered, and Thea Bowering was conceived either at the end of 1970 or the beginning of 1971.

I grew impatient with the industrial residue we found on our many windowsills every morning, so we shook the dust of Montreal. Angela and uterine Thea flew to the west coast in a B747, and I drove our six-year-old Chevrolet and two Chihuahuas across the country, and we took up residence in the commune on York Avenue in Vancouver.

I began writing instead of teaching, and every week we drove across Burrard Inlet to our birth classes. Eventually we got together with Dr. Herstein and Nurse Davidson and a lot of other people in the delivery room at Vancouver General, and had Thea Bowering. It was, as people such as we usually say, the best night of our lives. When that head and then the rest emerged the way they were foretold in the birth classes, I uttered those characteristic early-seventies words, "Oh, wow!"

I just now heard Thea Bowering leaving the house with her lifelong best friend. They are on their way to go apartment-hunting.

U MBRELLAS are not for men and boys to carry, I thought, so for my first two years in Vancouver I walked around city and campus in my old air force trench coat, my hair plastered to my skull. In semi-desert Oliver it rained about seven times a year, usually just in time to split the ripe cherries on the trees, for instance. If it started raining chances were that the sun was still out in part of the sky, and in half an hour you could go out on your bicycle or picking ladder again. When I came to the coast and it started to rain I would step into a downtown doorway to wait it out. I could have starved to death.

I saw male students holding big black umbrellas over them, but big city ways are the slope to dissipation, I reasoned. In Oliver I had never seen a man carry an umbrella. I had never seen a man push a shopping cart, either.

*"My ball team, the Granville Book Company Paperbacks; I'm instructing writer
and catcher Brian Fawcett," Woodlands Park, Vancouver, 1990*

After a couple of years of plastered hair I acquired an umbrella and an ability to be patronizing toward small semi-desert towns. Here is the way you acquired an umbrella: you went to the university lost and found; you maintained that you had misplaced an umbrella; when asked to describe it you mentioned that it was black with a brown wooden handle. Yes, that's the one, you said.

But I still hate the rain. I live where it rains forty or fifty centimeters a year, and I still take the rain, especially on a day when I am scheduled to play ball, as a personal affront. Once on a rainy day I enquired of my ten-year-old daughter: dont you just detest the rain? She replied: no, of course not, it's just the weather.

I do not carry an umbrella anymore. I have a rain hat and a semi-waterproof jacket. I am two men in one—I am the urbane man of letters who has read Roland Barthes profitably, and who is familiar with this city, perhaps with an earlier version of it. But inside that guy is the Oliver boy, a somehow more pure human being who was thrust up by a terrain that God had in mind—greasewood, sagebrush, pondero-

sa, cactus, sandy cutbank, quick diamondback in the garden.

I never used the word "garden" to refer to flowers until I had lived in Vancouver for at least a decade. Back home a garden is back of your house (sometimes in front, too) where the tomato leaves are prickly and fuzzy in the sun.

VANCOUVER is my home, though, and while it often crosses my mind to start living somewhere else, Toronto or Adelaide, for instance, there isnt really anywhere else that would be as good as this place. When I am in Arizona or New Mexico I have an odd feeling that that's where I was meant to spend my life. It must be the climate speaking to my subconscious, if I have one. But though I like to walk around in a T-shirt in Tucson, I do not like guns and jet fighter planes and atom bombs.

Visitors and the local public relations people often remark on Vancouver's natural beauty. But the longer people have lived here, the less natural beauty there is. Real estate monsters litter subdivisions higher up the mountains, and where the trees used to be, the rain-beaten earth slides downhill. In 1960 my girlfriend and I ran a boat to Passage Island and found the beach covered with condoms. I wondered how many sexually agitated people could have made it to that generally empty spot. She instructed me regarding toilets and sewers and ocean tides.

But if you like the margins of culture, while not desiring to flee it altogether, Vancouver is a good place to write. The novelists who most often make the covers of magazines, Margaret Atwood, Robertson Davies, Timothy Findley, Michael Ondaatje and Alice Munro, live in Toronto or a quick ride from that city. The most highly touted up-and-comers have arrived in Toronto from other places in the British Commonwealth of Nations.

Toronto is the centre of the country, and while it is no Paris, people who write with eyes for a career head there from the provinces. Vancouver tends to be a place for losers or people who cannot fit in or artists who want to protect their marginality. If you want a career in the magazines you have to put up with snow and hard winter wind off Lake Ontario, and sickening humidity in the summer.

Torontonians envy and pity Vancouverites, for their easier life and underdeveloped ambition. They say my, what a gorgeous little baseball stadium, and phew, how can you understand the poetry in that magazine?

So I continue to live in Vancouver, a kind of exile ameliorated by Air Canada and the Canadian Broadcasting Corporation. When I lived back east I got phoned a lot for "assignments." Here I find the time to write, and play ball in February.

WRITING is interesting. I mean the act, I guess it is, of writing. The fun we call the work, ever since André Gide called it that. Part of it is deciding how to write the novel or the serial poem, or say this alphabiography. This is being written by pen (Pilot Precise V5) double spaced in a series of university examination booklets with the covers torn off. I dont think that makes it academic writing, does it?

My father had a beaten old black portable typewriter with round keys, so I wrote my Oliver *Chronicle* baseball and basketball reports on that, typing with my middle fingers because my father did it that way, his right forefinger having been lost to a timber saw before I knew him.

A lot of corny movies about novelists, and the poetics learned from Charles Olson, persuaded one to compose on the typewriter, even poems, except those you wrote on the inside back covers of paperbacks at the Varsity Cafe. But in 1970 in an Irish section of London, England, I began to write a book that would

be called *Autobiology* (1972), and for a decade I wrote just about everything by hand, to slow me down. I just had to choose the paper to write on, sometimes a nifty sketchbook a friend brought back from Japan, or school scribblers (a lot of writers use those, I have found out), depending on the size of the "work."

For the novel *Burning Water* I went to Chinatown and bought a number of thick hardcover notebooks made in the People's Republic and called "Sailing Ship." Robin Blaser had showed me one at his house. They were perfect, because ten pages held a thousand words, a Trieste day's writing about George Vancouver's sailing ships. I decided to stay home and write my next two novels, the second of which was *Caprice*, directly into the word processor, my first computer, an Apple II expanded to 64K. People always asked whether it made a difference to the novel.

And so on. For a few years I was writing journalism and radio stuff on the computers, letters on my IBM Selectric typewriter, and poetry and essays by hand. Now while I am writing this piece by hand, I am also collaborating with Angela in a sequence of meditations on pictures. I am writing directly into my Macintosh Classic, and she is writing by hand on a pad of foolscap. We are also collaborating with Mike Matthews and David Bromige on a nostalgic novel. That is being done with a Mac Classic, an IBM PC, a NEC, a Mac SE, and three copying machines. Now that's fun.

XEROGRAPHY arrived during my writing lifetime, thank goodness. It made it possible for us to compose collaborative novels through the mail, of course. Marginalized poets could make local magazines if they knew someone who worked in an office with lax security. Writers who wanted to create text with a visual organization or disorganization could design manuscripts to challenge any publisher. But then unscrupulous schoolteachers could pirate our poems for the classes in contemporary relevancy.

We all know luddite writers who refuse even to teach themselves to type, who lock themselves into garrets and fashion sonnets or family chronicles with ostrich-plume pens by candlelight. But others among us cheer for every new magic machine that comes along to make text production less a drudge. I am known to be too shy to buy a new shirt, but I like buying gizmos when I get big enough chunks of sudden money. I've bought six personal computers and we still have five of them in the house (or in the car).

My old *Tish* friends Frank Davey, Fred Wah, and Lionel Kearns got their first computers as soon as such things became available, and I followed shortly. In the early 1980s they began a lovely experiment, something called *Swift Current*. Continuing our interest in innovative magazine creation, it was an electronic literary forum, a magazine fed by writers with modems. Subscribers could pick and choose from the menu, invent their own table of contents. Readers could print out their favourite material. It was a very democratic way of assembling a journal—especially if you were well off enough to get access to a modem. There were not many single mothers among the contributors.

Still, it was quite different from a glossy quarterly offering learned articles and new poems received at the editor's address a year or two earlier, written a year before that. In *Swift Current* you could read the review of a book before the book was between covers.

Xerography is probably the widest purveyor of literature, though. It can save time and effort and occluded texts. This week Angela used my home copier to capture Sheila Watson's 555-page 1965 dissertation on Wyndham Lewis. That dissertation is usually buried in the University of Toronto library. It

is longer than all Watson's fiction books put together, and nearly as heavy as the author herself. But she will never be duplicated.

YOUTH, just as they have always told us, does slip away. Writers, though, can keep on writing about their youth, even as their bodies fall apart around them. They can feed off it. While other people regret, they can exploit. What a peculiar Cartesian experience—look at Jack Kerouac, getting fat and big-nose and boozy while he wrote about Ti-Jean running beautiful down another track or football field. Samuel Beckett was notoriously bedeviled by Descartes. So all his "characters" are decrepit men and women, old as a soothsayer in a jug, even while Beckett was hopping down a Paris street.

Still, though it can be their bread and butter, writers I know miss their youth more than regular people do. I think it may be that being a mature author with a back-cover photograph proving one's august immovability from the literary scene has not proven to be as enjoyable as being a very little-known

George Bowering, 1990

poet or fiction writer with the ignited hope of dazzling people.

I cannot remember when journalists and editors stopped referring to me as one of my country's most promising new writers, and then one of my country's most accomplished young writers. I do recall that such nonsense went on longer than I thought it should. Now they always introduce me as a person who has won two Governor-General's awards, written an enormous number of books, and become some kind of illustrious gent. The part of me that is interested in my youth hates to hear that.

When I was fifteen, working in the orchard near Naramata, I stepped backward off my ladder with seventy pounds of apples in the picking bag strapped to my chest. I had forgotten that this part of the orchard was sloped toward the clay cliff overlooking Lake Okanagan. I stepped back farther than I expected to and cracked a lumbar vertebra. I had a sore back when I stood at attention in the air force honour guard, and now I have a sore back because I play second base. For forty years I have had a sore back every minute. Sometimes it gets worse, even ambulance worse. Sometimes it makes me walk like those old guys we have all seen walking past the bus station.

It's a legacy from my youth.

It goes away for a while when I am fast asleep. I have always refused to sleep in the daytime, because I hate to have hours of my life happen when I dont know about it.

But everyone has to sleep sometime. . . .

Z z z z z z

BIBLIOGRAPHY

Poetry; book-length poems:

Sitting in Mexico, Beaver Kosmos, 1965.

Baseball: A Poem in the Magic Number 9, Coach House Press, 1967.

George, Vancouver: A Discovery Poem, Weed/Flower Press (Toronto), 1970.

Genève, Coach House Press, 1971.

Autobiology, New Star Books, 1972.

Curious, Coach House Press, 1973.

At War with the U.S., Talonbooks, 1974.

Allophanes, Coach House Press, 1976.

Ear Reach, Alcuin Society, 1982.

Kerrisdale Elegies, Coach House Press, 1984.

Poetry chapbooks:

Two Police Poems, Talonbooks, 1969.

The Sensible, Massasauga Editions (Toronto), 1972.

Layers 1–13, Weed/Flower Press, 1973.

In Answer, William Hoffer, 1977.

Uncle Louis, Coach House Press, 1980.

Quarters, Gorse Press, 1991.

Do Sink, Pomflit, 1992.

Poetry collections:

Sticks & Stones, Tishbooks, 1964.

Points on the Grid, Contact Press, 1964.

The Man in Yellow Boots/El hombre de las botas amarillas, translations to Spanish by Sergio Mondragon, Ediciones El Corno Emplumado (Mexico), 1965.

The Silver Wire, Quarry Press, 1966.

Rocky Mountain Foot: A Lyric, a Memoir, McClelland & Stewart, 1969.

The Gangs of Kosmos, House of Anansi, 1969.

Touch: Selected Poems 1960–1969, McClelland & Stewart, 1971.

In the Flesh, McClelland & Stewart, 1974.

The Catch, McClelland & Stewart, 1976.

Poem & Other Baseballs, Black Moss, 1976.

The Concrete Island: Montreal Poems 1967–1971, Vehicule, 1977.

Another Mouth, McClelland & Stewart, 1979.

Particular Accidents: Selected Poems, edited by Robin Blaser, Talonbooks, 1981.

West Window: The Selected Poetry of George Bowering, General Publishing, 1982.

Smoking Mirror, Longspoon, 1982.

Seventy-One Poems for People, RCD Press, 1985.

Delayed Mercy and Other Poems, Coach House Press, 1986.

Urban Snow, Talonbooks, 1992.

Fiction:

Mirror on the Floor, McClelland & Stewart, 1967.

A Short Sad Book, Talonbooks, 1977.

Burning Water, General Publishing, 1980.

En eaux troubles, Editions Quinze, 1982.

Spencer and Groulx from the Forthcoming Novel Caprice, William Hoffer, 1985.

Caprice, Viking/Penguin, 1987.

Harry's Fragments, Coach House Press, 1990.

Short-story collections:

Flycatcher and Other Stories, Oberon Press, 1974.

Concentric Circles, Black Moss, 1977.

Protective Footwear, McClelland & Stewart, 1978.

A Place to Die, Oberon Press, 1983.

Criticism:

How I Hear "Howl," (chapbook), Beaver Kosmos, 1967.

Al Purdy (monograph), Copp Clarke, 1970.

Three Vancouver Writers, Coach House Press, 1979.

A Way with Words, Oberon Press, 1982.

The Mask in Place: Essays on Fiction in North America, Turnstone, 1983.

Craft Slices, Oberon Press, 1985.

Errata, RDC Press, 1988.

Imaginary Hand, NeWest Press, 1988.

Editor:

The 1962 Poems of R. S. Lane, Ganglia Press, 1965.

Vibrations: Poems of Youth, Gage, 1970.

The Story So Far, Coach House Press, 1972.

Artie Gold, *Cityflowers,* Delta Canada, 1974.

Imago Twenty, Talonbooks, 1974.

Red Lane, *Letters from Geeksville: Red Lane to George Bowering, 1960–64,* Caledonia Writing Series, 1976.

Great Canadian Sports Stories, Oberon Press, 1979.

Fiction of Contemporary Canada, Coach House Press, 1980.

Fred Wah, *Loki Is Buried at Smoky Creek: Selected Poems,* Talonbooks, 1981.

David McFadden, *My Body Was Eaten by Dogs: Selected Poems,* McClelland & Stewart, 1981.

The Contemporary Canadian Poem Anthology, Coach House Press, 1983.

Sheila Watson and the Double Hook: The Artist and Her Critics, Golden Dog Press, 1984.

Taking the Field: The Best of Baseball Fiction, RDC Press, 1990.

Author, with Robert Hogg, of *Robert Duncan: An Interview,* Coach House Press, 1971. Author of play "A Home for Heroes," which appeared in *Prism International,* University of British Columbia literary journal, 1962, and a television play "What Does Eddie Williams Want?," CBC-TV (Montreal), 1966. Also author of radio plays "George Vancouver," 1972; "Sitting in Mexico," 1973; "Music in the Park," 1986; "The Great Grandchildren of Bill Bissett's Mice," 1989.

Contributor to numerous anthologies, including *How Do I Love Thee: Sixty Poets of Canada (and Quebec) Select and Introduce Their Favorite Poems from Their Work,* edited by John Robert Colombo, M. G. Hurtig (Edmonton), 1970; *Ten Canadian Short Plays,* edited by John Stevens, Dell, 1975; *Introduction to Poetry: Canadian, British, American,* edited by Jack David and Robert Lecker, Holt (Toronto), 1981. Contributor of poems, articles, and reviews to numerous magazines, including *Atlantic Monthly, Canadian Literature, Poetry, Poetry Australia,* and *Walt Whitman Review.* Editor of *Tish,* 1961–63; *Imago,* 1964–74; Beaver Kosmos Folios, 1966–75.

Nicole Brossard

1943-

(Translated from the French by Susanne de Lotbinière-Harwood)

I have just finished writing this short autobiography and now I feel like starting all over again, in the present tense this time, because the present is the only time space where I have the impression of existing, of enjoying myself, of using all my faculties. What has been lived is lived. Sooner or later, whatever past lives on in me will, probably in spite of myself, find its way into the coming books, novels, or poems, will astonish me, amaze me, will dawn on the horizon of thinking like a discovery. It will propel me toward further enigmas to unravel, to unfold, it will come forth like a story to invent, it will stretch itself out inside me like a dreamed memory, it will lead me toward other norths, a thousand souths, it will come back to the present to seduce me in the suggestive guise of the word fiction. Whatever of the past still lives in me will resemble Montréal and Montréal will change once more in midsentence. What lives on will come back to inscribe its yes, a proud yes amid energy and anguish, at the heart of that which never changes inside of us for, as we know, the body never forgets that other very ancient body which obliges us to sign our very brief story in history.

There is in me a *too much to touch life as it should be approached when time comes to talk about myself.*[1] My resistance to anecdote has always been strong. For this reason I have always kept my distance from autobiographical writing, as if this raw matter of life called lived experience has no relevance until it has been transformed by creative energy, by the questions and the imaginary landscape it generates. I am a woman of the present, one who forgets the details as she goes along, retaining only the essential of my relations to others. Certainly the ties we weave with the world and with people are made of details, facts, and small gestures, but their importance stems essentially from the values and the intentions guiding us, from the imaginary space in which we insert them.

Writing an autobiography, no matter how short, is interesting to me only insofar as I can attest to the

"Reading within the reader," East Berlin, 1990

enigmatic process by which I become what I write. I am not unaware that, by definition, an autobiography offers a wealth of information which, as they say, sheds light on the work. I play this game of anecdote for myself first of all, a woman of the present, attracted by the *spectacle* of the child, of the teenager, and of the young woman I was in the Québec of the Quiet Revolution, in the geographical space of my Montréal urban reality.

I am not unaware also that my Québec literary and cultural references can be shared only if I describe lovingly, explain passionately, name precisely.

---

[1] In English in the original—SLH.

39

When daily childhood is nice and normal, memories are few. Some sensations, for example, the smell of earth when playing with little red cars under the balcony and filling your mouth with loud zooms and sudden braking sounds. The first scratched knees, a salty taste under the tongue when you cry. The delicate fabric of Sunday dresses, the patent leather of new shoes purchased for Easter, my mother's red coat. The mysterious sounds coming from the living room on the evening of December 24 when your imagination is all full of Santa Claus. The smell of fish on Fridays, of church incense, the heaviness of wet clothing on winter days. The first snake spotted in a field of buttercups and daisies.

*

I was born in Montréal, in an ultra-Catholic Québec, where social, cultural, and political life was largely controlled by the Roman Catholic church. No book could be published without the *imprimatur* of the archdiocese; from the pulpit, parish priests, who claimed not to be involved in politics, peremptorily asserted that hell was red like the Liberal Party and heaven blue like the "Union nationale" party. Social life was structured around the religious calendar. Pleasure led directly to hell.

Contrary to the practice popular at the time which incited people to marry very young, my parents got married at the age of thirty, on December 1, 1942, after dating for two years. All their photographs from that time were taken outdoors: in Montréal, in front of the Mary-Queen-of-the-World Cathedral where they were wed, in Québec City where they honeymooned, in front of Château Frontenac or in front of "la Porte St-Jean." Despite the warmth of their smiles, the violence of the cold is felt in small clues, like the way the shoulders are slightly hunched, the peculiar manner in which my mother is holding her bouquet. I was born on November 27, 1943, a few days before their first wedding anniversary. A difficult birth where I introduced myself into this world irreverently, that is, ass first. My mother has always taken this as a sign from

"My parents' marriage: Uncle Judge is left of my father, my paternal grandmother, Alice Delorimier-Gratham, is behind, and to the right of my mother, my mother's father," 1942

"My grandmothers Alice Delorimier-Gratham and Martha Chevrier-Matte," 1944

the gods, as a possible explanation for my rebellious, daredevil, mischievous character, and I confess that the hypothesis quite pleases me. Two years later my sister, Francine, was born quietly, earning her the reputation of a mild and easy child.

Of my early years, spent on rue Garnier in the northeast of Montréal, I have only a few memories: the daily walk from our home to my maternal grandmother's who lived on rue De Normanville; an attempt at fraud where I tried to pass off the sailor's cameo, which for generations has adorned all Player's cigarette packs, as a new stamp; a joyful masquerade where I showed up at home wearing enormous red wax lips purchased with money earned through the illegal sale of my fake stamps. False lips and fake stamps. A joker, this little girl already not such a little girl!

Obviously, I, like everyone, have a primary scene to recount. I must have been four. It was a lovely summer Sunday. I was quietly hanging about in front of our house, wearing a pretty dress on which I had pinned a sheriff's badge like those found in Cracker Jack boxes. A gang of kids was playing close by. I don't remember if I join them or if it is they who invite me to share in their games, but here I am among them. A simple game is proposed in which you have to jump over a little rope held taut by two boys. I am the first one to pass the test, apparently very easy. Too easy. Without warning, they lift the rope. I stumble, trip, and finally fall flat on the ground. On my knees, a bit of earth mixed with blood. The dress is intact. I don't cry but I run back home. There,

horror of horrors, I realize I have lost my badge. This is the only event I can remember from my childhood. It was my first encounter with deceit, meanness, stupidity. I came out of it furious and humiliated, having been deposed from the rank of sheriff to gullible and unwary little girl.

Then I entered St-Arsène school. A single memory: the ugliness of the boots I have to wear, the stiffness of the white plastic collar adorning, and the word is an overstatement, the compulsory black dress. Dozens of little girls all dressed in black. Nuns whose tone of voice rises as soon as we raise our voices, who threaten our lovely little hands with their clackers. Then one day, major sanction, here I am, imprisoned inside a locker for ten minutes. I can hear my classmates' chatter, the scraping of their boots on the floor. I don't know if I am really afraid. The noises comfort me. At the foot of the locker, a ray of light coming through gives me hope. This was in 1948, and today it amuses me to think that in those years of great darkness, known as Québec's *grande noirceur*, my ray may have connected with the one emitted by a group of artists who, gathered around painter Paul-Emile Borduas, published the manifesto entitled *Refus global* (Total Refusal): "The bounds of our dreams were changed forever (. . .) Make way for magic! Make way for objective mysteries! Make way for love! Make way for internal drives!" said the ray.[2]

When I turned seven my maternal grandmother bought a house and came to live with us, that is to say in her home. So we moved to the other side of town, to Earnscliffe Street, in the Anglophone district called Snowdon, in Montréal's westend. My mother took this as a sign of upward mobility. She liked to repeat that the English were nice people and that, being more educated than French-Canadians, they also had better manners. This surprised me, mystified me a little. Later on, she came back to the subject by insinuating that an English-speaking husband would make a much better match. This must have had a certain impact, for my sister later lived in England for seven years and my first boyfriend's name was Barker. My mother also never missed an opportunity to warn my sister and me against all those who spoke like "common people," meaning those who spoke that bad French those of my generation later called *joual*, and whose usage they politicized. The "common people" were represented by the garbagemen, the grocery store delivery boy, and the street-sweep-

[2]*Refus global/Total Refusal*, the complete 1948 manifesto of the Montréal automatists. Translation and introduction by Ray Ellenwood, Toronto: Exile Editions, 1985.

ers. The milkman and the mailman seemed to belong to a different class and found favour in my mother's eyes. Of course, proper people were the lawyer and his wife who lived across the street, a rich widow and her unwed daughter, our neighbours to the left whose son was a popular composer, and, obviously, our own family which had a judge, lawyers, and Jesuits. I don't know why but all these comments seemed to me profoundly unfair and, most of all, useless. The name of a street often came up, St-Lawrence Street, which my father often referred to as *la Main*. If you believed my mother, beyond St-Lawrence Street everything was murder, orgies, and women of ill repute. From now on, it was understood that my sister and I would be westend girls and that our territory would be defined by Morgan's huge department store located opposite Phillip's Square. And so the image of a city split into two cultures slowly took shape inside me. Over the years my mother's warnings against the east once and for all transformed that part of town into a vast wasteland of vague fantasies which, in time, found their echo in the characters of *Chiens perdus sans collier, Rebel without a Cause,* and *West Side Story.* James Dean became my hero, not in the silly way that girls get a crush on actors but, very simply, because somewhere inside me, I was James Dean.

Today I know full well the origin of my attachment to country-and-western music, to rock'n'roll, this fascination for black leather jackets, waitresses, and cheap bars. I also know that this imaginary space infused part of the atmosphere in my novels *French Kiss* and especially *Mauve Desert,* where melancholy and the "lust for life" work together as a duo, like an echo.

As soon as we arrived in the Snowdon area my mother registered me at St-Antonin school which, like all schools at that time, was run by nuns. I don't know why but once again my mother was thrilled that my sister and I were involved with les Dames de la Congrégation Notre-Dame, as if the word "dames" was going to ennoble us. I liked school and did well. My parents were not fanatic Catholics. They practiced their religion without extreme piety, without prudery, socially, as it were. I even suspected my father of being an atheist ever since I had caught sight of him sitting in a restaurant when, in principle, he was supposed to be attending mass. Of course I remember on a few occasions, and then only to please my grandmother, having to kneel on the kitchen linoleum floor to recite the rosary with "Le chapelet en famille," a radio program which was then broadcast live from the cathedral, featuring as its hero Cardinal Paul-Emile Léger, whose voice vibrated, droned, and rolled and droned on some more for a quarter of an hour in 99 percent of Montréal homes. So it was in school that I really learned about religious rites and was instructed about the variety of lapses and sins that even a young person such as myself was in danger of committing. Crucifixes, holy images, rosary beads; incense, organs, chalices, and ciboriums; another sermon, Lent, at last the month of Mary, May, lilacs, I experienced all of that, the host melting on the tongue, a little gluey, the dead flies in the holy water fonts, the darkness of the confessional where you had to tell all. At the age of ten I started asking questions during catechism class. I knew that something was weird in their system. If God was Almighty he could stop evil, suffering, and wars. He had no excuse, none, for not doing it. If the Pope had vowed poverty, why did we have to send him money? In short, where I sought logic and coherence in what I was being taught, I met with lies, hypocrisy, and injustice. Every contradiction heightened my sense of revolt and indignation. My inner desire for spirituality was offset by a feeling of danger about entrusting the salvation of my soul to all those old men: the Pope, the bishops, cardinals, parish priests, and vicars. Today when I happen to attend a baptism, a wedding, or a funeral, I concentrate on the architecture of the church, the smell of the flowers, and the music so as not to hear the officiating priest's sermon.

The nuns wore long black dresses which, when they kneeled down and stood up during chapel, produced a concert of soft swishing and rustling sounds that blended with the whispering and buzzing of praying mouths. Apart from the face, hands, and a few wisps of hair visible above their foreheads, their whole body was a mystery. While it had never occurred to me to imagine the sexual features of my mother's body, the nuns' bodies intrigued me. Some of them had an ample chest but we hesitated to conclude that this had anything to do with breasts. In sixth grade I fell madly in love with Soeur Sainte-Martha-Marie. I spent a good part of my time imagining her in a sundress, fantasizing about her beautiful black hair, and especially trying to guess what her life might have been before she entered convent. Had she known love? Might she be moved by the love I vowed her? Would she allow me to kiss her forehead? Such were my thoughts when during the month of May, the month of Mary, I chose the way of church instead of the street, so that I might for a moment meet her gaze. Chance moves in strange ways. On the last day of school, marking the end of elementary school for me, we had to return to our classrooms to wash out our desks and collect our personal belongings. That day we were allowed to listen to *La vie en rose* sung by the beautiful, passionate voice of Edith Piaf or the ever-so-sensual Silvana Mangano doing the theme song from the film *Bitter Rice*. After dusting, soaping, and wiping my desk, all the while swaying my hips left and right to the beat of the music, I went down to the toilet to wash my hands. Ghislaine B., a classmate who seemed a little more worldly than we were, was standing silently in the door frame. We exchanged a few words about our summer vacation plans and then without warning she took me in her arms, kissed me impetuously on the mouth, parting my lips with her tongue. Then she took off without a word. I have no idea how long that kiss lasted but subjectively speaking, it must have been everything and more than Hollywood had ever produced. Every time the memory of that kiss came back to me, my belly would catch fire in a way that made me quite ecstatic. The effect lasted very intense for over a week. Then it was summer. One beautiful July evening, at that hour of the day when all is calm without being voluptuous, as I sat with Jasmine Lamontagne on a bench in MacDonald Park, I tenderly put my lips on her lips. Jasmine seemed to enjoy it because when I opened my eyes, hers were still closed. Unfortunately, a few moments later, she nonetheless concluded that we had just committed a sin, probably a mortal one.

My father was a kind man, amiable and very gentle. He worked as an accountant for a collection agency. He worked in English. I felt him respectful of his bosses but he did not hesitate to speak up in favor of the French-Canadians who worked with him. He loved American movies of the thirties, stars, Hollywood, New York, downtown restaurants, horse races, and the fiery discussions after which you make up with an affectionate hug. I inherited his love of restaurants, of New York and feverish urban life, of fair argumenting.

There was my father but also the Brossard family, which we seldom saw but which played an important part in the idea I was to develop about my name. By listening to conversations between my mother and father, I came to understand that I would one day have to prove myself worthy of this name worn by a line of lawyers and judges. My father was the sixth in a family of eight whose eldest was a Superior Court judge. About this judge, his exploits (Rhodes scholar, Cambridge student, great sportsman), and his qualities, I heard enough so that the words personal discipline, honesty, integrity, as well as the Latin proverb *mens sana in corpore sano* slowly settled in my mind as an ideal.

The ban put on the east, its dangers and vulgarity, and the family example held up to me in time transformed themselves into a spirit of rebellion and transgression which, combined with an ideal of justice and intellectual probity, charted in me the traits of an identity which I would later sum up in the expressions "urban women radicals," *"fille en combat dans la cité."* But much earlier, I would probably have translated this double image as: James Dean versus the honest man of the Enlightenment. No female filiation whatsoever. No feminine face in the shaping of my identity. Yes, perhaps my paternal grandmother, Alice Delorimier-Gratham, when I learned that she had participated in the suffrage movement and that her name made me a descendant of the Chevalier De Lorimier who, following the Patriots' uprising of 1837, was hanged in 1838.

About the Brossard family I remember also the holidays, when the entire family gathered for Christmas and New Year's. While the children played downstairs, I often went up to the living room to listen to the adults talking. It was there I first heard the name of Maurice Duplessis, who was prime minister of the province for twenty years. Very quickly I concluded that this man was a treacherous and uneducated rogue. Though I knew nothing about political life, I learned very early on to hate this man and the narrow-mindedness he represented. I

"About 1947, already trying to move the earth"

"Me, my mother, and my sister," about 1953

promised myself never to vote for the "Union nationale" party he headed. One autumn evening in 1959, as the television news announced his death, I leapt up screaming with joy, exactly as I did when the Montréal Canadians scored a goal. I was undoubtedly not the only one to experience this feeling of liberation, for the departure of this man heralded the great changes of the Quiet Revolution.

From 1956 to 1960 I studied at Collège Marguerite-Bourgeois, located in Westmount, enclave of the English-speaking bourgeoisie. It was a large beautiful building surrounded by greenery behind which was an orchard where, in the spring, our young senses found a space for confiding and daydreaming. Inside, everything was spacious: the gymnasium, the amphitheatre, the cafeteria, the chapel. It was without a doubt a privileged place for young girls from good families. There I learned Latin, developed a passion for history and literature, and became interested in mathematics. My first year went by normally between studies, basketball, and hours spent in conversation with my best friend. Most of the girls around me were interested in boys. I don't know why

but there seemed to be an equation between the fact of having rich parents and the capacity for necking. I found the girls of my age a little vapid and was mostly interested in the older upper-grade girls. In the summertime I would spend two weeks at the Girl Guides' camp on Lac L'Achigan and then join my family at a nearby inn for the rest of the season. The days were paced by swimming, Ping-Pong games, reading detective stories about agent "IXE–13." The evening walk was followed by a stop at the snack bar where I played pinball like a maniac.

In 1958, o enigma, I don't know what happened but I was overcome by a profound and immeasurable melancholy. To this day I still don't know what caused this sadness which I would nonetheless qualify as existential. All the great questions about life and about death suddenly seemed to converge in my teenaged body. Was it the year I saw *Nuit et brouillard* (*Night and Fog*), the Alain Resnais film in which we are shown the huge mass graves discovered by the Allies upon their arrival at Auschwitz and Dachau? One thing is certain: when, in the comfortable middle-class living room of our home, I saw those heaps of corpses, of bones, of hair, and jaws, on that day, I became a philosopher. How could human beings, presumably endowed with a soul, have tortured, murdered, debased other human beings? The day I saw those columns of skeletal women, men, and children who could only still testify to their humanity through their eyes, I knew that never again would humanity be the same in my mind. Evil and violence existed. In becoming aware of this I felt despoiled, not of my innocence, but of that part of oneself which, no matter how tragic the human condition, seeks to exonerate the species for its animal ferocity. The species was beastly and I aspired to being an angel. Today I believe I understand the origins of the first lines of *Mauve Desert*: "Very young, I was already crying over humanity. With every new year I could see it dissolving in hope and in violence."

In the fall of 1959 I met Maurice B. He was a student at the Collège de Montréal. He was two years my elder. Friendly, good-looking, athletic, and romantic, he often alluded to his Irish origins on his father's side. I knew little about the Irish but was soon convinced they constituted a courageous people who loved life. Maurice also spoke to me about Lamartine, Châteaubriand, and Victor Hugo. He explained to me in detail the rules to observe if I should someday, following my heart's desire, wish to write a sonnet. He entertained me by reciting *Le Lac* by Lamartine and, in the same breath, segueing almost immediately into the first four stanzas of Hugo's *Booz endormi*. He wrote poems for me and I did the same for him. He introduced me to *Letters to a Young Poet* by Rainer Maria Rilke, a book which stayed with me a very long time and made Rilke one of my favorite poets.

I finished high school knowing I would not go on to college. Health insurance did not exist at the time and my mother constantly repeated that if anything ever happened to my father, no one would be able to ensure our survival. But if I were to take a secretarial course, at Notre-Dame Secretarial School for example, I would become an insurance policy of sorts for the whole family. And so for one year I disguised myself as a well-dressed young woman to take such courses, the majority of them given in English. I learned shorthand, typing, and the quality of discretion indispensable to any secretary. What could have been a fatal turning point in my life today turns out to be useful.

I worked as a secretary in an insurance company for two years. It was my entry into the real world: the women talked about marriage, children, and new curtains; the men about money and promotions. Only one of my colleagues, Elise, interested me. She spoke a beautiful French and read a lot.

In the spring of 1963 I quit my job with the intention of returning to university to finish my B.A. I had saved up a bit of money. On June 29, 1963, I boarded a Dutch ship, the SS *Ryndam,* for a six-week trip to Europe where I visited several countries. That trip was a true initiation to art history. Nothing escaped my curiosity, my thirst to know: vaults, naves, friezes; ceilings, flagstones, and gothic windows; tombs, bridges, and prisons; rivers, lagunas, lakes, and gorges; squares, boulevards, and piazzas; bistros, pubs, and trattorias. Everywhere culture had worked hard on nature, had carved marble and stone into the memory of queens and kings, the equestrian shapes of great warriors. Nature had let itself be changed into wines of every color and taste as well as into a wide variety of warm little bread rolls. The guts, limbs, blood, and fat of animals had become magical names on restaurant menus. Everywhere males looked for females—*"cherchez la femme"*—but *women, Frauen, donne* were in reality teenagers, wives, mothers, or old women. Yet men were finding woman for she was there, everywhere, sculpted, painted, photographed, well framed. I wrote in my personal journal every day, faithfully jotting down the names of the architects, painters, and works I was discovering. Sometimes when one dazzled me I would describe the feeling it had stirred inside me. I came back to Montréal with a head full of castles, cathedrals, gardens, with "fertile eyes" (Eluard). Going to university would now be imperative.

In 1963 one "accessed" the Université de Montréal via a long wooden staircase which, from Maplewood Street, today renamed rue Edouard-Montpetit, led to the main building erected in 1924 from designs by architect Ernest Cormier. Once you reached the top of the stairs, while taking the time to catch your breath, you could contemplate the northend of the city and, on clear blue days, watch the Laurentian Mountains undulating in the distance.

When recalling my years as a student at Université de Montréal, I easily confuse those spent completing my B.A. with those during which I did my B.A. in literature. The confusion no doubt stems from the fact that the friendships and extracurricular activities are what remain most vivid in my memory.

I involved myself in student associations as soon as I entered university. I worked at the newspaper *Le Quartier Latin* where, as a matter of fact, I published my first poems on March 3, 1964. A few months earlier I had met the poet Michel Beaulieu who was to become my first publisher. He is, I believe, the first poet I ever met. Whenever he opened his mouth it was to talk about a book of poems he had just read,

About 1960

about a poet, or about poetry in general. He spoke with equal fervor about the poems and the paper they were printed on. Having grown up surrounded by art in a family of painters, he dreamed of producing the most beautiful books of poetry. He introduced me to the painter Roland Pichet who in turn acquainted me with the work of printmaker Albert Dumouchel and of many other artists. It was during this same period of time that I met a student who turned me on to jazz. And so every Wednesday night during the winter of '65, together with some other students, we would head down to the Casa Loma, a Sainte-Catherine Street club which had had its heyday in the fifties and was now hoping to attract a new clientele by presenting live jazz. There I heard John Coltrane, Duke Ellington, Miles Davis, and so many others who never failed to amaze me. At about the same time I also frequented le Perchoir d'Haïti, where Québécois and Haitian poets gathered to read their work. I remember the feverishness of Juan Garcia, the immeasurable defiance of Gilbert Langevin, long conversations with poets Serge Legagneur and Roland Morisseau. Those evenings exuded a complex energy. The Québécois poets, whose political anger was on edge, scattered their poems with swear words, invectives, and political demands while the Haitian poets, exiled by the violence of the Duvalier regime, read their texts with an awesome, breathtaking intensity.

As I write these lines I am well aware that it was mostly men who, through their passion for an art form, imparted their love of art to me. That way of saying: "You see? Do you hear that? Read this!" with an ecstatic air as if suddenly the beauty of the world held wholly in a verse, a poem, a painting, a musical phrase. I discovered this passion only much later in women writers like Michèle Causse, Florence Delay, Marie-Claire Blais, Daphne Marlatt, Louky Bersianik, in the composer Micheline Coulombe St-Marcoux, and painters Francine Simonin and Irene Whittome.

But another passion had begun to reveal itself in Québec's social fabric: the passion for political realities. I am using the word "political" here because it allows me to encompass the signs of what was to give my generation a sense of history, nourish our will for radical changes, our desire for freedom. Something was at stake in our lives, and this meant reclaiming a country and a language as well as shaping our collective identity. We were working, so to speak, on four fronts: challenging English-Canadian political and economic domination, denouncing the exploitation of our natural resources by American multinationals, struggling against the power of the clergy, resisting the omnipresent influence of French literature.

In the early sixties, few Québécois novels and little poetry were being published. We did have our classics such as *Le Survenant (The Outlander)*, *Bonheur d'occasion (The Tin Flute)*, and *Les Plouffes (The Plouffe Family)*, but this was very little compared to the number of French books which constituted our main reading matter. The French *livre de poche* (pocketbook), which first appeared in 1953, had made the works of Camus, Sartre, Gide, and Malraux available to us. As I moved from one text to the next, the streets of Paris became more familiar to me than the streets and boulevards of my own city. We were like strangers to our own literature, to our own reality. For this reason, nationalist consciousness led to a growing interest for our own literature. Every book published by a Québec author constituted proof of our existence, contributed to widening the horizon of our collective image reservoir. At university, with Québec literature professor Réginald Hamel, we discovered our own early-century poets, as well as the reviews *Gants du ciel* and *Le Nigog* which had both since disappeared. Professor Hamel had set up a documentation centre on the last floor of the huge tower dominating the university. Great motivation was needed to get there, and ours was. Here we had access to the works of the past as well as to the current output which, thanks to reprint editions of the poems of Alain Grandbois and Anne Hébert, and with the publication of books by Jacques Ferron, Paul Chamberland, Hubert Aquin, Marie-Claire Blais, and Réjean Ducharme, was becoming increasingly stimulating.

This passion for our literature and this determination to make it known, combined with the new questionings about our language and about writing raised by the French *nouveau roman* and the journal *Tel Quel*, led Marcel Saint-Pierre, Roger Soublière, Jan Stafford, and myself to found *La Barre du Jour*, a literary journal whose first issue came out in the spring of 1965, a few days after the publication of my first book of poetry, *Aube à la saison*.

Nineteen sixty-six was a very full year. On January 22 I married Roger Soublière, exercised my right to vote for the first time, and published my second book of poems, *Mordre en sa chair*. Roger and I lived Québec's political and cultural reality to the hilt—demonstrating for a French Québec, against the Vietnam War, writing articles, studying. *La Barre du Jour* took up a considerable amount of our time: meetings, proofreading, meetings with poets of our generation as well as with those older than us who elicited our admiration. This is how I met poet Alain Grandbois. He was sixty-eight years old then and lived in Québec City. So Michel Beaulieu, Marcel Saint-Pierre, Roger, and I headed for Québec. Grandbois welcomed us. The man was small, frail, a fracture of the spine caused him great pain. And yet for over two hours he talked to us about his travels around the world, about his friends Breton, Supervielle, Picasso, about his library lost during the German Occupation. From time to time his wife Madeleine brought coffee and cookies. He would take advantage of her presence to confirm a date, a place. I have kept a slightly uncomfortable memory of this encounter. Was I too timid to really benefit from the conversation, was it the living room's cramped space, or perhaps quite simply the sensation that we were all fragile in the face of time and death? That same year we also visited Alfred Pellan, with whom we spent an entire night talking while continually circulating between his studio and the sitting room. From among all these encounters I have kept a vivid memory of the afternoon of June 12, 1968, spent at the home of Claude Gauvreau. Gauvreau was among those who had signed the *Refus global* and this impressed me. He was a greatly demanding man. Rebellion raged inside him, always seething just under the skin, and would surge out suddenly in a torrent of words. He had written a lot but most of his texts remained unpublished, which seemed scandalous to us. As a matter of fact, I was there to make sure he would give *La Barre du Jour* permission to publish an excerpt of his novel *Beauté baroque.* Behind all his resentment and verve I felt a tender man, hurt, highly intelligent. When time came to leave, he gave me a copy of *Le Vierge incendié* by Paul-Marie Lapointe and a copy of his book *Sur fil métamorphose.* I saw him several times after that, among others during that notorious "Nuit de la poésie 70," which would make its mark on a whole generation and make a hero of Gauvreau. He committed suicide in July 1971.

Meeting writers of a generation previous to mine, writers whose work elicits my admiration, has always moved me. Always I feel a sense of continuity, a pride in sharing as though the love of language and the passion for words traversed time, immutable, regardless of the obstacles encountered by each generation. There is nothing more magical than admiring the thinking and emotion of creators, than to be able to watch memory wending its way through years, cities, loves, between the morality and the aesthetics of an era, to see the reflection of this obstinacy, this ruse of the heart with which poets have always sought to renew the posture of both body and spirit in the face of anguish and solitude, amid planets and traditions.

I obtained my B.A. in literature in 1968 and started teaching in a high school in Ville Saint-Laurent where Roger and I were living since our marriage. I taught for a year, then the Canada Arts Council awarded me a grant allowing me to work on *Sold-out: Etreinte/illustration (Turn of a Pang).* Then came October 1970 and the declaration of the War Measures Act by the Canadian government headed by Pierre Elliott Trudeau, which served as a pretext to arrest over three hundred people, including many writers and intellectuals. The sight of the military on the streets of Montréal was a shock. The army had ceased to be a concept. Anger, panic, and a certain paranoia were setting in. The army's presence would only reinforce our determination to prepare the birth of a nation.

In the fall of 1972 I went back to Regina Mundi School. It would be my last year of teaching. I did not enjoy teaching and the days seemed to crawl by. But in early September I met a young gym teacher, Germaine, a tall woman with very black hair whose face pleased me and moved me instantly. This encounter would soon modulate the mood of my days. We saw each other every day, went to the restaurant, the movies, took day trips to the Laurentian mountains. In the summer of '73 we left for six weeks in Greece where we became lovers. On the terraces of the Plaka in Athens, atop the Metéora, on the boat between Mykonos and Hydra, at Epidaurus or at Delphi, we were goddesses whom no deity could separate. But, o the paradox, after returning home to daily life with Roger, I became pregnant. I remember

With Germaine (left) in Greece, 1973

during that whole period being seized with a frenzy of feminist readings. I read *The Second Sex, Sexual Politics, Amazon Odyssey,* and *The Dialectics of Sex.* Time was going by, my body and my thoughts were transforming. My body became round, pleaded in favor of inner peace, well-being, and indeed, I remained relatively calm, content mostly to assimilate intellectually the inflammable matter of my readings. I simply did not have the means or the energy to be nervous. I was a huge body full of life, I was circulating among the planets. I was cosmos, chemistry, flesh, blood, living cell in the enigmatic phenomenon of life.

When my daughter, Julie Capucine, was born on April 24, 1974, I had become like many other women, a mother; like some women, a radical feminist; and like a minority of women, a lesbian in love.

Then began the most exhilarating, the most difficult, and the most fruitful time of my life. I was finally going to start resembling my thoughts, my pleasure. But for this I would have to spend a few years outwitting the reality invented by men; I would have to venture, body and soul, into a semantic field strewn with countless mines, some already exploded in the form of everyday sexism, others, even more terrifying, the buried mines of misogyny.

I will never be able to overemphasize the turmoil of emotions, astonishment, distress, anger, deep joy that feminist consciousness produced in me. Between my readings and the encounters, discussions and gatherings with women, how to describe the irreversible transformation at work in me, the variety of emotions, the growing number of questions, an accelerated intersecting of contradictions and certitudes. What I was discovering was immense, terrifying, intolerable. How had I been so blind? How had I managed for such a long time to ignore this essential revolt of women, this indispensable solidarity between women? I was seized by a feeling of urgency. I wanted everything to happen all at once. We needed documents, proof of what more and more of us were discovering. We needed to reinvent our lives. To change the laws. We needed books to accompany us. We needed spaces where we could come together to talk about ourselves. We had to make over the world.

When I think back on all those evenings and nights spent in women's bars, Chez Madame Arthur on Bishop Street, Baby Face on Dorchester Boulevard, Gillie's, then Lilith and Labyris on rue St-Denis, it is like a dreamed life story. Every time I entered one of those bars I was filled with a feeling of pride. In just the time it took to find myself sitting at the bar once again among friends or among unknown women, I was already swept up by a current of energy, a

feverishness which, on the first beat, expressed itself in heated conversations and on the second, drove me onto the dance floor. I loved to dream our essential revolt in the rhythmic motion of bodies close to bodies, to feel the softness of cheeks against mine, the fragrance of my partners. "Women's arms, hope," I often said to myself in those days. I am well aware that bars, even those for women only, are not the best places to "hang out" in if one wants to be a good-looking old lady some day, but be that as it may I felt good there, happy. For me it was also an opportunity to meet women from all social classes, all walks of life, women whose words would have been inaccessible to me in the normal course of my writer's activities. There was something magical there, beautiful, an affirmation of our existence, a free circulation of desire, of solitude, of camaraderie, of despair, of hope, and of excess. This is what fascinated me, kept me awake nights, insatiable when encountering the singularity of each one of us, and our similarities. How many times when leaving a women's bar, as I found myself walking among heterosexual couples and late-night partiers, did I not experience the feeling of suddenly being thrown into an alien world, did I not feel reality suddenly taking a fantastic turn, becoming surreal, fictive, how many times did I not experience that sensation of a radical break between what made sense in the heat of the bar and what, once outside, seemed to me such an incongruity. Sometimes also a slight vertigo would come over me, a slow wavering which left me pondering, worried, nostalgic, alone, very alone, in the starry night.

In 1974, actress Luce Guilbeault, who was at the peak of her popularity, called me to talk about an eventual collaboration. Perhaps as research assistant, scriptwriter, or co-director. A project took shape: we would make a documentary film about the American feminist writers whose books we considered "must" reading for all women. We wanted to find out about the journey that had led these women to write their books and we were equally intrigued by their daily lives. So in the spring of 1975, Luce and I left for New York to do our preliminary research. We would interview Ti-Grace Atkinson (the amazon intellectual), Kate Millett (the thinking artist), Betty Friedan (the liberal bourgeoise), Rita May Brown (the radical lesbian), and Shulamith Firestone, but unfortunately we were unable to locate her. Through our research we met Margo Jefferson, Lila Karp, Kathy Sarachild, Jill Johnson, and many others, each one seeming more intelligent and courageous than the one before. The movement had undergone sufficient upheavals that some of them let show a certain disappointment, a slight bitterness, something which never failed to leave us puzzled. We spent most of our time in Greenwich Village and in SoHo, where most of the women we wanted to meet were living. We went to Lincoln Plaza to meet the pretentious Betty Friedan. The very moving Kate Millett warmly welcomed us in the Bowery loft she was using as a studio for her painting. In the evening we would return to our Fifty-seventh Street hotel exhausted and frenzied. We would have a last drink, smoke a last cigarette, and then each would go and let herself sink into the replenished stock of images and words gathered during the day.

During every interview we would ask a question about Simone de Beauvoir's *Second Sex* in order to determine what influence it had had on the American women. The radicals enthusiastically acknowledged the major role the book had played in their life while the liberals admitted to having been more influenced by Betty Friedan's *Feminine Mystique*. This is when the project formed to interview Simone de Beauvoir so as to find out if, in turn, reading American feminists had changed her perspective on the nature of women's struggle.

It was November 1975, the sun was shining brightly. It was ten o'clock in the morning. We arrived on Place des Vosges, where we were going to stay with actress Delphine Seyrig, a friend of Luce's. I will never forget our arrival. The entire Place was littered with autumn leaves violently blazing away in their many hues of red, yellow, and ocher. All we could see around the Place were coupés and convertibles from the twenties, some parked, others in motion. On the sidewalks, elegant ladies in long dresses are walking on the arms of men in frock coats. I mean I know that Paris is a dream, but please! Then someone warns us to walk close to the wall. We are in the midst of a movie being shot. Delphine gives us a friendly welcome. I cannot stop looking at her, her face is so beautiful, her voice carries me back so much into the atmosphere of *Last Year at Marienbad*. A few days later, Delphine arranges our meeting with Simone de Beauvoir. I am going to conduct the interview and I am very nervous. The evening before, an interview with de Beauvoir is broadcast on television. I think, "No body, only a mouth that speaks without fail and tiny little hands demurely placed on her knees and occasionally lifting up like little mechanical things. Such coldness. How am I going to be able to do this interview?" The following day, November 27, my birthday, we arrive at 11 bis Schoelcher with a team of French women filmmakers. Simone de Beauvoir opens the door. As the crew sets up, she disappears, then reappears for the interview.

She is wearing a turban like in most photographs. Her lips and nails are painted red. She smiles slightly. I ask my questions, she answers, and then, once the interview is over, disappears with a lady of her own age, I imagine to some café where they will talk for an hour or two while sipping a whiskey, perhaps a glass of Beaujolais *nouveau*.

I have kept a vivid memory of that stay in Paris for several reasons: the magnificence of autumn, the voice, beauty, and grace of Delphine Seyrig, Simone de Beauvoir's painted lips, and the perfect seduction scene played out for me by a novelist. She so seduced me that for months I dreamed that France and Québec were connected by an isthmus, and that by merely hopping into a taxi or onto a train, one could be in Paris.

Back in Montréal, something obvious leapt to my attention: ever since *Québécoises deboutte!* had folded, we had no feminist newspaper. This seemed unimaginable to me. We had to act. I talked to my friend France Théoret. Within a few weeks we had succeeded in putting together a team of five to work at publishing a paper we would call *Les Têtes de Pioche* (the hard heads) to indicate our stubbornness in defending our rights and the cause of women. The first issue appeared in March 1976, the last one in 1979.

Parallel to our film project, Luce Guilbeault had had the idea for a stage play. In the same way we had wanted to let intellectuals speak in the movie, we now wished to hear the words of female characters whose intimate thoughts we could only imagine, whose feelings we could only presume to know. And so profiles came to us, those of the menopausal woman, the actress, the prostitute, the worker, the lesbian, and the writer. Six characters, six monologues, six authors. Meetings, discussions, rehearsals. There was great intensity, everything was experienced passionately, raw on the skin, with a strong sense of solidarity between authors and actresses. I wrote the writer's monologue which was admirably performed by Michèle Magny. The play opened at Théâtre du Nouveau Monde on March 5, 1976. There was a full house for three weeks. On some nights we thought the room might explode the tension was so unbearable. The men were uncomfortable, impatient, the women moved to tears and vibrating at last with healthy anger. We knew that for many couples the evening would not end like an ordinary theater outing. After the show, actresses and authors would head for an Old Montreal restaurant, La Maison Beaujeu, which was owned by one of the actresses. There we ate, drank, talked endlessly. The artist's life attracted me, the theater excited my violent desire to

(From left) Pol Pelletier, Marthe Blackburn, France Théoret, Nicole Brossard,
Luce Guilbeault, and Odette Gagnon, 1976

amorously, fanatically place my words in another body, an actress's body which would be even wilder than my own. I believed I would need one, two, several bodies to express the excessive feelings in me. Then in time I return to this thought that desire can only find true appeasement in the body thinking through its desire.

During this time I worked on a text I termed "fiction-theory": *L'Amèr ou le Chapitre effrité (These Our Mothers; or, The Disintegrating Chapter)* published in 1977. It is, I believe, the book that cost me the most effort. Before that, my defiance, my transgressions were inscribed in the context of the defiant sons' struggle. So they could be playful, humanistic, subversive, or formalist and make sense in the grand patriarchal scheme of things. I was a bit like a woman who, believing her humanity to be an acquired fact in the eyes of everyone, passionately defends Hu*man* Rights without realizing that if she were to defend women's rights and their right to difference with the same vigor, she would be marginalized, thwarted, ridiculed. The time had come to enter the core of the feminine subject and to make sense beyond patriar-

chal meaning. Language was my ultimate ally, my worst enemy. Every word was double-edged. Contradiction was a permanent risk. I knew that if I failed my certitudes, if I held my anger back, if I censored the lesbian utopia within, I would be broken by a huge ground swell which I myself had unleashed. I had to be able to stand up to the terrifying wind of patriarchy's violent symbolic order and simultaneously be able to tenderly lean over the face of a child, lovingly embrace women's shape.

On December 22, 1978, Germaine, with whom Julie and I had been living for three years, accepted a dinner invitation at the home of a former professor of hers, Marisa, who was also living with a woman. In the car, we were singing, we were happy. It was snowing lightly. The city seemed in slow motion, calm. We were far from suspecting that, on that evening, the course of our lives would be changed. Destiny? How to name that attraction, that feeling slowly seeping into every one of our thoughts and which, no matter how meticulous the reasoning one might apply in pushing it back, persists, unskirtable. Sitting in the dining room, our conversation led us to Paris, to Italy, to New York where Marisa had lived, then back to Montréal where we discussed politics, the upcoming referendum on Québec sovereignty, and feminism. In short, a very civilized evening which in principle should not have changed our lives.

The four of us often got together afterwards. In July of 1979 we all left for Martha's Vineyard where we spent a month in a big house by the sea. The time went by pleasantly. By day I read Wittgenstein's *Tractatus logico-philosophus,* in the evening I entered the ineffable world of Djuna Barnes's *Nightwood.* Julie was introduced to the tender flesh of lobsters and played the little siren on the huge rocks cluttering the beach. That summer, Mary Daly, whom Marisa and I had met in Montréal that year during a lecture she had given on *Gynecology,* visited us for a few days and we had enthralling conversations. And then once

again the sea and love took up the whole space. *Amantes (Lovhers)* was gradually taking shape.

A year later, on the same date, Marisa bought a big house where we have lived ever since with my daughter, Julie. Our life organized itself around writing and research, in a content dailiness intercut by numerous trips. From this encounter came the books *Amantes* and *Picture Theory,* a large part of the texts which comprise *La Lettre aérienne (The Aerial Letter)* and *Sous la langue (Under Tongue).*

I remain relatively discreet about this love for a very simple reason: I have not yet found the words to express, to describe the fine fiber linking us together. Sometimes I say we have no merit in the matter, that it is all a question of biochemical compatibility. Sometimes I use the words crystal or diamond to translate the durability of my sentiment, to explain that neither words nor gestures repeated a hundred times over have succeeded in wearing out the essential passion of re/cognition we have for one another.

Writers and poets of Québec, 1981: (front row, from left) Marie Savard, Madeleine Ouellette-Michalska, Henriette Major, Janou Saint-Denis; (back row) Marie Uguay, Yolande Villemaire, Nicole Brossard, Louky Bersianik, Jovette Marchessault, France Théoret, Madeleine Ferron, Sylvie Sicotte, Marie Laberge, Madeleine Gagnon, Suzanne Paradis, Désirée Szucsany

In March of 1981 I went on a lecture tour in France, Belgium, and Italy. When I returned I left for Toronto where I was invited to participate in the "Writers in Dialogue" series organized by Betsy Warland. My partner in dialogue would be Adrienne Rich. This moved me deeply because I had the greatest admiration for her poetry and essays. A few hours before the reading we had coffee together to get acquainted a little. I talked a lot, asked a few questions about her texts, but Adrienne remained silent, thoughtful, preoccupied by the pain from the rheumatism she had contracted. Later on, when I joined her for the evening, she seemed to have regained some energy. The room was full. There was a wonderful atmosphere. I read excerpts from *L'Amèr* and from *Amantes*, which Barbara Godard had translated for the occasion. There, for the first time, I experienced the feeling that my texts were finding an echo, were making sense for a large number of women. I felt the force of the energy circulating in the room. I understood that this current of energy was composed of the values and experiences crisscrossing in all directions of our lives. This energy, I could hear it vibrating in each and every one of us. It came from our tears, our orgasms, our laughter, and our wounds. This energy, I could hear it healing our lives. The magic of words was operating. It was building bridges between us. And on these bridges, we were going forward to meet our lives.

When I returned I immersed myself once again in *Picture Theory*. Women's energy, Marisa's love, my fascination for knowing, my desire to unravel the great patriarchal enigma, everything converged on the page and incited me to recognize, to detect, in every single word, the matter favorable to the advent of a quality of emotion upon which the book's meaning depended.

On September 5, 1982, my father died of a heart attack. On October 29, *La Nouvelle Barre du Jour*, on the initiative of poet and critic Claude Beausoleil, organized a colloquium on my work, to be followed by the launch of *Picture Theory*. The two events short-

"October 29, 1982—date of the colloquium on my work: (front row, from left) Louky Bersianik, France Théoret; (middle) Normand de Bellefeuille, Louise Forsyth, Nicole Brossard, André Roy, Pierre Nepveu; (back) François Vasseur, Louise Dupré, Louise Cotnoir, Michèle Saucier, Yolande Villemaire, Suzanne Lamy, Claude Beausoleil

circuited each other. On the one hand the recognition of my peers thrilled me, on the other, my father's sudden death left me cruelly suspended between the world of the living and the obscure world which mourning was shaping inside me.

For the first time in my life I experienced anguish. And as anguish is a feeling that slowly, perniciously infiltrates the body and spirit, for four years I was unable to comprehend what was happening to me. I remember a panel discussion in Québec City where my texts were being discussed. I remember getting up twenty times to splash cold water on my face. I remember, in Rome in 1984, stopping in every café on the Piazza Navona, convinced I was going to faint every time. Between 1983 and 1986 I lived in a state of unspeakable sadness, inhabited by a strange melancholy, a deep nostalgia. All this seemed to me so improbable, so incompatible with my way of being, happy in the present, turned toward the future, filled with the certainty that life is worth living. All of this was not me and yet it was me. Somewhere in me fear, heat, and thirst were preparing the setting for *Mauve Desert*. Without realizing it, I was *living* grief, just like at fourteen I had, without realizing it, grieved for my faith in an intrinsically good humankind.

The more time went by, the more I became convinced I would never write again. I had experienced this sensation before but this time I had the impression it was accompanied by the sentiment that literature is derisory, that any writing is useless, that I had reached the extreme limit of playing with language and meaning. In any case, after Joyce, could anything worthwhile possibly be written? Little by little I displaced mourning for my father onto writing. And yet I continued to write. I wrote "Dont j'oublie le titre," a book of poems which remains unpublished. I published *Domaine d'écriture*, whose first lines, *"Rien ne pouvait plus s'écrire* (Nothing further could be written),"* are an accurate translation of my distress. I wrote a *Journal intime* for a radio series. All of these written with tears in my eyes. I did however keep up the good habit of closely observing my syntactical and grammatical behaviour. For example, I noticed the excessive use I was making of the pronoun *I* and of the verb *to be*, as if during that period of loss and mourning, I needed to insist, *I am*, to repeat *I am* to fully convince myself of my existence here and now. Little by little, I got caught in my own game and, convinced that the use we make of pronouns is not gratuitous, I became absorbed in reflecting on the internal laws that bring us to using pronouns according to our emotional needs. Today still, I remain convinced that when we use an *I*, a *you*,

With daughter, Julie, in Carmel, California, 1983

a *she*, or a *we*, we are simply responding to psycholinguistic laws active inside us, knowing mirrors of our inner states of being which are, each in their turn, demanding a little presence of self, dialogue, distance, or solidarity.

During this time I became passionately interested in translation. I had often worked with translators Patricia Claxton and Barbara Godard. I had seen their notebooks, noticed that in their hands my books had become manuscripts filled with annotations, underlined words, circled in pink, yellow, or blue. Whenever Patricia or Barbara came to my home for a work session, they questioned me about a word, an expression. I did my best to remember, to retrace the mental path I had travelled. I described the images, the settings hidden behind the words, the association of ideas, the value given to a certain word, my preference for this or that one. I was fascinated by what, in one language, did not exist and by what, in the other, was luxuriantly present. In my eyes translating became a complex act of passage which enflamed the mind and, like reading and writing, demanded great powers of concentration and decision-making. I thought that, in life, we were always translating our emotions, our sensations, our values, that the words of others could only make sense if we translated them through our own experience, our referents, that part of life escaped us because we did not have the words to name, to translate, that is to embed into our experience the sensations, the feelings, the concepts which seemed so obvious in another language. Later on I worked with Susanne de

Lotbinière-Harwood and Marlene Wildeman and this only reinforced my interest in the phenomenon.

One day after writing a ten-page poem I had the idea of rewriting every page to produce a version of it, similar and different. I made abundant use of synonyms, homonyms, played with rhymes and rhythm. The result was *L'aviva.* Then in 1985, Daphne Marlatt and I both produced "transformances." I transformed her *Characters* into *Jeu de lettres* and she turned my poem "Mauve" into another *Mauve.* These were not actual translations but rather a game of transformation where each one retains some room to manoeuvre.

My fascination with translation grew, transformed itself into the challenge and grand fantasy of translating myself from French into French. This is how the premeditated matter of the idea came to meet the hot emotional matter which for two years now had been preparing the tone, the setting, the atmosphere of my novel *Mauve Desert.*

Now enough about me, let's move on to the subject of travelling. Travelling is a large part of my life. Trips make me feverous, vulnerable, open, put me at once in a poetic state. Like a "sourceress," I walk, pen in hand, seeking out the café, the terrace where I can sit, ponder, write. I love feeling that everything is relative, that if in Paris people are going about their business in the rain, in the midday rush hour, there, at Ayers Rock, people are meditating in the sunset while looking at the enigmatic rock aflame with the most glorious mauves, that while I am visiting the Golden Pavilion in Kyoto, there, in San Francisco, Kathy Acker is reading an excerpt from *Don Quixote,* that if tonight in Helsinki day lasts all night long, there in Buenos Aires, I am walking on a street called Corrientes, my head full of tangos, that while I am making love in the great bed in Room 502 of the Curacao Hilton, over there, in Rome, Rosanna and Giovanna are proofreading the Italian translation of Jane Rule's *Desert of the Heart.* I love travelling because it is a sure way of understanding that there are many of us worrying, drinking, and laughing at the same time, giving different names to death, pleasure, the sun, and the sea. I love leaving because over there, one must visit cemeteries, ghettos, prisons, walk under arcades, look for a parasol, always wear dark glasses when coming out of a church. Because over there, one is easily mistaken about an address and a name, over there, one learns to say thank you and good-bye at the same time, one gets excited quickly, one looks everywhere, one is easily frightened. At night in hotels, one reads the Bible and drinks champagne before going to sleep. Over there,

it is tomorrow sooner or later here in your arms, there, it is still tomorrow since there are many of us dreaming. I love travelling, inventing sentences like this one, for example, where I can assert that contrary to what happens in North American cities where conversation almost always revolves around an anecdote, for the French the life of ideas seems to be an inexhaustible subject of discussion during which one eventually ends up talking about oneself anyway. I love travelling because it is easier to talk about oneself abroad. Now let's go and have a drink. I'm really fed up with this autobiography where the years follow all in a row like at a funeral. Let's have a drink at poet Claude Beausoleil's home. I'll explain why along the way.

Like travelling, *la fête* plays an important part in my life. Probably because I associate it with the spoken word, with the circulation of an energy which has, in the past, often transformed itself into projects, discoveries, ideas, seduction, into an urge for writing poetry. I cannot imagine *la fête* without an excess of words, without an overflow of meaning, in a word without fiction being involved.

Although writing is an act carried out in the greatest solitude, it nonetheless remains subject to the chance of our encounters, of our readings, of the day-to-day history of literary life. When I talk about *la fête,* I associate it with a moment when the very logic of time comes undone, reshapes, and comes to mould itself onto that part of us which chooses to exist in another dimension, that is to say, in the dimension of a desire, always the same one, restated like an existential ardor.

La fête weaves complex ties because it makes the *I* euphoric, enflames cultural matter, transforms the gaze. Paradoxically, *la fête* has meaning only if literature, ethics, the political, and memory agree to force us into asking culture the very best questions. *La fête* finds its full meaning at the heart of enjoyment, when we suddenly become aware of belonging to a short, very precise time in history.

Montréal poet Claude Beausoleil understood this dimension of *la fête* perfectly. Twice a year he would welcome fifty or so writers of every generation to his Parc Lafontaine apartment. In winter, we arrived in snow-covered coats, hands frozen, glasses all fogged up; in summer, we entered the house like a breeze, circulating, tanned bodies among the tender green of plants, the modernity of the paintings and posters on the walls, glancing furtively at the bookshelves then, between the tinkling of glasses and the cigarette smoke, here we were at last in the heat of action, in the midst of words. Here Gaston Miron is reciting an excerpt from *La Marche à l'amour,* there Yolande

Villemaire is inventing the Yellow Shadow game. Over there, Elise Turcotte and Carole David are discussing Louise Desjardins's latest poems. Here, the contagious laughter of Hughes Corriveau meets Denise Desautels's beautiful voice. There I am, pouring myself a glass of wine before explaining why the word Man makes women invisible, here Acadian poet Gérald Leblanc is describing the streets of Moncton as he quotes Diane Léger and Herménégilde Chiasson. Further on, rocker Lucien Francoeur is talking a lot about himself and a little about Jim Morrison and Rimbaud. Over there, Louky Bersianik is arriving at the same time as France Théoret, here Paul Chamberland is explaining the meaning he assigns to the word "geogram." François Charron and André Roy are discussing painting and film. When around midnight poet Jean-Paul Daoust starts singing *"Nous sommes tous morts à vingt ans* (We are all dead at twenty),*"* silence shrouds the room, a silence engulfing all our books, a silence from which Montréal emerges like a turn-of-the-century and our coming books in which we will dare all as long as *la fête* protects us against death. When Jean-Paul sings, I think of all the girls dead at five years of age, ten years later, always later, a whole life of pink ashes, to paraphrase the title of one of Jean-Paul's books, *Cendres bleues* (blue ashes). Then I imagine that the characters in our books will find a better way to tell about our sleepless nights, the celebrations and the wanderings, about our insatiable appetite for living among words, where life renews itself, literary in all its splendor.

*

It is almost midnight on Tuesday, December 31, 1991. I am finishing this short autobiography. I am alone, I am listening to the tangos of Susana Rinaldi and Astor Piazzola. I think of Gertrude Stein, who had the nerve to write *The Autobiography of Alice Toklas*, who had the sense of propriety to write *The Autobiography of Nobody*. I believe that solitude is a necessary state, fine proof of discretion and patience when, amid words, our whole body knows that nothing in the world will prevent us from inventing

"In the garden of Marguerite Yourcenar: Marisa, Nicole, Germaine, and Christiane," Petite Pleasance, Bar Harbor, 1991

reality as a door to the future, whatever of the past unfolds in fiction.

Reality is what matters and as a writer I have to deal with it as fiction because I know that twenty-first century reality will be about the worst and the best of our fictions.

BIBLIOGRAPHY

Poetry:

Aube à la saison (title means "Dawning season"), published in *Trois*, A.G.E.U.M., 1965.

Mordre en sa chair (title means "Bite the flesh"), Esterel, 1966.

L'Écho bouge beau (title means "The echo moves beautifully"), Esterel, 1968.

Le Centre blanc (collected poems), Orphée, 1970.

Suite logique (title means "Logical suite/sequence"), Hexagone, 1970.

Mécanique jongleuse, Génération, 1973, translation by Larry Shouldice published as *Daydream Mechanics*, Coach House Press, 1980.

Mécanique jongleuse [and] *Masculin grammaticale*, Hexagone, 1974.

La Partie pour le tout, L'aurore, 1975.

D'Arc de cycle la dérive (etchings by Francine Simonin), Edition de la Maison, 1979.

Amantes, Les Quinze, 1980, translation by Barbara Godard published as *Lovhers*, Guernica Press, 1986.

Double Impression: Poèmes et textes 1967–1984 (collected poems), Hexagone, 1984.

L'aviva, Nouvelle Barre du Jour, 1985.

Domaine d'écriture, Nouvelle Barre du Jour, number 154, 1985.

(With Daphne Marlatt) *Mauve/Mauve*, NBJ, 1985.

(With Marlatt) *Character/Jeu de lettres*, NBJ, 1986.

Sous la langue/Under Tongue, bilingual edition, translation by Susanne de Lotbinière-Harwood, L'Essentielle éditrices/Gynergy Books, 1987.

Installations, Ecrits des Forges, 1989.

À tout regard, NBJ, 1989.

La Subjectivité des Lionnes, L'arbre à paroles, 1990.

Typhon Dru (with photographs by Christine Davis), Collectif Génération, 1990.

Langues Obscures, Hexagone, 1992.

La Nuit verte du Parc Labrynthe, Trois, 1992.

Fiction:

Un Livre, Editions du Jour, 1970, translation by Shouldice published as *A Book*, Coach House Press, 1976.

Sold-out: Etreinte/illustration, Editions du Jour, 1973, translation by Patricia Claxton published as *Turn of a Pang*, Coach House Press, 1976.

French Kiss: Etreinte/exploration, Editions du Jour, 1974, translation by Claxton published as *French Kiss; or, A Pang's Progress*, Coach House Press, 1986.

L'Amèr ou le Chapitre effrité: Fiction théorique, Quinze, 1977, translation by Godard published as *These Our Mothers; or, The Disintegrating Chapter*, Coach House Press, 1983.

Le Sens apparent, Flammarion, 1980, translation by Fiona Strachan published as *Surfaces of Sense*, Coach House Press, 1989.

Picture Theory, Nouvelle Optique, 1982, translation by Godard published by Guernica, 1991 and Roof Press (New York), 1991.

Journal intime, Les Herbes rouges, 1984.

Le Désert mauve, Hexagone, 1987, translation by Susanne de Lotbinière-Harwood published as *Mauve Desert*, Coach House Press, 1990.

Radio plays:

"Narrateur et personnages," first aired by Radio-Canada, 1971.

"Une Impression de fiction dans le rétroviseur," first aired by Radio-Canada, 1978.

"La Falaise," first aired by Radio-Canada, 1985.

"Souvenirs d'enfance et de jeunesse," first aired by Radio-Canada, 1986.

(With Michèle Causse) "Correspondance," first aired by Radio-Canada, 1987.

Other:

"L'Écrivain" (monologue; first produced at Le Théâtre du nouveau monde, Montréal, 1976), published in *La Nef des sorcières*, Quinze, 1976, translation by Linda Gaboriau published as *Clash of Symbols*, Coach House Press, 1979.

(Editor) *The Story So Far: 6/Les Stratégies du réel* (anthology), Coach House Press, 1979.

La Lettre aérienne (essays), Remue-Ménage, 1985, translation by Marlene Wildeman published as *The Aerial Letter*, Women's Press, 1988.

(Editor with Lisette Girouard) *Anthologie de la poésie des femmes au Québec (1677–1988)*, Remue-ménage, 1991.

Work represented in anthologies, including *La Poésie contemporaine de langue française*, Saint-Germain-des-Prés, 1973; *Quebec mai francia Kolteszete*, Europa, 1978; *The Poets of Canada*, Hurtig Publishers, 1978; *Antologia de la poesia francesa actual, 1960–1976*, Editora Nacional, 1979; *Anthologie '80,* Editions le Castor astral, 1981; *La Poésie québécoise: Des Origines à nos jours,* Editions de l'Hexagone at PUM, 1981; *Lords of Winter and of Love,* Exile Editions, 1983; *Poesia del Quebec,* Editions Ripostes, 1985; *Sp/elles,* Black Moss Press, 1986; *Poésie du monde francophone,* Le Castor astral/Le Monde, 1986; *Émergence d'une culture au féminin,* edited by Marisa Zavalloni, Editions Saint-Martin, 1987; *Deep Down,* edited by Laura Chester, Faber, 1988; *Brise-Lames/-Antemurale,* Bulzoni Editore (Rome), 1989; *Cradle and All,* edited by Laura Chester, Faber, 1989; *Companeros: An Anthology of Writings about Latin America,* edited by Hugh Hazelton and Gary Geddes, Cormorant, 1990; *Lesbian Philosophies and Cultures,* edited by Jeffner Allen, SUNY Press, 1990; *An Intimated Wilderness,* edited by Judith Barrington, Eight Mountain Press, 1991; *Inversions,* edited by Betsy Warland, Press Gang, 1991; *Von nun an Nannten sie sich mutter,* edited by Uli Steib, Orlanda Frauenverlag, 1991; and *Resurgent,* edited by Lou Robinson and Camille Norton, University of Illinois Press, 1992.

Also associated with *Réelles,* Quinze, 1980. Contributor to periodicals, including *Opus International, Etudes françaises,* (also cofounder) *La Barre du Jour, La Nouvelle Barre du Jour,* (also cofounder) *Les Têtes de pioche* (newspaper), *Liberté, Possibles, Protée, Cross Country, Contemporary Literature, Exile, Room of One's Own, Journal of Canadian Fiction, Essays on Canadian Writing, Fireweed, Prism International, Island Ethos, Resources for Feminist Research, Cistre, Journal des poètes, Masques, Actuels, Action poétique, Fem, Liaison, Les Herbes rouges, Trois, La Vie en rose, Dalhousie French Studies, Tessera, How(ever), Writing, Between C and D, Notus, Estuaire, Die Horen, Vlasta, Oracl, Jungle, Chemin de ronde, Les Cahiers bleus,* and *Trivia.*

Ed Bullins

1935-

TWO DAYS SHIE . . .

When I was young, I was bitten by a dog. Not only was this experience frightening, it was surprising.

A cousin and I had been playing tag and hide-and-seek among the narrow alleys and side streets of North Philadelphia. Part of the terrain resembled bombed-out cities in Europe, post-World War II.

I recall escaping from my cousin through an alley which adjoined backyards of buildings which seemed abandoned.

Behind me, my cousin limped, having suffered a wound in the sole of his foot the week previously, from stepping on a nail. I enjoyed being able to keep easily ahead of him. Over my shoulder, I laughed and taunted him as I trotted ahead, leaving him in my imagined dust. My turned head saved me.

The big dog leaped from an overhanging porch, attempting to tear out my jugular, but my twisted jaw bone caused its fangs to slip off, and I lurched forward, away from sure death, and the beast's chain strangled and halted the animal, as I silently raced for home, with blood spilling down my chest, and my cousin screaming and crying somewhere behind me, from the terror of my escape.

Afterwards, over the years, I realized that was the first time I had realized that death could touch me personally.

My mother was given the name of Bertha Marie Queen at birth. She was born in Darby, Pennsylvania, just outside of Philadelphia, sometime around World War I. I am vague concerning the date because my mother was uncommonly closemouthed about things she considered "her business." She did tell me, however, that her birth records had burned up in a courthouse fire, and she had difficulty proving her birthplace to employers from time to time, always finally satisfying their queries, though I never saw any real documentation of her arrival on earth.

I think she was the third surviving child in her family. Over the years, at family gatherings for holidays or funerals, I have heard whispered refer-

Ed Bullins

ences among my mother, aunts, and uncle about stillborn deaths of their brothers and sisters, but, actually, I do not remember if these had been real conversations or dreams. Of course, I could interview my older relatives, but somehow my past attempts have left me frustrated and confused, so that I have usually allowed the past to be the past.

My uncle Reuben was the oldest. He left Philadelphia around Valentine's Day before I was born (two days shie of Independence Day) to go to New York City, where he lived in Harlem for many years, and to where I later went to visit him, first as a youngster. He has since returned to retire to a home owned by my cousin Florence.

Next came my aunt Bea(trice), Florence's mother, and matriarch of the family. She married and separated from a Frank Garrison, whom I was not old enough to remember, and her children carry that surname, but she again married, and later buried her husband Jack Williams and lives today as Mrs. Williams.

My mother followed, then my aunt Sarah, who was the real rebel and iconoclast of the Queens. She moved to Los Angeles, an unimaginable place to us then, and had a daughter, Cousin Charlotte, who still lives with her mother though she is nearing middle age. Aunt Sarah was short, under five feet, and even shorter than my uncle Reuben, who claims we are descended from Ethiopians. Where he got his information from is another family mystery; he would only whisper over a festive family punch bowl on rare occasions, with a sly twinkle in his eye, but giving nothing definitive. I have wondered if Pygmy descent was more apt, in regards to that segment of the family.

Aunt Sarah moved to LA in the late forties. Before then, in Philadelphia, she wore pants, as if she were still involved in the World War II effort, and had a reputation for slightly bizarre behavior. What this behavior was was never explained to me by my mother, but I remember Aunt Sarah turning up at one of our North Philly addresses one dawn, cursing and enraged. The top part of one of her hands had been nearly sliced off, leaving a dark-skinned fillet hanging onto a blood-gushing wound. Someone on Columbia Avenue, one of the North Philly meccas for the fast life of those days, had taken a switchblade to her to settle an argument.

At the St. Luke's Hospital Emergency Room I heard my mother repeatedly chastise Aunt Sarah over her choice of friends. Philadelphia was very territorial in those days. Some neighborhoods were worse than others, but any of them could conceive life-threatening situations if you were a stranger, or worse, if you were recognized as being part of a rival (and mostly warring) section, family, gang, team, school, or race. To part of our family, Aunt Sarah was kind of weird because she hung out sometimes in South Philly, but especially on South Street. We thought that any day she could be delivered on our steps in a potato sack, or when our imaginations really waxed lurid, we had visions of one of Aunt Sarah's ears, lips, or thumbs being thrown through the window inside of a gin bottle. I believe that Aunt Bea could concoct the most colorful and fanciful of the unseemly prophecies. But exaggeratedly violent or not, all of us in the family have collected our Philly street wounds, in one way or another, so those ghetto tall tales were usually based on how many stitches did one get, how close the blade or bullet nicked one, and other combat particulars, told matter-of-factly as part of the routine life-style, but great stuff at parties and dinners.

Soon after Aunt Sarah's hand healed, she began talking about moving to California. She said she hated the cold weather of the East, and Los Angeles was as far as she could go to get away from everybody she knew. She declared many times that we were fools for staying back there in the cold. Mother and Aunt Bea humored her as best they could, not believing her threats of self-exile, but shortly she boarded a train and was gone. Mother and I went down to Thirtieth Street Station. It was the first time I can recall being there. Years later, I worked for two years and a half across the street at the Philadelphia General Post Office. My subway stop was below, and I would come up the escalator and walk through the huge, high ceilinged marble waiting room. Sometimes I would linger in the exact spots that Mother, Aunt Sarah, and I had stood, remembering that day. And over the years I have since been through there numerous times—coming, going, to and from many points—but I think each time of when Mother and I went down and said our good-byes to Aunt Sarah. We all seemed happy then, but somehow since, things changed. I grew up and Aunt Sarah never really trusted me then; I became a man, and because of that, trust, and then love, were things to be withheld. I did not understand and was hurt when I discovered this years later, but that was all a part of growing up as well, I have since realized.

Aunt Sarah never returned to Philadelphia. My mother missed her a great deal; they had been running buddies when they were young. And in the mid-fifties, Mother did go and stay with Aunt Sarah for almost two years to nurse her back to health after Charlotte was born, but that part of the world did not suit my mother. By then, she was a power machine operator at the Quarter Master Corps in Philadelphia. She sewed army uniforms, duffle bags, and other GI issue, and when production slowed a bit after the Korean conflict, and I was away in the navy, she took a leave of absence to go out West. Her displeasure with Southern California had to do with the alien life-style in general—no snow in winter, too many cars, strange people—but she cited the facts that the unions were not strong in LA and that people there who were not citizens were working for "pennies." Besides, she was very lonely for the place she grew up in, so she returned to the City of Brotherly Love after Aunt Sarah was on her feet.

My aunt Sarah died not too long ago. I forget who told me, probably my cousin Florence. I remember talking to Florence on the phone. She was at home in New Jersey. And I do not remember whether I called her first, or she called me, but in any case, we talked about the death of Aunt Sarah.

Florence told me that Aunt Sarah had been dead for more than ten days. Her body was being held by the coroner and some things had to be explained to the authorities. Florence was fuzzy on the details, so she asked me to call her sister Dorothy in Los Angeles and find out what I could, and call her back.

From Los Angeles, Dorothy told me that she was confused and pissed off about what was going on. Aunt Sarah supposedly had died after arguing with her daughter, Charlotte. It seems that Charlotte had moved out of Aunt Sarah's place the week or so before. They had been angry at one another, but Charlotte visited anyway and they had some words. Charlotte's story was that she went into the kitchen to fix some tea and while there heard a gasp from the bedroom; when she returned, Aunt Sarah's eyes were rolled up into the top of her head, with the whites showing.

Lost Generations

Mother was born in Darby, I suspect, because it was an intermediate point between the family's rural beginnings in Eastern Shore, Maryland, and the northern migration to the metropolitan centers—Baltimore, Philadelphia, and the epitome of civilization for them, the Big Apple, New York City.

Mother's father worked on the trains that plied the Eastern Seaboard corridor, from Boston to Washington, D.C., and points south, I imagine, or it could have been cross-country, from Baltimore and Philadelphia, across Pennsylvania through Harrisburg and Pittsburgh, to the mid-West. Granddad must have been a porter, I have thought many times. He could have been other things, but my mind has been comfortable with me thinking of him as being a porter.

Granddad died in an accident on the trains. This much I have been told. And that my grandmother lost her house in West Philly, in a "good" residential area near Fairmount Park, and considerable property as a result of the stock market crash of 1929 when the banks failed. Soon she too was dead.

Years later, the lost house of 1929 was pointed out to me by one of my cousins, as we drove past it one day after attending a funeral. To me, the house looked like the place on Haverford Avenue in West Philadelphia, since demolished, in which Aunt Bea raised her children and partially me; it was a bit larger, but as shabby looking as the other one would have been if it had not gone to make way for a middle-income housing tract. The lost house off of Fairmount Park was one of those row houses that you find in many residential neighborhoods in Philadelphia and elsewhere. At the end of the 1920s the street was without a doubt on the edge of ritzy, a haven for more fortunate colored people, but by the late seventies it resembled many others of the deteriorated inner city. Only thing though, it fronted on the largest municipal park within the boundaries of an American city, Philadelphia's Fairmount Park. When I was a schoolboy, I took pride in these kind of Philadelphia things and vowed many times never to live anywhere else. More than once in my young life I have promised girls and young women that I would never under any circumstances ever leave Philly to live elsewhere. They soon quit me, not wishing to be trapped by a local yokel and condemned to spend the remainder of their sentences of life within that prison of the spirit, Philadelphia. Curiously, I left there, never to return for more than a weekend, while they have stayed in place.

Miles away to the east, across the park in North Philly, off of Diamond Street and near the serpentine Ridge Avenue, those kind of houses in the style of the ones mentioned fronted on the park, and were even larger. They too have fallen into disrepair, even while being tokens of past better times, especially for some people of color. Like a segment of the folks, our lost house and some of the present standing ones shared a history of mutual, extended collapse, total abandonment, and decay.

The lost house near the park had a wooden porch and steps with banisters. A picture window looked out on the porch, and two windows were upstairs over the sloping roof which covered the porch, where chaise swings were once moved by the gentle evening breeze and the toes of courting lovers. I had lived in these kind of houses in Philly and had seen and visited them in Baltimore, Wilmington, Cleveland, and other places in between. It is said amongst us that the Great Crash set our family back a couple of generations, and that we have never fully recovered. And some say we never shall, that we are a series of lost generations.

Banks closed, and savings were lost. Mortgage and insurance companies folded, and our assets vanished. There was little work for our people so eager to work. And the social impact of my mother and her sisters being part of the generation of the

"New Negro Woman" had its effect on our not so extended family as well.

Today, my cousin Florence is considered rich through her crafty real estate dealings and Johnson Products (or a like company) marketing, but she earned the down payments on her first properties from working at a laundry and saving as much as she could hoard.

The depression and five children with no man in the house at that time caused my aunt Bea to go on welfare for a decade until she went to work for an industrial laundry, taking most of her children into the plant with her as they grew old enough. Those former calamities—numerous mouths to fill and no breadwinning partner—were not so secretly seen by some as minor family disgraces, whispered about late at night by my elders when I was supposed to be asleep. But the social infractions did indeed prove minor, for Aunt Bea rose to be the backbone of the family by the time the forties faded with its war effort and air-raid drills. Before, within my memory, from the very late thirties until six months or so after FDR died, it was our aunt Margaret, sister in some way to my maternal grandmother. I say "in some way" because neither my mother, aunts, or uncle have ever consented to speak of those matters to me, and because Aunt Margaret was very fair-skinned, no doubt able to pass for white in some instances, and had the appearance of being rich, in the terms of those times—house in the suburbs of southwest Philly near the airport, farm in Lawnside, New Jersey, new shiny black Buick with chauffeur, and a live-in cook and handyman. But I shall speak of Aunt Margaret Mansfield later. Her sister, my mother's mother, was dark and very African looking from her pictures, with high "Indian" cheekbones. Her husband, my mother's father killed on the train, was dark also, but looked smaller than his wife, though she was not a fat type of person judging from the photos. Uncle Reuben seemed to have taken after his father in looks and stature, Aunt Bea and Sarah after both of them, but my mother was light brown with hair that did not kink so much and could grow down her back if she wanted it to. She was said to have a touch of Aunt Margaret's side of the family in her, I believe, or perhaps I only dreamt that someone told me this, and have kept it buried in my mind for nearly fifty years. But I do believe that my mother once mentioned that her father did not accept her as being his at first because she was too light-skinned, until Aunt Margaret got him straight. Or was this the tale about the Indian in my grandmother coming out in my mother? Nonetheless, I, myself, have closely questioned a couple of my wives when they produced lighter-than-

usual children for me, but I was reminded of my mother and Aunt Margaret and quickly dismissed the suspicions because most of my offspring have my mouth, probably inherited from my unknown father's side. The Garrisons, my cousins, are not a big-lipped clan, nor are any others of my generation or before, including my mother. In fact, when I was little and could not fight so well, my cousins teased me until I cried by calling me "baboon," even being lovingly prodded on by Aunt Bea.

Our family thought of themselves as Northern colored people, not ones to have broods of kids like Southern plantation Negroes. And we aimed to be the workers of the nation—railroad workers, construction workers, cooks, waitresses, janitors, guards, truckers, launderers, messengers, stock clerks, caddies, dish and car washers, yardmen, greens keepers, exercise boys, prize fighters, laborers, farmers, power machine operators, and, alas, even petty criminals. The threat of welfare, robbing us of our independence, was almost as ignoble as discrimination and segregation to most of us. But a few of the older generation fell victim to the dole so that the young could eat and grow out of poverty, though ever since the first acceptance of the government handouts, a segment of the clan has lived their cockroach existences in that way, while mainly being ignored and forgotten by the other branches of the family tree as those who lived and stayed somewhere across the proverbial tracks. Yes, those great social upheavals—the crash, the depression, wars—and their aftermaths helped disperse the Queen family and spread their seed to both shores of America.

There is speculation on my part that the name Queen was taken from Queen Ann's County, Maryland, at the emancipation time. The locale is part of the Eastern Shore region, east of Chesapeake Bay, I imagine, though I have not looked for it on maps in that regard since I was young when I looked for it as the ancestral plantation home of my imagination; and I also looked for Barkley, Henderson, Greensboro, and Goldsboro, homes of nubile Maryland farm girls that my puberty caused me to stalk like a critter in rutting season on vacations "down home." And I once looked for a horse-breeding place, Ellicott City, outside of Annapolis, I think, after I got out of the navy. A shipboard buddy, William Henry Jones, promised to teach me to tend thoroughbred race horses. I did not find that part of Maryland on the map, but perhaps I was looking on the wrong side of the bay.

I lived on the Eastern Shore for short times—summers mostly—but did attend Denton (Maryland)

Junior High School for a semester. My mother boarded me out with a rural family in Marydel, Maryland, for about half a dozen seasons, and after learning that the bay was a lot of miles away, it interested me even less. I was already used to two large rivers, the Delaware being the largest running through Philadelphia, the Schuylkill the other; and I knew that the ocean was on the other side of New Jersey around by Atlantic City. Perhaps twice a year the ocean was of concern—July Fourth and Labor Day, when a church or neighborhood bar excursion bus would take us, my cousins, friends, and me, on picnics and outings to the beach. And in Maryland I had even traveled to Ocean City and Atlantic City on old, rickety, yellow school buses. The bus company was owned by a black family, Pinkston, or something like that. But a bay was not quite an ocean, or at least my young imagination did not become excited by the Chesapeake.

Once my aunt Jessie, who was not my aunt at all but perhaps a fourth cousin through marriage, took me and some of her other charges to Royal Oak, Maryland, where we young ones swam in the bay, and we all ate crab at some rich white folk's place who were away. Aunt Jess had friends who worked for the rich people, and we were their guests. The place was right on the bay. It had a boat landing, a diving board, I think, and trees leaned over the water, some even weeping willows. The day was muggy and I became afraid of the jellyfish that were in the water; the older people kept trying to keep us clear of them, and after I learned that they gave an awful sting if touched, I came out and stayed out. The bay seemed very different to me from the ocean. It did not have waves at that location, but was at times still, deep, and menacing.

How my mother, Bertha Marie Queen, became Bertha Marie Bullins is a mystery to me. I accept it now as I did then as my mother's way—not telling me or most people her personal secrets, past actions, and private revelations. I have inherited a bit of this characteristic.

I have met my father a number of times, but his name by then was Edward Dawson. There is a dimly remembered story hesitantly told to me by my mother of my father escaping death in Georgia and coming to Philadelphia, Pennsylvania, where they met. (Or did they meet in Chester? But no, my stepfather, William Carroll, was from Chester, so my father would not be there, or would he?) My father worked until the mid-fifties as a cook in a Chinese restaurant on the Philadelphia main line, at a place close to the bus and rail terminal where people embarked for the southern suburbs, including Ches-

ter. Strange, I have often thought, my father having to change his name to elude Southern justice. And his ending up cooking Chinese food as good as I have ever tasted.

Frankly, this has all seemed at times farfetched to me, even while I experienced it, but my aunt Bea confusingly supports my version of the story, while missing parts, so her absentminded manner of telling her side gives me reason to think that she has gotten my father mixed up with someone else.

In any case, when I was twenty or so and out of the navy, a woman called me on the phone and said she was my half sister, my father's daughter, and invited me to visit her and my father's family. I promised to go, but did not, soon losing the address and number, and never regaining them. I have often thought about the possibilities of that moment in my life.

My mother was determined to have me become "a Great Negro Leader." When she took me to visit her friends, invariably I was stood in the center of the room, and asked, "Edward, what are you going to be when you grow up?" And my answer, which had been rehearsed since before I could speak, was even born, according to my mother, was "I am going to be a Great Negro Leader." The answer was always applauded, except when I visited my cousins, who would giggle and snicker until my aunt Bea threatened to slap them up aside their nappy heads. They especially laughed when I recited the entire version of "The Night Before Christmas" one Christmas eve, as they lay in their bunk beds in two adjoining rooms on the second floor of 4707 Haverford Avenue in Philly.

Forty-seven zero seven Haverford Avenue, West Philly, was an important address to me. It was my aunt Bea's house, or at least the first one I knew of, and my first vivid memory of it was when I was held in my mother's arms at night on the porch as she argued with a man whom I think was my father. He slapped her and my mother exploded, chasing him down the street, with me tucked under one arm and throwing milk bottles at him with the other.

My mother was all of five feet tall and very pretty. (My daughters Patsy and Cathy inherit her physical characteristics. My other daughters sometimes take more after me and their mothers.) She had a small waist and big legs. When I was very young, and she was a young woman, I remember her holding my hand as we walked down a street and her hand tightening on mine at the corner, where a group of men made remarks about her "big purty legs," and her "bein' built like a brick ——house, baby." I wanted to kill them, even though I was not yet old enough to go to school. I wanted to smash them. To

Bullins (left), Ishmael Reed, and Cecil Brown, 1988

close their filthy mouths. But my mother said to me, "Look, Edward. Look at the street light. When it is green, then it is time to go." And I remember when I was older, but still a small boy, my mother and I crossed Broad Street near downtown on a winter day when the ice had been rubbed into a sheen by cars. Mother slipped. Her feet went out from under her and she landed on her bottom with her legs kicking in the air. I was so embarrassed. I ran screaming with laughter to the other side of the street. There, I turned and cracked up as Mother, half slipping, partially sliding and crawling, made her way across the frozen street. When she got to the other side she looked ready to kill, but seeing me rolling in the snow from mirth, she broke into laughter too. We laughed together about that bitterly cold day for years.

Baseball Bill

I must have been less than ten years old when Bill began taking me to baseball games. Boy, did Bill know baseball. He was an avid fan. I hadn't heard of Jackie Robinson by then, and Bill was still kind of

carrying me around, so I must have been less than ten.

Bill was really my stepfather, sort of, though he and my mother never got married, for their own reasons that they never told me, though they did live together from the late thirties until the early fifties. Back in those days there was a real social stigma about men and women living together outside of wedlock. But we moved a lot in the early years, around that big, old, ugly, dirty city, so we were there, then we were gone. Sometimes, I was told to introduce Bill to my friends and the neighbors as my father, and sometimes my uncle, or a roomer, or just a friend of the family, until we moved to 1514 North Darien Street, in Philadelphia, where we stayed from 1942 to 1952, when the big breakup came, and after I had grown into a teenager and became aggressively hostile to my friend Bill.

But before then, Bill took my mother and me to baseball games at Schibe Park, probably between 1946 (after he returned from World War II) and 1949. He really did know baseball. We saw the Negro League teams—the Kansas City Monarchs, the

Homestead Braves, the Philadelphia All-Stars (at least that's what I think their names were). They were fierce rivals and played exciting, incendiary ball. Remember, this was before the time of TV. The first players I saw kicking sand on a black umpire's shoes were black players with names like "Boston Blackie Jones," or "Brown Bennie Blackwell," or "Slick Sonny Boy Scott." Of course those were not their real names—I've forgotten those—but their names had that type of colorful, suggestive alliteration. Like the Harlem Globetrotters whom I saw later, some of the black baseball players had specialty clown skills. Some shagged flies and grounders during the exhibition period with huge gloves, others did base-running routines or challenged horses to footrace them, and others did various entertainment bits. But the rivalry between the teams was fierce. I have seen bench clearing brawls at the black games more than once, when my mother would cover her eyes and Bill and I would be screaming for an early death to the ump.

Bill would come home from the railroad or stock shipper's job and pick us up and we were off to "Play ball!" times, catching the trolley car on Erie Avenue and whisking electrically to the game. The first several innings were played as the sun set over Fairmount Park, and then the game's lights were snapped magically on to our "ohhh's" and "ahhh's," mixed with the murmurs of thousands. What beautiful, hot summer nights, with Cracker Jacks, Dad's Old-Fashioned Root Beers, Coney Island-type hot dogs, beer and wine (for Mom and Bill, slipped in by brown bags and her straw purse), and smokes (they were both pack-a-day Camel puffers).

Oh, those happy, carefree summer nights. And so many black people were there. So many. More than at church. Or at camp meetings. Or at a Daddy Grace or Father Divine parade. . . . That was so long ago.

When I was ten years old, I was also in love with my elementary school teacher, Mrs. Woodward. She thought of me as special, and I was the only black male student in her class, and I loved it. Mrs. Woodward was my favorite, and still is. One day in class, she stopped by my desk and made an announcement. She said that that day I had become one of the most fortunate people in America because Jackie Robinson had been admitted to major league baseball. I didn't tell her that I didn't know who he was. Or that I was completely dumb to the significance of any relevance of Jackie Robinson to baseball.

Later, I asked Bill about these questions. And he took a big drag of his Camel and said: "Eddie, it's the beginning of the end." And I didn't believe him any more than I did when he returned from VJ-Day,

saying that the world would be destroyed in nine months or so, because the U.S. of A. had the atom bomb . . . and an itchy trigger finger (he was an artillery man at the Battle of the Bulge, I think); or later, when he stopped trading Mickey Spillane-type mystery stories, cowboy shoot-'em-ups, science fiction, and comics with me because I was reading a little of George Orwell and Thorsten Veblen, which meant that I was becoming a geek or a Communist, or worse . . . both. But Bill knew baseball, at least Negro baseball. Yes, my friend Bill knew what he knew. And the older I become, the more I think like my surrogate father.

Saved to Search

I was born and raised at the bosom of traditional black American religious belief and practice, but, paradoxically, circumstances prevented me from being or becoming a devout follower or believer. For one thing, my mother was rebelling against the church when I was born, and she continued to be an intermittent agnostic for the next twenty years, then gradually became a fundamentalist religious Pentecostal to such an extent that she alienated and shunned the whole of the family, except for me, who was by the time of her death rumored to be an atheist.

I always hated going to church. It was boring. Banal. Rigid and confining.

Also, early on, I found that the black Baptist, Methodist, and Presbyterian churches were hypocritical and crooked. To me, they became the seat of degeneracy and decadence.

At least the hustlers, gangsters, and street people were honest about what they were about, I believed.

Actually, I could write a book about this subject. It would be filled with nonbelief, though now I have come to believe that there is a great, divine mystical force in the known universe. Only thing though: man has not been able to identify it or incorporate this knowledge into a popular belief system.

I was made to go to church fairly regularly and did so until I was ready to get baptized. Then I rebelled. And my mother, aunts, surrogate matriarchs, etc., gave up on me. None of the other men of the family were made to go as soon as they approached manhood, so I was not going to go either.

My cousin Milford (a fourth or so cousin) was found in church every Sunday, but he was holding on precariously to life, so I guess he saw the church as his safety net.

Each preacher that I met soon became exposed as corrupt and two-faced. My mother would rail against their faults until she succumbed to their deceits. And I believed that I could detect their flaws even better than she could.

One preacher stole the church funds and started another church. But my aunt followed him. Another committed crimes and was given thirty-five years in prison, but I was told not to condemn him; it was the Lord's providence. The others seemed only jack-legged shysters, stereotypical slobbering pretenders and wimps, mealymouthed petticoat chasers, and worse.

Once, when it was almost time for my baptism, when I had to join and commit myself to their God and ways of worship, I was almost overcome by religious ecstasy, or the Holy Ghost, or whatever that ecclesiastical feeling could be called. The church was jumping, the singing, the preaching, the beat, the music. And I felt I was losing control, being taken over by a celestial power, but I rebelled. I escaped. I ran from there. I would not become another Cousin Milford, old and drooling senselessly in messianic revery. I would not become the preacher that my mother prayed I would. I would not become a hypocrite. I would rather martyr myself on the streets of the ghetto, in the den of thieves, in the diseased wombs of whores than become that.

Later, I explained away my near possession as a phenomena of audio hypnotism. Perhaps a lame excuse, but I feel saved in order to keep searching.

Unsexy Sex

I am convinced that I have already written about my initial sex encounters much better than I can do now. For one thing, I was younger when I wrote them (the experiences), so the moment was closer to my recall. Then too, I was attempting to write "Serious" stuff, with a big "S"; so sex had its own importance, among the other rite of passage memorabilia—first big fight, first time away from family alone, first kiss, etc.

The first sex experience really had two parts, one half preceding the other by some years. At first, there were the childish years of wonderment and curiosity about the whispered thing—sex. This was the time of probing through children's games of "house" and "doctor" and peeking at whatever a little girl would let me if the occasion arose. Then came the inexperienced attempts, which were never satisfying or even known if done correctly.

Then by the time of puberty, an older girl took me, led me into the initiated, and made sure I accomplished the real deal.

But I was still new, though I didn't understand that. I thought because I had done the act at a relatively young age for the western world, that I was nearly a man of the ghetto. How long ago that was for me.

Conformity/Nonconformity

I have always been a nonconformist, even when I was adhering to the social/political/artistic norms of the conformist. Being an only child of my mother's, I learned early to set my own priorities. To a casual observer, these objectives may not have seemed determined, nor of value, but they were mine, so they mattered.

My cousins were always together, a family, and I was part of this family; however, I was still the cousin, close, but not a brother or sister, so I was perceived as different from them, and was.

I remember the year I broke away from my neighborhood group and joined a street gang, the Jet Cobras, across town. Much was made of this by the homeboys on my block, even though they were not fighting with the Cobras. No, the Cobras were too far away for much to be known about them in that section around the corner from Eighth and Jefferson; even so, my friends turned on me and fought me for leaving them.

But I needed the Cobras. My new girlfriend lived in the center of their territory, so I joined them for that reason, plus I liked being in with an older, tougher crowd.

This nonconformist streak followed me through a few failed marriages, the service, and into the arts.

I did not want to be like everyone else, so being an artist was fine with me. My family finally made their psychological peace with me and became proud that I was different.

Now, at my present age, I try and act like a surface conformist, but am not. I thank my luck that science has not found a way to read minds yet. If so, I know I would be lynched, burnt at the stake, or exiled to the far side of the society for my anarchistic, antisocial, nonconformist thoughts, which I cannot even mention.

Not that I am a freak, or creep, or geek, or pervert, or psychopath—I am just a simple nonconformist, or that is my pet conceit.

Take school. I dropped out of high school. No one in my family of working class, depression era (post slump), blue collar folks had gone past the tenth grade, but I dropped out and later went into the navy. I did not stay in the navy ("What, you quit a lifetime job, boy!"), but went back to school. Soon, I got a job at the post office, but quit after twenty-nine months. ("You crazy fool! You gave up another lifetime job!") No one understood that I did not want a lifetime job. Or that I found value in learning things for the pleasure of doing.

I used to lament that so many people misunderstood me, that I was outside the norm of society, but later I derived value from that character flaw. I gained recognition and status for being nonconformist. I became a leader of nonconformist thought and behavior. Now, few would accuse me of being an ordinary conformist. Actually, I am now an ordinary nonconformist, but I conceal this gift of American democracy usually by hiding.

Having written over fifty plays, I became concerned early in my career with the stylistic aspects of my plays. I did not want them to be apparently in the same or similar genre; therefore, I have experimented with various modes, hopefully giving my work some literary range.

I have been categorized as a writer of realistic black ghetto dramas. There is some truth in this, since many of my more well-known plays fit that description, even while containing nonrealistic elements. Some of these plays are "Clara's Ole Man," "The Corner," "Daddy," "The Duplex," "The Fabulous Miss Marie," "Goin' a Buffalo," "In New England Winter," "In the Wine Time," and "Street Sounds."

Some of my work falls into the categories of surrealism/symbolism and are some of my personally favorite works: "C'mon Back to Heavenly House," "The Devil Catchers," "Dialect Determinism," "Dr. Geechee and the Blood Junkies," "The Electronic Nigger," "The Gentleman Caller," "High John da Conqueror," "How Do You Do," "Jo Anne!" 'Pig Pen," "The Psychic Pretenders," and "The Taking of Miss Janie."

Avant-garde is a sort of catch-all category for pieces of my work. In fact, it is not really a category that I can truthfully use, though elements of the absurd and craft tactics of the artistic and philosophical fringe can be found in various works of mine.

The overriding theme or subject matter in my body of work is the African American diaspora of Northern America, especially the black urban dweller of the industrialized Northeast and Western coast— their displacement in the twentieth century, their migrations, and social and class conflicts.

My series of plays, "In the Wine Time," "In New England Winter," "The Duplex," "The Fabulous Miss Marie," "Home Boy," and "Daddy," deal with an extended family of modern African Americans from the underclass of America's ghettos. I call this series "The Twentieth Century Cycle."

In the early fifties, for the black working-class American, the drug of choice was alcohol, usually cheap wine for the more economically marginal and youthful. Nevertheless, the aspiration to break the generational problems of national oppression and historical prejudice lived in the dreams, hopes, and lived-out and acted-out myths of the ghetto. These plays are an attempt to illuminate some of the life-styles of the previous generations of the black underclass, some of whom were the forebears of today's crack, ice, and substance-abuse victims. These plays demonstrate that, intentionally and unwittingly, a few did escape the cycle of destruction with dreams of building a better tomorrow.

"Pig Pen" and "The Taking of Miss Janie" are a pair of plays which build an interracial scenario of the 1960s, during the Civil Rights/Black Power/Viet-Nam/Flower Power/Sexual Freedom/Drop Drugs/Love Generation era.

The plays "The Devil Catchers" and "The Psychic Pretenders" are mystical/ritualistic pieces, containing voodoo practices (rites), Sufi esoteria, farce, myth, comedic oral folk literature forms, puns, and games.

The plays "The Mystery of Phillis Wheatley" and "I Am Lucy Terry" are written for young, middle-school audiences. They are based on historical characters but depart sometimes to an almost Alice-in-Wonderland style.

"High John da Conqueror" and "Dr. Geechee and the Blood Junkies" share a mode that could come from an African trickster deity, if they (the plays) were inspired enough.

The reason why I began my present theater, the BMT Theater, is because I want to show my work to a new, vital audience, in a part of the nation which is essentially new to theater. The West Coast is a near cultural vacuum, as far as theater, and especially black theater, is concerned. Some blacks are its worst enemies.

Whatever my faults, I am indeed an American writer, an African-American writer, who has something to say to all of America. My work is real, not only to me, but to my found and unfound audiences, who feel its sweat, its cries, its bleeding, its loves and hates, and its fights for what is right and good, even though it sometimes fails through its own excesses of bad taste, bad blood, and poor judgement, but righteously so, even innocently so. I feel that I am a writer quite unlike any other American writer and, through a retrospective deja vu of my staged scenarios, some sense of this can be displayed. I am an artist of the theater; my canvas is the theater, and my scope is as wide as humanity will allow.

My philosophy is simply to write the best works that I can. To write the story is my goal; to show truth through the mythic play form.

My ideology is to be as good as I can while I can, and to try to make the world a better place through theater—my art.

The Metaphoric Club

The metaphoric club that I am closest to is the dart game at a friend's house that I visit a couple of times a week.

The game is about two years old. It started with two brothers and spread through an extended group, mostly men, which now includes a few women.

Almost every night the game goes on. The players vary, except for the houseman. He stays confined to his house, caring for his invalid mother. His brother had shared the house as well, even though he was living with his wife not too far away and divided his time between the two addresses. But he developed a heart condition and was resting in bed the day that the big earthquake of 1989 struck in the Bay Area. He became frightened, got out of bed, tried to climb out of a second-floor window as the house and street swayed, and fell back into his bedroom, knocking himself unconscious. Soon afterwards, he died. But the dart game has continued even though one of its founders passed on.

I am in the inner circle of the dart game. It is an organization which has circles trapped within circles. There is the houseman JW, and there are EH, JD, DW, KW, and myself, EB. Also MM, RN (a woman), and RM. I place myself near the center of the group, which extends in orbits around this core group. Dozens of players frequent the game.

I value the game because of the camaraderie, the pseudo status it gives me on a social level, and for the group, which acts as my support cadre. So I am happy with this game, for the time being.

Occasionally, I become bored and restless. I feel that I have opted for a stifling routine, that the voices at that place sound alike, saying the same things over and over. I promise to break away, not to return for a good while, but I seldom keep my promise for as much as a week.

"At my graduation party from Antioch University,"
San Francisco, 1989

The dart game has cable TV, so the major prize fights and sports events are routinely shown. Also, the newest movies and other TV fare.

Being that I drink less and less as I grow older and older, I have stopped drinking at the game.

This metaphoric club—the dart game—will probably continue until something in the life of the houseman changes. Whereupon, only memories will remain, but they will be mainly positive.

My Place

My writing place. Where is it? . . . Years ago it was any table, mostly a kitchen table, where I could park my typewriter. Usually, it was a young woman's table. In college, young women, many times but not always white young women, would think it romantic or revolutionary or artistic to have a young black unheard of "wannabe" writer in their kitchen, pounding the manual or decrepit electric keyboard until late into the night when the neighbors would pound on the walls and ceiling and floor, or ring up on the phone, anonymously, and then curse about black bastards keeping them awake before suddenly hanging up.

This would be my signal to retire to the waiting bed and make love until dawn, before the young lady departed for work, so that I slept through the day until night, when I pounded the keys of the machine on the kitchen table, producing writing.

Now my writing place is my room above my theater. I have been here almost two years and I am just beginning to make it my own. Nearly ten years ago, in New York, I lived so long at home with my wife and kids that I almost forgot that I had written in other places, many other places. Breaking away from there and taking my two youngest children with me somehow turned something around in me, and it has been hard, but not impossible, to write since.

There have been other tables, tables of women no longer quite young but attractive, however, it was hard to adjust. I was a family man without a home and on the road with a family. Everything was familiar, but nothing the same. And writing became less important than the survival of my children and myself, or at least I give this reason.

Presently, home to me is my rented mailbox and the trailer where I keep my phone, typewriter and books, tax files, and business records (BMT Theater, etc.), plus two radios and two TV's (part of the salvage from passing through children), and a crowded assortment of flotsam and jetsam that I have gathered in the nearly ten years I have been in California.

As for sleeping, I sleep in San Francisco, at my girlfriend's home. But it is not my home.

For years I used to say that wherever my typewriter is, that is my home. That was when I was reaching for the self-conviction of being a writer. And had to live it. So it has almost come to pass again. Even while this rented typewriter is bound for the repair shop, I am attempting to make it a central focus in my daily life rhythm.

When I die, will my out-of-date IBM Selectric be fixed and permanently in place, instead of rented? When I die, will this thing contain my spirit? Will it house this soul of an American black man, even though it is an apartheid South Africa supporting machine?

BIBLIOGRAPHY

Published plays:

How Do You Do?: A Nonsense Drama (one-act; first produced as "How Do You Do" in San Francisco at Firehouse Repertory Theatre), 1965, Illuminations Press, 1967.

"In New England Winter" (one-act; first produced Off-Broadway, 1971), published in *New Plays from the Black Theatre,* edited by Bullins, Bantam, 1969.

Five Plays (includes "Goin' a Buffalo" [three-act; first produced in New York City at New Lafayette Theatre, 1969], "In the Wine Time," [three-act; first produced at New Lafayette Theatre, 1968], "A Son, Come Home" [one-act; first produced Off-Broadway, 1968], "The Electronic Nigger" [one-act; first produced at American Place Theatre, 1968], and "Clara's Ole Man" [one-act; first produced in San Francisco, 1965]), Bobbs-Merrill, 1969 (published in England as *The Electronic Nigger, and Other Plays,* Faber, 1970).

The Fabulous Miss Marie (one act; first produced at New Lafayette Theatre, 1970), Doubleday, 1970.

"The Gentleman Caller" (one-act; first produced with other plays as "A Black Quartet" by Chelsea Theatre Center at Brooklyn Academy of Music, 1969), published in *A Black Quartet,* New American Library, 1970.

The Duplex: A Black Love Fable in Four Movements (one-act; first produced at New Lafayette Theatre, 1970), Morrow, 1971.

The Theme Is Blackness: The Corner, and Other Plays (includes "The Theme Is Blackness" [first produced in San Francisco by Black Arts/West], "The Corner" [one-act; first produced in Boston], "Dialect Determinism" [one-act; first produced in San Francisco, 1965], "It Has No Choice" [one-act; first produced in San Francisco by The Playwrights' Workshop], "The Helper" [first produced in New York by New Dramatists Workshop], "A Minor Scene" [first produced in San Francisco by Black Arts/West], "The Man Who Dug Fish" [first produced by New Dramatists Workshop], "Black Commercial #2," "The American Flag Ritual," "State Office Bldg, Curse," "One Minute Commercial," "A Street Play," "Street Sounds" [first produced at La Mama Experimental Theatre], and "The Play of the Play"), Morrow, 1972.

Four Dynamite Plays (includes "It Bees Dat Way" [one-act; first produced in London], "Death List" [one-act; first produced in New York by Theatre Black at University of the Streets, 1970], "The Pig Pen" [one-act; first produced at American Place Theatre, 1970], and "Night of the Beast" [screenplay]), Morrow, 1972.

Best American Short Plays, 1990 (includes "Salaam, Huey Newton, Salaam," [first produced at Ensemble Studio Theatre, New York, 1990]), Applause Theatre Book, 1990.

Unpublished plays:

(With Shirley Tarbell) "The Game of Adam and Eve," first produced in Los Angeles at Playwrights' Theatre, 1966.

"Next Time . . . ," first produced at Bronx Community College, early 1970s.

"The Devil Catchers," first produced at New Lafayette Theatre, 1970.

"Home Boy," first produced in New York, 1972.

"The Psychic Pretenders" (A Black Magic Show), first produced at New Lafayette Theatre, 1972.

"House Party," first produced at American Place Theatre, 1973.

"Ya Gonna Let Me Take You Out Tonight, Baby?," first produced Off-Broadway, mid-1970s.

"Judge Tom," 1992.

Other:

(Editor and contributor) *New Plays from the Black Theatre* (anthology), Bantam, 1969.

The Hungered One: Early Writings (collected short fiction), Morrow, 1971.

To Raise the Dead and Foretell the Future (verse), New Lafayette Publications, 1971.

(Editor) *The New Lafayette Theatre Presents the Complete Plays and Aesthetic Comments by Six Black Playwrights* (anthology), Doubleday-Anchor, 1973.

The Reluctant Rapist (novel), Harper, 1973.

Work is represented in *New American Plays,* Volume III, edited by William M. Hoffman, Hill & Wang, 1970, and in *Black Thunder: An Anthology of Contemporary African American Drama,* edited by William B. Branch, Mentor, 1992. Editor of *Black Theatre,* 1968–72; editor of special black issue of *Drama Review,* summer, 1968. Contributor to *Negro Digest, New York Times,* and other periodicals.

Austin C. Clarke

1934-

Austin C. Clarke

Rediffusion is the name we gave to it. It was a square speaker, nailed high above my head by the man who worked for Rediffusion "in town." "In town" was where everything in my life that was important and exciting and expensive was sold, and happened, and bought. The man might have been in a hurry to go to the nearest rum shop to buy his liquid lunch of Doorley's Rum, to be helped down by a bread-and-fish. But when he had nailed the Rediffusion box out of my reach, and had hooked it up, and had left in his green van, the words poured out in a marvellous avalanche of foreign English accents, covering me with the things they wanted me to know. And I took in everything; and later in life, at Harrison College, I sifted through the English chaff intended to educate me, but not always successful in discovering for me the germ of wheat of my Barbadian self.

And the lamp with its chimney of cleaned sparkling glass, "Home Sweet Home" printed on it like italic frost, contradicting both the comfort and the structure of the house in which I began my life, would set off its glow in a selected portion of the quiet room, like a spotlight in a theatre of swallowing darkness, showing only the interminable, indestructible insects: moths, mosquitoes, "blasted bugs," as my mother called them in her nightly torment, "crawling all over my body, worse than the blasted flies during the day"; and in the wholesome swallowing darkness, the smell of a woman's perfume, the smell of her hair lathered in coconut oil, the smell of flowers just outside the front door, and the smell of the night just after a hard rain, hitting the body like pellets, soaking the only change of clothes, and the voices in cadence, in tales, in horror, superstition, and bragging; idolatrous and Christian, working out in the skeins of their voice and memory all the scandals of the village, scaled down from the larger scandals of the island, going on and on, as I sat near my mother, in fear and in wonder from their storytelling.

In this small house, at the beginning of my memory of autobiography, was one book. The Holy Bible. It was always kept on a "centre" table (which was never placed in the centre of the "front house" that we called the parlour) made of mahogany, polished until you could see your teeth and lips in the wood as you passed, a thousand times a day, obedient always to the sharp remonstrance not to brush against it with your clothes or put your dirty paws "on my table." The Book was always lying on a white piece of crocheted white circle; always with its silken cloth cross marking the spot. The present spot was Revelations. I would read from this Book every night to my mother before the neighbours, aunts, and girlfriends visited to compete in their idolatry of ghost stories. Perhaps this is why I never wrote mystery or detective stories. I could never reproduce the torment and the curdling of thin blood in the meandering tales, as they sat, always, in a rough-formed circle, with the wick of the lamp lowered for atmosphere and for economy during these years of the "War up in England."

England, like the words from the Rediffusion box and the smudged print of the *Barbados Advocate* newspaper, the *Beacon,* the *Herald,* and the *Observer,* like the kerosene oil lamp, was the maker of things, of everything in my life.

And then, all of a sudden, above and beyond my small comprehension, we became respectable: with servants, maids, a man working the ground: planting canes, eddoes, sweet potatoes, corn, cucumbers, and other vegetables in a kitchen garden which it was my job to oversee; we became the inhabitants in a big house "with 'lectricity, oh my God," my mother said, complimenting her own good hardworking fortune and moving up with the Yardes "out the front road," which was the most prestigious place to live; and the women, aunts, and girlfriends stopped coming. It seemed as if their never-ending ghost stories could not withstand the harshness of the electric light shining down upon us, as if the elements were confused, as if it were always midday under the sun. And with this sharpness, with this new definition of things, the crochet on the white cloth on the mahog-

any table still placed like a sentry in the centre of the room, this time a real parlour, was white as snow, the shape of the table itself now plain as day was a heart made under another mahogany tree, in a yard of the joiner shop miles from our new prowess and progress up the slippery ladder of Barbados's social class. And still, there was only one book in our house. The Holy Bible. Bigger now. Newer now. Blacker now in its leather-bound cover. With its leaves trimmed and painted in gold. And, marking the spot, was the cross made from the leaf of a coconut palm, toughened and almost brittle with time, left there, still in the pages of Revelations, from Palm Sunday at the St. Matthias Anglican Church.

I was now a cub. "Ah-kay-lah, we'll do our best. Dib. Dib. Dib-dib. Dob. Dob. Dob-dob . . ." And a choirboy. With black cassock and white surplice starched lightly and shining like the old shade with "Home Sweet Home" in the old, smaller house; and in my right hand, placed sanctimoniously under my right armpit, the Psalter, tormenting and confusing with its psalms numbered in Roman numerals; the Book of Common Prayer, in which I could never find the "order" of things, and sometimes when I found it, that part of the ritual of the Church of England was already completed; and the book *Hymns Ancient and Modern* in which I revelled.

Ride on, ride on, in majesty
In lowly pomp, ride on to see.

And I was attending the second-best, second-grade, secondary school, in the island Combermere School for Boys. There had been an examination taken by boys who were bright from all over the island, with a scholarship attached to it, called Junior to Second Grade. There were twenty-four places, the winners of which would get their geography book *Dudley Stampp,* free; *Virgil Aenid, Book One,* free; the *Acts of the Apostles,* free; geometry and algebra books, free; and an exercise book for each of these subjects, with a colour for each subject, all free. The only colours of our exercise books that I remember now are the grey-green for geography, and the red for English.

"Once upon a time, and a long time ago, there was a man who had three heads . . ." This was the beginning of the first short story I ever wrote in my red exercise book.

There were twenty-four places. I came twenty-fifth. My mother had therefore to pay for my education. And I went, five days a week, bright and early for nine o'clock, dressed like a British soldier, complete in starched khaki, three-quarter khaki socks, brown John White shoes, and with a book bag

Of a times, when decency was decency. When a man knew his place. Whatever that place maybe. When things was in order. And nothing could be out of order. In them times, boy, a man who was a man, make-sure he had a roof from the lumber-yard, or at least a roof in mind, to provide his be-trothed with, before he come talking 'bout the sins of the flesh. All that, all that brand of life this semi-American, John Moore Adams, contrabanded. Contrabanded. And now, for me, a Thorne from Sir-Joseph to see that man passing in front the house in his American car, and in his American clothes, and me, to be renting a house from him who con-trabanded our entire family, boy, in all fairness, it is more than a Christian can take. But. Where there's a will, there's a way. I am glad enough at the way you growing-up, the way you learning yr lessons, and the chances you have in life. And I prays every night, that you will do the right thing. Namely, leave this damn place. The first chance you get. I do not know toomuch about learning. And particular, the learning I understand you are learning at the College.

Manuscript page in the author's distinctive calligraphy

that contained all the volumes of textbooks I owned; with a pencil box, made in England; an Easterbrook fountain pen, made in England; a blue school blazer, replete with school crest, made in England; and its motto, made in Latin (we never thought of Italy when we read of Rome): *Religione. Humanitate. Industria. Combermere School, Barbados, founded in 1819 . . . ,* founded by an Englishman. And in an elliptical shape, inside the name that bordered it, two of the tallest stalks of sugarcane ("Juice-nine-tray-five": J–935; the sweetest also); an opened book, and below the book on the left, an ink stand; and on the right, a quill pen. Armed and equipped like this, collared and tied with a tie of woolen knit, in blue and gold, how could I not succeed?

This was the background against which I learned, and was made to learn, the fundamentals of an education not invented for me, invented and made in England, but which, in the stubborn determinism of my mother and other Barbadian mothers, we moulded to our own use and usage, because they knew—even if I did not, and even if I merely wallowed in the aristocratic and prestigious symbolism of being a "high school boy," a member of the new black elite—they knew it was the surest passport to success. Success meant a job better than being a sanitary inspector. Than being a cash boy in Cave Sheperd, Haberdasher. Than being a messenger boy in a large bank, Barclays Bank: DCO. It took me until the Third Form—3-A, the form of the bright-bright boys who were younger than the average age for this form—to realize that DCO was not an academic degree. Yes, a job better than a messenger boy, in Barclays: Dominion, Colonial, and Overseas. Or working on a plantation, even in a job to be envied in those days, as an overseer, dressed still in a khaki suit, khaki sun helmet, brown boots, and a whip, riding between rows of young J–935 sugarcanes and the "slips" of sweet potatoes, and rows of young men and women, perhaps my own mother, or uncle, and certainly, many cousins. "They can't tek it outta *there,* son!" my mother always said, pointing to her head, and meaning the storehouse of the "learning" I was getting at Combermere, that it was beyond theft. I wonder now, at this age, in this place far from Barbados, in these times of Barbados independence, whether I understood the radicalism in her statement. Did she, could she have experienced an occasion when someone tried to extract from a young Barbadian like her son, the knowledge he had acquired? Did she, and could she have understood the extent to which "them in power" would have attempted to deny that that young man, like her own son, had in fact acquired the knowledge necessary to

pull him from the open-pit toilet, from the rich, powerful, and subduing soil of the plantation, from the grease round the axle of English cars which he would have been bending down to, to repair in years of unpaid apprenticeship, "Take this shilling and see what you can buy with it!" since he had never been a "high school boy." She certainly must have known, from her own experience, that all those jobs were jobs "whiching you have to bend-down to do. Is time you learn to stannup, hear me? *Stand-dup!*"

The background also coincided with a new politics of national independence. But looking back, I did not need the manifestos of former Combermerians and zealots, those soaked in the *Communist Manifesto* and in the lectures of Professor Harold J. Laski of the London School of Economics, which was in time going to be my destination to understand her harder lessons. It was my mother who, in her amateur but wholesome way, exposed me first to the meaning of independence. But hers was a personal independence. A dream of manliness, manhood, and success.

I was too young at this time to understand and, if I did understand, to be able to put into effect my mother's oppressive sense of responsibility. But if, at the risk of reminiscence and of rationalizing through hindsight, there is any means an author has of pointing back over that dark time of youth and adolescence—both of which in my case were peppered with gaiety and joy, privilege and the enjoyment of materialism—to seek out the "catalyst" or the "thing" which caused me to be an author, I would have to say it was a man, Frank Collymore, who taught me English language and literature with more success than he was able to drum into my head the exercises in French: *je suis, tu suis, il suis,* and *nous sommes!* I liked the sound of *nous sommes;* and I blurted it out with colonial pride, without having realized the two previous mistakes I had made. Perhaps Mr. Collymore, after whom a hall in Barbados is now named, understood that the heavy accent of my bilingualism, Barbadian-English and Barbadian-Barbadian, were the two cultural determinants, too cultural and too determining, for me to be able to catch on to another light-tongued culture. Culture is the word. He taught me, in later years when I submitted my first efforts in the short story to his literary magazine *Bim Literary Magazine,* that the Barbadian dialect was not only a rupturing of English, but a profound expression of a culture of a people whose way of saying things required the similar formality of style, construction, and visual presentation equal to the respectability reserved for the English language pouring through the Rediffusion box. There was nothing in my life, nothing in my environment, nothing in my dreams at this time to tell me, without the claim of hindsight referred to earlier, nothing to prepare me for the profession of being an author. But as I think of this, at this moment, I know that it is not really the truth. Everything in that time, the sum total of my life and existence, provided the raw material which I have reconditioned into the prose of my novels and short stories. And as I think of these things and of these times, it would be futile of me not to admit that it was precisely this background, Combermere School, and later, Harrison College, which was to be the social and psychic spine of my book *Growing Up Stupid Under the Union Jack,* a memoir, as my publishers called it, but which is really the first volume in a planned three-volume autobiography.

Writing had not become by this time even an interest; although I was beginning to be fascinated by the Sunday broadcasts from the British Broadcasting Corporation which flung back into our faces the literary expressions of West Indian men like ourselves who were either living at that time in London, or at home; some few, brave enough to represent for a foreign audience the peculiar meaning of life in the Caribbean; and this reflection from a reputable authority that had obvious colonial credentials of the highest order told me, in my innocence, that something very important was happening through the speakers of the radio of our public-owned system, Rediffusion, made also in England. But more than this authorization was the surprise that we in the West Indies were capable of putting down our thoughts in literary measure and theme, so that my innocence turned to arrogance and told me that I, too, could one day write a poem different from the *Ode on a Grecian Urn* or *Hyperion* and just as good, that contained the smells and the rhythms and words I was living with and hearing every day around me. My schooling in English literature was basically the ability to memorize large portions of the "best" literature written by Englishmen and Englishwomen. We had, for centuries before, because of the literary imperialism of the time, ignored completely American literature. As a matter of fact, the term "American literature" was never used in Barbados during the years I received my formal education. There was no thought given to that vast country to our north, no association with the finer things in life, nothing except the possibility, with little virtue and creative tact, of making large sums of money in a very small time.

In the village in which I grew up, although we did not use that term—we used "the area," or more often, the "neighbourhood," with great stress placed upon "neighbours"—in the neighbourhood in which I grew up, there was already the landscape that was similar to that in England, the roll of the land, the trees on the hills whose colour changed in the distance and in the weather which did not change too often, the skies, the sea, and the sun with its heat which could do things to a person's head and a person's brain; and of course the people, but in my young mind people meant boys and girls, and you would be in love with the girls, and have the boys, their brothers, to help you out in your dramatic and puerile encounters of the heart. One such boy was the brother of a girl with whom I was probably in love, as love is known in these heart-wrenching circumstances. But what is more important about that love is that I wrote a poem about this boy and called it "The Ballad of Bandy James." He walked with his knees touching each other. I certainly must have been affected by my reading and memorizing of the *Ballad of Reading Gaol,* although at that time literary expression and literary criticism had not yet descended into that fascinating sphere of the psycho-literary. But there was ease in expressing admiration for Bandy James in rhyming couplets, the arrows intended for his sister; and the subject himself provided unquenchable inspiration, because each time I saw him, or thought of him, meaning that I was thinking of his sister, I would write two more stanzas. This then, with an inspiration that is natural, the effect of a woman upon a man, was the cause of my first serious and nonserious adventure in writing.

And when James ceased to be important, and his sister faded as a literary source and as a person, and the landscape had become more pronounced in its effect upon my consciousness, I tried in other poems to reproduce that sensual symbiosis between my young life and the "neighbourhood."

Still, writing as a profession was not in my mind. I wanted to be a politician. And I wanted to be a barrister-at-law. And I knew that I would go to England, taking that consistent, sure, time-honoured journey of the colonial to the Mother Country, and give authority to my "higher" education in the same way as the broadcasts of West Indian poetry and short fiction on the BBC's "Caribbean Voices" had done in the sphere of my cultural education.

I was being prepared now for this journey during my years at Harrison College, a school for the bright, a school in an island with a literacy rate of 99.8, the highest in the world; and there could then be no thought that I would not succeed, for we considered ourselves not as black Englishmen really, certainly not as Negro-Americans, we considered ourselves as the

Austin Clarke
A responsive candidate in Oakwood

A prospective voice at Queens Park

"My political campaign poster when I sought the nomination for the Ontario riding of Oakwood for the Progressive-Conservative Party," 1977

best in the world. The education at Harrison College was similar to that at Combermere in the sense that much had to be learned by rote, but instead of classes in form rooms, we were now being prepared for Oxford University and Cambridge, with seminars in each of the two or three subjects in which we specialized. I chose Modern Studies. But since at Combermere history was not taught, I chose Latin with Roman history to back up my intensive "learning" of English. Whereas, for instance, at Combermere we were given thirty lines of Latin verse to learn—to memorize—as homework for the weekend, at Harrison College, it could be as much as three hundred lines, and certainly not less than one hundred. Intensity therefore became the character of my life. Everything was done in larger, deeper, more compelling measure.

And here, in a different atmosphere, where our masters wore academic gowns while they taught, where there were richer boys with richer, bigger, blacker Humber Hawks driven by bigger, blacker, liveried chauffeurs and the level of noise in the Yard

under the sandbox tree was lower than at "ten minutes" break at Combermere—separated by a wire fence through which we crawled, but in one direction only—where the uniforms were distinguishable so that the whole world of Barbados knew from a glance that you were a "College boy," my life took on an ease distinguished by the intensity of the work we had to do and read. I was relaxed in these circumstances; now leading a life waiting like someone who knows he shall inherit some throne, or come into a large inheritance, waiting only for the time to take the boat across the Atlantic and take my rightful place beside some other student, from some other country, and compete with him, on equal terms, and return to Barbados as a barrister-at-law, armed with a degree in political science and economics, which in plain simple terms meant a politician.

Politics was the rage then. The African colonies with their severe yoke of cruelty and disenfranchisement, the West Indian colonies with politicians who were magicians with words, foremost amongst whom was Eric Williams, and an atmosphere of a brightening of things brought into our homes, ironically, by the same BBC; all this created horizons in the minds of us young men and young women, an enthusiasm which could no longer be circumscribed by any kind of liberalism cautioning temperance or tolerance or a slower rate of shaking off the shackles of colonialism. I must say that even though I had my own arsenal of words aimed at the destruction of colonialism, I did not and could not know the indelible effect upon my own psyche of that political and psychological conditioning. For when I looked round, as all of us did then, even in the vortex of a colonial administration that encompassed every aspect of our lives, we still were able to feel that we were the privileged, the new elite, and we gave thanks in an ironical ceremony and celebration of the things we knew, and the people we were: to the British. *Growing Up Stupid Under the Union Jack* tries to face that psychological ambivalence.

I did not choose Britain. I was not so lucky. Lack of funds and lack of the power of information about living conditions and studying in Britain were not within my reach and prevented my taking the French Line's trans-Atlantic boat; and in that disappointment I was saved from the bitterness of damp weather and cool hospitality which greeted my neighbours who went to the Mother Country.

I chose Canada. And I stress "chose" now, even if I did not then, because as I have lived in this country with its own national unmannerliness, of being less than courteous to immigrants and other strangers, I want to stress that my presence here is voluntary, so that in the prevailing crisis we have in my adopted country that touches the place, the plight, and the role of the immigrant, and the reaction and the perception of the immigrant and the stranger in the new vortex of multiculturalism and its worst apprehensions, I must always remember that I made the choice to be here. I cannot therefore give the wrong answer, or make the wrong argument, when I am trying to describe my place and presence in this vast, complicated, and self-destructive land.

Still, at this point, I did not think of writing. Although I had in my enormous leather bag a tiny collection of poems, actually rhyming words about love, which I had dared to call *Pensamientos*. That a West Indian who speaks English and writes his poems in English would call his first self-published literary work *Pensamientos*, the language of another European conqueror and colonizer, was to me exotic and romantic; but when it is regarded in a more serious manner, as these things have a way of being done by scholars and academics, it is reasonable to infer that during these days of decolonisation, which I left at the height of their vociferousness back in Barbados, we were not unaware of another world to our south. And it could be said that in my small way I was conscious of the regional or federalist consciousness that we in Barbados, even though we often considered ourselves to be the centre of the world circumscribed by our Britishness, were nothing more than a haphazard pebble strewn into the vastness of the Caribbean Sea.

I had visited Venezuela, Caracas to be exact, for my memory of the former is formed by my touching the exotic, passionate, sensual parts of the latter, like a starry-eyed young tourist; but I had seen a part of the world, unknown previously and thrust upon me like any sailor on board a galleon sent out from Spain and Portugal. It has had a lasting impact upon my memory and upon my recollecting of wondrous days. This followed me to Toronto, where I came to be educated at Trinity College in the University of Toronto, eager as members of my generation were to read economics and political science. It was a glamourous course of study. For in it we expected to find all the answers to the multitude of social and economic problems—none of us had pondered for a moment upon the psychological and cultural problems—by studying and then using methods and methodologies of systems which were by definition inappropriate to our political and economic constitutions. But the glamour spread itself over the irrelevancies of this education just like the memory of Latin America in its proportionate short visit had done, to delude me that I knew everything about the Caribbean region.

Here, to my great surprise, my small collection, *Pensamientos*, became large, judged by an authority similar in its acceptability as the two hours of broadcasts of West Indian literary expression, each Sunday for a season, on the BBC's "Caribbean Voices." It may be said, therefore, that I had found my voice. And found it in the most unusual place, Toronto, Canada. But I was not thinking of writing. The fact of *Pensamientos* being chosen as the "prize contribution"; the fact that the prize was five Canadian dollars, a fortune in 1956; and the fact that I bought a bottle of Gordon's Dry Gin, a bottle of Schweppes Tonic water, bottlers by appointment to Her Majesty (or was it His Majesty?), and a package of Players, perhaps also the tobacconists of majesty; the fact that I was a poet, even if only a university poet of the highest calibre for that academic year, did not provide the enthusiasm or the creative force to make me want to put down the large intractable volumes on the *British Constitution*, on the *Price Theory*, the *Principles of Economics, Economic History of the Middle Ages*, and other readings in the British Constitution and take up the pen. And the fact that the things I could purchase with this small fortune were precisely those goods I had purchased in Barbados told me that Canada was the same colony as the one that I had left, for the furtherance of education, growth, manhood, and nationality. And this apprehension of a very serious fact, that my presence here could not be interpreted as a cultural shock for Canada was the same little place as Barbados, would be reworked by me over the years to understand the difference between an immigrant—and what that means in the vortex of psychoracial recriminations—and someone, as I see myself, who *chose* to come to this country.

All around me, in these days of the middle fifties, I saw the first presence of peoples who were not Canadian by birth, who knew nothing about Canada, until their boats, the SS *Displaced Persons*, the SS *New Canadians*, and the "coloureds," who were not honoured by any such means of transportation, arrived on these shores. I watched them; and I watched the hosts, as they were mistakenly called, for they showed not much civility to these strangers; and I watched the interaction of strangers and host. But my main interest lay in those women immigrants—who were called "domestic workers"—whose status was officially "landed immigrants" or "immigrants reçu" (satisfying the bilingualism of the country) who arrived in wonder and in bewilderment, in escape from the crushing poverty and the poverty of achievement back home, in hope and with a stronger sense of civic duty than one is moved to say of recent and contemporary immigrants from the same islands in the West

Indies. I saw these women on Thursdays, the traditional day-off for domestics; I saw them used and misused by their fellow West Indian men, who in order to protect themselves from the stigma of racism and wanting to be seen differently by the host, relegated these beautiful women to a social status not known before in the West Indies, but manufactured here, where both the domestic women and the student men were lumped in the same bag of cotton, some of us tarred, all of us feathered by the same encompassing definition: "coloureds." We protested in several ways and got that appellation changed to "Negro." There were, however, a few references to "boy" and "girl"; but these were personal and individual eccentricities which could be corrected by a surreptitious slap in the face, or a box to the ears. But what I saw was the humiliation of these women in the homes to which they were "schemed" to work for about two years, before they could go out into the wide blue yonder and make their peace and their fortune as any strong, able-bodied immigrant is driven to do.

"In my study when I was teaching at Yale and The Meeting Point *had been published," 1969*

This watching was more rewarding than the reading of those large, black-bound leather texts on the principles and theory of politics and economics, which are nothing more than a study of life. I had found something to which to rivet my wandering attention; to indulge in; to dream about; something that bound me in a strangling necktie to the experiences of these women. And from this mortar and pebbles and rock-stones came the pestle, things I would write in my first serious novel, *The Meeting Point*. It was an obvious title. One with no pretension to symbol and metaphor. But one which I later found out has a more significant meaning: it is the native Indian word for Toronto. What *was* that meeting point between the native Indian and the English and the French, in those days before an Ontario Human Rights Commission? What was it like when the first native (and perhaps naive) Indian ventured beyond the limits of his reservation and dared to cross the boundary of the English encampment? And what civility characterized their first intercourse? What were the size and the durability of the Bibles distributed in exchange for blankets? What was it like? If I was interested, if I had had time to be circumspect, if I really wanted to know that history which does not exist and which was not thought about in the living rooms and editorial rooms of the host, all I had to do was slacken my pace at any of the major (and minor) intersections of the city of Toronto to see, in summer and in fall, in spring and in cold, the bodies of these native Indians prostrate, not quite asleep, not quite frozen by their nearness to the inhospitable concrete, frustrated and humiliated in their drunken quest for equality and out of their wits through cheap drink, unable any longer to stand and face the meaning of that first meeting, on that first meeting point. And I decided then, that I shall never be an Indian, native or immigrant, in Toronto.

I often wondered what would happen if twenty of them, noble even now from the memory of themselves in books of Indian bravery, were to drink enough and have enough of this "fire water" in their system, to quell the previous and recent historical disposition towards surrender, and instead walk in a line to the building that houses the Ontario Legislature and exhale like dragons this "fire water" and burn the place down? I wondered if there was no Martin Luther King amongst their ranks? And when they would lift their heads up to me and plead "Brother," a new, uncomfortable term of closeness, and then temper the term with a mendicant request "Spare a quarter?", I would quicken my pace and walk out of their nickel-and-dime social demand.

We, who were not born here and did not want to, were asking for much more; *asking;* which is not the attitude requisite to dignity and the possession of rights; but we were asking for more, although our "more" was just as undignified and humiliating. WE asked to be able to sit at the same counter to eat a hamburger, which most of us did not consider appropriate or desirable diet; we asked to be able to walk into a barbershop and have our hair cut by a barber, who was not schooled in the intricacies of the kinkiness of our hair; we asked to be able to rent a room, infested with foreign smells, cold in the basement, restricted from having a bath more often than on Sunday nights (for a people who grew up with water surrounding us!); we asked to be able to sit in a cinema with other persons who were different in colour, but who, in the tomb of the darkness looking up to a kind of fantasy, were buried in the same blackness anyhow; and we asked them to sit beside us on the public streetcar and bus and, later on, on the subway train. We had been asking them, before this ritual of bequests, not to call us "nigger," or "boy," or "girl," or "coloured," and to train and discipline their curious children, as we had been disciplined and trained by our mothers, to respect those older than ourselves, and oh my God, please prevent your little white boy or little white girl from pointing her lollipop-smeared finger and saying for all the world to hear, "Mummy, look, a chocolate man!"

Smudged by that chocolate, those amongst us of lesser durability, those who had misunderstood the meaning of their presence in this cold place, cowered for nights in the cold basements with the dripping iron pipes, and amused themselves with memories of pleasanter times and pleasanter persons, listened to outdated West Indian calypso music, and killed the foreign fumes of dank subterranean living spaces with a new incense, a new essence of curried chicken and rice. Those of us who had arrived, fat from the indulgence of maids and servants in our homes; those who had left behind the chauffeured, black Humber Hawk; those who could walk with a high head and talk man-to-man to priest, parson, prime minister, chief justice, pimp, and pauper found in our social restrictiveness that we were losing our ability to speak. There was no one with whom to speak. And in our introvertedness, we became introspective; some lost all hinge with the mind; and all of us became soliloquizers. Perhaps that is why, amongst my generation, we held *Hamlet* in such reverence. And do not at all find trivial the simple mirror-mirror of "to be, or not to be," a question of self-examination which when posed in the private coldness of my basement can be answered with violent certitude because the

condition of its posing has not been assuaged. The question is the nightmare of purpose: the unanswerable reason for my being here.

But being here is not, in spite of all this skepticism and doubt, a transitory matter. Being here is the deliberate positioning of the artist inside the locus of his inspiration; and since it is inspiration and since it is in a real sense also the centre of dislocation, the positive aspect of his existence in this condition must supersede most, if not all, of the disadvantageous nature of the dislocation itself. The inspiration is the shield; and it becomes the justification, if not the rationalisation of what one other West Indian novelist, George Lamming, calls "the pleasures of exile." I myself have never accepted that the condition of my being here is an exile. And I do not subscribe to the contention that exile, even without the unmannerliness of racism, can ever be "pleasurable." Not the inherent contradiction so much as the implied masochism warns me to eschew this definition of my condition; that to succumb to it, or to regard it as tenable, would tend to place upon the observations I make about the placing of immigrant beside host, in other words, the explanation of the relationship, a too great cynicism, if not to say, anger.

Anger is one of the things I tried to inject into my writing. I was impressed by the use of anger in the works of Richard Wright, Countee Cullen, Langston Hughes, James Baldwin and, later on, LeRoi Jones (Imamu Baraka); to say nothing of the jazz expressions of Miles Davis, John Coltrane, and the better blues singers and bluesmen, like Louis Armstrong. It was a property in their work which in these days, now the sixties, seemed to give the work meaning, having already imbued it with its form. "Functionalism" and "racialistic responsibility" were the two terms encouraged by those of us who were "blacker" (also a new word) than others, to be the measuring rods of any artistic expression that was going to be meaningful, also a new term, to suggest functionalism in our art. And I tried, as I said, to inject this anger into my work, with the disastrous effect that, like the theories I had studied in university and had forgotten to alter and modify before I tried to apply them to my sphere of experience, it was jaundiced; and plain bad art. Not that anger itself could not have been used by me, the artist, to fashion if not to pepper what I was saying about my character and my location. But it had to be a different anger. In America, in the hands, and in the reeds, and in the chords of Wright, Baldwin, and Baraka, anger was part of their psyche. It could not be otherwise; and to have ignored it, or to have ascribed a tolerable role to its impact, would have been cultural treachery. The anger in being here was more diplomatical, more sophisticated, meaning not more indelicate or couched in niceness, but undefinable and unseen, more often than not.

The two novels that followed *The Meeting Point* were *Storm of Fortune* and *The Bigger Light.* In them, I tried to place this anger correctly into its Canadian perspective: to differentiate this North American (and therefore British) malady from the American virus. I have probably imbued into this second and third novel (the three now called the *Toronto Trilogy*) too much hope of improvement, too much hope of curing, too much hope that once the virus had been properly diagnosed and treated in some of its anatomical constitution even by necessary surgery, I was deluded into believing that the curse in the malady was repudiated and eviscerated. This was not the case. This is not the case.

So, during the middle years of the sixties, years of excitement for every political mentality, I was forced to visit the mecca of this political excitement; but not before I had armed myself with a knowledge of Frantz Fanon, W. E. B. Du Bois, Kwame Nkrumah, Aimé Césaire, Martin Luther King, Jr., and, to a lesser degree of acceptance (implorations for rights had never taken root in my intransigent soil which assumed that I possessed these rights the moment after my navel string was cut and buried in the soil of Barbados), Malcolm X, the nation of Islam, and the entire movement in America brought about by African-Americans and called "black awareness." The movement, and the real meaning of it, posed a different question from the one with which I had to wrestle; that is to say, it changed, and was forced to change from "to be, or not to be," to one which I was equally forced to face, if not to answer: "Who am I?" But it was not such a simple question, suggesting individuality. It was more a matter, in those days, of the group, the tribe, the "race." There was a further responsibility of replacing the myths invented by others and forced upon us by myths of our own invention. There is, of course, a definite danger when one deals in myths. But as my mother would say, "Boy, this is life." And if we are numbered amongst the living, we are different in that categorization from those in the *quick.*

This "black awareness" was depressive, oppressive, and freeing. And I think that in this denouement lies its significance; that any movement intended to bring dignity, to define, and to remind of forgotten worth, must have as its result the freeing of the bondage that was the previous self and the previous characterisation.

It was therefore a joyous time. The bullets were flying; the buildings were burning; the bull-whips were swinging (and some bodies too, on sycamore and magnolia trees native to the South), we were beaten, trod upon by horses, and made hoarse in the repeated and sometimes seemingly futile rendition of a wish: "We Shall Overcome." But it was now impossible to be beaten down. Our lives were filled with joy: the anticipation of an Elysium which, even if it were short-lived, at least provided the pie and the symbiotic violence in the pie, which we were now demanding. Demanding. A far cry from asking.

I celebrated this awareness, this new time, this spiritual discovery by writing a collection of short stories, my first, with the title *When He Was Free and Young and He Used to Wear Silks.* Academicians, that breed of literary detectives, have been asking me since 1971, the year of its publication, what is the meaning in the title? Does it have a hidden meaning: are we to think of anything specific, that is, personal, from amongst its words? Are we to ascribe some linkage with liberation and the spirit of youth, that is itself liberating, to the words in its title? There was no such dramatic or academic purpose in its choosing. I

"At my desk at the time when When He Was Free and Young and He Used to Wear Silks *was published," Toronto, 1972*

had been doodling one night . . . when words had become difficult and thoughts chilled by the Toronto winter, ruminating upon the "lessons" I had learned from my frequent trips to America, meaning New York City where I worked as a free-lance radio broadcaster for the Canadian Broadcasting Corporation, during which incursions into the belly of America, now being eviscerated by hatreds, I had met and had interviewed all the prominent and significant leaders of this "awareness" movement . . . doodling away time, as any author understands to be the days of prebirth, the lonely waiting days and hours, when the muscles in the stomach become tight and tenseness overtakes the entire body, waiting for the delivery of a book.

When we were sitting in those humid afternoons in the Modern Studies Sixth Form, dreaming of places beyond the one hundred and sixty-six square miles that are the dimensions of the land known as Barbados; when we jumped over those turnstiles that roped us in, only in a physical manner; and when we accorded and conferred upon ourselves academic degrees from the world's highest seats of higher learning, I, like the others, and perhaps not to be outdone, in my always unharnessed imagination, became A. A. C. Clarke, Esq, BA (Oxon), MA (Cantab) LLD (Lond). But I knew, as we all did, that Oxonford, Cantabria, and Londonensis sounded better, and displayed us as being bright-bright-bright, as several Latin-fools, Greek-fools, Mathematics-fools and, dare I say, English-fools, than if we had merely written behind our names, Oxford, Cambridge, and London. We all lived in those afternoons the future we wished and invented for ourselves. WE could behave like this, because we had the education; and an education, as I have said earlier, not invented and certainly not intended for us; but in a country with a literacy rate of 99.8, where in those days, the forties, there were five daily newspapers in a population of just under two hundred thousand, but an education which our mothers knew the worth and value of. So, we wrenched from those sessions of memorization and learning by rote, subjects and topics which bore no faint relation to our lives in the "neighbourhood" to our own use and usage. That, my mother would say, is what education means. I had forgotten it for a time when I arrived at Trinity College. Needless to say, I have not attended Oxonford, Cantabria, nor Londonensis. But Trinity was sufficient. It was a colony's memory of the architecture and ruins of the first of those two seats of learning.

"Always buy the best." I think she meant, always buy the best your pocket can afford. So, following my mother's philosophy, I have always yearned for the best; studied for the best; worked for the best. The best of wherever I am. "And eat the best." We could do that in Barbados. So, the precept was necessary, if absurd. "And wear the best." English cut. She did not have to say, "Work for the best," meaning for the best salary. But I knew that on my own and would yearn also for the days when I would be armed with a British degree, warmed by an English suit, no less than Savile Row, and with a wallet bulging with Yankee dollar bills. And not to forget the meaning in my choice of the title *Pensamientos,* the sensuality, in music or of the flesh, of something Spanish. *Hippa; Hippa! Ai Carramba!*

This was the time of a political euphoria, of a different nature that capsized the country of my adoption. And the fact that it had nothing, in specific terms, to do with racism, caught me up in its vortex and I, like millions of Canadians, relished in this national excitement and worship of a political leader with whom I could identify, precisely because he possessed some of the charismatic qualities of those West Indian politicians I had left behind. It was called Trudeaumania. And even though as a liberal I could not subscribe to his strictly Liberal political policies, he caught me in his wrapped embrace by means of a plank in his political platform: "The Just Society." This just society was intended to mean the granting of individual rights which he felt were better endowments than the parochialism of something called nationalism, or antifederalism. It became for me an adjunct to the bitterer struggle being waged to the south of us. And it was easy to apply the more racially nationalistic aspects of the one to the other. It was as if I had found my political identity, and that identity brought me into agreement with a land, though adopted, and with which I could make my peace.

In this new national pride, being a Canadian, I could more easily accept an appointment as Visiting Lecturer in the English department and the American Studies Program at Yale University. In Barbados, I mimicked the mannerisms of the masters who were my favourites, though not necessarily the best imparters of knowledge, and likewise at Trinity, I aped the eccentricities of two dons, whose life seemed to be full of fun, the fun of teaching learned concepts, the fun of travelling to foreign countries during the long vacation, and the fun of poring over books, drinking sherry, and indulging in intellectual chatter. And, of course, they all dressed like Oxford dons.

At Trinity, I soon eschewed the intractable theories of political science and of economics, and spent more of my time in the company of the "divines," theological students (not really wanting to

The launching party for The Prime Minister, *1976: "The novel was banned in Barbados, is
still not sold there, and I, myself, was made persona non grata for many years." (From left)
Jamaica High Commissioner to Canada; agent, Dennis Strong; the Hon. William Davis,
Premier of Ontario; daughter Janice Elizabeth; the author; daughter Loretta Anne."*

be one), those older, maturer men whose skin did not
see the tan of summer, cloistered as they were with
their moral, ethical, and theological studies, made
digestible and soothing as their voices would intone in
their practice of the Canticles and the Order of an
Anglican service (high Anglican, of course!), with
generous portions of the best sherry, every afternoon
at four. I was in the pickle of form and of condition to
assume the frightening appointment in one of North
America's ivied seats of learning. Combermere and
Harrison College had prepared me for this eventuali-
ty. In the English department at Yale, I taught a
course in creative writing along with the distinguished American poet and novelist Robert Penn
Warren, with whom I spent many leisurely luncheons
in the Yale Faculty Club. It was he who introduced
me to bourbon and branch water, after having first
explained what "branch water" meant. My course
was called Daily Themes, or something like that. And
just as close in his cordiality was a Southern historian,
he and Mr. Warren both displaying a splendid aspect

of Southern charm that had nothing to do with
"white liberalism"; and he a man of tremendous
intellect and understanding of the conflict then
overtaking the country of America and called, mistakenly, a Southern problem. This was Mr. C. Vann
Woodward.

Elsewhere, the cities in the North and some in
the South were burning. Black Power was raging.
And it was felt that this burning nationalism would
come to Yale University, as another aspect had
already visited Columbia University and made heroes
of that university's radical students. But within Yale,
with its ivy, and its thick brick, and with a somewhat
progressive attitude and understanding of "what the
Negro wants," an attitude better than Harvard's,
than Smith's, better even than Columbia's, we would
sit and discuss with fierceness and frankness, in
college suites, in masters' lounges, in the dining halls,
and at Mory's, beating our arguments, like pieces of
iron toughened in this fire of discussion, preparatory
to publication in books, in magazines, in journals, and

in learned papers. I received more education listening to these men, authorities of world renown in their respective fields, than I was imparting to my own students, than I could have received had I been a Yalie chained to the books in the Beinecke library. These were hectic times: of intellectual brilliance, of the joy of drink, dinners, talk, talk, talk, while watching the country disintegrate into pieces, and quiver at its foundation, as we sat silent for nights and nights in front of the television screen. Walter Cronkite was more lugubrious then. And the black students, the first large bunch, insecure, shy, confused about the "relevancy" of being at an Ivy School, Jack!, instead of being in the ghettoes with the brothers. "Yale be a motherfucker!" Mistaken and ignored by the campus police, harassed by the New Haven police, mistaken sometimes for members of the labouring class, all of whom were black men and black women. But when all was said and done, they were Yalies, as they themselves boasted in the better moments of their presence upon this frightening, sturdy campus.

It was as if I had fallen into the best-stocked library in the world, these men with whom I talked and talked and talked: my still good friend, Robin Winks, master of Berkeley College, detective and historian; William Sloan Coffin, the chaplain; A. Bartlett Giamatti, with whom I had many pleasurable scotches and no talk about baseball; John Hersey, the novelist and master of Pierson College, who drank only beer at his dinner parties and drowned me in my new-found bourbon and branch-water; J. W. Hall, master of Morse College, who had invited me the term before as a Hoyt Fellow in the company of Alexander Calder, the man who made mobiles; Professor C. A. Walker, with whom I shared a passionate interest and love for Dylan Thomas and with whom I ate lunches at the High Table, while the disbelieving black students sat in sullen silence at the "Black Table," wondering, as I drew near enough to hear their disapprobation, "How the brother could stand that motherfucking Southern accent!"; Professor R. W. B. Lewis, the biographer of Edith Wharton, in whose college lounge I spent most of my time, awake and sleeping, and of which college Norman Mailer and I were Fellows.

Norman had come up to defend his latest piece in the new journalism craze of an article on civil rights, published in *Look* magazine; and I must say he took more unnecessary shibboleths from the black students than he deserved and from which he could duck. I am not sure that he blocked all the punches thrown at him, some of which were boiler-house punches. But we met many times afterwards, in the best living rooms on Park Avenue, in the home of John and Dominique DeMenil of the Menil Foundation, later to be the publishers of *The Image of the Black in Western Art.* And after our soirees in Park Avenue, at which personages like Andy Warhol were present, Norman and I went to Houston, Texas, for the launching on the moon, guests of the DeMenils, and in the company of Dacia Maraini and Alberto Moravia, Italian novelists.

In this fortune of being placed at the centre of things intellectual and cultural, I was able to penetrate one myth which demanded, in its puritanical nationalism, black authorship of black subjects. William Styron had got himself into some hot water, by this raging black nationalism, for daring to write about a black man, recently resurrected by this school of nationalist thought and by this fierce cultural radicalism into the status of hero from the plantation field, and the *Ten Black Writers* (did in fact) *Respond;* but it was an uneven and not too scholarly rebuttal, primary among which was the piece by Mike Thelwell and then the contribution of my friend, John Henrik Clarke (no known relation), editor of the rebuttal, and more worthy to be known as the editor of the black affairs journal *Freedomways.* I made the effort to invite both Styron and Clarke to my class in Afro-American literature at Yale. But not at the same time. Bedlam nevertheless broke out. Not on both occasions. But it was the manifestation and the real meaning of the university, and of scholarship, and of something which is now under equally fierce criticism as the theory of black authorship for black works, something called "freedom of expression." Styron was not permitted to think that he could use this "freedom!" when he was messing with blacks; nothing in his arsenal of good writing could qualify him in his daring, his presumption to be able to be aware, to "deal with," for this was the real meaning behind the controversy, nothing about Styron a white man and, God forbid, a Southerner to boot, to make him capable of understanding to the satisfaction of the rising mood of pervasive black cultural-nationalist Black aesthetic, to portray a black slave. And Styron made the mistake, corroborated by the original document on which *Nat Turner* is supposed to have been based, that it was poor Nat's love for the white girl of the plantation which caused his hesitation to strike the match which caused the rebellion to fail. This psychosexual syndrome, and the reaction to it by black cultural nationalists, was something Styron was not to touch. That document bears the imposing title: *The Confessions of Nat Turner, the Leader of the Late Insurrection in Southhampton, VA, as Fully and Volun-*

tarily Made to Thomas R. Gray, in the Prison Where He Was Confined etc., etc., . . . published in 1831.

Understandable that, in these times, the national image of blacks had not improved from that portrayed in Western art from time immemorial; so who needs a man with the wrong colour to reemphasize this stereotype and dare to write about a black man, and not make him wholesomely positive? Who shall respond to Alice Walker's portrayals of black men in *The Color Purple?* Who shall dare to lift a pen and respond to Toni Morrison's *Tar Baby?* Styron's *Nat Turner* was published in 1967, and responded to in 1968. We are still waiting for ten brave, brawny, black writers to respond to the Misses Walker and Morrison. Is black literature too inordinately political for the wrong reasons?

The same approbrium did not greet Eldridge Cleaver's *Soul on Ice,* a nasty overrated book, misunderstood by all of us black intellectuals, and given too inordinate scholarly significance. But I understand now, as I taught it then, that it was a necessary political tract in this scheme of myths. But the humanism is not there, even in an argument of black upliftment. Imagine practising rape on white women (his enemy in the terms of Black Muslimism) to perfect it on black women, whom he had the audacity to call "his sisters"! The rage was pervasive, and in many cases became, because of that rage itself, irrational, and crude, truculent, and barbaric. These were some of the mistakes in criticism that I myself made. For we were all caught up in the present controversy which demanded answers to be given immediately, sometimes even before the questions were posed; perhaps because we felt, at that time, convinced of the prophesy in the front-page story in *Esquire* magazine, that we were indeed facing a "Second Civil War." And we were not appeased, soon afterwards, by James Baldwin's apocalyptic title *The Fire Next Time.* Many more of us thought for sure that we would at any random moment be shot dead in this civil war; and whether or not we escaped this judgement, either through the pragmatism of an Uncle Tom or by pulling a Nat Turner, or through discreet emigration to Cuba or Algeria as Cleaver himself did, it was going to be a fiery furnace: "Can you dig it, brother?"

Simultaneously with Yale, I was asked to be a Visiting Professor in English at Brandeis, to occupy the chair of the Jacob Ziskind Professor of Literature, which took me to Waltham just outside Boston. In Boston in those days, taxi drivers did not stop for blacks at night. And I froze for two hours once while trying to be cheerful and laugh at the stupidity of racism, a futile diversion, until a brother came along

and took me to the black ghetto in Boston's "violent neighbourhood."

We were like academic guerrillas in those days: flitting all over the Eastern seaboard to impart a black wisdom, a black aesthetic to liberal minds. And my own ambivalence was rooted in the fact of my birth, and in the fact of my meaning I was a Barbadian. How close should I be to these black American nationalists and extremists, the various Karengas and Bobby Seales? Could I dare make that distinction on a purely cultural or intellectual basis: confess to the British in me, and bring down the wrath of thundering racial irresponsibility upon my head? Should I take the bread and run? Should I give an intellectual reason to racism; rationalise the treatment of blacks—meaning only American blacks? Should I eschew my obvious difference? Some answers came from Imamu Baraka, and some from Malcolm X. "You sure didn' come here on the Mayflower!" The punctuation mark behind the reminder, in one case, was "Brother." Malcolm wanted me to understand the history of my people. Behind the other reminder, less a reminder and more an upbraid, was "Motherfucker!"

I learned my lesson well, and retired to Toronto in 1971. But I was called back soon afterwards, to Williams College, as the Margaret Bundy Scott Professor of Literature, where I cooled my head for one semester; and satisfied, intellectually and materially, I once again retired to Toronto; to be recalled to Duke University, because of racial and collective accountability, "Motherfucker, you was in the Ivy Leagues. We read about you when you was at Yale, and Brandeis and Williams, can you dig it? So, bring your black ass down South, to see the real action, motherfucker! It be Dook (Duke), this time, bro'. In the Deep South. Can you handle this shit?" And Duke, in North Carolina, it became.

The South was beautiful. The South was safer than the North. Not so stimulating as Yale; but culturally rewarding in a shocking and ironical way: I felt as if I was back in Barbados, while I was in Durham. Perhaps it says something about Barbados. Then again, it may equally be a reminder of the other. The smell of pachouli; the grease of fried chicken from Chicken Box Number One, which I shared with Norman Mailer on one of his jaunts through the South, to lecture and tell jokes at Chapel Hill and at my home university. I can hear Malcolm's voice as I write this. *"Your* university, brother? *Yours?"* No, I did not come to America on the Mayflower!

Plots and schemes of great works equalling the majesty of William Faulkner's prose went through my mind; and I made notes, none of which I have so far used. But the experience cannot be eradicated from my mind; the feeling of relaxation, mixed gently with the possibility of danger, like being in love with a lovely wrong woman, that first touching of the limbs, that exhilaration, that quintessence of sensations, walking in the peculiar darkness a minute after dusk, as if the sun had never risen, smelling of pachouli and the burnt oil from the chicken, and the smell of mentholated cigarettes, and monuments of magnolia trees, hanging low to the ground like testicles of black men raped in rage, covered in white tablecloths and sheets, "strange fruits" according to Billie Holiday; and remembering, and remembering. I passed a graveyard—built in mortar and marble as if it was intended for some plain in ancient Greece—twice each day on my way to the university and back; and passed it four more times each day of the weekend, on my way to the Chicken Box Number One, and to the tuck (confectionary) shop which cashed cheques for professors. Pecan pie. And ice cream. And watermelon, eaten with a vengeance in that homogeneous, disregarding blackness of myths. And I even

In Las Vegas

tried Ripple wine with some black students from North Carolina State University, who used me as a role model for their own personal aspirations. And made me welcome. And made me see myself, in a different wholesome manner from the consciousness I had been imbued with in the North. But I yearned for the North. In the darkness, which is every night, a bullet may miss its target, and all of the blacks in the blackness of the Southern night "are the same motherfucking victims, Jack!"

It was time to leave America. I had seen enough. I had received an education unequalled in any university. I had collected in my mind the raw material for three novels which would require the minimum of time to be put down on paper. I was like a winter animal, with enough subsistence to last me through the cold of the author's precariousness with money, without having to work. And I was at peace with myself: I had seen Black Power, had seen the Muslims in America, had seen the mountaintop. It was time for home. Canada. Little, Brown had brought out *The Meeting Point* and, a year later, *Storm of Fortune,* and then *The Bigger Light.* And they had also brought out *When He Was Free and Young and He Used to Wear Silks,* my first collection of short stories. I thought, with no reservation, that I had reached the mark set for myself by myself. Little, Brown refused to change the title from the Canadian one, even though their edition contained a few different stories, replacements for some published before in the Canadian edition. Or I was like a cow, having shaved the green lawn down to the precision of the Latin American gardeners I had seen in River Oaks in Houston, machete in hand, sombrero protecting their sweating backs from that torture of sun, and now in the shade in repose to chew the cud in satisfaction, like a soldier retired from the trenches.

I had thought that I would write a Southern novel. At least to set part of the action in the South. But I could not recapture the South: not its smell, not its nuance, not its spirit. And so my great Southern novel became a nonfiction of observation along the lines of a psycholiterary commentary on LeRoi Jones's play *Dutchman.* I dissected the play, put it against the background of the civil rights movement in all its various nationalisms, and when I thought I was writing about the South, I was really writing about New Haven and Yale. I called this manuscript "God and Mammon at Yale." It also dealt with the threatening visit, and the threats in that visit, of the Black Panthers to Yale. We all thought the fire had come. And we had buttoned and holed the black female students at Yale in certain "tombs" and secret society basements against the rage of those whom we were sure would bring harm to these young ladies. The Panthers did come. And so, too, the Students for a Democratic Society. And when they left, all that was lost was the annual day of merriment and hot dogs and hamburgers burnt in the quadrangles of the colleges, and the beer spilled on the spot by enthusiastic amateur hands of brewers, and the dances that go with that Homecoming, or College Day. I am not sure we learned anything from this lesson in economy. I am not sure we learned anything from the pallour of lingering eye-searing pellets of tear gas, fired from guns of the Connecticut National Guard.

I have used portions of "God and Mammon" at readings at conferences and in lectures. But I was not able to write my Southern novel. The aspiration turned to desperation. And years later, perhaps ten, I discovered the manuscript among other discarded projects, turning yellow through lack of interest and competence to complete them; but furious at this literary failure, I tried to do the impossible: change nonfiction into fiction. But in my attempts, I discovered that it was not really an attempt to do the impossible. I discovered that fiction is closer to nonfiction in the hands of a novelist than most would admit. For after all, I was merely putting into conversational writing those parts of the book which, when left untouched, could be regarded as discursive parts of a novel. And I called it "American Dutchman." You can assume the apologies to LeRoi Jones! In passing, I ought to say that I know LeRoi very well, having interviewed him in Newark, which he used to call New Ark during his Spirit House days, just before he became the Imamu, after he stopped writing the poetry that dubbed him greater than Ginsberg, as a Beat poet. And of course, at Yale, I taught his excellent book *Blues People*, which to me has not received its due attention as a document essential to the understanding of blues and the psychoracial implications in that music.

Once, on the way to Princeton with LeRoi, or as he was called by his close friends, Roi; in the company of Larry Neal the poet, and accompanied by my agent—my black agent—agent to H. Rap Brown and all of us, we decided to have breakfast in Grand Central Station before setting out to Princeton. I was fully acculturated by appetite to the South. Larry ordered juice and toast. My agent, thin as if perpetually on a diet, ordered nothing. Roi ordered orange juice. And I, tea, toast, bacon, fried eggs, hash browns, and grits. I had covered every vicissitude and nuance of ethnic dietary eccentricity. And as I cut the first morsel of egg and bacon, ready to lift it to a hungry mouth, Roi said, as if he was talking to someone sitting at the other table, "Brother, do you eat the *piiiig?*" For five years the *piiiig* never crossed my lips. And it was not only because he had taken from his briefcase a pamphlet put out by the Muslims, showing in graphic words and compelling illustrations the depravity of slaughter evisceration and devouring of this animal so precious and essential and fundamental to the diets of millions of peoples of the Southern Hemisphere. I remember Malcolm X castigating Martin Luther King and lumping his civil rights philosophy to the things he and his ilk ate. "Pork-chop-eating Baptist ministers." Roi said, after I had left my breakfast untouched, as if it had been afflicted by a plague, "You are *what* you eat."

But it was the attraction, like a call that cannot be ignored. It was as if I had left America without having written the conclusion to my life. It was as if Toronto had become dull and unexciting in my absence. It was as if the new collection of stories I completed after Duke, *When Women Rule,* was not enough to keep me content. It was that the march on Washington had, mistakenly, solved all further need of demanding civil rights.

I was asked to be a Visiting Professor in the Black Studies Department at the University of Texas at Austin. And not having known that a city had been named after me, and having received the telephone call at eleven o'clock at night, and not wanting to be raised from my lethargy and third retirement, I thought there was some good fortune, some fatalistic message in the identicalness of names. Austin goes to Austin. And to Austin I went. And just before I left Austin, I was appointed Cultural Attaché for Barbados at our Embassy in Washington, D.C.

Looking back over this small slice of my life, I am struck and made small by my presence in a certain place when world-shattering events have taken place. I am made small in the significance of these events. And made small also because of being chosen, perhaps, to be so placed: for when Kennedy was shot in Texas, I was riding the subway in Toronto, back from the main post office, with the cheque, in English pounds, in my hand, the advance on my first novel, *The Survivors of the Crossing.* When Martin Luther King was shot, I was in the masters' lounge at Calhoun College, drinking bourbon and milk. When Malcolm X was shot, I was in the living room of my cousin's in Toronto, drinking scotch and soda. And when Governor Wallace was shot, I was approaching a turnstile on 95 North on the way from Silver Springs, Maryland, in a Mercedes-Benz, to Toronto.

Austin was vast. And the campus vaster. And I relished in the materialism of America and this centre of Johnsonian bigness and extravagance. The stores were open twenty-four hours a day, a splendid phenomenon, particularly as I lived alone and had no routine. And they sold champagne and wines in the same store as lamb chops. The Right Honourable Errol Barrow, my Prime Minister of Barbados at the time, visited me in Austin and gave a lecture and talked too long answering questions for the students, and I had to take him to my townhouse beside the lake and, through the convenience of twenty-four-hour stores, was able to cook him these lamb chops, frozen when we arrived, succulent when they were taken out of the oven, and being too late to think of sleep, we talked till morning came.

Morning came in the harsh form of personal social commitment. University life, shoulder to shoulder to academicians, could only be a hiatus in the more ordered life of an author. And the too close positioning of myself to that life of books and casual ideas, to that unreal environment, unreal in the sense of not having to face the ordinary, bothering minutiae of life.

And now, I am embarking on a new life. A new life, in the full sense of that term. I have been lonely and monastic, inhabiting a house of ideas with only books and music to talk to; but satisfied, as I had thought, by this habitation and conquest of personal environment, until I met her. She is young. And what does this mean? Does this mean I am her teacher, recapturing events and experiences, and shedding them to her under a low glow of lamp, with lighted candles adding to the atmosphere, and spinning my own tales of demons and superstition, and frightening other episodes from a time she does not know, a child as I was, in that humid cathedral of deal-board and galvanized tin in Barbados when my mother would punctuate her stories with hands flung at those "damn bugs"? Does it mean I have emptied myself of the demons that live in the mind and soul of every novelist: expiation the only prologue to a new drama of irony? Or is it the completion of one circle and the drawing of another? Whatever it is, she is here. French, German, Irish, and Canadian Indian—why not Chinese?—all wrapped tight in her face and high cheekbones, inscrutable as her anger can become, staunch as her love is; virile, if you can call a woman that; virtuous to tormentation, and with the width of her ancestries only one dimension of her attentiveness. I call her by one of her names. Her mother called her by all five. I think I am right. I do not think her mother was wrong. For from that beginning, that root, rooted in a history of fierce fighting for dignity, and flight from reservation, and perhaps before that grandeur in her mother's struggle was realized by her, it might have been a fighting for mere existence.

The author in 1990

So that spirit of redoubtableness, indomitable as the Indian spirit that comes from her birth somewhere in the North, she, woman, takes now the stage in this new drama that shall spin its own lovely tales of life. And life is . . .

And now, as a "judge" of the Convention Refugee Determination Division of the Immigration and Refugee Board of Canada, I give a new life to those who seek refuge in this country of marvellous humanitarian spirit.

BIBLIOGRAPHY

Poetry:

Pensamientos (collection), self-published, 1950.

Novels:

The Survivors of the Crossing, McClelland & Stewart, 1964.

Amongst Thistles and Thorns, McClelland & Stewart, 1965.

The Meeting Point, Macmillan, 1967.

Storm of Fortune, Little, Brown, 1973.

The Bigger Light, Little, Brown, 1975.

The Prime Minister, General Publishing, 1977.

Growing Up Stupid Under the Union Jack (autobiographical novel), McClelland & Stewart, 1980.

Proud Empires, Gollancz, 1986.

Short Stories:

When He Was Free and Young and He Used to Wear Silks, Anansi, 1971, revised edition, Little, Brown, 1973.

Nine Men Who Laughed, Penguin, 1986.

Short Stories of Austin Clark, 1984.

When Women Rule, McClelland & Stewart, 1985.

Other:

Contributor to numerous anthologies, including *Canadian Short Stories,* Macmillan, 1973; *Canada in Us Now,* NC Press, 1976; *Many Windows, 22 Stories from American Review,* Harper, 1982; *Confrontations, Brooklyn & World,* Nos. 25–26, Long Island University, 1982; *Journal of Caribbean Studies,* Vol. 3, 1983; *Chelsea 46, World Literature in English,* Chelsea Associates, 1987; *The Oxford Book of Canadian Short Stories in English,* Oxford University Press, 1986; *Contemporary Caribbean Short Stories,* Taber & Faber, 1990; *Exile, A Literary Quarterly,* Vol. 13, 1988; *From Ink Lake,* Lester & Orphen Dennys, 1991.

Also contributor of articles to various periodicals including *Canadian Literature, New World Quarterly,* and *Studies in Black Literature.*

Scriptwriter of "Myths and Memories," "African Literature," and other filmscripts for Educational Television (ETV), Toronto, 1968.

Hal Clement

1922-

REALITY INTERFACE

Record and prediction. History and hope. Biography and ambition. Fact and fiction. Memory and imagination. Past and future.

Nice, sharply distinct pairs of concepts, if one doesn't examine them too closely; helpful, clear-cut aspects of reality, if one is careful but not too critical; and also, of course, carefully avoids that uncontrollable power mixer called *dreams*.

I'm a writer; I remember and imagine, record and foretell, so I do steer as far as possible from dreams.

But how far is that? How much of the semirandom search and careful reassembly of units of memory and imagination which I'll be describing for the next few pages will actually avoid that scrambler? Am I really in good control of these abstract operations? I can't guarantee my own objectively; I'm human, as far as I know. You'll have to decide for yourself how much of what follows is memory and how much imagination.

At a certain moment somewhere around 1950, I was certainly feeling in quite close touch with reality. The roar of the engine was coming directly to my ears, making a two-link connecting chain of sensory impulse and interpretation (computer-based terms like "interface" were still years in the future). Visually I was a little more separated, my eyes sweeping over instruments which registered altitude, heading, airspeed, rate of climb, rate of turn, and various subtle facts about the internal behavior of my engine. Since I understood how all these devices worked, however, and was accustomed to their use, there were not too many links of sense and inference in even the longest of the visual chains.

The other auditory connection, the hum of the radio beam in my earphones, was certainly the longest and probably most tenuous. The present clear steadiness of the sound meant little by itself. It had to be merged with memory of its changes over the recent minutes and with my grasp of the underlying science at several physical levels to provide the set of mental

Hal Clement, pseudonym of Harry C. Stubbs, 1982

symbols, whatever they might be, which I equated with knowledge of the airplane's location and actual direction of travel.

Since the weather was clear, I could have linked myself much more closely with these last two aspects of reality—that is, formed a shorter and much stronger chain—with eyes instead of ears by looking outside the cockpit, but this was against the rules. The canopy was blocked by an opaque hood which I was not supposed to open. I was on an instrument practice flight, and only the safety pilot in the other cockpit was allowed to have a quick-interactive reality link

"Flight-suited and parachuted before a Vultee BT-13," Gunter Field, Alabama, about 1943

and to be "directly" aware of such things as other aircraft on a collision course.

To me, the connections I did have with the rest of the universe were perfectly satisfactory. I understood the instruments and I trusted the other pilot. The Boston area was as usual fairly crowded with other aircraft, but there was nothing to be really afraid of. I felt no psychic warning and wouldn't have believed it if I had. I am much more mechanistic than mystical by nature and had settled for myself well before 1950 that warning hunches are a feedback phenomenon related to worry, and that they are wrong or at most self-fulfilling much more often than they are useful alarms (I still feel that way, if you're a mystic hoping to read here about my conversion). I had disposed of worrying even earlier; somewhere in my teens, during the late thirties, I had firmly decided that whatever I died of was not going to be ulcers. Take reasonable precautions about the future,

Hal, but don't stew about the ceiling's falling in (though I'd seen that happen).

I knew about the human sense of humor, of course. I like to think I have one myself, but there are some things I can't see as funny. I know, about the way I know I'm going to die fairly soon, that certain people find "practical jokes" amusing, but I can't recognize such people by sight and have never formed the habit of testing those I meet for this quality. I haven't even developed a test I would trust.

I was therefore quite surprised when my connections with outside reality suddenly snapped, and the universe of my cockpit separated completely from the larger one beyond.

My seat lurched downward and sideways as though trying to leave me sitting on air. The control stick jerked from my hand. The turn needle went all the way over to the right, airspeed dropped abruptly and alarmingly, the artificial horizon rocked to the left and then jerked as though it had hit something hard. The gyro compass spun wildly. I realized later that the radio beam had continued its steady hum, but the other events took my attention completely away from that reality link.

Much of my personal body control disappeared. The microphone had flown from its hook, and with an odd feeling of detachment I watched my hands jerkily and helplessly batting it back and forth. Neither could catch it for, I would guess, fully a second. I still don't remember which one finally did.

Then things quieted down again. The airplane seat was pressing my parachute once more, inertial effects became normal, and my training could take over at both reflex and conscious levels. I reset the tumbled gyros, hung up the mike, watched the turn and airspeed indicators come back to normal.

And since I was an experienced and well-trained pilot, I figured out correctly what had happened even before the sadist in the front seat who had snap-rolled the trainer began laughing into my earphones. A mind-set which automatically rejects the supernatural has its advantages; at least, it can save time.

The airplane was a North American AT-6, one of the best aerobatic machines ever built, and my "safety" pilot had violated no regulations in stunting it—merely most of the rules of humanity, under the circumstances.

I've been afraid plenty of times, of course, both before and since that event. Never before or since, however, had or has fear come with so little warning and separated me so thoroughly from the nice, regular, orderly reality I've now spent nearly seven decades trying to understand. Never before or since *as far as I can remember*—a key point for the rest of this essay—have I been even nearly out of physical control from outright terror.

It was scary at the time and remains both scary and infuriating in retrospect. I couldn't get at the guy—he was out of reach in the other cockpit (they're fore-and-aft, not side by side, in the AT-6). Back on the ground there was nothing to do; we were of equal rank, physical altercation is unseemly between officers, and anyway he was a good deal bigger than I. Complaining or being anything but a "good sport" would, for emotional rather than logical reasons, have redounded more against me than against him. Take reality as it comes, Hal.

That's how I *think* I remember it—the way it reads now over forty years later, off the more or less hard disk somewhere between my ears. I even remember the fellow's name, though I'm not going to give him the satisfaction (if he's still alive and still likes practical jokes after forty-odd years of maturing) of mentioning it here.

But I'm not sure it's pure, undiluted memory. Why not?

There are several image-producing faculties besides memory in the human mind, and it's not always easy to be sure which is responsible for a particular picture. We wish, we imagine, we plan, we dream. All these things produce records which may or may not reflect reality at all closely; and while we do indeed remember, we do *not*, whatever the scientologists may claim, record in complete detail every bit of sensory input. First, on the theoretical side, I don't see how one could possibly have enough recording material—"tape"—to do any such thing. Second, observationally, most of the data seem to me to indicate very much the contrary. This is not just in my own personal case.

Sometimes the evidence is humorous. In the fall of 1940, the beginning of my sophomore year of college, a year before Hal Clement had sold any stories so I was still plain Harry Stubbs majoring in astronomy at Harvard, I had solar expert Donald H. Menzel assigned as my faculty adviser. What he remembered of the introduction was evidently a picture; I was Mr. Butts the next time we met. I don't remember our discussing the matter, but he presumably used a picture scheme to help him recall personal names. A decade or two later, when the computer people were getting serious about mechanical translation between languages, a story began making the rounds. It may be apocryphal but I find it very believable, and it certainly supports the point I'm trying to make (which does not, of course, support the story; I have as low an opinion of circular reasoning as

the "scientific creationists" claim to have). As the tale goes, someone tried to translate the highly idiomatic phrase "out of sight, out of mind" from English to Russian by whatever program was being worked on at the moment, and then before having the Russian product checked by a person familiar with the language (or at least, if this was done, it didn't get into the version of the story which reached me) have the program turn it directly back into English. What came out was "invisible moron."

It seems to me that the same sort of thing went on in the mind of the solar expert and the processing of the computer. Items were categorized, stored, and treated as members of classes, not as unique bits of information. It also seems to me that that's the best either of us, person or robot, can do. There are far too many bits to deal with. I suggest that a key problem in memory, translation, and even basic comprehension is the establishment of criteria for sets to which words and ideas can be assigned. (If this is already an obvious or familiar fact to psychologists or philosophers, sorry; I'm poking around in a lake of experience just past my tiptoe depth.)

The classification itself is a problem which we don't all solve the same way, of course. Some of us index concepts according to their emotional content, such as the uncontrolled terror of nightmares and the horror of a Stephen King story or a splattergut movie, opposed to the pleasurable thrills of watching and hearing *Fantasia* or experiencing a love dream or viewing the landscapes at Zion Park. Others try to pigeonhole them according to degree of realism ranging from solidly objective memories through firm plans for the future down to daydreams, sleep dreams, and nightmares. Others may use ease of recall as the guide, or relative uniqueness, or any of scores of other criterion sets.

I haven't solved this problem to my own satisfaction and don't expect to, partly because I can't always decide objectively whether I'm dealing with pure memory or imaginative editing at a given moment. As a result I don't trust my recollections too far. Most of the time I'm fairly sure of *recent* actual memories, but as the years go on . . .

There's another entity inside my skull besides the recording disk, and don't get the idea I'm complaining. Years ago it would have carried a blue pencil; now I suppose it has a keyboard. I wouldn't want to live without it. It's provided most of my entertainment since early childhood as well as earning me a modest fraction of my living since I sold my first story fifty years ago. However, it has to be disciplined, another key point for the rest of this essay and, even with the firmest control I can supply, it sometimes gets at my memory storage. I am quite certain that I am not alone in this, and if you think it doesn't apply to you, you're a lot more religious than I am. Also, I'm fairly sure, more naive.

Imaginations, by nature, are editors. They are not the same thing as memory, but they share quarters with it. Information, factual and fictional, flows both ways between the two. Imagination gets its initial working materials from the memory disk, but it also likes nothing better than to juggle those materials until what writes out on playback is something that didn't happen at all. Usually the editing is arranged to make you feel better about yourself (all right, speak for yourself, Hal).

There's a common belief that a dying person sees his or her whole past life flash by. I doubt this seriously. I wouldn't try Russian roulette to check my own biography because I don't believe it would work, not just because I'd be doubtful of surviving (and I suppose you'd have to be really doubtful for it to have any chance of working. Blanks wouldn't get you scared enough). I just don't believe I'd see the true story.

It seems far more likely that imagination has already done its editing and the memories wouldn't be very accurate, though this might not make them any less interesting. I don't mean that the reworking is complete, of course, since I can recall a good many embarrassing incidents of my own life. I *may* be frank about some of them here as I go along, but don't expect a detailed, honest, and objective history of Hal Clement's world since May 30, 1922. I don't suppose I could provide such a thing with the best of intentions.

More practically, as an observational basis for my doubt that breathing into a plastic bag would help my memory, I've *really* been scared almost out of my wits several times, quite scared enough to expect death, and at least once for quite long enough to let a good section of the life tape scan if it were going to. No biographical review of the sort happened.

As far as I remember. Maybe, of course, *that* memory has been edited. But you could check; there were other people there.

September 17, 1944. A lot of paratroopers and gliders had landed in Holland that day, though I didn't know it yet. There was a shortage of transport aircraft to keep them supplied; I didn't know that either. I did know that on that afternoon the Forty-fourth Bomber Group (Heavy) of the Second Bomber Division of the Eighth AAF was ordered up on a *low-level formation* practice flight over East Anglia—Liberator bombers flying one wingspan off the ground,

less than one wingspan apart, scaring the hockey out of the local horses and me, and no doubt adding the phrase "Damn Yankees" to the Midlands farmers' vocabulary if it wasn't there already.

That evening we learned about the Eindhoven business (*A Bridge Too Far,* if your history comes from Hollywood) and could guess what was coming. It came. The next day, September 18, 1944, the first anniversary of my first solo flight, they loaded the Forty-fourth's bomb bays with parachutes carrying K rations, howitzer ammunition, and similar goodies, added a C-47 drop specialist to our briefing staff, and spent much time explaining why we should stay within a hundred feet of the ground until we reached the drop zone. It was to make things difficult for ground gunners—they'd have to pan too fast to have much chance of hitting us. We had to admit this seemed a good idea, whatever else we might think of low-level formation flying.

They had modified the usual formation arrangement. The normally low left and high right V's were to fly level with the lead one, and the slot element, ordinarily lowest of all, was omitted since it would have spent the entire time over target in the lead V's propwash (and wingwash, which has a strong downward bias). Hence there were only nine aircraft to each flight. Our plane (for the occasion; the idea that the same crew "owned" and always flew the same bomber is strictly Hollywood, in my experience) led the right V. Since Barney, my pilot, would have to spend most of his time looking left to keep us in position, it would be up to me, in addition to watching the engine instruments, to keep one eye forward and tap him on the shoulder if I should notice anything like a church steeple or power line that seemed to be higher than we were.

Preferably soon enough to lift over it.

After an only mildly eventful takeoff and join-up (there was a fire in the number two—left inboard—supercharger which the engineer extinguished with little trouble), we crossed the North Sea at a comfortable thousand feet and began to let down when we saw the Dutch coast. My nerve tension went up, not down. I have *never* liked low flying. I was reprimanded in twin-engine advanced training for being in a climb all the way through what was supposed to be a river-level flight through the Delaware Water Gap. I still get uptight landing from or taking off to the north at Washington National Airport, which involves low turns in airplanes much heavier than any I ever flew myself (my mind knows the pilots know what they are doing; the lower levels of my nervous system are less certain). I have a strong sense of self-preservation and a clear grasp of the general physical

"Official group shot of our crew in front of a B-24 just prior to going overseas. I am standing far left, next to Barney, our pilot, the tallest of the bunch," Westover Field, Massachusetts, June 1944

laws governing the behavior of airplanes, including the one which does not permit two solid objects to occupy the same space at the same time and the one that says that in a coordinated turn the wing loading goes up inversely as the cosine of the bank angle. These are simply more links in the many chains which I like to believe connect my mind to reality.

(Side point: I will continue to use the word "reality" throughout this composition. I know that some philosophers and most acid-droppers insist that there are many realities. I resent, subjectively, the use of the word in this way; I believe quite firmly that there is one and only one genuine, objective, actual reality—the one, to quote one of my students of many years ago, which you can reasonably expect to kill you if you take your hands off the steering wheel and tromp down on the gas pedal. I don't say that humanity is completely familiar with it yet, but it's the one the physical scientists are trying to get to know, and which we hard s-f writers—mostly—like to believe we are working with.)

I did not get a very good look at Holland, though I saw enough from a hundred feet up, in occasional glimpses, to appreciate its flatness. I really did esteem that quality at the time and under the circumstances; I found years later, gadding around with wife and kids in our Microbus, that the much less flat Wyoming and Utah have far more beautiful scenery. This is a matter of subjective taste, of course. I was not being subjective over Holland, except in the matter of preferring to live.

There were some complaints over the intercom from the waist section of the plane; it appeared that there were indeed German gunners popping at us from crossroads, and our crew couldn't shoot back, not because of our speed but because around each German were dozens of Dutch civilians jumping up and down waving welcome. I sympathized and told them so but had my own troubles. I kept swinging my eyeballs from engine instruments to terrain ahead and trying to breathe.

Then the oil and fuel pressure gauges all went out, number two engine began to act up again, and smoke started to curl up from under the flight deck. I assumed that whatever had started the original fire was back at work with additional support, though that didn't explain why *all* the pressure readings had gone. I reported on intercom; Barney kept flying, since there was really nothing else he could do, I kept looking ahead for the same reason, and Ken Waitt, our engineer, ducked out of his top turret and down through the flight deck hatch. It transpired that a bullet had cut number two throttle cable, wrecked one of the inverters which furnished alternating current to my instruments, and shorted the other. I cut them off at Ken's direction, and the smoke stopped. At intervals for the rest of the flight he'd call from underneath, "Turn 'em on!" I'd get a quick oil and fuel pressure reading, a puff of smoke would come up through the hatch, and Ken would yell, "Turn 'em off!" leaving me to hope the readings I'd just taken would remain valid for a while.

This all between looks for church steeples, of course.

No such structures showed up until we reached the "chutes away" point, pulled up to slow down, and dropped our load. Then I did see one which prevented our staying with the formation in its left turn back toward England. We had to make a wider turn than

"Back home at 7 Story Street, Cambridge, Massachusetts," summer 1945

the rest of the flight to avoid it, and never did catch up again. This was something of a relief for me since Barney could share in looking ahead, and positively relaxing after we left the coast and could climb to a decent height.

Now, there's a point to all this. I suppose the low-altitude run lasted fifteen or twenty minutes, though I have no objective record and it certainly seemed longer. Flying a thirty-ton airplane about one wing-span off the ground gives essentially *no* time for corrective action if anything goes seriously wrong, or even if one merely hits the wash of a plane ahead. I was fully entitled to be scared stiff, and I was making every use of this right. I have not, however, any recollection of seeing scenes of my past life flickering between me and either the engine instruments or the Dutch landscape at any time during those minutes. There wasn't time to look at such pictures if they were there, of course; I was far too busy.

I'm admitting this may be an edited memory, since it makes me look better—I kept doing my job when the going was rough. This was over forty-seven years ago as I write this. I don't know how much editing that little guy behind my eyeballs has been doing with his keyboard during all that time, but he's certainly been busy enough in other ways.

He didn't make a complete hero out of me, if that means anything. I do remember coming close to panic as we landed. We'd used number two engine all the way home in spite of the cut cable because the throttles on the B-24 were springloaded at 65 percent power, but of course we did have to shut it off and make a three-engine landing. When we touched down, we found that the left main tire was flat. All I could think of was how fast we were decelerating and how fast the plane coming in behind must be closing on us, and yelled to Barney to get us off the runway; he, six years older than my excitable twenty-two, calmly held the "Puritanical Witch" straight until she had almost completely stopped and then allowed her to ground loop to the left. We came to a halt safely off the runway, facing the way we'd come from, with what looked like a tangle of rubber bands around the left wheel hub.

At least I didn't panic enough to grab controls. Not done. (Once I did, actually; on one takeoff Barney's seat came unclamped, and he slid back out of reach of the wheel. I didn't wait for orders that time.)

There are people still alive—Barney was, at least a few months ago, and probably a lot of the rest of the crew—who could give their own versions of this story. It would be interesting to see how much editing actually has been done on my disk. Granting that the real universe does include its own past, I still feel a good deal more confidence in my mental images of its broad, basic rules than in those of the details of what's happened to me so far. (Say it simply and directly, Stubbs: You like and trust science much more than you do history, even if they're both supposed to be representations of reality. Better still, I trust my scientific "understanding" much more than my memory.)

But should I? Even learning the rules, which is the central activity of science, still involves imagination. And imagination is known for its creative power, isn't it?

Well, surely real experience, and hence memory, must make more clear, more intense, more vivid images in the cerebral disk than imagination can, mustn't it?

Really? How? In what fields?

Comprehension of events and principles—of underlying reasons? I doubt it. Le Châtelier's principle is very, very clear to me. But emotions like horror and fear (are they quite the same)? Maybe, but I *don't* remember being "horrified" by anything which has actually occurred to me, by anything I have read, or even by some of the splattergut movies I've seen (not many–no moral objection, they just don't send me). I felt nauseated at spurting arteries in my early, military first-aid training films, but quickly got over it. I am disgusted by things like supernaturalist propaganda and stories of child molestation, but this seems to be intellectual and not to affect my heart action, blood pressure, or retching reflex; if anything it seems to go along with the feeling of contempt, something I try to keep under control—after a few years of even indirect confrontation of Hitler and his works, I'm afraid of feeling personally superior to anyone. Too dangerous to the ego. This all seems to be more imagination than memory, though, so I'm still not sure which is more intense with me.

I mentioned earlier about not being familiar with horror. This is true as far as clear detail and waking experience go, but I have dim, remote recollections of nightmares in my childhood. Researchers can, if they like, pin down the date better than I; I would guess at 1927 or 1928, when I was five or six. The nightmares were connected with Harold Gray's comic strip; Little Orphan Annie's orphanage burned down over a period of two weekends in the *Boston Herald,* and on the second Sunday I couldn't find the funnies. I asked my mother where they were, and she said she had hidden them; the fire was still going on, and she didn't want me to have any more bad dreams. I presumably argued, but don't recall who won.

"Mary and I gloating over our firstborn,"
Albuquerque, New Mexico, 1953

A fire, of course, is as reasonable a fear as crashing a low-flying bomber, but I'm not sure fear is the same thing as horror (I've talked shop once or twice with Stephen King, but neither of us feels really comfortable with the other's thing). On the other hand, a man of twenty-two has or should have a better visualization of the real universe than a boy of five or six, and certainly has more experience, both personal and vicarious. I'm still trying to decide here whether imagination of something terrifying or horrible can be more intense than an actual memory thereof; and having related what promised to be another good argument, I realize now that it proves nothing. Dreams are admittedly imagination—wholly undisciplined imagination—but it was the *memory* of the dream which was terrifying me. Or was it? I presumably woke up already scared, if my mother was moved to hide the cause. I give up on this point; it's another of things I don't know.

I have not, until very recently, used any of my flying experience in science fiction writing, so my imagination has not been consciously drawing from that area. On the other hand, I've had as much practice as anyone making excuses and I have remembered, or daydreamed, about the old days over Europe, so the editor has had every chance to get at the material. Let's analyze this aspect of daydreaming a little less mercifully; it is, after all, another mental activity with a strong connection to writing and some to the real universe. How close? (Remember, the writing has been a self-supporting hobby with me for half a century.)

I was writing before I was flying, and reading science fiction well before either; just how early depends on how one defines science fiction, I suppose. My earliest relevant memory—which seems not to have been much edited, because I have been able to verify it objectively—is of a Buck Rogers comic strip panel in which someone is waving at a vanishing space-ship and saying, "They're headed for Mars, 47,000,000 miles away. It will take them twenty days to get there even if they go 100,000 miles an hour." This strip appears in the first volume of Buck Rogers reprints to be published, in 1969. My copy has an inscription by one Tony Goodstone, a representative of the publisher, saying "the first copy sold anywhere" and dated November 15 of that year. The date of the strip in question is not shown, unlike the usual ones of today, but is certainly in 1930 and pretty certainly sometime in February (the strip number is 360 of the "Tiger Men of Mars" episode, if that helps anyone's research). This would be three months or so before my eighth birthday. I had never heard of Mars, and the numbers were a little surprising for one of my age at that date, so I asked my father. Dad didn't know either (he was an accountant who had never attended college) but knew what to do. He hiked me down to the local (Arlington, Massachusetts) public library, and I came back with a

popular astronomy book under one arm and Jules Verne's *Trip to the Moon* under the other.

A couple of years later a friend of my own age named Roger Hotaling introduced me to the science fiction magazines which he kept in his cellar and which his parents, I now feel fairly sure (editing?), pretended not to know about, and I became quite firmly hooked on the genre. I began buying the magazines regularly as soon as I could afford them, at about the age of twelve (my first purchase was the December '34 issue of *Amazing Stories,* on Thanksgiving Day of that year. My aunt, whom we were visiting for the day, made no secret of her disapproval—less, it seemed, of the subject than of spending twenty-five cents for a magazine. I had the quarter, and the issue contained a Professor Jameson story; I had already read one of these in Roger's cellar in the October '33 *Amazing,* so I was meeting an old friend).

Certainly these publications were largely responsible for some aspects of my imagination such as my mechanistic view of the universe, at first so extreme that I honestly believed science could accomplish *anything* sooner or later. I was even less critical than I should have been about the Hugo Gernsback masthead "The Magazine of Prophetic Fiction" in, I think, *Wonder Stories.* I developed rather quickly into one of those obnoxious goggle-eyed brats (yes, I did wear glasses) who make life difficult for any teacher who makes a minor slip in class. Don't take it out on me now; I've paid for it since during forty years of teaching. I also, like most juveniles, developed a very high opinion of my own knowledge and competence, and either lost sight of or was shamefully slow in grasping the distinctions between my imagined (daydream?) universe and the real one. At least I can honestly claim it was not a supernatural one, though.

On the other hand, I did gradually develop critical powers, a key part of the discipline in anyone's imagination, and the science fiction helped there, too. Even in my early teens I could occasionally see that some of the things which happened in the stories I loved so much were, to put it mildly, improbable. The description of the invisibility device in John Russell Fearn's "Liners of Time," serialized from May to August 1935 in *Amazing Stories,* was sheer gobbledygook, and I could see this at thirteen. Even the time-travel technique itself was unconvincing to me (time was a *gas,* the time machines made of a metal which *floated* in it). By the time Professor Jameson and his Zoromes reached the slab-shaped planet fragment (1937 or so), I not only knew that such a body was unlikely—sorry, I still have the early s-f fan's distaste for the word *impossible*—but I knew why. I was also

Clement (left) with Groff Conklin, editor of The Best of Science Fiction, *at the World Science Fiction Convention, Cleveland, Ohio, 1966*

firmly convinced that I could write stories complete with strange worlds and stranger life-forms without making such blunders.

I did have a notion of the difference between "could be" and "is," so I grasped that science fiction was indeed fiction, but I had the very common teenage misconception of just how closely my own imagined reality matched the real one.

Naturally, I prefer to believe that I was never as bad as the so-called "scientific creationists." I *think* my mother had brainwashed me against the supernatural when she thought my sister and I were taking the radio show "Chandu the Magician" too seriously, years before. She had seen us making magic rings and performing magic passes, uttering chants beginning with "By the Power of the Three times Three" and similar nonsense, and was mildly scathing about it. ("You're just *playing* with that stuff, aren't you? You don't *believe* it, I hope?" We hastily assured her we didn't.)

I realize that my mentioning Chandu and the Institute for Creation Research in practically the same breath will annoy members of the latter group. I regret the fact, mildly, but can't help it. There is a strong basic resemblance between the two, though as a teenager I could never have stated it at all clearly. It involves one aspect of discipline of the imagination— the ability to recognize and avoid wishful thinking. It is therefore quite relevant to the hard science-fiction writer's line of work.

Science necessarily assumes that the universe runs by law, with the corollary that the nature of that law may be inferred by watching things happen and thinking along cause-and-effect lines. The supernaturalist and mystic assume at least tacitly a universe of whim, run by the will of one or more beings not subject to law. Admittedly we may indeed be in such a universe, since there is no way either to prove or disprove it, but the scientist can *never* fall back on the supernatural as an "answer." It may just conceivably be the truth some time or other, just as there may conceivably be a better explanation than the roundness of the earth for all the basic numerical astronomical observations or a better explanation than evolution for the observed nature and distribution of life-forms on our planet. However, there is no way to be even moderately sure by any objective standards whether or when the supernatural is true; for the round earth and evolution, if a better explanation ever turns up the fact will be obvious.

Also, while anyone with even a fairly good imagination can build an indefinitely large number of supernatural scenarios to "explain" any set of observed facts, there is never any *objective* way of deciding among them. While I had not reached this level of lucidity in my teens, I did have a safely solid prejudice against mysticism.

This, unfortunately, carried over into fantasy stories (except for some reason the Oz books and Dr. Dolittle, which I read with great glee in my youth. These may have saved me from total fossilization) and still does to some extent—while I have learned to enjoy reading fantasy, I still can't seem to write it. I never bought *Unknown* magazine while it was on the stands; the copies I now own were acquired from used-book dealers at collector's prices (lack of foresight carries its own penalty, obviously; someday it will kill me). When my own first story was published in 1942 and the fan group called the Stranger Club drew me in, I never took full advantage of Bob Swisher's then *complete* collection of the s-f and fantasy magazines. I filled in on the Doc Smith and John Campbell superscience tales I had missed, as Stranger Club meetings tended to consist largely of silent reading sessions at Bob's house interrupted when his wife served refreshments, but I passed up Lovecraft and Howard. I considered, I now sadly confess, that fantasy meant improperly disciplined imagination. I did not yet realize, in spite of my sales, that the mere composition of a good story of any length called for more discipline than I yet possessed.

I've matured and mellowed to some extent. I now greatly enjoy Terry Pratchett's Diskworld tales and Howard and his successor's Conan stories. I prefer the earlier Conans, actually; I'm a bit old-fashioned in matters of sex, which has been getting more blatant in the recent ones. I've always felt that this was an individual's private business *unless and until* it risked babies and diseases which the said individual couldn't pay for him or herself. Realistically I knew that Conan would have been enjoying himself unrestrainedly with the girls all along and probably leaving offspring all over the Hyperborean world, but I saw no point in mentioning it. I didn't miss the omitted sex in Howard's stories, and I don't use it in my own. Science fiction is supposed to stimulate the imagination, but anyone whose imagination needs assistance in that direction is probably beyond my help. At least, that's my excuse; it's true that I was brought up in a quite Victorian style. I have no trouble keeping my characters wrapped up in environment armor, not in the scenarios I enjoy setting up.

What happens in my own imagination is another matter, but still my own business. However, to get back to the point, I am more tolerant now of fantasy and even enjoy it.

As I say, though, I can't seem to write it. Whenever I try, the result is science fiction. Years ago I was asked to do a vampire story for a proposed anthology. I had read *Dracula,* and assumed I knew all that was necessary about vampires, so I gave it a try, but the result was not fantasy. My "vampire" was a retired Roman army doctor of about the time of Galen who had sired four hemophiliac sons, of whom only one six-year-old was still alive at the time of the story. The father was trying to solve the problem of blood transfusion a couple of thousand years before there was any real chance of anyone's doing so; my story dealt with his detailed efforts. Their effect on the ideas of his neighbors was left pretty much to the imagination (I still think it was one of my better early efforts at characterization). The original collection never appeared, but the story was published eventually in a horror anthology under the title "A Question of Guilt." (Nothing about it horrified me.)

I have, then, been all right on "could be" and perfectly aware of its difference from "is" or "was." I've been fairly well linked with reality since—well, let's say the end of my undergraduate days, or perhaps the end of my service in World War II.

As my memory now claims, of course.

I majored in astronomy at Harvard, finishing in February of 1943—most of us had speeded up our course work because of Pearl Harbor—and immediately joined what was then the Army Air Corps Reserve. It was already obvious that I was not going to be an astronomer, since my math was too weak (if Dr. Bart Bok, who wrote my general exam, had included a question about the method of least squares I probably would not have graduated. I still don't really understand it). I went back to college, Boston University this time, on the GI Bill after the war and picked up an M.Ed. and settled down as a high school teacher. Some years later, during the *Sputnik* panic, I got an M.S. in chemistry from Simmons College, doing summer work on a National Science Foundation grant. Thanks, fellow taxpayers. I had been writing all this time; I was still an undergraduate when John Campbell bought my first story in October 1941, and another a few months later. My parents had also become reconciled to science fiction; the $245 grossed by the two stories had made a very large dent in Harvard's $400 annual tuition. More to the present point, the course work *and the writing* had between them combined both to stretch and to *discipline* my own imagination. Painful as the realization was, I had come to admit that some things were really impossible even though there was no way of being absolutely sure what all of them were,

and *I* could make major mistakes even in writing, just as my predecessors had. Another strong chain or two had been formed between me and reality.

John Campbell caught many of the mistakes; readers caught others. I was just another member of the crowd. It was very good for me.

I remained firmly attached to my mechanistic idea of reality. I still do. I don't know if it's possible to rescue me, you well-meaning mystics. I'm not sure my sanity would survive proof that tarot, or numerology, or spiritualism, or "scientific" creationism, actually had significant truth hidden in them except in the most figurative sense. I now know, however, that my picture of the real universe is (*a*) extremely restricted, so I would *not* be too dismayed (though quite surprised) to learn that telepathy or ESP actually worked in some way I don't yet understand. I also know (*b*) that my picture is very blurred at the edges and probably elsewhere. I am even ready to admit that it may be grossly wrong in what seem to me to be clear and plain details here and there, but I would need voluminous and weighty evidence to be convinced in any specific case.

I have no trouble believing in quantum mechanics even though I don't understand *why* it works, because it clearly does—its prediction batting average seems to be as good as or better than Newton's. I can believe in the possibility of a pinhead-size computer able to outperform the Cray because I have a general understanding of how such a device *might* be made—it's no longer my childhood fannish faith that science can do anything.

But I did *not* take seriously the book *In His Image,* which appeared several years ago, in which a wealthy man had himself cloned, because I believe I have a fairly accurate idea of the difficulty of such a job and am sure we're not able to do it yet. This does not mean I regard it as intrinsically impossible—after all, we do make children, even if we don't consciously control all steps of the process. Mary and I have made three ourselves. I just think I know about where we are now in cloning engineering practice.

The believers of *In His Image,* as well as those in numerology, tarot, and other forms of magic, will claim that I lack an open mind. I disagree; I consider it as open as is safe. I wear with glee—am wearing as I write the first version of this page—a button which says, "There's a Difference Between an Open Mind and a Hole in the Head."

I'm not bothered in the least by the fact that practically no two people would agree just what the difference is. One has to form one's own opinions, and accept responsibility for them. I have done both.

With Isaac Asimov, receiving the Skylark Award at the "Boskone" Science Fiction Convention, Boston, 1969

Or, to stick with the analogy of this essay, one has to forge one's own links to, or specify one's interface with, reality. Naturally, one hopes the links aren't personal fetters.

I started this work with a description of fear, a situation in which there is a tendency to lose various kinds of control, and mentioned a little farther on the need to control the imagination, or at least subject it to some kind of discipline. I know some people disagree that this need is real, and like to "expand" the human consciousness regardless of results. I have been asked whether I have ever tried any of the chemical and emotional pathways to this sort of "liberation," such as alcohol, rock festivals, LSD, or religious revivals, and have admitted that I have not. I am afraid of such tricks, and consider them superfluous anyway. . . .

There is one minor exception: in my late twenties, on a single occasion, I ingested enough ethanol to make me aware that my eyes and feet were not in complete agreement about the details of my connection with reality. I disliked the sensation intensely, and do not intend to repeat the experience. I don't

like not being in reasonable control, though I realize that no one is ever in *complete* charge of things. I am not particularly religious, but regard prayer as a valuable reminder of this fact (when the prayer degenerates to a magical ritual intended and expected to produce observable results on the real universe, such as an exorcism or a rain dance, I become much less sympathetic). Similarly, I do not intend ever again to ride a roller coaster, however safe my intelligence tells me the activity may be. This attitude may have contributed to my strong reaction against the practical joke I described at the beginning of this account.

Naturally, I have fairly often been given the "Don't knock it 'til you've tried it!" line. My standard answer is "And what's *your* opinion of potassium cyanide?" I've observed plenty of victims of ethanol and other drugs—one of them very intimately and for quite a number of years—and am neither too stupid nor too unsympathetic to be able to learn from the experience of others. If this and my earlier remarks about sex make me sound prudish, Victorian, or even right wing, I'll have to live with the reputation. There are worse things than being self-

With Poul Anderson, award-winning science fiction writer, and his wife and collaborator, Karen Anderson, at the World Science Fiction Convention in the Hague, Netherlands, 1990

controlled or even being scared of some aspects of reality.

I've had a lot of fun out of life, in spite of the fact that I am afraid of alcohol and other drugs as well as casual sex. I still want to stay in control, though; my mother was an Alzheimer's patient for her last few years. . . .

So I've seen what happens when the wiring breaks down and will do nothing intentionally to hasten the process. How well I can face up to natural failure is another matter. I don't and presumably can't know how far this has gone now or at any other given time. I've been *told*, once, that I had hallucinated. It was very long ago, and at ten or eleven years of age I was able to reject practically anything unpleasant without even bothering to find a reason.

I was home briefly from school with some illness or other. I don't remember what, I don't remember the symptoms or even whether they included fever; but I was being kept in bed. I do recall very clearly—it must have scared me even then—my father's coming into my room at one point and claiming that he had been there a few minutes before and that I had insisted he was Miss King, my current (fifth grade) teacher, and was talking to him on that basis. I did not remember the phenomenon then, and have never remembered it since, but have no reason to doubt my father's word.

Something that happened so long ago without later consequences doesn't scare me now, but if it

happened again tomorrow I would very much want some concrete explanation like a few degrees of fever. *Something*, at least, that would let me regard it as temporary. Lacking that, I fear I might start to violate my personal rule against worry, or possibly even start to build some sort of denial mechanism. I hope I wouldn't wind up convincing myself that someone was trying to make me doubt my own sanity, but don't really know that I'm safe from paranoia.

This point leads in at least two other directions; I'm sorry, but words are not ideal communication tools, and probably won't be so as long as sentences tend to be linear structures. Right now I'd like to follow both paths at once, but will try to be clear instead. They'll have to come one at a time.

Route One: I am reminded of a story by, I think, the late Eric Frank Russell in which an organization named, as I recall, the Norman Club had the tactless habit of asking candidates for membership, "How do you know you're sane?" The group had some sort of black box for finding the answer in each case, but the story left me wondering at the box's criteria. When faced with that question myself I have another stock answer: "I *don't* know. It's just a convenient working assumption designed to let me get things done." I can believe that, intellectually; subjectively, I feel as certain of my own sanity as anyone reading this does of his or hers, but I wouldn't swear to it in court.

Route Two: I am also reminded, though the connection may not be as obvious, of a faculty meeting at the beginning of a summer school at which I was the science teacher. Each of us outlined briefly what we hoped to accomplish in our few weeks with the kids, and when I had finished the art teacher expressed disappointment with what I had said. He had been hoping that I would stress the "sense of wonder" in my pupils, whereas I had concentrated on matters of understanding—quite basic understanding, in my opinion.

Now, I have heard much about this "sense of wonder" in my four decades of science teaching and even more in nonscientific conversations. The impression I get is that people don't always mean just the same thing by the term and don't even always know exactly what they do mean, but that the *surprising* nature of the universe we live in is commonly what they have in mind.

Now, it seems to me that we are most surprised when we know the least. A good stage magician who appears to be violating the natural laws we think we know arouses our wonder because we fail to predict what's about to occur. Someone who had never seen a bird might be surprised to see it fly, and might reasonably wonder how it did so; but reasonable (by my standards) familiarity with physical phenomena and laws would remove the second mystery.

Nevertheless a creative imagination could still wonder why the laws exist at all and why they have the form they do.

If this is what my friend had in mind I apologize to his memory, but I was not about to try to get to that level with a bunch of fourth, fifth, and sixth graders. What I was tempted to say in response to my artist friend's criticism (no, let's be honest: actually I wasn't tempted at the time, it was one of those things you think of long afterward and wish you'd said) was that in effect I was going to teach the kids about pigments, perspective, and brush strokes and felt sure that this would help their appreciation of paintings.

My own surprises—failed predictions—have tended to be scary, in the hundred-feet-above-Holland and AT-6-cockpit sense, and I certainly didn't want to scare my students. In the second sort, this lasted *until* I realized the things that were happening and could explain them. In the first, of course, the fear continued as long as I was facing an inherently unpredictable situation; I had no way of knowing when or whether we'd hit something or be hit by something. In both cases I was scared by the unknown or unknowable. I have found that I don't like to be scared, in a trainer cockpit or anywhere else. I don't think scaring kids is a good way to teach them.

I have also found that I am generally least scared when equipped with a nice, solid, coherent, material, mechanistic view of the situation even though this leaves me fully aware that I'm going to die fairly soon. It's just more predictable.

In March of 1953 I was in a five-foot-deep trench at Yucca Flat, Nevada, looking up at a predawn sky streaked by contrails from several aircraft which were already lit by the nearly risen sun. Four thousand yards away was a steel tower containing what was euphemistically dubbed a "nuclear device." I was at the time teaching a course in weapons effects at the Special Weapons School at Sandia Base in New Mexico, and it seemed appropriate to the authorities that I should have a good look at some of the effects.

A loudspeaker was holding forth on what was expected to happen and what we should do, such as stay down on one knee and not put our heads above the edge of the trench until we were told to or, if the public address system failed to survive, until after the sound wave had passed us. I was quite able to figure that the wave should reach us about eleven seconds after the blast, although there were special physical effects which *might* cause it to arrive a trifle sooner.

On the whole, I felt reasonably safe until the final countdown started and even most of the way through that. However, at minus two seconds I remember saying to myself, "Stubbs, this is an *experimental* device. Nobody knows just what is going to happen. What are *you* doing here?" Another of the times I can remember sudden, extreme fear, again of the unpredictable and unknown.

Since the trench seemed the safest reachable place to be in any case, this realistic reflection did not cause me to panic and I stayed where I was, looking down at my luminous watch dial as the count went to zero.

Suddenly I could see the whole watch face; the sky was essentially daylit, though the color was wrong—more like burning magnesium than sunlight, and I could easily see the second hand move and judge where it would be when the sound wave arrived.

It moved about two seconds, and I got my first "wonder." The entire trench rocked back and forth under me.

And I had not predicted it.

Now, I had had a perfectly good undergraduate course in seismology about eleven years before, under one of the pioneers in the field, L. Don Leet. It took me essentially no time to realize what was happening, and to kick myself metaphorically for not expecting it to happen. How I would have reacted without the benefit of Dr. Leet's course is an interesting matter for speculation, though of course I was protected from many possible panic sources by my antisupernatural conditioning. At any rate, I had now felt and recognized a seismic wave.

The sound wave arrived on schedule and contained another unpredicted item. I had been taught in physics at both high school and college level that the longitudinal motion of the molecules in a sound wave is negligible; they travel a microscopic distance forward while the pressure is rising, and then a microscopic distance back while it is falling. It is only the *wave* that really travels.

No one had discussed waves with a period of over a second. The forward motion this time lasted long enough for the wind—the moving molecules— to sweep a considerable amount of dirt onto me from the front of the trench. The dropping pressure phase lasted even longer and swept still more dirt from the back; I was longer figuring that one out (excuse: the pressure curve was asymmetrical. It was possible for the pressure to get farther above fifteen pounds per square inch than it could get below that value. PV energy was conserved, so it spent more time below atmospheric pressure). By that time the loudspeaker,

"With Mary by the 'Red Wagon,' a mounting I improvised to hold three cameras at once for eclipse photography," Kona, Hawaii, July 11, 1990

of the nasty facts about *that* inosilicate were revealed; I travel, commonly by jet, to two dozen or so science-fiction conventions a year and presumably get a good dose of cosmic rays; I live in New England, with its goodly supply of granitic rocks (about ten grams of uranium per ton) and soils derived therefrom; and Mary was a smoker for the first thirty-two years of our marriage (she quit a year before my sister, also a smoker from her teens, died of lung cancer). So if you're a taxpayer, don't worry; my own hospital insurance will have to cover whatever happens to me.

That's another aside. The main point of this long Route Two is that the more you know and the better you understand the real universe—yes, I'm using that word again—the less scared you're likely to get; and if wonder is still important to you, you can still have it at a really high level like "why does the universe seem to run under a single, consistent set of laws?" Knowing things, no matter how much the detail, will never spoil that, as far as I can see.

I am not all that different from the nasty little ten-year-old I described some pages back. I'm a little more cautious, because experience has taught me that I can be wrong, but I still have on the disk between my ears a fairly extensive and detailed description/picture set of the real universe. I know it's less than complete. No doubt it's crassly wrong in spots. A professional who should know told me recently that a satellite in geosynchronous orbit tends to work up to an orbital inclination something like sixty-eight degrees from Earth's equatorial plane, because of high-order effects from our equatorial bulge.

I doubt this strongly. I don't feel sure enough of my own mental picture to call him wrong, and of course it's possible I misunderstood him, but I certainly don't see any mechanism which would produce this effect. It has not occurred for the moons of Mars or the inner satellites of Jupiter, all of which are in the equatorial planes of their primaries where I in my innocence would expect them to be, and both primaries (especially Jupiter) have equatorial bulges.

I realize that the mathematical weakness which caused me to end up as a high school teacher rather than an astronomer may be entirely responsible for my failure to grasp this situation. At the same time, I spent that career working out verbal and pictorial analogies for concepts which are normally handled mathematically, because my teenagers did not usually have the math. I got quite good at this and know very well that a lot of other people are at least equally good. I can't help hoping, therefore, that something of the sort can be done which will let me see what the story is about this orbit plane. If any skilled professional—he or she will have to be a teacher and a

which had survived, told us we could get up and watch the mushroom cloud and what was left of the fireball, and twenty or thirty minutes later we all rode buses into the site where the tower had been to get our lecture material. Everything else was reasonably predictable, rather than "wonderful."

For the record, I also knew a good deal about ionizing radiation. I knew I was picking up a modest dose. Mary was already pregnant with our first child at that time, but we had two more afterward. As far as anyone can tell, they are normal. If, four decades or more later, I come down with cancer, there is no way I will feel free to soak the taxpayers for it. There are too many other possible causes. I taught high school chemistry for forty years, and have been exposed to goodness knows how much lead, mercury, and even nastier things like cadmium and nickel; I've worked with benzene and some of its derivatives before people had put most of them on the carcinogen list; I made salt wicks for Bunsen burners out of asbestos as a simple source of monochromatic light before some communicator, not just an astronomer or mathematician—can help me, I'll be most grateful. I wouldn't mind, of course, being convinced that I'm right. Math makes stronger links between mind and reality than words, but of course even mathematical symbols are still only analogies. Mathematical models are not foolproof; it's too bad, but we still need even animal experiments at times.

There is at least one more reason for my preference for control and discipline. I've mentioned the roller coaster and my one experience with ethyl alcohol, but there is another and fairly common phenomenon wherein the imagination seems to run totally out of control. This can be fun, but can also be scary.

Dreams. I do have these occasionally. I seldom remember them in detail, and can say with assurance that none of them has ever helped me solve either a real life or a story plot problem. Usually what little I recall has been pleasant, but there are such things as nightmares. And I don't want to be out of control before I get scared.

There are none in my recent memory, but perhaps they get edited out before I even wake up. Mary has never reported my showing any signs of my suffering that way during our nearly forty years of sleeping together, so I'm more curious than worried. I did mention the Little Orphan Annie nightmare of decades ago. But I can reasonably hope that young children, with their lack of knowledge, may be more vulnerable to nightmares.

I keep telling myself. Then I recall the delightful dreams of flying with the aid of a coffee-can lid when I was young, and I certainly knew better even then . . .

Maybe I'm actually nightmare proof now. In that case, I'd have to admit I don't know why.

Realistically, I am much closer to death now than I was then, and I now have much less confidence in any sort of afterlife than I probably had as a child. I should logically be *more* scared of the unknown. Shouldn't I be dreaming more about frightening things now? Or am I, and simply getting it edited out of memory even before I wake up?

Maybe I should have taken more psychology courses.

But let's stick to the rule. I refuse to worry about it. I can't see dreams as useful links in any of the chains between me and reality. If they happen, they happen. If one should provide a seed for an idea, fine; I'll gladly use it; but I see no more reason to take any dream more seriously than the layout of a deck of tarot cards. There is to me simply no obvious connection between either one and what I consider reality. I'll concede, just as I will concede that the earth may not actually be round, that such a connection may conceivably exist; but it is up to the believers to provide a good, detailed, unambiguous demonstration supported by unimpeachable records and repeatable experiments. Anecdotal "evidence" alone doesn't count.

I've heard about plenty of "fulfilled" and "accurate" horoscopes, tarot readings, and numerological analyses.

I've also heard several plausible accounts of sailors who had fallen overboard or had their ships sink under them being helped ashore by dolphins.

Without seriously disputing any of the tales, I would not form any conclusion about either dolphin intelligence or the general dolphin attitude toward humanity without a good supply of data on the sailors who have been helped in other directions than shoreward.

And I don't see where I'm likely to get this, any more than I'm likely to get an honest report of his or her annual prediction batting average by a professional astrologer.

The author at home

There are people, including some I greatly like personally, who will regard this attitude as a bulwark between me and reality rather than a product of links connecting me with it. I'll have to live with this. They may be conceivably right. The universe may really be supernatural.

The evidence, though, says otherwise. I can't be absolutely certain of anything, but I can be happier with the odds provided by physical evidence and coherent reasoning than with a coin-toss choice between the Elder Edda and *Bulfinch's* (or anyone else's) *Mythology*.

I don't feel a *need* to be absolutely certain of anything. If I did I could choose, or invent, a religion and fall back on faith. I'm quite satisfied with my confidence in the published predictions of the next solar eclipse. Understanding how an orbit is calculated and why that method works makes a strong enough chain to reality for me. At least I'm reasonably safe from writing a story in which a myopic character lights a fire by letting the sun shine through his glasses.

And I hate paying sucker's prices for a good mineral specimen because of "crystal power." Decent fossils cost enough without competition from Chinese medicine men.

BIBLIOGRAPHY

Fiction (under pseudonym Hal Clement):

Needle (first serialized in *Astounding Science Fiction*, May-June, 1949), Doubleday, 1950, published as *From Outer Space*, Avon, 1976.

Iceworld, Gnome Press, 1953.

Mission of Gravity, Doubleday, 1954, reprinted with an essay, "Whirligig World," by Clement and an introduction by Poul Anderson, Gregg Press, 1978.

The Ranger Boys in Space (juvenile), L. C. Page & Co., 1956.

Cycle of Fire, Ballantine, 1957.

Close to Critical, Ballantine, 1964.

Star Light (sequel to *Mission of Gravity*), Ballantine, 1971.

Ocean on Top, DAW Books, 1973.

Left of Africa, Manuscript Press, 1976.

Through the Eye of a Needle (sequel to *Needle*), Ballantine, 1978.

The Nitrogen Fix, Ace Books, 1980.

Intuit, New England Science Fiction Association, 1987.

Still River, Del Rey, 1987.

Contributor (under pseudonym Hal Clement):

Reginald Bretnor, editor, *Science Fiction Today and Tomorrow* (nonfiction), Harper, 1974.

Bretnor, editor, *The Craft of Science Fiction* (nonfiction), Harper, 1976.

Bretnor, editor, *The Future at War*, Volume 3: *Orion's Sword* (nonfiction), Ace Books, 1980.

Harlan Ellison, editor, *Medea*, Bantam, 1985.

Other:

Some Notes on Xi Bootes (nonfiction), Advent, 1959.

(Under pseudonym Hal Clement) *Natives of Space* (short stories), Ballantine, 1965.

(Under pseudonym Hal Clement) *Small Changes* (short stories), Doubleday, 1969, published as *Space Lash*, Dell, 1969.

(Editor under pseudonym Hal Clement) *First Flights to the Moon*, introduction by Isaac Asimov, Doubleday, 1970.

(Editor) George Gamow, *The Moon*, introduction by Isaac Asimov, Abelard-Schumann, 1971.

(Under pseudonym Hal Clement) *Left of Africa* (juvenile historical fiction), Aurian Society Press, 1976.

(Under pseudonym Hal Clement) *The Best of Hal Clement*, edited by Lester Del Rey, Ballantine, 1979.

Contributor to periodicals, including *Astounding Science Fiction, Satellite Magazine*, and *Sky and Telescope*. Also author of column on children's science books, under name Harry C. Stubbs, in *Horn Book Magazine*, 1969–84.

Calvin Forbes
1945-

Calvin Forbes, 1991

In 1945 Langston Hughes said in one of his most popular poems, "Life for me ain't been no crystal stair," and I guess there's little argument about the downside (is there ever an upside?) of being born poor, especially for one who hopes to become an artist, since it's generally accepted in a bourgeois culture that most artists flee from the middle classes.

Class distinctions shouldn't be taken lightly, but they're about as useful as racial differences. With this in mind, I hesitate in stating I was born poor. Neither mark of shame nor badge of honor; merely a fact. My mother denied it while she lived, and she no doubt denies it still, saying correctly (or so I was taught to believe) that there is a poverty of the spirit and a poverty of material needs. A poverty, in the postin-dustrial world, that is the result of the lack of hard cold cash, needful on winter nights in Newark, New Jersey, where I was born in the City Hospital (now part of the Rutgers University Medical School complex) in 1945 and raised in a cold-water four-room apartment at 95 South Fourteenth Street, where all my seven sisters and brothers, save the oldest, Jacob, who was born in North Carolina, were born and raised to adulthood, for a grand total of six boys and two girls. That house, as well as another house I grew up in during the last stages of my teenage years, is no longer standing. The first is a parking lot, and the latter was torn down to build an expressway overpass. Such absences must be symbolic of something or other.

Father, Jacob Forbes, late 1940s

There were six apartments at 95 South Fourteenth Street, three on either side of a stairwell that always seemed poorly lit, with long hallways full of shadows. It was a ramshackle wooden-framed building that should have been torn down years before I was born. It was a horrible place to live, though some of our neighbors were worth more than gold and, to paraphrase a line by Robert Frost, they made all the difference.

The apartments were all of a kind called a railroad flat, four rooms one after another like railroad cars, similar to what folks in New Orleans call a shotgun house; all of us managed to live in four small rooms, from the kitchen (shot) straight through to the living room, past my parents' bedroom, past the only other bedroom in the house, the bedroom I would in time share with two sisters, one older, one younger, and one older brother, though two of my older brothers, grown men by then, also stayed with us when they were home on leave from serving in the army, Germany and Korea, in the middle or late fifties.

In the bedroom I shared with my siblings were two twin beds, each lumpy mattress narrowly sleeping two of us. No central heating, only a kerosene stove in the living room and in the kitchen a wooden stove converted to a gas oven to keep us warm. Certainly cash was needed to buy the kerosene, to pay the rent, the gas and electric bills, to feed and clothe the eight children my parents raised to adulthood, none of us ever getting into any real trouble, my mother was proud to say.

Robert Hayden's poem "Those Winter Sundays" comes to mind, where he speaks "of love's austere and lonely offices" and how the child in the poem can't help but misunderstand his father's expression of love, the father rising early to stoke the wood-burning fire, then demanding that the child also rise early, but in the comfort of the now heated room, to prepare for Sunday school. Several poems from my first book of poems, *Blue Monday,* also come to mind, most notably "God Don't Like Ugly."

Looking back, I see that *Blue Monday* is full of references to my growing up. Strange, because I have always debated the value of autobiography, whether as a critical tool or as a source of creativity. I prefer to see poetry, as Wallace Stevens suggests, "as the supreme fiction." Poetry as a higher form of fiction, telling a story, like history, like myth, but not just my own personal story.

There are poems in *Blue Monday* whose sources are sermons I heard as a child, songs, verbal games and words, whole phrases even, gleaned from neighbors and family and friends, almost all of them Southerners transplanted from the small towns and farms of the South. After leaving home, after I had gotten some of what the old folks called "book learning," I would come in time to refer to these gifts as part and parcel of the African-American oral tradition. These folk forms would become the bedrock of my poetry. And since reading has always been a big part of my life—books, memories lifted from printed pages—reading has meshed with the folk culture of my youth in making me the kind of poet I am today.

I have always loved idiomatic language and other turns of speech. Take the title "God Don't Like Ugly." It's hard to translate. Such an expression resonates deeply in people who are familiar with its complex associations. Doesn't Robert Frost somewhere mention that poetry is untranslatable? Isn't the heart of poetry untranslatable? We get the literal meaning easily enough, say, when reading a poem translated from the French or, for that matter, when reading Shakespeare, but for the rest we usually have to rely on footnotes.

"God don't like ugly," my mother would say, admonishing me for some ugly deed or word I had ushered into the world. It's an old expression, and when I read that poem aloud to audiences, I always garner a few sighs in recognition. Perhaps they are recalling some incident, or a caring face. Nonblacks too respond, since the feeling behind the words is universal.

Besides the oral tradition, the blues, not just the music per se but the lyrics and the wry philosophy underpinning them, had a major impact on my conception of the kind of poem I wanted to write. Gospel and (rhythm and blues) music were all around me when I was growing up. My brother Charles played the piano and the saxophone, and my sister Betty sang in all-girl groups locally that were modeled after such well-known national acts as the Marvelettes.

Except for the mantelpiece, which stood like a shrine in the living room complete with a clock my brother James had sent home from Korea and rows of family photos and other family heirlooms, the only other furniture I can recall fondly from that house on Fourteenth Street is the upright piano that belonged to my brother Charles who, along with my brothers James and George, was away in the army during most of those years. I really got into the blues years later, though, belatedly realizing their cultural importance. I quickly made up for lost time, digesting their lyrics and images and wisdom like a hungry man. I remember meeting and listening to Mississippi John Hurt at the Newport Folk Festival in the mid-sixties and being awed by his presence. I was eighteen or nineteen, discovering old and new worlds. Growing up, the music, the folk culture, was like a piece of pottery lying around the house, paid little attention to until somebody hipper came along and pulled your coat— an old African-American idiomatic expression— about the valuable object collecting dust within your reach.

Going to church and listening to gospel music were regular events for us. My older sister, Betty, would eventually switch from rock and roll to gospel. Gospel music, which is akin to the blues, and the whole church experience have had a powerful influence on me. Two poems from *Blue Monday* reflect my background in the church: "The Middle Life," which recounts the times after church when we were expected to put our minds on God and not on playing outside with our friends or listening to music, except maybe the gospel music being aired on WNJR, and "Sunday," which I dedicated to the poet Samuel Allen, an elder statesman of African-American poetry, who befriended me during my Boston years. "Sunday" recounts a visit I made when I was home once and went to church with my mother for the first

time in many years. Through Sam I met Sterling Brown, another elder statesman whose work I admired, and Gwendolyn Brooks, another trailblazer.

The title *Blue Monday* stems from another old expression, popularized by great R & B singer and piano man Fats Domino. As a kid I remember asking my barber why he wasn't open on Mondays, and he told me because he didn't work on Blue Monday. I was half thinking of his remarks when I wrote the title poem for *Blue Monday*, though I had the book's title in mind way before I wrote the poem. My barber, a friend of my father's, suffered from the malaise of living for the weekend. Mondays always brought back reality with a bang.

There were few if any books in the house, except for the Bible. Yet, up until the age of twelve or so I read a great deal, mostly borrowing books from the nearest branch of the Newark Public Library, maybe two, three miles away, in a mostly white section of town. I recall reading short stories in the *Saturday Evening Post*, too, which I bought with the pocket money I earned doing whatever odd job I could in

Mother, Mary Forbes, early 1970s

the neighborhood, or working with my mother and father who opened a small restaurant when I was in the seventh grade. We ate better, and now my clothes were no longer secondhand, but we continued to live at 95 South Fourteenth Street, not moving up until my first year in high school, and then only a few blocks away, to 27 South Thirteenth Street.

One of my favorite books from my high school years was *Exodus* by Leon Uris. I often wonder whether some writers are bred more on the Hardy Boys than on Thomas Hardy. I was also very impressed with *Bread and Wine* by the Nobel Prize–winning Italian novelist Ignazio Silone. Another novel, *A Tale of Two Cities,* knocked me out and the essay I wrote on it enabled me to graduate from high school. Several teachers from high school and junior high school years stand out: Mr. Wacker, who once told he could never make up his mind about whether I belonged in the advanced English class or the remedial class, and Mr. Martin, a music teacher, one of the few black teachers yet he taught us no black music. There were others: Mrs. Goldberg, who would befriend and encourage me and advise me even after I graduated; Mrs. Mandel, who praised me to high heaven, the first teacher to do so, yet she dismayed me when she advised me not to hang out with certain of my black friends and classmates because I was smarter than them; and another, a history teacher who had seemed so liberal, yet who shunned me when I went to him after graduation for guidance regarding my protest against the Vietnam War when I was considering turning in my draft card.

The only black writer I recall reading in high school was James Weldon Johnson; his poem "Go Down Moses" was included in one of our high school literature textbooks. He was an important African-American intellectual and activist writer before World War II. He wrote "Lift Every Voice and Sing," known as the Negro National Anthem, as well as a novel and other books. I wished I had been exposed to his and other African-American writers' works a lot earlier. We never studied Johnson's poetry in class, though he was the only African-American writer I recall ever being included in any of the textbooks we used. How then did I come to be a writer, bookish, when, as I said before, books and book reading were not a given in my home, and I was offered no role model in school or elsewhere?

I wasn't what you would call a good student, if you measure such things only by grades. My grades went up and down, and I was once threatened with being expelled for "hooking" school, though I was in a few advanced English classes and did well on the English and math sections of standardized tests like the SAT and the PSAT. One of my buddies who scored the highest in the city on the math portion of PSAT, Pops we called him, dropped out of high school, and may not ever have graduated. The memory of his lost life and many others like him still haunts me. Surely, I too could have been one of the casualties. By sixteen I was heading for trouble, hanging out on the street corners, doing my best, in spite of Mrs. Mandel, to be one of the fellows.

Before street life laid claim to me, many of my future best friends enjoyed teasing me, calling me a bookworm, or worse. My father, too, doubted the wisdom of book learning, echoing the popular belief that book learning would sooner than later get a black man nowhere, or that too much book learning would render you not quite black or mannish. Once, my father even threw some books of mine away. Sad to say, such views are still common in much of the African-American community today. But my father and my peers had little to worry about; by the time I was in my teens, the street corner life had a hold on me. By conforming to the sadly unchanging harsh code of conduct offered to a young black male growing up in what some call the inner city, and by playing sports (basketball became my passion, even upstaging my budding interest in girls for awhile), I did manage to avoid the nerd syndrome. Too many bright young black children, perhaps especially males, are either alienated from the black urban (folk?) culture, or sucked hopelessly into its worst pitfalls. I was lucky. I was the first of the six boys in my immediate family to graduate from high school, though the others completed their education in the army and have done well, owning their own homes and so forth. Today I am a college teacher and a writer. Having survived with my roots unsevered, this foundation saved me as a person and a writer. It kept me sane. It plugs me into the language and style of even this generation's urban black culture, empowering me to feel it in my bones. But, like I said, I was lucky. The balance could have swung the other way.

The neighborhood itself was my home away from home. In the apartment across the hall from us lived a family equally as large as our own. We visited freely back and forth. Their cousin Jimmy Barnes came to live with them around the time I was eight or nine. It was during the summer and we were sitting on the porch. Jimmy had a book of poems, don't ask me how or why; I believe it must have been an anthology. I asked to see it and I read a poem by John Donne, the great sixteenth-century English poet, "Go and Catch a Falling Star." It's my first memory of reading a poem, of even knowing such a thing existed. I told Jimmy I could write something like that. I could make words sing on a page, in the mind, like Donne's words had for me. Keep in mind that I didn't understand completely what I was reading, but I felt it, enjoyed the poem's music. I wrote something, long lost and forgotten, and showed it to Jimmy. From that day on I was smitten. I count it as one of the turning points in my life. It was magic.

I always knew Jimmy Barnes had gotten me into poetry. But I was surprised to find out that he was aware of his input. After we moved away I didn't see him again, except maybe once or twice at the most, until I had already published *Blue Monday*, when I was in my late twenties. His cousins, the Hawes, had moved too, after their mother, Jeannette (she was the only adult I was ever allowed to call by her first name), had died. Hers was my first encounter with death, and it's a complex memory that has stuck with me all these years. I tried to write a story about her once; maybe I'll try again. She was one of my mother's best friends, and I loved her too, like a second mother. She was so full of life, but cancer took her, leaving her husband, Freddy, to raise the rest of the eight kids not yet out of the house as best he could. I met Jimmy again at a reunion of the old neighborhood, held by one of the Hawes now living successfully in one of the suburbs of Newark. Jimmy showed up and asked me directly how come I hadn't sent him a copy of my book since he was the one who had got me started. I was shocked speechless. I will never underestimate the value of personal influence, what some people like sometimes to call having a role model. You never know who's watching you, listening to you, learning from you, in the most casual of circumstances.

John Donne remains one of my favorite poets and his style, his use of imagery, has had a major impact on my work. Specifically, I liked the way Donne used a central metaphor to structure his poems. When I was in my twenties, I sat in on a class on sixteenth-century English poetry taught by Professor Edward Taylor of Columbia University at the Bread Loaf School of English. Taylor's class opened my eyes to Donne, Jonson, Marvell, and other poets from that era. I even showed him some of my poems, including "For My Mother," one of my first attempts at writing seriously, which he liked; he pointed out what was false and what was real in my work. The poet Robert Pack, who taught at Bread Loaf and nearby Middlebury College, also offered criticism along with carefully considered advice.

My job as a child was to go to the corner store to pick up and "carry the kerosene can back home," as I wrote in "God Don't Like Ugly." I hated

Calvin, thirteen years old and in the eighth grade

doing it, because the kerosene can would invariably spill, and the smell of the kerosene would stick to my clothes and skin and invariably stink.

But similar to the character in Robert Hayden's poem "Those Winter Sundays," I had little awareness as a child of how my mother and father suffered, working hard for the meager heat and rations that were our lot. When I became aware of the immense shortages we endured as a family, compared to the world outside my neighborhood, it was the beginning of my maturity. I became aware of the tremendous sacrifices my parents made to provide for us, yet I also was becoming acutely aware of what we lacked. I remember speaking on this topic to a friend. I was eighteen or so, feeling high off myself, ready and eager to join the civil rights movement that was swirling around me; I was taking classes at Rutgers University, the Newark campus, and working downtown at the Newark Public Library (where I truly learned to read while stacking books), finally financially ready and eager to move out of my mother's house to my own apartment, my first, in downtown Newark. I thought I was bad. I was, like the old folks used to say, smelling myself.

I told my friend there were people who never had to worry where their next meal would come from, worry whether they could afford to go to the dentist, the doctor, or buy a pair of cheap shoes. Worry can kill you just like cancer. Some people call it stress. My mother could worry herself to tears.

Most of the people I grew up with were more or less in the same boat I was in. Nobody pulled a yacht. I have always wanted to write a poem that began "the poor are always with me / because I have been poor." I never could complete that poem because I never knew what else to say, or how to express my thoughts in a form that would be poetry for me. I never wanted to write prose broken up into little lines. A poem, for me, has to have form, structure, and it has to sing.

Some people reading this might say I am indulging in a bit of self-pity, maybe even romanticizing my past, asking for sympathy. (A reviewer once made such a statement about *Blue Monday*. I am grateful that his opinion wasn't shared by any of the other reviewers of my work.) But I don't see myself and my work that way at all. I long ago learned that the circumstances of my past are not unique. There are a whole bunch of poor people in the world, of all creeds, nationalities, and races. It's just that my youth marked me, for better or worse. I believe my story is a universal one, certainly one shared by many African-Americans of my generation. In spite of the hard times, it was rich in love, though I didn't always recognize the love around me as such. Lucille Clifton in her fine poem "Good Times" captures this feeling very well.

I try to stay in touch with my past in order to mine its resources for my future work and growth as a person and an artist. What more can a poor boy from Newark want? I surely never wanted to be president of the United States.

Today, I basically earn my living by reading and writing. Though it may not be cool to admit this, I am middle-class, by income if not attitude, a college English professor, a writer, living a life I doubt my parents could have ever dreamed. My children are well within the middle-class comfort zone, though I am unmarried now and separated from their respective mothers. My daughter and son will never experience the world I lived in, though they won't always have the material things they covet.

When I was living in Hawaii, I sent my father and mother an article I had written on B. B. King. It was one of the first things I ever published. My mother was proud. My father, if I recall my mother's words correctly, said I was lost. Lost? Meaning what? Gone out of the circle of 95 South Fourteenth Street

forever? What was gained, if something was lost? Such questions still haunt me.

My mother and father were born in 1914 and 1917 respectively in the Greenville area, in the eastern part of North Carolina. My first published poem, "For My Mother," recounts something of their courtship and how they came north.

> Pale as the familiar cream and tea, you
> Float past history and into a cup; before
> My birth, a time so unreal I imagine
> Helen stealing your thoughts while you
> Decide to climb down for the favors
> Of my father: he insisted that you charm
> The sheriff and harness a mule for a free
> Ride north. One brother was born already.
>
> Drowning now as tired
> dreams like hands
> Lift the fallen gay parade, you drink to a mad
> Life father led leaving you always pregnant and poor.
> Some sons went unborn. I was out on the final knot
> Of promises, as your citadel collapsed in old age
> And my lonely father became a fabled and alien man.

The Helen I am referring to is Helen of Troy. I wanted to have the allusion of Helen of Troy being abducted by Paris and contrast it with an image of my fair-skinned mother, who was middle-class (her father was an undertaker), running off, eloping with my father against the wishes of my maternal grandparents. My father was certainly not middle-class. To be sure, I have "fictionalized" this story somewhat, as indeed my mother might have when she told me the bare bones of it. I sent her a copy of the poem, which was published in 1969 in the *American Scholar*. When I asked her if she liked the poem, she said *oh, it sounds so pretty.* Her comment remains for me very telling. For I believe what she meant was that the poem had music, that it sang, that it made sweet sounds in her mind. This quality of words as music, the orchestration of metaphorical language, is what I aim for in my work.

"For My Mother" was my first published poem in a national magazine. By the time it came out, my father was a sick and tired old man. No longer the vital aggressive man I knew, he would die within the next few years. I write about him in several poems in *Blue Monday:* "My Father's House," a poem that began in my mind while I sat in church listening to the minister preaching over my father's casket, and another poem, "Father," grows out of that time as well. My father was a strong and very intelligent man, with only a grammar school education, who while struggling to own his own business was often out of work, but wouldn't work for white people, and was always dreaming of making big bucks. I can't say when I was wrestling with memories of my father because I still am. There were countless numbers of African-American men like him of his generation; strong men who rather than buckle under to the system of racism dropped out and made their living on the fringes of society. He always wanted to be his own boss, to own his own business, and had several, all of which he lost. Maybe he would have been more successful if he had had the opportunities I had. I plan to write more about him and the many men like him I've met over the years. I used to count my mother as the major influence on my life; yet my father's can't be discounted, though I long ago leaned away from him, perhaps misreading my past as a consequence. I have several newer poems, not yet published, about being a father myself.

Another poem I wanted to write, but never could quite finish, began "since I left my mother's house." It was to be a poem about my travels, both spiritually and physically. I was living in Hawaii when I first started to break through with my writing to something approaching art. I had tried my hand at poetry and fiction before, publishing a poem in the Rutgers University student magazine. A line from that poem, which I regret I have lost, seems to have heralded much. "I thought too much of baggage and such / and lost you along the way."

Up until I was about thirty I was always on the move, crisscrossing Europe and America, hitchhiking once coast-to-coast, living much of the

California, 1960s

time out of one suitcase, with a sleeping bag and a portable typewriter additionally weighing me down.

Always in the back of my mind was the thought to become a writer, even when my friends laughed at me back home in Newark when I said I wanted to be a writer, while standing on the corner one evening. They laughed, but they would have fought for me, with me. In my neighborhood, that's how friendships were sealed and measured. My friends laughed at my ambition, saying, "Whoever heard of a black writer?"

If my story resonates it's because it's one of many, of African-Americans who like myself leap-frogged into the middle class by dint of the civil rights movement and its successes. The poem "For My Mother" is not only about my mother but also about the period known as the Great Migration. My parents and countless other African-Americans left the South between World War I and World War II, seeking a better life up North. Many of them departed with a sheriff at their back, similar to a Robert Johnson's blues "Hell Hound on My Trail," whose lyrics are as metaphysical as John Donne's, and whom I would listen to and learn from in order to get that blues feeling in my poems.

My mother told me a story of seeing a black man dragged down the street behind a car. She was a child. What had he done? She didn't know. I think of Richard Wright's great short story "Big Boy Leaves Home."

But times have changed, my life was different, my children's lives will be different, better.

Within a year after graduating high school, which I barely finished, I became active in the civil rights movement, joining the Newark branch of CORE, the Congress of Racial Equality. I got a job at Western Electric, one of the major employers then in the Newark area. It was decent work, good paying, and not of the backbreaking kind. I was a file clerk and, believe it or not, the first African-American in my section. My older brother Charles worked at Western Electric, and so did a friend from high school, though he was more my sister Betty's age, a few years older than me. He would go on to become one of the first African-Americans to make it as a male model. Today he's still frequently pictured in fashion ads in major national magazines.

I was taking classes at Newark Rutgers and hanging out with the college kids on the weekend, already a step removed from the safety and danger of my old neighborhood. One of my most important friends from that time, the person who first introduced me to the world of modern poetry, was the poet Sotere Torregian. Sotere wasn't a full-time student, either, I don't think, but he was always hanging around, like I would be doing soon after I left my job at Western Electric. Sotere introduced me to all the modern poets: Pound, Eliot, Williams, Spender, and Auden, and to the work of the new, younger poets like John Ashbery and Frank O'Hara. Sotere would take the 118 bus to New York and go down to the East Village and listen to the poets read their work. I tagged along with him, awed by the New York scene. Eventually I would move to the East Village, living on East Twelfth Street, between Second and Third avenues, and work at the New York Public Library, and Brentano's Bookstore, both on Fifth Avenue, all this time taking classes at the New School for Social Research with the poet Jose Garcia Villa who taught me the basis of all I know about poetry. A poem from *Blue Monday,* "The Russian Poets," features a line from a poem that I wrote for that class. "Coo wild bird . . ." I only saved that line, in a notebook. I try to salvage lines, words, phrases for later use so I won't lose anything worthwhile. Jose and the class had laughed at my first poem, yes, a crude poem I see now, though their laughter hurt me to the bone back then. But I learned my lesson, heeded Jose's advice, and came back two weeks later with a poem that everybody praised. I became one of his special students, and I would gather with him and the others after class to drink beer and eat in a local bar, a dive, Smiths on Sixth Avenue where beer was cheap, and listen to Jose speak to us on poetry and life while he sipped martinis. He had known all of the poets whose work he championed in class: E. E. Cummings and Dylan Thomas were two he often mentioned.

Once, I heard Amiri Baraka speak at Rutgers. His play *A Dutchman* was a hit in New York. He was so cool. Known as LeRoi Jones then (I always dug that capital R) in his shades, seersucker jacket, and bow tie. He was smoking those French cigarettes whose name rhymes with galoshes. I talked to him afterwards. He's from Newark, a homeboy, and I respect the many changes he's gone through in his life and work. He is capable at any time of exploding, as he has in the past, into something quite brilliant, so I always listen out for him and read him, even today, though I am often disappointed in some of his views.

Another time, I heard Langston Hughes read in New York City, at New York University. In *Blue Monday* there's a poem "Reading Walt Whitman" that compares Whitman to Langston Hughes. Hughes's work, especially his short stories about the character he called Jesse B. Semple, means a lot to me, and some people have said a series of poems I wrote about a black folk character, Shine, reminds

them of Hughes's work. But I have in the past been ambivalent about his stance as a poet. That day when I heard him speak he said to the audience that modern poetry was too complex. Yet I was learning through my readings and contact with other poets just the opposite. It was very confusing. In many ways he might be like Louis Armstrong, whom some younger jazz musicians sometimes have a hard time accepting, not because of the music per se (or, in Langston's case, the poetry) but in the almost jester-like figure he often cut, maybe for the benefit of the (white?) buying public. I was living in New York City then, soaking up everything I could that would teach me anything, trying to find my voice. I took part in some of the open readings at St. Mark's Church, one of the landmark centers for artists in the East Village.

I have always been a reader, even in my hanging-out-on-the-corner days. When I committed myself to becoming a writer, I also became a devoted listener. To the conversations of my friends, who opened the books inside their minds up to me. To music. European classical music. East Indian music, gaining popularity in the mid-sixties when I came of age. To jazz. Birdland. The Village Gate. The Five Spot, the legendary club on St. Mark's Place where I first saw Charlie Mingus play. I was only eighteen or nineteen and could legally drink in New York City, a short forty-five-minute bus ride away from my mother's house. The legal drinking age in Jersey was twenty-one, but I had been hanging out in bars since I was fifteen or so and drinking some before then; maybe I looked older. Certainly much of my maturity was a facade. Another example of a life my children won't experience. I grew up too fast.

Moving out of my mother's house was the first of my relocations. I had two apartments in downtown Newark, one with a roommate on James Street, another by myself on Bridge Street. I was working then at the Newark Public Library and could walk to work. After awhile I got the heart to move to the Big Apple, because riding the 118 bus back and forth was getting to be a big drag. That was the start of my sojourn, moving to The City. I stayed there a year. Then came California. Haight-Ashbury. Vietnam War. Vermont. Hawaii. The Black Panthers. I didn't know what I was doing, but I survived. That's my general feeling about that time. That and disappointment.

Black Power was on the rise. But I was a renegade by then, a rogue Negro. My friend Sotere Torregian, who had by then published a poem of his, one of my favorites, "Kool Aid" in the *Paris Review,* was a Communist and a religious Catholic. He didn't see any contradiction. His heroes were the Catholic

With son, David Askia Forbes, Jamaica, 1987

Worker people and the Berrigan brothers. He reminds me of Whitman's famous words about entertaining contradictions: "I contain multitudes." Sotere said he kept his poetics (he would probably disdain that term) separate from his politics, which is something I learned from him. His religion too was in another sphere. When I first travelled to California with my ex-roommate, I stayed with Sotere and his wife, Kathy, in Palo Alto, home of Stanford University, about thirty miles south of San Francisco. I lived in California off and on for two or three years and worked several jobs, mainly at the Stanford University Press as a draftsman. Sotere was a very special person, and meeting him was a milestone on my path to becoming a poet. He saw himself as a Surrealist as early as the 1960s. The Spanish variety of the 1920 surrealistic art movement in Europe would become a major influence on American poets in the 1970s when an earlier generation of Spanish poets were being translated and read by American poets. The Chilean poet Pablo Neruda had recently won the Nobel Prize. I read him with great zest. Around that time W. S. Merwin published a book of poems called

The Lice, which was also a knockout. Merwin, an American poet who was into something different from the standard fare of Robert Frost or Robert Lowell, was somebody Sotere turned me on to. While I was living in Hawaii, I got a chance to hang out with Merwin when he came to the University of Hawaii to give a reading. I think he lives in Hawaii now.

Someone asked me the other day if I thought my poetry was political. No, not if by politics you mean advocating an ideological position. I try to write about the people I have known, in the real-life circumstances that I have observed. The poem "Maybelle" from *Blue Monday,* for instance, might strike someone as political or sociological, but hopefully there are readers who can recognize it for what it is. When I was growing up on South Fourteenth Street in Newark, neighbors and friends during the summer would gather on the porch, as others did up and down the block, to talk and laugh into the late hours of the night because it was usually too hot inside their apartments. There were a few owner-occupied homes on the block, some two-family dwellings where one floor was rented out, and some single-family dwellings. These houses followed the same pattern. People would visit back and forth, as long as they were on speaking terms, which was usually the case. Memories of those times are among the happiest of my childhood. Kids would be playing hide-and-seek and jumping double-dutch under the streetlights, or sneaking to listen to some of the more raucous talk of the adults who usually sat in chairs drinking beer or lemonade. The poem "Maybelle" imagines me sitting on such a stoop, one of the adults now, with a childhood schoolmate. The real Maybelle is someone I haven't seen since the sixth grade.

> Squeezed next to her sponge cakes
> I hold my nuts too tight.
> Her children dance before us
> Rising like vapors
> From the summer sidewalks.
>
> There's not much room
> On the steps and we're crowded
> Together like peas
> In a pod; childbirth made
> Her soft, fat, and easy to get along with
>
> As she nurses her fifth
> Child, a boy who sucks like a plunger.
> We're protected just by being
> Here; if a bomb fell
> There would be no survivors.
>
> These night people will keep me
> From myself; good barbecue
> And beer, late mornings, moon sweat,
> Lay ahead. All I remember is
> The hop-scotch pattern of her braids.
>
> Sister now five times a momma
> Dreaming of hitting that magic number,
> A combination. Her name
> Isn't Maybelle but it might as well be.
> She was/is so fine
>
> Yes indeed I wanted her to be mine
> Her breasts are like crows
> And her nipples aren't pink
> But are more like sweet raisins
> Dark against her son's darker mouth.

"Maybelle" was an important poem for me to write. I am very pleased when African-Americans (and nonblacks too) tell me that they know the people in my poems, especially the one just quoted. The poem has the colloquial and idiomatic language I like to use, which gives it that homespun feeling. It paints a picture. People say they can see these people, the scene on the stoop. One reviewer, though, said I showed a racial preference in the last stanza when I mentioned dark nipples. As a child I remember seeing women breast-feeding their babies, though they were always exceedingly modest; a woman would take a towel or a cloth diaper, cover her breast, and proceed to feed her baby. It wasn't a sexual moment for me. Yet its memory is sensual. And it's no more racial than Wordsworth or some other English poet celebrating the pale beauty or rosy cheeks of some lass or other.

One of the qualities I wanted to achieve in my poetry was the tension between the folk elements and the formal ones. This desire began to take hold in me when I lived in Hawaii and crystallized when I lived in Boston, where most of *Blue Monday* was written. I lived in Honolulu, in a house with several people who taught at the University of Hawaii. Through them I joined a writing workshop of people who met at each other's homes to read and critique each other's work. The workshops proved invaluable to me. When I lived in Copenhagen in Denmark in 1975, I took part in a workshop which was also an important learning experience for me. In Hawaii I worked several odd jobs, sweeping floors, washing windows, and my favorite: working in a zoo, in the mountains above Honolulu. These jobs not only earned me money, but they also put me into contact with people I wouldn't have met otherwise.

The poet Phyllis Thompson was one of the founders of the workshop in Hawaii. She's published a book of poems entitled *The Creation Frame*. She was teaching English at the University of Hawaii. I believe she was originally from upstate New York. Through Phyllis and my other friends I met W. S. Merwin, Kurt Vonnegut, and the Japanese novelist Yasunari Kawabata, who won the Nobel Prize for Literature (1968), all of whom came to read or lecture at the university that year. I was reading a great deal and listening. Many of my ideas about literature and race were formed during my stay in Hawaii. I liked Kawabata's work, and perhaps that was the start of my interest in things Japanese; learning even a little about another people's culture helped me to learn my own. In high school I had read a little about Buddhism, and it being the '60s Eastern culture was very in. In the back of my mind the trip to Hawaii was merely a stopover on my way to Japan to study Zen Buddhism. Perhaps my interest in Eastern culture was occasioned by my reading Hermann Hesse's novel *Siddhartha*, very popular in the '60s. But my mind always stayed tuned to the issue of race.

Two examples stand out. I like writing in a series and at that time I had decided to write a series of poems I called rough sonnets because they wouldn't rhyme but would otherwise follow the sonnet form. I planned to use Greek and African myths as part of the structure of the poems. The poem "For My

Mother" would be the only one out of that series I would keep out of the several I wrote, though I published two of these rough sonnets in the *American Scholar* in 1969.

I submitted early drafts of the poems to the workshop. One of the members, an Englishman living and teaching in Hawaii, asked me why I wanted to use an African motif in the poems, since I knew nothing about Africa. I heard him loud and clear, yet my reply didn't reveal my churning thoughts; for I soon realized that I could learn about Africa the same way I had learned about Plato and Homer and Keats and Pope and Chekhov. The list is endless. If Africa was outside my personal experience, then what was my experience? It was from that inner dialogue that I began to think of my folk heritage as a source and to see that what Yeats and others (the Japanese writers) did with their folklore, I could do with mine. I was reading a lot of Yeats at that time and learning a great deal about Irish folklore and history. Africa is as much a part of my heritage as ancient Greece or England, if not more so.

Another incident also proved noteworthy during my stay in Hawaii. I was meeting a lot of native Hawaiians, Japanese Americans, and other Asian Americans. Being in that sort of society helped me see race in terms other than black or white. Soon after I arrived in Hawaii, I went to a party where a group of Hawaiians were performing native Hawaiian songs, accompanying themselves with guitars. This wasn't the commercial stuff of Don Ho. It was the real thing. Their folk music, their blues. One of the musicians asked me if I wanted to perform. I can't sing or play and said no. But it's the way he asked me that's important. He asked me if I wanted to sing my people's music. Not his exact words, but close enough. I was taken aback. My people's music, my culture. Was African-American culture something of value that people in Hawaii, thousands of miles away from its roots in the churches of the urban North and dirt farms of the South, could treasure? Inside of me the thought began to form that I had a culture, not just a pathological response to racism that many textbooks claimed. I came to realize that gospel music, the blues, the preaching and oral styles of African-American people are at the roots of my culture (though I won't negate the impact of European culture on me). I began to explore those ideas in my work. I still am searching out the nuances of those values I inherited from my family, my people, back through slavery to Africa, and to the future, to rap, a folk expression gone high tech, advancing the tradition.

At Yaddo, Saratoga Springs, early 1980s

Because of my love of the great Irish poet W. B. Yeats, I was especially happy to visit Ireland several years after my time in Hawaii. I walked the streets of Dublin and caught a performance at the Abbey Theater, all the time thinking of Yeats and the Irish writers I had come to admire through him: Synge, O'Casey, Joyce, Donleavy, Frank O'Connor. From Yeats I learned the value of tradition. Yes, in Hawaii it all came home. So besides being a slice of paradise where I met some wonderful people, Hawaii was very important for my development as a poet. Sometimes you have to leave home to appreciate it. Because of the time I spent in Hawaii, I was asked to contribute to an anthology of Hawaiian poets published by the University of Hawaii Press. The book was coedited by John Unterecker, who coincidentally had written a major biography of W. B. Yeats. Unterecker had taken up residency in Hawaii and was teaching at the University of Hawaii.

After Honolulu, Hawaii, my next stop was Boston. It was the '70s. The focus of young African-Americans had shifted from the civil rights movement to the black power movement after Dr. Martin Luther King's death. Malcolm X's influence was peaking (it's on the rise again) and on college campuses across the country black students were protesting what we now know as the Eurocentric bias of much of the educational system. Feeling renewed after Hawaii, I decided to get involved in the black movement again, this time in the black consciousness movement, what some people call black nationalism. I wanted to become involved in the black movement and in the antiwar movement. The Vietnam War was still happening. One of my most vivid memories of those times is the shootings at Kent State University of the antiwar protesters by the Ohio National Guard units. Still, very little of my political involvement came into my poetry. My major personal protest was filing for noncombat status with the draft board in Newark. I did that in 1966, when I still lived in Newark. The FBI investigated me, talking to my mother, neighbors, shaking everybody up. When my mother told me those white people won't let you get away with that stuff, I knew right away I had to keep doing what I was doing. Besides, a friend of mine

from high school was killed in that useless war. His name was David. I named my son after him.

After a few months in Boston, I got a job at Emerson College teaching African-American Literature, part-time at first, but by 1970 I was teaching full-time. I have taught since then, except for periods when I dropped out to renew myself.

I published some poems in *Poetry* magazine that first year in Boston. *Poetry* magazine was at one time the most prestigious place to publish poetry in the United States. One of the poems was "Poem on My Birthday," written in Hawaii and changed somewhat from the version in *Poetry* magazine when I republished it in *Blue Monday*. It was an important poem for me because it was one of the first poems I ever wrote where I broke through to a freedom of language and metaphor that was at the heart of my feeling for poetry.

I wound up staying in Boston, except for several trips during the summers to Europe, for about eight years. I lived in many places in Boston and nearby Cambridge, moving quite a bit. During my time in Boston I met a lot of poets and writers. Sam Cornish.

As speaker (standing) on a Howard University panel with novelists Gloria Naylor and Julian Mayfield, 1986

Tom Lux. Jim Tate. Russell Banks. Many of these writers I met through Bill Corbett, poet and teacher at Emerson, and Jim Randall, who also taught at Emerson and ran a small press called Pym-Randall with his wife. Pym, I believe, was the name of their cat. Today Emerson College has a very fine creative writing program which got its start around the time I was in Boston.

In 1973 I started teaching at Tufts University. By 1974 *Blue Monday* was out, published by Wesleyan University Press. Wesleyan University Press was a much-respected publisher of poetry, publishing many of the leading poets of the '70s: James Wright, Robert Bly, James Dickey. I was flying high, in good company, and very pleased.

In 1975 I received a Fulbright to teach at the University of Copenhagen in Denmark as part of a teacher-exchange program the University of Copenhagen had with Tufts. Looking back, I see that many of the places where I lived and worked and that were important were islands, or near the water: Oahu; Hvar, Yugoslavia, where I spent a summer; Jamaica; Denmark; and the Eastern Shore of Maryland. Yet I can't swim.

I taught courses in literature to Danish students studying English and lived in an old section of Copenhagen with a canal, with boats going up and down it outside my living room window. There were a few other English-speaking writers around: John Barnie from Wales, Richard Thomas from the States, and Bruce Clunies-Ross from Australia. Together we started a workshop, meeting irregularly at each other's homes, drinking beer and eating, and going over each other's work with a fine-tooth rake. The poet Rita Dove was in Europe then and we met several times to talk and exchange ideas. She would later win the Pulitzer Prize. I also lectured in England and France on that trip.

Being a part of the workshop was a great experience for me. I started a novel, only to abandon it within a year, and wrote many of the poems that would form the core of a series called *From the Book of Shine*. John Barnie later on would found a small publishing company, Razorback Press; and he would publish fifteen of these poems under the title *From the Book of Shine*, in 1980 in Wales. Burning Deck Press would first publish the same poems under the same title in 1979 in the U.S.A. Both were limited editions, the first twenty-five being signed by me. They were both printed on really fine-grained paper and hand tied and bound. The books themselves are representative of the printer's art and are good-looking. Shine is an African-American folk character, one I first heard about as a young boy. I have modernized him

With son, David Askia Forbes, Washington, D.C., 1991

somewhat, making him surreal in some ways. I gave him an "old lady," Glow, who's completely my own invention, and a son: Shade, son of Shine. I like these poems very much. There are now about twenty of them and they form the nucleus of my new book of poems, "The Shine Poems."

There were a lot of jazz musicians living in Copenhagen then; the best known was tenor man Dexter Gordon. He and I met a few times and chatted and he left an enduring impression on me. He starred in the film *Round Midnight* about a jazz musician living in Europe and died a few years back. He was one of the last of the giants among us who had a hand in creating modern jazz. One day I've got to write about him. Not him really, but my impressions of the life musicians of his era lived, based on conversations I had with Dexter.

I stayed in Copenhagen a year, returning to teach at Tufts and to go to grad school at Brown University to study with John Hawkes and Keith Warner. Michael Harper was a big factor in my going to Brown. While I was in grad school I continued to teach at Tufts where Denise Levertov and X. J.

Forbes and his daughter, Jahia Forbes, Eastern Shore, Maryland, 1989

Kennedy were my colleagues. Kennedy has edited several well-known textbooks on poetry. He chose one of my poems, "The Chocolate Soldiers," for a book he edited called *Messages*. At Tufts I helped organize a conference of writers of African descent from around the world, with a French teacher from Trinidad by the name of Wilbur Roget. Indeed my world was expanding, but it was shrinking as well. My father was already dead; within a few years two of my brothers would die. And in 1984, my mother.

Nineteen seventy-four was a watershed year for me; a beginning and an ending. My first child was born, David Askia, my first book of poems was published, and one of my brothers, Richard, died, beaten to death in a robbery. Another brother, George, had died a few years before in a crazy car accident. I wrote a poem, "Hand Me Down Blues," about George before he died. I used to get his old clothes, hence the title. But I refused or couldn't write about Richard's death. That refusal set the stage for a war within that would eventually tear me apart. The fight was about the use of the autobio-

graphical. For example, how should I write about my father? Should I disguise him? What is the truth, anyway? Something strictly fictional seems to have more integrity. It's a battle still waging, though I believe I have the upper hand right now. Fiction—as in myth, history, the tribal stories told around the camp fires—interests me more than the merely true. Truth is something higher, more noble. Truth doesn't have to be true, as in the daily news. Leastwise that's what I believe today.

In the late '70s I sunk into a major crisis, one that would last and deepen over several years. I stopped teaching for a while, taking other jobs, finally moving to the Washington, D.C., area in 1978 where, soon after becoming restless with the nine-to-five routine, I took a job at Howard University. It was my first experience in a mostly black institutional setting. Living and working in a majority black setting prepared me for my journey to Jamaica. In 1982 I won a National Endowment for the Arts fellowship and went to live in Jamaica. There I began to heal and to write again. I started working on a new novel. I always wanted to write a novel, and I recently finished the one I started during those months in Jamaica. I also have completed a new book of poems, "The Shine Poems," mentioned already. After a long dry spell, the spirit, or the muse if you prefer, has come back to me.

Living in Jamaica was one of the best things that ever happened to me. I lived mainly in Kingston, the capital, but I hitchhiked around the island and even got a chance to travel to Trinidad and Barbados. The writers and artists and the everyday people I met there were very welcoming (in Denmark this was true as well; the same for Yugoslavia the summer I spent there), and it was a pleasure to live in a place far away from the daily grind of racial tension so much a part of life in America, maybe for white as well as black people. I couldn't have found the same peace in Europe; in Europe I would have stood out like a sore thumb, still a minority. In Jamaica, I didn't seem any different from the vast majority of Jamaicans until I opened my mouth. Sometimes there is a definite comfort in being anonymous. I thought about living permanently in Jamaica, but I couldn't find a job, though I did teach part-time at the University of the West Indies in Kingston. My year in Jamaica introduced me to the wide variety of West Indian writers, in person and through their books. Earl Lovelace, Erna Brodber, Lorna Goodison, Mervyn Morris, to name a few, are people I read now and teach to my students. The study and teaching of West Indian and African literatures (African literature written in English, not traditional languages) enabled me to see new possibilities for my own writing. C. L. R. James and Chinua Achebe are two writers whose work guided me down a new path. James's novel *Minty Alley* was really an eye-opener. He wrote about black people but not about racism. Racism and its effects are typically the main topics for black writers in America, and not black people per se being their own human selves. Very few black American writers are free, and I think that's the right word, to not write about racism and racial conflict. Equally important for me were two books by African-Americans: Zora Neale Hurston's *Their Eyes Were Watching God* and Charles Chesnutt's *Conjure Woman.*

Yes, I have been very lucky. I have managed to survive as a writer though I haven't published or written much in the past several years; yet, I have a mountain of experiences to explore. I just hope it won't be all uphill from here.

While living in Washington, D.C., I became deeply involved in the cultural life of the city, helping to start several organizations, namely the Black Film Review, with the writer David Nicholson, and the African-American Writers Guild, with the novelist Marita Golden and Culbert Simpkins, who wrote a biography of John Coltrane. I also worked with the Institute for the Study of African-American Literature. I lived in Washington, D.C., for about eight years. Living there was the one of the most solid things to happen to me since my youth; it allowed me to reconnect with the front-porch people of my childhood, to become part of a neighborhood again. Besides teaching at Howard University, I taught at Washington College on the Eastern Shore of Maryland, fifty miles from D.C., and the University of Maryland, Baltimore County, and the American University.

Going to Jamaica gave me a new resolve to continue to write and a renewed faith in the meaning and value of culture as a healing force. It's good to know where you came from, to know your past is of value, in order to chart new directions. I see myself and my work as an artist in many ways as someone who spreads that good news. T. S. Eliot, in his essay "Tradition and the Individual Talent," says much the same thing.

While I was back in Jamaica for a visit in 1984, my mother died, something else I haven't been willing to write about. And my youngest child, an angelic girl child, Jahia, was born in 1988. Today, I am single, finished with the inner struggles that kept me from writing, and eager to move forward. I want to write a play about my father. I want to write a series of essays, semi-autobiographical. The novel that I've recently completed is part of a series of several that I will write concerning four friends, tracing their friendship over the generations. As I said before, I like working in series. I used to worry about running out of things to write about; now I worry about running out of time. One of my favorite poets, the British writer Philip Larkin who died a few years back, didn't publish that much. I am all for quality over quantity. Poetry may not be a calling, but it's certainly not a business or a career. Today many of my poems are being reprinted in anthologies, and I receive several letters a year from young poets and just plain readers (once, from as far away as Albania; another time, India) who have read my work. So I try not to worry about publishing more.

I am currently living in Chicago, teaching literature and writing classes at the School of the Art Institute of Chicago, and writing more and better, or at least I think so, than I have in a good while.

BIBLIOGRAPHY

Poetry:

Blue Monday, Wesleyan University Press, 1974.

From the Book of Shine, Burning Deck Press, 1979.

Contributor:

Arnold Adoff, editor, *The Poetry of Black America: Anthology of the Twentieth Century*, Harper, 1972.

Abraham Chapman, editor, *New Black Voices*, New American Library, 1972.

X. J. Kennedy, editor, *Messages: A Thematic Anthology of Poetry*, Little, Brown, 1973.

Miller Williams, editor, *Contemporary Poetry in America*, Random House, 1973.

Daryl Hine and Joseph Parisi, editors, *The Poetry Anthology, 1912–1977*, Houghton, 1978.

Frank Stewart and John Unterecker, editors, *Poetry Hawaii: A Contemporary Anthology*, University Press of Hawaii, 1979.

Keith Waldrop and Rosemarie Waldrop, editors, *A Century in Two Decades: A Burning Deck Anthology, 1961–1981*, Burning Deck Press, 1982.

Dave Smith and David Bottoms, editors, *The Morrow Anthology of Younger American Poets*, Morrow, 1985.

Sascha Feinstein and Yusef Komunyakaa, editors, *The Jazz Poetry Anthology*, Indiana University Press, 1991.

Wilson Harris

1921-

I live now in Essex with my wife Margaret. It is some thirty-odd years since I emigrated from Guyana, South America, to the United Kingdom. I was thirty-eight when I left British Guiana (as Guyana was then called) in 1959. An English friend tells me that the marvellous glow one sees sometimes--particularly at the end of the day—across the rolling Essex countryside is known as the East Anglian light. He claims that this radiance is due to a pattern of rainfall that is adequate but not excessive in this corner of England and also to the open vistas and skyscape that run from the sea miles away on the distant East Anglian coast of Norfolk.

All this is of great interest to me for landscape/skyscape/riverscape/seascape (and their intermingled bearing on each other which transcends immediate locality) have been a living text—if I may so put it—in the way I read and reread the elements (as if the elements were a book) when I lived in South America and travelled from the Atlantic coastlands into the heartland of the Guyanas.

Now I sometimes find that the rolling Essex countryside reminds me of an aspect of the savannahs of the Guyanas. I dream of the survey expeditions I led there and into the rain forests as a young man for fifteen years or so.

Peculiar as it may seem, those expeditions through the coastlands into the rain forests have enriched my appreciation of the Northern world. Likewise my experience of East Anglian light gives to memory's return to the Guyanas a rhythm and counterpoint, a spatiality, that affects, for instance, the narrative shape and imageries in the passage below that comes from my latest published novel *The Four Banks of the River of Space* which appeared in 1990.

Wilson Harris with wife Margaret, on edge of rain forest in Australia, 1986

Our guide was signalling to us. The mouth of the trail had been cleared and we climbed and entered the Bush. The fantastic, planetary greenheart trees rose into marvellous silvery columns on every hand. Clothed in water-music. The trail was narrow. We walked in single file. The cracked silvery veil of greenheart possessed the texture of slow-motion rain falling within the huge Bell of a still Waterfall in which whispering leaves of fluid sound ran up into veil within veil of Shadow-organ gloom towards the highest reaches of the Forest and the slits of the Sky far above. Subtle fire-music.

I had never before seen the shining bark of greenheart columns in this slow-motion raining light (nor the Sky clothed in frail ribbons of fire-music within the lofty gloom of a Bell) in all my remembered Dream of Forests I had travelled in my youth. How young was I, how old was I? We had entered it seemed—the Macusi guide first, Penelope second, Ross third, I last—an innermost chamber of the magical Waterfall beneath god-rock. It encompassed the globe, the ancient world, the modern world. As if the Waterfall had been uplifted from the river and transferred within us in the music of space, around us in

Shadow-organ imperceptible (not wholly imperceptible for we were aware of it) dance of genesis.

(From *The Four Banks of the River of Space,*
pp. 132–133)

There was a large black trunk in my mother's bedroom which she opened for the first time in my presence on the day the news came that my stepfather had disappeared (presumed drowned) in the rivers and rain forests of Guyana. The year was 1929. I was eight years old.

My stepfather's death or disappearance was the second crucial bereavement my mother suffered in six years. My father had died suddenly in 1923, and my memories of him were therefore quite naturally void or hollow, though on seeing the contents of the large open trunk he seemed strangely alive in my aroused imagination because of books of his my mother held up, a photograph to which she pointed in which he stood between two companions, and a horse carven from a greenheart tree.

A subconscious thread or connection was woven then with the South American heartland of the Guyanas into which I was to lead many survey expeditions as a young man. The impact of the forests and savannahs on those expeditions was to become of profound value in the language of the fictions I later wrote. My stepfather's disappearance in that immense interior when I was a child was the beginning of an involvement with the enigma of quests and journeys through visible into invisible worlds that become themselves slowly visible to require further penetration into other invisible worlds without end or finality. All this was to loom in the drafts and revisionary scope of poems and novels I embarked upon in the 1950s. The heartland of South America was as remote in the early and mid-twentieth century to my relatives and friends as if it existed on Mars.

In 1929—the year of the opening of the trunk—we were living in Georgetown (the capital of British Guiana). We had moved there from New Amsterdam (the other township on the coastlands some sixty miles away) in 1923. My father's estate had yielded enough for us to buy some property. But economy and prudence were needed, indeed essential. My father had been a successful businessman—particularly in the insurance field—but had entertained lavishly and run a chauffeur-driven car.

The shocking news of my stepfather imbued my mother—I was to learn later—with a conviction of bondage to fate. She felt herself fated to bereavement. Yet she retained in some degree a rebellious mind. She longed to travel, to go abroad, to leave the country, but circumstances made this impossible.

*Mother, Millicent Josephine (Glasford) Harris,
Georgetown, British Guiana, 1929*

When I emigrated to the United Kingdom in 1959—eight years after her death—I felt the shadow of her approval. I was doing in a sense what she had desired in the late 1920s after losing two husbands.

I had just come in from cycling, lifted the bike up the stairs into the gallery of the house, when I heard what had happened. Even now after all these years I remember someone passing on the road singing "Gal me lover letter loss." It was an old river song. And I thought he dived into the river to find it and would never come back! The bike was a gift from him I had received on Christmas Day, 1926. The wonder of glittering wheels, the shining machine, have never entirely left me. Memory is enriched by shadows of ecstasy, Christmas ecstasy. He had wheeled me around the drawing room and into the bedroom where my mother now stood three years later beside the open trunk. Those three years from 1926 (the shadow of the bike) to 1929 (the year of the drowned man in the river) are an eternity.

As such it makes vivid the day of all days my mother opened the trunk and revealed to me its contents. She was weeping to break her heart. "They belong to *your* father," she cried, "the books, the horse." I felt grief and limbo yet light as a feather as if I were still being wheeled around the room on Christmas Day.

"They belong to your father," she repeated. A peculiar and a positive statement! Peculiar rebellion against fate? She was confused, distraught. My father was no longer here to own anything. And yet he was closer than he had ever been as I touched the books and the horse. There was reproach in my mother's voice directed at my vanished stepfather. She was reproaching him for abandoning her. *My* father would never have left her had he lived. She was confused. I was confused by a tide of emotion within her. Confused by memory's trunk, memory's open grave it seemed. She turned and left the room abruptly.

So little one knows about oneself. So much one is afraid to acknowledge. The moment of birth, of issuing from a woman's body, lies in a void. The birth of the imagination may terrify but it lies in some degree within a theatre of recollection. A realm enriched by uncertainties. Uncertainty, yet one touches the threads of the gestation of idea and vision by which unconscious memory erupts into the subconscious and conscious body and mind. In my latest published novel, the character Anselm retraces his steps to arrive at a capacity for revisionary judgements of the nature of reality within and without himself. He is told by Canaima, his guide, that such revisions make him "a medium of the dance" of time. Make him also the "carnival heir of the dance." Anselm is astonished. He had never seen himself in the light of a carnival heir and he records in his book of dreams that the shock of such disclosure leads him to contemplate alternative or parallel existences in himself. How strange is one to oneself? How many quantum strangers does one bear in oneself?

My first acquaintance with Homer's *Iliad* and *Odyssey* arose from the books in my father's trunk. Ulysses returned to his home, to his wife, to his son, disguised as a beggar, after twenty long years, ten on the plains of Troy culminating in the belly of the great wooden horse (the womb or foetal masquerade it provided the Greeks to outwit the Trojans), ten in foreign lands and upon the ocean wave. As I look back across the seas of time into the harbour of my childhood, it is not easy to disentangle the impact the Ulyssean beggar made on me, when I read the *Odyssey* with my mother's help, from an encounter I had with a Georgetown beggar a block or so away from our home. I came upon the Georgetown beggar the very year my stepfather disappeared. We lived in a good

and quiet neighbourhood, and it was unusual to come upon beggars so close to home.

He was leaning against a red-flame flowering tree that grew on a parapet against a canal. Dusty. Ill-kempt. But his face and eyes upset me most of all. They looked so porous yet masklike. When I got home I could not eat. I saw those extraordinary, unsettling features on my plate on the dining table. Nausea, hollowness, engulfed me. I lost all appetite. Hollowness. But a sensation of being sculpted arose in that hollowness, shaped within, born to imagine, to visualize, strangers at the gate of the self.

Across half-a-century and more a shadowy surfeit, sickness, emptiness returns to instil traces of my encounter with the beggar. The fabric of his face upon a floating tide of sorrow is stitched into Homer's beggar within a tapestry of gestating vision. . . .

This is December 1991 as I write this essay. I look back into the body of a century and am aware of the difficulty of pinning down the origins of imaginary identity one shares with others, those one meets on the street who are real yet unreal, others who are equally problematic but real even though they come from an ancient world and from the dusty covers of a book; from the shelf of a library or from a grave, from one's father's trunk, from a river or an ocean.

The age of five is a shadow in the past but inexpressibly real. The age I floated upon the saddle of a bike and the ground seemed to tilt. The age in which I was initiated into the terrors of school. The age in which I was part of a shadowy congregation witnessing Latin theatre, the stations of the cross, the pièta.

It happened this way. Next to the school was a Catholic cathedral established by the Portuguese in British Guiana in the 1920s. They were an influential minority at the time in the heterogeneous population of the Guyanas. The school and church were in Main Street. My mother had misgivings for—unlike my stepfather—she was not a Catholic. She was Congregationalist. My stepfather, who was of mixed Portuguese descent, was a strong Catholic. He chose the school. I felt frozen, unable to move, as I stood in a stream of indifferent bodies and faces pouring into classrooms, but was helped by my stepfather's niece, a tall, thin, gentle girl, who introduced me to the headmistress. It was the Easter term in 1926 when I joined the school. And on Good Friday we were led by the headmistress into the cathedral. I watched the stations of the cross and felt the wooden Christ come alive when he was taken down into the arms of his mother. It was not wood I saw but the life of sculpture metamorphosed into a mystery of flesh-and-blood.

Portraits of Wilson and Margaret Harris, 1954

I am not myself a Catholic. The dogmas of the church, its rituals, its infallibility, are coercive and unhelpful to me. But its music and the descent of the imagination into the life of sculpture were poignantly active that Good Friday afternoon in the reality of living objects and in the beauty of the sacred. Something in me that was half-frozen, half-fluid child, foetal spirit, susceptible to metamorphosis, responded to the spaces of a carnival theatre, carnival wood, carnival masks, the birth of associations imaginary and real. A few years later—after my stepfather's disappearance—I began to read the *Odyssey* with my mother's help. We read it together. I read of the Trojan horse. But it revolved in my mind and took on quite different proportions. For I saw it in the light of my own father's horse carven from a tree in the Guyana rain forests. I was in it, secreted within it, a splinter of "mother-horse, father-horse," a splinter in an inimitable cathedral of reality that threatens to enclose, to dominate, but also brings a taste of a dialogue with truth beyond coercion, a dialogue with the living arts of freedom one pays dear to exercise, so dear it is as if blood oozes from an axed tree, the radiance of the sun from the soil of memory.

The Portuguese were renowned for the Carnival theatre they staged at Easter. The Good Friday Christ was nailed into, then taken from, the cross. The painted blood on his hands and feet, and in his side, seemed astonishingly real. I was struck, however, less by the painted blood than by the gloom and shadow, the radiance and dazzle, of glass windows arching up to the roof of the world. I was in the mutuality of the divine, I was in mother-horse, I was in father-glass, father-horse, mother-glass, I ascended, descended, into a mysterious constellation of evolutionary spaces.

(From *Carnival,* p. 122)

That passage appears in the novel *Carnival* and it invokes the seed of *Latin* theatre in which I was immersed at the age of five some sixty years earlier in the colony of *British* Guiana; a seed that caught the light of the descent of the imagination into objects that seemed to me then (and now) mysteriously potent and alive. One may not remember the hour of one's birth but the livingness of glass and wood and sacred space is a surrogate dimension of emergence from a womb of flesh-and-blood into the body of the mind. That surrogate body with its spatial antennae reaches into unconscious memory of light and darkness in the hour one was born, subconscious intimacy with the density and fragility of things one touches as if they grow out of one's fingertips. . . .

Perhaps it is now clear that this autobiographical essay is, at one level, a retracing of my steps backwards into the past with the help of linkages in the fictions I have written. At another level it is a quest for "father-glass, mother-glass" in which particles of memory accumulate again into reflections of the mind's grasp of a procession of objects and masks that are native to the birth of vision and inimitably alive.

I stressed "*Latin* theatre on a Good Friday in *British* Guiana" a moment ago in order to illumine the diverse and paradoxical roots of my colonial heritage. I myself am not of Portuguese descent as my stepfather was. But there was an object-kinship between us. The wheeled machine he gave me was touched by the riddling light of Christmas ecstasy even as the painted Christ in the cathedral was born of Good Friday theatre. All these extremities of marvel and touch, the trade of things truly given, truly accepted, become the realization of a thread that runs through his blood and mine. Kinship is the realization of the object-miracle of life that has its roots in old and new worlds encapsulated in a box, or a book, or a cross, or a pattern of technology that illumines a shared passion rather than ideological greed. The object-miracle is alive also within diverse step or dance. The 1920s and 1930s were decades when masked dancers of African descent danced through the city on tall stilted amazing limbs. Special holidays were set aside for such dances. They too were family—they subsisted upon a thread of metamorphosed object-kinship in that their flesh-and-blood was living sculpture in the dance. They were daubed sometimes with Hindu motifs—perhaps dancers of Indian descent were amongst them—as if to announce a shared dynasty of festival with Lord Shiva of Asian/Indian epic.

I knew that my father who had died when I was two was of mixed blood but I lost touch with his relatives, so that my family tree on his side remains obscure. The carven horse in his grave (so it seemed) of a trunk that my mother opened was threaded into Homer's giant horse when I read the *Odyssey* as a child, but it was also to be resurrected many years later and to be ridden by the character Donne in my first published novel *Palace of the Peacock*.

> A horseman appeared on the road coming at a breakneck stride. A shot rang out suddenly, near and yet far as if the wind had been stretched and torn and had started coiling and running in an instant. The horseman stiffened with a devil's smile, and the horse reared, grinning fiendishly and snapping at the reins. The horseman gave a bow to heaven like a hanging man to his executioner and rolled from his saddle on to the ground.

(From *Palace of the Peacock*, p. 19)

Donne is a conquistadorial horseman, the wild twin brother of the I-narrator who is nameless in the novel. Identity becomes a twinship in the terrifying, ecstatic life of the family of humanity to which we all belong, in which we are all reflected in the heights and in the depths of history. My grandmother on my mother's side was half-Arawak, half-European. The Arawaks were a gentle, very gifted people but they were called savages. My grandfather (my mother's father) was Scot and African. Such a family tree is not unusual in the South Americas. I perceive my antecedents within dimensions of dual and multiple theatre. In other words, even if they were not my biological folk—or if I were in pure (so to speak) lineal descent from one or the other ethnic ancestor—I would still claim them all within a descent of the imagination that links the animality of the painter Titian to the scored visage of a sculpted Benim priest or to a pre-Columbian Arawak/Carib infant riding a jaguar steed against the sun. Jaguars were children of the sun in ancient American legend.

Georgetown was known as the Garden City of South America in the 1920s. It was famous for its Botanical Gardens, its flowering, exotic trees, its elegant colonial houses not of stone or Grecian marble but of hardwoods and softwoods transported down the Demerara and Essequebo Rivers to the low-lying coastlands from accessible forests beneath the rapids and waterfalls some sixty miles upriver from the sea.

There, at those rapids and waterfalls, the landscape began to change profoundly and dramatically. The land began to rise. The rivers were now above the reach of the Atlantic tides. I remember the great cathedral forests and how they rained gently at times with splintered leaves and sun. Parrots wheeled at sunrise and sunset above the wide rivers as if they were blind yet steady as a clock. I used to set my watch by them on expeditions into the heartland of the country.

The inaccessibility of the Guyana rain forests in the 1920s, '30s, '40s, '50s—the difficulties exploitative agencies encountered—helped to stave off further decimation of the descendants of pre-Columbian peoples living there since the sixteenth century when the Spanish conquistadores Cortez and Pizarro penetrated Mexico and Peru. It helped also to protect invaluable flora and fauna, chattering creatures, and rare birds. I remember on my first expedition in the 1940s being greeted by the cry of the "who-you" bird as it was called by an old bushman in my party. WHO-YOU? WHO-YOU? WHO-YOU? As I listened and wondered how to respond, the interior seemed a million miles away from Georgetown.

And yet it was as if that cry had been heard on the coastlands. It was the theme of a ballad or calypso played by the tall stilted dancers who danced through the streets. The mimicry of birds by humans requires a far-reaching chapter in the psychology of music. Likewise the links between dance and architecture have not as far as I am aware been explored. Do dancers susceptible to the tremor of earthquake regions follow in some degree, subconsciously, unconsciously, the rhythm of a vessel sliding on a wave? The tall dancers in the streets of the Garden City danced in midair with a slightly rolling motion as upon an invisible tide. Their lofty station—the elongation of their bodies into artificial stilts and legs—

reflected the great skill of the dance. It was curious to see them—how their pillared being achieved a counterpoint to the equally pillared slender columns upon which the houses in the city stood and appeared to sail motionlessly, as it were, above the ground. For in point of fact the ground of the city was beneath sea level. The houses therefore were uplifted as a precaution against flood waters from ocean and river.

I remember how the dancers would bring their masked features close to windows and doors, proffer an agile fist or a begging-bowl, and appeal for a fee for their extraordinary performance.

I did not realise fully then—though I sensed it in the marrow of childhood—that the dancers were performing a parable of a flood. On the western boundary of the town lay the mile-wide estuary of the Demerara River against which earthen dams, in need of continuous repair, had been built. On the north, conjoint with the river's estuary, lay the Atlantic Ocean.

In the heavy rainy season the pressure on the dams became ominous when it was reinforced by high spring tides from the sea. The Dutch, who were

"The sculpted head is by Susan Jones," University of Texas, 1982

colonial masters of the territory in the eighteenth century, had built a sea wall against the ocean. I remember walking upon this when the tide was low and the ocean glistened half a mile and more in the distance.

On the other side of the wall, as one moved east, were football, tennis, and cricket pitches stretching to the edge of the residential areas.

A word now about the Demerara conservancy or reservoir on the south and the southeast of Georgetown. For this may help me to extend, I hope, the parable of the flood, of the vessel and cradle of revisionary resources that the complicated Guyanese landscape was and is for me as I retrace my steps into the past in this essay.

The conservancy had been designed in the nineteenth century by English engineers to supply the city and various settlements and sugar estates upriver and to the east with drinking water and irrigation water.

I became acquainted with it for the first time in 1932 or '33 on a picnic with a couple of friends. It appealed to me as a benign, dark stretch of water that seemed to burn in the sun. Stately palm trees grew close to the empolder dams. There were one or two fishermen on the dams with outstretched rods. It was a scene that could have been painted by Constable. The conservancy reached for miles it seemed and occupied an apparently level expanse of partly wooded, partly savannah countryside submerged to create a reservoir.

It was not until the late 1940s that I learnt—as a member of a land surveying team carrying out a new penetrative reconnaissance of the Demerara catchment—of an oversight in the construction of the conservancy. Straight-lined dams with occasional changes of bearing and parallel works—laid out more or less with indifference to the subtle gradients of the topography and to the incremental buildup of contours higher up the river—constituted an economic model for the needs of industry in the *immediate locality*.

We are now coming abreast of the pollution of environments in the late twentieth century. But apart from this the object lesson of the conservancy for me was the mirror it held up to the life of great rivers—such as the Demerara, the Essequebo, the Berbice in the Guyanas—which have their rushing headwaters in untamed and peculiar regions. A frame of settlement and reservoir on the Atlantic coast—however remote it appears from such headwaters, however fortressed to serve its own ends—may become a trigger of environmental crisis within a system of intricate forces and dimensions extending into the body of a continent.

That continent may be despoiled. The dangers as our century draws to a close are manifest in Brazil and elsewhere. The consequences would be dire for humanity. Then the tyranny of immediate gratification or parochial blindness to the mysterious book of landscapes would have triumphed. It has not yet happened. There is still a chance. Landscape is not a passive creature. It is a series of revisionary texts within nature and psyche, the nature of psyche, the psyche of nature, revisionary insights into the problematic reality and spirit of the arts and the sciences. My experience in and perception of South America is such that I could never take these for granted whatever gloss or lustre or privileged status of persuasion was placed upon them.

In 1973 I was invited to speak at a conference at the University of Kansas, Missouri, and I spoke there of a narrow escape from drowning I experienced twenty-five years earlier just after the end of the Second World War.

> We were gauging the Potaro River for hydro-electric power and had chosen as our station a section where the river narrowed and then opened up again to run towards the Tumatumari rapids a mile or so away. We set up a base line on one bank with alignment rods at right angles to this. We were thus able to align ourselves and anchor our boat in the river, one anchor at the stern and another at the bow. Then with a sextant we took a reading in order to calculate distances from the bank as we made our way across the river. The Potaro River is strangely beautiful and secretive.
>
> When the river falls, the sand banks begin to appear. At the foot of the Tumatumari rapids or falls the sand is like gold. Above, an abrupt change of texture occurs—it is white as snow.
>
> When the river runs high the sand banks disappear. We were—on the particular expedition to which I am referring—gauging the river at a very high and dangerous stage. The water swirled, looked ugly, and suddenly one of the anchors gripped the bed of the stream. The boat started to swing around and to take water. We could not dislodge the anchor. I decided that the only thing we could do was to cut ourselves free. So we severed the anchor rope and that was the end of that. Two or three years later, gauging the river in the same way, the identical impasse happened. Once again the anchor at the stern lodged in the bed of the stream. And this time it was much more crucial because the boat swung so suddenly, we took so much water, that it seemed to me at that moment that we were on the point of sinking. I am sure I couldn't have swum to the river bank if the boat had gone down because at

that high stage I would have been pulled into the Tumatumari falls and decapitated by the rocks. As the boat swung I said to a man behind me: "Cut the rope." Well, he was so nervous that he took his prospecting knife and all he could do was a sort of feeble sawing upon the anchor rope as if he were paralysed by the whole thing, the river, the swirling canvas of the stream. And then another member—the outboard mechanic—gave a sudden tug and the anchor moved. The boat righted itself. Half-swamped as we were, we were able to start the outboard engine and drive towards the bank. We began pulling up the anchor as we moved in. We got to the bank and then were able to bring the anchor right up when we discovered that it had hooked into the one we had lost three years before. Both anchors had now come up.

It is almost impossible to describe the kind of energy that rushed out of that constellation of images. I felt as if a canvas around my head was crowded with phantoms and figures. I had forgotten some of my own antecedents—the Amerindian/Arawak ones—but now their faces were on the canvas. One could see them in the long march into the twentieth century out of the pre-Columbian mists of time. One could also sense the lost expeditions, the people who had gone down in these South American rivers. One could sense a whole range of things, all sorts of faces, all sorts of figures. There was a sudden eruption of consciousness, and what is fantastic is that it all came out of a constellation of two ordinary objects, two anchors.

(From *Explorations,* pp. 59–60)

Is autobiography an art? I do not know. Does retracing one's steps imply an oscillation? Does it imply a cyclical as well as a spiralling vision? Does it imply a pendulum that moves from side to side as well as forwards and backwards within a clock and calendar of space? With the mysterious death by drowning—if he did die by drowning—of my stepfather, my mother, my half-sister, and I went to live with my grandfather. He was a retired civil servant. I idolized him. He seemed so secure, so wise, so strong, so kind. With hindsight I think he would like me to accept the fact that he was a child (as much as an old man is a child) of his century—more nineteenth than twentieth century—a child of the Garden City. He was approaching eighty when we went to live with him in 1929. His wife—she was his third wife—was not my grandmother. I never knew my grandmother but learnt she had died when my mother—the last of four children—was born. There was no offspring of my grandfather's second marriage, and his third to a woman of his own age did not occur until he was in his sixties and in retirement.

My cousins were all some fifteen years or so older than I. My mother, Millicent Josephine, was younger than her brother, Edwin, and her sisters, Beatrice and Lucilla. Lucilla died before I was born. Beatrice became the wife of the distinguished politician and historian A. R. F. Webber.

My mother, unlike Edwin and Beatrice, married late. She was thirty-seven when I was born. My father was in his middle fifties when he died.

The stay with my grandfather lasted close on eight years. He was immortal. His secure roof seemed paradise. I tried to banish the thought from my mind that he would die. But when it happened in 1937 I was not stricken or overwhelmed as I thought I would be. He had been ill for a year and I witnessed the crumbling of a monument then. He was vulnerable, he suffered. And when he died I was astonished to experience something akin to relief. I released him in my imagination from pain. He released me to live and remember him for what he was, a mortal man. It was his blessing.

Dostoevsky is the genius of possessed character in the nineteenth-century European novel, possession that crumbles within the cul-de-sac of imperial order. He has written somewhere (I think it is in *The Brothers Karamazov*) of a saint who dies and is expected by everyone to smell of roses. It does not happen. My interpretation is that the blessing one receives from the dead and from the complex life of spirit in nature is not in a perfume or in the conscription of a rose. My grandfather believed in the resurrection of the dead and I have wrestled with this theme in my novels. Wrestled with it through alterations in narrative shapes in which the eye of the mind recognizes what it thinks it knows or remembers, what it forgets, what it remembers in a new and original, revisionary light.

In an interview in August 1990 by the Scottish poet Alan Riach, I was questioned about this. And I approached the enigma of the resurrection of Christ by referring in the first place to Sophocles's *Antigone* in which the status of death is absolute. Hades triumphs. I referred to the action of blind fate superbly dramatized in the play, the blind seer Tiresias whose counsels about the sacred necessity to bury Antigone's brother, not to leave his corpse exposed on the street, fail to plant seeing eyes in the heart of Creon, king of Thebes. Tiresias's prophetic blindness which sees but fails to enlighten the king becomes a counterpoint to Creon's spiritual blindness of heart. Oedipus himself—Antigone's father and the father of her dead brother—was blind. The entire cast is submerged in a tragedy of restrictive vision. At the dawn of the Christian age we find that classical

"Reading for the British Council in Paris, (from left) Professor Jean-Pierre Durix of the University of Dijon (French translator of my novels), myself, and Professor Michel Fabre of the Sorbonne," 1991

blindness inserted into the textuality of the Gospels. The resurrection therefore is not a rhetorical proposition. It takes up afresh the burden of classical tradition. The disciples and Mary Magdalene fail for some time to recognise or see the shape and features of the resurrected Christ.

Yet a change was occurring in the frame of classical tragedy. The absolute status of Hades, of death, was changing. The change occurs in the life of problematic texts, the mystery of language within which the dawn of a new age cannot be taken for granted for it brings veils which part and yet through which one sees with difficulty. The restrictive vision of the past cracks a little in a wholly new way. The narrative is suffused with new particularities that conceal at one stage what is before us. But we begin to recognise what at first is unrecognisable. We recognise the unrecognisable by plumbing, in some degree, new particularities inserted into the body of tradition. The link with the resurrection is born then, I would say, out of potential that has been bypassed or eclipsed within texts of classical order, a link that

begins with uncertainty to break certain formal assumptions and to disclose a deeper originality or thread or continuity running out of the past into the present and the future.

My grandfather loved his small garden with its roses and sunflowers. He was the child of the aesthetics of the parochial Garden City. He was blind to the threat of endemic flood built into the settlements that surrounded him. Yet not entirely unseeing. We were all, in some degree, passive creatures and victims of habit. Now—so long after his death—I would inscribe upon his grave a new epitaph that may do justice to his faith in the resurrection. That epitaph would imply links between imageries, yet differentiation in imageries, to bring home a wholeness beyond immediate or partial grasp. A ROSE IS A PARTICLE IS A WAVE.

Queen's College in Georgetown was the premier educational institution for boys in the 1930s from preparatory school age, around nine or so, to matriculation or preliminary degree stage, seventeen or eighteen. I was a student there from 1934 to 1938. Fees were high and it was rather a strain on my mother, particularly after my grandfather's death. No statistics may explain the curious phenomenon Queen's College was, the voyage upon which it was embarked as a vessel of learning linking old worlds and new. It is easy, for instance, for me to quote from a dusty archive of memory and say I left at the end of 1938 with credit or distinction in English, Latin, history, and mathematics. The last was not my favourite subject, but I could enjoy the elegance of geometric and algebraic proportions, and at a time—when unemployment was endemic in the colony—it became the basis upon which I was able to study the trigonometric properties of land surveying (astronomy, geomorphology, hydrography, engineering-surveying, topography, etc.) under government auspices as was the custom—though one could also prepare for the stringent territorial examination with a private tutor—in the British Empire in the 1930s and 1940s.

Later it became more prestigious for young men to study at a university abroad or at home. The

"My daughter, Denise," Essex, 1990

University of Guyana was not founded until the late 1960s.

Having paid due regard, as it were, to archival statistics, I return to the peculiar—even somewhat precarious—microcosm Queen's was in the 1930s. It was never quite the same, I believe, after the Second World War with the eruption in its wake of fanatical racism and the ideological and implacable confrontations that were enshrined and embalmed between East and West in the late 1940s and the 1950s.

I retrace my steps into Queen's in my novel *Carnival* within the shadow of a boy called Everyman Masters, who is being educated to climb upon a mule or horse as a prince or overseer of the plantation world of the Guyanas. When he eventually leaves Queen's and becomes an overseer, he is mistakenly identified for a treacherous lover by a peasant woman of his estate, stabbed by her, drawn in anguish to experience his first metaphorical death—the woman's knife in his ribs—within a "twentieth-century divine comedy of existence."

Though the section in my fictionalisation of Queen's is a limited area of the novel, the implications of linkages between dimensions of a twentieth-century *inferno, purgatorio, paradiso* are subtly there within a cradle of learning that involuntarily perhaps breaks a ghetto-fixation with an absolute *inferno* and an absolute *paradiso.*

Everyman Masters becomes a Virgilian guide after his second, real death in London, England, to which he emigrates from Guyana with his young friend Jonathan Weyl. He returns in Weyl's dreams. Let us remember that Dante's Virgil was forbidden entry into the *paradiso* because he had been born in a pre-Christian age and was therefore a pagan. This taboo or sanction of fate is fractured when Everyman Masters as a boy in 1931 enters Queen's through a gateway or door over which is inscribed:

THE AION IS A BOY WHO PLAYS

PLACING THE COUNTERS HERE AND THERE

TO A CHILD BELONGS THE COSMIC MASTERY

Who is that child? What cross-cultural medium or microcosm of universal being does he bear which is to exact a price upon him in an altered fabric or narrative of tradition with its linked dimensions of *inferno, purgatorio, paradiso?*

Long before the United States was to embark upon desegregation in its institutions of learning, no barriers existed in Queen's, in classrooms, upon playing fields, between students or masters of different ethnic background. There were English masters and students, there were masters and students of African descent, Asian descent, Portuguese, Chinese, Welsh, Scottish. There were students and masters of mixed descent.

The inscription above the gateway through which Everyman Masters passes in *Carnival* is attributed to Heracleitus the Obscure. It seems apt to me for a variety of reasons. Greek was still being taught at Queen's in 1931, though by 1934 when I became a student there it was no longer in the curriculum. Nevertheless, though we read Shakespeare, Donne, Milton, Pope, Coleridge, Tennyson, Wordsworth, we also read Latin texts, Ovid, Caesar, Sallust. But that was not all. In the college library I remember coming upon a slightly terrifying, gripping, marvellous picture of the sculpture of the birth of the maize god. An arm's length away was another volume with a photograph of the ceiling of the Sistine Chapel. True, I grant, the ceiling was painted a decade or so before the conquest of ancient Mexico and Renaissance Europe's encounter with the maize god. But many who were to worship there in succeeding decades and generations—including Michelangelo himself who died in the middle of the sixteenth century—were to experience a blossoming, a flowering of creation, a new genesis, when the food supply of sixteenth-century Europe was virtually doubled (according to the American historian George Vaillant) in the wake of the conquest of the ancient American cultures and civilizations.

There was something prophetic, I am inclined to say, in Michelangelo's intuitive choice of genesis, of creation themes, in his great paintings upon the ceiling of the Sistine Chapel. These are I think a symbolic inscription, a wonderful gesture pointing backwards into Biblical legend, forwards into the New World. Indeed Columbus had already sailed upon what is now known as the Caribbean Sea, but the conquistadores Cortez and Pizarro had not yet encountered the god of maize and his irrigation systems of genius that sustained a variety of fruit, vegetables, potatoes, tomatoes, all exciting and unknown to Europe at that time.

The birth of the maize god portrays the labour of the creaturely sculpted woman from whose body we see an infant child emerge. A curious counterpoint to the fatherhood of the universe painted by Michelangelo, but a valid and creative one it has taken centuries for our civilization to take on board on the male-dominated ship of the globe.

Queen's College did not have actual courses that dealt with the Americas as a whole but there was no overt censorship of books in the college library nor in the public library in Main Street—a stone's throw from the Catholic school I attended at the age of five—endowed by Carnegie.

My curiosity was aroused as never before during those years at Queen's. I grew aware of ambiguities and questions I could barely frame to myself in the 1930s, questions that were to haunt me in the years that followed. Questions that are at the root of novels I did not yet dream I would write, though their shadow may have been there (who knows) for I have not forgotten—it was sealed into my mind, a wondrous compliment and prophecy one cherished—an occasion when my English master said to me when he had read a story-essay I had written, "One day, Harris, you will be a novelist." I could not believe my ears and floated for the rest of the day in space. I remember certain things about him vividly. He was scrupulously fair in marking papers and had no favourites which made his remark all the more telling. He smoked hard—pipe and cigar—I could smell the strong tobacco on his breath when close to him. His skin was very pale, hair black as coal. He tended sometimes to come into the classroom unshaven but extraordinarily alert and sensitive to the needs of the students.

There was an irony, a humour, about his approach to books. He would comment wryly on the nature of censorship, the way censors could promote best-sellers. For instance forbidden books! Have them on your drawing room bookshelf, read or unread, at any price. It was the surest way to impress your friends at a Sunday morning cocktail party. He had sought out Aldous Huxley's *Brave New World* in the first place because of a rumour that it had been banned in Australia though no one had the slightest notion why. He had lost his copy and asked us—the students—whether any of us had seen one around. He had been unable to obtain it in the public library.

Forbidden books were good business. They were projected around the globe by way of rumour and legend. Books were intricate and complex commodities and sometimes works of genius fell to the bottom of the pile, lost, forgotten, and yet they returned and survived against the greatest odds. The funny thing is that I knew he meant it, that despite his wry humour he was serious about the life of the imagination.

I formed the impression that this master was not popular with his colleagues and that he resigned or was sent packing.

In *Carnival* I fictionalised him into the character Delph: *not* by any means an identical portrait. Nevertheless, there is a correspondence that is drawn from his inspirational practice in the classroom. He used to ask us to write narrative that incorporated various motifs or symbols or objects he would list on a blackboard. He was the most imaginative English teacher I had at Queen's, and his transposition into Delph—half-human, half-oracle—is set out at one stage in *Carnival* in the following passage:

> In 1931, as if he anticipated the sack, Mr. Delph gave Masters several *As* for English composition. His habit was to inscribe a list on the blackboard and to request his students to incorporate it into a story. One such prophetic list, straight from the oracle's blackboard mouth . . . ran as follows: marble woman, burning schooner, crocodile, milk, Magna Carta, Bartleby's widow.

(From *Carnival,* p. 75)

The resources of "divine comedy" in our age may lie, I feel, in the way we relate the ancient to the modern to illumine the enigma of prophecy that teases the imagination in Delph's list. The founding of a colony in the ancient Greek world was a sacred matter. Take the crocodile. Ponder on the peculiarity of its eyes. The Delphic imagination may lift those eyes from the margins of the world—from what nowadays we would call a mere colony—into the milky way. The crocodile's eyes, hidden in the darkness of a creek at night, glow astonishingly when they are addressed by a pencil of light issuing from a torch in one's hand. They become stars in an underworld sky. They witness to a link between creature and constellation. Such linkages—as in Quetzalcoatl, the god-man of ancient America who is flanked by coatl, the snake, symbolising the earth, and quetzal, the bird, symbolising the heavens or the sky—are native to Amerindian myth and legend.

Such linkages are inscribed as well in the constellations of the scorpion, the bear, the dog, the horse, the wolf. It is as if, I suspect, there is a therapy in such creativity, a numinous inoculation of the body of the mind which may heal us of dread forces or implacable animality within ourselves.

I return to the inscription above the gateway in my fictionalisation of Queen's College: *The Aion Is a Boy Who Plays / Placing the Counters Here and There / To a Child Belongs the Cosmic Mastery.*

Perhaps the ancient author of that inscription possessed his blackboard on which he chalked a variety of counters to be moved here and there. Perhaps he was involved in a dimension of oracle in which an equation exists between a child's cradle and the birth of language. In every culture around the globe that equation exists in diverse and sometimes not easily recognisable forms. Hermes speaks to his brother Apollo on the day he was born. Or is there a

"Receiving book of essays on my fiction from Professor Hena Maes-Jelinek," Paris, 1991

tongue in the wood of the cradle? Does the rhythm of the tides in our blood infuse the vibration of the harp in the skeleton-tree in our flesh? Does the whisper of a leaf spell out the astronomy of dust? Every ventriloquist of spirit becomes in turn the instrument of what he mimics to break the mould of purely human pride or purely human discourse.

In the 1930s, it seems to me, curiously marginal or colonial institutions (such as Queen's College) in empires that were to crumble after the Second World War were aligned to unconscious/subconscious oracle. Guyana itself was a paradox. A doomed plantation economy yet one of the legendary sites of El Dorado. It was to experience decades later a vestigial dimension of holocaust in the sinister Jonestown massacre triggered by a group of American cultists during the Forbes Burnham regime when Guyana had become a republic.

The Jonestown disaster was headlined around the world in newspapers and magazines though it happened in a remote forest. One wonders in 1992—the quincentennial year of Columbus's voyage into the New World—whether the enslavement of the

Amerindians by the conquistadores who came in the wake of Columbus will receive the analysis it deserves in the world's press. The malaise of El Dorado is sometimes bleakly visible at the extremities of a civilization: the malaise of paradise, the malaise of gold. . . . Perhaps this is inevitable. The centres of a civilization are linked to extremity, extreme hope, extreme crisis. How can they evade, or escape from, dilemmas they have themselves helped to fashion across generations and centuries? Dilemmas, yes, but resources as well at the heart of history for revisionary momentum within an inner/outer voyage of the imagination. . . .

My own voyage outwards was consistent, I am sure, with my expeditions over many years along the coastlands and into the interior of Guyana. A landscape—a theatre of psyche and nature—I was to return to again and again in my dreams. I emigrated to the United Kingdom in 1959. There was an inevitability about this. The voyage out, the sense of the action of memory across distances, the sense of nonlocality (or intense spatiality with its roots everywhere), had become an asset in unravelling restrictive orders or blindnesses. An asset and a key into the

dimensionality I sought in the fiction I was beginning to write.

"Inevitability"—to which I referred a moment ago—implies a spectre of inner/outer consistency or necessity that may shape one's birth, the strangers one encounters at the gate of self. The Indians in India would call it karma. I prefer "freedom" one scarcely understands since "fate" and "freedom" are twins and can change one into the other.

My first marriage had ended in divorce. My ex-wife remarried and we remained on good terms until her death in 1964. I remarried in England in 1959. I met my second wife for the first time in 1954. I never dreamt we would see each other again. It was my good fortune that we did. Without her help over difficult times in the 1960s and '70s, I do not think I would have survived as an imaginative writer into the '80s. I owe much to her love and comprehension, and it was as if our relationship had been shaped by forces deeper than ourselves.

It was her second marriage as well. She was born in Edinburgh, Scotland, and had left in the 1940s to work in London. Hers was a singularly independent mind. In the winter of 1962 she collaborated with a

"Descending the Pyramid of the Moon," Teotihuacan, Mexico, 1972

young American composer as librettist in a television opera based on Charles Dickens's *A Christmas Carol*. Her libretto was highly praised by critics. She has had ten radio plays produced by the BBC. She is also in my view a fine poet.

We secured a flat in the Holland Park area in 1959. I had never been into the park or grounds of Holland House and was to have what I may only describe as a psychical experience there. My wife Margaret and I entered from Holland Park Road. We ascended a gentle incline which brought us to the edge of a pond. I stopped with a sudden, utterly startling impression. It was as if a host of persons unseen yet real came out of the trees calling, "Come in, come in, you are welcome here." I was taken aback, astonished. The impression was concrete though no one was in sight. Not a sound. And yet I heard voices of silence clearer and deeper than sound. They passed and I told my wife. The happening drove us to do some research about Holland House in the Kensington Library. We discovered that it had been the home of a famous English family who were renowned for their hospitality to writers, thinkers, poets, and politicians. Had I been privileged to hear an echo of that hospitality? I was never to have that experience again though Holland Park became a favourite retreat of ours in the heart of the city. I listened many times but never again did the host of place, the voice or voices inscribed into place, speak. One welcome, one invitation, was enough perhaps and indeed I never felt less than welcome in the beautiful grounds surrounding the ruins of old Holland House bombed during the Second World War and converted later into a student hostel and an open-air theatre.

In 1977 my novel *Da Silva da Silva's Cultivated Wilderness*—which has a setting in Holland Park—appeared. In the passage I shall now quote, the painter da Silva writes to his wife Jen who is away visiting her sick father in Peru:

Today's one of those rare days that are so marvellous. I wish you were with me. Quite flawless, the light. What light. Subtle, translucent waterfall. No, tide, an ebbing and a flowing. Sun glints on leaves. Wind appears to stream through them until one catches a glimpse, the wind I mean, it's liquid. I would give my right arm to paint such light, the essence of unselfconsciousness. . . . The weather's so lovely I've taken my easel. . . . I think of you and hope the ordeal of your father's illness will soon pass. I entered the Park from Abbotsbury Road, ascended the avenue of limes to the statue of Lord Holland with the pond at his back. Paused for a while to make a sketch of green-headed ducks. The place is unique. Oaks, birches, chestnuts, cedars. Priceless woodland. And through a crack in the painted wood on my canvas I see peacocks and cranes. Took the paved path through rose bushes lit like lamps, curled flame, then across the stretch of green with its gnarled sentinel tree, down into the old Dutch Garden and on to the fountain under the clock. Fish in the pond there were darting gold, red, silver. A sudden bird flew through the fountain with a human voice, wing touching water, floating voice, sprinkle, close as the rooted hair on one's hand.

(From *Da Silva da Silva's Cultivated Wilderness*, p. 27)

Da Silva da Silva was an acknowledgment on my part of the hospitality that the host of place—the invisible host—had bestowed upon Margaret and me within the grounds of old Holland House. The book did not sell well. And yet something odd occurred ten years later. Channel 4 of Independent Television set out to make a film on my work in 1987. Colin Nutley, the director, chose to base it on *Da Silva da Silva's Cultivated Wilderness*. I grant that within the limited budget at his command, it would have been impractical for him to take a crew into the landscapes of South America to film—let us say—*The Guyana Quartet*. Yet it gave me a strange feeling to find myself (I made two or three fleeting appearances in the film) standing in the eye of the camera close to the pond where Margaret and I had stood in 1959 and I had heard the echo of a vanished age and felt the warmth and the embrace of living absence or invisible presence.

I was to take occasional critics and scholars who came to see me into the grounds or park. There were excellent seats close to the old Dutch Garden and within tree-lined avenues. I remember taking Hena Maes-Jelinek there in the 1970s. Hena's background is European Jewry. She is a brilliant and unusual critic. She lives with her Belgian husband René in Liège and is Professor of Commonwealth and English literatures at the university there. Her interest in my work has continued across the years and is profound. She edited a remarkable book of essays by generous critics, scholars, poets—entitled *Wilson Harris the Uncompromising Imagination*—that was presented to me (it came as a total surprise, even my wife kept the secret) in Paris on my seventieth birthday in March 1991. I must confess I was pleased by the diversity of contribution from writers such as Margaret Harris, Kathleen Raine, David Dabydeen, Michael Thorpe, Fred d'Aguiar, Kirsten Holst Peterson, Anna Rutherford, Michael Gilkes, Michel Fabre, Mark Williams, Alan Riach, Gareth Griffiths, Stephen Slemon, Joyce Sparer Adler, Russell McDougall, Gregory Shaw,

Nathaniel Mackey, Helen Tiffin, Louis James, Mark McWatt, Mary Lou Emery, William J. Howard, Al Creighton, Desmond Hamlet, Jean-Pierre Durix, Michel N. Jagessar, and Hena Maes-Jelinek.

On certain occasions, not often, I have tended to discuss with Hena the haunting reality of the mystery of evil. She lost close relatives and friends in the holocaust. This is so unbearable that the imagination (whether philosophical or creative—and the two are linked) is challenged to the core of its genesis, *unfinished* genesis, I believe. I—on my part—am aware of the numinous and hidden scars on the body of cultures in South and Central America and in the Caribbean.

Our dialogue has been fruitful. It has helped in the creation of an understanding of cross-cultural parallels and the deep bearing these have in overcoming implacable opposition and divides within a tormented world.

In this autobiographical essay I have attempted, in some degree, to illumine some of the forces and currents that bear upon the gestation and birth of a personal vision. I stress *personal* for I embrace no dogma, I have no absolute theories.

I close this essay with an unforgettable experience of a trip Margaret and I made to Mexico. We were able to go there in 1972 when I was a visiting member of faculty at the University of Texas at Austin.

Black Marsden—a novel which has much of its setting in Edinburgh (my wife's birthplace)—had been published that very year. The visit to Mexico was to provide me with a curious sequel called *Companions of the Day and Night.* The title is drawn from motifs of the great calendar completed within Montezuma's reign—a decade or so before the Spanish Conquest. That a fiction set in a layer of Mexican landscape and tradition should prove a sequel to a work largely set in Scotland raises for me a personal and private sensation of cross-cultural links between Celtic numinous darkness and pre-Columbian/post-Columbian uncertainties in the soil and ethnicity of all immigrant peoples in the Americas across the centuries. Africans possibly before Columbus, certainly through the Middle Passage, Scots after Culloden, Irish at the time of the great famine, Poles, French, Jews, English fleeing to the New World from persecutions. . . . Indeed a trigger of memory in

With Margaret, Essex, 1991

135

me was fired by faces of Mexicans I encountered, reticent, slightly withdrawn, mixed ancestries, all pigmentations: faces in one focus stoically Indian/Aztec/Toltec perhaps, in other foci resembling my own mixed relatives and friends in Guyana. I remembered my own daughter, Denise, of whom I am very fond. She has something of that expressive spirit of curiosity blended into restraint and solitude that I glimpsed in some of the passersby in the Avenida Juarez. (I see her now afresh in my mind's eye as I write. She lives in New York and visits Margaret and me in Essex virtually every year. She is writing a novel.)

As we moved through Mexico City—its marketplaces, its museums, its halls, its churches (it was close to Easter when Margaret and I were there) in which Christ and his disciples were carven and painted in the colour and shadow of stranger gods, stranger sacrifices—the past seemed subtly alive.

The very dust that swirled on the road out of Mexico City to ancient Teotihuacan (which means "the place where the gods are made") seemed a sprinkling, a powdering, of a vanished reappearing dimension of fossil light. We passed convents on the way, ruins, the mouth of a tunnel into a mound or hill upon which a Catholic church stood. That tunnel led to a hidden Toltec shrine that had nestled in the earth for four-and-a-half centuries in concealment from the eyes of the conquistadores and their descendants.

We came around noon to Teotihuacan. We had read about it and knew it had been abandoned by its inhabitants—because perhaps of famine or crisis or some other circumstance unrecorded in the history books—long before the Aztecs arrived two or three centuries before Cortez. They named it Teotihuacan for they did not know its original name.

We set out to ascend the pyramids of the sun and the moon after exploring ruined shelters and palaces and corridors inscribed in places, it seemed to us, with child deities in swaddling clothes. Some had the head of young lions and birds. And there was a profusion of butterflies.

When we gained the height of the moon it seemed to us that if we gazed hard enough into a faint cloud of dust we would see the pointillist swaddling clothes—uplifted from the paintings beneath the pyramids of the sun and the moon—and this would tell of infant astronauts and the astronomy of long-vanished yet subtly alive poets and painters and sculptors and priests in space and in the memory of time. The light of the mind was their epitaph and our cradle.

BIBLIOGRAPHY

Novels:

Palace of the Peacock, Faber, 1960, reissued as Book I of the *Guyana Quartet*, Faber, 1985.

The Far Journey of Oudin, Faber, 1961, reissued as Book II of the *Guyana Quartet*, Faber, 1985.

The Whole Armour, Faber, 1962, reissued as Book III of the *Guyana Quartet*, Faber, 1985.

The Secret Ladder, Faber, 1963, reissued as Book IV of the *Guyana Quartet*, Faber, 1985.

Heartland, Faber, 1964.

The Eye of the Scarecrow, Faber, 1965.

The Waiting Room, Faber, 1967.

Tumatumari, Faber, 1968.

Ascent to Omai, Faber, 1970.

Black Marsden: A Tabula Rasa Comedy, Faber, 1972.

Companions of the Day and Night, Faber, 1975.

Da Silva da Silva's Cultivated Wilderness [and] *Genesis of the Clowns*, Faber, 1977.

The Tree of the Sun, Faber, 1978.

The Angel at the Gate, Faber, 1982.

Carnival (see below), Faber, 1985.

The Infinite Rehearsal (see below), Faber, 1987.

The Four Banks of the River of Space (see below), Faber, 1990.

Carnival Trilogy (includes *Carnival*, *The Infinite Rehearsal*, and *The Four Banks of the River of Space*), forthcoming in paperback.

Short stories:

The Sleepers of Roraima, Faber, 1970.

The Age of the Rainmakers, Faber, 1971.

Poetry:

(Under pseudonym Kona Waruk) *Fetish*, privately printed (Georgetown, Guyana), 1951.

The Well and the Land, Magnet (Georgetown), 1952.

Eternity to Season, privately printed, 1954, revised edition, New Beacon Books (London), 1978.

Nonfiction:

Tradition, The Writer and Society: Critical Essays, New Beacon Books, 1973.

Explorations: A Series of Talks and Articles, 1966–1981, edited by Hena Maes-Jelinek, Dangaroo Press (Denmark), 1981.

The Womb of Space: The Cross-Cultural Imagination, Greenwood, 1983.

The Radical Imagination, University of Liège (Belgium), forthcoming.

Contributor to *Poems from the West Indies,* edited by Jose A. Jarvis, Kraus, 1954; *Caribbean Rhythms: The Emerging English Literature of the West Indies,* edited by J. T. Livingston, Washington Square Press, 1974; *Enigma of Values: An Introduction,* edited by Anna Rutherford and Kirsten Holst Petersen, Dangaroo Press, 1975; *Critics on Caribbean Literature: Readings in Literary Criticism,* edited by Edward Baugh, St. Martin's, 1978; and *The Literate Imagination* (essays on the novels of Wilson Harris), edited by Michael Gilkes, Macmillan (London), 1989. Also contributor to *Literary Half-Yearly, Kyk-over-al,* and *New Letters.*

Rolando Hinojosa-Smith

1929-

Rolando Hinojosa, 1986

I was born in Mercedes, Texas, a small agriculturally based community in the Lower Rio Grande Valley. It lies three miles north of the Rio Grande and forty miles west of the Gulf of Mexico. Rural and with ample rich farmland, the Valley also enjoys semi tropical weather which allows for a twelve-month crop system.

The area has been part of the United States since the state's annexation to the Union in December 1845. Prior to annexation, the people there had been Spanish subjects, Mexican citizens, and Texans. In 1860, they became citizens of the Confederacy and underwent Reconstruction as did any Southern state.

In 1749, the area was settled by Spanish subjects; there was no army, but also no presidios, and no church missions according to the first census in 1750; by contrast the first U.S. census took place in 1790. The names on the rolls are still found with great frequency on both sides of the Rio Grande. Intermarriages between the people on the southern and the northern banks of the Rio Grande have been and remain part of the culture. In brief, a stable and, oftentimes, isolated community.

On the maternal side, the Smiths arrived there in 1887; my mother was six weeks old at the time. Her father, Abraham Neumann Smith, was the postmaster in Progreso, a settlement, and her mother, Mary Phillips, taught school in a one-room country school.

My father, Manuel Guzmán Hinojosa, was born on a farm just north of Mercedes; the farm and the neighboring family cemetery are within two miles of each other. Recently, the state of Texas designated the cemetery a landmark and has taken over its maintenance.

The above are cold facts and there's no way to make them sound otherwise, or any need to, either.

Additionally, the area is also bicultural, and, as a borderland, the ties between Texas and Mexico are psychological, economic, historic, and, because of time, bound by blood relations. The ties were established early and maintained by years of isolation from both Mexico City and Washington, D.C. The emphasis there has been on family structures.

The youngest of five children, I too attended school in Mercedes and must have occupied the same seats as my brothers and sister who preceded me. The town remains much the same: small and with a conscious sense of continuity. At age seventeen, I found it stifling and left for army service two months after my high school graduation.

Irony, that great stuff of life, comes into play here: after years of zero productivity and publication, I found that Mercedes and the Lower Rio Grande Valley were what I knew best. To my fortune and happiness, I found this out after a lifetime of reading, living, and a questionable amount of formal and self-education. Lest I sound romantic here, I knew I wanted to write; it was the *what* that was missing.

What I took with me when I left was a love of reading. Fostered in a home, where everyone read, I was also encouraged by the example of three teachers: Alma Whatley, Merle Blankenship, and Amy Cornish. With Miss Whatley, I wrote and edited the eighth-grade newspaper; with Mrs. Blankenship, I was taught how to memorize passages, how to remember from close reading; and with Miss Cornish, writing. I entered writing contests as a junior and as a senior. Five of the honorable mentions and selections form part of the Mercedes High School library.

As for the army service, I later found it no different from what my friends told me: dull and boring during periods of inactivity, feverish and exciting the other times. I was no hero; I was—to quote from Luke 17:10—a useless servant who did no more than was commanded of me.

The G.I. Bill followed, and I graduated from the University of Texas in 1953. I married for the first time in 1956 and worked as a high school teacher, as a laborer in a chemical plant, as an office manager for a work-clothing manufacturer, and then went back to high school teaching before quitting that to earn money as a civil servant, which enabled me to work on my master's. There was a divorce and there was a son, Robert Roland; I did not see him from 1959

Rolando in 1932

until 1986 when his mother relented and told him where I was. Ours was a happy, nervous reunion full of surprises and discoveries. We've been working on our relationship ever since, and I don't suppose this presents anything new to those familiar with this type of reunion. Needless to say, I'm very proud of him, and I've also reminded him that his adoptive father is both remarkable and generous to have raised him in a way I was not prepared to.

I remarried in 1963, and with an M.A. from New Mexico Highlands University, I entered the doctoral program at the University of Illinois.

Those were five long, study-filled, hard-working, happy years. Upon completion of my doctorate, my wife Patti and I returned to Texas; Clarissa, our oldest daughter, was born in Urbana in 1966. I taught at Trinity University (San Antonio) during 1968–70. I then became chairman and, subsequently, dean of the College of Arts and Sciences, and Vice President for Academic Affairs at Texas A & I University (Kingsville) during 1970–77. At that time, my wife decided to enter law school. In 1977, I took a position at the University of Minnesota; Patti enrolled in law school and won her degree in 1981. Our second daughter, Karen, born in San Antonio during my Trinity days, was twelve years old at the time.

In 1981, I had the choice of remaining at Minnesota or taking a job at University of California at Los Angeles or at the University of Texas. We chose Texas, and Karen counts this as one of the best decisions we've ever made. For me, the jury is still out on this verdict; Karen, though, is a Texan and adamantly so.

Patti worked for the Railroad Commission and for the Attorney General's office before becoming an associate in private practice. She specialized in domestic law and was very good at it.

In 1988, out of the blue—for me, at any rate—Patti filed for divorce and moved to California. Clarissa had graduated from Texas that spring and went with her. Karen, a senior as I write this in the fall of '91, expects to graduate next summer.

That has been a part of my life not known to most of my readers. It should prove to be of little interest as well.

Young Rolando (right) with friend Malcolm Robinson, Fort Eustis, Virginia, 1947. "Sitting on the doorstep is Freddie Silva, the model for the character Pepe Vielma."

On the writing side, this begins seriously in the early seventies. Events and circumstances of the times conjugated into a period of productivity for me. Vietnam was still with us and there was a renewed fervor of civil rights by the Mexican-American citizenry; one of the avenues open for me was the example set by Tomás Rivera and his prize-winning novel . . . *y no se lo tragó la tierra*. Here was a work published in this country, in Spanish, and by an independent Mexican-American house, Quinto Sol Publications. This enterprise began as a graduate, undergraduate, and professorial endeavor at the University of California at Berkeley.

Its journal, *El Grito*, carried the subtitle *A Journal of Contemporary Mexican American Thought*. The journal was a mixed bag: articles on history, economics, sociology, anthropology, social work, but it also included poetry and narrative prose fiction. It was a free enterprise and not dependent on any grants from any quarter. It was also very good.

Within three years of publication, Quinto Sol announced a literary prize for fiction; Rivera was the first winner (1970), and I won it in 1972 for *Estampas del valle y otras obras*. Two Texans and both works in Spanish; the 1971 winner was Rudolfo A. Anaya (New Mexico) for *Bless Me, Ultima*. This impetus and these examples were enough for me; I've been writing and publishing my works ever since. My first check from Quinto Sol was for thirty-five dollars; I both remember and treasure it still.

The first two works, *Estampas* and *Klail City y sus alrededores*, were written in Spanish. The translations were done by Gustavo Valadez and José Reyna, and by Rosaura Sánchez, respectively. Subsequently, I did two English renditions of the same works, *The Valley* and *Klail City*. These were followed by *Korean Love Songs*, in English, *Mi querido Rafa*, an epistolary novel using both languages, and then *Rites and Witnesses* and *Partners in Crime*, both in English, and the bilingual edition of *Claros varones de Belken (Fair Gentlemen of Belken County)*; Julia Cruz did the English translation for this one. I then did the English version of *Dear Rafe*, taken from *Mi querido Rafa*, as well as the Spanish version of *Becky and Her Friends*, *Los amigos de Becky*. It's confusing, true, but bibliographers are magicians at sorting these things out. *Korean Love Songs* has an announced publication date of October 1991, in German, with the title *Korea Liebes Lieder*. The English version appears on the facing page. The effort here is due to Wolfgang Karrer of Osnabrück University who, aside from his native German, has mastered English and Spanish. Our conversations, to any bystander, innocent or not, are bound to be baffling as we go from one language to the other, to the other.

The series is called the "Klail City Death Trip" series and it is based on Mercedes and the other communities in the Lower Rio Grande Valley of Texas. The works deal with Mexican Americans, but not exclusively. There is also the Mexican national side of things represented as well as the Texas Anglos who share space with the Texas Mexicans.

Favorable newspaper reviews on the series are pleasing, but articles where the writers spend over a year thinking about my work are closer to the mark. Their reputations as scholars rest on these articles and hence this material is serious. M.A. and doctoral theses on my work are likewise gratifying, whether written here or abroad as in the cases of scholars in Sweden, Italy, Spain, Germany, etc. Articles from France and Hungary and elsewhere are also pleasing; it is further gratifying to talk with scholars who take as much interest in the doings of the denizens of Belken County as I do.

My writing habits are, as most habits, subject to change. But there is one unalterable habit: I write something every day. It's good practice for me, and it is also a good practice for any writer.

Reading and teaching also take much of my time, but I find both to be fruitful and engaging. I find myself rereading favorite books and writers (essays, biographies, history, and some frivolous writing, too). (I must admit that the pervasiveness of free baseball is a great temptation; nothing, though, beats a live performance in a major-league park for me.)

Students. I wish they would take pride in their spelling. I also wish they would write stories about their characters instead of dwelling on *characterization*. This last may be a product of our creative writing classes. In this regard, I must also take partial blame: I am the director of the Texas Center for Writers at the University of Texas, a program generously funded by James Michener. (Jim and I team-teach a course, and I think he and I have as much fun as the junior writers who take the course with us.)

As for the junior writers, the up-and-coming writers, they may be better than we were at their stage. I find, though, that they do not read many European writers; this goes for students wherever my readings take me: Stanford, Yale, Harvard, and the smaller, lesser-known schools. Writers, though, are writers, and they do not necessarily have to come from any particular school.

Because of my background (family, social circumstance, geographic origin, the military, education, work experience, etc.), I refuse to accept cate-gorization of any kind. I say this since artists—and particularly writers—are subject to commentary by those who seek to explain what we do in and with our work. It's a normal rejection, I suppose, and certainly not unique on my part. Still, uninhibited assertions by those who seek to explain writers cannot go unanswered. This if only to satisfy myself, but it will also help me to say what I have to say unequivocally.

Having said this, I can only imagine—but I *can* imagine—the headshaking of those who say writers are not to be trusted. Maybe we are not supposed to be trusted, but, if so, who among us should be? The government? Our established religions? The other institutions which seek to control our lives? Who?

It's a broadside question and not one which seeks an, or any, answer. Rhetorical, then. But, put here for this purpose: my life—as that of most people's—is so filled with contradictions that it is impossible to be comfortable with any categorization. My life is mentioned but not spelled out in my writing. Both my life and my writing are parts of who and what I am and have become, but only parts and not all of that which functions consequently or, as is often the case, with any degree of consistency. And, it also happens that different stages of one's life are considered, accepted, or rejected, and, if rejected, appear again at another time and perhaps in another novel. And let's not talk about the subsequent and many rewrites which will then cause the writer to say: "All bets are off. I've changed my mind about this and that (at *this* time and for *now*), and I'm just lucky as hell to have finished *this* novel."

Am I asking for a cessation of the study of literature by scholars? No. I believe in research, in investigation, and in the publication of such findings. What I ask for—demand, really—is that they do not look at one's latest work in isolation from the previous works. Since writing is often a compendium of the whole of one's background, and since any individual novel fails to cover the whole of one's life and one's work, then patience, hard work, and reason should also be present and at one with knowledge and the necessary tools to bring everything to bear upon that novel, but only in the light of the whole.

My *Klail City Death Trip* is an interrelated series of works, and I'm presenting it as one novel; both the series and the novel it seeks to finish are incomplete. Since this is so, it could be called a dialectical series, I suppose.

Does this mean that no critical work should be attempted until the work is completed? The answer again is no, since one should not put an end to a discussion that seeks, by reason, an intellectual investigation. Each new addition takes its place in the series and the investigator should catch up with it with the understanding that the search is not over.

M.A. and doctoral theses as well as articles or monographs show this to be the case: they begin at a determined point (*Estampas del valle*) and end at another determined point, for the time being; in this case, *The Useless Servants,* which is the next work in the series and in preparation still.

But isn't this what we are doing now, scholars will ask? In many cases, yes, and I read with care what investigators say. What I am saying as clearly as possible is that what the characters say or do at one point may be contradicted by the characters themselves at another point. This, to me, is the stuff of life: contradictions and the apparent, the evident, truth which must be dug out. Truth may be a constant, but human views are not.

To my good fortune, most critical scholars do look critically and in sequence, and this is a blessing. And yet, there are still those who see each work as independent instead of examining it as merely one more link in this chain I've been forging since 1973.

To seek perfection in any sphere is illusory, of course, but one can always use a forum such as this one to counsel patience to those reviewers and critics whose job is to explain what one is doing.

Does this sound as if I want to have my cake and eat it too? I hope not. If it does, however, and worse, if it's true, then perhaps I shouldn't be trusted. After all, the world and I and the readers have been altered by time. So too, then, have the characters changed. And there my writing stands, but does it? No, it's more of a moving target and one which I will try to keep on the move.

A question often asked is why I publish with a small house. First of all, I'm convinced that big houses and their imprints are not interested in what I do. I see nothing to add to that. Second—and this is important to me and to all writers—small houses are more patient; sometimes it takes them three years to sell a first run, and this creates a backlist of my works.

With three exceptions, all of my work is available and for sale. Of the exceptions, two, *Estampas del valle* and *Klail City* (which is being titled *El condado de Belken;* space does not permit a full explanation), are to be released soon by Bilingual Press, Arizona State University. The third exception is *Korean Love Songs,* but, as mentioned above, a German translation is forthcoming.

Backlists, for me, are far more important than a transitory blockbuster which leaves little when the dust settles. The money is not comparable either, but if I were going solely after that, I would have had to give up my teaching (which I will not), and I'd most probably have to change my way of writing to suit a mass audience (which I won't). I'm raising a false issue here since no major publisher is interested, and there it stands.

A careless reader may suspect I'm resentful, but if so, then the reader is, in a word, wrong. To have published as much, to have travelled as much, and to have had the opportunity to help others came about because of my writing. How could one be resentful?

One of the bonuses in writing is being invited to do a reading of one's work. The invitations have taken me abroad (Cuba, France, Germany, Mexico, Panama), and in this country to universities and colleges as diverse as the Ivy League, and some not-well-funded schools in Texas and in other parts of the United States.

I still have energy for travelling and consider what I do as part of an instructional bent in the fostering of Mexican-American literature. It's just one part of general American literature, but not as well known or as publicized as, say, Afro-American literature.

The audiences have been varied, needless to say. The places, though, do bear mentioning: I've read from the back of a pickup truck, to driveways near some family's lawn, to living rooms with kids rolling on the floor while I plowed ahead. If one can read in this atmosphere, one can read anywhere: I once read to a group of helicopter mechanics in a hangar. It's become a source of pride that I will read just as enthusiastically for 20 as for 200 or 300 people.

Just recently, a budding Mexican-American civil service employee group asked me to read at a public library. Counting me, there were eight, and we had a grand time. The reading also allowed me to meet that fine singer Tish Hinojosa. Between her singing and my reading, the one-hour scheduled meeting ran for two and a half hours.

This wouldn't have done, I'm sure, at some rigidly structured conference. These, however, can be fun, and because of them, I've been able to meet mainstream writers and poets such as Ed Doctorow, Kenneth Koch, and William Gass. What I've learned from these writers is their unfeigned congeniality. They, I'm sure, had no idea who I was, but it didn't matter to them: I was there, I was introduced as a writer, and therefore I had a right to be there.

Stories come out of these meetings at times. Stories not for publication or for insertion in some novel, but stories which can be passed on to others. Here's one: In 1988, and thus a year before the Tiananmen Square massacre, a group of us from the States were invited by University of California at Los

Hinojosa (left) with author Julio Cortázar, Carol Cortázar, and Fernando Urrea,
Cienfuegos, Cuba, 1980

Angeles to meet and talk with some Mainland China writers. Both groups submitted samples of their writing and abbreviated vitae to translators.

UCLA was a most gracious host and provided some form of entertainment nightly. At one of those functions, we were entertained by five women dressed as Texas cowgirls. The numbers were old-timey ones ("I'm an Old Cowhand," "Don't Fence Me In," etc.), and the singers and musicians were very, very good. During a break one of them asked me who the Chinese guests were, and I explained.

She called the other members of the group. It turned out they'd been interned in Shanghai, of all places. I happened to remember that the poet Carolyn Kiser, one of the ten writers invited by UCLA, had a Chinese connection: her father had worked in Shanghai, and so I got the musicians and Kiser together.

Talk about coincidences. Her father had befriended these women and had sheltered them in Shanghai during those perilous times. The women were Ashkenazim, living and working in Shanghai at the time.

There's a novel there somewhere, but not for me to write. What struck me, as always, was the smallness of the world. Who or what forces brought all of these people together for a moment of genuine pleasure, of recognition, of gratitude?

A night later, at a Hollywood party (whatever that means or implies), Martha Scott, always a favorite of mine, walked in with her husband. She was quite excited about a school for young actors she was heading and we talked on that awhile. Then her husband started playing the piano, and what piano! "Who's your husband?" I asked. "Mel Powell," she said. Mel Powell; this brought back memories of big-band days, and I already knew of his association with the Yale music department and his work on films and as an arranger.

Not only is he a marvelous pianist, but also a wide reader. Bill Gass came up to me and said, "He's a fan!" Powell had read Bill's *Omensettler's Luck* and had commented with sagacity and pinpoint accuracy on the merits of that difficult book.

A recurring question came to me, as it usually does in these affairs: What's a Mercedes, Texas, boy doing in a place like this?

Other parties have been more modest, but I'm continually taken by people's generosity of spirit. They usually say I seem to be having a wonderful time, and I correct them to drop the *seem* since I *am* enjoying myself.

Something else I enjoy—and this keeps me in my place in the world—is that after having been picked up at the airport and delivered safely wherever I'm going, after the work, the food and drink, and my name on posters all over campus, I get to stand in line at the airport counter. Flying coach, of course. I say I enjoy this comedown of the amenities because it keeps me from getting too big for my britches. If that's the phrase.

There's nothing like anonymity to put one's writing accomplishments in a 20-20 perspective.

One last story: Amy Ling and I once worked at Harvard with James Baldwin. It was a gray, cold, and rainy Sunday afternoon. The next day's baseball opener had been cancelled. This was the year Detroit reeled off that incredible streak before the other teams could even catch their breath.

The three of us read and talked with the packed house at the JFK Building. Amy's reading was first-rate, and I remember a mother-daughter dialogue which formed part of her performance. I glanced at the crowd; not a peep out of them. Riveted, that overblown word, described the audience's attention. Baldwin followed her and it was difficult to top what Amy had done.

He didn't even try. He read in that measured tone and he too had them eating out of his hand. And now, the Texas Mexican. Baldwin smiled and said, "Here's Rolando."

That's all, that short phrase, and it got the crowd's attention.

The subsequent conversation and the rapport with the audience were on target. If writers are accused—and some of them should be—of egotism, or of not earning their fees at such events, that wasn't the case there. Unfortunately, Baldwin died soon after, but his kindness, his friendly courtliness, to both Amy and me served as reminders that here was James Baldwin, a writer unassuming and genuine.

When I started out to write (and to have work published), I obviously had no idea what would be in store ten to fifteen years later. Indeed, to have thought of meeting other writers could not have entered my mind. I'm sure it didn't. This makes me sound like a "gee whiz" guy, and I suppose I am. Does it matter?

Readings, for me, are usually enjoyable. I find people to be unfailingly courteous and kind. The questions, and every writer has heard them, run to a pattern: When did you first begin to write? When did you first decide to be a writer? What writers influenced you the most? What books do you read and have you read?

There are also questions regarding the technical part of writing: Do you follow a schedule? Is there a special time you prefer to write? Do you use a computer? How do I get an agent? And so on.

The object of the questions, I think, is that one's answers may produce some key to unlock a magic room that has all the answers on "how to write." The questions are earnest enough.

My answers are also usually the same: Much reading, and a desire and an urge to write, perhaps even to show off. As for writers who have influenced me, for good or ill, their names are legion. I believe that one is influenced daily, and not only by writers. How one acts or reacts to those influences is another question entirely. This, to me, depends on one's experiences, or lack of them. I, too, do not possess the key to that magic room.

At one time in my youth, I read interviews. I found them instructive and entertaining. How much they influenced my writing, I cannot say. But influence me they did, because I now have been interviewed several times. I hope what I've said in these interviews and in future ones will be of some benefit. As always, it's hard to know what comes from all or any of this.

Jealousy. I've not yet suffered writer's block, and I wonder if this is so because I worry more about my characters than I worry about what other writers are doing. I publish with two small presses (and they have those backlists I mentioned), and consider myself blessed. Many acquaintances—writers—publish with mainline houses or their imprints, and their conversations usually run to: "they're not spending money to publicize my book."

This is more likely the case than not. Publishing is a gamble. The publishers have to pay rent and taxes, illustrators, printers, binders, and God knows what else. After this, they pay shipping costs (and when the books are remaindered, and they are, they also pay the postage). In this regard, I'll quote Mr. Knopf, who said: "Gone today, here tomorrow."

There is much prestige in being a book publisher, and many take beatings on some of the work they publish, but the stakes (and the prices of books) being what they are, a few hardback blockbusters can show a healthy profit. A New York City reading audience that can gobble up 200,000 hardbacks in a week brings in a healthy sum of money for everybody.

But what if the book is a bust? (And I'm speaking of novels, not cookbooks, self-help books, etc.) Then the publishers have to swallow hard and keep going. And what of those writers who complain that their books aren't being publicized? Well, I wonder if they consider what the shelf life of a novel is in any of our national retailers? Probably not or, if they do, they probably think it wouldn't, it couldn't, apply to theirs. As in everything, it depends on the public too. The public may be fickle, it may be anything the writer wishes to call it, but it is the public who buys the book.

When that disappointment comes, that momentary awe of having had one's book accepted by a major house (or imprint) fades; I imagine this is the time when one becomes a bore.

Now, my work is difficult to read at times. It isn't that I come up with high-blown concepts; it's that I don't write that familiar object, the nineteenth century form of the novel. Also, my novels are short—too short for most publishers, I've been told. (Told, by the way, by academic critics who, God knows how, have that information at their fingertips. They may be right for all I know.)

Mi querido Rafa

última novela de

Rolando Hinojosa

Klail City Death Trip Series

Cover of Mi querido Rafa

About three years ago, I was called by a very junior editor from Random House. Did I have anything? No idea how she got my name (I've no agent), and I said that what I wrote was not what her house would be interested in. She was kindly insistent and said she'd still like to see some books; I sent her three and never heard from her again. (I wish I had the books back; I paid my publisher for them, and since I don't use the university's money to send my stuff out, that little change, too, came out of my pocket.)

Understandably, she was beginning her job with them, and she was drumming up business for the house. Nothing wrong with that since publishing is a risky business. It happens, though, that what I write could not possibly interest the general reader. And no, it isn't that I'm a snob; it's a clear personal recognition that what I do has limited appeal, even if, as Jim Michener says, a respected one. I thank him for that, of course. He, in truth, is both generous in his actions and acute in his knowledge of the market.

I've no idea how many pages I've published, but I would hazard that two of Jim's books cover as many pages as my eleven books. Two different writers and audiences. I find it fortunate I recognize what it is I do.

Another friend, Tony Hillerman, read some of my work, and he took time both to write and encourage me to submit my manuscripts to two agents he knows. This was some time ago, and I didn't follow through. But can the reader of this imagine what a boost to my ego Tony's kindness generated?

Editors. I'm told that great editors have disappeared from the big houses. This may be so since I've no knowledge or experience in this regard. Too, it may be that writers can employ their own editors. What I do see a need for is proofreading. That errata are to be found in most books is now commonplace. A shame, but true. I've made mention of our students' poor spelling, and since junior editors come from those ranks, what can one expect? It is my conviction that writers are responsible for errata, and they should see to them.

I suppose one can put this down as but one more example of the sloppiness, the lack of pride one witnesses daily in all manner of services in our country nowadays.

As I reread that last line, I think: "Spoken like a true mossback." But is it so? Am I a mossback or is the country's general attitude one tending to sloppiness and mediocrity?

These are important matters, of course, and meat for any writer. But is it the country's mood to read this type of novel? Do people care? I think they do, but even if they don't, writers care and, eventually, it's the writers who force us to look at ourselves. Not always a pretty or an exemplary picture, but writing about this and similar matters is worth the candle.

Doubt. Maybe this is another part of the writer's block. Doubt is like fear, and fear, as Faulkner reminds us, is a luxury a writer cannot afford. A lack of self-confidence in any endeavor (pitching a change-up instead of a high hard one on a 3-2 pitch) is a killer. Doubt may exist and may prove beneficial if the writer seriously questions that he has done the best there was to be done. If there is doubt, rewrite. And rewrite until you are satisfied, until all doubt is removed. To be sure, this is easier to say than it is to carry through.

One thing about writing, though: people may not care if one begins to write or if one stops writing. The writer, then, must care, and caring enough about what one does is a firm step in removing doubt.

A few words on jargon and age. A recurrent phenomenon, the mid-life crisis, passed me by. If it comes at age forty-plus, then it is a matter of luck: I published my first book (*Estampas*) when I was forty-four. Perhaps it will come after I'm through writing, but I don't know when that will be.

From the evidence around me, most of my friends and colleagues, men and women, have been divorced at one time or another. Is divorce part of the mid-life crisis? I can't offer expert testimony; what I do see is general unhappiness. But this, I think, is a product of unadaptability to increasing age, to a recognition of a certain erosion of one's energies, and to certain limitations in spheres which, when one was younger, one gave no thought to. Perhaps unadaptability is that which is now called the mid-life crisis.

Words, as writers know, have come into our lexicon, some to stay, others for brief visit, until replaced by a permanent one, or by another exciting but likewise transitory word or phrase.

For now, *dilemma* is quite popular, and chances are that it could fit here: "He's facing a mid-life dilemma." Why not? I remember when *viable* (in the 1960s) was as common as dirt on a farm. And remember *co-opted* and *non-negotiable demands,* and all the other handy, off-the-rack, ready-to-wear words and phrases? For the past ten years now, *basically, in terms of,* and *early on* have been riding high; perhaps as high as *mid-life crisis.*

I think that English—and it *is* a grand language—will survive those other pedantic usages: *probably* and *seems,* among others, which parade as

Cover of Dear Rafe, *Hinojosa's translation of his* Mi querido Rafa

learned pronouncements. They are neither the former nor the latter.

Writers, then, not only care about words, we also put them to work; and, it is work which keeps words alive and kicking up a fuss. Clichés don't bother me as much as they bother my teaching colleagues; if properly used, clichés can produce some readable scenes in the midst of arid prose that poses as those learned pronouncements.

So, no mid-life crisis for this writer, who remembers a word from his childhood: *melancholia.* This is now described as a manic-depressive psychosis. And who am I to argue with the coiners of phrases such as that one? They, I'm confident, will forge another to replace manic-depressive psychosis soon enough.

My freshman English Merriam-Webster's of forty years ago did not list *manic-depressive psychosis* (MDP) in its list of definitions; instead, it gave us *sadness, brooding,* and so on. (Words usable to writers.) My up-to-date Merriam-Webster's (the ninth edition, 1985) includes MDP; it doesn't talk about a cure, though.

*Hinojosa (right) with authors Ron Arias
and Tomás Rivera, Claremont, California, 1981*

I cannot pretend to take anyone to task here, but if English has survived, it's because of its resiliency and that of folk who use it and who refuse to water it down with jargon. Still, jargon does reflect the times, and if jargon is a key to characterization, no writer will hesitate to have his characters use it to develop characterization and background.

The latest example of jargon I've run across was on a Delta flight. It came in the words used for airsickness. The German stuck to *Luftkrankheit*. The two telescoped words *Luft Krankheit* tell us the bag is for airsickness. Delta, a fine airline but a namby-pamby user of English, went with the PR people and claimed that the bag was for "motion discomfort." I don't need a bag for discomfort.

The French, linguistically conservative as ever, say that the bag is for *mal de mer,* even if we're flying some thirty-six thousand feet above the *mer*. What rankles, though, to use a Bushian phrase, is the discomfort thing.

The above, and its tone, are inherited traits. My parents had a scant formal education, but both were great readers. My brothers and sisters followed suit, and so, I thought, that was the way of the world. (And yet, how many of us have been in houses which possess no books or magazines but, in their place, find all manner of electronic equipment? A form of compensation, I suppose.)

As for the tone, it may be termed cranky, although it's closer to a niggling impatience with people who possess a reasonable education but who can't, or won't, speak and make themselves understood clearly. Who prefer circumlocutions and euphemisms when straight talk—or writing—is called for.

To be raised by two strong parents can be deleterious for some children. And mine were strong and held strong opinions; there were, however, no lectures on right or wrong, on honesty or dishonesty, and the like. They led straight—and economically straitened—lives, and we consciously or unconsciously tried to emulate them. Added to this, there were no spankings.

Both, too, were great narrators; performers, really. Some of the stories were folktales, but some, the fantastic ones, must have been of their own invention. As for jokes, puns, and word games, they were at it all the time, it seems, and one was allowed to participate. They laughed just as hard as we did, but the loudest yells or shouts would be for those going from Spanish to English and vice versa.

A close family, and one also addicted to card playing. And now, despite our father's death over forty years ago, we, the children, all adults and some of us grandparents, remember him during our conversations and phone calls. He died of a stroke, instantaneously. As our mother described it a day after the funeral, she was removing his shoes and he had started to tell her a joke when the stroke hit him.

Our mother died in 1974, at age eighty-eight, and she too remains a frequent topic of conversation. Because of this, the grandchildren still speak of Gramma Carrie; not all knew or remember their grandfather, but because of our stories about him, he is someone who died only recently. (One of the reasons for this closeness may be due to the life one led in a small town.)

Gramma Carrie was a remarkable woman. On a sidenote, she was also an indifferent cook. I don't mean she couldn't cook (or bake, or baste a ham, etc.), it was that household chores were a matter of complete and studied indifference to her. Her cooking and her baking were first-rate, but she took no pride in them. Tasty stuff? Oh my, yes; but, for her, this was merely something she did. It wasn't her life.

My father, indeed all of us, were not indifferent eaters, and I was and remain finicky. More so now since she died; as indifferent as she was to cooking, she could prepare anything: biscuits, scones, flour gravy, soups, etc. Not her kind of life, though.

She behaved (and I believe I told my oldest sister this) with all the hauteur of a bullfighter. She'd place the food on the table and walk away from it as if she had had nothing to do with it.

She was also a major-league smoker; as most smokers in their sixties and seventies, she'd fall asleep, and one of the five of us was always on the lookout for her.

My father smoked occasionally. His drinking consisted of one beer now and then, and usually with food at home. Because Mercedes was a small town, I, at age ten or so, could buy the beer to bring home.

Although born in Texas, as were his parents, grandparents, and great-grandparents (going back to 1749), he—because he was a Texas Mexican—was issued a pass card to return to the United States whenever he crossed the river into Mexico. Mercedes is but a few miles from the river, and the family did much of the grocery shopping in Mexico, especially during the Depression and World War II.

Among the personal effects I was given at his death was this pass card issued by Immigration and Naturalization.

I thought the card a piece of racist nastiness. For starters, his eyes were listed as black when they were as blue as my mother's, as mine, and as his own mother's. His skin—he was a red-faced man—appeared as medium-dark. He was also listed as short when he stood near six feet, and the hair was wrong, too. What one reads is a stereotype; what one sees in the picture is something else.

Truthfully, and unfortunately, racism has never been far from the core of many Texans.

One last word on my mother. She cared about my university grades (they were high), and she told me so in the spring semester of my last year at the university. I was surprised she even mentioned grades since, as an adult, I received my grades at my university address. One of my sisters probably kept her abreast of this part of my life. It's not important, I don't think, but going to school was my job, and my responsibility, and had nothing to do with her, as she would have put it.

Regarding me, one of her proudest moments came when my brother-in-law, O. B. García, an attorney (a man whose food I ate before, during, and after my college work), told her: "That boy can do anything. If he says he's going to be a writer, a college professor, he'll find a way. No need to worry about him." She quoted O. B. years later, and she said: "That's why I've never worried about you."

With that backing and confidence in one's abilities, I saw no obstacles I couldn't handle. My father too felt that way about me, about all of us, and he must have been a bit of a bore when he talked about us to his friends. We learned of this weakness after his death, and I can only hope that my children know how proud and confident I am of them.

Before this gets too treacly, however, I should say I don't go propping up my children after every

lapse in whatever they attempt. They know I'm in their corner, and we let it go at that.

Before I settled down to write about the place I was born in, my writing was a series of fits and starts. My mind was like an engine that needed a serious overhaul, a tune-up of some sort.

It was clear I wasn't going to die of hunger, not in this country, and not with my education. I'd had all sorts of jobs, but not one that showed me what I wanted to be engaged in for the next thirty to thirty-five years. One of the jobs was interesting: I worked as a shift-work laborer for a chemical plant (baccalaureate degree in hand). It was there I met a class of people I'd not known of: old oil-field hands and plant workers who stuck to their jobs despite plant closings and an unsettled life, having to move every two to three years. I also taught in a high school and found this challenging up to a point. The pay, by the way, was half of what I earned at the chemical plant. I also worked for a work-clothing manufacturing company and served first as office manager and later as sales manager. I was competent but, like my mother and her kitchen chores, that wasn't my life. The last job was as a claims representative for the Bureau of Old Age Survivors Insurance under the Social Security Administration.

In the fall of 1963, I was admitted into the doctoral program at the University of Illinois. I had been so intent on studying, teaching, and reading that I finished the degree with no idea one could teach and write as a professor. My education had been in literary criticism, but my heart wasn't in it. My professors never knew since I worked just as hard as anyone. I did tell one classmate that I wanted to write fiction, not literary criticism. In his opinion, I'd never earn tenure that way. Luckily for me, I had only a vague idea what tenure was, so it wasn't a concern. Come to that, tenure has never been a concern.

It was also my fortune to run across Robert Lopez Flynn at Trinity University in San Antonio. Bob was the writer-in-residence, and his first novel had just been published by Knopf.

Skipping Wednesday morning chapel, mandatory at the time, I introduced myself and told him what it was I wanted to do as a college professor: write. His encouragement was of great help to me and now, some twenty years later, I remind him of that every time he and I read at some college or another.

Here's another story. In 1986 or '87, Bob served as moderator (coincidentally at Trinity University) for a panel consisting of Jim Michener, Ted Fehrenbach (who also comes from a family of old Texans), and me. The theme was on myths, and the three of us were flailing away at Texas and its myths when a member of the audience (and it was a large audience) came running at us waving a placard or a package of some sort. Now, Jim Michener enjoys rude health and was in rude health then, but his physical reactions have slowed down, understandably. Somehow I found myself on my feet and rushed to meet the woman and to put myself between her and Jim. Not five seconds later, members of the audience came and led her away. It was a sad case all around. None of us knew then or later how we had insulted her or our state. We never did find out. Some years later I was being interviewed on the Public Broadcasting Service station in San Antonio, and someone mentioned the incident and the woman. Luckily, this was off camera, and I learned that she had caused similar scenes elsewhere. Anyway, the incident did provide for a lively icebreaker at dinner that evening. With the years, Jim makes my role in the affair bigger and more important than it was.

I seem unable to come to the point in this part of my life that has to do with my writing. Nevertheless, it started this way: a student at Texas A & I University

handed me a story by Tomás Rivera. (He'd been awarded the Quinto Sol Literary Prize the previous year, 1971.) The piece I read was enough for me to decide what I needed to do: to write about the people from home, the Lower Rio Grande Valley of Texas.

I began to write (in Spanish) about the lives lived in Spanish for the most part. Characters and events came spilling out; not quite like dictation, but they did come at me at a rapid clip. A chance meeting took me to San Marcos, Texas, and Daniel Rodríguez, a friend and former colleague, introduced me to Tomás. We didn't attend another meeting and we also skipped the formal luncheon, and later that evening I drove with him to San Antonio. We talked as if we'd known each other for years, and our friendship was to endure until his death in 1984.

He knew literature, and he too had received his degree in literary criticism, but his heart belonged to creative work. Unstinting in his encouragement, he asked me for a sample, and I mailed it to him a few days later.

By the time the piece was published, I was some three-quarters done with *Estampas.* Rudolfo A. Ana-

Rolando Hinojosa, Tony Hillerman, and Gabrielle Cosgriff, Tucson, Arizona, 1985

Hinojosa (center) during the shooting of the PBS television program "Birthwrite," 1989

ya won the 1971 Quinto Sol Prize for his *Bless Me, Ultima,* and I won it the year after that.

I had written on my hometown and the rest of the towns and small cities that stretched along one hundred miles of the Rio Grande from Brownsville to Rio Grande City. But I also had Mexico, the southern bank, on my mind. A shared history, psychology, and blood relationship had kept the people together; for them, the Rio Grande was a jurisdictional barrier, not a cultural one. And, while Tomás had concentrated on the life of the Texas Mexican migrant farm laborer, I placed my attention on life in the Valley; a settled, established community which, for the most part, did not follow the migrant trail the way Texas Mexicans did in Tomás's territory, the Texas Winter Garden area.

It was only after the second novel, *Klail City y sus alrededores,* and its success (the Casa de las Americas Prize) that I decided I was writing a series, the "Klail City Death Trip" (KCDT) series.

For *Estampas* I had drawn a map and populated it with small towns. The county seat, Klail City, was modeled after but not copied from Mercedes; the biggest city, Jonesville, was my relative Américo Paredes's invention for his hometown, Brownsville. The county, Belken, was a composite of the three lower Valley counties: Hidalgo, Cameron, and Willacy.

Since I was writing some of the works in Spanish and others in English, most academics didn't know what to do with me. Too, they didn't agree on whether I was writing a novel or vignettes or short stories or what. I continued to write, content that the material was being published and sure that the mystery of its genre would sort itself out when the scholars reached an agreement among themselves. I think it has, although I think of the KCDT series as *one* novel with many parts or books.

To help me along, I have used prose fragments, feigned newspaper accounts, dialogs, monologs, stories intercalated between chapters of a novel, and I've used the detective genre once, so far. I also have used the epistolary form and reportage. In short, I'll use whatever I can to help me tell my story, as in *Korean Love Songs,* a book of narrative prose in verse form dealing with four young men from the Valley who find themselves in the Korean War. Currently, I'm at work on another part of the series, and once again I'm using still another form to tell my story. My two publishers, Arte Público Press (University of Houston) and Bilingual Review/Press (Arizona State University) are quite generous, and eclectic in their taste, and probably wonder, from time to time, what I'll come up with next. Publishers have different worries from writers; I think they worry about money *and* writers. Writers usually start to worry about their next book about the time the current one is winding down. That's probably the way it should be. It's no secret that small publishers do not pay the money one reads about regarding advances. But smaller houses have other advantages, as I mentioned earlier.

My characters, since the work is a series, recur now and then and some reappear quite often. I find it interesting that I see them at different ages in their many lives with their dreams alive for some, their hopes dashed for others, but all in there, living and dying in that small, restricted area I've carved for them.

As the real Lower Rio Grande Valley changes, so does my Belken County, although usually some twenty to twenty-five years behind the current times. To bring the series up to the present time holds no fascination for me. Some of the characters still recall the Spanish-American War and the Mexican Revolution; some remember World War I and World War II and the younger members may have fought in Korea. Some, and this is a very oral culture, talk of the mid-eighteenth century in vivid terms and likewise of the Mexican War and the American Civil War, a contest which saw some Texas Mexicans fighting for the Union while others supported the Confederacy.

It isn't that war plays an important part in the series, it's that I have found wars to be a handy device through which to track generations, events, changes, and so on. It works for me.

I should like to close this with my parents. My father worked as a farmer, as a gandy dancer, as a shepherd in Wyoming, and fought in the Mexican Revolution and remained involved with it, in one way or another, until 1933. He also gambled for a living, owned a dairy farm, two or three dry-cleaning shops and, when I was growing up, served as a policeman in our small town. A full life, and an active one too. Obviously, such an active man needs a strong wife, and he was lucky to have fallen in love with my mother. (Later on, when I learned the meanings of *bulwark* and *stalwart*, my mother's face came to mind.) She was, and not incidentally, a beautiful, autumn-haired woman who never wore lipstick in the forty years I knew her.

As for me, and I've revealed more about me and mine than I thought possible, I must have been destined to be a writer. With the family and the times I was born into, I couldn't help it.

BIBLIOGRAPHY

Fiction; all under name Rolando Hinojosa, except as noted:

Estampas del valle y otras obras (first novel in "Klail City Death Trip" series), Quinto Sol, 1973, bilingual edition with translation by Gustavo Valadez and José Reyna published as *Sketches of the Valley and Other Works*, Justa Publications, 1980, revised English language edition published as *The Valley*, Bilingual Press, 1983.

Klail City y sus alrededores (second novel in the "Klail City Death Trip" series), bilingual edition with translation by Rosaura Sánchez, Casa de las Américas, 1976, published under name Rolando R. Hinojosa-S. as *Generaciones y semblanzas* (title means "Biographies and Lineages"), Justa Publications, 1977, translation by Hinojosa published as *Klail City*, Arte Público Press, 1987.

Korean Love Songs from Klail City Death Trip (novel in verse form; third in "Klail City Death Trip" series), illustrations by René Castro, Justa Publications, 1978.

Claros varones de Belken (fourth novel in "Klail City Death Trip" series) Justa Publications, 1981, bilingual edition with translation by Julia Cruz published as *Fair Gentlemen of Belken County*, Bilingual Press, 1987.

Mi querido Rafa (fifth novel in "Klail City Death Trip" series), Arte Público Press, 1981, translation by Hinojosa published as *Dear Rafe*, 1985.

Partners in Crime, Arte Público Press, 1985.

Rites and Witnesses (sixth novel in "Klail City Death Trip" series), Arte Público Press, 1989.

Becky and Her Friends, Arte Público Press, 1990, translation published as *Los amigos de Becky*, 1991.

Other:

Generaciones, notas, y brechas/Generations, Notes, and Trails, (nonfiction; bilingual edition), translation by Fausto Avendaño, Casa, 1978.

(Author of introduction) Carmen Tafolla, *Curandera*, M & A Editions, 1983.

(Contributor under name Rolando Hinojosa-Smith) Alan Pogue, *Agricultural Workers of the Rio Grande and Rio Bravo Valleys*, Center for Mexican American Studies, University of Texas at Austin, 1984.

(Translator from the Spanish) Tomás Rivera, *This Migrant Earth,* Arte Público Press, 1986.

(Contributor) José David Saldívar, editor, *The Rolando Hinojosa Reader: Essays Historical and Critical,* Arte Público Press, 1985.

(Editor, with Gary D. Keller and Vernon E. Lattin) *Tomás Rivera, 1935–1984: The Man and His Work,* Bilingual Press, 1988.

Also author, under pseudonym P. Galindo, of "Mexican American Devil's Dictionary." Work represented in anthologies, including *Festival de flor y canto: An Anthology of Chicano Literature,* edited by F. A. Cervantes, Juan Gomez-Quiñones, and others, University of Southern California Press, 1976. Contributor of short stories, articles, and reviews to periodicals, including *Texas Monthly, Texas Humanist, Los Angeles Times,* and *Dallas Morning News.*

James D. Houston

1933-

WORDS AND MUSIC

All music is what awakes from you
when you are reminded by the instruments.

—Walt Whitman's "Song for Occupations"

My Father's Passion

I was up in Round Valley not long ago, north of San Francisco, visiting some friends. It's a bowl of mountains surrounding what used to be a lake bed. In midsummer the sky turns light around five, and I was out walking very early, along the gravelled road that cuts through their acreage. On a nearby hillside sprinkled with oak and madrone, I saw some movement. A buck bounded into the open, evidently stirred by my approach. When I stopped, the buck stood his ground watching me, his head turned, waiting, a two-point buck in elegant profile against the tawny summer grass.

For five minutes, at least, we watched each other, while my mind wheeled back forty years and more to the days when I had come into this valley, and into others like it, with my father, in search of animals just like that one. I was thinking how such a sight, for my father, in those days, would have filled him with the huntsman's excitement and erotic rush. To see such a creature poised, with the chest exposed, the buff coat glowing, almost shining, as if polished, this was completion, this was fulfillment, this was what gave meaning to life. He would have raised his rifle, and he would have aimed just behind the shoulder, hoping to penetrate the heart and see the buck drop where it stood.

He had grown up in east Texas, the son of a cotton sharecropper and itinerant blacksmith. During the 1930s he moved to California among the many thousands on the road in search of better luck, better weather, better jobs. By the time I am describing here, the years right after World War Two, we were living in San Francisco, where I'd been born. He had found work painting houses, and now he was an independent contractor with a couple of pickup trucks and usually a crew of three or four men to

James D. Houston

manage. These trips into the northern counties were his way of getting some relief from the paint and the thinner and the dropcloths and the ladders and the city.

We would head across the Golden Gate Bridge, through Marin County, which was still mostly dairy country then, on toward Petaluma, which called itself "The Egg Basket of the World." ("I'd just as soon not have to drive across a basket full of eggs," he would say. "Once them shells start breakin', you're gonna have nothin' but a mess, the way that egg yolk will get up around your axles and your tie rods.") Beyond Willits we'd bear right, heading inland, and follow the Eel River over twenty miles or so of dirt

"My paternal grandparents, John James and Ruth Hooper Houston, in east Texas after he had retired from blacksmithing and farming," 1935

road and find our spot and park and set up camp with the other men who had come along, other contractors, or journeymen painters my dad had hired, sometimes my uncle Jay, who was also from Texas and managed a Union Oil station—working men taking a few days off to roam the back country.

There would be steaks and potatoes and beer and whiskey, but not too much whiskey, not the first night, at any rate. We would sleep in sleeping bags, in a tent if the weather turned bad, and be up at dawn for more food, sausage and eggs and bitter coffee and toast half burned over the grate. Then we would load the rifles and move out in pairs, in search of fresh tracks and droppings.

"You head over that way, Jimbo, along that draw, up toward them trees. See the ones I'm talkin' about? I'll head over yonder, across that clearing, and maybe we'll scare something up. They've been through here already, but they're not far off. I believe we're gonna get us one or two before the day is out. I just feel like this is gonna be our day. The

thing is, don't get jumpy. And don't yell or do anything sudden. Just take your time . . ."

We would split up, stepping quietly, watching out for sticks and anything else that might snap or crackle, using hand signals. I'd walk and squat a while, sweat and wait, and look to see where Dad was. I can see him still, across the draw, his jeans belted high, his red billcap, his twill shirt patched with sweat, hunched like a soldier on patrol. He loved it out there. It was his passion.

Do I mean the killing was his passion? Or do I mean all the rest of the things you did to reach the moment when you pulled the trigger—the driving and the joking and the beers and the open-fire cooking with the shadows sliding toward you down the darkly burnished slopes, and the knowledge that these hills and groves went on for miles and the land you had entered was as thick with wildness and roaming creatures as the late-night sky was thick with stars?

In his case I think he needed them both, the wildness and the rifle that would give him some piece of it to bring back home, antlers, the side of venison, a glossy hide. In my case, it was something like Christianity, which has been my mother's passion. I had never liked the Sunday morning meetings much, the sermons that went on forever, and clothes I didn't want to wear. And yet I inherited the words to three or four hundred gospel songs and learned to love the language of the King James Version of the Bible, and after many years of downgrading Jesus and the irrational notion that anyone could be resurrected from the dead, I rediscovered the wisdom of his teaching and came to appreciate the many ways there are to die and somehow return to life.

I guess I was ten when Dad gave me my first rifle, a .22. It was the first year he took me hunting, which was also the first time I watched an animal die at close range. Not a major animal, just a gray squirrel I took a shot at because I wanted to please him. It fell from a pine limb into the blanket of needles beneath the tree and twitched a few times. Watching the blood trickle, I knew I was supposed to feel strong and proud. This was what I had been practicing for. This was why he had bought me the rifle. As Dad hunkered to inspect the hole, I felt no pride. I felt shame and loneliness. He said it was not a bad shot at all and said we should keep the tail, which we did. It hung on the wall of my room for years—for him the emblem of someone he hoped I would become, for me the emblem of something I'd hoped I'd never have to do again.

Travelling with him through the mountains of northern California, I never took to the killing. I am not sure why. Maybe it was growing up a city kid. Maybe if we had truly needed the meat it would have been a different story.

Forty years later, as I stood transfixed in the cool morning air of Round Valley, it occurred to me that this deer I'd been watching was surely a descendant or distant relative of one my father had shot, or shot at. Silently I asked the buck for forgiveness. In the same moment I gave thanks that my father had brought me out to places like this at the time in life when whatever is presented to you leaves its mark, its indelible and ineradicable imprint. Killing for sport had not appealed to me at all. But thanks to him I discovered the many wonders of the long Coast Range, the tawny humps above the oak-scattered valleys, the wildness of the back country, the boot crunch of soil under still madrones, and the rusty curl of madrone bark under the arid, pale blue sky.

In search of game we travelled north and south of San Francisco, as I have continued to do throughout my life, exploring this region I now look upon as my natural habitat. And by that I do not mean California. Not all of it, from border to border, from Berkeley to Tahoe. As a subject, or as a vast network of interlocking subjects, California can give you a lifetime of things to think about, and write about, and wrestle with and brood about. But as somewhere to regard as your habitat, it's just too big. There's too much to grasp. I tried to grasp it once, tried to claim it all, you might say, in a book called *Californians: Searching for the Golden State.* One thing I learned from that experience is that our nervous systems are not designed to identify with something as large and diverse and contradictory as the state of California. Along the eastern seaboard it would encompass everything from Boston to Cape Hatteras. It would include the Adirondacks and parts of Appalachia. The Coast Range itself is various enough; but in this long wrinkle bordering the continent's western edge, there is a continuity of terrain that has helped me stay located, both physically and spiritually. It is a subregion of the far west, stretching from Eureka in the north to Point Conception in the south, including the ridges and ranges between the Pacific shoreline and the western foothills of the Central Valley. The mountain chains are called Yolla Bolly, Diablo, Santa Cruz, Gavilan, Santa Lucia. Between the ranges there are long, fertile valleys called Anderson and Napa and Sonoma and Santa Clara and Salinas. There are mineral-rich mudbaths at Calistoga, and the wilderness Zen center at Tassajara Hot Springs down inside a gorge behind the drop-off cliffs at Big Sur, and the old mission towns of San Juan Bautista and San Miguel. A couple of missions still stand out there by themselves, among the foothills and the oaks—San Antonio de Padua, La Purisima—restored adobe relics from the days when this stretch of California was the farthest outpost of the Spanish empire.

And there are the cities built on hills and slopes and sprawling across the one-time fields and dunes—San Francisco, my birthplace; San Jose, where I finished high school and went to college and met my wife; the city/state called Stanford, where I went to graduate school and later spent a year as a Stegner Writing Fellow; and Santa Cruz, where we have raised our three children, where we've been living for almost thirty years now, where I have, for better or for worse, done most of the writing on all my books.

I have lived in other places and travelled around quite a bit—in Europe, in Asia, in Mexico, and among the Pacific Islands. But I have always come back to this region I consider my habitat. I call it my place, this long string of places. Again I thank my father, and my mother too, for the choices they made that brought us here and kept us here. Given the

"My maternal grandmother, Alta Nora Belle Gulley Wilson, at age twenty-one," Huntsville, Alabama, 1909

general restlessness and slippery temporariness that characterizes so much of life along the western shore, I consider myself lucky to have anywhere at all to feel connected to.

These places, in turn, have connected me to certain travellers and storytellers and poets who have touched me in a very visceral way. I think first of the chanters and legend-makers from the coastal tribe whose creation story begins like this:

Water covered all, they say.
Only peaks remained, they say.
Here eagle and hummingbird and coyote took
    refuge,
    they say.

I think of Fray Juan Crespi whose *Diaries* describe the trailblazing overland expedition north to San Francisco Bay, led by Captain Portolá in 1769, and Robert Louis Stevenson, who passed through here in the 1880s, wrote for the papers in Monterey, later travelled through what is now known as "the wine country" and left us *The Silverado Squatters.* There is Jaime de Angulo, and Robinson Jeffers, and William Everson, and Lew Welch, and most immediately John Steinbeck. In their works I have felt a compelling territorial kinship.

Nowadays I can walk down to the sandstone bluffs a block from where we live, and I can look across the waters of Monterey Bay and see the outlines of the region they call "Steinbeck Country." Did I have such a view in mind when we chose to live here thirty years ago? Not at all. Not consciously. But as it happens, he *was* the first novelist who caught me and really held me. And as it happens, on almost any day of the year I can see the low place in the shoreline, the broad delta where the Salinas River spreads out and meets the bay. I can see the mountain ranges he describes in the early pages of *East of Eden,* representing for him the polarities of light and shadow, the sunny Gavilans to the east of his home valley, and to the west the Santa Lucias, shaded in the afternoon, less knowable, more foreboding.

I was seventeen, just starting college, when I came upon *Tortilla Flat,* then *Cannery Row,* then *Of Mice and Men.* By that time we had moved south from San Francisco into Santa Clara Valley, which could still claim to be the world's largest orchard—six million fruit trees, their springtime blossoms adding to the lower end of San Francisco Bay an inland sea of pink and white. As I read his books it did not occur to me that the Salinas Valley, another hour south by car, was also framed by parallel ranges and opened onto a bay. It did not occur to me that the hills and

mountains hovering around his stories were parts of this continuous terrain I had inhabited all my life. At no point did I think or say aloud, "I *know* this place. I *know* these people." Yet that was how his stories affected me—at that level of implicit recognition. As I read *The Long Valley* and *The Pastures of Heaven* and *In Dubious Battle,* these were the valleys where I had already spent summers picking apples and apricots and peaches. These working stiffs were the men who had worked with my dad before and after World War Two.

Am I saying Steinbeck has been an influence on my work and on my way of seeing? I have never been comfortable with that use of the word *influence.* The most you can say is that you have your favorites. There are writers you admire, for the skill or for the art or for the level of inventiveness or for the professionalism of a career well spent. And there are writers—sometimes the same ones, sometimes not—to whom you are powerfully attracted, for reasons that may or may not have something to do with literature and literary values. They speak to you, or speak for you, sometimes with a voice that could almost be your own. Often there is one writer in particular who awakens you, who is like the teacher they say you will meet when you are ready for the lesson. In my case it was John Steinbeck. He spoke to me from a landscape and a history that I knew before I knew *about* it.

Land of Two Promises

In an interview someone once asked a well-known novelist why he had chosen this particular career. "It allows me to use the word *work,*" he said, "to describe my greatest pleasure in life."

"You mean writing," the interviewer said.

"No, I mean brooding, and pacing back and forth, and staring out the window."

Sometime early in 1964, soon after I had finished Stanford and we had moved from the peninsula over the hill to the coast, I was doing just that— brooding, and pacing back and forth, trying to finish a short story I had started during my air force time in England, some four or five years earlier. As I paused to stare out the window, I noticed a candy store that stood on a corner about a block away, on the far side of a large open lot, empty except for a few neglected fruit trees. We had been living in that house for a couple of years, and I had been visiting the town of Santa Cruz off and on since high school, so I had seen this candy store a hundred times, perhaps a thousand times. Yet I had not seen it. I had never looked at it—

a fixture in my daily life, so familiar it had gone entirely unnoticed. As I studied the details—the whitewashed walls, the corny Dutch windmill—something began to buzz, the tingling across my scalp that I now refer to as the literary buzz, a little signal from the top of my head that there is some mystery here, or some unrevealed linkage that will have to be explored with words.

I sat down at my typing machine and began to describe the candy store. By the time I finished, fifteen pages later, I had described the stream of cars along the coastline road that runs through the neighborhood, I had described the town, and where I thought it fit into the larger patterns of northern California, and I had begun to examine, as well, why I had chosen the town and this stretch of coast and the elderly, windblown house we still occupy.

The result was an essay both regional and personal. In terms of my perception of myself as a writer and what I could write about, it was a small but crucial turning point. It was my first attempt to write, not only *about* this part of the world, but to write *from* this part of the world. (My original title, which did

"*My father, Albert D. Houston, with the U.S. Navy in Honolulu,*" 1925

not last very long, was "From Here.") This was also the first piece I sold to a national magazine—it came out in the now-defunct *Holiday,* in May 1967—and the first piece that earned anything like a significant amount of money, six hundred dollars, which was a decent fee for an essay, back in the mid–1960s, and a bonanza for us, in the days when four hundred was our monthly budget.

Several years later I saw something else for the first time. Like the candy store, this too had been waiting outside the window. I had of course heard the legends of the San Andreas fault. I had drunk from the reservoirs of water stored in long depressions created by the movements of the continental plates. I had crossed the rift zone countless times in my travels up and down the coast. So in one sense I had been seeing it all my life. Yet I had not seen it, not until I read an article in *Scientific American* about a recently verified theory called "Continental Drift." This astounding vision of global geology was just then going public. In the air for decades as a theory, it had not been universally accepted by geology professionals until the late 1960s—which had given rise to a spate of articles such as the one I'd come across. I was electrified. Here was one of the most influential natural features of the western American landscape. I had lived within four or five miles of it since birth, yet it had been virtually invisible to me, a legend, a folktale, an elaborate rumor.

I had to know more. I called my friend Gary Griggs, Professor of Earth Sciences at the University of California at Santa Cruz. He had studied these things. For one of the courses he was teaching back then he had already designed a fault-line field trip. A week later we were climbing into his pickup truck, with a six-pack of beer and some country western music on the radio, heading south from Santa Cruz toward Watsonville, then following the Pajaro River east along Highway 124.

The river has carved a trough through that fold of the Coast Range, a trough called Chittendon Pass. It's a place where the river crosses the San Andreas, which in turn marks the zone where two pieces of the earth's crust meet and grind together, the Pacific Plate and the North American Plate. Thanks to deep cuts by road crews in the 1930s, we could stand there and see these two massive slabs spread before us like an open-faced sandwich—on one side, a chunky wall of granite, overgrown with brush and eucalyptus; on the other, a brighter wall of buff-colored shale, stratified at a steep angle pointed up and west, as if the granite sides were nosing in under the shale. Above this layering there was a dip in the ridge, the

159

kind of low spot that makes the trace line visible from high altitude.

We followed the fault line for fifty more miles, past sag ponds, and little avalanches, and displaced creek beds. In Hollister, Gary turned onto a side street lined with Victorian cottages and farm-town houses. Down the center of this street we could observe the tar line, which was offset about eight inches. Hollister sits right in the rift zone, as does the La Cienega branch of the Almaden Winery, a few miles farther south. The winery was being gradually torn in two. For students of ground flow it is a historic site. It is where the fault line's pattern of steady creep was first identified, back in 1958.

By the end of this day I felt as if I'd flown a light plane from Mendocino to Tehachipi. I was imagining the long crease, a diagonal seam through the north/south flow of ridges. I saw how all the places I had known and cared about were in some crazy, fearful, and fascinating way stitched together along this seam. And I had begun to see how the forces that came pushing up against the continent to make the lovely and inspirational mountain ranges and to shape the valleys between the ranges—these same forces also accounted for the rift zone that had triggered so much damage in 1906 and in 1928 and 1968, and could jump and jolt again at any moment. The sources of creation and the sources of destruction, or rather, the ongoing threat of massive upheaval, were one and the same, and this realm so often called the Land of Promises was really a Land of Two Promises that had been coexisting in the earth for a long long time.

I had recently completed my third novel, *A Native Son of the Golden West.* That day I felt again the buzzing across my scalp. Not long afterward I began to enter the lives and histories of the fictitious Doyle family, whose inherited acreage happens to border the notorious fault line. I had embarked upon a long exploration of the yin and the yang of coastal geology, which you might say continues to this day, since the Coast Range has its place on the so-called Ring of Fire that encircles the Pacific. This Ring, sometimes called a Rim, is seismic and economic and political and multicultural and mythological, and sacred too, with sacred craters here and there around the huge circumference and shrines of every type.

The day I made that trip with Gary Griggs, I began to feel a tension pulling. I could not then have put it into words. Indeed, if I had been able to, I doubt that I would have plunged into the making of a story that became the novel *Continental Drift.* But looking back, I believe it might be described as a tension between the fertile and abundant and essen-

"A wedding portrait of my father and mother, Albert Dudley and Alice Loretta Wilson Houston," San Francisco, 1932

tially pastoral landscape of my youth, and the continuous presence of an unpredictable subterranean power. It was of course tempting to regard this in the Biblical way, as some version of the tension between good and evil. Many were already doing so. In those days it was fashionable to predict that the San Andreas Fault would sooner or later crack wide open and everything west of it would drop into the ocean. Such an event would not simply be a geological misfortune, it would somehow be fit punishment for accumulated sins. But sin and retribution did not interest me nearly so much as what this famous fault line can tell us about the great wheel of earthly cycles and the coexistence of opposites.

My Mother's Voice

I started with places. I could just as easily have started with words. Perhaps I should have. If you are a writer, these are the primary tools. But why? Why do you choose one set of tools rather than another? I have played a lot of music in my life, acoustic guitar and upright bass, a little piano. I've made some money at it too. Why didn't I choose music as my principal line of work? Why not sound? Why not stone? Why not a hammer and a chisel and a saw? Why not paint, and the brushes and the ladders and the drop cloths, like my dad?

I have mulled this over for quite a while, and I trace it back to the church I grew up in. I won't say which church, except to note that it was Christian and fundamentalist, so that all our religious activities and all our efforts to communicate with God consisted primarily of words.

"Fundamentalist" means you look to the letter of the New Testament for guidance, and nowhere else. We were so fundamental that almost everything had been stripped away from the worship service. In such a world, think of the role that words can play. Think of their power, when all other enticements and sensual attractions are gone. In the meeting halls of my youth there was no incense to entertain the nostrils, no stained glass or statuary to beguile the

"Family portrait of my father and mother, my sister Gloria, age nine, and me at twelve," San Francisco, 1946

eye. There were no robes or hats or sceptres, no gleaming pendants or rich brocade to appeal to your sense of theatre, no bells or chimes or gongs, not even a piano or an organ to help the spirit soar. According to the logic of our elders, the New Testament made no mention of stained glass or carved statues or upright pianos, and if it was not right there in front of you in God's own words, you'd better not presume to be dressing up the worship service just because it seemed like a good idea.

God's word was the measure, and if you hold to the letter of the New Testament, you do not have much left *but* words to express the longings of the human spirit:

Words in the form of scripture readings from the pulpit.

Words in the form of prayer, both public and private.

Words in the form of sermons and exhortations and invitations to come forward and be baptized in the name of The Father and The Son and The Holy Ghost. The fact that all our preachers and deacons and elders had come from somewhere in the South or Southwest seemed to give the words more weight or more zeal in the delivery. They all had ties to Texas or Oklahoma or Arkansas or Alabama or Tennessee. The voices carried a mix of drawl and old-fashioned oratory that seemed to sharpen the effect of the King James Version, when it was quoted or read out loud. They savored the archaic terms, as if it were a private language that somehow belonged to them, to us. Words you never heard anyone else use, they would utter with special relish, words like "viper" and "begat" and "smite thine enemies," and "raiment" that could be "girded about the loins."

Songs unaccompanied by musical instruments would have to rely totally on the voices delivering words of praise to the Lord.

Even at meal times the words came first. Give thanks to God with your voice, *then* eat.

And sometime after dinner, in my earlier years, one of the women's voices would begin to read from the New Testament, or from the Old. Sometimes it would be my mother's mother, Alta Nora Belle Gulley Wilson, born in the Cumberland Mountain region of Tennessee in 1888, a good-hearted country woman if ever there was one, a seamstress by trade, who had followed her daughter out to the coast. After three years of elementary school she'd had no further education. She was working in a textile mill in Huntsville, Alabama, when she met the man who would become my grandfather, an itinerant millhand, good-looking and footloose. They had two children, and then he disappeared, went back to Georgia where he'd come from, some people said, though his movements have remained elusive to this day. Grandma never talked about him much. As far as I know, he was the only man in her life. In later years she preferred to call herself "a widow." Her spare time was devoted to church work. She studied the Bible every day. It was her solace and her reference and her inspiration, and all of this was carried in her voice, carried across the continent from where she started life, Van Buren County, in the mountains of eastern Tennessee, and into our front room there in the Sunset District of San Francisco, as we listened to her read aloud the stories of David and Goliath, Jacob and Esau, Joseph and the Pharoah, Paul and Silas, the parable of the Prodigal Son.

Sometimes it would be my mother doing the reading. She was born in Huntsville, raised in Texas. She'd had two years of college when she met my dad, doing field work one summer outside the little panhandle town of Quanah. They ran away together to California. He was the hunter in our family. She was the reader—of books, stories and poems, and all forms of scripture. She always did the best she knew how, passing on to me and my sister whatever she had learned from her mother to share with her kids, and how can you not listen to your mother's voice, when she is reading to you from Genesis, reading from the Psalms, reading how flames appeared upon the heads of the Apostles on the first day of Pentecost after Jesus ascended, and how they spoke in tongues, with miraculous command of new and unknown languages.

Eight or ten years of this, when you are young and impressionable, can have a powerful and lasting effect. It all sinks in. The words sink in, the very sound of the words and, at some level or another, the potent message they carry. In the Gospel According to Saint John, there is one sentence that spells it out:

*In the beginning was the Word, and the Word
was with God, and the Word was God.*

Quote a verse like that and you run the risk of sounding self-congratulatory, as if you have hit upon some true path to salvation via the sacred calling of prose or poetry. I wouldn't want to go that far. And I certainly don't want to sound religious here. I don't think of myself as a religious person. I associate religion with institutions and organizations. This is much more personal. The point I want to stress is that, long after I left home, at age eighteen, and left the family church behind, the role of words and the appeal of words stayed with me, the idea that words themselves can somehow provide an access to the

higher power, whatever name you choose to give it. I had started out writing newspaper stories in high school and, eventually, short stories. That seemed to be the motive for quite some time—getting the story told, and hoping to see the words in print, and, later on, hoping to get some money for the effort. But writing has turned out to be a good deal more than that. I have come to rely upon it as a line of work with a spiritual dimension. In Zen terms you might call it a form of practice. Just about any type of creative work can be described this way, work that allows you to travel both outward and inward.

Where Strangers Meet

Now I see that I must start a third time or, rather, go back again to San Francisco and start at a different place, since it all begins there—the journeys with my father, the Biblical journeys with my mother and grandmother, and eventually the ways the city prepared me to travel through the world I live in now.

When they packed up their suitcases and left west Texas behind, my mom and dad were immigrants from farming and ranching country where the land was wearing thin. The community they joined had a lot in common with the one they'd left, composed mostly of transplanted southerners and southwesterners, Anglo and Protestant, who had all come west in the 1930s, or soon after the outbreak of World War Two when the Bay Area's shipyards started working double and triple shifts seven days a week. They all clung together, as immigrants usually do. Not until I entered high school did I begin to see beyond this community and to grasp the range of histories that had shaped the city of my birth. These histories were shaping me too, but in ways I would not understand until many more years had passed.

Lowell was the city's high school for the college bound. It was located about midway between Ocean Beach to the west and the Embarcadero to the east, the long row of shipping docks that poked out into the bay. A four-story redbrick building, vintage 1912, Lowell drew students from all parts of town. It cut across district lines, which meant it also cut across culture lines and ghetto lines. Suddenly I found myself sitting in classrooms with Japanese kids and Hispanic kids and Jewish kids and Italian kids. I recently glanced through the yearbook from 1949, the year I left Lowell. I see the photo of a kid who had just transferred in from Teheran.

For the first time I was watching and admiring athletes who were Asian American. One of the

"With my wife, Jeanne, on Maui, before hiking down into Haleakala Crater, where we spent one night of our honeymoon," April 1957

lightweight basketball teams had a very good season, according to the yearbook—13 wins and 4 losses, "paced by forwards John Chin and Yukio Isoye." They were graceful and quick, and during the warmup games, before the varsity took the floor at Kezar Pavilion, they were counted among the heroes.

I remember a husky fellow named Allen Gan, president of the scholarship society, who also threw discus on the championship track and field team. I remember Rudy Suarez, soft-spoken and swarthy, a loping right end, as well as a varsity basketball sharpshooter. If he had not graduated at midyear he would have made All-City. I remember that the student body president in 1949 was a track star named Jim Plessas, listed in the yearbook's "Hall of Fame" as the All-American Greek. He broke two city records that year, in the low hurdles and the broad jump, ran the relay anchor lap, and was generally regarded as the man who led the track team to its fourth straight city title.

I don't mean to suggest that Lowell High in the late '40s was a model of cross-cultural harmony. It was a midcity American high school with in-crowds and out-crowds, nerds and primadonnas and rivalries and status symbols and graffiti in the locker rooms and fights in the park two blocks away. But looking back, I see that it had a profound effect on the way I would come to perceive the world. Though I usually entered the old brick building full of teenage fears

and doubts, I nonetheless took it for granted that a high school could have a Japanese forward, a Chinese discus thrower, a Jewish halfback, an Italian quarterback, a Greek student body president. For a couple of formative years I had the chance to walk the hallways of a little city-within-the-city where people with all these histories had found a way, at least part of the time, to get along.

I had to leave California to find out how rare Lowell was for that day and age. I was midway through my junior year when my family moved south to Santa Clara Valley, where I finished high school. From there I was sent to Texas for a short-lived football career at a small Christian college. This was a family idea. My mom and dad wanted me to get to know the old country, to see the skies and listen to the winds of their younger days. And we had a cousin who had the ear of a coach, who wangled me a scholarship.

I have a yearbook from that campus too. It is fascinating to scan the faces. This happened to be a school where almost everyone came from Texas or Oklahoma. They were all white, all Protestant. In short, they all looked much like me and my relatives, a yearbook full of almost-kinfolk. Texas was my almost-homeland, and this was my natural tribe. Yet something was missing. I would not have been able to say quite what. Not back then. I was a freshman, running on hormones. But now, looking back, I see that the monocultural climate already seemed as odd to me as the arctic.

I made some friends there, met up with uncles and half-cousins I might otherwise never have known. But a year later I was back on the coast. I had transferred to San Jose State, where I soon met the woman I would eventually marry. Her background was Japanese. Her father had grown up near Hiroshima. Her mother's parents were immigrants from Niigata, in northern Japan. Jeanne herself was born in southern California, and her parents had moved north from Long Beach a few years after the World War Two internment.

We arrived at that campus on the same day, with the same major, journalism, and the same minor, Spanish. It was a much smaller place than it is today, about one fifth the size. In 1952 there were six thousand students, and we were the only two with this particular major/minor combination. During the first quarter we had five classes together. Everywhere I went I saw this radiant young woman of Asian descent. You can call it coincidence. You can call it luck. Or you can call it destiny. In any event, once we started going together, we did not see ourselves in sociological terms. She was Jeanne and I was Jim, and we could not stay away from each other. It was much later, when someone would say, "What was it like to be dating an Asian American?" or "There couldn't have been many interracial couples back then . . . ," only later did I begin to think about the sequence.

If I had been born in Texas, or if I had stayed there, chances are much slimmer that I would have stepped across such a border. But in the mid-1950s Santa Clara Valley, like San Francisco, was already a multicultural region, and I had already come to think of the world as a place where cultures could intermingle.

To cross this border, of course, was to enter a realm I knew almost nothing about. I was very

"Videotaping the 'Today Show' after the 'Farewell to Manzanar' teleplay won a Humanitas Prize, July 1976. Seated: Director/Producer John Korty, who helped write the script; Jim; Jeanne; Larry Gelbart and Jay Presson Allen, who also won script prizes; NBC's Bob Abernathy. Standing: Charles Williams of the Lilly Foundation, Ray Bradbury, and Father Ellwood P. Keiser."

innocent back then. My view of cultural intermingling was very narrow. This view began to change on the day I met Jeanne's father, a man I only saw once. We were never introduced. Jeanne was afraid for me to meet him, knowing how deeply he would disapprove. She too had taken a border-crossing step, the first in her family to do so. There were ten brothers and sisters. She was the youngest, and she was the renegade.

Soon after we started dating, I drove out to her family's house, south of San Jose. It was a Saturday afternoon. She had said she'd meet me in town, but for some reason I insisted on picking her up. Maybe I saw this as the chivalrous thing to do. Or maybe I knew this was the only way I'd ever have a chance to look him in the eye.

Her father was working strawberries then. The house was off to the side of his field, among some outbuildings. As I pulled into the yard, he appeared on the porch, in jeans, an old felt hat. I was driving a 1938 Chevy sedan. He looked first at the car, with grave doubt, then at me. He had a thin black moustache and a weathered, aristocratic face. When I told him why I was there, he shook his head and seemed to cough. He stepped down off the porch, stood with his feet planted and his hands on his hips, holding me with his gaze in a way that forced me to look at him.

In that brief exchange, at the edge of his acres of immaculately tended strawberry furrows, I saw a man, or felt the spirit of a kind of man previously unknown to me, a man from Asia, a man from Japan. I would later learn that he had lost most of his relatives in the bombing of Hiroshima. Thirty years before I was born he had immigrated to the United States, to work, to live, to make a fresh start. He and my father had at least that much in common. His home region was in a deep depression when he left Japan, at age seventeen, heading east on a steamship bound for the Land of Promise. He had worked as a lumberjack, a cook, a farmer, and eventually as a fisherman based at San Pedro. After the attack on Pearl Harbor he was arrested by the FBI, falsely charged with delivering fuel to enemy submarines off the coast of California. He lost his boat and he lost a career sitting out the war in an internment camp called Manzanar, not far from Death Valley. He had been so scarred by that experience, he stopped speaking to Caucasians. It was a point of honor. Now, into his yard had come a suntanned Anglo fledgling with scales on his eyes and lust in his heart, driving a neglected '38 Chevy and looking for his daughter, the youngest, the first to go away to college.

All this was in his face. Though I could not have known it, I must have felt it. I felt something coming from him, and it was not hatred or bitterness. What he projected was the hard-won toughness of a man who had survived everything America and Japan had thrown at him, who had preserved his dignity and found a way to continue.

That was 1953. It was almost twenty years later when Jeanne and I began taping her recollections and the vivid childhood memories that would become the book and then the television drama *Farewell to Manzanar*, the story of her family's experience during and after the World War Two internment of Japanese Americans. Three decades after they had all been loaded onto busses in downtown Los Angeles and ferried north to the Owens Valley in the high desert east of Mount Whitney, she finally reached a point where she wanted to talk about what had happened there. She needed to talk about the events—the evacuation, the details of life inside the camp, as she remembered them from age seven and eight and nine. More importantly, she was ready to give voice to her deepest level of feeling and emotional knowledge. For each of us, for our different reasons, writing that book and getting that story told was a way of paying tribute to her father and her mother, to their lives and the remarkable spirit that carried them through those years.

After that meeting next to his strawberry field, I never saw him again. The year before we were married he passed away. But as I came to know the clan he had left behind, Jeanne's nine brothers and sisters and their families, and as I learned to be the new uncle to thirty-six nieces and nephews, and heard the many family stories, I continued to think about that afternoon and this man who is the grandfather of our three children. For me it was a moment of awakening, the beginning of an education that continues to this day. A window had been opened, for the first small glimpse of another world, another way of being in America, another way of seeing the white world I had, until then, pretty much taken for granted.

My Mother's Voice, My Father's Passion

My mother was the reader. She was also the singer. She had a bell-like alto voice, and she could carry a tune because she had grown up among people who entertained one another with singing. She sang in church—always sitting down close to the front, so she could make eye-contact and harmony-contact with the songleader—and she sang around

"Our children Joshua and Gabrielle are twins, seen here at seventeen"

the house. This was before we had TV sets going day and night. Maybe she sang to fill the spaces we now fill up with talk shows and daytime serials. She sang gospel tunes—"Rock of Ages" and "When the Roll Is Called Up Yonder." She sang western swing tunes like the ones being made famous by Bob Wills and His Texas Playboys. She sang old favorites such as "You Are My Sunshine" and "Oh! Susanna" and "Camptown Races." These and much older tunes she had learned from my grandmother who, in her day, had been a singer too and who still knew some of the ballads she had grown up with as a girl in the Cumberlands.

My mother provided the lyrics, you might say, while the accompaniment was provided by my dad. He was not a singer. But he was a devoted picker, practicing every time he had an hour or so to spare. His main instrument was the steel guitar, which he had learned to play while he was in the navy during the 1920s. He joined right out of high school, looking for a way to see somewhere else in the world besides east Texas. The next thing he knew he was in the Hawaiian Islands, stationed at Pearl Harbor with a submarine crew, where he spent three years.

I know very little about what happened to him there. He never talked about it much, partly because he never talked about anything much. But something had made those years important for him, given them a shine. My guess is they were magic years. The islands have quite a bit of magic, even now, in spite of the crowds and the prices and the traffic. Hawaii is still the northern point of the Polynesian triangle. From a cobalt sea the emerald mountains still rise to cut their jagged edge against a technicolor sky. Imagine what it was like seventy years ago, before statehood, before tourism, before the mega-hotels went up, before the planes had started crisscrossing the Pacific. He was eighteen, nineteen, twenty. The steel guitar was a new instrument then, invented by Hawaiians, and introduced to the world not too long before he got there. He fell in love with the picks and the strings and the sliding steel bar and the sweet music they could make.

In one of my earliest memories, my father is down on his knees in front of the radio. We had one of those oldtime radios made of dark carved wood, with a curving top and cloth over the speaker, a piece

166

of furniture large enough to dominate the room. Set against a wall by itself, it had a strangely compelling presence. When three or four of us were gathered in front of it gazing at the speaker and listening to one of the evening programs—"One Man's Family" or "Suspense"—you might think it was an altar to the Deities of Sound.

Kneeling there alone on a weekend afternoon, he would hold his ear up close to the cloth and fool with the dials, trying to bring in a show known as "Hawaii Calls" that used to be broadcast live from the lanai of the Moana Hotel. This was when the Moana and the Royal Hawaiian were the only two hotels at Waikiki. The MC was Webley Edwards, and he would always find a way to remind you of the climate you were missing out on. With a mike down close to the shore-lapping surf, he would say seductively, "Temperature of the air here at Waikiki is 76, temperature of the water is 74." The musical director was Al "Kealoha" Perry. Sometimes Lena Machado, known as "Hawaii's Song Bird," would sing, sometimes the great falsetto artist George Kainapau.

My father would wait all week for this. Some Saturdays the shortwave signal would be so faint it was nothing more than a thin and lonesome trickle struggling to make it across 2400 miles of open water. Every once in a while, if the weather was right, you could hear the songs and the voices loud and clear, the ukes, the rhythm guitars, and somewhere behind the music the lapping surf. Then my father would set back on his heels and listen reverently.

That is what I remember. Anything that brings your father to his knees is going to make an impression on you, and this was what could do it: the sound, or the very hope of hearing the sound of "Hawaii Calls."

When the show was over he would plug in his amp and hook up his steel and spend an hour working on one of his big production numbers, such as "On the Beach at Waikiki," or "The Hilo March," upbeat, full of slides and chimes. His finger picks would flash, and the strings would whine, and at these times you did not interrupt him. If you tried to get his attention—"Hey Dad, Mom says dinner is almost on the table"—he would show no sign that he had heard you, as if he were in another room, or on his own private island. If you tried again, "Hey Dad . . . ," you might get a scowl, but not a glance, since he would not lift his eyes from the strings and the picks.

Why the scowl? He was practicing. What was he practicing for? He had a band, he would tell you later, and in a couple of days they were going to be rehearsing again. But it was more than that, much more. I know now that the tunes kept him connected

to a time and a place in his life he always dreamed of getting back to and never could, except via the radio and the transporting powers of the music itself.

He always had a band when I was growing up. They didn't play for money, they just played for the pleasure of it, and for parties now and again. They practiced in our living room because he had speakers and a couple of mikes and the most space. These were all men from Texas and Oklahoma, bringing along their Gibson guitars, a fiddle, a banjo, or a mandolin. It was mainly a western band, with this island flavor contributed by my dad and his amplified steel. His all-time favorite tunes were "The Hilo March," which he delivered with bravado and many flourishes, and "The Steel Guitar Rag." Running a close third was "The San Antonio Rose," usually sung by my mother. She had carrot-colored hair and fair skin that would turn pink with tearful happiness as she stood by his speaker and sang this song from the homeland they had left behind, a song of yearning for those "lips so sweet and tender / like petals fallin' apart . . . "

As a kid I resisted the sounds of their repertoire. To my ears then, it was cornball music. It was "Okie"

"Our older daughter, Corinne, age seventeen"

167

"With Wallace Stegner (middle) and Al Young (right) at a reception celebrating forty years of Stanford's writing program and the Stegner Fellowships," 1989

music, and I was not an Okie. I was from San Francisco, the city by the Golden Gate, where you saved your paper-route money to buy a cashmere sweater and combed your hair into a ducktail.

But maybe it all goes back to nights such as those, and to the three kinds of music I grew up with— gospel, and country, and Hawaiian.

I have written a novel called *Love Life,* about a woman who is guided by the voice of Hank Williams and has a not-so-secret desire to be a country singer. I have also played in a lot of bands myself over the years—dance bands, bluegrass bands, jazz combos, and in piano bars—and I wrote another novel, called *Gig,* about the night-club world as seen from a musician's point of view. And something about those island tunes my father played and loved and listened to—and listened for—has sent me across the water time and time again, to live a while, to write a while, to listen. After numerous essays and articles, two video documentaries, and the two novels I have located there (*A Native Son of the Golden West* and the newest work, called *Angel's Cord*), I still have not had my fill of the place.

I think of the Coast Range as my base and habitat. I have come to see Hawaii as a heart-land, some form of older spirit-home. And why should that be so? I am still not entirely sure. Jeanne and I like the multicultural mix—that is part of it—the faces and the voices and the foods and the races that gather there from all parts of the Pacific region. In the histories of our two families, the islands stand as some kind of meeting ground or intersection or crossroads. They hold a position, both geographical and symbolic, out there in the middle of the ocean midway between California and Japan. Jeanne's grandparents came to Hawaii as contract laborers, and her mother was born on a Kaua'i sugar plantation in 1895. Her father spent time in Honolulu on his trip across the Pacific in 1904. We were married in Honolulu in 1957 and spent our honeymoon hitchhiking around the outer islands, visiting the craters and old temple sites and ghostly valleys and meeting people who have become lifelong friends.

At the time I had already been out there for about six months. After we graduated from San Jose State, I had some open space in front of me. I saved

168

enough money for a one-way ticket, thinking then that this was an original idea for an expedition. I was so busy setting out on my own, I had not stopped to remember the sound of my dad's guitar or where he had learned to play it. But I hear it now—"The Hilo March"—and I am wondering if he himself ever got to Hilo. He could have, though he never mentioned it. There's no way to know for sure. There were so many things he never mentioned. Maybe this song was in the air. Most Hawaiian songs pay tribute to a specific place, a bay, a mountain, a point of land, a town. Maybe he had heard the 1920s recording that first made it famous, a steel guitar version by Pale K. Lua. Maybe he just heard it, and it worked on him the way it worked on me.

Thirty-five years ago the trip took fourteen hours from San Francisco. En route I was dreaming of beaches. But I soon found myself drawn inland, toward the mountains and the chain of craters that bear witness to Hawaii's volcanic origins. Like a chain of stop-time photographs, they chart the history of the earth, from Kaua'i in the north, the oldest island, with its razor cliffs worn down by wind and endless rain, to Hawaii in the south, the Big Island, the youngest and still growing, each time new lava steams into the sea, spilling outward from the region Hawaiians call "The Navel of the World."

This is the island I most prefer to visit now. Hilo happens to be its principle town, a port town on the windward side. The Big Island has produced many talented musicians and composers, some great dancers and chanters. The best slack-key guitar players have come from there. I like to go into the high country and sit for a while among the plains and heaps of old dark lava and listen to the stillness of the craters; then come down into town and listen to the music, always listening for some note I must have heard once, or more than once, or maybe in between the notes he was picking on the silvery strings that held him captivated after he had switched off the radio and sat down to practice on those long-ago Saturday afternoons.

Santa Cruz, California
February 1992

BIBLIOGRAPHY

Fiction:

Between Battles, Dial, 1968.

Gig, Dial, 1969.

A Native Son of the Golden West, Dial, 1971.

The Adventures of Charlie Bates (short stories), Capra, 1973, enlarged edition published as *Gasoline: The Automotive Adventures of Charlie Bates,* Capra, 1980.

Continental Drift, Knopf, 1978.

Love Life, Knopf, 1985.

Nonfiction:

(With wife, Jeanne Wakatsuki Houston) *Farewell to Manzanar: A True Story of Japanese American Experience during and after the World War II Internment,* Houghton, 1973 (also see below).

(With John R. Brodie) *Open Field* (biography), Houghton, 1974.

Three Songs for My Father (essays), Capra, 1974.

Californians: Searching for the Golden State, Knopf, 1982.

One Can Think about Life after the Fish Is in the Canoe, and Other Coastal Sketches (bound with *Beyond Manzanar and Other Views of Asian-American Womanhood,* by J. W. Houston), Capra, 1985.

The Men in My Life, and Other More or Less True Recollections of Kinship (personal stories), Creative Arts, 1987.

Editor:

Writing from the Inside (textbook), Addison-Wesley, 1973.

(With Gerald Haslam) *California Heartland: Writings from the Great Central Valley,* Capra, 1978.

(Also contributor) *West Coast Fiction: Modern Writing from California, Oregon, and Washington,* Bantam, 1979.

Contributor to anthologies:

Year's Best Science Fiction, Delacorte, 1965.

Stanford Stories 1968, Stanford University Press, 1968.

Capra Chapbook Anthology, Capra, 1977.

Yardbird Lives, Grove Press, 1978.

Borzoi College Reader, Knopf, 1980.

Unknown California, Collier/Macmillan, 1985.

California Childhood, Creative Arts, 1988.

West of the West, North Point, 1989.

Writers and Their Craft, Wayne State University Press, 1991.

Television and screenplays:

(With J. W. Houston and John Korty) *Farewell to Manzanar* (two-hour screenplay based on book), Universal Studios, produced and directed by John Korty, NBC World Premiere Movie, 1976.

(With J. W. Houston) "Barrio" (four-part television series), developed via Henry Jaffe Enterprises and ABC, 1978 (as yet unproduced).

"Lia: The Legacy of a Hawaiian Man" (one-hour musical documentary), directed by Eddie Kamae, via the Asian-Pacific Foundation, Honolulu, premiered at Hawaii International Film Festival, 1988.

"Listen to the Forest" (one-hour environmental documentary), directed by Eddie Kamae, via the Asian-Pacific Foundation, premiered at the Hawaii International Film Festival, December 1991.

Other:

Contributor of short stories and articles to *Bennington Review, Honolulu, Los Angeles Times, Manoa, Mother Jones, New York Times, New Yorker, Playboy,* and *Rolling Stone.*

Jeanne Wakatsuki Houston

1934-

COLORS

Jeanne Wakatsuki Houston

Colors! Seeing the stages of my life as colors. Where did I get such an idea? I trace it back to 1956, when I was twenty-one years old working as a group counselor in a Northern California juvenile detention hall. It was my first full-time job. I was supervising teenage girls brought in for violating probation, running away from home, and sometimes more serious crimes. But most often the offense was "incorrigibility."

Jessica T. (fictitious name) was a racial mix of Philippine, Samoan, and French. One of the "incorrigibles," she was brought to the hall for breaking probation or, more precisely, for getting into a fight.

Jessica was well-known to the staff at Hillcrest. She was sixteen and, since the age of twelve when she was booked for running away from a foster home, had been a frequent visitor to the hall.

When I came on shift one afternoon, the other supervisors were chatting in the lounge about Jessica, lamenting her fate, which they believed would be a sentence to CYA (California Youth Authority). I had never met her, but surmised from the tone of talk she was someone special, someone I would have to contend with in a serious way.

"Now, don't let her looks scare you," said one of my colleagues. "She can grimace like a gorilla, but she's really a teddy bear."

*"My mother and father, Riku and
Ko Wakatsuki," Spokane, Washington, 1916*

By the time I unlocked the door to the rec room where the girls enjoyed free time outside their otherwise locked cubicles, I was anxious about meeting Jessica. A blast of music greeted me. I looked around the lively room. She wasn't hard to miss. Big, almost six feet tall, wiry black hair frizzed out in a halo (unusual hairstyle in those pre-sixties days), she stood away from the group, tapping her feet and snapping fingers to Elvis Presley and "Blue Suede Shoes."

I introduced myself. "I'm Miss Waka. You must be Jessica."

Jessica glared. "How come you're *Miss* Waka?" She emphasized "Miss." Her voice was melodic and didn't match the piercing hostile eyes.

I waited for her to grimace, trying to remain calm and in control of the situation. All the supervisors shortened their names. Mrs. Finlof was Finney; Mrs. Sullivan was Sully; Mrs. Coulter was Coulty, etc. Since I was so young, only a few years older than some of the girls, the staff thought it would be more appropriate that I be called *Miss* Waka, instead of a

nickname. I thought fast. "Well, can you think of a good name to call me?"

Her eyes flickered, met mine, and looked away. Then she broke into laughter, a light tinkling sound incongruous with her bulky body.

"I sure can." Her eyes now were friendly. "I know you must really be crazy to work in a place like this . . . really crazy. So, you should be called Wacky."

From that day on, I was known at Hillcrest as Wacky. There was some talk among staff that the nickname could be construed as disrespectful, but since I was not offended, the question was dropped. The truth of the matter was I liked being seen as "fun" and "unserious," which the nickname implied. It was very sober business trying to maintain a "homelike" atmosphere in an institution with locked doors, high cement walls, and regimented routines. I wanted to seem frivolous, to lighten the responsibility and authority so loudly announced by the ring of keys jangling from my belt.

Jessica and I became friends. The court date when she would learn her fate was late in being set, which meant she remained at the hall for an unusually long time. I was then part-time, but worked some day shifts, allowing closer contact with the girls once they were out of school (held at the hall). I discovered Jessica had unusual artistic talent. I encouraged her to spend spare time drawing and painting, which she plunged into with great enthusiasm. Even though I knew very little about art, artistic subjects became our mode of communication.

She would say, "Wacky, today is a green day, so I'm painting landscapes . . . you know, like Picasso or whatever his name . . . even though I'm feeling blue." Then she'd laugh, her big full-lipped mouth open, exposing white gapped teeth.

I'd say, "Well, Jessica, make good use of your blue period." And I'd drop some artists' names I really knew nothing about ". . . like Rembrandt and Monet. They used blue."

When she was upset and angry, usually after a visit with her probation officer, she would stomp down the hall muttering, slamming a fist rhythmically into her open palm. Her face would be dark and ferocious, and she'd pass me saying, "Don't come near me, Wacky, I'm really muddy." Even though I was sure she would never turn that wrath on me, I heeded her words, warned by the tattooed letters L O V E on the fist smashing into her open palm.

I brought her paints and paper and books on art. In a way, I was educating myself as well. Soon, the rec hall and her room's walls were covered with paintings, splashes of vivid colors—rainbows, flowers, butterflies, jungle animals. The pictures were not what one expected to see from a person who looked like Jessica. With her wild hair, powerful size and often tough vocabulary, she kept the other girls at a distance. But with the staff, particularly me, she was gentle and humorous.

One day I was called into the front office and mildly reprimanded by an uncomfortable administrator who said that it appeared I might be practicing favoritism. Perhaps I was identifying with Jessica. Since I was at least a foot shorter and sixty pounds lighter, I was nonplussed by the remark. "What do you mean 'identifying' with her?" I asked innocently.

He cleared his throat. "You're both Asians, you know. You don't want the other kids to think you're favoring her because of race."

I was astounded. This hadn't entered my head. Speechless, and also too unconscious then about my own identity as an Asian-American to respond indignantly, I only nodded my head and left his office.

I was the only Asian group supervisor working at the hall during the day (a Japanese-American male worked the graveyard shift). Asian delinquents were rare. "Orientals," as we were called then, were the model minority, hiding in the closet of "respectability," hoping to become invisible in a society still reeling from the Second World War and Korea.

Angry at this accusation, but still too young and inexperienced to fight back, I decided to deal with the situation by withdrawing from Jessica. I tried to do it subtly by working the graveyard or mornings, or if I was on shift during the afternoon, I would become involved in other activities. This didn't affect her.

"Hey, Wacky," she'd say, friendly as ever, "when are we going to paint a mural together? Let's do Chicano . . . like Diego Rivera!" It was as if she knew my plight, understanding institutions and group behavior better than I.

Then the day arrived when she was sentenced to the California Youth Authority, the last stop on the road that had begun in a foster home, spiraled down to a convent, and then juvenile hall. Her probation officer came to see me. "I'd like to ask a very unorthodox favor of you," she said. "Jessica will be transported to Sacramento next week, and we're afraid she's going to bolt. We hate to handcuff her in the car . . . and she said she wouldn't run if you could accompany her."

Miss Brown was a tough P.O. but also had a heart. No one wanted any juvie to attempt an escape while being transported to CYA. The consequences could be formidable. I agreed to go.

We left San Mateo at midmorning, timing it so we could stop for lunch at a popular restaurant outside of Davis. Somewhat like the final supper for convicts in death row, lunch at the fine restaurant was a last meal on the "outs" before the kids were locked up by the state. They could order anything they wanted—which was usually a hamburger, fries, and coke. Jessica ordered a shrimp salad.

"I'm really scared, Wacky," she said with a trembling voice. Tears rolled down her cheeks. The driver of the car, another P.O. returning to Sacramento, dabbed her own cheeks with a handkerchief. She was crying as much as Jessica. I later learned this was not uncommon among officers having to transport delinquents to CYA. To them, as far as rehabilitation was concerned, it might as well be death row.

I didn't cry, remembering the warning not to identify. Then Jessica said, "You know, Wacky, I understand. You used to be such bright colors. You were red and orange and purple and turquoise. And now you're fading . . . you're like a color that's fading away."

By the time we dropped Jessica off in Sacramento, I was drained. After leaving the restaurant, she had wept the whole time, her large body shaking as if she were riding a motorcycle. My final words to her were, "Don't be afraid, Jessica, Van Gogh was crazy and Gauguin had leprosy. Look how famous they are!" The absurdity of my statement made her laugh. She relaxed and was actually smiling when she walked haughtily toward the building with the P.O. Before entering she waved and yelled, "Bye, Wacky. Stay colorful."

RED

The color RED pervades my earliest memories of childhood. Primary and powerful, its hues are vibrant, lighting up a time that was grounded in family.

The youngest of ten children, I was born in Inglewood, California, on September 26, 1934. At the time, my father was farming what was then the outskirts of Los Angeles. Today, huge airliners streak across asphalt runways which cover the rich soil where he raised strawberries, green beans, and lettuce.

I have no concrete memories of that time, only stories told within the family of life on the farm. My older brothers and sisters talk about how I used to get lost in the bean patch, wandering for hours amidst tall poles of green beans, a barefoot waif wailing in the succulent forest while the rest of the family searched.

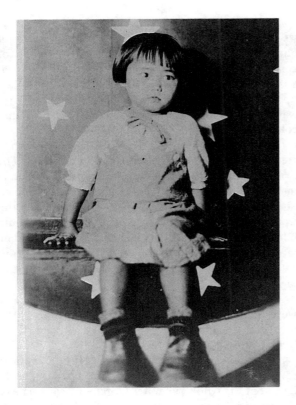

Jeanne, about five, at the arcade on Ocean Park Pier, California, before the war

I don't remember this and, in a way, I am glad. My family refers to the thirties as the dust-bowl period of *our* history, dull and grey instead of the bright red I remember.

"You're so lucky, Jeannie," they say, as I cringe with guilt. "We had to eat cabbage sandwiches and line our shoes with cardboard to cover the holes in the soles."

So, I was born during the Great Depression. But when I was two my father turned to commercial fishing, and we moved to Ocean Park, a small coastal community whose main attraction was its amusement pier. Ocean Park Pier, now long gone, was our "playground." It was a magical place. With sweet vanilla perfume from cotton candy, candied apples, and salt-water taffy wafting around the noisy shooting galleries, and thrill rides, neon lights, and freak shows bombarding my senses, it is no wonder my memories remain so vivid. The pier was my nursery school, the amusement attendants my sitters. The neighborhood kids and I spent most of our days there.

The roller coaster, shoot-the-chute, and ferris wheel were forbidden territories, which was all right with me, since I saw too many dazed revelers screaming with terror and throwing up after rides. It amazed me anyone wanted to be thrilled like that. The freak shows and tunnel of horror were more my speed. Although I wasn't supposed to go, I would sneak in, wrapping my arms around someone's legs while I stared at the bearded lady and Siamese twins. I see a sharp picture of the pinhead dressed in a Japanese kimono, nervously twisting a sequined purse with thin blue-veined hands. He especially intrigued me because he was small, not much taller than I, and wore heavy make-up, bright lipstick and face powder which failed to cover the purple five o'clock shadow of his lower face. His hair was swept up into a small bun from which dangled Japanese ornaments.

One day, as I gazed at him—more awed than curious—he looked me straight in the eyes. I remember being shocked, feeling a pang of pity, feeling badly and not understanding why. I know now those beady black eyes had drawn from my childish heart its first feeling of compassion. I never went back . . . even when the neighborhood kids and the rest of the family came ranting home one day, excitedly describing the "geek" who bit off chicken heads. I had no interest, and as it turned out—so the story goes—my sister Lillian got too close to the wild man and he tore out a clump of her hair.

The merry-go-round was my favorite. Giant roan stallions with flowing manes and jeweled saddles. I watched them gallop past, forelegs bent gracefully in the air, rising and falling in time with the nickelodeon music. I fell in love with the marbled stallions, never missing a chance to ride them, which was often, since the attendant let the gang ride free. I can still feel the smooth cold porcelain of muscled flanks which I stroked and petted after a day's hard ride.

I was faithful to my inert friends for many months until a new concession opened at the end of the pier. It was a live pony. A little white horse tethered to a stake posted in the middle of a circle. After riding around the circle, children could then be photographed, posing in cowboy hats and chaps or fur hats and muffs. I was enthralled. A real live horse that could respond to my passionate devotion!

But it was expensive. I nagged and whined at Mama to let me ride the pony. Finally, she gave in, but only after deciding a picture in my new red coat she bought for my older sister's wedding would be worth it.

As "karma" would have it, my infidelity had its consequences. After riding around in circles, proudly displaying my new coat, we stopped for the photo. For some reason, the pony bucked. I flew off the saddle onto the ground. Screaming, I rolled in the manure-laden dirt, more terrified by the shouting adults and Mama's cries than by the fall. But it was traumatic. The smell of horse manure can still accelerate my heart beat. I have never ridden a horse since . . . except at fairs and amusement parks where those shiny porcelain horses beckon like long-lost lovers.

YELLOW

The Second World War is a swirl of yellow. Yellow for the hot, dusty desert where I spent three and a half years in an internment camp for Americans of Japanese ancestry. Yellow for stinging whirlwinds and fierce duststorms that pricked the skin like needles and coated everything, including our lips and eyelashes, with thick ochre powder.

When Japan bombed Pearl Harbor on December 7, 1941, I was seven years old. The FBI came to our house and arrested my father on false charges that he was supplying enemy Japanese submarines with oil from his fishing boat. He was incarcerated in a federal prison in Bismarck, North Dakota. We didn't see him again for a year.

In April 1942, my mother, nine brothers and sisters (some married), and I arrived at Manzanar, located off Highway 395 in eastern California be-tween Death Valley and Independence. The book *Farewell to Manzanar*, authored by myself and husband James D. Houston, relates in detail my remembrances of camp life.

But the book was written twenty years ago, the writing of it releasing and thus healing the deepest wounds of that experience. Since then, other memories have risen to the surface. Only after that project was completed did I recall that my first experience with books occurred in Manzanar.

Before going there, I remember having a fleeting acquaintance in kindergarten and first grade with readers and children's picture books. In our home at Ocean Park there were few books. Thus, it was with incredulous astonishment that I viewed a huge pile of hardbound books mounded in the center of a fire-break near our barracks.

In the first months at Manzanar, there were no schools or libraries. And so, it seems, some charitable organizations, apprised of this, had sent truckloads of books to stock a library. Unfortunately, there were no available buildings to shelter them, so they were dumped in the middle of the spaces between barrack blocks—bleak, sandy acres left open in case of fire.

The pile was a jagged mountain range as huge as a two-story building. I had never seen anything like it and scrambled up the peak with other kids, sliding over slick pages, jamming legs between crevices. We played mountain climbing and war, throwing books at

Manzanar barracks, internment camp for Americans of Japanese ancestry during World War II, Owens Valley, California, 1944

Group picture of internees in front of Catholic Church in Manzanar. Jeanne, age ten, is in front row indicated by arrow.

each other and hiding in foxholes dug into the sides. It didn't occur to us to read the material which provided us with such a wondrous playground. But after a week or so of diligent mountaineering, a few thunderstorms and dust storms dampened our enthusiasm. The book heap, now worn down to a hill, was abandoned.

One sunny afternoon, as I walked across the firebreak, a glint caught my eye. The book graveyard was still except for pages fluttering in the wind like earthbound kites. I soon discovered the source of light. Framed in shiny gold gilt, a scene of Rapunzel letting down her long hair from a tower's window shone from a book of fairy tales. I was entranced. Who was this beautiful lady with long yellow hair? I leafed through the book and found I could read the print. That afternoon I sat down amidst the torn and water-stained wreckage and read every story in Hans Christian Andersen's *Fairy Tales.*

Until the books were removed to the empty barrack which became our library, I explored the mountain again and again, no longer adventuring, but searching and scavenging for more stories of fairies, and princes, wicked stepmothers, and gem-studded kingdoms. Like a prospector seeking a second strike, I jealously guarded my stake, rummaging and examining until I found dozens of fairy tale books and took them home to our barracks.

This was my initiation into the imaginary world of written words. From fairy tales I advanced to mysteries—Nancy Drew became my idol. I read about Katrina, the Russian ballerina who rose from a starving peasant background to the Czar's palace. I read some classics—*The Scotsman, The Deerslayer, The Pathfinder,* and even attempted *Wuthering Heights.* At age nine and ten, the mind is resilient. It is open and inquisitive. It is also bent on survival. Books became my major form of recreation, my channel to worlds outside the confined and monotonous routine of camp life.

ORANGE

I look into the kaleidoscope and see the period after Manzanar as essentially the color orange—intense, concentrated, and rich—rich with memories of awakenings, of social interaction outside the family. Puberty and hormones. Adolescence and social initiations.

When the Second World War ended with the bombing of Hiroshima and Nagasaki, we were relocated to a defense housing project in Long Beach, California. Ironically, it was only a few miles from Terminal Island, the Japanese fishing community from where my father last fished before he was picked up by the FBI. For many years Terminal

Island had been a unique ghetto populated by Japanese fishermen and their families. Today it is part of the port of Long Beach and a base for the navy.

Cabrillo Homes was a large cluster of brown square buildings, some two-storied with eight apartments and the others long, low bungalows of four. They were federally built for defense plant workers and families who swarmed to California during the war, drawn by work in the shipyards. When the war ended, some returned to their homes in the South, Midwest, and East, but many remained, still living in the housing project.

What a different world! From a racially homogenous one-mile-square community, I entered a multiracial and cultural matrix, a ghetto where our only common denominator was poverty. It was my first experience living among African Americans and Latinos. In Ocean Park, we had lived in a Caucasian neighborhood, mostly Jewish and Italian. At Cabrillo Homes, I met, for the first time, Americans of Polish, Cuban, and Mexican descent. I heard for the first time the twangs and drawls in the language of Oklahoma, Texas, Missouri, Georgia—even the clipped whine of Boston.

Ah! Cabrillo Homes! Crossroads for America's hopefuls—halfway house for America's economic and political refugees. We were an early experiment in cross-cultural living. At Manzanar, Glenn Miller and the rising young swooner Frank Sinatra were our musical idols. In the housing project, country western music and Mexican rancheras blared from open windows. I became a fan of Roy Acuff, Red Foley and Bob Wills, and the Texas Playboys. I learned to sing in Spanish, delighting my Mexican friends with renditions of "Tu Solo Tu" and "Ella," popular rancheras sung by Jorge Negrete and Pedro Infante. At age eleven, I was thrust into this varied environment—a new stucco landscape, strange and somewhat fearsome, but alight with bright orange.

My first boyfriend lived across the street from me. Green-eyed, blond, and freckled, Billy Fortner was the archetypal "boy next door." He was an only child whose parents had come to California from North Carolina to work for the navy. When his mother called from their upstairs apartment "Billeee . . . Bil-leee" in her soft southern drawl, I envied him and wished my mother would call for me with such tenderness and gentility. But, my mother, of course, would never dream of calling for any of us publicly; she never even raised her voice in the home.

I learned to play post office and spin the bottle with Billy, Doris Jean, and several other adolescents in the neighborhood. I mention Doris Jean because she was the spunky ringleader of our clandestine

games. She lived in the apartment underneath his, part of a large compound of buildings from which I felt excluded. Our apartment was in a long, low bungalow. Where the kids across the street played seemed out of bounds for me, a private club whose membership mandated living in that complex. The main reason, though, was that the families who lived there were all Caucasian and from the South.

But one day, Doris Jean knocked on my door and, after introducing herself, asked if I wanted to work with her and some other kids for her father. Flattered by the invitation, I enthusiastically accepted without even asking what the job would be. It turned out Doris Jean's stepfather operated cigarette vending machines which he placed in restaurants and bars around town. In those days, a pack of cigarettes cost about twenty-two cents. The machines took quarters, which meant the customer's change should be three cents. Because the machines did not make change, our job was cutting a slit in the side of the cellophane wrapping around the pack and sliding three pennies down its side. He paid us ten cents a carton.

Doris Jean's parents usually were absent on Saturdays. When they were gone we worked fast so we could play the games wily Doris Jean had learned in Texas and magnanimously taught us. Although Billy was part of the neighborhood gang, he didn't stuff pennies, since he was a few years older and had a paper route. But he joined our afterwork soirees, which thrilled the girls who all had a crush on him.

I experienced my first kiss playing spin the bottle. It was Billy's spin and the bottle stopped, pointing at me! I remember apprehension, excitement, curiosity and fear churning within as we entered the bathroom and closed the door.

"I don't know how to kiss," I whispered.

"Don't be scared," he said. "Just close your eyes."

Shaking, I squinted my eyes tight and waited for what seemed like hours for the touch on my lips that was supposed to change my life forever. It was disappointing. His lips could easily have been the back of my own hand.

But I liked the game, mostly because of its secretiveness. Even though Billy's kiss never sent me into ecstacy, I loved him wholeheartedly. He was always kind, and since I didn't have a bike like most of the other kids, he would take me for rides and even offered to teach me how to maneuver one.

I was shocked a few months later when Vernon Hicks came to our apartment with a message.

"Billy's leaving this afternoon, goin' back to North Carolina," he whispered conspiratorily, "and wants to kiss you good-bye."

I ran across the street thinking there was going to be one last game of spin the bottle at Doris Jean's house. But Billy was standing by the stairs, dressed in new going-away clothes. He beckoned for me to come behind the building. It was clear there wasn't going to be any game. At first I hesitated, terrified by the thought of being kissed by choice rather than by chance. But love for cavalier Billy overcame my timidity, and I joined him. Neither of us said a word. I closed my eyes and with pursed lips waited for the usual brush, the sweet but impersonal touch. This time it was different. Gently he cupped my face with his hands and kissed my lips . . . not once but three times . . . softly and slowly. I remember thinking this was the way they kissed in movies. Then his mother's soprano voice called, "Bil-leee . . . Bil-leee . . . we're going."

"Good-bye," Billy said, squeezing my hand.

He hesitated, waiting for me to say something. But I couldn't respond. I was frozen. I finally uttered, "Good-bye, Billy." That's all I said. To this day I have regretted never saying what I wanted to . . . like "write me" or "where are you going?" or "I love you and thanks for being such a great first-kisser."

Billy disappeared from my life in a suitcase-laden taxi—his father seated in front with the driver and he with his mother in the back seat, waving to me even as the orange-and-black cab rounded the corner a block away.

Whenever I hear a soft Southern drawl or anyone mentions North Carolina, I wonder about Billy, my blond and freckled first love. I wonder where he went, what he became—and if he ever remembered me.

I was still living in Cabrillo Homes when the idea of becoming a writer germinated. I was in the seventh grade. Our junior high was new and didn't have a journalism class from which a newspaper could be written and published. A search for writing talent began by having students write an essay about a memorable event in their lives. The winners would form the journalism class—if they wanted—and publish the school paper and annual.

I wrote about hunting grunion in Ocean Park with my family before the war. On full-moon nights when the tides were high, the grunion would "run." Small, silvery fish about the size of anchovies, they would fill the waves, fluttering and flipping, glinting in the moonlight as my family scooped them up with buckets. We cooked and ate them there on the beach, the bright moon and bonfire turning night into twilight, while a balmy Southern California breeze cooled the summer air.

On the strength of that essay I was asked to join the journalism project. Until that moment I had no idea what the word "journalism" meant. But I was intrigued and enthusiastically plunged into the new class. I soon became editor in chief of the school paper, which we called the *Chatterbox*.

The step from reading fairy tales to editing a newspaper was a big one, and, I see now, this experience in junior high school was one of the crucial events in my life. That I could write was clearly programmed in my mind by a wise teacher who knew about validating youngsters, about directing them to higher goals—even when circumstances did not seem to support it. In the late forties, with the Second World War barely over, who would encourage a young Japanese-American girl living in a ghetto to work toward becoming a writer? Only an idealistic, fair-minded person. I was lucky to have met such a person in junior high school, my English teacher.

Jeanne, about fifteen, a junior at Long Beach Polytechnic High School

She planted the seed, but it didn't really sprout for many years. Although I continued to write for my high school newspaper in Long Beach and majored in journalism for the first two years at San Jose State University, I had no tangible goal. In those days, Brenda Starr was a comic book character who was a glamorous newspaper reporter. In a childish way, she was my idol. Somehow I was going to be a newspaper journalist like her! This was fantasy, of course. In my second year of college, reality set in.

One day I went to see the journalism department head for advice about my major. I didn't know him very well, having taken only one class from him, "Press and the Public." I used to see him rushing around campus, in his navy blue suit and tie, looking like he had just scooped the story of the year. I heard he had been a rather famous newspaper correspondent before he came to San Jose State.

I sat down in his office, a messy room with yellowed newspaper clippings on the wall and scattered over his desk. A small Persian rug, grey with lint, covered part of the floor.

"Now, Jeanne, just what do you intend to do with a journalism degree?" he asked.

"I really don't know," I answered. "That's why I've come to see you. I guess I would like to be a reporter."

He peered at me with steady blue eyes. "I'm going to be honest with you, my dear. Newspaper-writing jobs are hard to come by for men. For women, it's almost impossible."

I was crushed. I had known it was a tough field for females since only a few of us were majors, but I wanted to believe becoming an Asian Brenda Starr was possible.

"You might think of switching over to advertising." He continued when I didn't respond, "It's still in the journalism department."

My heart sinking, I said, "Oh, I don't think I'd like advertising."

He scratched his curly brown hair, grey at the temples. Without looking at me, he said, "I can only tell you that you would have a very hard row to hoe trying to land a job with a newspaper. Believe me." He hesitated. "You're a woman . . . and you're oriental. That's double tough."

At first I didn't know how to take his words. Was he racially prejudiced himself? Or was he being kind, trying to help prevent a more disastrous disappointment later on?

Gently, he said, "Maybe you should think about changing your major. You're only a junior now, so it won't be a problem."

Fighting back tears, I thanked him and left the office. After a few days, I realized he spoke the truth. All the Asians on campus were majoring in "invisible" fields—lab techs, engineering, nursing, occupational therapy, secretarial—fields open to Asians for jobs. I decided to change my major to sociology and social welfare.

GREEN

Three years before I had that conversation, my family had moved from Cabrillo Homes up north to San Jose where my father tried for the last time to find a future in farming. San Jose in 1952 was the center of a lush agricultural region. Prune, apricot, and cherry orchards crisscrossed the Santa Clara Valley, carpeting it with fragrant blossoms in the spring. Compared to the tough streets and bare landscape of Cabrillo Homes, San Jose was gentle and quiet, a midsize farming community enjoying its organic wealth.

My father raised strawberries—in the beginning as a sharecropper with Driscoll Inc., and later on his own. At the housing project, my friendship with two Mexican sisters and with members of a car "gang" called the King's Men had given me some training to communicate with my father's farm workers. They were braceros from Mexico and spoke no English. I could speak some Spanish, mostly street "argot."

When we first moved up north, I was devastated. I liked the fast street life and found farming dull and "unsophisticated." I missed my friends. When the Mexican braceros arrived to pick berries, I found comfort in speaking with them and singing the Mexican songs I had learned at Cabrillo Homes.

Looking at the green memory fragment, I think of Calistro. Jovial, good-humored Calistro! Middle-aged and married, he had left his family in Chihuahua to earn money in El Norte. He had four children whose picture he proudly showed to everyone he met, and he was a good musician, strumming an old cracked guitar during lunch hour to entertain the other workers.

One day I noticed him sitting barefoot by the irrigating flume. I thought he was cooling his feet in the water flowing through the open wooden trough. As I approached him, I saw he was lining his shoes with cardboard to cover large holes in the soles. I remembered my older sisters' and brothers' stories of the Depression, how they too had re-soled their worn shoes with cardboard. I had always felt guilty for not suffering the deprivations they had to endure. When

I saw Calistro re-enacting that potent family story, I decided to atone. I bought him a new pair of boots.

Needless to say, he became a devoted friend. When I revealed I could sing in Spanish too, our friendship was sealed. As we picked strawberries under the relentless California sun, we sang to alleviate the hardship of stoop labor and heat. He taught me a cheerful song called "Mi Cafetal," which I can still sing today.

Aunque la gente vive griticando
Me paso la vida sin pensar en na
Pero no sabiendo que yo soy el hombre
Que tenga una hermosa y linda cafetal . . .

"Although people live criticizing the life I lead so idly, they do not know I am the man who has a beautiful coffee plantation. . . ."

He loved bologna sandwiches, and I liked the hot burritos the braceros were served for their noon meal. We traded lunches. I always added a thick onion slice to the bologna sandwich, which he greatly appreciated.

By befriending the workers, I eased through the first summer away from Long Beach. When autumn arrived and the braceros began leaving, I had grown to like the pastoral pace, the clean green world of Northern California. But, I hated saying good-bye to Calistro.

The day he left he brought me a gift. Wrapped in newspaper, it was a matchbox with a tiny worn crucifix tucked inside. The figure of Christ was silver, delicate and smooth, and the cross was fashioned out of dark wood. I knew it was probably Calistro's most valuable possession. I still have the crucifix, safely stored with other good-luck fetishes I have collected over the past years.

BLUE

Marriage. Blue diamonds, sapphires, sparkling turquoise light. The colors radiate from deep pools and surging surf, mountainous coastal valleys, lush rain forests—the jeweled landscape of the Hawaiian Islands.

At San Jose State I met Jim Houston. We were both journalism majors with Spanish minors, and thus had all the same classes. We began dating. After graduating from college, Jim went to Hawaii, and I remained on the mainland, working at Hillcrest Juvenile Hall.

After six months in the Islands, Jim sent me a Valentine. It was an unusual card, a long slender Ti leaf with BE MY VALENTINE inked on one side and WILL YOU MARRY ME on the other. I later learned the Ti leaf was used in Hawaii for ceremonial purposes, the belief being it had powers to bless and consecrate. In those days mail from Hawaii took at least two weeks. By the time the Valentine arrived, the usually lush green leaf was a brownish husk. But the message printed on it had not lost one bit of its luster.

Within a month, after a thirteen-hour flight from San Francisco, I arrived at Honolulu at 7:00 in the morning. We were married that evening during a spectacular sunset at Kaiser Lagoon, now part of the Hilton Hawaiian Village complex in Waikiki. Jim and his friends had made all the arrangements weeks before so our only task was to buy a ring, which we hurriedly did that morning.

We were married on the beach where the only person wearing shoes was Reverend Sam Saffrey, who was fully attired in black robe, tie, and suit. Bible in hand, the sunset glinting off his glasses, he officiated the "traditional" part of the wedding.

For the Hawaiian part, Winona Beamer and Ed Kenny, professional singers and dancers whom Jim had befriended in Kona, performed a ritual of chants, drumming, and symbolic rites. Both Ed and Winona are steeped in their Hawaiian heritage and have worked at reviving Hawaiian culture for many years. When we married in 1957, respect and acknowledgement of indigenous cultures was not as prevalent in the public consciousness as it is today. In fact, Winona recently revealed ours was the first wedding ceremony she had chanted for.

It was hauntingly beautiful. They blew conch shells—to the East, West, North, and South. They rattled gourds and planted a Ti leaf in the sand. A burnished brown calabash held kukui nuts, rocks, and shells, which Winona gracefully retrieved, each one symbolizing a quality bestowed on our marriage— kukui nut for strength, shells for protection, lava rock for union. The final rite was the draping of a long maile lei over both our shoulders. Maile is a vine that grows in high rain forests, mostly in the Big Island and Kauai, and is prized by Hawaiians for its fragrance. Like the Ti leaf, it is often used to bless ceremonies. We have been married now for thirty-four years. Perhaps their "mana," spiritual power, flowed through that maile lei, binding us together in a strong and unusual way.

After the discouraging conference with my journalism teacher at San Jose State, I gave up hope of becoming a writer. I plunged into psychology and

Jeanne and James D. Houston at their wedding on the beach in Honolulu, with Ed Kenny and Winona Beamer performing a Hawaiian ritual, 1957

sociology and wanted to become a field probation officer, those P.O.'s who worked in the community supervising delinquents on probation. Ironically, the same argument by my journalism professor to dissuade me from a writing career was also used by the head of juvenile hall when I asked to apply for a job in the field.

"This county is not ready for an 'oriental' P.O. . . . especially female," I was told by an honest administrator. "You're better off as a group supervisor back in the unit."

Jim's intention, as long as I had known him, was to be a writer. By the time his request for marriage came, I was ready to hand over all my ambition to him and to vicariously experience his writing career as a "support" person. Besides, I was a "female of the fifties" . . . and an American with a Japanese cultural background. It was not odd to "live in the country of his shadow"—a phrase I remembered from a Japanese poem.

The seed to become a writer, planted by my English teacher in junior high, was nurtured through high school and for two years in college became dormant. It remained dormant for many years as my priority shifted from career for myself to wife and mother. It was not until 1971, fourteen years after our marriage on the beach, that the thought of writing resurfaced.

With Jim's encouragement and help, the long buried seed came to life. *Farewell to Manzanar,* our collaboration, was my re-entry into the world of writing other than as Jim's most avid fan. Later in this essay I relate in detail how and why this change came about.

GREY AND LAVENDAR

Jim held an ROTC commission from San Jose State. Our honeymoon in paradise ended when he received orders from Texas to report for training at Lackland Air Force Base, after which he would be sent to England. That fall, I took a train across the states to New York, where I boarded a Dutch liner for a five-day crossing of the Atlantic and my first visit to Europe.

After the tranquil blue of Hawaii, England was sharp, provocative, and heady. Elegant silver, delicate lavender lace. In many ways I found England to be almost overwhelmingly strange. Weather was a big factor. Except for the three harsh winters in Manzanar, I had never experienced such damp cold that penetrated through layers of wool straight to the bone.

It was the East Anglian fog—thick mist rising from bogs and marshes, shrouding the countryside, sometimes never lifting for weeks at a time. I was used to sandals and tennis shoes, cotton shorts and t-shirts and spending most of the day outdoors. I had to buy a new wardrobe, unaccustomed accessories such as scarves, gloves, woolen underwear, and fleece-lined boots. There were days when I never ventured outside, loath to leave the warm hearth of the kitchen fireplace.

Our first home in England was a ten-room, four-hundred-year-old townhouse. Called "The Roost," its rooms were small, some the size of large closets. Jim had to duck to pass through doorways. It was my first acquaintance with coal fires, musty oriental rugs, and antique furniture. The crooked, creaked floors and dark hallways reminded me of scenes from *Great Expectations,* and I fully expected to see Miss Haversham sitting in one of the bedrooms—or the ghost, perhaps, of Mrs. Hawker, the lady of The Roost who had died there two years before.

When we moved into our home, we had agreed with the rental agent to continue allowing a photographer the use of a small hut in the backyard as a darkroom. For several months we never laid eyes on our phantom neighbor. Then one rare warm and sunny day, I sat outside in the yard. A very tiny woman emerged from the shedlike building and, seeing me, approached shyly. She had short greying hair, thick and curly, and a smooth olive complexion. Even from a distance I was drawn to her smiling eyes, twinkling hazel eyes that looked both mischievous and curious.

As she walked toward me, I noticed she limped. Her back was deformed, causing her to appear stooped. "I must take your picture!" She almost shouted. It was as if lightning struck! Before I could answer or even say "hello," she had whirled around and in a flash had re-entered the darkroom. When she emerged again, she carried a square box camera a little smaller than a shoe box. Dancing around me like a drunken elf, she snapped pictures, all the while chattering in heavily accented English.

"So, you are the Americans," she said, looking at me through the camera lens. "But, you are different, yes? You don't drive those giant cars, so much they look like tanks. And where are you from? China? Japan? Shangri-La? Oh, what a lovely picture this will be!"

Jim and Jeanne with close friend Corinne Kong (for whom daughter Cori is named) and date, New York City, 1958

Occasionally she would look up from her lens, not at me, but at the sky. I later learned she was famous for the soft natural quality of her work. She never used artificial lighting, depending fully on the light from the sun.

"It's nice, too, that you shop at the green grocer's and Mr. Kincaide's butcher store. Most Americans shop at your base and, really, they keep their homes much too warm. It's not healthy. By the way, dear child, my name is Bertl . . . Bertl Gaye."

I was delightfully dumbfounded by this spritely woman. When I recovered enough to tell her my name, she said, "But, what a strange name you have . . . you don't look like a 'Hooston'," she prolonged the "oo's." "Are you not a Chinese princess or a samurai warrior?"

I laughed and told her my father was actually from a samurai family in Japan. "Then, I shall call you 'Sami'," she said. "It suits you better."

We had no previous idea who our resident photographer was, nor had we made any inquiries. Yet Bertl seemed to know about us, about Americans. After we became friends, I learned the airbase was not very popular among the villagers—especially when Americans brought huge cars, Buicks and Hudsons, that hogged their narrow roads, oversized refrigerators that blew out wiring. And, of course, there was the terrifying possibility the shrill jets streaking overhead, sometimes breaking their centuries-old windows, could be carrying nuclear bombs!

Bertl lived across the street, alone except for holidays and summer when her son Adrian, then fourteen, came home from boarding school. I spent many afternoons and evenings in her spare but tasteful house. I helped garden, sipped afternoon tea, and enjoyed many delicious meals with her. She introduced me to classical music . . . Bach, Schubert, Dvořák, Brahms. During many bitterly cold evenings, Jim and I huddled with Bertl in her small living room, playing Scrabble while Mozart's "Eine Kleine Nacht Musik" warmed our spirits.

Near the end of Jim's tour in England, she moved to Cambridge, where she leased a large flat with rooms she could rent to students. That summer she decided purposefully to board two German students attending English language classes. I happened to be staying with her while Jim was traveling on the continent.

"This is a lesson, Sami. Watch what happens," she said. "They will wonder if I am a Jew, but I will not tell them unless they ask. Then we can have a talk." She said this without malice. I knew Bertl had fled Austria in the thirties and that her family had died in the death camps of Germany. She never

Oldest daughter, Cori, with Al Young, writer and longtime family friend, 1991

talked much about her past. But sometimes she would reminisce about her youth in Berlin, mentioning acquaintance with Oppenheimer, Teller, Planck, and Szilard. At the time I didn't recognize the importance of these physicists, and Bertl never dwelt on their fame. But I knew she was a pacifist and strongly opposed to nuclear development.

Bertl cooked the two German students tasty meals. She assisted with their English language studies. She took them to concerts and picnics. I could see they were growing fond of her, enjoying her wit and wisdom as I did. But the charged question never came up.

Then the last week of school arrived. Bertl said, "They will ask me tomorrow, Sami."

They did. At breakfast Mara, the dark-haired one, hesitantly asked Bertl if she was a Jew. When Bertl confirmed she was, both girls began to weep.

"Why do you cry?" she said gently. "It is not your crime. But you must go home and tell your parents you have spent your summer with a Jew, a Jew who didn't spit at you and treated you well. Then, they can cry, not you."

They embraced Bertl. "How you can show respect for me is to fight against nuclear bombs. No bombs! Go back to Germany and protest this madness!"

Years later I heard from Bertl that Mara had become a peace activist. I now see my time with Bertl taught me to be an activist of another kind. I, too, believe in peace and abhor nuclear weaponry. But Bertl's greatest lesson for me was about forgiveness, about understanding, and about "passing it on." Today, I try to express these values in my writing. In my life, I try to live them.

Bertl Gaye, my Austrian bodhisattva, will always remain a shining silver light in my memories of England.

VIOLET

In 1961 we returned from Europe after three years in England and nine months in Paris, France. Our eldest child Corinne was born and six years later the twins Joshua and Gabrielle. When Cori was eighteen months old, we moved from Palo Alto, where Jim was attending graduate school at Stanford, to Santa Cruz, where we still live today.

One day my nephew who was going to University of California-Berkeley came over to visit. It was 1971. He was taking a sociology course and, for the first time in his life outside of talk in the family, had heard about Manzanar.

"Aunty," he said, "You know I was born in Manzanar and I don't know anything about the place. Can you tell me about it?"

"Sure," I said, "but why don't you ask your folks?" I felt no hesitancy in talking about the internment camp and wondered why he couldn't get information from them.

"I have, Aunty, but they seem reluctant to talk about it. Like I shouldn't be asking or there's some skeleton in the closet."

That's strange, I thought. I then began telling him about life in camp—about the schools, the outdoor movie theater, baseball games, judo pavilion, dances, and beautiful rock gardens. Whenever my family got together and we happened to talk about camp, we would joke about the lousy food, the dust storms or the communal showers, or we talked lightheartedly about recreational activities. I reiterated the same stories to my nephew in the same superficial way.

He looked at me intently, as if never seeing me before. "Aunty, you're telling me all these bizarre

"Our twins, Gabrielle and Joshua, with friend Rebecca at Cori's wedding in Santa Cruz," 1991

Jeanne and Jim on their twenty-fifth wedding anniversary, 1982

things. I mean, how did you *feel* about being locked up like that?"

For a moment I was stunned. He asked me a question no one had ever asked before, a question I had never dared to ask myself. Feel? How did I feel? For the first time I dropped the protective cover of humor and nonchalance. I allowed myself to "feel." I began to cry. I couldn't stop crying.

He was shocked. What had he done to send me into hysterics? I was embarrassed, and when I gained control of myself, told him I would talk to him some other time. But now I understood his parents' reluctance to discuss too deeply the matter of the internment.

At the time, I was "aunty" to thirty-six nieces and nephews. Seven had been born in camp. I realized none knew about their birthplace, Manzanar. Since it seemed too painful to talk about it, perhaps I could write a memoir, a history—just for the family.

I had not written for years. I tried to begin. But I found myself in tears, unable to concentrate. Was I having a nervous breakdown? It was apparent my nephew's innocent question, a question he had a right

to ask, had opened a wound I had long denied ever existed.

I turned to Jim. "I'm having trouble writing this memoir."

"What memoir is this?" I hadn't told him about my project. "What seems to be the problem?"

Embarrassed, I explained, "I can't stop crying whenever I try to write about Manzanar. I think I'm going crazy."

"Let's talk about it," he said, now intrigued.

Through tears I told him what I could. I was emotionally honest for the first time. I remembered feelings—of loss, of shame and humiliation, of rage, of sorrow. He sat quietly, listening. Then he said, "I have known you for almost twenty years, married to you for fourteen . . . and I never had any idea you carried all this around. This is not something to write just for your family. It's a story everyone in America should read."

Thus began our collaboration of *Farewell to Manzanar* and my return to writing. We spent a year working together; I talked for hours into a tape recorder; we interviewed family and other internees; we researched the libraries.

When the book was published in 1973, my life changed. The year spent delving into those three years of my childhood and its aftermath was as powerfully therapeutic as years with a psychiatrist. I reclaimed pride in my heritage. I rediscovered my ability to write. I realized I could no longer hide "in the country of my husband's shadow." With Jim's encouragement and support, I left the comfortable safety zone of domesticity and ventured out into the open field. I began to write again.

Violet. Ah! Violet. My favorite color. A mix of red and blue. How fitting that the red of my happiest childhood memories and the blue of Hawaii and marriage should fuse to produce the "violet" period of my life! Red for groundedness, strength, yin power. Blue for expression, communication, yang power. Violet for spirit, the fusion of yin and yang.

I don't know whatever happened to Jessica, my friend from Hillcrest Juvenile Hall. I hope she is an accomplished artist someplace. Wherever she is, I wish her a "colorful" life and thank her for the friendship which inspired this memoir.

BIBLIOGRAPHY

(With husband, James D. Houston) *Farewell to Manzanar: A True Story of Japanese American Experience during and after the World War II Internment* (nonfiction), Houghton, 1973.

(With Paul G. Hensler) *Don't Cry, It's Only Thunder* (nonfiction), Doubleday, 1984.

Beyond Manzanar and Other Views of Asian-American Womanhood (bound with *One Can Think about Life after the Fish Is in the Canoe and Other Coastal Sketches,* by J. D. Houston), Capra, 1985.

Contributor:

Ethnic American Woman, Kendall-Hunt, 1978.

Asian Americans: Social and Psychological Perspectives (Science and Behavior Books), 1980.

Ethnic Lifestyles and Mental Health, University of Oklahoma, 1980.

Common Ground, Scott, Foresman, 1982.

Crossing Cultures, Macmillan, 1983.

American Childhoods, Little Brown, 1987.

Racism and Sexism, St. Martin's, 1988.

A Gathering of Flowers: Stories of Being Young in America, Harper, 1990.

American Mosaic, Houghton, 1991.

Also author of screenplay with J. D. Houston and John Korty "Farewell to Manzanar," Universal and MCA-TV, 1976; and teleplays "Barrio," with J. D. Houston, developed by National Broadcasting Co., 1978, and "The Melting Pot," developed for David Obst in conjunction with Paramount Pictures, 1980. Contributor of essays, articles, and reviews for magazines and newspapers, including *California, California Living, Der Spiegel* (Hamburg), *Dialogue* (international edition), *Los Angeles Times Sunday Magazine, Mother Jones, Reader's Digest* (Japan edition), *San Francisco Chronicle Sunday Book Review, San Francisco Review of Books,* and *West Magazine.*

Joanne Kyger

1934-

When fairies go flying in circles
They look like rainbows in the hills.

At the age of five my first poem was published in the literary and news magazine of the Naples Elementary School in Long Beach, California. I closed my eyes and told it to the teacher, who wrote it down. The only one in kindergarten to make it in print that year.

My family had been circling around a lot. From Vallejo, California, where I was born on November 19, 1934, to China six weeks later, to Pensacola, Florida, two and a half years later, where my sister Margaret was born, and on to Long Beach, California, where my mother's family had located in 1918, down from the Saskatchewan cold. Sister Evelyne was born there.

My father was a career navy officer from a small town in Virginia—Elkton, Virginia. We were all living in Lake Bluff, Illinois, a few years after my print debut. My father was stationed at the Great Lakes Naval Training Station nearby. I was listening to the radio one day when an announcement happened. "Daddy, Daddy, the Japanese have bombed Pearl Harbor." "You've been listening to too much Jack Armstrong." We didn't see him for three years after that.

Lake Bluff, on the shores of Lake Michigan, was a wonderful small town for a child to spend time in. I learned to do important things: read, write, ride a bike, swim. Wonderful, mysterious walks in the woods, the ravine, along the lake. Learned to play the violin, oh horror. My white cat, Pussums, returned after being dropped off at a new home forty miles away, but chose to reside at the fire station instead of our house from then on. Gradually able to read more and more, a delicious escape, traveling by train to the next town to get the newest Oz books.

Then the war was over and wounded father back, and we moved to Drexel Hill, Pennsylvania. And then after four years, back to California, to Santa Barbara, to a white house with a pink band around it. My parents separated—a relief not to hear the fights. In high school I was academically superior but socially inept, lacked cashmere sweaters and

Joanne Kyger with Arthur Okamura, 1978

socks. The poet Leland Hickman and I wrote for the school newspaper's feature page. He was sophisticated, worldly to me, but was also able to laugh at my pieces, like "From Dinah Shore to Dinosaur," about Mr. Meen, tracer of lost bones.

Henry Brubeck, brother of the famous jazz musician Dave Brubeck, directed the high school band and orchestra. I was still sawing away on my violin, second violin, and playing in the orchestra was a social godsend for me. I never was asked out on a date in high school. More social life came from the Congregational church group I attended. Dr. Norman Gable, a professor of anthropology at Santa Barbara College, assisted with some of the youth groups at the church and showed us old Native

California Chumash campgrounds. He had assisted with the excavation of King Tut's tomb in Egypt as a young man. I became aware of how recent the Anglo history of California was. He was also patient with my growing dissatisfaction with God, and my efforts to prove to him the lack of existence of same.

I was working part time at the Santa Barbara Public Library by now, and one of the librarians, under oath of secrecy, gave me Jean-Paul Sartre's *Existentialism* to read. I didn't really understand it too well, but it fueled my doubts about the Congregationalists. And when the minister had an affair with a married woman and left, well . . . hypocrisy. And church was over for me.

Santa Barbara College, located on the Riviera overlooking the town, had a beautiful small campus and cost $57 a semester, so I could afford to attend. I really was interested in learning "things of the mind" now. Many of the students were Korean veterans on the GI Bill and it gave the campus a more adult tone.

Philosophy taught by Paul Wienpahl caught my heart and attention. Armed with rebuttals for the classical proofs for the existence of God from Bertrand Russell's *History of Western Philosophy*, I made a last foray on organized religion and made an appointment with a Franciscan father at the large Santa Barbara "Mother" Mission. He told me I needed "faith," so I was never part of that grandiose edifice.

I was meeting some exciting students who believed in "art." "My brother is a published poet, Victor M. Di Suvero." I had never heard of him, but I was impressed. Mark Di Suvero and I competed in philosophy class and fought over books on reserve in the library. Even though he was more bohemian, I had a more subtle understanding, thought I, and stopped riding around in his funky truck. I got an *A*, and he got a *B*. He moved into a tree house and started being a sculptor.

I met the Mountain Drive people north of Santa Barbara who pressed their own grapes by jumping up and down naked in a huge vat of them. A definitely more relaxed way of living; they were glamorous artists.

*

I am not doing very well in freshman English. I have a snotty little column I write for the college newspaper called "Easy Come." My English teacher, Hugh Kenner, takes one of them personally:

> I had a most enlightening conversation the other day—in fact it was a turning point in my IQ—when I learned about the Real and Finer things in life. Through a professor I became involved in conversation with a real Intellectual. I know he was a real one because 1) he hadn't washed or shaved, 2) he wore sandals without socks, 3) his sweater, which he had on inside out, looked like it had housed a homecoming game for some moth colony, and 4) over the sad depression of his nose, he wore horn-rimmed glasses.
>
> I was wonderfully and fearfully awed. This caused me to leer in a manner which I was sure would impress even the most forlorn Existentialist. To place myself on intellectual ground, I started to meander glibly about a well written story I had read. His pipe froze momentarily in mid-air when I asked him if he had seen it. Whereupon he crisply told me he never read anything but imported magazines and added that he didn't read well written stories—it just isn't done. Are streams of consciousness well written? No. Well that's what truly artistic pieces are and it takes real feeling to understand them. It's not everyone that can understand bastardized Joyce.

In Shanghai, 1937

I am not thinking of Hugh Kenner at all when I write this, but he gives me a *D* anyway, because I cannot spell, do not proofread my papers, and write down the first thing that comes into my head. Later on, when I have learned some self-discipline, he is more accommodating in terms of grades, and I learn some Ezra Pound and Yeats from him. T. S. Eliot has already become my favorite writer because of his world-weary attitude. Thoreau's "lives of silent despair" also fits nicely into my scheme of things.

A group of students get together to start a literary magazine, but I am too shy to show my rough, emotional outpourings. I have no skill in channeling this energy, but poetry appeals to me. I am, however, vociferous about everyone else's work, and a small magazine does get published.

*

The campus had moved to Goleta by the fall of 1954 and become part of the University of California. One of the first buildings erected there was the library, a big, spacious, modern building. I worked part time there until they told me I was not librarian material, which I wasn't. But I had moved out of my mother's house when I was nineteen and needed a part-time job to support my frugal student existence. So I went to work for an insurance company and held this job until I graduated. Although I didn't really ever graduate, being one unit short. I had held off taking biology until my last year, a graduation requirement, but could not pass the biology laboratory class. I was ready to go to San Francisco by then, so just went on. It turns out I never needed that degree for any job I ever applied for.

My interest in philosophy continued in school, especially the works of Heidegger and Wittgenstein. I was able to write short, concise papers for my teachers. A small group of the faculty with similar intellectual bents met together and advised a small group of students. I was one of these students in the tutorial program. I could choose a subject and find a teacher to meet with. It was casual and easygoing, which biology lab was not, being composed of items to memorize.

Another marvelous teacher for me was Howard Warshaw of the art department, and part of the group of cubist painters who gathered around Rico Lebrun, in California. The first and only painting class I took of his, he asked us to paint an object in the cubist manner. I didn't know how to, so I asked my friend Nemi Frost to do it for me. She had taught herself how to draw and paint and had a playful primitive manner with a tinge of Aubrey Beardsley, which I much admired. "This is not cubism!" said Howard Warshaw. So I traced a few Picasso drawings and was able to execute my favorite ceramic pitcher in the approved style. I was much enamored of Warshaw's manner and sophistication. Fortunately his wife was amused and worldly. I certainly would hate being a faculty wife. From my journal: *"He says he likes to draw me. I wonder how he feels."* Someone told me they had seen one of those sketches of me in New York City last year, wearing my grey Lanz dress and black Capezio slippers. *"His sketches make me look long and magic. He says he is studying El Greco. I kept smiling to myself today and had a difficult time keeping a straight face thinking about last night. Nemi and I went to Jerry's house, who is a potter on Mountain Drive. We all stayed, drinking red wine, because his wife Bonnie was away on her vacation. A very German friend named Albert came over and became very drunk and drew Nemi's portrait in the front of Jerry's new Morris Graves book, with a toothbrush dipped in ink. 'What have you done to my book?!' 'You should be honored.'"*

I had found an apartment in San Francisco, over La Rocca's Bar on Columbus Avenue. Packing up an old borrowed station wagon with all my books and precious objects, but no furniture, I drove up one day in January 1957 with my Siamese cat. I got a job at Brentano's at The City of Paris in downtown San Francisco. I wore a hat and gloves when I applied for the job to work as secretary to the manager.

I met my first San Francisco poet, Kirby Doyle. We went to see Lawrence Ferlinghetti read his poem "Autobiography" at the Poet's Follies. Then Kirby wrote his autobiography which sounded just like Ferlinghetti's and got very mad when I told him so. So we didn't speak for a year.

*

The *Howl* obscenity trial is happening, spring 1957. I visit City Lights Bookstore and buy a copy and fall in love with the writing, the tone, the truth. I read *On the Road* while a friend drives me in his car out of San Francisco up to the Russian River into the redwoods. I look out the window occasionally but I am too busy reading this wild adventure to notice much my first trip north.

The Beat Generation, the San Francisco Renaissance, is dramatically in the air, most especially in North Beach, which I visit every night in my red Capezio slippers with silver buckles. I have them reheeled every two weeks. I drink devastating martinis and hear Kenneth Rexroth and Lawrence Fer-

Halloween, 1957: Ebbe Borregaard, Jack Spicer, Joanne Kyger, and Joe Dunn

linghetti read poetry with jazz at The Cellar. My friend Nemi Frost has moved up from Santa Barbara. Nemi has lived in Mallorca and met Robert Creeley and the painter John Altoon, and tells me mad stories of her adventures there. I am starting to get a picture of a certain kind of world.

A friend from The City of Paris, a young painter named Jerome Mallman, takes me to The Place, a famous writer and poets' bar run by Leo Krikorian, formerly a student at Black Mountain College. This is where it's really happening. Champagne $4 a fifth and beer 25¢ a glass. Black Mountain College in North Carolina had closed the year before, which brought a group of young writers to form a group around Robert Duncan and Jack Spicer: John Wieners, Joe Dunn, Michael Rumaker, Ebbe Borregaard. And Paul Alexander and Tom Field, painters. Also, George Stanley from San Francisco, Russell Fitzgerald from Pennsylvania, Harold and Dora Dull from the northwest, and David Meltzer up from Venice, California.

Joe Dunn and John Wieners nickname me "Miss Kids" because I call everyone "Kids" and invite me to the Sunday afternoon poetry group that Jack Spicer and Robert Duncan were "teaching." They usually went like this: Jack and Robert would read whatever current work they were writing. Sometimes Robert would be writing a poem while Jack was reading. Most often, Jack's poems would be addressed to someone there in the group, some of whom had been in his Magic Workshop class earlier that spring. Then the younger writers would read whatever they had

written. Jack was a serious listener and the poem would be read two or three times. Does it sound "true"?

David Meltzer, who was involved in the poetry and jazz scene at The Cellar, wrote rather long and somewhat undisciplined pieces at that time. One poem was so long he had to stand on a chair to read it. When he turned it over to read the other side, Jack and Robert rushed forward and set the bottom of the page on fire. These meetings were very lively, with large amounts of red wine being consumed in whatever containers were available—jars, saucepans, etc. Then I was told by George Stanley that "some people are just coming here and treating this like a party." That was me and my friend Nemi Frost. "You can take a girl out of Santa Barbara, but you can't take Santa Barbara out of a girl," Jack was always saying. These poetry occasions were not to be considered frivolously. If I was to participate, I would have to read my poems.

I had been hesitantly writing the past nine months, simple pieces, childhood memories. The reading was at Ebbe Borregaard's the Sunday afternoon I read. I remember James Broughton was there and, when I finished reading, said, "Wonderful." Spicer said, "What are your plans for poetry?" Harold Dull said, "Shh, leave her alone." One of the most important initiations I ever had. After that I wrote "The Maze," the first poem in my book *The Tapestry and The Web*. I had attained a "voice."

Jack Spicer was very anti-Beat, disliking the publicity he thought they were seeking. When Allen Ginsberg read from *Kaddish* to a large gathering sponsored by the Poetry Center, we all attended. Jack said to me, "You like this stuff?" and made us all walk out! This was Allen's return to San Francisco after *Howl*, and the exit gave him a nervous breakdown—Spicer's little saucy, campy group. Spicer also didn't believe in publishing in any of the new magazines which were appearing, except for Don Allen's *Evergreen Review*, #2, on the San Francisco Renaissance. Don Allen was an editor at Grove Press and an old friend of Spicer's from Berkeley days. Jack didn't believe in City Lights Bookstore either, and refused to let any of his White Rabbit Books or *J* magazine, when he started to publish them, be distributed there. They were disseminated from his base camp, The Place.

Joe Dunn founded the White Rabbit Press, at Spicer's suggestion, to print the work of the group, using the AM Multilith at the Greyhound bus lines press building. From November '57 to September '58 he produced ten titles: the works of Steve Jonas,

Robert Duncan, Harold Dull, Richard Brautigan, Helen Adam, Charles Olson, and Jack Spicer. Though not fine printing, they were of artistically high standard with covers and illustrations by Robert Duncan and Jess Collins. *J* magazine was mimeographed and contained the work of Ebbe Borregaard, Richard Brautigan, George Stanley, Jim Alexander, Helen Adam, Ron Loewinsohn, Don Allen, John Ryan, Robert Duncan, etc., and myself! My first real poem in print! The world changed. I thought people on the street looked at me differently.

*

So sometimes at The Place it is 25¢ for beer and sometimes 25¢ for poetry, the price of the White Rabbit books. Tour buses go by The Place at night to watch the Beatniks. Alfred Aronowitz of the *New York Post* comes out to do a series of pieces on the Beat Generation writers. He interviews Ebbe Borregaard at The Place who says, "You see that table? That's called the Poet's Table. That's because all the famous poets of the San Francisco Renaissance sit there. Jack Kerouac used to sit there. Allen Ginsberg used to sit there."

At the Poet's Table on this night are several persons, only two of them poets. One is a girl, blonde and beautiful. She sits at the head of the table talking incessantly, not caring who is listening to her, and often not listening to herself. "Oh, I hate repartee," the girl is saying. "It's so wasteful. . . ." "She doesn't stop talking unless she's reading her own poems," the poet puts in.

"Why is it," the girl asks the poet, "that I never see you and Robert at the same time?"

"That's because he's an extension of my personality," the poet answers.

Soon another poet, young and lithe, walks in and draws up a chair next to the girl. He is followed by several others, all similarly young and all similarly lithe. They sit about the girl, talking to her, seeking her attention, diverting it from the others. Soon she rises and leaves with them.

"They're not trying to make it with her," one of the group says. "They're faggots. She's a queen bee—you know, a faggot's moll. I have a theory that all of San Francisco is a faggot's moll. They're only attracted to her because they want to *be* like her."

*

I felt this a dreadful portrait of myself. Hell-bent, the times escalated for me. Especially the time of

Jack Spicer, Ebbe Borregaard, and Joanne Kyger

night I went to bed, not wanting to miss a single thing. And then up to work in the morning. Eventually I ran down Telegraph Hill and broke my ankle, and had an enforced retirement in a cast for five months. Thus I was unable to flit around and met Gary Snyder, after he had returned from his first trip to Japan, in a seated position in The Place, with crutches and a painted cast halfway up my thigh.

Gary came to our Sunday poetry group and read from *Myths & Texts*, sitting cross-legged on a table, with Jack Spicer sitting cross-legged *under* the table, like a troll under a bridge. Jack decided Gary's poetry more than "passed" although he still considered him a "Boy Scout." But I think Gary's poetry is wonderful, grounded, healthy.

I soon visited Gary's Mill Valley cabin, home of the Dharma Bums and Old Angel Midnight. It was a beautiful, rustic, restful place. San Francisco was wearing me down, my first experience of living in a city. My apartment over the bar had accordion and piano music rising through the floor every weekend until two A.M.. And old Papa La Rocca, of the old world, gave horrible penetrating stares from the bar window every time my "lithe" friends went in and out of my entrance next door. John Wieners, whom I called Pip, visited and stayed with me a lot, making toast, and giving himself facials and trying on my sandals and scarves. He was a most accomplished and soulful lyric poet and typed out his *Hotel Wentley Poems* there. He was my most tender friend, giving me Charles Olson's *Projective Verse* to study. He thought that in madness was freedom and magic, and stepped across the edge and couldn't speak to me or anyone else for a long while. "Oh for the days of Marie Laurencin. Oh for the days of 'Miss Kids,'" he would shout.

Lew Welch arrived one day when I was at Gary's cabin and hung up his wedding ring on a nail by the door. "That's over," he said. Energetic, funny, sharp, we liked each other at once. He offered to read and critique my poems. "He isn't interested in your *poetry,*" Gary said. An attitude he never entirely lost.

"Wait until you meet Philip Whalen," Gary said. Lew, Gary, and Philip had all roomed together at Reed College. My first meeting with Philip was disastrous. We went to a Chinatown restaurant, Gary and I, with Philip just after he had come down from Washington State. I was prattling on about how to use chopsticks and Philip stormed out saying, "I cannot stand girls like you, sorority type," etc. Food was a serious matter with him. I wasn't sure what I had done but apologized abjectly the next time I saw him and we became friends forevermore.

*

Gary moves into my apartment after the first of the year, 1959, to find a boat to work on that will take him to Japan. I have many debts to pay, like a huge charge account at Macy's, but after I have paid those and gotten a ticket, we decide I will come to Japan and study Japanese and Zen. An undertaking not to be taken lightly, I must "earn" my way there. For my fractured consciousness, Zen Buddhism seems to me the only path out of the "nothingness" of Western philosophy. I *need* to find that discipline, that art form.

After Gary's going-away party the La Rocca brothers, mounting the steps shoulder to shoulder to my apartment, tell me I am too noisy and must leave. I decide to move to the East-West House, a communal house over on California Street, where people interested in going to Japan live. They have a small library of Buddhist books, share cooking, and divide up expenses at the end of the month. It is very economical. Lew Welch is already living here, along with some other friendly people.

The most important thing to happen to me before I move is my first public poetry reading—part of a series at Pierre Delattre's Bread and Wine Mission on upper Grant Avenue. Saturdays at nine, during February and March 1959, feature Jack Spicer, Daniel Langton, Robert Duncan, Lew Welch, and myself. I go into a frenzy trying to figure out what is suitable to read. I write to Philip, who has

gone north again, about my predicament of standards. He writes back saying he is returning to the Bay Area to institute an era of "kindness and good will" and will try and be there for my reading. And at four o'clock on the afternoon of March 7, the day of the reading, he presents himself in my doorway, green pineapple in hand, "come to San Francisco forever." It is a festive afternoon and evening as I write of it in a letter to Gary:

> . . . Tom Field was there buying imported beer and wine all day to keep the spirit high. He and Philip had a fine time eating raw hamburger and drinking while I in a last minute sensibility was typing some of my poems into readability. I began to have apprehensions when Jack Spicer and Ebbe Borregaard came over to "help" me get to the reading. Jack was trying to convince me that it was "fashionable" to be late for one's own reading. All he really wanted to do was stay and drink my "fashionable" Madera Rainwater. But at last all six of us got on our way. Except that after I shut and locked the door, Jack Spicer found the telephone cord still wrapped around his leg, which he thought was spaghetti. Stan Persky had arrived an hour before and Philip threw the new *Evergreen Review* at him because he was asking too many questions. I was exhausted when I got there because Jack Spicer had his arm around my neck all the way up Greenwich Street. But the reading was just fine. Your mother was there, and she wanted to have a reading too. And she showed me her photographs—many reflections in mud puddles.

A lot of my attention in learning to write poetry had to do with the line, how to get your voice on the page. I wrote, *"Finding your voice in poetry is equivalent to finding yourself."* I had read William Carlos Williams's *Patterson,* Book V, which made a great impression. Finished reading it standing up on the bus home from work. *"He allows the poem to contain so much, letters, quotations, poetry of others, and it works so beautifully!"* I was moved to start a letter-poem to him, but never sent it, and went on to write more poems, clinging to his relevant soul of beauty.

I paid $15 a month for my tiny room at the East-West House which I filled with plants and flowers, even though it was rather dark. Shared cooking expenses came to about $36 a month for the dinners we took turns cooking. I really didn't think I could cook, but tuna casserole seemed to be acceptable to them. I learned how to sit Zen-style meditation. The Buddhist church nearby had a new priest from Japan, Shunryu Suzuki, who had a very early morning meditation class. Although Suzuki couldn't speak English then, his sweet and active pantomimes showed us what to do. Bill McNeill, another former

Black Mountain student, brought me over there and introduced me at 5:30 one morning, and I presented him with some small pink rosebuds. Bill kept on studying with Suzuki Roshi and finally went on to Japan where I met up with him a few years later. It was often hard to get up in the morning, especially since I found the social life of the East-West House fascinating. Living there at the time were Philip Whalen, Gai-fu Feng, Claude Dahlenburg, Lew Welch, Mertis and Brian Shekeloff, Albert Saijo, and many visitors. It was far away from North Beach, but still active in late-night conversations. So many people moved into the house they started an overflow house a few blocks away on Buchanan Street called the Hyphen House—the hyphen between East-West.

Our Sunday poetry group gradually dismantled. Robert Duncan and Jess Collins had moved to Stinson Beach and nobody wanted to ride the bus all the way over to California and Fillmore, where I lived. I did say, "Look, we can do this without Spicer," since he was so solidly in North Beach, but it didn't work. By now, any time Philip would write something in his notebook, I would read it as soon as he left the room.

His writing became a focus for me. What was he talking about, was it about me? Why did it sound so graceful and funny, how did he do it, what was the shorthand? And Lew Welch polished his lines out loud, over and over, spoken speech.

During this year Ruth Fuller Sasaki, who was Gary's sponsor in Japan and ran the First Zen Institute in Kyoto, which hired him part-time, made it clear that I could not come and "live" with Gary. We would have to marry. So he proposed marriage in the mail and things seemed to be a little more formal for the future. I bought a black wool dress with a scooped neckline for a wedding dress. Practical basic black so I could wear it many times over.

Leaving for Japan was a big step for me, leaving all my friends. I packed a big trunk, including my collection of Capezio shoes in labeled boxes (which were to prove utterly unsuitable), and boarded the *Nichiharu-maru* in Long Beach on January 29, 1960. It was a twenty-two-day crossing and a good transition time, complete with Japanese baths. The only other passenger on the freighter was a young Japanese girl who had been going to school in California. She was

At Nemi Frost's painting show, Buzz Gallery: Ernie Edwards, Bill Brodecky, Paul Alexander, Joanne Kyger, Jack Boyce, (seated) Nemi Frost

Joanne and Gary Snyder, 1961

very droll and explained to me that "in Japan you eat with your eyes" when everything fell out of my chopsticks.

When we docked in Yokohama, Gary came on board and gave me a big kiss. I hadn't seen him for a year, although our correspondence had been intense. We went back to his little cottage in the countryside near Kyoto, and were married three days later at the American Consulate's office in Kobe. Five days later on Sunday, February 28, we were married again by Gary's Zen teacher Oda Roshi, Chief Abbot of Daitoku-ji, a large and beautiful complex of temples in Kyoto. Madame Ruth Fuller Sasaki had rebuilt and refurbished one of these temples which became Ryosen-an, the home for the Zen Institute in Kyoto. There was a small *zendo* in which foreigners could practice meditation, a library building where the translation projects she was involved with went on, and her own comfortable Japanese-style home. Buddhism in Japan usually had nothing to do with marriage ceremonies, which traditionally took place in a Shinto shrine. Buddhism took over the ceremonies of the last rites for the dead. This was true to

such a degree that Buddhist priests were often facetiously referred to as "high-class undertakers." But Oda Roshi had devised a simple ceremony which took place in the monastery's main Buddha hall.

I arrived on the back of Gary's motorcycle in my black dress and pearls, early enough to dab off the dust. We knelt on red brocade cushions and then Oda Roshi read from a large sheet of heavy white paper, an announcement in formal language addressed to the founder of Daitoku-ji and the successive patriarchs of the line, the guardian gods, and our ancestors, that this union was to take place. "You must never be forgetful of the benefactions of the nation or of the Buddha." Only I couldn't understand what was going on since it was spoken in Japanese of the most formal sort. There was a flower arrangement on the altar of pine boughs and spring flowers.

The reception was next door at Mrs. Sasaki's. In her words, we had a traditional American wedding menu—chicken salad, crab-meat salad, many kinds of sandwiches, coffee, fresh strawberry ice cream, and wedding cake—the traditional cake four stories high and topped with a miniature bride and groom. Mrs. Sasaki was a great "traditional" cook from Evanston, Illinois.

A little earlier, at the monastery gate, photographers were waiting. Somehow both the Japanese and American press had gotten hold of the news of the wedding, which was unusual for its time. It made the wire service in the United States and there were lots of articles: BEATNIK POET TAKES U.S. BRIDE IN JAPAN, S.F.'S GARY SNYDER MARRIED IN JAPAN, POET MARRIES VALLEJO GIRL IN ZEN RITUAL, LOCAL GIRL MARRIES S.F. POET IN JAPAN, EX COPY BOY PENS POEMS GETS MARRIED.

"Snyder lives in a three-room Japanese house on the outskirts of Kyoto. He draws water from a well and cooks with a wood stove. He chops the wood himself." And from the English-language newspaper in Japan, the *Mainichi*--YOUNG U.S. COUPLE GO NATIVE TO LEARN ZEN, LOCAL CULTURE. "There is no gas or running water. The simple farmhouse Joanne now lives in is a far cry from her home in America which she left only a few weeks ago. It was quite a change for Joanne, but she is determined." We were a part of a small foreign community in Kyoto studying the Japanese arts who often lived a more primitive life than the modern-minded Japanese—trying to shut ourselves off from the "material" world to study traditional culture.

So I studied Japanese conversation, flower arranging, practiced meditation, and visited with other members of the foreign community there. I didn't have a lot of Japanese friends, language was always a problem.

My friend Bill McNeill moved to Kyoto from Eiheiji, head temple of the Soto Zen school, where he had been ordained as a monk. He had been feeling isolated and needed some of the cultural liveliness of the city. Bill loved to party and I remember he arrived with a friend once just as a major typhoon was about to hit, with supplies for a big celebration. I was too worried to do that. Roof tiles flew off, the fence blew down, windows broke, the house shook, it was scary. By this time Gary and I had moved from the country house to a place north of Daitoku-ji with running water and electricity. We shared it with Mrs. Hosaka, who lived quietly in the upstairs room and studied tea ceremony. She was formal and always wore kimonos and must have thought I was a bossy American woman. I was quite outspoken in discussions with Gary and far away from what was traditionally expected of Japanese women. She now lives sometimes at Green Gulch Zen Center near Muir Beach and teaches tea ceremony there in a Japanese-style building which incorporates some of the decorative wood pieces of the Kyoto house. Dick Baker, then abbot of the San Francisco Zen Center, spent some time in that Kyoto house before it was torn down to make room for an apartment building. He rescued those architectural details and brought them along with Mrs. Hosaka to Green Gulch. She was always very tenacious about living in that place.

I taught conversational English for a living, as did many of the Americans there. Occasionally I had an English-speaking part in the low-budget Japanese films that were being made around then. Once I was a nun in a film about gangsters and spoke in Japanese. In another I was a belle of the last-century Meiji period and sang ballads in a Yokohama saloon until there was a barroom brawl and the scene ended. I sang, "At night in bed, I sought my love, I sought him but could not find him," etc. I didn't sing very well. The director was either laughing or crying, his shoulders shaking. Lotte Lenya through the meat grinder.

In December of 1961 Gary and I took off for a six-month trip to India. We had prepared for the trip for some time, planning an itinerary which took us through the historical Buddhist sites in Ceylon, India, and Nepal. "Don't go with the stink of Zen," Gary's teacher told him. A French passenger line which stopped at ports throughout Southeast Asia and India provided a reasonable bunk and lots of food. I bought a smart, French yellow raincoat in Hong Kong, a stylish mistake. I was always washing it, along with my one black drip-dry outfit. We traveled with rucksacks and sleeping bags.

We planned to meet up with Allen Ginsberg and Peter Orlovsky, which we finally did in New Delhi at the end of February. They both had let their hair grow very long, a new style. We traveled to Rishikesh and then Hardwar, where we saw hundreds of naked *saddhus* covered with ashes, parading into the Ganges. Then up to Almora to visit Lama Govinda, a German who followed the path of Tibetan Buddhism, and then on to Dharamsala to meet the Dalai Lama. India was so unexpectedly beautiful, exotic, historical, wonderful. It wasn't until I left that I understood that the beggars holding out stumpy fingers had leprosy. But constant traveling was tiring and we were happy when we docked on May 8, Gary's birthday, at Kobe, and caught a train home. Kyoto did seem like home. This trip has been detailed in Gary's *Passage through India* and my *Japan and India Journals*.

*

Later on that year Don Allen, who has just edited the *New American Poetry,* visits Kyoto. He is marvelous, witty company. We admire each other's treasures. I have become very interested in Mingei, or Japanese folkcraft pottery, and buy a beautiful big blue bowl with red spots which Don still offers to baby-sit when I go on trips.

Philip Whalen asks me for some poems for *Foot* magazine, edited by Bill Brown and Richard Duerden, and they get published immediately. I am still not sure what makes a poem "good" or not, but my line is confident and that to my mind is what differentiates one poet from another.

Cid Corman is living in Kyoto during this time, publishing *Origin* magazine, which could be had for "love not for money." He is very particular about his editing, finding poets whose work is not always available and publishing large chunks of it—Lorine Niedecker, Louis Zukofsky, Gary. I give my poems to Cid to read and receive a strict and unenthusiastic critical response. I am devastated. "I told you not to," says Gary.

Allen Ginsberg arrives in the rain one day in June for his first trip to Japan on his way back from India. Mrs. Sasaki takes to him at a dinner at her house, even though she has been critical of the Beats and their "fox" Zen. He has already eaten one dinner before he arrives so he can talk more. But he is sincere and sits meditation with the monks in the monastery *zendo.* When it starts to get to be too much for him he sings the "Star Spangled Banner" at the top of his unvoiced lungs.

Gary and I decide to return to the United States for a year and I embark on a President Lines ship on January 20, 1964, four years after I have arrived. Gary will follow later, and find a boat on which to work his way across. When I land in San Francisco, Philip Whalen is there at the dock, and I am knocked out by all the California faces. Fantastic culture shock—I am no longer in the minority and too tall. I hear from Don Allen, who wants to print a book of my poetry. I am lauded and feted.

The Beatles are in the air. Richard Brautigan and I sit at Vesuvio's and memorize their names and pictures—that's John, and that's Paul. We write a letter with Jack Spicer to Ringo Starr. Everything is hilarious and fun. My tension, my ulcer, go away. I don't think I ever want to return to Japan. I'll never be disciplined enough to follow the strict path Gary is on. Japanese culture at this time is restrictive for me, but I realize Gary has a feeling and commitment to

what he is doing there in his Buddhist studies that are not accessible to me. So we separate once he returns and get a divorce. The lawyer gets my story mixed up with his other client at our court date with the judge. *She* is the one who had to carry seventy-six buckets of water from the well to the bath. I never minded doing that, but one had to have a reason in those days besides mutual consent.

Stan Persky starts publishing his magazine *Open Space* once a month for the year of 1964. I go back to the Odyssey and write a series of poems based on that Homeric adventure, mixing it with mine. "I think you're still in the maze," Spicer says. Gino and Carlo's in North Beach is now the center of the poets' scene and new faces have arrived. Larry Fagin tells me he has been rehearsing how to meet me. He has been considering a water pistol filled with black ink. Stan Persky is now living with Robin Blaser, having resolved his sexual identity. We had had long talks about it four years before. It is a very talkative, political time, with schisms and nasty poetry infighting. An anti-Don Allen anthology parody is published in *Open Space.* Gary goes over and takes a poke at Stan who is bartending at The Anxious Asp, defending Don's honor as editor.

Bill McNeill has returned from Japan and is making a movie, but the plot keeps changing and no one can figure out what it's about. Helen Adam is a star. I do something like acting covered in green taffeta by the ocean with some scuba divers. Bill is sharing a place with the painter Ken Botto, Lew Welch, and his buddy Jack Boyce. The latter two had met up in the Trinity Alps where they had gone to get away from the pressures of civilization. Jack and I get along well and we get a place together near Bill's. Lots of comings and goings of poetry friends. We listen to Robert Duncan read his long piece on H.D. "What do you want from me?" she asks him, now an old woman in her seventies.

The Buzz Gallery opens in Japan Town, next door to the old Hyphen House, run by Paul Alexander and Larry Fagin, where they put on a series of painting shows and poetry readings. I read there and Jack Boyce has a show of his paintings.

I work hard on getting my book for Don Allen together, *The Tapestry and The Web.* It has been set somewhat randomly by linotype and each line has to be cut out and pasted up again, a laborious tapestry-maze. It is displayed in City Light's window in the fall of 1965.

I have almost daily conversations with Richard Brautigan on the telephone, listening to what he has just written, discussing his future. Sections from *Trout Fishing in America* have been published in various magazines and *A Confederate General from Big Sur,* published by Grove Press in 1964, is being nominated for a prize. The phenomena of the Beat Generation writers springing into instant fame after publication is on his mind, and we are sure the same thing will happen to him once he wins the prize. And that life will never be the same for him and we will never have these ordinary conversations again. But he doesn't win the prize and with some embarrassment life goes on as usual. He goes on to write *In Watermelon Sugar,* which he dedicates to me and his other daily phone touchdowns, Don Allen and Michael McClure. His "fame" comes a few years later with the rise of the hippy reader.

*

About this time Dick Baker, working with Tom Parkinson, professor in the English department at Berkeley, Don Allen, and Robert Duncan, started to plan the Berkeley Poetry Conference, and invited me to read. It was fraught with poetry politics from the beginning and it was only through Baker's diplomacy that it happened at all. A few years ago a woman writer told me, "I hated you, you were the only woman invited to read." However, Lenore Kandel was later included in an open reading. About thirty-four poets participated in lectures, symposiums, and readings. Among them Allen Ginsberg, Gary Snyder, Robert Creeley, Charles Olson, Jack Spicer, John Wieners, Richard Duerden, Robin Blaser, and George Stanley. Philip Whalen and Michael McClure had been invited to read only, and not give a lecture or be on a symposium. Michael thought that not seemly in terms of their experience, and persuaded Philip to drop out with him. I had been scheduled to read with Philip, but now I was to read with Lew Welch. Lew, when he got emotional over his writing often used to weep, and I didn't want him to ruin the reading by crying. I begged Philip by phone to reconsider, Dick Baker at my elbow, but he had made his decision. And Lew didn't cry. The Poetry Conference, July 12-24, 1965, was described as the greatest mass gathering of poets in the history of the country. I met and heard for the first time Ted Berrigan, Ed Sanders, and Jim Koller. A time of cross-current excitements. Charles Olson performed his great filibuster at his "reading." He and John Wieners had just flown in from Spoleto's Festival of Two Worlds, where they had read with Ezra Pound. John brought me a photograph of all these beautiful profiles—himself, Pound, John Ashbery, Bill Berkson. Olson's energy was very unfocused, although tremendous,

and he never seemed to finish a thought or sentence, and never completely read a poem all the way through. It was rather unnerving as a power bid. "I'm right here, Boss!" shouted Ed Sanders. It went on until the university guards turned off the lights and closed the building.

Jack Spicer's reading at the Berkeley Poetry Conference was his last public reading. He died at San Francisco General Hospital, August 17, after being found in a hepatic coma two weeks earlier. We had visited him in the hospital, but he was delirious and spoke cryptically. He was only forty years old, and was my first important teacher, friend, who had ever died. There was a wake at Robin Blaser's and we met Jack's mother and brother, who put us at our ease, they were so sweet and normal. Richard Brautigan called and asked me to take a perfect rose to Mrs. Spicer since no one had personally invited him, and I told him he had to bring it himself. Jack had helped him considerably with *Trout Fishing in America,* polishing those short turns of phrases. Jack was a wonderful teacher—original, brilliant, impossible. "Poetry is only for poets."

Robert Duncan had submitted a poem of mine he thought very successful to *Poetry* magazine, which they accepted. A rendition of Circe and her pigs, mixed up with a camping trip to Yosemite. I felt quite firm-footed in poetry now, with a very successful reading at the Berkeley Poetry Conference, my own book published by Don Allen's Four Seasons Press, and the ultimate classic literary magazine *Poetry* accepting my work.

I read in November at a Vietnam Day Committee poetry reading at Longshoremen's Hall in San Francisco. A cross-grouping of poets focused on "Love not War," bringing together the artists and the "politicos," the beginning of flower power and "love generation" happenings.

*

Bob Dylan comes to town and plays with an *electric* band. A big change, since folk and social issue singers *had* to be acoustic before then. There is a big party after the concert at Bob LaVigne's painting studio with an expanded cast of guests invited. Ken Kesey is sitting on a couch watching his "own" movie. LSD has started to arrive socially, along with the Hell's Angels and Joan Baez. Dylan doesn't speak to anyone when he arrives and closets himself with Michael and Joanna McClure. What a snob, I think, and stop admiring him. He names his favorite poets as

San Francisco, 1969: (front row) Claude Dahlenburg, Gary Snyder, Magda Cregg,
Jim Koller (with glasses), Lew Welch, Zoe Brown, Bill Brown; (back row) Masa Snyder,
Jack Boyce, Joanne Kyger, Don Allen, Cass, Margot Doss, Philip Whalen

Rimbaud, Smokey Robinson, W. C. Fields, and Allen Ginsberg.

Philip Whalen is going to Japan, at Gary's invitation and his own initiative. Lawrence Ferlinghetti decides it would be a good time to have a group picture of the poets in front of City Lights Bookstore, since Philip is leaving. I invite Philip over for lunch before the grand occasion. Then we go to the bus stop and wait and wait and wait. When we finally get there all the pictures have been taken already. Andrew Hoyem, printer, arrives in a rented ambulance and is wheeled out on a stretcher. Then someone calls the fire department and two fire trucks arrive with sirens screaming. Vesuvio's next door does a lot of business with poets who just want to watch.

Philip's going-away party to Japan, the Philip-a-Go-Go, is another grand social event. Mod is in, clothing looks colorful and great, and there is lots of dancing, like the watusi. Don Allen shows us how to "get down."

In February of 1966 I traveled to Europe for six months with Jack Boyce. It was like going to the History of Western Art School. I wanted to see what Europe was like, where my "western culture" had come from. I also wanted to pursue the art of Paolo Uccello. I had seen a copy of his picture *The Hunt in the Woods* when in Japan and written a poem about it, published in my first book. A gentle movement into dimension, the first invention of perspective, and a way-out-of-the-flat tapestry of writing I felt involved with.

*

I travel with an Olivetti portable typewriter and write poems along the way. *Coyote's Journal* had been formed the summer before by Bill Brown and Jim Koller, and they want to publish any poems I can send them.

We travel through Spain, France, Italy, Greece, Germany, England. In Paris I receive a note from

Tom Clark, who has written me expressing interest in my work. He is working at the *Paris Review* and staying with Ron Padgett and his wife Pat, who are in Paris at the time. Tom is amusing, and very bright, and very curious about the poetry scene in San Francisco. Larry Fagin is also there and wants to show and give us his grand rap on the famous salon paintings in the Louvre before we make any opinions of our own.

I buy a little alcohol burner stove and cook in our hotel room. We stay for the month of April and I write a little novel—one chapter a day for a week. A mixture of dream continuity and everyday happenings, with some Tibetan tantra tanka's, which I have just seen, mixed in. Link Martin, another San Francisco poet, is in town, and I do a little formal reading in our hotel for him and Larry, with candles and wine. This piece is included in my next book of poems, *Places to Go,* along with a series of poems written in Rome.

In Greece, a place of much fantasy myth for me, I find the country is not green and frolicsome like I had imagined, the country where I had put Pan in a landscape of mischief. I copy down a translation of the Prayer of Socrates in the National Archaeology Museum in Athens: "Socrates: O beloved Pan and all ye other gods of this place, grant to me that I be beautiful in my soul within and that all my external possessions be in harmony with my inner man. May I consider the wise man rich and may I have such wealth as only the self-restrained man can bear or endure. Do we need anything more Phaedrus? For me that prayer is enough."

This reaches out of ancient time to me. It's religious. But just as I have finished copying it down in my notebook, the guard catches me by the arm and shouts that I must leave! No copies, photographic or otherwise. We go on to the place of the Eleusinian mysteries. I peer into an old cave, beer cans tossed about. Is this where it all happened?

In London I buy a Carnaby Street outfit and am ready to land with style in New York City. We have decided to stay there for a year so Jack can check out the painting scene. We stay with my old friend Bill McNeill who lives on the lower East Side. What a depressing place! Worse than Calcutta or Naples. I never get used to New York City.

After much searching, a loft space is found in what is now the Soho, a floor beneath the experimental filmmaker Jack Smith. I get in touch with Lewis Warsh, whom I had published when I was guest editor of *Wild Dog* magazine in San Francisco, and go over to his apartment on St. Mark's Place. Ted Berrigan is sitting there with Jim Brodey, and soon

Anne Waldman bursts in the door. Here is a poetry scene, which gives me some succor during the year I am there. But I can't find any *ground.*

Jack Smith is always pounding about overhead doing strange things. One day I am asked to sit in during a day of filming the magnum opus he is working on. I am taking the place of Charles Henri Ford, and sit in a wheelchair with a black veil over my head. Irving Rosenthal is dressed in diapers like a baby, laying in a crib, while two naked men toss him with a six-foot-long salad fork and spoon. This really increases my surreal sense of New York, which is going through its acid-generation phenomenon, one step behind the Summer of Love in San Francisco. Keith Lampe, whom I knew in Kyoto, is here, involved in anti-Vietnam War demonstrations. After the Great Human Be-In in San Francisco's Golden Gate Park happens, we decide we will have a New York City version in Central Park, which we call a Spring Out. It is highlighted for me by smoking banana peels among thousands of people.

And where is the voice of poetry coming from now in the confines of New York City 1967? Some ponderous notes: *"The linear aspect of the poem is merely a suggested voice line to take one from beginning to end, but suggesting no such consecutiveness in thought with all its layers. The area that is the poem is able to contain all elements, for what one can recognize and adhere to is the continuity, no matter where it comes from."*

Dick Baker visits with Suzuki Roshi, his teacher. They want to buy land in California, and think we may be interested in participating in buying a large tract of land in what is now called San Juan Ridge, near Nevada City. A large commitment to building a community. We don't buy this land, but Gary and Allen Ginsberg do, and Gary raises his family there. When I ask Suzuki Roshi some question during the lunch I am serving, about Buddhism, he very charmingly puts his napkin on his head and continues eating his soup. I wish I could remember the question.

I remember one grand social event in the loft when Ted Berrigan plays the tape of the interview with Jack Kerouac he is doing for the *Paris Review.* Andy Warhol comes and I show him how I have painted many things with aluminum paint, just like in his studio. He is very sweet with a shy smile. This memory gives me the patience to sit all the way through *Chelsea Girls,* watching for ages as Nico trims her bangs, one hair at a time, while talking to Gerard Malanga.

In August 1967, Jim Koller came in his pickup truck and drove us back to California. Bill Brown was living in the small coastal community of Bolinas, where he had built a house. We stayed a few days there, the first of many visits to this place which was to become my home a few years later.

I was immediately offered a year's job working on an experimental television project at KQED in San Francisco. The idea was to see how artists could translate their creations into the medium of video. At that time the equipment was quite bulky and one could not actually use a TV camera because of union regulations, so ideas had to be translated to the TV crew. Producer Brice Howard had also invited Bill Brown; Bill Allen, a painter-sculptor; Richard Felciano, composer; and Loren Sears, a filmmaker. A lot of the techniques and effects we discovered were visually startling—feedback, tape delay, etc.

My most successful piece was an eleven-minute translation of Descarte's *Discourse on Method* into video, using various techniques to visualize thoughts. "I think, hence I am. Get the picture?"

Charles Olson and Robert Creeley were also invited for a few weeks in March of 1968 to do whatever they wanted in the TV studio. Charles envisioned himself like the poets of old, tapping out his own particular voice beat with a staff. He read his more recent poems and watched himself on a monitor, which showed visual delays of a few seconds, and occasional feedback of his reading layered in. "Feedback is a whore," he said.

A little after I had returned to San Francisco, Richard Brautigan took me to Haight-Ashbury. I had left before this place had become the focal point of the hippies, and returned after it was all over. We attended its "death," a large coffin being carried up Haight Street. And what had happened to the poetry scene in San Francisco, in North Beach? Definitely very quiet. Richard had finally found his fame, though.

The next move was *where* to move in 1968. After a time in Lagunitas and Bodega Bay, we decided to buy land in Bolinas. We kept visiting friends there, Bill Brown, Dr. John, and Margot Doss. A small community was already existing there. And when Tom Clark with his wife Angelica bought a small house, we saw the beginnings of literary adventures. Arthur Okamura, painter and teacher at the California College of Arts and Crafts, had been living there with his wife, Liz, raising a family of four children since the late '50s. He and Liz had spent time with Bob Creeley in Mallorca a few years earlier. Arthur did the illustrations in a collaborative book with Bob in 1970, which ended with the lines, "I want to go home." So Creeley moved to Bolinas, which became

his home for a while, with Bobbie and their three daughters.

I was at this point sharing a house with Bill Berkson in downtown Bolinas. Bill was freshly arrived from Manhattan. Jim Herndon, an old friend of Jack Spicer's, who came out to fish, said, "Joanne, why are you hanging out with all these *New York* poets?"

By this time, Ebbe Borregaard, who was not a New York poet, was living there and building his boat, actualizing a dream which had been sitting in his Berkeley backyard for some years. Also Lewis and Phoebe MacAdams, Duncan and Genie MacNaughton and their three children, David and Tina Meltzer, Lewis Warsh, Ted Berrigan and Alice Notley, Jim Gustafson, Sara Schrom, Jim Carroll. And the literary dean of New American Poetry, Don Allen, himself, riding a bicycle.

Philip Whalen spent some years here, on and off, and shared a house one memorable summer with Joe Brainard. John Thorpe and Rene lived a real homesteading life on the mesa, raising chickens and vegetables. Aram and Gailyn lived here, moved away to live in a teepee in the wilderness, and came right back again. And Richard Duerden, Larry Kearney, Michael Wolfe. And more. But as you can see, it was very literally dense.

It was a time of inventive country living, dirt roads, no street lights, interesting plumbing, and an hour away over the coast range for shopping. Robert Duncan called us the Bolinas bucolics.

My second book, *Places to Go,* was published in 1970 by Black Sparrow Press. A few fairly good reviews. Alicia Ostriker noted in the *Partisan Review,* "Risking folly, let us propose that Joanne Kyger is a genius, though a weird one. Handling her work is like handling a porcupine traveling at the speed of light. She is not 'disciplined' but is a radically original combination of symbolist and comedienne."

This was followed by *Joanne,* a small book published by Angel Hair Press, a "novel from the inside out." During that time in the early '70s I was living in such a novel, dramatic form that writing was only in short "inner" notations: "Well I just want you to / know the truth." The cover is a Polaroid shot by Bill Berkson of me with long hair, Indian bedspread pants, and bare feet.

In 1972 I made the first of many trips to Mexico. To San Cristobal de las Casas in the state of Chiapas. A beautiful high-mountain colonial town, surrounded by various Mayan-speaking tribes whose stories were full of men who could fly and hurl thunderbolts, protected by their animal-spirit companions who lived on the mountain nearby. These people had survived the Spanish-European invasion, unlike most of the

Brighton Street House, Bolinas, 1970: Bill Berkson, Lewis Warsh, Joanne Kyger, Andrei Codrescu

native peoples of North America. Their existence helped me when I returned to California and started to search for the religious and cultural remnants of the indigenous people here on this part of the coast. Some of these Coast Miwok stories were eventually published in my book *Up My Coast.*

Bill Berkson had started Big Sky books and magazines. He published *All This Every Day* in 1975 which depicts the spacious spaciness of that time in Bolinas. Rochelle Ratner said in her review of it, "Had she put in just a little bit more effort, she could be one of the best poets writing. The frustrating point is that she seems to understand exactly what she's doing even though she can't yet rise above it."

> . . . *So*
> *much I want to drift into story land, take life*
> *a little easier.*

Having an overactive brain with nowhere to go with the overactive "stuff" of it was part of learning to live in this rural moment of "now." Bolinas was being "invented" for me, along with sterner ways of adapting to life on the land—septic tanks, town government enacted through the water board; a water moratorium with the resultant cessation of any new building permits. A small town's efforts to become politically and culturally self-suffi-

cient with awakened awareness towards the land. Bolinas became an intersection for me in which eastern and western sensibilities centered over the millions of years of unrecorded history where I was standing. So my focus and ear became attuned to this place. What *is* the ocean saying? When I first lived here I thought the sound of the ocean crashing on the reef at night was saying "Boxcars, Boxcars, Boxcars."

In October of 1974 I was invited to participate in a poetry reading in San Francisco by Chogyam Trungpa, the young Tibetan Rinpoche teaching in the United States. Allen Ginsberg had conceived of this reading in connection with a visit from Gyalwa Karmapa, the spiritual head of the Kagyu order and Trungpa's teacher. It was a large, highly charged reading, and signaled the growing of Tibetan teachings in the United States. The dramatic nature of Vajrayana Buddhism contrasted with the more somber and sober demeanor of the Zen Center in San Francisco with its Japanese-based teachings.

Naropa Institute in Boulder, Colorado, became the center for Chogyam Trungpa's teachings. Poetry was also to be part of this school, and Allen Ginsberg and Anne Waldman founded the Jack Kerouac School of Disembodied Poetics. I was invited to be an occasional teacher there, with its increasing accommodation of the lineage of "the New American Poetry." Teachers were asked to speak about themselves, their interests, and demonstrate their own personal direction and voice. It remains the most lively and contemporary school of poetry in the United States today.

It was while teaching at Naropa in 1978 that I met Donald Guravich, a writer and artist from New Brunswick, Canada. When I returned to Bolinas he joined me and we have shared a household since then.

In 1980 Kenward Elmslie published *The Wonderful Focus of You* from his Z Press.

> *Something will happen if we let it*
> *Everything happens no matter what we decide*

—my daily working philosophy.

The cover of the book is a picture taken by my neighbor Nancy Whitefield of myself at the Bolinas Sun Festival, a yearly celebration and parade in honor of our sewer ponds. We followed a route from the old downtown sewer outfall pipe at the mouth of the lagoon, paraded through town in great costume, and went on up to the mesa land, where the sewage was pumped into a series of recycling ponds, and had a party. This project was the great feat of the young, newly elected water board of the '70s, who under mandate from the state found a million-dollar solu-

Joanne Kyger and Donald Guravich, 1985

looking rather doleful, which hangs in the Bolinas Library today.

Bill died when I was on that trip. My journal from that time was published as part of the "Curriculum of the Soul" series, outlined by Charles Olson and published by Jack Clarke and Al Glover in Buffalo.

*

Most recently, Black Sparrow Press has brought out *Just Space*, a collection of my writing from 1979 on. Really a local story, mostly about what I do here. I work on the town newspaper which has come out three times a week for the past seventeen years—a kind of glue that keeps the town informed of itself. It is a place which is absorbed with itself, discouraging the casual outside visitor by lack of a road sign which says "Bolinas."

Poetry readings at the library and large group readings still happen, although the writing community is not as vibrant as it was a decade ago. Robert Grenier is among some of the more recent writers who have moved here, and a small group meets weekly with him to read new books of poetry and reread the classics. Friends move away and come back, children grow up and go away to school. A few have become poets. The weather is still the main topic of conversation.

tion for the 265 houses downtown that had heretofore dumped their effluent into the ocean.

Lewis MacAdams, also an elected water board member, and I performed a play at the main pond, when the system was officially opened. We had spent about a month writing about the history of the project and the massive oil spill that preceded it. But when we read our play, the wind whipped the words out of our mouths and no one could hear a thing. One of the more ephemeral performances, we proceeded on for twenty minutes. Finally we progressed to the champagne in the ceramic toilet container someone had brought as a celebratory gesture.

In 1984 I went with Donald on a trip to the Yucatan. My old friend Bill McNeill was very ill when I left. During his frequent visits to Bolinas he always painted. He did a life-size portrait of me outside one afternoon, posed in a long red dress, hand on a red chair, and one foot lifted, prepared to stomp down on Ignorance and Sloth. It was executed before a party of friends, Bobbie Creeley calling out the constant injunctive, "Change that tone of red!" Among his many other portraits is a large one of Robert Creeley,

BIBLIOGRAPHY

Poetry:

The Tapestry and The Web, Four Seasons Foundation, 1965.

The Fool in April: A Poem, Coyote Books, 1966.

Joanne, Angel Hair Books, 1970.

Places to Go, Black Sparrow Press, 1970.

Desecheo Notebook, Arif Press, 1971.

Trip Out and Fall Back, Arif Press, 1974.

All This Every Day, Big Sky, 1975.

(With Larry Fagin) *Lettre de Paris*, Poltroon Press, 1977.

The Wonderful Focus of You, Z Press, 1980.

Japan and India Journals 1960–1964 (with photographs by Gary Snyder and Allen Ginsberg), Tombouctou Books, 1981.

Mexico Blondé, Evergreen Press, 1981.

Up My Coast (adapted from the stories of C. Hart Merriam; illustrated by Inez Storer), Floating Island Books, 1981.

Going On: Selected Poems 1958–1980, Dutton, 1983.

The Dharma Committee, Smithereens Press, 1986.

(With Michael Rothenberg) *Man-Women* (illustrated by Nancy Davis), Big Bridge Press, 1988.

Phenomenological, Institute of Further Studies, 1989.

Just Space: Poems 1979–1990 (illustrated by Arthur Okamura), Black Sparrow Press, 1991.

Contributor:

George Plimpton and Peter Ardery, editors, *The American Literary Anthology,* Random House, 1969.

Anne Waldman, editor, *The World Anthology,* Bobbs-Merrill, 1969.

Laura Chester and Sharon Barba, editors, *Rising Tides,* Pocket Books, 1973.

Contributor of poems to periodicals, including *Coyote's Journal, Paris Review, Poetry, Rockey Ledge, Turkey Buzzard Review,* and *World.* A collection of Kyger's work is held at the Archive for New Poetry, University of California, San Diego.

William F. Nolan

1928-

A LIFE IN WRITING

William F. Nolan, a portrait sketch by Donn Albright

Psychology tells us that no memory is ever lost. We retain every moment of our lives, each hour, day, and year, from birth to this immediate second, recorded and stored within the mysterious, complex computer of the human brain. Much of this memory-detail remains unavailable to us on a conscious level and there's a reason. If we remembered *everything*, we'd suffer an emotional overload. Thus, individual memory becomes highly selective.

I'm writing these words on Christmas Eve, 1991, which is appropriate, since my first vivid childhood memory concerns this annual holiday.

It was December 1929, in Kansas City, Missouri. I was a year and ten months old. Mom took me to

Montgomery Ward's Toyland to have my picture taken with Santa Claus. I believed in him implicitly, and I can still remember my sense of shocked awe as I sat on the Great Man's lap. He'd come all the way from the North Pole just to let me pose with him. For young Billy Nolan, the magic was totally real.

Christmas Day was always the best day of the year when I was a child. I'd drift off to sleep on a snowy Christmas Eve in my little back bedroom on Forest Avenue, knowing that when I awoke in the morning there would be a tall, brightly lit, beautifully decorated floor-to-ceiling Christmas tree in our living room with a spill of gaily wrapped presents laid out beneath it. All thanks to jolly old Saint Nick, who personally visited our house between midnight and dawn.

Of course, it was Mom and Dad who worked so diligently through the long night hours to make all this happen for me, savoring my delighted cry of joy when I entered our magically transformed living room on Christmas morning.

I grew up in the midst of the Great Depression and times were tough. My father was often out of work. Mom earned $100 a month as a stenographer at the post office, and lack of money was always a source of pressing concern. I recall one year when we had to rent out the front part of our tiny house for $25 a month in order to buy coal for the winter.

But Christmas was the one time of the year my parents determined to make perfect. They always succeeded. Those magical Christmas mornings have remained with me down the decades; they represented the deep and abiding love of both my parents for their often overindulged only child. . . .

In truth, I was not my father's only child. He had four other children by an earlier marriage, but I didn't learn this until I was fourteen. I was stunned. Wasn't Mom the only woman Dad had ever loved? No, first there had been Clara. . . .

Michael Cahill Nolan was fifty years old in 1928, when I came into the world, and he'd lived a wild, adventurous life before becoming my father.

He was born in Canada (the seventh of ten children) near the St. Lawrence River, in Toronto, Ontario, on November 19, 1877. His mother was Canadian-born, his father was an immigrant from

"My father, Michael Nolan, as a pioneer 'pathfinder' in 1910—after driving the first automobile over the Santa Fe Trail"

Ireland. In 1884, when he was seven, the family moved to Kansas City. Dad used to tell me about driving a horse-drawn milk wagon as a boy.

A month before his twenty-fourth birthday he married Clara Rieke, who had just turned nineteen. They eventually had four children, three boys and a girl. Clara's family had a great deal of money which gave Dad the means to enter a variety of business ventures. However, his main enthusiasm centered on that turn-of-the-century phenomenon, the automobile. In 1908, at thirty, he became a racing driver, competing in a Stevens-Duryea, and was soon running a dealership for these cars in downtown Kansas City. Among many athletic endeavors, Dad was active in baseball, track, and tennis. But the motor car remained his primary passion. In 1910 he was selected as "Pathfinder" for the Star Cup Tour, pioneering a cross-country motor route into New Mexico in "Old Betsy," his big, six-cylinder Stevens-Duryea, the first automobile over the historic, wagon-rutted Santa Fe Trail.

Always keen for new adventure, by 1916 Dad had become a gun-toting cavalryman under the command of legendary "Black Jack" Pershing. He rode into the mountains of Mexico in pursuit of Pancho Villa, the notorious bandit who had been raiding American towns across the Rio Grande. This campaign proved to be the last major engagement for the U.S. Cavalry.

My mother, the youngest of four surviving children, was born Bernadette Mariana Scholastica Kelly in Kansas City, Missouri, on March 12, 1894. Her father, Michael Kelly (the only grandparent I ever knew from either side of my family), came from southern Ireland at sixteen to work as a railroad laborer in St. Louis. He married Katherine Flynn, a St. Louis public school teacher, in September of 1879, and they moved to Kansas City where he eventually opened a small grocery store in the downtown area. They had eight children, four of whom died near birth.

In 1902, at the age of eight, my mother moved with her parents to a new one-story frame house at 3337 Forest Avenue. Unhappily for her, she was not allowed to grow up there. Her aunt was the Mother Superior of a posh girls' boarding school in Maryland and, because of her aunt's position, my mother was sent there as a charity case. Painfully out of place among the snobbish offspring of the nouveau riche, my mother was haunted throughout the rest of her life by the trauma of being sent to that strict (and often abusive) convent school from age eleven through sixteen.

"In my first year, with my mother, Bernadette Kelly Nolan," Kansas City, Missouri, 1928

At twenty-one, back in K.C. (having become a piano teacher), she met Dad. He later claimed that "I fell in love with Bernie at first sight," but it took twelve long years before he was able to obtain a divorce from Clara. By then, my mother was thirty-three and, by her own admission, "desperate for children." Unable to wed within the Church (since Dad was now a divorced man), they were married by a Justice of the Peace in April of 1927.

Temporarily, they moved into the Forest Avenue house with Grandpa Kelly (who owned it), and Mom soon became pregnant. She was overjoyed at the prospect of motherhood.

As William Francis Nolan, I was born at St. Luke's Hospital on March 6, 1928—named after my grandfathers *William* P. Nolan and Michael *Francis* Kelly.

When I was just two months old, Dad invested all of his money ($15,000) in a large stone-and-wood house on Blue Ridge Road on the outskirts of town. The purchase included ten acres of land on which he intended to raise chickens for commercial sale. Although I have no conscious memory of this period, we lived on Blue Ridge through 1929, until disaster struck: nearly all of Dad's chickens died during the winter. We were forced to move back into the small house on Forest Avenue with Grandpa Kelly—who was with us there until his death six years later.

Grandpa and I were very close. Each day, in his deep, Irish-accented voice, he'd read me the latest rabbit adventure of "Uncle Wiggily" from the Kansas City *Star*—my first exposure to prose fantasy. And when I began attending St. Vincent's Academy (a parochial school) at age six, in 1934, he would always walk me to and from school. His death the following year, from pneumonia, left me stunned and shaken.

My parents tried the cafe business twice; both times they lost money. Finally, Dad obtained work with one of his brothers, Theo Nolan, as a fire insurance adjuster. On occasion he'd leave K.C. to settle an out-of-town claim and bring me back abandoned toys from the fire site. For years I played with toys smelling of smoke and ash.

My lifelong addiction to films (I still see more than fifty a year) began in 1935, when I was seven, with *The Miracle Rider,* a Western serial starring Tom Mix. The Isis theater (at Thirty-first and Troost, just three blocks from my home on Forest) ran a special children's matinee each Saturday. For a dime you got two feature films, a pair of cartoons, a newsreel, a short subject (usually a comedy), and a weekly installment of a "thrilling new serial." For many years thereafter, I never missed a Saturday matinee and my wife claims that the Isis was my "real alma mater." She's right; my career as a professional storyteller was definitely launched at Thirty-first and Troost.

I've always been blessed with fabulous health. In fact, the only time in my life I've ever been a patient in a hospital was in 1936, when I was eight. I had an operation on my left eye to correct a cross-eyed condition and I've worn glasses ever since.

In 1937, at nine, I wrote my first poem on a scrap of school notepaper, and a year later I plunged into fiction, filling two blue-lined Big Chief nickel notebooks with a lurid array of stories featuring cowboys, G-men, magicians, and air aces. Reading them again, these many years later, I shudder at my youthful

"Almost two, on Santa's lap at Montgomery Ward's," 1929

ineptitude. In a word, my stories were dreadful. Nonetheless, the seeds had been planted.

I was a typical boy of the times, addicted to red-and-black jawbreakers, collecting penny charms, sailing boats on Troost Lake, trading Indian cards for marbles, digging caves in vacant lots, sledding in winter, roller-skating in Gillham Park, reading Big Little Books, swimming at the YMCA, making model planes, playing pirate from a tree house in our backyard pear tree, riding my bike fourteen miles on a Sunday, and conducting desperate gun battles in the kitchen with toy cap pistols. Don Miller and Jack Morgan were my best pals and they shared all my passions.

In those pre-television days, every kid I knew loved radio drama; we'd rush home from school to tune in "Jack Armstrong," "Renfrew of the Mounted," "Captain Midnight," "Dick Tracy," "Little Orphan Annie" . . . And I was a real nut for "Lights Out!" and "I Love a Mystery."

I was reading Tom Swift and book series featuring "Bomba the Jungle Boy." I was also into heroic dog stories, having discovered a dusty copy of *Kazan* by James Oliver Curwood in a corner of our basement—the first "adult" book I remember reading. *White Fang* and *Call of the Wild* (both by Jack London) became special favorites.

My first job, on weekends, was hauling groceries in my red metal wagon for the customers of a store at Thirty-fifth and Troost. At ten cents a trip, I averaged a dollar a day, which was good money by Depression standards. Back then you could buy a full meal, with dessert, for a quarter (thirty cents with the tip), and postage stamps were a penny.

I joined the Boy Scouts in 1940 but was never able to progress beyond the rank of Tenderfoot. My fires always went out and I kept getting lost in the woods.

Of course, I was raised an Irish-American Catholic. (Forest Avenue was located in a working-class parish which was overwhelmingly Irish-American.) At twelve, I served as an altar boy at St. Vincent's Church.

My mother was a devout and deeply loyal Catholic. However, because she had married a divorced man (a mortal sin), she was, by Church standards, excommunicated—no longer allowed to receive the sacraments. In particular, and to her enormous distress, she was not allowed to receive the sacrament of Holy Communion. When she married Dad, she thought she could live with this sacrifice, but as the years went by she found herself in a state of steadily increasing inner turmoil.

"Lost in the adventures of Tailspin Tommy *at ten, when I began writing stories of my own," 1938*

Finally, our parish priest offered her a deal: if she would agree, under penalty of eternal damnation if she ever broke the promise, to never again have sexual relations with my father, she could continue to live with him in the same house *and* receive Holy Communion. Reluctantly she agreed, taking what were called, in those days, "brother-sister" vows. Part of the deal was that she and Dad would never again sleep in the same room, be in a state of undress in front of each other, or indulge in any physical affection beyond a simple (and nonsexual) kiss. Dad loved Mom so much he went along with her wishes, but I always felt that one of the reasons he took to drinking heavily every weekend was due to Mom's bizarre arrangement with the Church, a prime example of religious blackmail and a perversion of normal human relations.

I was never entirely happy as a Catholic. As the years went by, I learned more about the history of the Church, about its hypocrisy and abiding lust for power and wealth. I witnessed its cruel manipulation of guilt and "sin" as weapons to subjugate its members. But it took me decades to leave. I have said

"At seventeen, about to graduate from Lillis High in Kansas City," 1945

many times in recent years that—as a bitter ex-Catholic—I fully acknowledge the good *people* in the Church, but the institution itself is corrupt. I am well and happily out of it.

In June of 1941, at thirteen, I graduated from seventh grade at St. Vincent's and, that fall, enrolled at nearby Lillis High within easy walking distance of my house on Forest. It was, of course, a Catholic school. (Catholic parents in those pre-Vatican II days were required by Church law to send their children to Catholic schools. In truth, the idea that I might just as well have gone to public school was so unthinkable that it never entered any of our minds.)

Three months into my freshman year, Japan attacked Pearl Harbor and I was destined to spend the four years of World War II as a high school student.

I must mention, at this point, the influence of comic book heroes in my young life. I was an avid collector and eventually amassed some 430 comic books (through 1943), with complete runs of Superman, Sub-Mariner, The Human Torch, Captain America, Captain Marvel, Hawkman, and dozens of others. Batman was my prime favorite and I would spend hours at home in the evening drawing these comic book characters, adding many new ones of my own invention ("The Blue Sparrow," "The Golden Star," "The Red Cape," "The Silver Bullet," "The Purple Dynamo" . . .). In 1944, convinced that I was now "too old" for comic books, I dumped my entire collection for five dollars, which turned out to be a serious error in financial judgment. Yet who would have dreamed that in the nostalgic 1980s a single issue of Batman would sell for $80,000?

I'd been drawing since I was old enough to hold a crayon and at Lillis I became cartoonist for the school paper, winning (in my senior year) first prize in an all-city high school competition (for "Freshman Frankie," my serial comic strip in the *Lillistrator*). I was also staff artist for the Lillis Yearbook. It seemed, at that time and for many years thereafter, that I was headed for a career in commercial art. But there were other factors in the equation . . .

In March of 1942, on the occasion of my fourteenth birthday, Jack Morgan gifted me with a copy of *The Rancher's Revenge* by Max Brand, a writer I'd never heard of. His real name, I later discovered, was Frederick Faust. It is impossible to overemphasize the influence of Faust in my life. I credit him, in large part, with my having become a professional writer. Printed beneath my senior photo, upon my graduation from Lillis, were the words: "To carry on for Max Brand." (He'd been killed as a war correspondent in Italy.) Prophetic words, indeed, as future decades would prove. I would later find myself, as an adult professional, editing Faust's stories for publication! But as a schoolboy I was strictly a Max Brand fan and by 1948 I had collected more than a hundred of his books; I was also writing about him for amateur magazines. I'll come back to Faust later; there are still vital subjects to cover relating to those formative Lillis years.

Such as girls. Ah, girls! How I loved and feared them. I was desperately shy (which I masked by wild humor), and the fact that I suffered from a severe case of acne didn't help the situation. In fact, it was not until well into my senior year that I had my first date. Her name was Betty Brown and she was editor of the *Lillistrator*. When I took Betty to the senior prom, I let her go inside alone while I spent the evening clowning around in the hall; I'd never learned to dance and I was too mortified to let anyone know. In a male-female dating situation, I had zero self-confidence.

I wrote a lot while I was at Lillis. As a result of my verse, I was elected to Quill and Scroll and my grades put me into the National Honor Society. In

1944, at sixteen, I was working on my first novel (never finished) and I turned out many stories and poems that year (a total of 25,000 words). I'd discovered Ray Bradbury in *Weird Tales* and I was also reading the horror fiction of H. P. Lovecraft. In fact, I became an enthusiastic horror buff during this period, happily devouring such macabre anthologies as *Sleep No More* and *Tales of Terror*.

I was *terrible* in school sports. Just couldn't hit a ball or sink a basket, and my glasses and skinny frame kept me from trying out for football. Dad, the ex-athlete, calmly accepted the fact that his son was no sportsman; he was actually quite proud of my creative ability in prose, verse, and art. Even when we'd go camping, each summer, at the Lake of the Ozarks, I'd be stretched out in the rowboat reading H. G. Wells while Dad did all the fishing.

My best friend at Lillis was Bill Hennessey; he was also my worst enemy. How could this be? Well, Bill would often torment, tease, and bully me, but just as often he was great fun to be with. We shared many good times. We wrote and performed plays on the Lillis stage, double-dated the Brown sisters (Bill with Edith, me with Betty), and were fellow artists and collectors. I'd known Bill as a schoolmate since my early years at St. Vincent's and now he's my oldest friend. We see each other once each summer when he visits Los Angeles; the "bad times" are now forgotten and only the warmth and nostalgia of a longtime friendship remains.

I often worked weekends and summers during the Lillis years: at a paper box factory, as a theater usher, as a parking lot attendant, and (during Christmas) as a helper in the post office. Thus, I was paying a good share of my expenses and taking pressure off my parents. Actually, we were doing okay financially. Pearl Harbor had brought the Depression to a close, and Dad (now in his mid-sixties) was earning $2,000 a year at a defense plant; Mom brought in another thousand from her clerk-typist job. Three thousand was a solid annual income in the early '40s and living money was no longer a family problem.

In June of 1945, at seventeen, as a member of my graduating class of 149 students, I received my diploma from Lillis High. That summer I went to work for Hallmark Cards as a cartoonist/writer, but it was obvious I needed more art training. In October, I left Hallmark to enroll at the Kansas City Art Institute. One of the classes was Life Drawing and I recall the utter shock—and delight—of seeing my first naked woman! (There were no nudie magazines on the stands in those days.)

Although I did well enough as an art student, I wasn't satisfied with my potential; I lacked major talent. In a 1946 diary note I vented my frustrations: "I'm an oddity . . . I live life out of books. I'm drifting . . . must find my place."

I knew that the "place" wasn't Kansas City. I had taken my first trip (by train) to New York that year and, while the giant metropolis dazzled me, I was sure that I'd never want to live and work there. So . . . where?

In January of 1947 my aunt Grace (Dad's sister) provided the answer. She wrote from California asking Dad to move the family out there and take over the management of her lemon grove in Chula Vista (south of San Diego near the Mexican border). She would provide a house for us to live in and a salary of $100 a month. (By then, Dad was earning $3,000 a year, but the lure of a "new adventure" in California was too tempting to resist.)

He flew out to the West Coast (still a fairly unusual way to travel in those days) while Mom and I arranged the sale of the Forest Avenue house (for $6,500, including the furniture). I was glad to bid farewell to our Victorian Midwest neighborhood and, at nineteen, strike out for an expansive new life in the West.

I'd learned to drive the family car (a 1936 Dodge) and, in June, Mom and I headed for California along Route 66, a week's run that gave me my first view of a mountain. (Not equal to the impact of a naked woman, but impressive, nonetheless.)

I began day classes at San Diego State College that summer while Dad managed the lemon grove for Aunt Grace. But he soon discovered that the trees were unproductive, the soil overworked, and the profits practically nonexistent. In 1948 the grove failed and Mom was forced to go to work at the Veteran's Administration in order to support the family. The following year Dad moved us all to San Diego where he opened a small tobacco-and-candy stall. He was seventy-one and this would turn out to be his final business venture.

Meanwhile, at San Diego State, I had won first prize in an all-campus art competition (for a watercolor painting) and cartoons of mine were appearing in *Cacti*, the college humor magazine. I also received the top grade in English (earning the only "E"—for Excellence—in the class). My teacher told me I had "the makings of a writer," but I was still firmly aimed at a career in art.

In September of 1948 I ended my formal education; I left college to become associated with a group of young San Diego artists. I had my own art studio at the Spanish Village in Balboa Park where I sold watercolors; I also painted outdoor murals for a pet shop and a miniature golf course. My one-man show drew heartening praise from the director of the San Diego Fine Arts Gallery, who wrote of my "beautifully painted watercolors" (one of which had won a cash award at that year's County Fair).

I worked for my father at "Mike's Smoke Shop" through most of 1949, trying to help him make a go of the business, but he was forced to close down in March of 1950.

For me, the highlight of 1950 was meeting Ray Bradbury at his home in Los Angeles, just two months after his publication of *The Martian Chronicles*. At twenty-nine, he was the hottest name in science fiction and it was through Bradbury that I became an avid SF fan and reader. Ray and I have been close pals ever since that first meeting—a friendship that has extended through more than forty years.

That summer, a month after meeting Ray, I got my first decent-paying job ($100 a week) at Convair Aircraft as a parts inspector on B-36 bombers. By the following year, at the age of twenty-three, I made an important life decision: I would abandon art as a career. The money just wasn't there and I felt that I had no productive future ahead of me as a commercial artist.

Then what *would* I do with my life? I had begun what I inwardly termed "serious writing" (which included several months of work on a booklet, the *Ray Bradbury Review*, tracing Bradbury's first professional decade), but I didn't feel that I could earn a living by way of the written word.

Still, I loved to write. I sent my first typed story out to market in 1952 while I was still working at Convair. It didn't sell, but then I hadn't really expected it to; the satisfaction of having completed a story I felt worthy of professional submission was reward enough.

The San Diego years were about to end. In September, anxious to try life in San Francisco, I quit my job with Convair and headed north. For the next three months I lived in a fog-damp San Francisco hotel on Market Street. I joined the (unpaid) staff of *Rhodomagnetic Digest*, an amateur SF publication, writing and illustrating several pieces for them, but I was unable to find a paying job in the city. I ended up in Los Angeles in 1953, working as a credit assistant at a downtown paper company—and hating every minute of it. I knew that office work was no answer; I wanted to *write*. But even though I had managed a first book appearance (in a volume on Max Brand), and had self-published my booklet on Bradbury to

some fine reviews, I was still unable to imagine how I'd ever make it as a professional writer.

Then Charles Beaumont entered my life. Actually, I'd met him the previous year when I'd stopped by Universal Studios to have lunch with Bradbury on my way to San Francisco. We'd been joined by Beaumont, who was then running a mimeo machine in the studio's music department. He, too, wanted to write for a living, and Ray had been reading his manuscripts, offering professional advice.

Now, early in 1953, Chuck Beaumont and I got together again at his apartment in North Hollywood and an instant friendship was born. Here was a young man (he was twenty-four) of wit, integrity, and driving ambition, who had determined that nothing would keep him from achieving great success as a professional writer. He was just the tonic I needed to help me launch my own career.

Chuck had a four-story head start on me, having made his initial fiction sale in 1950; I was still a full year away from mine. Through Beaumont, I also met and became friends with beginning writers Richard Matheson (then working for an aircraft plant), John Tomerlin (a radio sportscaster from Bakersfield), and Chad Oliver (who was then working toward a degree in anthropology at UCLA).

On weekends, we'd often sit up all night in twenty-four-hour coffee shops, talking intensely into the dawn about our work, arguing story points, dissecting plots, sharing our dreams of "a life in writing." I recall these all-night sessions with fond nostalgia; they helped shape my creative life and gave it meaning and direction. It was a vital, exciting time.

I was living in Culver City, a few blocks behind MGM Studios, and regularly attending meetings at LASFS—the Los Angeles Science Fiction Society. (Later, I would write for their fan publication.) Bradbury was in Ireland, working on the screenplay of *Moby Dick* for director John Huston; before leaving, he had told me that when I felt I had a top quality manuscript polished and ready for market, I was to send it to him first, for advance criticism. Late in 1953 I sent him a 5,000-word science fiction story, "The Joy of Living." Its plot revolved around a man who falls in love with the humanoid robot he has hired to take care of his children. At the end, I had him drive her back to the factory and sadly return home alone. Ray loved the story, but felt my ending was "all wrong." He told me to *reverse* the situation and have the man accept the love offered by this perfect mechanical woman—otherwise, he told me, the reader would be "emotionally let down." Bradbury was right. I made the change and sold "The Joy of Living" to *If: Worlds of SF* in February of 1954. (I still have a photo copy of the $100 check they sent me.)

By God, I was a professional!

Chuck Beaumont proposed that I leave my office job and that we team up to write comic book material, mainly Mickey Mouse adventures, for Walt Disney's Whitman Publications. I agreed and for the next four months we turned out stories for Mickey and Pluto with titles such as "The Giant Pearls of Agoo Island" and "The Mystery of Diamond Mountain" (the latter being an open "steal" from F. Scott Fitzgerald's "The Diamond as Big as the Ritz").

Unfortunately, the money I earned from Whitman did not cover my living expenses and I was forced once again to seek office work. That summer I was hired by the California State Department of Employment as a job employment interviewer.

In 1955 a consuming passion for auto racing was ignited when Chuck and I witnessed our first sports car event in Palm Springs. (I remember that actor James Dean was competing there.) I'd purchased a British Austin-Healey, and Chuck had a Porsche Speedster. Along with John Tomerlin, also Porsche mounted, we became instant fanatics, attending weekend sports car events from Pebble Beach to Santa Barbara.

By the close of the year I was selling to some of the second-grade men's magazines (*Escapade, Nugget,* etc.), but my breakthrough came in February of 1956 when a story I'd written on a Sunday afternoon sold to *Playboy* for $500. Bolstered by this triumph, I took my dive into the cold sea of full-time writing; on April first of that year I quit my job with the Department of Employment. My financial security was a cash reserve of $1,000 in savings.

I flew to Chicago to meet *Playboy* editor Ray Russell, then on to New Orleans to write a crime tale set in that city. My time was my own and I could travel as often as my funds allowed. Working for myself was a heady, wondrous feeling. By year's end, in nine months, I'd written thirty-seven stories and articles, one per week. And I'd sold nearly all of them.

I was now a columnist for a sports car publication, reporting on monthly races, and I'd moved up to a faster Healey, the Le Mans 100-M competition model. In October of 1957, at twenty-nine, I ran the 100-M at the Hour Glass Circuit near San Diego and came home with a class trophy.

By December, Chuck and I were in New York where we tied down a book sale with G. P. Putnam's Sons. Together, we would edit a comprehensive motor racing anthology titled *Omnibus of Speed.*

In May of 1958 I celebrated my hundredth sale and that summer took off for Connecticut to work with John Fitch on his racing autobiography, *Adventure on Wheels,* already presold to Putnam's. (I'd met Fitch in 1957 when I'd covered Nassau Speed Week in the Bahamas.) With the publication of *Omnibus of Speed* in November, I had a hardcover book to my credit. And when the *New York Times Book Review* gave it high praise, I knew my career was off and running.

I didn't own a television set until 1956, but within three years I had decided to write for this relatively new medium. It was a fresh way to challenge myself creatively and my pals Beaumont, Matheson, and Tomerlin were already selling teleplays. In 1959 I wrote and sold scripts to *One Step Beyond* and *Wanted—Dead or Alive.*

However, auto racing still occupied most of my attention and by the end of the year I was at Sebring, Florida, representing *Motor Trend,* watching California ace Phil Hill drive in the first U.S. Grand Prix. I'd met Hill at previous competition events, and we formed a bond of trust that resulted in my doing many magazine pieces on his career, capped by his biography two years later and a motion picture sale of the book to Warner Bros. in 1991.

"Being congratulated for a trophy-winning run by (from left) John Tomerlin and Charles Beaumont in my Austin-Healey Le Mans 100-M at the Hour-Glass Circuit near San Diego," 1957

Dad was very proud of me for my work in the automotive field, the only sport we'd ever shared as father and son. By then, of course, he was far too old (in his eighties) to attend any races with me, but he enjoyed telling me stories about his own speed career, in the days when he'd competed against such stars as Barney Oldfield. I was amazed. I hadn't realized that Dad had actually raced against this legendary speed king. Oldfield had helped launch the Ford Motor Company when he drove Henry Ford's tiller-steered "999" to victory at Grosse Pointe, Michigan, in 1902.

That afternoon I went to the library and asked for a book on Barney Oldfield. None existed. Well then, I told the librarian, I guess I'll have to write one. Which is what I set out to do.

I spent most of March and April of 1960 on a cross-country research trip gathering background material for the Oldfield book—visiting the automotive library in Detroit, the Library of Congress in Washington, then on to Barney's hometown of Toledo, Ohio.

My research was interrupted by a whirlwind trip to Europe with Beaumont and Tomerlin. Chuck had talked *Playboy* into sponsoring a trip to Monaco, for the Grand Prix of Monte Carlo; he was to write up the race for them.

We booked passage on one of the last piston engine flights to Europe (jets were replacing them)—and almost didn't get there. One of the plane's engines failed over the trackless tundra of Greenland, and we had to make a forced landing for a new engine.

The Monte Carlo event was one of the high points of my life—with Grand Prix machines roaring through the narrow city streets at full throttle and a fabulous post-race gala with Princess Grace (Hollywood's own Grace Kelly!) in a shimmering white evening gown on the arm of her Prince.

The trip was capped by five days in Paris (my first visit there) and a flight back to the States in a safe new 707 jet.

Some good news was waiting for me; the American Library Association had named *Adventure on Wheels* as "one of the year's best books for Young Adults." The citation was *most* welcome.

I became a film actor in 1961.

Beaumont had written a screenplay for producer-director Roger Corman based on Chuck's novel *The Intruder,* and he was going on location in Missouri to play a school principal in the production. Did I want to test for the role of "Bart Carey," the town bully? You bet! Corman signed me on immediately. As a Missouri "cracker" I was a natural; I'd grown up

"With fellow actor Ocee Ritch as I portray a nasty screen villain in Roger Corman's The Intruder *on location," Missouri, 1961*

listening to such accents and I certainly was familiar with the local culture.

We shot *The Intruder* in eighteen days in the sizzling heat of summer in humid southern Missouri. The film starred William Shatner as a man who attempts to manipulate the then-volatile issue of school integration to gain personal power. He hires me to beat up a liberal newspaper editor and blow up the town's Black church. Sullen and unshaven, with a wooden stick match at the corner of my mouth, I made the most of a juicy role.

That November saw publication of my *Barney Oldfield* biography. By then I'd sold my first film treatment (in collaboration with Richard Matheson) to American International Pictures. Financially, 1961 was my best year yet as a professional writer.

On a personal level, however, at thirty-four I was still not ready for a serious relationship. While filming *The Intruder* I'd been involved with a local Missouri girl, but it had been a classic "location romance," based on a lot of fantasy and very little reality.

The following summer I began dating an extremely attractive young woman named Marilyn Elizabeth Seal whom I'd met through Richard Matheson (she'd once been a baby-sitter for his children). She was engaging, bright (with a genius-level I.Q.), and had ambitions to be a writer. In fact, she already had an impressive list of credits, beginning with her first "professional" sales to Archie Comic Books as a ten-year-old fifth grader. We enjoyed going out together, but after three months we both decided it was best to go our separate ways since I really didn't want to commit to anybody. I was afraid that if I got sidetracked into a deep relationship, possibly leading to marriage, I'd be putting my writing career in jeopardy.

By December I was in New York where I sold *Impact 20*, my first book of fiction, to Warner Paperback Library. It was mainly a collection of SF and fantasy, with a scattering of crime tales. Bradbury agreed to do the introduction and, fittingly, I dedicated the book to him.

The roots of *Logan's Run* extend back to mid-1963. Chuck Beaumont was teaching a class in science fiction to beginning writers at UCLA and he invited me there as a guest speaker. On the way, in my car, I tried to think of a simple way to demonstrate the difference between straight fiction and science fiction. I recalled the cliche "life begins at forty." Ah, *that* was it!

As I told the class, if a man turns forty to face a mid-life crisis, and decides to quit his job and leave his wife, you have *straight* fiction—but if a man turns forty and is pursued by police in a future society that does not *allow* anyone to live past that age (due to overpopulation), then you have *science* fiction.

I had generated this concept only to make a point to Chuck's class, but later that night I jotted down the idea for my files, thinking it might form the basis of an interesting short story. Then I promptly forgot about it.

I was concerned over Chuck. At thirty-four, he was now drinking heavily (which he'd never done in the past) and his behavior was becoming erratic. The headaches that had plagued him through the years of our friendship had worsened. Something was *wrong*.

I had just signed on as managing editor of a new SF/fantasy digest, *Gamma*, and I wanted a Beaumont story for the first issue. Chuck wrote "Mourning Song" for me—a grim narrative about a man who could not escape from a death-figure who waited for him, even beyond his prison cell, at the story's end. I had no idea at the time that the plot mirrored Chuck's own deepest fears: that Old Man Death was soon coming for *him* and there was nothing he could do to avoid the encounter.

"Mourning Song" was the last story Chuck wrote. Within weeks after completing it, he was into the early stages of a disease that first robbed him of his mental powers, then destroyed him physically. Indeed, something was *very* wrong. But what?

In 1964 doctors at UCLA provided the shocking answer: Charles Beaumont was an early victim of Alzheimer's Disease. There was (and is) no cure and, by February of 1967, he would be dead at thirty-eight. I was losing my best, my dearest friend . . .

My career was progressing steadily. I was SF book reviewer for the *Los Angeles Times* and had been selected for *Who's Who in the West*. Two of my books were published in 1964, and four more in 1965, including *John Huston: King Rebel*, the first full-length biography of the controversial film director.

I'd taken my concept of a man running from police in an overpopulated future society to writer-friend George Clayton Johnson, asking him what he thought should be done with the idea. George and I had written and sold a teleplay (unproduced) to *Twilight Zone*, and I knew we could work together. He felt that the plot should be developed into a screenplay, that it would make a very solid film. That's fine, I said, but first it should be done as a novel, *then* as a script. More money that way, and more creative control. He agreed—and, in August of 1965, in a rented motel room near the beach at Malibu, George and I wrote the first draft of *Logan's Run* in three weeks. All the elements were there, with many effective scenes, and the basic idea had been strengthened: we'd lowered the compulsory death age to twenty-one and added a strong love interest. In our science fictional future, when a citizen's crystal "palm flower" turns black (on his or her twenty-first birthday) that citizen must seek out a sleepshop for a quiet, easy death. The alternative was to become a "runner" and be hunted down and painfully terminated by a Sandman (a future cop). Logan is a cop-turned-runner who fights his way to love and final sanctuary.

Neither of us had ever written a novel, but I had much more experience with prose than George, who was mainly into scripting, so I told him I wanted to take the manuscript to San Francisco and rework it alone, giving it a cohesion and polish it now lacked. (I'd often go out of town to work in those days; such "isolation" helped me concentrate.) I redid the entire manuscript in San Francisco, bringing it into submission format. I felt it was original and striking, a very strong first novel with major potential.

Dad had been taken to the hospital while I was gone and I drove back to find that doctors had removed a malignant tumor from his bowels. At his advanced age, the operation was too much for him and he slipped into a coma.

My father died a month short of his eighty-eighth birthday, on October 9, 1965. But while he was still conscious at the hospital, I'd had a final chance to tell him how much I loved him. And he understood. . . .

Novelist E. L. Doctorow was then an editor at Dial Press, in New York, and he bought hardcover book rights to *Logan's Run* early in 1966. The film rights were optioned to producer Stan Canter: $10,000 down against a total pickup price of $100,000. Once we'd locked up these deals, George and I rented an office in West Hollywood and wrote the first draft of our screenplay, based directly on the novel.

In March of 1966 I made a long-delayed change: I became an ex-Catholic. I was finally free. It was a decision I have never regretted.

I'd been regularly selling material to *Playboy,* and now they bought a novelette of mine, featuring hard-boiled L.A. detective "Bart Challis," for $3,000 as lead fiction. Based on this, I decided to build a series of novels around Bart's adventures.

My career was almost terminated (along with my life) that December when I sold a screenplay (based, fictionally, on the life of actor James Dean) to up-and-coming director Billy Friedkin—who was to gain fame with *The French Connection* and *The Exorcist* in later years. Billy wanted to fly down in his private monoplane to San Felipe, on the Gulf of Mexico, to scout a possible location for our film and he asked me to accompany him. I've never liked flying in small planes, but I agreed—and our trip down went smoothly. We made extensive location notes and set out to return to Los Angeles.

At Calexico they told us that an incoming storm would make flying conditions "very hazardous" for light planes. Better to rent a car and drive. No, Billy insisted we take off into the storm—and it was a doozy. By the time we got close to the Palm Springs airport, the winds were slapping our plane around like a tennis ball. Visibility was minimal and I figured we'd never make the airport. We did—by a hair—moments before it was closed down.

I never flew in a private plane again.

In March of 1967 I phoned Marilyn Seal. She was working as a purchasing clerk at Capitol Records and, by this time, had sold several articles to mainstream publications. We saw each other briefly that spring, but again, we drifted apart. She was looking for marriage; I wasn't.

Logan's Run was published that September to excellent reviews. Stan Canter's option was up; he had failed to raise the remainder of the money. He offered us a flat buy-out for another $40,000, but we said no. Our price was our price. George Pal, a well-known SF producer, was very high on doing *Logan* for MGM and that's where we took the project on a new option deal.

My first major horror story, "The Party," was printed in *Playboy* that year (April 1967). It was later selected for several "classic" anthologies and named, by *Newsweek,* one of the century's seven most effective horror tales.

Approaching the age of forty, in 1968, I decided that I was finally ready to form a permanent relationship. I had been dating Carol Soucek (who would later become editor of a major architectural magazine), but it was obvious that we were not destined to spend our lives together.

Through the Mathesons, I once again contacted Marilyn Seal. No matter who I'd dated, she was always at the back of my mind. No one else measured up. Now a full-fledged professional writer, Marilyn was editorial assistant for a chain of three teen publications with the responsibility of writing the equivalent of a complete magazine every month. Her name, however, had changed. Because of her teen readership, she needed a more "with it" byline on her work, so she was writing under the name "Kam Lytton." (Never comfortable with her birth name, she would later go through the process of legally becoming "Cameron.")

Our emotional rapport was stronger than ever. Now that I'd left the Church and made the decision to settle down in my personal life, we were free to enter into a serious relationship. Cam was the woman I was destined to marry . . .

My first Bart Challis mystery thriller, *Death Is for Losers,* was published that year, along with another of my SF anthologies, but my deepest satisfaction came from acceptance in the literary magazine *Prairie Schooner,* who printed a four-page poem of mine on Hemingway, "Now Never There," in their fall 1968 issue. This was proof that I'd come a long way with my verse.

By the end of the year the Nolan/Johnson team had triumphed. Metro-Goldwyn-Mayer paid our full price of $100,000 for film rights to *Logan's Run* (with our revised screenplay accepted as part of the deal). On the MGM proceeds, I bought myself a new 911-T Porsche sports car and, for Mom, a Magnavox color television set.

Indeed, for me, having found Cam and with *Logan* off and running at MGM, life *did* begin at forty!

Dell brought out the first paperback edition of *Logan's Run* in 1969 and my second Challis novel, *The White Cad Cross-Up,* was published by Sherbourne Press. I'd made a deal with this local Los Angeles house for the entire series, at one a year, and I was already working out a plot for "The Marble Orchard," Bart's third adventure. But Sherbourne was in financial trouble and, before any more Challis books could be issued, they were out of business. When they died, my series died with them.

I had discovered the work of Dashiell Hammett in the early '60s, shortly after his death, and was shocked to find that no one had ever undertaken a full-length study of his work. I determined, as I had done with Oldfield, to fill that gap. My critical/biographical/bibliographical study, *Dashiell Hammett: A Casebook,* was published in April of 1969. It contained the first complete listing of his work for *Black Mask,* the magazine that had printed all of Hammett's early classics, including his masterwork, *The Maltese Falcon.* I was gratified to see the book win an Edgar Allan Poe Special Award from the Mystery Writers of America (MWA).

Cam had never been to Kansas City and I wanted to show her my hometown: the schools I'd attended, the streets I'd run and biked and roller-skated over, and the house in which I'd spent my childhood.

That winter, therefore, in the new Porsche, we drove cross-country to Missouri—my first trip back to Kansas City since I'd left twenty-two years ago. Everything had changed. My old neighborhood was now a slum, an area of trash and broken bottles, cracked walks, crumbling houses . . . a dying section of the city that had once been golden in my memory. Indeed, you *can't* go home again. . . .

"With my wife, Cameron Nolan, a year after our marriage," 1971

The big event of 1970 was my marriage to Cam. We wanted to make the wedding simple and uncomplicated, so we drove to Las Vegas and were married at the Little Church of the West, the nicest wedding chapel in town. She looked beautiful that day, and she still is—the best, the brightest, the most important person in my life. Years later, when I put together my first book of verse, I wrote the dedication poem to her, expressing my love.

> *For My Wife*
>
> You stretch
>   my mind
>   my mental muscles.
> You show me places
>   I'd never known
>   but go
>   because of you.
> You make demands
>   creatively
>   that I pridefully fulfill.
> You demonstrate
>   what goodness is
>   and care
>   for every creature.
> You carefully move
>   the sidewalk snail
>   to safer ground.
> You flood life's darkness
>   with your light.
>   Because of you
>   I'm me.

We bought our first house that fall, in the western San Fernando Valley of Los Angeles, in Woodland Hills where Cam had been raised (and where, as a teenager, she had baby-sat for the Mathesons—the root beginning of our relationship). We were to live in that house on Cavalier Street for the next eleven years.

Over that 1970–71 period I had five more of my books published, four anthologies, and a novel, *Space for Hire,* a wacky send-up of SF and the hard-boiled mystery. In it, I introduced my series detective "Sam Space," who gets involved with three-headed females, attends his own funeral in a parallel universe, is transformed (temporarily) into an egg-laying Zubu bird, and fights a fire-breathing robot dragon. It reflected the zany side of my writing persona and, happily enough, was selected as one of the year's five best original paperbacks, winning me my second Edgar Allan Poe Special Award from MWA.

Late in 1971 Cam and I flew to Toronto where, for two weeks, I worked with radio great Norman Corwin on his new television show, *Norman Corwin Presents.* He had selected my first printed professional story, "The Joy of Living," for TV dramatization and

I was there to polish my script and oversee its production. A remarkable, exciting experience.

The major phase of my television writing began the following year, in 1972, when I had a meeting with producer/director Dan Curtis (who'd just come in from New York after completing his *Dark Shadows* series). Dan and I hit it off immediately.

My first of many Curtis script assignments was a Movie of the Week for NBC, *The Norliss Tapes.* No sooner had I finished this teleplay than I was in Taos, New Mexico, for a month, writing a two-part adaptation of the Henry James ghost classic *The Turn of the Screw.* (Both scripts were put into immediate production, with the James teleplay filmed in London, starring Lynn Redgrave.)

From time to time, I had spoken before a variety of groups, at colleges, creative writing classes, and during fantasy conventions. Now, in 1972, I was asked to address a meeting of the Young Adult Librarians of Los Angeles at the downtown public library. I chose to deliver a short history of science fiction, a speech successful enough to warrant its printing in a magazine. For me, public lecturing is akin to acting; I am enough of a "ham" to enjoy relating to an audience.

My enthusiasm for the sport of motor racing had waned. With the publication of my biography *Steve McQueen: Star on Wheels* (intended for young adults), and a collection of my racing essays *Carnival of Speed* (due for release the following year), I was closing out this era in my life. As a writer, I felt I had said all I wished to say in the genre.

Late in 1973 both of the TV/film industry trade papers (*Daily Variety* and *The Hollywood Reporter*) ran banner announcements to the effect that MGM was "making its return to major production" with a new high-budget film adaptation of the novel *Logan's Run.* I was surprised, amazed, and delighted. The book had been sold to MGM six years before and I had given up hope that the film version would ever be made. Once George Pal's connection with the project dissolved, *Logan* had been dropped from the Metro production schedule, yet here it was, touted as the film that would "save" MGM!

My association with Dan Curtis had moved into high gear and I was working with him at his office during the week and at his home each weekend. I was under pressure to complete the script on a period gangster project *Melvin Purvis, G-Man,* for American International Pictures; it would be released as a feature film in Europe and as a Movie of the Week for ABC here in the States. Dale Robertson was set to play the legendary FBI man, and shooting was scheduled to begin in Sacramento on the day my script was completed. A crew of a hundred was on standby. The pressure was so great that I was forced to write forty pages of script in one night in order to meet my deadline. (This, by the way, is a speed record I've never matched since!)

In February of 1974 I was on location in Sacramento, in northern California, with Dan and the crew, doubling as writer and actor. I'd been assigned the role of a triggerman in Machine-Gun Kelly's gang. In the climactic roadhouse shootout with the FBI, I'm blown away by Purvis as I'm firing a submachine gun at him. I was frustrated by the fact that no one in the States ever saw my bloody death scene; it was cut from the ABC version and was used only in Europe, where the film was released as *The Legend of Machine-Gun Kelly.*

I was red-hot in the industry—five film/TV offers arrived in one month. I juggled two scripting jobs simultaneously, writing the teleplay for NBC's *Sky Heist* while turning out a screenplay for United Artists on the Bette Davis film *Burnt Offerings.* In researching *Sky Heist* I got a chance to fly with the Los Angeles Sheriff's Department Aero Bureau, in their chase helicopters, on night patrol into the San Gabriel Mountains. To me, they seemed much safer than Billy Friedkin's private monoplane—and we *didn't* fly in storms!

By 1975 several more of my books had been published, including a chapbook on Hemingway, but my main activities remained centered in the entertainment industry. Three of my Movies of the Week were telecast that year: *Trilogy of Terror, The Kansas City Massacre* (another Purvis venture), and *Sky Heist.*

In May I received an honorary doctorate from American River College, delivering an address at the ceremonies, and by the following month I was in Dallas, Texas, on location for the MGM filming of *Logan's Run* (at last!).

I spent two weeks in Dallas with the Logan crew. British stars Michael York and Jenny Agutter played Logan and Jessica, and they were superb. Less superb was the final shooting script by David Z. Goodman (the screenplay George and I had written had been scuttled). Logic and cohesion were missing from the Goodman version and the final molasses-slow third of the film bore no relation whatever to our fast-paced novel. Nevertheless, some effective scenes from the book *were* recreated for the movie, the most spectacular of which was the collapse of the gigantic ice cave and the death of Box the robot. Back in Culver City, on a huge sound stage, an army of studio technicians had labored to build the ice cave. Entering it for the first time, I felt a bit like God. It is strange and

"With (from left) actor Carl Betz, executive producer Joel Katz, actress Vivian Reis, director Ted Post, and creator/producer Norman Corwin for the production of my first solo teleplay 'The Joy of Living,'"
Toronto, Canada, 1971

wonderful to see a purely imaginative concept rendered into three-dimensional reality.

Paperback rights on *Logan's Run* had reverted to us and George and I, in collaboration with Dial Press, now sold softcover rights to Bantam for a $55,000 advance against royalties (their edition would eventually earn $90,000).

Later that year (1975) I was featured speaker at the thirty-year Lillis High reunion dinner in Kansas City. I'd graduated three decades earlier as a boy with his head full of unrealized dreams; now I'd returned as the "class celebrity." It was a triumphant evening.

In June of 1976 MGM's *Logan's Run* opened across country, becoming the hit of the summer, while Bantam saturated bookstores with 450,000 copies of the paperback edition. The film I'd written for Bette Davis, *Burnt Offerings,* was also released that summer to excellent box office. I had two back-to-back hits.

I'd approached MGM with the idea of a big-screen sequel, having written a forty-page outline on *Logan's World,* but they had other ideas. MGM

wanted to sell Logan directly to television, and CBS agreed to back the series. I was asked to develop the pilot episode with producer Saul David. Since our script was later butchered by the show's ultimate producers (Ivan Goff and Ben Roberts), I determined to have nothing more to do with the ill-conceived series. (It was axed by the network after only thirteen episodes.)

In March of 1977 I rented an apartment for two months on the island of Coronado (across the bridge from San Diego) to write a novel for Bantam Books. They had offered me $50,000 for a sequel to *Logan's Run;* I transformed my forty-page film outline for *Logan's World* into a 50,000-word novel. While I was in the area I lectured at San Diego State University (called San Diego State College when I attended in 1948) and had my picture taken with the members of LROF—Logan's Run Organization of Fans.

It was a prestigious year. Both *Logan's Run* and *Burnt Offerings* won Golden Scroll Awards from the Academy of Fantasy and Science Fiction as Best SF Film and Best Horror Film of 1976, and (for my pioneering work on Hammett) I was given the Maltese Falcon Award in San Francisco.

This was also what I have called "The Year of the Mummy." It is a Hollywood story I tell at almost every lecture—about how I was hired by ABC to script a modern version of *The Mummy* and how they kept asking for more and more changes as the outline progressed, how the Mummy himself kept getting stronger with each draft, until—at the final network meeting—they happily informed me that, at last, I was "green-lighted" for the teleplay. They just wanted one final change. I said sure, tell me what you want, I can handle anything. We want to drop the Mummy. But that was the whole *idea* of the thing! No, not at all, they said. They wanted me to write a script about how these five characters defile the Mummy's tomb at the beginning of the story and how they all get knocked off, one by one, until at the end there's just a big question mark left on the screen. Did they die of natural causes, or did the "Curse of the Tomb" do them in? I said thanks but no thanks—and that ended the project.

"Delivering my acceptance speech upon receiving an honorary doctorate from American River College," 1975

Logan's World was selling well for Bantam and with *Logan's Run* into its sixteenth printing, they offered me a contract for a third novel in the series. Since I had always felt that Logan's full story should form a trilogy, I signed the contract and began laying out the plot for *Logan's Search.*

After working on a film treatment at Universal that spring, I moved over to a new production company to script a science fiction epic for them. Big plans, big budget. But they closed down their operation before the film could be produced and, much later, I was told they were actually in business as a front for the largest cocaine ring in the San Fernando Valley! Of course, having had nothing to do with drugs in my life, this news really floored me. Working in Hollywood, you never know *what* to expect.

In October I made my second trip to Europe as part of the "Scene of the Crime Mystery Tour." (A good friend of mine, Ruth Windfeldt, who owns the Scene of the Crime bookshop, had put the tour together and she went along as our guide.) We all had a grand time in London, Cambridge, Oxford, York, and Edinburgh. (The highlands of Scotland were particularly impressive.) During this trip I was able to visit the offices of one of my British publishers, Corgi Books, where I arranged for the subsequent publication of several of my SF titles.

I returned home from Europe to find that my mother was very ill. Her health had been in a steady decline for over a year and now (in late December) she was taken to a Culver City hospital for emergency treatment. At eighty-four, she was terribly thin and frail. I was told by her doctor that there was practically no chance that she would survive. I loved her a great deal and it was hard facing the fact that her time had come. There was nothing I could do to save her.

Mom died shortly after midnight on January 4, 1979, of heart and kidney failure; she also had congested lungs and an aortic aneurism, among other serious problems. I knew it was best for her to move out of this life. I'm convinced that there is no final death of the spirit. In 1980 I dedicated *Logan's Search:*

FOR MY PARENTS

Michael Cahill Nolan (1877–1965)
Bernadette Kelly Nolan (1894–1979)
who are alive, somewhere, in this universe—
with love and gratitude.
Because of you, Logan runs.

In 1979 I'd been selected for inclusion in *Who's Who in America,* and soon thereafter my short story

"Saturday's Shadow" was voted one of the five best horror stories of the year by the World Fantasy Award Committee.

In February of 1980 Robert Easton, Frederick Faust's son-in-law, offered me the chance to edit the first in a series of *Max Brand's Best Western Stories* for Dodd, Mead. I was less than a month away from my fifty-second birthday—which made the offer ironic and somewhat startling. Why? Because when Faust ("Max Brand") died back in 1944, he was exactly my age, less than a month from *his* fifty-second year. Thus, just as my high school yearbook had prophesied, I was "to carry on for Max Brand."

Eventually, I ended up doing three of these Dodd, Mead collections of Brand's best (into 1987), along with a biographical/bibliographical study, *Max Brand, Western Giant,* for Bowling Green State University Popular Press. I had paid my debt to Frederick Faust.

I can't write about my life without writing about my cats. Prior to the 1980s I was strictly a dog lover; I'd owned dogs off and on since boyhood, but I had never liked cats. They were unresponsive; they chased birds; they yowled at night. Then, in July of 1980, my wife found an abandoned kitten hiding under a tumbleweed near a laundromat in Salina, Utah. She brought the cat home, but we didn't know what to call her. Cam had written a book on ancient Egypt and knew that the Egyptians of those times loved cats. So we named ours after Sekhmet, the lion-goddess.

Sekhmet proved to be only the first of our well-loved felines. As I write these words in my working office at home, cats seem to be everywhere. At the moment we have five (Sekhmet, Sasha, Buffy, Muscles, and Tiger), all strays who needed a home. As every socially responsible cat owner should do, we've made sure that all of our animals are spayed or neutered. It's the only way to solve the serious and increasing problem of pet overpopulation.

We love our cats for their special personalities; each is unique. I've discovered that they are continuously fascinating, as well as being extremely loving and responsive. Ours don't chase birds. And they don't yowl at night, either. They're too busy sleeping on or around our bed.

Cats and writers go together; their ultra-cool feline demeanor is comforting in times of stress. There's a reason why cats are so often pictured on the desks of writers: by their very presence they contribute to the creative process.

Yes, I confess it openly: I have become a dedicated cat lover.

By 1981 I had sold a new short story, "The Train," to *Gallery* magazine. The story had come to me in a dream and concerned an old steam train that, over a slow century in the mountains of Montana, gradually transformed itself into living flesh. Once its passengers are on board, the train-thing devours them.

The hero of my story must battle this creature and destroy it before it destroys him. As with *Logan's Run,* at first I considered this idea no more than the basis for an effective short story—but it lingered in my mind over the next decade until (after a research trip through Montana) I expanded it into my first horror novel, *Helltracks.* Now, finally, I have put that nightmare to rest.

In April of 1982 I accepted a new challenge: I taught a creative writing class at Bowling Green State University in Ohio, a brief but exciting experience. Much later I was offered another teaching job at UCLA Extension, but I turned it down. It would have taken time away from my writing, but the temptation was there; reaching out to touch the minds of others is a heady feeling. I was able to pass along some of my hard-won knowledge of professional writing in 1990 with my book *How to Write Horror Fiction.* The feedback on this one has been very satisfying. Many people, both professionals and amateurs, have told me that it's the only "how to write" book they've ever read that actually *does* teach a person how to write. Gratifying words, indeed.

Through the years I had been gathering material on Dashiell Hammett; I wanted to follow up my earlier critical study on this writer with a full biography. In 1983 this ambition was realized with the publication of my *Hammett: A Life at the Edge,* and I appeared on radio and television in New York that year, promoting the book. This experience intensified my interest in hard-boiled literature, leading, in 1985, to *The Black Mask Boys,* featuring my extensive history of *Black Mask* magazine (the birthplace of the hard-boiled school).

Earlier, in 1980, superstar Steve McQueen died of lung cancer. I had published a book about McQueen's racing in 1972, and we'd always assumed I'd wind up writing his full-length biography as well. There was so much in his colorful rags-to-riches life and career that I had not put into print. By January of 1984 my biography, *McQueen,* was in the nation's bookstores and I had embarked on a cross-country promotional tour. Over the next three months I appeared on twenty-one radio and television shows, from *Entertainment Tonight* to *Good Morning, America.*

It was this latter show that had me sweating. Normally, I am not nervous on television, but this one was different: the show's legendary interviewer, Barbara Walters, could be intimidating, and I knew that many millions of people would be watching me intently. It did not help my state of mind when I was scheduled to go on directly following former President Gerald Ford, sitting in *his* still-warm chair, staring into the probing, totally professional eyes of Ms. Walters. When she asked me the first question, with the cameras rolling, my throat locked and I could barely whisper a reply. Then, abruptly, I gained emotional control, saying, essentially, the hell with it, Nolan, you're on the air and you'd better shape up and not make a damn fool of yourself in front of the entire country. The rest of the interview went smoothly.

One of my primary ambitions was realized that year when several of my stories were adapted to comic-book format by Pacific Comics; top artists were employed and one of them, Al Williamson, had long been a favorite of mine. Having Williamson illustrate one of my stories was a genuine thrill. Now, in the 1990s, Malibu Graphics has embarked on a two-year series project in which they are adapting all three of my Logan books into comic-book format, using dialogue and descriptions directly from the novels.

My first hardcover collection of shock fiction, *Things Beyond Midnight,* was published late in 1984, establishing my credentials in the genre, paving the way for *Helltracks* and an anthology I would edit in 1990, *Urban Horrors.*

The year 1985 was highlighted by a location trip to Arizona and by my third excursion to Europe.

First, a bit of history. When the British decided to tear down London Bridge in the 1960s, a rich American entrepreneur purchased the historic structure and had the stones carefully numbered so that they could be properly reassembled in the States. Then he shipped them (all ten thousand tons!) to a stretch of raw desert at Lake Havasu, Arizona, near the California border. There, over the next three years, the 900-foot span was rebuilt, with a section of the Colorado River diverted to flow under it. Next, an authentic English village was laid out around the bridge to create the perfect atmosphere. Lake Havasu now had itself a star tourist attraction.

Returning to Los Angeles from a cross-country trip, Cam and I stopped to see it late one evening. Staring up at the dark structure I got an idea. Surely Jack the Ripper himself must have walked over this bridge some hundred years ago. What if he suddenly reappeared to begin his savage killing spree anew in our century? What if a final stone is found at the bottom of the Thames River in London containing the "essence" of the Ripper, and what if this missing

"Two examples of . . .

stone is brought back to Arizona to be fitted into the bridge? A tourist cuts herself on the stone and her blood revives the killer. Rising out of the stone comes Jack the Ripper!

This idea grew into a two-hour teleplay. In May of 1985 my script went into production in Lake Havasu. Cam and I spent several weeks there, on location. I did final polish work on the teleplay as it became a Movie of the Week for NBC. (Originally telecast as "Bridge Across Time," it was released in Europe, and later in the States, as "Terror at London Bridge.")

In the summer of 1985 I was called in by New World Television and ABC to write a Movie of the Week tailored to the disparate talents of Gary Coleman (star of "Diff'rent Strokes") and Angela Lansbury (of "Murder, She Wrote"). The network wanted to team them in what ABC termed "some kind of a train mystery."

I came up with an international thriller set in Europe called "Murder on the Istanbul Train." Coleman would be seeking a lost treasure, the Cross of Constantine, aided by Lansbury—who would, at the climax, turn out to be the villain. (Actually, my wife originated this plot which I gratefully appropriated.)

The ABC executives liked the basic concept and asked me to develop it. For research purposes, I told them, it would be necessary for me to go to Europe, join a tour group in London, and personally ride the new Orient Express from Paris into Vienna. They agreed and I took off for my third European jaunt (first class, of course) funded entirely by the network and New World Television.

It was a total success. I made copious background notes, returning to the States with all the plot holes neatly filled.

In one of my notebooks I recorded some shorthand impressions of this trip:

> Out of London's Victoria Station to the Devon coast . . . the wide-winged gulls, like a drift of pale confetti against the chalk-white Cliffs of Dover . . . the choppy waters of the English Channel on the crossing to France . . . into the bright, busy harbor at Boulogne . . . skimming past summer-fresh countryside on the long, drowsing afternoon's train ride to Paris, the City of Light, aburst with energy . . . the cross-babble of many languages . . . the narrow, climbing streets of Montmartre . . . and the tourist-jammed cobbled square beneath the domed shadow of Sacré-Coeur . . . the thrusting soot-blackened gargoyle faces of Notre Dame . . . the smart, expensive, bright-awninged shops along the Champs Elysées . . . the awesome splendor of Versailles with its golden rooms and veined marble . . . the bitter-smoked steam engine pulling us out of the Gare de l'Est . . . the immaculate white tablecloths laid with sun-dazzled silver in the vintage wagon-lits restaurant car with its etched white-glass nudes . . . the night trip through Germany with a hushed 3 A.M. depot stop in Stuttgart, a city sleeping beneath its blazing 3-pointed Star of Mercedes . . . the morning run through Austria, passing flower-decked cottages . . . into the gold-blazed richness of Salzburg, dominated by its mountain fortress . . . and, finally, through the storied Vienna woods, rising in a green-black tide to rolling hills . . . then crossing the Danube into Vienna itself, the *Third Man* city, with its under-street Hapsburg crypt, and the silver-scrolled coffins of Emperors . . . to the Palace of the Hapsburgs and its vast formal gardens . . . to a concert hall alive with violins . . . and darkness, with memories of Mozart currenting the steepled streets . . .

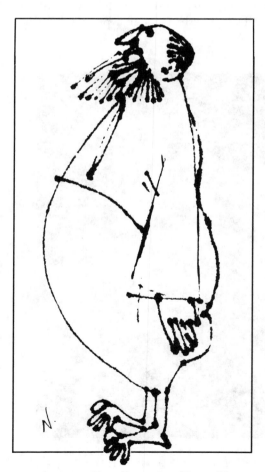

what my wife calls my 'napkin art'"

Unfortunately, although my final script was enthusiastically approved by the network, *Murder on the Istanbul Train* was never produced. On hiatus from her series, Angela Lansbury decided to go with a soap-opera miniseries instead of my international thriller.

By this time, my second Sam Space novel, *Look Out for Space,* was in print. It will be supplemented (in 1992) by a third entry in the series, a collection of shorter adventures, *Three for Space.* I'm quite fond of Sam and I have some future plans for him that will involve a much wider audience. I'm convinced that he has major potential.

Since I had grown up with radio drama, I was particularly gratified to have "The Party" dramatized for world presentation as part of the UNICEF Halloween Show in October of 1985. The adaptation was based directly on my printed story, and I was proudly on hand that evening for the broadcast.

Another lifelong ambition was realized in 1986 when a book of my best poems, *Dark Encounters,* was published in a beautifully bound limited edition. My poetry has always been a very private part of my life and my output is sparse. I'm hypercritical regarding my verse and, in fact, have written just one poem since 1986 that truly satisfies me—a rumination on the suicide of novelist/poet Sylvia Plath.

Final Exit

The dark yew tree
    Partnered with night
Slumbered her.

The mouthing rose
    Seeping its brows of blood
Soothed her.

Until life (O shock of waking!)
Swarmed finally free
    From her cell-walled hive
Of self.

I was able to exercise my art talent once again in 1986 for a collection of the three Logan novels, *Logan: A Trilogy,* which Maclay and Associates published in a special hardcover edition. I designed the cover, turned out three full-page ink drawings (one for each novel), and provided an illustrated frontispiece.

In July of 1988 I was accorded the honor of contributing to a "Special Nolan Issue" of the small-press magazine *The Horror Show.* I had become quite active in the genre (being on conference panels titled "Modern Masters of Horror" and being represented in such anthologies as *Masters of Darkness* and *Great Tales of Horror and the Supernatural*) and I was making a concerted effort to build a reputation for quality terror-suspense fiction.

Still, I could not resist the chance to widen the scope of my work. In 1989 I was given the opportunity to write *Rio Renegades,* dealing with an outlaw band roving the Rio Grande border country in 1876. My novel was part of a Western series written by several other authors, so I used the publisher's "house name" of Terence Duncan. However, I made sure that I was firmly attached to the book by a tongue-in-cheek dedication:

> To WILLIAM F. NOLAN
> without whom this book
> could never have been written

In my career I've used such pen names as "Frank Anmar," "F. E. Edwards," and (thanks to my father) "Mike Cahill" on various magazine pieces, but thus far *Rio Renegades* is one of only two books which I have had published under a pseudonym (the other

"With my early mentor and longtime pal Ray Bradbury," Los Angeles, 1986

being *The Work of William F. Nolan*, my bibliography, on which I used the name "James Hopkins" as co-compiler).

I responded to a creative challenge of a different kind in the summer of 1989 when I entered a professional recording studio in Hollywood to tape a dramatic reading of my novel *Logan's Run*. The audiocassette resulting from this session was commercially released by Dove Books on Tape.

That same summer, producer/director Dan Curtis once again entered my life. Dan had spent most of the decade working on his monumental TV adaptations of Herman Wouk's related novels *The Winds of War* and *War and Remembrance*. Now he was anxious to get back into production with some less serious material; we worked together for several weeks on a Movie of the Week sequel, *Trilogy of Terror II*.

In 1991 I supplied eleven pages of art for a booklet of mine, *Blood Sky*, and another thirty pieces of art to the magazine *Threshold of Fantasy* for an interview profile. This, however, was all free work.

I *did* get paid for some new art which I supplied to *Weird Tales* for their "Special William F. Nolan Issue" in the fall of 1991 (another honor for which I am most grateful), but I have long since reconciled myself to the fact that I'm *not* a professional in this field and never will be. My art, these days, is pretty well confined to coffee-shop napkins.

I have chosen to call this essay "A Life in Writing" and the title is particularly apt, since I cannot imagine life without words. Words . . . waiting inside my head . . . waiting to be put to paper . . . waiting for me to give them a unique life. And we *are* unique, each of us, each writer on this planet. No one else has my exact background, my particular experiences, my way of looking at people and places and objects. There was a Hemingway world, a Faulkner world, a Scott Fitzgerald world . . . and there is a Nolan world. This is the world I intend to keep exploring as I enter my thirty-sixth year as a full-time professional writer. I have a long way to go. There is much more ground to cover, many stories left to tell.

Someone once asked me at a lecture: "Mr. Nolan, why do you write, write, write?" I replied with a question of my own: "Why do you breathe, breathe, breathe?"

That says it all.

BIBLIOGRAPHY

Fiction:

(With George Clayton Johnson) *Logan's Run*, Dial, 1967.

Death Is for Losers, Sherbourne, 1968.

The White Cad Cross-Up, Sherbourne, 1969.

Space for Hire, Lancer, 1971, reissued with new introduction, International Polygonics (IPL), 1985.

Logan's World, Bantam, 1977.

Logan's Search, Bantam, 1980.

Look Out for Space, IPL, 1985.

Logan: A Trilogy (collection), Maclay, 1986.

(Under the pseudonym Terence Duncan) *Rio Renegades*, Zebra, 1989.

Helltracks, Avon, 1991.

Short-story collections:

Impact 20: Excursions into the Extraordinary, Paperback Library, 1963.

Alien Horizons, Pocket Books, 1974.

Wonderworlds, Gollancz (London), 1977.

Things Beyond Midnight, Scream, 1984.

Three for Space, Gryphon, 1992.

Six in Darkness, Pulphouse, forthcoming.

Poetry:

Hemingway: Last Days of the Lion (poem with essay), Capra, 1974.

Dark Encounters, Dream House, 1986.

Nonfiction:

(With John Fitch) *Adventure on Wheels: The Autobiography of a Road Racing Champion*, Putnam, 1959.

Barney Oldfield: The Life and Times of America's Legendary Speed King (biography), Putnam, 1961.

Phil Hill: Yankee Champion (biography), Putnam, 1962.

Men of Thunder: Fabled Daredevils of Motor Sport (collection of profiles), Putnam, 1964.

John Huston: King Rebel (biography), Sherbourne, 1965.

Sinners and Supermen (collection of profiles), All Star, 1965, reissued as *Legends and Lovers*, Borgo, forthcoming.

Dashiell Hammett: A Casebook (critical study), McNally & Loftin, 1969.

Steve McQueen: Star on Wheels (biography), Putnam, 1972.

Carnival of Speed: True Adventures in Motor Racing (collection of essays), Putnam, 1973.

The Ray Bradbury Companion: A Life and Career History, Photolog, and Comprehensive Checklist of Writings, Gale Research, 1975.

Hammett: A Life at the Edge (biography), Congdon and Weed, 1983.

McQueen (biography), Congdon and Weed, 1984.

The Black Mask Boys: Masters in the Hard-Boiled School of Detective Fiction (collection of profiles/anthology), Morrow, 1985.

The Work of Charles Beaumont: An Annotated Bibliography and Guide, Borgo, 1986, revised and expanded edition, Borgo, 1990.

(Under the pseudonym James Hopkins with Boden Clarke) *The Work of William F. Nolan: An Annotated Bibliography and Guide,* Bongo, 1988, revised and expanded edition forthcoming.

How to Write Horror Fiction, Writer's Digest Books, 1990.

Editor:

Ray Bradbury Review, privately published, 1952, revised and updated edition, Graham, 1988.

(With Charles Beaumont) *Omnibus of Speed: An Introduction to the World of Motor Sport,* Putnam, 1958.

(Anonymously coedited with Beaumont) *The Fiend in You,* Ballantine, 1962.

(With Beaumont) *When Engines Roar,* Bantam, 1964.

Man Against Tomorrow, Avon, 1965.

The Pseudo-People: Androids in Science Fiction, Sherbourne, 1965.

Three to the Highest Power, Avon, 1968.

A Wilderness of Stars: Stories of Man in Conflict with Space, Sherbourne, 1969.

The Future Is Now: All-New, All-Star Science Fiction Stories, Sherbourne, 1970.

A Sea of Space, Bantam, 1970.

(Anonymously edited) Chad Oliver *The Edge of Forever* (collection), Sherbourne, 1971.

The Human Equation: Four Science Fiction Novels of Tomorrow, Sherbourne, 1971.

(With Martin H. Greenberg) *Science-Fiction Origins,* Fawcett Popular Library, 1980.

Max Brand's Best Western Stories (collection), Dodd, 1981.

Max Brand's Best Western Stories Volume II (collection), Dodd, 1985.

Max Brand: Western Giant: The Life and Times of Frederick Schiller Faust, Bowling Green University Popular Press, 1986.

Max Brand's Best Western Stories Volume III (collection), Dodd, 1987.

(With Greenberg) *Urban Horrors,* Dark Harvest, 1990.

(With Greenberg) *The Bradbury Chronicles,* Penguin/ROC, 1991.

Screenplays:

A Dream of the Stars (documentary), Dollens Productions, 1953.

(With George Clayton Johnson) *Logan's Run,* MGM, 1967.

(With Ray Russell) *Dorian Black,* printed in *The Book of Hell,* Sphere (London), 1980.

(With Dan Curtis) *Burnt Offerings,* United Artists, 1976.

Also author of twenty television scripts, including *The Turn of the Screw, Sky Heist, The Kansas City Massacre, Bridge Across Time,* and *The Black Summer.* Contributor of short stories, articles, artwork, and poetry to 225 periodicals and newspapers, including *Prairie Schooner, Sports Illustrated, Playboy, Los Angeles Times, Alfred Hitchcock's Mystery Magazine, Road and Track, Films and Filming, Weird Tales* (special Nolan issue), *The Horror Show* (special Nolan issue), and *The Writer.* Contributor of fiction and nonfiction to more than 200 anthologies and textbooks, including *Adventures for Americans, The Fitzgerald/Hemingway Annual, Masters of Darkness, Best Motor Racing Stories,* and *A Treasury of Great Horse Stories.* Several Nolan works have been selected for tapes and video.

Nolan has also published several short-story pamphlets, including "The Dandelion Chronicles," and "Blood Sky." He has served as columnist, *Badge Bar Journal,* 1956–58; book reviewer, *Los Angeles Times,* 1964–70; contributing editor, *Rhodomagnetic Digest,* 1952; managing editor, *Gamma,* 1963; West Coast editor, *Auto,* 1964; associate editor, *Motor Sport Illustrated,* 1964; and contributing editor, *Chase,* 1964.

Jay Parini

1948-

MY LIFE SO FAR

There is something irresistibly seductive about the prospect of visiting one's past in memory, about moving through that pre-verbal jumble of images and feelings that surfaces in nightmares, in daydreams, in sleight of thoughts. Freud talks about remembering the past in order to "burn it up," as if that would do it. It won't. The past is obstinately pre-verbal; indeed, the unwritten world is not erased by the written word. It is merely shadowed by it, or limned.

The treasure-house of images that constitute a sense of one's self-in-the-world is stunningly resilient and productive. One can go back to it again and again, for stories and poems, for essays. And every attempt to capture it—to arrest and reify a little piece of it—seems just wrong enough to warrant another try. And this keeps us (if I may speak for other writers as well as myself) writing.

How does one begin to describe the curve of one's private memory, the history of one's heart? The first thing I remember, or imagine I remember, is sitting beside my father in a blue 1950 Chevy. I was two, and it was one of those red-letter days that sticks out in memory because it was different from the others. We went over to a Chevy dealership in West Pittston owned by a man called Roy; the dealership was on the banks of the Susquehanna River in West Pittston, Pennsylvania. Our double mission that day was to pick up the new car and drive to the hospital, where we were picking up my mother and my new sister, Dorrie, who had been born a few days earlier. She was born, like me, in the old Pittston hospital, which looked out across the river.

What I recall is leaning against my father's strong, hairy arm as we drove. It was August, bright and hot. And that wonderful smell briefly in the possession of all new cars filled my head: an odor of plastic, squeaky clean glass, hot leather, and oil. To this day I never see a 1950 Chevy in one of those antique-car dealerships without finding myself breathless with adoration. One day I plan to buy one.

I spent the first four years in Exeter—mining village near Pittston—then in Scranton. The imagery

Jay Parini, 1990

of anthracite mining was all around me: abandoned coal breakers, with their thousands of tiny windows long ago smashed, the clapboard siding weathered gray much like the barns of New England. Culm dumps were heaped around the edges of the towns, burning a bright vermillion-blue at night; when the summer winds drew across them, they filled the air with a sulphurous smell that struck me then as natural. It was what air smelled like.

Here and there one could actually find abandoned mineshafts, with hexing crosses nailed over the entrances saying "Danger" and "Keep Out." I was deeply attracted to those mines: the idea of tunneling

At ten months old with his father, Leo Parini, 1948

backward into time. My uncle Gene was a miner, and my paternal grandfather had been one, too, although briefly. Indeed, my uncle Gene was among the last miners killed in the anthracite mining region: on the day I graduated from high school in 1966. The mine caved in on him, crushed him, leaving his widow with five young children. I wrote a poem about it called "The Miner's Wake"—

The small ones squirmed in suits and dresses,
wrapped their rosaries round the chair legs,
tapped the walls with squeaky shoes.

But their widowed mother, at thirty-four,
had mastered every pose of mourning,
plodding the sadness like an ox through mud.

Her mind ran well ahead of her heart,
making calculations of the years without him
that stretched before her like a humid summer.

The walnut coffin honeyed in sunlight;
calla lilies bloomed over silk and satin.
Nuns cried heaven into their hands

while I, a nephew with my lesser grief,
sat by a window, watching pigeons
settle onto slag like summer snow.

The sense of having come from a family of Italian immigrants on my father's side was always strong. My mother's family were from England— working-class WASPs. So I felt, in a way, tugged (not torn) between two worlds. On alternate Sundays I would visit my Italian grandmother, Ida, who would serve me a wonderful plate of homemade pasta with her own rich tomato sauce or visit with my English grandmother, Ruth Clifford, who cooked dumplings and roast beef and delicious blueberry pies. (My mother, Verna, cooked plain old-fashioned food: ground beef and mashed potatoes, string beans, iceberg lettuce.)

There was a good deal of suspicion of the ethnic Italian world on my mother's side, but my father, Leo, had been transmogrified from a threatening little Italian guy who had never graduated from high school into an upwardly mobile businessman who had joined the Baptist Church and now taught Sunday school. The story of my father's climb to the respectable middle class is one of the central stories of America in the postwar era.

He was one of five brothers, the son of a small-time hood who dabbled in cards, dice, race tracks, and various traditional cons; he worked in the mines only when he was desperate. "Pop" had come from Rome, and in his late twenties he was married by prior arrangement to a fifteen-year-old girl from near Genoa—my grandmother. The children came quickly, five kids in five years, but my grandfather was no family man. He took off, returning every now and then from Miami or New York to say hello in a broad-brimmed fedora and chocolate-brown suit. His gold-toothed smile is the only thing about him I remember (and the fact that he carried a pistol in a shoulder holster).

In the mideighties, while living in Italy, I wrote a poem about my grandmother and her boys: an idealized version of what heaven might be like when they are all home for Sunday dinner. It's called "Grandmother in Heaven," and it sums up my impression of that particular family:

In a plume-field, white above the blue,
she's pulling up a hoard of root crops
planted in a former life and left to ripen:
soft gold carrots, beets, bright gourds.
There's coffee in the wind, tobacco smoke
and garlic, olive oil and lemon.
Fires burn coolly through the day,
the water boils at zero heat.
It's always almost time for Sunday dinner,
with the boys all home: dark Nello,
who became his cancer and refused to breathe;
her little Geno, who went down the mines
and whom they had to dig all day to find;

that willow, Tony, who became so thin
he blew away; then Julius and Leo,
who survived the others by their wits alone
but found no reason, after all was said,
for hanging on. They'll take their places
in the sun today at her high table,
as the antique beams light up the plates,
the faces that have lately come to shine.

The contrast with my maternal grandparents, who lived around the corner from my house on South Rebecca Avenue in West Scranton, was extreme. Grandpa Paul Clifford worked for the telephone company as a lineman. He put up wires all over northeastern Pennsylvania, and he liked to smoke stogies and sit in his undershirt and listen to ball games on the radio. He had little to say, but he had a rather kindly gruffness about him. My grandmother, Ruth, was large and sweet, a diabetic farmgirl from near Altoona whom my grandfather had met by chance while on a job. She spent her life longing, I suspect, for the simple life of the farm she'd abandoned. Her gentleness was inspiring, and she and I formed an extremely close bond, especially after she lost her legs from the diabetes when I was twelve. I spent hours sitting and talking with her in the few years she had left.

My parents were molded by postwar mores. My mother had worked in a shipyard with my father during the war, but—like all American women of the time—she was herded back into the home, where the idea of being a "housewife and mother" was glorified by the magazines and, more importantly, by television, which hijacked the nation's collective mind in the early fifties. I don't think she ever really liked being a housewife, and as soon as Dorrie and I left high school, she rushed eagerly out to work.

I was among the first generation to be raised by the shiny little screen. Howdy Doody, Captain Kangaroo and Mr. Greenjeans, the Mouseketeers: these were my friends. I loved Walt Disney, and I envied him. The idea that he spent his time thinking up cartoons and movies like *Parent Trap* and *Davy Crockett* struck me as the ideal life, and I determined at the age of six to live by the imagination. I wrote to Walt Disney, and he (or his studio) sent an autographed photo that I pinned above my bed. It stayed there until I left home for good in 1966.

I was a daydreaming, nervous child with no friends to speak of. I loved baseball, but I couldn't hit and I couldn't catch. I did not like school. My mother told me what to do and when, and I did whatever I was supposed to do on the surface and did what I wanted to do behind the scenes. My body was going through

"As Little Leaguer," 1960

the motions of daily life, but my heart and head were powerfully elsewhere. I learned dreadful habits of dissociation from the world around me that I have to fight against now rather painfully. And I rarely win this fight. My natural state is dreaming, and I find the imagined world preferable in most cases to the "real" world, though I understand that the imagined world depends upon and springs from the real world—a subject contemplated with infinite sophistication by Wallace Stevens in his poems, which have meant a great deal to me over the past two decades. (I keep thinking of two lines from "Man with a Blue Guitar"—"I cannot bring a world quite round, / Although I patch it as I can.")

My father was successful as an insurance salesman, and I became very enamored with the image of success. It was part of the American story, and I liked that story. I still do. I watched my father energetically perform his work and learned by imitation to perform well in whatever work I had at hand. I determined to get out of what my mother called "my shell." To make friends. In the seventh grade I bought Dale Carnegie's *How to Win Friends and Influence People,* and I memorized his rules for social interaction. I put them into practice. To my astonishment, I found I could actually make friends quite easily; people were hungry for attachments, for recognition, for an audience. I became a reasonably good listener, and I still listen with attention to my friends.

My father, in his late thirties, was converted to a Fundamentalist brand of Christianity, and one of the positive side benefits for me was a thorough introduction to the King James Bible. Every morning my father would read a chapter to us, and I loved to hear him linger over the biblical rhythms and quaint diction. The language of Bible was imprinted on my brain, and I still feel those rhythms as I write: the slight pitch toward formality undercut by a startling draft of ordinary speech. "I will lift up mine eyes unto the hills, from whence cometh my help." There is no better prose than this.

For reasons involving family dynamics too complicated to explain here, I could never abide being told what to do. At school, I resented any assignment and would read only books not suggested by a teacher. This resistance continued through college, and it continues today. I have to struggle to read even the books that I assign my own students! And I do not easily follow instructions. Nothing gives me more pause than a booklet full of instructions that must be followed: how to assemble a fold-out bed, how to put together a stereo system or install a new program on my computer or get my fax to work. The result of this deep-set resistance to being told to do anything was that my high school and college grades were, given my natural bent toward reading and writing, comparatively low.

Still, I managed to get into Lafayette College. As the first person in my family ever to attend college, I felt amazingly privileged and proud. And Lafayette impressed me deeply with its traditions, its idyllic campus on a hillside overlooking the small industrial town of Easton, Pennsylvania. One of America's oldest colleges, founded in 1826, Lafayette still had the aura of the twenties clinging to it, with football games attended by gentlemen in fur coats, with rich and drunken alumni staggering around the campus on weekends.

I took to college life with relish, even though I had to struggle horribly with issues of authority and self-discipline. I got a *C* in freshman English my first semester, but I liked the course, and I began to write poetry and prose in my spare hours. In the spring of my freshman year, I saw that an open poetry reading was being held at the coffeehouse on campus sponsored by the chaplaincy, and I appeared with a trembling sheaf of a dozen poems in hand.

My turn came, and I took the stage in front of a sizable crowd and two well-known English professors, W. W. Watt and James Lusardi. My poems were terrible in almost every way, but they showed a certain affinity for verbal expression, and I was encouraged by the response of the audience and, in particular, Dr. Lusardi. He took me under his wing, and that made all the difference.

My career plans were uncertain. I had imagined that, somehow, I would become a lawyer and politician, running for Congress or some such thing. Those ambitions harked back to my "successes" in high school as class politician, actor (I was actually quite good, I thought, in *Our Town* and *Camelot*), Eagle Scout, and Boy Most Likely to Succeed. Public life had seemed possible, and it was even comfortable. I could escape into an image of myself thrown upon the screen of society. I imagined it was not impossible that one day I might become President of the United States.

But the truth was I preferred reading and writing poems to almost anything else. And my "real" self, the person I meet in the dark, in silence, walking in the woods or sitting by a pond, has little interest in publicity, power, or "politics" in the conventional sense of that much-abused term. It did not take a genius to see that American politicians were hollow men in suits, and that they made little dent on the imagination, the emotional, or spiritual life of the people they "represented."

I entered college in 1966, and I recall seeing my first demonstration against the Vietnam War during the early part of my freshman year. I watched a dozen or so upperclassmen (there were no women at Lafayette then) holding up protest placards, all led on by the college chaplain, F. Peter Sabey, who later became a good friend. I remember that water was dumped from a window of a dorm onto their heads by some fraternity boys, who snickered and jeered. Until that moment, I had vaguely thought the war was a good thing. In high school, I had actually led a march in favor of the war (and received a gold medal from the American Legion for my efforts!).

I was, briefly, on the brink of having to go to Vietnam myself. My draft board called me up, and I went on an early-morning bus to Wilkes-Barre, where I stood in line, naked, with a hundred other eighteen-year-olds. The horror of that day comes back to me with dream-exactitude. The innocence of those boys, all joking about "killing gooks," still saddens me. I did not want to kill anyone. And I did not want to see them, my countrymen, killed.

A turning point for me was reading Noam Chomsky's essay on "The Logic of Withdrawal" in *Ramparts* in September of 1967. The magazine was sitting in the chaplaincy office, and I took it back to my dorm. I realized then what a mistake the war was, and how American power had been thoroughly

Jay with his sister, Dorrie—Scranton, Pennsylvania, 1966

medieval haze. A city wall surrounded the town, centuries old, protecting it from the ravages of modernity. Students wore long scarlet gowns to class, and the lecturers wore black gowns. Time could not penetrate that atmosphere, and I sunk happily into a solipsistic life of the mind, reading poetry with the excitement and vengeance of first acquaintance.

A seminal moment came in a long British bathtub in St. Regulus Hall, where I lived in a damp basement room. I had just bought a paperback edition of the selected poems of Gerard Manley Hopkins and I opened it in that tub, reading "The Windhover," "God's Grandeur," and the "Terrible Sonnets" for the first time. When I closed that book, I knew that I would spend the rest of my life making poems. It was one of those strange, ecstatic hours. I was lifted; my soul felt as if it had been rinsed.

I could hear in Hopkins a voice that wakened my own voice: the hard alliterative drive, the linking sound of vowels chiming on vowels. A friend gave me a copy of T. S. Eliot's poems, and I now read "Prufrock" and "Burnt Norton" for the first time, then I turned to Wallace Stevens, Frost, Yeats, Whitman, Wordsworth, and Keats. Under the patient guidance of a young don at St. Andrews by the name of Tony Ashe, I learned what poets one might read and how one might talk about what one read. My own poetry came alive. I wrote day and night, trying my hand at sonnets, villanelles, and rhyming couplets. I wrote elegies, nature poems, verse epistles to friends in the manner of Pope, even ballads. It was a thrilling time for me.

I also gathered a circle of friends, mostly British. I went to tea parties, I walked along the West Sands and watched the cormorants grazing for herring on the cobalt waves, and I sat for hours on the pier looking across the North Sea. I walked in the woods nearby, once coming upon a whole field of bluebells in spring. The texture of British life was deeply moving to me, and it remains so: the smell of tea, the stone walls, the damp gardens, the tight smiles of the people, the lilting voices. I was fairly ignorant then of class differences, so I was not bothered by the snobbish aspects of life in Britain that would later come to upset me.

I did not, indeed, forget about the Vietnam War entirely. I argued against the war constantly with my friends, and I attended a rally against the war at the American embassy in London. I travelled to Paris, where I met a number of young Americans who thought like I did about the war. These were heady days, and I really did believe that a revolution had occurred; that the people of my generation would never again let wars and oppression, racism, econom-

misused. The country had been hijacked after the Second World War by "the best and the brightest," a small group of men who were using anticommunism as a way to create a huge national security state, complete with a secret police on the domestic (the FBI) and international (the CIA) fronts. That we were interfering in a civil war in a remote land by dropping endless bombs on children in tiny jungle villages was intolerable. This essay is no place to rehash my objections to the Vietnam War and what it symbolized; let me only say that I found myself deeply at odds with my country. I became a skeptic about America and its purposes in the world, and I have never lost that skepticism. I felt just as angry when we dropped all of those "smart bombs" on the innocent people of Iraq, thus increasing their already mammoth suffering.

I fled America in 1968. I went to Scotland, where I'd been accepted for a year abroad at the University of St. Andrews, an idyllic place if one ever existed. The oldest university in Scotland, dating back to the twelfth century, St. Andrews hung in a ic injustice, and all the bad things happen, and the hypocrisy and ignorance that seemed to occlude the minds of the generations ahead of me would be banished forever.

Another guide for me at this time was Bertrand Russell. I read his *Autobiography*—still one of my favorite books; it's a splendidly clear and moving book, and the first volume culminates with his imprisonment for protesting the First World War. The senselessness and barbarism of that war paralleled, for me, the Vietnam War, and I was inspired. I bought a multivolume collection of Russell's essays, and I found in his reasonable tone and liberal attitudes a home of sorts. Russell became a hero. I wrote to him in Wales, asking if I might come and visit, and he wrote back: "Dear Parini: Were I not ninety-six and at death's door, I should certainly welcome you to tea. Alas, we shall have to meet in the next world. Good luck to you." It was signed merely "Russell."

I went back to Lafayette College with reluctance. St. Andrews was difficult to leave. But the academic year of 1969–1970 was a zinging one: Kent State, the bombing of Cambodia, the full dithyrambic dance of the sixties. I found myself marching on Washington, making speeches to student groups, leading demonstrations. I debated the war on local television with a right-wing student. And I continued to write and read poetry. James Lusardi, with whom I was now studying Milton, read my poems with an intensity and affection that amazed me, treating my imperfect and jejune efforts as if he had just stumbled upon "Tintern Abbey." He gave me the confidence to declare myself, to my family and friends, a poet; he also suggested that I pursue graduate study in literature.

My academic career gathered momentum now, for the first time. I got an *A* in every course, and I did an honors thesis on Hopkins that won a prize. I was given a fellowship from Lafayette to be used for graduate study anywhere I chose. At the same time, my draft lottery number was promising, and—in any case—I was not opening any letters that arrived from my draft board. I simply took off for Scotland, unsure of when or if I would return. (When ominous-seeming letters from my draft board arrived, I dropped them into the fireplace unopened.)

M̲y stay in Scotland lasted through 1975. I lived, first, in the freezing attic room of a house owned by Tony and Sue Ashe. Tony remained my closest friend and academic counselor throughout my years in St. Andrews, and I learned from him and Sue what conversation sounded like. We had long lunches

every day, and these were attended by friends and colleagues; we traded witticisms, talked about politics, books, films. I learned the complicated ins and outs of the British class system.

For all its positive sides, my first year back in Scotland was difficult. I fell into a bleak despair, and I would spend hours simply staring into the fire in my room. I walked the beaches at night, alone. I felt isolated, frustrated, confused. I thought I was going to die, and I took to reading Buddhist and Christian scriptures with a vengeance. At night, in bed, I felt like I was dropping through a dark and windy void. The "Terrible Sonnets" of Hopkins became my life, with lines like "I wake and feel the fell of dark, not day" echoing in my head.

After six months or so, the depression passed. I turned my attention to my work, studying a little Latin and less Greek. I read everything I could lay my hands on from Chaucer and Wyatt through Shakespeare, Donne, Jonson, Dryden, Byron, Arnold, Joyce, and Beckett. I studied mythology, religion, and art—all in the rather haphazard way characteristic of British education—to my mind, the best way to do it. I always had the impression that my counterparts in American graduate schools were being too systematically "trained." They left with Ph.D. degrees from Yale and Stanford somehow believing they knew more than they did, feeling that their education was

On a beach in Crete, Greece, 1973

over. I knew this was just the beginning, and that I would never really "catch up." One never does. Indeed, I find myself endlessly circling back, encountering favorite literary works as if for the first time and wondering where I was when I first read them.

I was writing poems and, sometimes, stories in addition to working on critical research projects on Hopkins and, later, Roethke. It was in 1971 that I happened to meet Alastair Reid, the poet and essayist from the *New Yorker*.

Reid was a graduate of St. Andrews (his studies had been interrupted by the Second World War, in which he served in the Pacific), and my former history tutor—Miss Anne Wright—was a friend of his. When I confessed to her my poetic ambitions, she said, "Ah, you must meet Alastair." She called him, and we met in a pub in the center of town. He invited me to come to his house the next day with a batch of poems.

Reid and his son, Jasper, lived in a glade just off the Royal and Ancient Golf Course—the oldest golf course in the world. His house was called Pilmour Cottage, and it was nestled in a small copse of trees filled with rooks. One could see and smell the North Sea from his kitchen. I used to go jogging along the golf course, and I did so that day with a packet of poems in a manilla folder. I knocked anxiously at his door.

"Ah, the poet," he said.

"Yes."

"Come in."

I followed him to the kitchen, and we sat at the table and he worked systematically through my poems, crossing out words, whole lines and stanzas, adding words and phrases. He said almost nothing. Just "corrected" the poems.

"I used to work with Robert Graves," he said. "In Majorca. I translated *Lives of the Noble Caesars* with him. I'd provide a rough translation—though I never thought it was rough at the time. And he would simply revise it, changing what struck him as wrong. He would add this word or that phrase. It was how I learned to write." From then on, I brought him poems on a regular basis. And he would change things. We became fast friends, and the friendship continues to this day.

I learned a great deal from reading Alastair Reid's poetry, too. His mellifluous style, his idiosyncratic syntax, his tone of amazement: I picked all of this up from him. Reid got me interested in Yeats, in Dylan Thomas, in Graves, in Auden, and John Crowe Ransom. He also introduced me—quite literally—to Jorge Luis Borges and Pablo Neruda, both of whom he translated. Borges came to St. Andrews in 1972,

and I spent many hours listening to him. In London, that same spring, I met Neruda. It was all immensely terrifying and exhilarating. Ideas and influences were coming at me from every direction, but I liked it.

In 1974, a local bookseller told me he was starting a poetry press, and he asked to see a manuscript. I eagerly cobbled one together from poems I considered finished at the time, and he quickly agreed to publish it. *Singing in Time* appeared in a hardback and paper edition, with a tiny print run. My friends all dutifully purchased or bummed a copy, and I was happy to see my poems in type. It was about this time that *Scottish International*—a "real" magazine—accepted my first poem. I also began reviewing poetry for *Lines Review*. Not surprisingly, my first article was a survey of the poems of Alastair Reid.

I should add that Alastair wasn't the only writer I knew in those days. Two poets who lived together in Glasgow became good friends: Anne Stevenson and Philip Hobsbaum. They were both immensely kind to me and helped me. I would take the train to Glasgow for the weekend, attending their informal seminars on Sunday evenings. Hobsbaum introduced me to his former student, a young poet called Seamus Heaney, who was about six or seven years my senior. I invited Seamus to St. Andrews, where he read at a poetry festival I had helped organize. Later, I visited him a couple of times in Dublin. We shared a commitment to clear, imagistic poetry written in a concrete, musical, and alliterative style. My second book of poems, *Anthracite Country*, is deeply indebted to Heaney's early work.

The chairman of the English department at St. Andrews was a weathered and eccentric little man called Alec Falconer, who had been a naval officer during the war. His main interest was Shakespeare, and he had spent a lifetime studying Shakespeare in relation to the sea. He was convinced that during the Bard's lost years he must have been an officer in the Royal Navy. His masterwork was *Shakespeare and the Sea*, which he followed with *A Glossary of Naval and Gunnery Terms in Shakespeare*—two of the oddest pieces of literary scholarship ever produced.

Falconer was known only as "the Professor," and indeed each department had only one professor. Everyone else was a "lecturer." The poor man did, as it were, go completely insane in his latter years, and while he was my supervisor he was clearly suffering from paranoia and something like encroaching senility. But we got along well, and I liked sitting in his vast office discussing history, politics, and literature. He adored "Sir Winston," and he disliked "newcomers." C. S. Lewis was "that odious fraud." James Joyce and D. H. Lawrence were anathema. The great modern writer was Hugh Walpole. He was deeply conservative, but he was not an imperialist. He thought the Vietnam War "an ignominious war" because it was not fought among equals for reasons of self-defense.

I finished my thesis on Hopkins and the meditative tradition for Professor Falconer, then turned to my study of Theodore Roethke, which involved a summer of research in Seattle, where I systematically ploughed through the poet's working notebooks, which were housed in the Special Collections department of the library at the University of Washington. I loved doing research and writing criticism because so many different things came together as one proceeded. Working on Roethke, I had to grapple with the entire English poetic tradition, with Jung and Freud, with the mystical writers from St. John of the Cross through Evelyn Underhill.

My thesis work was also my education as a poet in the formal aspects of the craft. Roethke tried his hand at everything, and it was fascinating to read through his notebooks and to see how a great poet worked through many drafts, arriving in the end somewhere that could never have been foreseen. I noticed, for instance, that a phrase like "a sidelong pickerel" smile cropped up in poem after poem for two decades before it found its perfect and final resting place in the famous "Elegy for Jane." Roethke's notebooks became a model of sorts, and I still am never without

Parents, Leo and Verna Parini, 1989

a notebook. Mine is full of ideas for poems and stories, phrases, rough drafts, titles, favorite lines from other poets, fragments of conversation overheard in a diner. I quarry these notebooks regularly for poems and essays.

In retrospect, I feel gratitude to Falconer; he saw me through the complicated process of Scottish postgraduate study, and he was unfailingly kind. Most of the graduate students I knew in St. Andrews never finished their theses, for all kinds of reasons. The temptation to do little or nothing was overwhelming. But Falconer did not encourage meandering and laziness, and my instincts were in any case to forge ahead. I managed to have the doctoral thesis done by autumn of 1974, and I had the degree a year later.

I began tutoring and lecturing at St. Andrews from the moment I returned as a postgraduate student, and by 1974 I was pretty much accepted as a member of the teaching staff. My habit of writing in the morning and teaching in the afternoon evolved during that time. After breakfast, I would go to a building adjacent to the University Library that once housed the Scottish parliament—long before Scotland ever succumbed to English rule. There was a huge room on the top floor that seemed perpetually empty, and I found a niche there where I could work in peace. I began writing a comic novel about a young Canadian archaeologist who came to St. Andrews to do research on medieval castles. Written in the style of Evelyn Waugh, my favorite novelist at the time, it grew to some five or six hundred pages in manuscript. I would read it in the evenings to friends, who loved the *roman á clef* aspect of the story. We all had a good time, but the novel did not hang together, and I decided not to try to publish it. It still sits in my attic, a neat bundle of semifictive madness never quite realized.

In my last couple of years in St. Andrews I rented a little house on a lovely backstreet. I shared the house with close friends, and quite an energetic social life emerged: the usual big lunches, dinner parties, dance parties. I entertained various poets: Hobsbaum and Stevenson, the brilliant and blind John Heath-Stubbs (who spent a week with me once). I met Auden, just before he died, in Oxford. I continued my friendship with Alastair Reid, who had moved away from St. Andrews for a year or two, then returned. Once I made a pilgrimage to the island of Orkney—far to the north—where my object of veneration was a wonderfully original and affecting poet and novelist called George Mackay Brown, with whom I have occasionally kept in touch by letter.

The option of staying on in St. Andrews presented itself, but it was never really a possibility. I missed

Jay Parini and Devon Jersild, at their wedding, 1981

the United States—my family, especially. My parents were desperately eager for my return, and I had begun to tire of the British class system, which pervades and determines all aspects of life there. I applied to various colleges for jobs and was hired by Dartmouth, in New Hampshire. I left Scotland, in midsummer of 1975, for a new life.

I remember so well getting onto the train at Leuchars Junction, a few miles outside of St. Andrews. Tony Ashe drove me to the station, and I boarded the train with my head full of unrelinquished tears; I looked balefully out the window at the bright passing landscape of Fife, its green rolling pastureland, the sudden sky-blue glimpses of the North Sea, the tight-woven little copses. I had learned a great deal in Scotland, had grown up there in fact. Even after the six-month downward spiral in autumn and winter of 1970–1971, I had brief periods of being miserably depressed, but I always pulled through and learned something from the depressions. As Roethke once wrote: "In a dark time, the eye begins to see."

The idea of living in New England had always been attractive to me. Once on a family vacation in the early sixties, I had passed through Vermont and New Hampshire, and I recalled having thought these states would make a fine place to live. Robert Frost had been a particular favorite of mine ever since I first read "Birches" in the ninth grade, and I was much taken with the fact that Frost had gone to Dartmouth (though he dropped out quickly) and often lectured there in his later years. He had spent a rather bleak period as a farmer in New Hampshire, and had written affectingly about the stony landscape of the region.

I rented from Dartmouth a small apartment just off the campus on an elm-lined street. It was exciting to have a "real" job and to have my very own place to live in for the first time. The first years in Hanover were dizzying. I sat through endless academic dinner parties. I was involved in inviting visiting writers to the campus to give readings, so I quickly met dozens of poets and novelists. My senior colleague was the poet Richard Eberhart, a kind-hearted and generous man who, with his wife Betty, became surrogate parents. I settled into a rather comfortable life.

My daily ritual involved getting up about eight, then walking uptown to Lou's Restaurant for breakfast. At Lou's, I would settle in with my notebook and write poems. Midmorning, I would return to my apartment, type up the poems, rewrite them, and send them out to magazines. I would prepare classes, teach them, and meet with students in the afternoons. Evenings were spent reading or socializing with friends.

It all sounds very cozy, but there was a darker side. Dartmouth was stuck on itself, and there was a certain amount of silly snobbishness around that upset me. I found many of my colleagues difficult to talk to. Long-standing factions existed in the English department, and one had to put one's money on this or that horse. I tried to fathom the games being played, but I didn't get whatever it was that was going on. Quite naturally, I was deeply resentful of having to play games at all. On the other hand, I wanted to succeed at these games. Many nights were spent lying awake and fretting over what I'd said or not said to this or that colleague.

I was also lonely and sexually frustrated. Most of my real friends were, in fact, students, and in 1978 I met Devon Jersild, a beautiful and intelligent young woman from Illinois. She came into my office to ask if I would read her poems. I did. One thing led to the proverbial next thing and, by 1980, we had decided to get married soon after she graduated. My colleagues, alas, took a dim view of my relations with a student.

My feelings of resentment toward Dartmouth had been growing, and in 1979 I sat down in a fever of composition and wrote a novel called *The Love Run*— an immature thriller with a satirical underlining. The book was accepted by Atlantic-Little, Brown, with an advance of $12,500. I was amazed and delighted. (I also sold the movie rights and did a screenplay version, which—like most screenplays— was never produced.)

The novel was set at Dartmouth, and my contempt for certain aspects of the college was evident on every page. The sexual frustrations I'd experienced in painful ways during the first few years at Dartmouth were similarly unconcealed. I have never been able to keep a secret. I wrote what I felt, and the book contains many explicitly erotic pages that, in retrospect, I find embarrassing. Still, the book is cleanly written, has a fairly absorbing plot, and I will not disown it. One's books, like one's children, have a life of their own; one must not judge them too harshly.

Meanwhile I had published my thesis on Roethke, which I'd rewritten in substantial ways. *Theodore Roethke: An American Romantic* appeared in 1979 with the University of Massachusetts Press. It was well received, with reviews in the usual academic journals. And my poems, essays, and reviews were being published here and there: the *New Yorker*, the *Atlantic, Poetry*, the *Sewanee Review*, the *Hudson Review*, the *New Republic*, the *Nation*.

I felt very good about the poems, in particular. Coming back to the States had reawakened memories of childhood, and I wrote a lot about the mining region of Pennsylvania that became the first section of *Anthracite Country*, which was taken by Random House and published in 1982. Those poems were mostly short lyrics with a tight narrative and a concretely imagistic texture. One of my favorites is "Coal Train," which is about a young boy lying in bed listening to the train as it passes his house:

> Three times a night it woke you
> in middle summer, the Erie Lackawanna,
> rung to the north on thin, loud rails.
> You could feel it coming a long way off:
> at first, a tremble in your belly,
> a wire trilling in your veins, then diesel
> rising to a froth beneath your skin.
> You could see the cowcatcher,
> wide as a mouth and eating ties,
> the headlight blowing a dust of flies.
> There was no way to stop it.
> You lay there, fastened to the tracks
> and waiting, breathing like a bull,
> your fingers lit at the tips like matches.
> You waited for the thunder of wheel and bone,
> the axles sparking, fire in your spine.
> Each passing was a kind of death,
> the whistle dwindling to a ghost in air,
> the engine losing itself in trees.
> In a while, your heart was the loudest thing,
> your bed was a pool of night.

With the anthracite poems, I felt I had suddenly come into my own as a writer. I had swallowed up the voices of Hopkins, Roethke, Heaney, Frost, and others; I had digested them. What came out of all of this digestion was a new thing: my voice. The poems felt right to me, and real.

My personal life grew richer and richer. Having found Devon, I suddenly had a friend: someone I could talk to, share everything with. I also became close friends with Sam Pickering, a colleague at Dartmouth who wrote familiar essays and criticism. Most nights I would drop by his apartment across the street and have a drink. We shared war stories about the college, we talked about writing. In winter, we would ski through the woods together along the

With Ann Beattie, 1981

Connecticut River. In summer, we would go swimming in the ponds hidden in the woods around Hanover.

It was also during these years that I met Ann Beattie. She had written to me, having read some of my poems in magazines. It turned out that she lived near my sister, just outside of Boston. We met, and we have remained close. Ann was just beginning to publish stories in the *New Yorker,* stories that caught the frustrations and disillusionment of our generation with astonishing wit and artistry. I was, indeed, visiting her in Connecticut when she was just finishing her second novel, *Falling in Place,* and I read those pages in rough draft with admiration and awe. The absurdist note in her work—a peculiar mix of despair and wry humor—is part of Ann's way of being in the world. And I've watched her change and grow from book to book.

I could write a whole book about my friends. In the old days, as it were, extended families offered a kind of emotional life insurance. One's children moved among relatives. And neighborhoods. I grew up in that kind of world, having lunch at my grandparents' house, dinner with an aunt, and so forth. My neighbors on South Rebecca Avenue in West Scranton all knew me intimately; the mailman, for instance, was also my Sunday school teacher, and he awaited my letters of acceptance from colleges as

eagerly as I did. It was an intimate and protected world. But it was not the latter half of the twentieth century.

Dislocation, separation, and isolation are part of contemporary life, and my generation has been unusually dependent, I think, on friendship. We talk on the phone, visit each other, even travel together. Perhaps I am more inclined this way than others, but I rely on this contact with friends. It has been sustaining.

The Love Run was published in late spring of 1980, and the Dartmouth community did not like it one bit. Hate letters poured in from loyal Dartmouth graduates who loved their school and couldn't bear to hear a word said against it. With regard to my job, the timing could not have been worse, since I was up for tenure the next fall term. Needless to say, I did not get tenure—even though I had overwhelming support from the English department (much to my surprise). I was sent packing, and it was not an easy time for me.

Devon had graduated, and she was teaching for a year in Boston at the Commonwealth School. I would drive back and forth between Hanover and her apartment on Commonwealth Avenue nearly every weekend. I still recall the bleakness of that winter and spring of 1981. Where would I go? Was my academic career finished? Should I give up the idea of teaching altogether and simply write? It was a letter from Seamus Heaney, telling me not to dwell on external signs of accomplishments like teaching positions, that freed me. Seamus said, "Write your books. That's where your life is." And I did.

I buried myself in my work now, beginning a novel in Boston called *The Patch Boys,* having just finished *Huckleberry Finn.* I wanted to do a Huck on the Susquehanna, to write a novel that invoked the atmosphere of the anthracite region: the beauty of the natural world, the warm spirit of the people, and the sense of what William Carlos Williams once called "a new world naked." I was also eager to write a novel that would be as good as my poems, that would incorporate the lessons I had learned as a poet about imagery and tone, clarity and fidelity to one's innermost experience.

My father was always full of stories about growing up in Exeter, the little mining town outside of Scranton where I spent my first four years. I knew the place well, since my grandmother lived there until her death in 1979. I loved swimming in the river, with its mossy banks and slippery stones; I loved floating in the tepid ponds nearby. I loved the abandoned breakers, the ramshackle houses, the

Alastair Reid with Will Parini, Vermont, 1982

crooked streets that seemed to tumble in upon themselves. I loved the sense of neighborhood and family. And I wanted to get all of this into *The Patch Boys.*

I was married to Devon in Moline, Illinois, in June of 1981. We left the day after the wedding for Umbria, where we rented a tiny, stone farmhouse that was four hundred years old. In that village, called Torre Gentile, I lived blissfully with Devon, working several hours a day on my portable Olivetti. *The Patch Boys* grew and grew, although it would not see the light of day until 1986.

Torre Gentile was just outside of Todi, one of the classic hilltowns of Umbria. We made lots of friends that summer, and we grew to love Italy, the gentle rhythms of daily life there, the aura of the past that seemed to hang in the air like a benevolent shadow. The Umbrian hills were visible from our terrace, and we'd sit there sipping wine into the night with the violet hills spreading their long thin arms in a hauntingly open gesture. During the day we took long hikes in the woods nearby, which were full of wild boars. I think I could easily have stayed on in Torre Gentile for the rest of the year, but my final commitments to Dartmouth had to be fulfilled.

The final year at Dartmouth was, in fact, a pleasant experience. I was married now, very happy, and Devon became pregnant with Will, our first son. I

was still hammering away at *The Patch Boys,* making progress. And I found that nearly every job I applied for yielded a request for an interview. In order to stay in northern New England, which I adored, I took a job at Middlebury College, which was just over the mountain in Vermont.

Again, I seemed to be following in the footsteps of Frost. Frost lived in Ripton—near Middlebury—for a good part of his life, and he was a founder of the Bread Loaf School of English and the famous Writers' Conference there, which are both part of Middlebury College. Frost loved Middlebury College, and he often lectured and read there. He had many friends in the area who were still alive in 1982 when I pulled into town with Devon, who would soon give birth to Will.

I was pleased to discover that the departmental *angst* that everyone took for granted at Dartmouth was alien to Middlebury. My colleagues got along rather well. I quickly felt at home.

We bought a small house on a wide, tree-lined street called South Street—a street right out of Sinclair Lewis. I would write every morning and teach in the afternoons, often wandering into the town to write poems while sitting in a diner. The poems that came out of my newfound status as *paterfamilias* and local *burger* were gathered in a volume called *Town Life,* published by Holt in 1988. Those poems are about fatherhood, about marriage, about living in a town. But that speaks only to their surfaces. The poems reflect a deepening of overall tone and effect. I'd been reading Wallace Stevens again, and I became enamored of the way thought— its looping interlocking circles—had been embodied by Stevens in a language that was witty and resonant. I tried for something like the same effect. While there is still a concreteness and narrative motion in those poems, I think—or I imagine—there is an openness and freedom of association which occurs that had not found its way into my work before. There is a lot of attention to nature as an emblem of mind, a searching out of Emersonian "correspondences." Every natural fact is taken as a sign that points inward, then outward. As in "The Function of Winter," which I take to be characteristic of the voice emerging in *Town Life:*

> I'm for it, as the last leaves shred
> or powder on the floor, as sparrows find
> the driest footing, and November rains
> fall hard as salt sprayed over roads.
> The circulating spores take cover
> where they can, and light runs level
> to the ground again: no more the vertical
> blond summer sheen that occupies a day,

but winter flatness—light as part of things,
not things themselves. My heart's in storage
for the six-month siege we're in for here,
laid up for use a little at a time
like hardtack on a polar expedition,
coveted though stale. Ideas, which in
summer hung a crazy jungle in my head,
subside now, separate and gleam in parts;
I braid them for display on winter walls
like garlic tails or onions, crisp bay wreaths.
One by one, I'll pluck them into spring.
If truth be told, I find it easier
to live this way: the fructifying boom
of summer over, wild birds gone, and wind
along the ground where cuffs can feel it.
Everything's in reach or neatly labeled
on my basement shelves. I'm ready to begin
to see what happened when my heart was hot,
my head too dazzled by itself to think.

Town Life also includes a poem about one of the two trips I took, on journalistic assignments, to the Far East in the mideighties. Called "This Kampuchea," the poem returns to the Vietnam imagery that continued to haunt me from the sixties and still does. I recall flying over Vietnam for the first time and seeing the endless acres of permanently destroyed forests and thinking again about the hideous abuse of power—economic and military and political—represented by that terrible war.

A growing influence on my poems in the eighties was Robert Penn Warren, whom I had met soon after coming to Dartmouth through the good offices of Richard Eberhart. The friendship with Warren and his family grew, and Devon and I would visit the Warrens often at their house in West Wardsboro, Vermont, which was not too far away. Warren, called "Red" by his friends, would read my poems and offer suggestions. We would go for long walks in the woods and sit, over dinner, talking about literature. One of the things that attracted me to Red was the way he had moved so easily among the genres, writing poems, stories, novels, book reviews, essays—even plays! And he did this while teaching at Minnesota and Yale. He was a man of letters in the old sense of that term, and I admired that.

I once asked him about the way he moved from genre to genre, and he said, "Poetry is the great schoolhouse of fiction." I've never forgotten that. My novels would be incredibly different had I not been a poet, too. My sense of language is rooted in the traditions of English and American poetry, and my sense of narrative structure owes as much to *Paradise Lost* as to *The Great Gatsby* (I often, as a kind of private joke with myself, bury quotations from favorite poems in my novels).

I had a sabbatical leave from Middlebury in 1985–1986, and we took ourselves to Atrani, a small town in southern Italy along the Amalfi Coast. We were lucky enough to find a villa overlooking the sea. The town of Amalfi was a mile or so away—a pleasant walk—and Devon and I would go into town every day and write in cafes, which had come to expect us. Our second son, Oliver, was only six weeks old when we arrived in Italy, and we attracted attention simply by having a small baby. The Amalfitani would pass Oliver from arm to arm, sometimes kidnapping him for the whole day.

A local family adopted us, and they would look after the boys in the morning and bring us hot meals at midday and see that everything in the house was operating smoothly. For the most part, it was. But the transition to Italian life was hard for Will, who was only three and had a new baby brother. And the weather in winter—drizzly, cold, and windy—affected us deeply. The villa was unheated, so we crammed around a kerosene heater to get warm, inhaling its noxious fumes as rain beat against the shutters. Spring seemed reluctant to find us, which is not the

Robert Penn Warren, 1988
(photo taken by Jay Parini)

With Gore Vidal, Ravello, Italy, 1986

way we thought it was supposed to work in southern Italy.

For me, one of the great pleasures of the Amalfi Coast was getting to know my neighbor Gore Vidal. Gore lived in a luxurious villa called "La Rondinaia" which clung to a steep cliffside like a swallow's nest. We could see his villa from our terrace, and every day he would pass our house on his ritual walk into Amalfi to buy his newspapers. One day I left a note with the newsagent, saying that I was an American writer and was living temporarily in Atrani. He called immediately, and we soon became friends. We saw each other often, and we still talk on the phone every week or so. I've been back to Amalfi nearly every year to visit him.

It was Vidal who gave me the idea for *The Last Station,* my novel about Leo Tolstoy's last year. I had been reading and thinking about Tolstoy for some time, and after I read Henri Troyat's biography I got the idea for writing something about that intense and surreal last year, in which Tolstoy runs away from home and dies in the little railway station at Astapovo. My original thought was to make a book-length poem

or play out of it. But reading Vidal's *Lincoln,* I fell upon the idea of trying my hand at the historical novel.

Everyone in the Tolstoy circle, including Tolstoy, kept meticulous diaries of their daily life. As I collected and read through these diaries—those by Tolstoy, Sofya Tolstoy, his wife, Valentin Bulgakov, his secretary, Sasha, his daughter, his publisher Chertkov, and so forth—I realized that a kaleidoscopic novel was presenting itself. I decided to preserve the diary-like form, writing the novel from six or seven different viewpoints, one of them my own. In the original draft, there were long chapters by "JP" that reflected on the ongoing action in a discursive manner. I also wrote some fifteen poems during the composition of the novel, and these were included as part of the original, much longer, manuscript. I was eventually persuaded to drop the "JP" meditations and cut the poems back to the three that survive in the final book.

The novel was published in the summer of 1990, and the reception took me rather by surprise. The *New York Times Book Review* put it on the cover, as did

Newsday and many other papers. I was besieged by interviewers and invitations to do this or that. It was at first exhilarating, and heartening; soon, as one might well imagine, I grew tired of talking about the book. A couple of months after it was published, however, a phone call from Anthony Quinn, the actor, came one night after dinner. Quinn apparently had a passion to play Leo Tolstoy in a film; he wondered if I might like to do a screenplay version of *The Last Station*.

The many months that followed—a year and a half, in fact—were somewhat exhausting at times. Tony Quinn likes to wrestle a bear to the ground, and I spent countless long weekends in New York, where he lived, engaged in amusing battle. We would sit across from each other at a dining-room table in his studio, imagining scenes. I would go away and write them, then Tony and I would act them out. At one point I complained: "How is it that you always get to play Tolstoy, and I have to play Mrs. Tolstoy?" Quinn said, "Because you are playing Sofya in the film."

Jay Parini with actor Anthony Quinn, New York City, 1991

While the screenplay was underway, I was simultaneously writing poems in the morning, often for an hour or so after breakfast, and writing a new novel, *Bay of Arrows*. Once again, Alastair Reid was instrumental in my life. Devon and I had taken the boys for a winter holiday to the Dominican Republic in 1989, the main purpose of the journey being to visit Alastair, who was living in Samaná, a remote area of the island not far from the Bay of Arrows, a beach where Columbus was showered with arrows by the Taino Indians in 1492. Indeed, this small inlet was the first point of conflict in the New World between the Europeans and the indigenous population—a tremendously symbolic place.

Alastair, like Robinson Crusoe, had fashioned a life for himself out of very little there in the jungle. The two small houses he'd constructed, with help from a few local carpenters, were perched on a slope overlooking the sea and surrounded by tall palm and coconut trees. There was no running water, no electricity, little in the way of civilization. So Alastair collected rainwater in a cistern for drinking and cooking. He dug a latrine. He imported solar-powered generators to provide enough electricity to run a small refrigerator, some lights, and even a computer. His library was growing slowly, and it was filled with books on Columbus. I lay in a hammock reading.

I had always been interested in Columbus. My grandmother was born and raised in Savona, the town outside of Genoa where Columbus and his parents moved when his father decided to expand into the wine-and-cheese business. I used to sit in Scranton's Courthouse Square contemplating a huge statue of Columbus. (I even wrote a poem about him that appears in *Anthracite Country*.)

One thing led to another, and I found myself writing this novel that shuttled back and forth in alternate chapters between 1492 and 1992. The contemporary sections are about a man called Christopher Genovese, or "Geno." He is, in a sense, the reincarnation of Columbus. I stole countless little and large details from my own life to portray Geno—he's an English professor at a small college in Vermont, his wife is a writer, he has two boisterous sons. And Geno lives in a rambling midnineteenth-century farmhouse much like the one that we moved to, just outside of Middlebury, in 1989. But the parallels are all superficial. The personality of Geno is utterly his own. He is much more headstrong than I am, more sexist (I would hope), less willing to see beyond the patriarchal society around him. He is, like me, interested in radical politics, but his politics are terribly hypocritical.

One of Geno's interests is Noam Chomsky. As I have said earlier in this piece, Chomsky was a crucial figure in my early thinking about the U.S. in relation to the outside world, and I returned to reading Chomsky in the mideighties, frustrated by Reagan's brutal war against the Nicaraguan people. I found myself repoliticized, and angry. I could see that we had learned nothing as a nation from the Vietnam War. Our leaders were essentially bought men (and I do mean men). They owed their allegiance to the wealthy corporations who had sponsored them, and one of their chief purposes in life was to maintain a status quo in which American power was not questioned anywhere on the planet. They had, somehow, to justify a mammoth defense budget which was simultaneously pushing millions of Americans into a condition of poverty.

How does one restrain oneself? I wrote, on a whim, to Chomsky from Italy, and he replied at great length in a kind and thoughtful letter. When I returned from Italy, we met. (I did an interview with him for *Mother Jones* magazine.) We became friends. And I still find myself returning eagerly to his twenty-odd books on American power.

The novel *Bay of Arrows* grew out of my life in the late eighties, reflecting a wide range of my daily interests and concerns. As with *The Last Station*, it contains poems which are used to break the pattern of the driving prose narrative. Always, in writing, the pace of a narrative changes as one proceeds, moving between poles. On the one side, there is narrative momentum: the sheer delight of the story itself; on the other, there is lyric intensity, those passages where language takes on a strange concreteness. Often in writing I find myself so moved by a particular scene that I break from prose into poetry. By making the "hero" of this book a poet, I was able to use the urge toward lyric-making to my advantage, I think.

But book-making is a peculiar occupation, one that often seems at odds with teaching. Nevertheless, I find myself happily oscillating between the classroom and my study. The books I teach at Middlebury often inspire me to write something of my own. I enjoy talking to students, many of whom become friends. I like the notion of a community of scholars such as that described by Paul Goodman in his book of that name. In Goodman's vision, the academic village is a place where professionals work with apprentices in the mutual pursuit of knowledge. I do find that it works that way in writing seminars. My students, most of whom will never go on to write professionally after college, are nevertheless hopeful that this might happen. I have read a lot of poems and stories, and I can help them with theirs.

Life is so brief. I see the children growing fast, and it seems heartbreaking. I try to savor their sweet lives, but I feel this life spilling through my fingers like water. Poems—more often fragments of poems—accumulate in my notebooks, a kind of diary of my emotional life. The novels, written and unwritten, capture my imagination for a period, then subside. I like to think of the unwritten novels (there are about three or four in my head) as planes waiting for permission to land. Meanwhile, books for review cross my desk. I get the urge to go somewhere, to interview someone, or write about something. I wonder how to engage myself more directly with my wife, with my boys, with my community. I wonder how to use what talent I have to effect change in the larger political sense. I try to read, to think. All of this happens against a background of the shifting seasons: the lyric bloom of summer, the slow but unmistakable descent into fall, into winter's lockgrip, with snow muffling and blanking out whatever I thought I knew. I wait impatiently for spring, and it emerges slowly—with the hillsides turning from cobalt gray to a faint rouge as the buds swell. I go for long walks in the countryside, thinking. The wind that crosses my face is very much the world's breath, the *spiritus*. I know that soon enough I will return to the energy of the world in a much-reduced state, having finally learned (I hope) exactly how one lives in, around, the silence at the heart of what is real.

BIBLIOGRAPHY

Poetry:

Singing in Time, J. W. B. Laing, 1972.

Anthracite Country, Random House, 1982.

Town Life, Holt, 1988.

Fiction:

The Love Run, Little, Brown, 1980.

The Patch Boys, Holt, 1988.

The Last Station, Holt, 1990.

Bay of Arrows, Holt, 1992.

Nonfiction:

Theodore Roethke: An American Romantic, University of Massachusetts Press, 1979.

An Invitation to Poetry, Prentice-Hall, 1987.

A Vermont Christmas (with photographs by Richard Brown), Little, Brown, 1988.

Editor:

(With Robin M. Barone and Sydney Lea) *Richard Eberhart: A Celebration,* Kenyon Hill, 1980.

(With Robert Pack and Lea) *The Bread Loaf Anthology of Contemporary American Poetry,* University Press of New England, 1985.

(With Pack) *The Bread Loaf Anthology of Contemporary American Short Stories,* University Press of New England, 1987.

(With Pack) *The Bread Loaf Anthology of Contemporary American Essays,* University Press of New England, 1989.

(With Pack) *A Donald Justice Reader: Selected Poetry and Prose,* University Press of New England, 1991.

(With Pack) *A Nancy Willard Reader: Selected Poetry and Prose,* University Press of New England, 1991.

Writers on Writing, University Press of New England, 1991.

Gore Vidal: Writer Against the Grain, Columbia University Press, 1992.

The Columbia History of American Poetry, Columbia University Press, 1993.

Contributor to language and literature journals. Co-founder of *New England Review,* co-editor, 1977–1978; advisory editor, 1978—.

Antonis Samarakis

1919-

(Translated from the modern Greek by Penny Apostolidis and Andrew Horton)

I regret that, for reasons beyond my control, my autobiography does not include an important, crucial, I would say, event in my life: my death. A self-respecting autobiography should, of course, be made up of all those details that, in the author's opinion, shed light on his journey through life. And that inescapable darkness which we call "death" can often cast light on a person's life. A beautiful and defiant death gives a new dimension to a life that had a few good moments which honored the human condition including the moments of shared brotherhood, that is, those values which justify our journey on earth, but which also had many rough moments—cracks in the integrity of our character and in our resistance to the powers of this world.

But there is another reason I have regrets about the absence of my journey's end in this autobiography. I have often loved to use flashbacks in my writings. But here this trick is impossible. It's a pity, for I see death as some destination we all reach having travelled from nonexistence only to return to nonexistence.

At any rate, since human life is as it is (who knows what science and technology have in store for us), it is not possible for one to speak honestly about one's death and to describe it. Thus I too must go along the usual track. Nevertheless, I will deviate a little. I won't follow the cold procedure of an ID card: place of birth, date of birth . . . because we all arrived sometime somewhere in this world, and we had no control over these facts. I should add, I have always considered autobiography as something foreign, a little ridiculous, and egotistical because it seemed as if one were saying, "Look at me! I am different from you, superior, better than you." But I am now asked to compose my own autobiography as a distinguished personality, as some sort of "superman," and so I too have slipped into the genre though I tried to avoid it. The fact that I have accepted to write this autobiography signifies, I fear, that I have slipped into the deceitful fascination of the egotistical. It means that at seventy-three, I find old age begins to keep company with an inflated ego.

Antonis Samarakis

"Watch it!" cries a voice within me. But it's too late. I've already been carried away and given away my exact age.

I will begin with the formal stuff. I arrived on August 16, 1919, in Platia Vathis, a working-class neighborhood of Athens called Metaxourgio, close to the Larissa train station. I first saw the light of day at night, as my mother, Adriana (her name was Adriani, but I always called her Adriana, not "Mother," just as I called my father by his name, Evripidis, not "Father"), gave birth at 3:30 A.M.

This earth-shattering event happened at home, at 50 Maizonos and Chiou streets. I was delivered with the help of Kyria (Mrs.) Vasso, the kind-hearted midwife. There was no electricity in our house, so the light I first saw was from a gas lamp which gave the room the atmosphere of a thriller, foreshadowing a life that was destined to pass through many thrills. The twentieth century has been and is such a thriller which was greeted when it began with the hope and conviction that it would be the new Golden Age. But it didn't take long to reveal itself as not being made up of the gold of joy, peace, freedom, and justice for all. Rather our century was black gold, pitch black, and mournful, the gold of pain and heartbreak and death. At the dawn of our century, while all the world awaited it eagerly, dancing and singing, only one voice dared speak and say "no" to the frenzied crowd. It was a prophetic voice, the voice of a poet (who else can it ever be?). It was Thomas Hardy, the great poet, novelist, and thinker, who said that we were entering centuries of barbarism. What has followed has sadly justified his words. Among the hardships destined for us in this notorious century have been two world wars and, who knows, possibly a third one before the century expires.

A child of the period between the two world wars, I took my first steps with a wise mentor at my side: the street. The street taught me more about life than the schools I went to or the university. The streets of Athens meant as much to me as they did to Maxim Gorky in his novel *My Universities*.

From the age of seven or eight, I went out every day and even at night and roamed the streets and alleys. Adriana, my mother, who was the chief executive in our house (and so had the twenty-four-hour right to whip me while Evripidis, my father, never raised a hand against me), couldn't stop me. What did I do as I wandered the streets? What all children of the world do. I played, I had my friends, and, of course, I had my eyes wide open. I looked around, listened, understood more and more, felt and sensed the characteristics and essence of those I saw and, above all, I tried to grasp something of the mystery of life.

What amazing power of observation children and even infants have. Nothing escapes their view. But children also store up impressions, sizing us up, checking us over, judging us, tying us into their consciences. What a dangerous mistake it is for adults to say, "He is only a child," or "She doesn't understand."

When I was a child, Athens was not the noisy megalopolis of four million it has become today. Athens then was humane, the capital of Greece but yet friendly, gracious, with only a few cars. So we children were the masters of the streets. My teacher, the street, taught me to share everyday life with the other simple people, to take an active part and not be passive, to taste the here and now, and to live for the moment.

I said earlier that I would not proceed in the cold manner of an ID card or a bureaucratic form. I regret that without realizing it, I went astray and started to tell you when and where I was born, to talk about my mother, Adriana, and my father, Evripidis. But I haven't yet mentioned the other person in this quartet. We became a family of four when my brother, Costas, was born June 10, 1925, in the same house I was born.

My family was poor. My father was a low-level employee at the Ministry of Finance. His salary was very low, and so he worked afternoons and nights until the early hours of the morning. He was an entertainment tax collector, working cinemas and nightclubs. It is questionable whether he slept more than two or three hours a night, after which he would go to the ministry early in the morning again until late in the afternoon. But the other people in my neighborhood were poor too. They were workers and low-level clerks, some of whom had small workshops. So I knew poverty. But there was also the joy of home and of happy celebrations. Our problems were many, especially when illness struck, when a doctor and medicine were needed but we had no means to pay, not to mention what happened when we needed a hospital or an operation. Medical care for the poor in Greece was and still is today an unfortunate thorn, an open wound.

But did I not see and experience loneliness and alienation? I knew people who were locked up, who were barricaded inside themselves, figures carrying a dark night permanently in their souls. Most of the houses where I was born and lived until I was sixteen were single dwellings with courtyards, and I would go in and out of them often. I remember courtyards with small rooms surrounding them, and in each room there was a different case. Sometimes a man alone or even a whole family crowded together. I would start talking with them, and they would open their hearts to me as they confided their troubles and secrets. But, you ask, why would they do this with a boy? Yes, to a boy. Why not? With whom do you want a simple man of the street to have warm and direct human contact?

Ah! You, Kyria Katina, who lived alone in that tiny courtyard with the rosebushes and the carnations and the potted geraniums and the cans of olive oil. You, Kyria Katina, plump, round, but with a heart that was extremely sensitive and full of tenderness, the heart of a child. You who would share with me, nine-year-old Antonis, your bitterness and suffering ever since the Turks uprooted you from the ancient Greek soil of Asia Minor during the catastrophe of 1922 which was carried out with the guilty complicity and cooperation of the so-called "Big Allies" of Greece: England, France, and Italy. You would recount your loneliness to me, Kyria Katina, and your heartbroken memories, and you would offer me bitter orange preserves, and you would tenderly tell me in Turkish, "My little Antonis, *oglou benimi!*" which meant, "My little Antonis, my own son!" Whatever happened to your beautiful feathered fan which you forever waved across your face scarred by suffering? As you always said to me: "Aah, I have hot flashes!"

You will ask and you are right to do so, "Did you also go to elementary school or did you just roam the streets? When did you ever study?" Did I study? Of course I did. But above all, I studied the life that surrounded me. I studied eternity in the everyday. I also studied something else besides what I have mentioned: I looked at blind fanaticism, hatred, the persecution of simple people by the state's abuse of power. Then in my early childhood, in 1929, a law

Father, Evripidis, and mother, Adriani

was passed, strangling individual and civil freedoms. This was the notorious "Idionymo." With this law and without much legal protection, progressive, free-thinking people of the Left were persecuted for their beliefs. There were endless arrests around the clock, endless beatings, and castor oil dosages. People were jailed by the hundreds and exiled to barren islands. Every now and then I would see the police raiding our neighborhood. The secret police would barge into houses and, intoxicated, drag out of basements and first floors and out of some small printing shops that were there these poor people bound with handcuffs. These were the "terrible" criminals who were not charged with any specific acts except for their political beliefs. And to think that this very harsh law had been put together by the great free-thinking liberal politician, and a liberal at that, Eleutherios Venizelos. I must have been nine or ten when I set out from our house and went far away to the Plaka area of Athens, where today's tourists hang out unconcerned. I went to a small narrow street in Plaka, Nikodimou Street, to a wretched building which was the transport unit of the police and which gave "hospitality" for short or long terms to those citizens whom the police had arrested and were intending for exile or prison. Outside the building, overlooking the tiny sidewalk, were two or three small windows with thick iron bars. Through these I tried to see the people held prisoner in the basement. They were a mass of human souls, piled one on top of the other in pitch darkness. The only thing I could make out were vague figures, some hands. . . . I couldn't stay there long. The cops grabbed me, picked me up, and, of course, "anointed me."

I'm afraid I've said too much about my early childhood. But I believe that these are the decisive years for everybody. It is then that one's inner world is formed. Our innermost vision of life and society takes shape. All these things I lived through as a child were my initiation into the world, but at the same time they were also the origin of my writing. Yes, I was ten when I wrote a poem, my first. Gradually other poems followed. They were awkward first fruits, but with a feeling of protest, a child's voice of revolt was expressed against the panorama of social injustice and political intolerance which I had experienced and continued to feel in the neighborhood. At first I kept these humble poems secret. The first poem from this young literary effort was published in the Athenian monthly magazine *Xekinima* (Beginnings). It was in issue number eleven, November 1933 (I had written it the previous year), and I was thirteen. It was called "Thanatos (Death)":

Death

My days have shortened even more,
life fades at every breath with sighs
and death's wings on the closed door
mournfully, my last moment signifies.

Solitary figure in a void, the triple darkness
deep
encircles me; the lips unquenched are burning
and in the dark corner where we keep
the holy icons, a faint light from the oil lamp
is pouring.

Alone; upon a chair the candle flickers,
in vain the unutterable agony of the soul
it strives to clear; death lingers,
the body sweats while the room is cold.

Wind at the window—the final weeping;
darkness—the candle is out, outside the portal
the dog is barking, and from its corner,
in sad tone acute
"good journey" echoes the cracked lute.

Before this, in 1930–31, I had sent poems to two children's magazines, *The Child's World* and *The Edification of Children,* and they were published there. I had to have a pen name for the collaboration with these two magazines, so I requested and received the pseudonyms "Ideal" and "Bright Darkness." *Xekinima* was an adult literary magazine.

When I began writing poetry, something else happened that played a very important role in my life. I fell very ill. The doctors called my case adenopathy, "a pre-tubercular state." In those days, Greece was held hostage by two nightmares: tuberculosis and malaria. I remember vividly the kindhearted neighborhood doctor, Mr. Gounelidis. He came to our house late one night to examine me and stated firmly that the next morning I should move to the country, to a dry climate, without humidity, and stay there eating nourishing food and breathing fresh air. His order was that I should stay in the countryside for an extended period. So it happened. The next day the four of us left and we went to Halandri, a small rural town ten kilometers from Athens full of pine trees. But where did we stay? For two years we lived not in a house but in an army tent my father had kept since the Balkan Wars of 1912–13 when he was wounded (I remember him telling us that they had donated tents to some of the wounded soldiers).

I had to stay in bed most of the time. We had camp cots since a regular bed wouldn't fit in the tent. Also I would lie on a deck chair. And since I was inactive, time did not pass easily. What a fate for me who, from a young age, was all energy and perpetual motion. The only thing I could do during those endless hours was read, which was exactly what I wanted to do. Reading always fascinated me. It has been my passion since childhood. So strong was my passion then that I would not have found it strange if someone watching my birth had told me I came into the world with a newspaper in my hand.

So for two years of enforced immobilization, Evripidis, my dad, commuted daily to the Ministry of Finance and lugged home to the tent everything that could be read—newspapers, magazines, books—and not just those "suitable for children." Besides the current news, besides the major and minor events of the day which interested and moved me, I gained a broader and deeper understanding of Greek and foreign authors, including the works of both poets and prose writers. I felt particularly close ties to those authors who were concerned with the fate of simple people, of those wrongly called anonymous. I felt close to those who instilled in me a sense of social thinking, who were genuine, down-to-earth, and committed to dedicating their work to the struggle for a better world. These authors expanded my horizon, added new dimensions to my life. Dostoevsky, Chekhov, Tolstoy, Gogol, Mayakovsky, Pushkin, Lermontov were and are even today my greatest loves. Not of course that I understood much of their work at the time, but I had at least an idea.

Meanwhile I finished elementary school with the disruptions caused by my illness and went to high school at Varvakeion, a state school but a model one, perfectly organized. We had a student community with a student elected president, and students on the student council. During the student community meetings of each class, the student president sat at the teacher's desk running the show while the actual teacher watched from a chair, and if he (the real teacher) wished to speak, he would need permission from the student president.

Thanks to this atmosphere at the Varvakeion school, a student had the chance to develop a broad personality. We used to issue a magazine called *Student Life* which was actually reproduced by a printer. Varvakeion had a stage for plays, a large hall for cultural events, an amphitheater for art courses, drafting, drawing, physics and chemistry labs, a music room, a geography room, and a geology lab. I note all this because our school was something unique for a Greek public school at that time. But the most significant point was the exceptionally rich intellectual and cultural life at Varvakeion. Within such a framework, from the fourth year of high school (there are six years in a Greek high school), my classmates voted me in as president of the student body and this continued until we graduated. At the same time I was one of the chief editors of *Student*

Life. I published poems and short prose pieces there. I also directed theater performances and acted. I was almost always the one to deliver the official addresses on national holidays and on other special occasions, especially during my senior year. My classmates were the first to hear drafts of speeches of all the candidates, but in the end they always voted for me. At the same time many of my poems and the "Hymn of Varvakeion" were set to music by our music teacher, the late Ioannis Margaziotis, when I was still in the third year. And the other children in school would sing them. I also read, read voraciously, not just literature, but socially committed books and magazines from the Left and from the Communists.

This was my life and "career" at Varvakeion when . . . one day during the fifth class in 1933 when I was fourteen, my classmate Argyris Petrounias came up and said, "Antonis, you are a person who writes such beautiful compositions and reads them to all of us in class. You impress us greatly not only with your talent but with your social awareness and your harsh criticism of the social injustices. I think, Antonis, that you should not remain alone but should join a movement that has as its goal the smashing of social injustice and the fight for a better world. Only by a united struggle can we hope to achieve something worthwhile."

So, I joined the Left wing movement "Social Solidarity," which was headed by an exceptional man, writer, and journalist, Nikos Karvounis. Throughout his life, Karvounis fought for justice and humanity. At first I was just a member in the student division. The section included the schools of Athens, Piraeus, and the suburbs. The organization was, naturally, illegal, and so we held gatherings in the most unlikely places. Sometimes we met in houses, at other times outdoors. The regular police and the secret police were after us, but they never managed to catch us. A little later my comrades voted me in as secretary of the student section. I then had greater responsibilities but also more trouble with the police. We were very active, organizing events such as student gatherings to force the state to give students free transportation and to provide other facilities including scholarships. We used to stir up other worthy trouble as well, but it was not apparent to the public that the Communists were behind our activity.

My work at "Social Solidarity" lasted for about two years. It was there, in the office of the organization, which was a small room in an old building at the corner of Soratous and Lykourgou Streets on the first floor (an unmarked door), that I first met Yiannis Ritsos, the great Greek poet of all-embracing works, including prose and plays which have been translated around the world. My acquaintance with Yiannis Ritsos is deeply engraved in my soul, indelible forever.

While I was working at "Social Solidarity," I read more revolutionary literature. Certainly nobody at home or at school knew or suspected my illegal activities. Only my mother, Adriana, with her fantastic intuition had caught wind of something and was worried but didn't know exactly what was going on. I continued to write poems within the frame of protest and rebellion.

Shortly before I graduated from Varvakeion in June 1935, I went through a horrible crisis. I felt I could no longer work for "Social Solidarity" because I was obliged to follow the "line," that is, to follow directives from above. Within the organization I could not have the vital freedom I needed. An event that happened in connection with a poem I had written decided all. I had sent it to the Communist youth literary magazine and eagerly awaited their reply in their correspondence column. This is what appeared: "Our young comrade, your poem is fine and has intellectual and social concerns. However, we will not publish it for the following reason: is it right for a young comrade of fourteen to write poetry in such a melancholy manner?" This upset me and I began to question them. I wondered why a comrade, a young man, couldn't experience a wide range of emotions including sadness and bitterness. Must a believer be a robot or a goose-stepping soldier at an official parade? If I wished to be on good terms with my conscience, I had to leave. And so I did. I wrote to them in a letter full of agony that I could no longer stay there. I told them the reasons why I was leaving, explaining that I considered it my moral duty to return to my solitude.

But then what happened was hard to take. It was as if I had no ground to stand on, as if the carpet had been pulled from under my feet. I experienced a nightmarish confusion of conflicting feelings. For us then, the youth, this ideology was our whole life, friendship, romance. Everything was incorporated into this ideology. We devoted hours and hours to the cause at the risk of being caught by the police, with personal deprivation and sacrifice. Whatever pocket money we had we spent it on the organization. We bought Marxist books, magazines, and in a thousand ways we tried actively to contribute. So, when I found myself alone with poetry as my only channel of expression, I had difficult days and nights. I seriously contemplated suicide. How can I reproduce in words that cruel time? Yet it is so alive within me, as if it happened yesterday.

In such a confused mental and emotional state, I finished the Varvakeion high school with honors. I hate to say this, but this fact is important for understanding what follows. I was preparing myself for the university entrance examinations while working various jobs at the same time to help out the meagre family income at home. Even when I was younger, I used to do a lot of odd jobs on the way to school. I remember that among the many tragicomical things that happened to me then, my father gave me forms from the tax office to distribute to displeased residents. Seeing such a small kid "offering" them this ominous document, the poor people up in the hills and mountains along my route would chase me away. Women would scold me, half-joking but half-serious, chasing me with the pestle they used for washing clothes. Other times they would let loose the dogs on me, and I would reach home running between dogs and thorns with one or both of my pant legs torn.

So when I finished high school in June 1935, at the age of fifteen and a half, I wanted to go to the university and work at the same time, but to work at a better job since I now had my high school diploma. One day I read in the newspaper that an independent Ministry of Labor was being established in Greece for the first time. Up till then labor affairs had come under the Ministry of National Economy. This news found me at a stage when I had "past experience" in social issues dating from my first years of childhood. It was a past experience which I owed to the panorama of social and personal pain I had come across. I had been directly exposed to this panorama in my neighborhood, while reading had built in me a mental and spiritual world and a specific pattern of behavior. The works of those authors and thinkers who spoke to my heart had moulded me, and I had also learned a lot in the two years I had worked at "Social Solidarity." Therefore, I thought that if I got a job at the Ministry of Labor, a department principally concerned, in theory anyway, with the handling of social conflicts, I would find a good basis for my own desires to help the "humbled and scorned." I was given a job at the Ministry of Labor on November 20, 1935. I was sworn in as an entry-level clerk at such a young age because in those days you could work without having finished your army service.

The Ministry of Labor was situated in a building at the corner of Bouboulinas and Tositsa streets. Many years later when the ministry was no longer there, I found myself again in the same building, but under different circumstances which I will mention later. I went to the ministry with a dream of a life and a career in which I would have the chance to do something for mankind. A few months later, on the morning of August 4, 1936, I saw soldiers with bayonets and tanks at the street corners as I left home for the ministry. I did not ask what had happened. I knew it was a military coup since I was used to this spectacle ever since I had been a child. Every now and then a general or colonel would carry out a coup to grab power. He would use the young draftees entrusted to him by the people for his own gain. He would elevate himself to the title of "Savior of Greece." But soon he would be toppled from power because somebody else, another Savior, would come onto the scene, again with the army and tanks, to oust his predecessor. And so, with all of these successive military coups, the question arose, "Who will save Greece from her Saviors?"

But this new coup arriving on the morning of August 4, 1936, was not destined to fall so quickly. It was the dictatorship of General Ionnis Metaxas, who held Greece in his power for over four years until January 1941.

As was natural, the shadow of the dictatorship lay heavy over the Ministry of Labor. It was a totalitarian regime which was a reflection of Hitler's Nazi regime. And it was a copy of Mussolini and Franco's fascist regimes. Problems began at the ministry for many of my colleagues and myself, until the time came when I could no longer bear it and so I resigned.

Being unemployed then, I continued my studies at the university and also did whatever jobs I could find. As for my poetry, I wrote once in a while, but I seldom sent poems for publication. I never regarded myself as a real poet, that is, one who would one day publish a book of poems. Yet in those poetical moments, I felt the freedom of the explorer because I was an amateur.

Up till now I have hidden my emotional feelings. From time to time I fell in love, at least that is how it seemed to me. My first affair was in 1930 when I was eleven. I used to go three nights a week to English classes at the YMCA (HAN) located at 38 Mitropolis Street. There were lots of young people in the various sections, all of them boys. A very beautiful girl caught my eye there; she must have been two or three years older than me, and she used to accompany her two younger brothers. I never dared speak to her, nor did I ever find out her name. I was very attracted to her. I thought of her all the time, and I began to follow her as she left with the two boys just so I could see her, even from a distance, and see where she lived. Her home was a small two-story house on the very human scale we used to have in Athens. She lived on

Geraniou Street near the corner of Agios Konstantinos, near Omonia Square in the center of Athens. Hidden in the evening darkness, I would follow her the three times a week she and her brothers had English. Fortunately they were the same nights and hours as my English class. I watched all three entering the house, saw the light go on the upper floor where they lived, and stood for hours on the opposite side of the street, unseen, under an awning. Soon after I would enjoy the piano that my love would play. She was my secret passion. She played so beautifully, so beautifully. Perhaps it was not her at all, but that was the way I wanted it to be in my mind. Very romantic, you will say. Why not? I wish I could relive those hours when I was eleven and when my soul flooded with the light which this superb creature, "my girl," radiated in the night. But one day the story came to an end. I don't remember exactly how. I think that the two brothers left class. Maybe something else happened, maybe I simply stopped following my love at night. I am not sure. But what I am certain about is that I had a wonderful feeling that my life was illuminated by these moments and even now, when recalling my experience in 1930, I am overwhelmed by a strange, deep, pure emotion.

After I resigned from the Ministry of Labor, I began a new era of poverty and deprivation. Whenever I found a day's work, I did it no matter what was required of me. Meanwhile my studies at the law school were nearing completion. Then the war between Greece and Italy broke out on October 28, 1940, with the surprise attack on Epirus by Mussolini's fascist forces. Thus Greece entered World War II which had begun a year earlier elsewhere in Europe.

In February 1941 I received my law degree. When the Italians struck on October 28, 1940, and war began, I had immediately volunteered, but they did not take me because as a student I had already been selected for the reserve infantry at the rank of second lieutenant, and I was supposed to go to a special army school. If they had taken me as a volunteer, according to the regulations, I would have been a regular foot soldier. They refused because they desperately needed reserve officers. But because of the war, the reserve officers' candidate school was continuously put off. Finally I was not called up because the war took a more serious turn with the German attack on Greece which began April 6, 1941.

The Nazi hordes marched towards Athens despite the heroic resistance of our army and people. Since the time I was very young I detested fascism. After all I had been, as I said earlier, an active fighter

for democracy. As a matter of fact, at high school one morning the principal at Varvakeion called me into his office to tell me that I could learn German for free on a scholarship offered by Hitler's regime at the German school in Athens. There were many such scholarships and grants handed out by Hitler to high school and university students, secondary school and university teachers. University and post-graduate education was offered in Nazi Germany for free with additional stipends. This was a fiendish propaganda. In this way Hitler was preparing his future agents, the notorious Fifth Column which was going to serve his purposes triggering, as he had already planned, World War II. Of course I rejected the scholarship that the Nazis wished to give me. In fact, I felt such a revulsion that I have never since wanted to learn German, even though I thirsted for foreign languages.

As soon as the German forces attacked Greece, I arranged, through secret connections, to leave for the Middle East. I kept all details of my escape a secret from my family. I had not told my father, mother, or brother what I was planning to do. And when everything was ready for my departure, the German Stukas bombed Piraeus and sank the ship *Hellas* on which I was booked.

So I didn't leave Greece. On the morning of April 27, 1941, I saw my first Nazi units entering our Athens on Patission Street, by Koliatsou Square near my house. I sank into black despair. I locked myself up in the house in my bedroom, and for two to two-and-a-half months, I did not go out. I could not bear to see the Nazis in Athens. Gradually, due to hunger, I too became the ghost of my former self. But I had to do something about work. I could no longer remain unemployed. One morning near the end of June, I left my home for the first time since the Nazis arrived. I was looking for work. I had nothing particular in mind. I didn't know where to go. While I was leaving Panepistimiou Street and entering Ippokratous Street, dragging my feet due to my terrible weakness, I heard a car behind me slamming on its brakes. As I walked on the street I saw out of the corner of my eye a Nazi army car, ten yards away. One of those horrible cars, this one was black. And inside the car I saw one of the three or four high-ranking officers gesturing to me. I was overcome by fear. Then I was shocked to recognize the face of the officer gesturing to me as that of Fritz Pommerenke. Years before I had met him at the Ministry of Labor where he had come as a young man, blond, likeable, with small glasses, speaking fluent Greek, to ask for a work permit as a foreigner. He stated then that he wanted to be a bookseller and, indeed, he later opened a bookstore at 15 Ippokratous Street on the ground floor of the university club building. Fritz was an intellectual with a rich cultural background. He also wrote poetry if I remember well. But how could he then be wearing the uniform of a Nazi colonel? He himself immediately explained: he got out of the car and started talking to me while passersby looked suspiciously at me and while I prayed for the earth to open up and swallow me! He asked why I was so thin. What a question! Then he asked if I had a job. He said he would be happy to find me one immediately. He spoke to me softly, telling me he was one of the staff officers of Marshal von Liszt, who had conquered the Balkan countries and Greece. So he had been a spy all of those years! He had been one of the many who had come to Greece under disguise. He gave me his unlisted telephone number and insisted I call him. I never did.

Why do I mention this incident with Fritz Pommerenke? First because it shocked me. I shuddered at the sight of the real Fritz Pommerenke. But I also wanted to point out how totally the August 4th totalitarian regime had corrupted Greece with fascist spies. But wasn't the August 4th regime also a fascist government? In fact it was a Hitler-modelled fascist totalitarian cancered government, one of many, unfortunately, then and now.

Time passed with all of us in deep agony, plagued with problems, the most pressing of which was hunger and famine. As for me, I found a job in a lawyer's office working for a lawyer who handled only penal cases. My salary was ridiculous, almost nothing. And he loaded all of his cases on me because he was busy with other things. I should note that I was working as an apprentice lawyer. Right from the start, I was sent by my boss, a lawyer himself, to the courts to defend our clients, but since I didn't have the necessary license to practice law (you needed two years of practice in a law office and to pass a difficult bar exam), I was continually doing something illegal by appearing alone in court acting as a defendant instead of standing by as an apprentice while the regular lawyer spoke. But how could I refuse when I had such a great need to earn a living? I used to catch an illegal ride on the tram to the office from my home at the other end of Athens and return late at night with my bag full of briefs so that I could work at home late at night. I would hold onto the outside of the tram facing the trams coming in the opposite direction, along with many others doing the same thing on all trams. We were in constant danger, of course, of being hit and crushed under the wheels of the other tram passing right next to us with just as many illegal riders hanging from the side. And as an

illegal lawyer, I was in danger of finding myself in the defendant's chair receiving a long sentence. The cases we had in the office were all of the worst kind, with one worse than the next. I was aware that I was lying in order to protect felons and criminals. I did not last long at the job. After three months I suffered emotional fatigue. I felt disgusted with myself and gave up. My dream of becoming a lawyer, of fighting for justice, had been irreparably tarnished. So I reluctantly abandoned the field of law and again was unemployed.

I worked here and there, wherever I could at odd jobs, anything that provided me the means to buy a piece of bread. In the winter of 1941, that ghastly winter of the great famine, I worked as a day laborer in the central vegetable market. One day, when we were being given our daily portion of "food"—bean soup with a few olives—I had a disagreement with another laborer over a single olive. Either he or I had taken one olive too many and the disagreement became a fight in the mud. Obviously the bean soup and olives were destroyed.

People soon began to organize a resistance against the conqueror. How could anybody remain indifferent? Of course those in the Greek establishment, the eternal establishment, absorbed in their deep apathy, were far removed from the agony and struggle of the Greek people. The leaders of the political and ecclesiastical bureaucracies, the university professors, the members of the Academy of Athens, the pseudointellectuals, were all Dead Souls. There were, of course, a few bright exceptions. But those who struggled and gave their youth and their lives as a sacrifice for freedom were mostly the simple people together with the young—the boys and girls of Greece who were in the front line.

In 1942, I joined EAM, the National Liberation Front, the largest and strongest and most militant resistance organization. I had my first discussion about joining with the late Markos Avgeris, an excellent writer, poet, literary critic, and an extraordinary person. He was a doctor as well and I knew him for many years, feeling honored to be a friend. Markos Avgeris was his literary pseudonym: Giorgios Papadopoulos was his real name. He talked to me one morning about the National Resistance and the EAM, and towards noon we met again by chance outside the sweets shop Inomena Voustasia on Panepistimiou Street. Thus, I joined the National Resistance along with hundreds of other patriots. I was just a member, not doing anything special. Because I could not accept the communist ideology—the Communists were the founders of EAM—I asked to work in the

The author, 1963

National Solidarity, the purely humanitarian section of EAM. I had come to know the communist perspective on life as I have mentioned earlier during my childhood. On the one hand, of course, I could not possibly have stayed out of the National Solidarity. But on the other hand, being true to myself, I didn't wish to be part of the EAM section I had contributed to since I would be judged as having accepted communist ideology.

On the 5th of March 1943, I took part in the large bloody demonstration in Athens against the Nazis and their plan for civilian call-up. Every now and then I would take part in similar demonstrations and carry out a variety of assignments for the National Solidarity, naturally on an underground basis. At this demonstration, I was caught by quislings—the Greek traitors and collaborators of the Germans, the so-called Special Security. They were dressed in police uniforms. Some were real police officers while others were civilian traitors who had joined up. They shoved me into a small car, one of those black German army cars, and pushed me into the backseat with two criminals. They took me to

Kyriakou Square, and we drove down a narrow side street that came out on the Square. At the end of the street was the headquarters of the Special Security. There they conducted interrogations and tortures of citizens they caught every day. That was one place of torture along with the SS headquarters on Merlin Street and elsewhere. Most of the National Resistance fighters who were taken to Special Security were then executed or thrown out wounded and maimed.

The Special Security headquarters building was, I believe, a three-story structure. They took me to a room on the top floor, left me there a long time with one guard who sat across from me in a chair. At times he turned his pistol on me as if he were playing a game. He never said a word. Suddenly I heard horrible shouts of pain, moans coming from another room. God knows whom they were torturing at that hour of the night. But the sound was horrifying, frightening. I lost control and shouted, "Is this the way you torture those you capture? So savagely?"

He looked at me as if he couldn't understand what I was saying. "What do you mean?" he asked. "I mean what you too can hear. The man you are torturing is howling with pain." He looked at me again with a sarcastic grin. "Ha! You fool, nobody's howling, you idiot! Don't you know the people we treat haven't the strength to open their mouths?" I was literally at a loss. The screaming hadn't stopped for a moment. "But then, I don't understand. Who is it who's screaming like that?" "The torturer, you jerk! The guy who is now torturing somebody is screaming with pleasure, pure delight with his work, you get me now?" What could I say? When I finally left Special Security, alive, but wounded from the fierce beating, my feet dragging, I reached the corner and saw the street sign:

Hope Street

I shuddered. So this street in purgatory where there was no hope for those who passed into Special Security was Hope Street.

Twelve years later in 1954, when I was ready to publish my first narrative prose, a collection of twelve short stories focusing on the postwar quest for hope, my first thought was to give the collection the general title of Hope Street. But I finally chose a title which was that of the last short story: *Wanted: Hope.*

In April 1942, I went to Karditsa, a city in Thessaly. My beloved father was from a village in the area, Morfovouni or Vounesi as they used to call it in the past. My late father's village is mountainous, high on the Agrafa range, over two thousand feet high. There are villages in the plains of Thessaly also, but there is a sharp division between those who dwell in the mountains and plainsmen. There is a chasm even in their costumes, but above all in their mentality.

My mother and I arrived in Karditsa one night, and we rented a small room in a ground-floor home. My father and brother were still in Athens. I had found a job in Karditsa even though it was my first visit there and, in fact, my first trip into the provinces away from Athens. Working there I had the chance to visit many villages. And that gave me the opportunity to talk with the villagers about the need for a resistance. But mainly they talked to me about the National Resistance. Thus I made many new friends in the villages, mountains, and plains.

It was exciting and touching to see how these people yearned for the liberation of Greece from the Nazis and organized themselves within the Resistance, risking their lives daily in daring acts of self-sacrifice. To me, they were an invaluable example of an active resistance and a free, uncompromised conscience. Feeling I was parting with brothers, I said good-bye to them in November 1942 and hoped that we would meet again in a free Greece. I definitely had to return to Athens at that time.

We left Karditsa that cloudy morning, Adriana, my dear mother, Evripidis, my dad, who had come to see us for a few weeks, and myself. We travelled to Paleofarsala, a village, on November 25th on the Thessaly railroad which operated only within Thessaly. From there we could catch the international train running from Thessaloniki to Athens. But when we got off at Paleofarsaia we found out that there was no longer a train for Athens. The day before, Resistance fighters, risking their lives, had done the seemingly impossible. They had blown up the big bridge at Gorgopotamus where trains passed to and from Athens. Normally, with the sudden lack of transportation, I should have gone back to Karditsa. But all my life I have been unable to go back once I have started out for somewhere. So I left my parents in Paleofarsala to return to Karditsa, and I continued on foot to Farsala, walking for hours, and from there I set out for Athens, on a long trek of many more miles.

Exhausted by the dreadfully tough walk, I met a big open truck with a trap over the back headed for Athens after I had already walked about twenty kilometers. One of the two men sitting next to the driver, aged forty or more, dark with big thick eyebrows, gestured to me in a friendly manner, studying me through my road-weary mask. When I told him I was walking to Athens, he said, "Boy, are you nuts? Jump in. We're also going to Athens. Nea Filadelfia, to be exact." How could I ever forget the kindness of this man named Nikos Trypias? After the

war he was elected mayor of Nea Filadelfia. I read it in the newspaper one day. He has been dead for several years. I never saw him again after that meeting during the Occupation. Thus, I made the long journey in the night of the Occupation, in the back of the truck since there was no room in the front, but it was comfortable considering conditions at that time. I touched bodies as the truck rocked. They were almost human as they hung there dripping blood, slaughtered by man's hand, suspended from the roof. There were over thirty harmless young calves with me and they were all dead, but I was alive. They were in the meat business.

I did not imagine back in November 1942 when I said good-bye to my friends in Karditsa and the surrounding villages that my wish to meet them again would materialize about two years later, June 1944, in such an unexpected way and in circumstances that were highly dramatic and unbelievable. The story happened as follows . . .

So June 1944 was the last and the worst year of the German Occupation. At that time the Nazi monster, seeing that gradually the game was getting out of hand, started preparing to disengage itself from Greece and the Balkans and was thrashing wildly in every direction. Roadblocks were set up everywhere in our country. Arrests, tortures, executions by the hundred took place. No, by the thousand. Whole villages and cities were burnt to the ground and left in ruins.

It was the 4th or 5th of June, early on a Friday morning when I left home at 39 Ippolytou Street, near Koliatsou Square, to meet a twenty-year-old girl before going to work. We were to meet at the Larissa train station, and from there she would be leaving for Karditsa. She was headed there on a Resistance mission which I was also involved in.

I said good-bye to her, and as the train was pulling away, at the last moment before it picked up speed, I suddenly jumped aboard to head for Karditsa too. My move was spontaneous, unplanned. They had no idea at home that I would not return at noon.

In order to travel outside of Athens, I had to have a special permit from the Germans in addition to a ticket. I had neither. But I managed to hide during the trip, and, at noon the next day, Saturday, I got off at Paleofarsala to catch the Thessaly train for Karditsa. But we had a delayed arrival, and I feared that I would miss the Thessaly link. There was only one train per day, so I jumped from the train before it stopped, and with the girl following at a distance, I ran through the fields towards the Thessaly station to get our tickets. Suddenly in the middle of the wheat field, a tall armed man in civilian clothes leaped on me and aggressively demanded to know where I was headed. When I told him, he commanded, "Go to the EASAD garrison for a travel permit."

The EASAD was one more criminal organization that the Nazis had created with the aid of traitors and other shady types, and it was only active in Thessaly. The initials stood for National Farm Union of Anti-Communist Activity! Behind this ridiculous and pompous title were hidden the dregs of society who were after patriot Resistance fighters, sending them to their deaths. They did not have to give any account for their acts.

Up till that moment I had no idea that EASAD existed. But it wasn't long before I got a taste of their hospitality as I went up the stairs of the small two-story house where the "garrison" was located. I went into a room which served as their office. There were two small tables and two young men with greasy hair. They asked me where I was going. I told them. They looked me over carefully and, upon hearing my name, beat me up and threw me, covered with blood, into the basement which they used as a jail cell. It was

a room some six hundred feet from the "garrison," a dreadful room without windows. It was dark and contained men, women, children, and even babies as prisoners. The EASAD had mangled all of us in its gears. I was accused of being a Communist and was set up for trial the next morning, Sunday, along with the others. I was to be put through a "court martial," which is what they called their court. While I was being led from the "garrison" to the dungeon, I saw over ten dead patriots hanging from trees, the work of the EASAD criminals. Was this to be my fate as well?

It was now Saturday afternoon. The dungeon was crammed with human beings. Every once in a while the door would open and the EASAD traitors would throw in yet another prisoner. It was so dark in the dungeon that you could not see the face of the person pressing against you. And something else made us shudder: you couldn't really be sure who was a real prisoner sharing your fate and who was really spying on the group, ready to report anything subversive or against the EASAD.

"With my wife, Eleni, my great friend Graham Greene and his wife, Yvonne, in Mikrolimano, a small port near Athens," 1976

And then suddenly someone else was thrown in. The door opened for a minute, he was pushed in and collapsed on top of all of us, and he began to whimper. He told us that he was a travelling salesman with one of those large tricycles, I believe he said, who went around from village to village selling hairpins, combs, and such. But the EASAD monsters caught him. "You are a Jew," they told him. The poor man beat himself in despair and tore at his ragged clothing declaring that he was a Greek Orthodox Christian. How in the world could anybody call him a Jew! In fact, he said, his uncle was a practicing priest. No, they told him dryly. "You are a Jew and here is the proof: the SS has given us this book with Jewish noses shown in it and your nose fits perfectly with nose number seventeen."

The afternoon passed and dusk approached when the alleged Jew, perhaps to emphasize his claim of Christianity, asked us if we would be in favor of asking our guards for permission to go, under guarded escort, of course, to the only church in the village so that the priest could bless us and pray for us. So that the priest could pray to God to save us from the danger of death which we were about to face on Sunday, the next day, at the EASAD "court martial." When seven or eight of us agreed with him, he took the initiative and spoke to the guards. And in fifteen minutes we were on our way to the church with armed guards to our right and left.

Summoning all the strength in his soul, that kind priest whom we met for the first time in the church, begged God to save us from our imminent danger. I had never seen such a wonderful priest. He was very thin, with his eyes and face reflecting the refinement of his soul. In other words, he radiated light in the terrible darkness that surrounded us. We tried to persuade him to accept some money which was the custom to give him. Afterwards the guards took us back to the dungeon, immersed in our misery, awaiting Sunday and the "court martial" which would mean death. Unless the priest's prayers were successful . . .

I don't know what time it was, perhaps 3 a.m.—certainly it was in the dead of the night—when the door swung slightly open and a rough voice called out, "Samarakis! Out! . . ." I had no idea what was awaiting me. As I came out of the dungeon, somebody could have killed me. After all, they were all vicious. And of course I could hardly say, "Sorry, fellows, I'm sleeping now. Don't disturb me. Come later."

It was then that I saw a man, very tall and very armed, with guns, hand grenades, and other such encouraging weapons. He told me sharply, after dragging me three or four yards from the door, that his intentions towards me were not pleasant ones and that he had no sympathy for my approaching end. But then here is what happened: it turned out he was at the time serving as an assistant to the EASAD leader having previously abandoned his position with EAM. Because of this defection, the EAM took his wife and two small children hostage on the mountain. He told me that I would surely die and that when he had found out about my arrest, he had asked for me to be handled as a special case. He requested that there be no court martial for me on the following day but rather on that very same evening. Furthermore, he asked for me to be sentenced to death, but that he would take me under his own watch and on Sunday, the next day, would escort me on the Thessaly train to Karditsa. For what reason? So that, handcuffed, I could meet my friends and comrades from EAM who now held high positions. I would then offer my own life for the release of his wife and children. He made this proposal to me because, he said finally, he had information that I had important contacts with EAM.

I was bowled over, but didn't show it. How could I possibly have influence with EAM? Nonsense! I was just a young man who did whatever I could for the National Resistance. But I immediately grabbed for this unexpected luck, pretending that he was right and that things were as he said they were and that I could play a decisive role in solving his problem. I was lying at that moment, I must confess, but I had to pretend since such an unexpected chance had appeared before me.

When I agreed, he went to speak to the "court martial," while I was thrown back into the dungeon. Within half an hour he returned with two armed men and took me to the trial. They took me to the same house, the so-called "garrison," to the same room where they had beat me up a few hours before when I had gone to get a travel permit to Karditsa.

Things had changed this second time I entered the courtroom. The two small tables I had seen on Saturday afternoon were now joined together to serve as the "desk" for the "court martial." There was no electricity in the room, and an oil lamp gave out light that was felt as yet another threat, as an element of danger. Two or three Nazis, some other armed EASAD members, and my would-be savior himself stood in the corners of the room. The "judges" sat behind the joined tables. They kept most of their weapons on the table ready for use. In the center was the presiding judge, the most inhuman of all. But when I saw him, I froze. Who do you think it was? The priest! Yes, the kind and compassionate priest who had prayed with all his soul, who had prayed to God for all of us to be spared from death . . . that very death which he knew while he prayed that he himself would deal out to us in a few brief hours. What a thriller! . . .

[A brief footnote here. During the Occupation, the Greek clergy fought on the side of the people. This was especially true in poor towns and villages. Many of the priests were caught by the Nazis and also by the fascist Italians and the Bulgarian oppressors who were in partnership with the Germans. Many priests suffered unspeakable tortures and gave their lives without flinching as a sacrifice for the common struggle for freedom. This case I experienced in Paleofarsala was a deplorable exception to the rule.]

They tried me, they sentenced me to death with the priest up front as the best of them, rather, I should say, the worst of the lot. Dostoevsky was right when he commented, "Nothing can be more unbelievable than reality."

On Sunday morning a few hours later, the plan hatched by the National Resistance renegade proceeded as mapped out. We went to Karditsa . . . and finally he himself hid me away, counting on my alleged power to intervene in the higher echelons of EAM in Athens to get him through since I had managed to convince him that I had such influence, but everything I told him was a pack of lies. I also

With his mother, Adriani

played my part in Karditsa, for now I was bolstered by desperation and anxiety in the face of danger.

I arrived home in Athens after unimaginable adventures. I arrived terribly worn out on Tuesday or Wednesday morning around 6 A.M., and, as I opened the gate to our home, I saw my dear mother, Adriana. Because she had supposed for days that I had been completely lost, she hugged me tightly, smothered me with kisses, and ordered me to leave at once and vanish. Someone from EAM had been there the day before warning me to hide. The Nazis and their collaborators had found a list of names of those in the Resistance including my own. All I had time for was to kiss my dear father and brother good-bye.

From then until the liberation of Athens on October 12, 1944, I stayed in hiding, living in fear in a deserted warehouse without windows about ten miles from Athens. Only a nineteen-year-old girl, a student at the school of philosophy at the University of Athens, knew where I was hiding, and, risking her own life, would send me bread, cheese, and potatoes every three or four days.

But I was not alone there, for an army of rats paraded by my feet and kept me company, showing no fear themselves. It was only me who was afraid. I was scared they would bite my nose or fingers . . . thus half my food went to the rats as they quietly and patiently waited in a semi-circle around me for their share.

I wrote my last poem sometime around 1951. Then around 1953–54 I started working on my first book of narrative prose: the twelve short stories that became *Wanted: Hope.* The book was published with my own money because I did not have a publisher willing to do so. It had been very difficult, if not impossible in Greece, then and now, to find a publisher willing to back a young emerging author. My salary at the Ministry of Labor was not enough to cover these publishing expenses, so I had to work at various odd jobs in the afternoons and evenings, mainly in printing offices correcting and proofreading. In August 1954, I received my first copies of *Wanted: Hope* from the printers.

Before I go on with a brief account of what happened to the first copies of *Wanted: Hope,* let me just say a few words about how I was motivated to write these stories. What had I been until then? A certain person, a certain simple individual who had lived his childhood and youth intensely, with much experience and adventure. I had also lived through the war and the German Occupation. I was one of the many throughout the world who had fought, each in his own way, for a dream of a better world, filled with hope, honestly believing that after the world holocaust and the sacrifice of hundreds of thousands of people, the postwar world would be a world of peace, freedom, and social justice. Unfortunately the denial, the falsification of hopes and expectations soon followed. This is what I wanted to capture in *Wanted: Hope.* But there is also something implied in the title and in the last story: the continual quest for hope, the thirst and desire for hope. Thus the overall feeling of the twelve stories is not of desperation and hopelessness, but on the contrary, it is rather an optimistic realism. I'd even say it is a realistic confrontation of everyday life, society, and the postwar world with both feet on the ground.

The title alone, *Wanted: Hope,* summarized my own evaluation of the situation. It shows a man— myself since I am in and behind these stories—who doesn't give up, who won't passively accept the gloomy horizon of the world around him, but who fights for hope. And where are we at that point? In 1954 then and 1991 now, this priceless virtue which should be with us everywhere in full abundance like the air we breathe is, alas, very rare or perhaps it has almost passed away. We have reached such a point that the old assumption "while I breathe, I hope" is no longer appropriate. Rather we must come up with a variation: "as long as I fight for hope, I can hope" or "as long as I strive to believe that somewhere there is hope which I may find in my struggles, I can hope."

Now I can return to the story of these first copies of *Wanted: Hope.* It was an August afternoon in 1954 when I received fifty or sixty copies from the printer. I put them in an old battered briefcase and started walking towards Omonia Square, one of the two main squares of Athens, and from there I continued up Stadiou Street, Panepistimiou Street, Academias Street to reach the main bookstores located on these streets, giving each of them two or three copies. Not that I had any expectation to be paid for these first few copies. All I wanted was that they would accept to have them on the shelf, in the basement even, or the warehouse. Because when a book, especially a work of literature, is printed, it must be seen in bookstores if it is to have the good fortune of being sold.

What was the outcome of these first visits and pleas to these more than Athenian bookstores? Nothing. Zero. They didn't even bother to look at my book. Everywhere I was received with an icy refusal. Not a single copy of my fifty or so was taken.

Dispirited and upset, my briefcase still full, I passed Syntagma (Constitution) Square, the last stop on my futile tour, and went into the Cafe of Paris. Situated on the corner of Mitropolis and Nikis streets, on the ground floor of a beautiful neoclassical build-ing, this popular cafe was frequented mainly by middle-class men, most of whom were workers hardened by life. They would talk over coffee or ouzo or cognac and play backgammon or cards. I used to go there almost every afternoon around sunset, from the age of fourteen. I would drink my ouzo and afterwards stroll uphill to Plaka, the old neighborhood of Athens which was very beautiful then with its peaceful cobbled alleys, its acacias and myriad other flowers in the small courtyards, windows, and balconies of its two- and single-story homes. I would stroll there every night after being at the Cafe of Paris and I would find my friends, the simple folk like myself who included among them poets and painters and we would drink in Plaka's small tavernas.

That particular afternoon, after a couple of sips of ouzo, I stared at my old briefcase leaning against my chair with all of the untouched copies inside, and without knowing what had happened, I started crying like a child as all the bitterness welled up inside me and choked me. Those around me stared on good-naturedly but obviously amazed that a man of thirty-five was crying this way. They looked at me with that special compassion and tenderness that only the tormented common people have who are not, of course, intellectuals and officials of every ilk. In a minute I picked up the briefcase, opened it, pulled out a copy and nervously, feverishly, dedicated it, the first dedication I had written, to Antonis, to myself:

> *To Antonis Samarakis*
>
> *Courage!*
>
> > Antonis Samarakis
> > Athens
> > 8/18/54 9:30pm
> > Cafe of Paris

I had sent copies to a few newspapers. Two weeks after that night at the Cafe of Paris, the first review appeared in the morning paper *Kathimerini* on the Thursday literary page. It was written by Cleon Paraschos, an excellent poet, essayist, literary critic, and prose writer. His review had warm praise, and my joy was boundless. This was the first review of my first book: how could I not be overjoyed?

A few days later I had a second joyful surprise. Returning home from the ministry one afternoon, I found a postcard pushed under the gate by the mailman. On the back was an incredible text, handwritten and signed by Evangelos P. Papanoutsos, a first-rate personality, famous in Greece and abroad, a professor at the teaching academies, a thinker and philosopher, and a commentator every Thursday for the daily morning paper *To Vima*. I didn't know him personally, but he had read my book, he wrote, at the newspaper office where I had sent it, and he rushed to tell me that he loved it with all his heart and wanted to do something for the first time as feature writer in *Vima,* although he himself never wrote literary book reviews. His articles in the paper were always on the front page and were on broader topics such as philosophy, aesthetics, education, and social problems. His intention to write a review of *Wanted: Hope* was going to be an exception, precisely so that he could project his feelings on reading my book. But, he continued on the card, before writing his article, he wanted us to meet and he provided his address and phone number.

In forty-eight hours I was at his house, a modest home in Pangrati, Artotinis Street, in a middle-class section of the city. It was afternoon and he greeted me with warmth. We sat on his balcony overlooking the small garden in the courtyard. We sat for hours, perhaps six or seven, until night came and, without turning on the light, we talked on. I did most of the talking. He told me that he wanted to listen.

On Thursday, September 30, 1954, very early in the morning, much earlier than usual, I went to Koliatsou Square and eagerly bought *Vima.* My hands were trembling, and there, on the first page down to the right, was his article.

This was not just deep joy, it was absolute happiness. There were tears in my eyes. I was floating . . .

And that same afternoon there was a sequel. My phone went crazy. Who was it? Oh! The same bookstore owners who a few days before had kicked me out so rudely, uninterested in even looking at the cover of *Wanted: Hope.* And they even complained to me that I hadn't had the courtesy to send them copies of my book and so they didn't know what to say to customers who were looking for it! Now they all wanted my book because they had read the article by Evangelos P. Papanoutsos. The booksellers, of course, didn't even remember that I had already come to them. And I of course didn't tell them about the failure of my first visit. All I did was thank them and send them copies. Thus from one minute to the next the career of *Wanted: Hope* took a 180-degree turn and the copies of the first edition soon sold out. This miracle occurred because a personality such as the late Papanoutsos could acknowledge with amazing love this poorly printed book of seventy-six pages by a totally unknown author appearing in print for the first time.

This act of love and support by Papanoutsos was a turning point not only in my literary career but also in my life. Because right now, thirty-seven years later

since that Thursday, I am deeply overcome with emotion and gratitude when I recall him and his article which was published on the front page of *Vima.* Allow me to insert a piece of the article:

Intellectual Matters

A Prose Writer

I consider it my duty to call the attention of the reading public, and particularly those who from their critical standpoint follow the course and progress of our Letters, to a small, poorly printed book currently in circulation containing twelve short stories by Antonis Samarakis. The title, *Wanted: Hope.* There are just seventy-six small-sized pages. I may be mistaken in my excessive enthusiasm. I may be reacting to my indignation at the piles of literary books with "high claims" that seem to multiply every day. But I do not think that this small book should pass unnoticed. It convinces even the difficult and demanding readers that here is a man (in fact a young man who appears for the first time in our Letters) who really has something to tell us and who knows how to say this something without chattering, without superfluous embellishment, but in simple, brief, clear words (how admirable brevity is!), strongly and dramatically.

As a first effort, as a beginning in the difficult field of narrative prose, Mr. Samarakis's book has already achieved an encouraging and very promising success.

It is his world, his emotional world that wins over the reader, moving him deeply. It is a world tormented by the dreadful contradictions of our time. The world he depicts is turbulent, confused, yet full of courtesy and tenderness and imbued with a sense of calm, blessed compassion that even in ultimate desperation loves and respects mankind, turning away from hate, vulgarity, hypocrisy and lies.

In his story "The River," two soldiers on opposite sides come face to face with each other while swimming in the same river and rush to shore, frightened. They run for their rifles but our hero will not shoot: "But he didn't pull the trigger. The Other was there, naked as he had come into the world. And he was here, naked as he had come into the world. . . . Two naked men. Naked of clothing. Naked of names. Naked of nationalities. Naked of their selves. He couldn't pull the trigger. And naturally he gets killed because in the meantime the other has fired . . ."

Elsewhere in the book the speaker at a ceremonial gathering notices a boy in the back rows, a young boy listening with his soul in his eyes, and he stops his pompous talk about the rosy future that awaits the world after so many sacrifices: "No, he could not expound the usual philosophies in front of a child, he could not lie, he could not but be his true self in front of this boy. A voice within him cried: I cannot! I cannot!"

In the last story in the collection, the cry which has been building throughout, soft and controlled in many previous pages, breaks out in a tone of tragic irony. The hero here is the author himself, this time fully exposed:

"He glanced at the newspaper again: Indochina, the "Social Column," the piano recital, the two suicides for lack of money, small ads . . . WANTED typewriter . . . WANTED record player . . . WANTED jeep in good condition

WANTED genuine Persian rug. He took out his pad, tore off a sheet and wrote with his pencil: WANTED hope. He then added his name and his address. He called the waiter. All he wanted was to pay, to go directly to the newspaper, to hand in his ad, to beg, to insist that it get printed in tomorrow's paper without fail."

That the curtain falls upon scenes of such dark colors is not, of course, the fault of our narrator. It is our disillusioned world, as it prepares for suicide, that is at fault . . .

Mr. Samarakis has written a book of great promise.

E. P. Papanoutsos

Although I had written the stories in *Wanted: Hope* only to capture some thoughts and feelings with no intention of continuing to write, the flow of events made me change my course. In subsequent years I wrote the novel *Danger Signal.* The story takes place in Farsala, a small town of a few thousand inhabitants in Thessaly, and, towards the end, the action moves to Athens. I spoke previously about Farsala, when I recounted my adventures during the Occupation. It was precisely this memory that made me settle on the story of Farsala.

Danger Signal came out in November 1959. In this novel I tried to convey how our everyday life has been corroded and undercut by oppressive fears. Two in particular: the fear of war and the fear of hunger. The subject of war has tormented me since childhood. In the course of man's presence on earth, war has been everpresent: blood, sacrifice, disasters . . . whether under this excuse or that argument, every so often a new war erupts, men against men . . . Why? What for?

Agonizing questions were swelling up inside of me. The thought of war always tyrannized me. What worried me was not just war itself but the frightful effects ensuing from each case of warfare—the dead, maimed, wounded, physical, emotional, and moral wrecks, social and economic disasters, desertion, and much else. I was also worried about the disastrous effects that the prospect and fear of a new world war, capable of erupting at any moment, has on everybody's daily life and on our relations with others, a fear that is perpetually fanned and which haunts us by its constant presence.

I thought continually about these things and inevitably the time came for me to try and express them in writing. Thus *Danger Signal* was born. My aim was, by means of the narrative, to provide a measure of how the fear of war, the phobia I would say, undermines individuals and society as a whole.

There is an element of suspense in this novel supplied by the evasive presence of a "Monster" that is terrifying the city. The suspense is carried over as the narrative later continues in Athens, no longer through the shadow of the "Monster" but through the various adventures of the two main protagonists. I would say that the principal message of *Danger Signal* is that in a world so turbulent and contradictory as our present world is, we have no right to stay content, apathetic, or indifferent to our shared fate.

In November 1961, my third book came out, the eleven short stories in *I Refuse*. In *Wanted: Hope* the dominant theme was the agonizing search for hope in a postwar world corrupted by the false hope that after the holocaust the world would become a better place. In *Danger Signal* the probing moves in a positive direction: "I have no outlet, I have no hope. My only hope for expression is to be restless and more restless. As long as I am restless, I can hope. As long as I have restlessness, I hope. As long as there are restless people in the world and as long as there is restlessness in our world, there is hope . . ." I wrote also in *Danger Signal* that ". . . a serene man in our times is an unnatural man. Over and above the danger of war lies the danger of remaining unconcerned in the face of war. Over and above the danger of hunger lies the danger of being unconcerned in the face of hunger. Yes, here is the danger, the fundamental danger, the slipping away of restlessness from the hearts of people, the passing away of Holy Restlessness."

The stories of *I Refuse* present a more substantial pattern of protest and rebellion. The characters in these stories, and especially in the last one, "I Refuse," live out their own powerful refusal to accept the craziness of daily life such as it is when others control its course and fate for sinister reasons. Ultimately the characters in "I Refuse" discover a solid base as they establish a firm foundation. "Even though you may have nothing else in life, you will always have that certainty that somewhere there is someone you can make less unhappy, less lonely. This is a certainty you cannot ignore, a certainty which nobody, nothing, and no one can deny you!" And further on in the same story I wrote, "You have no right to go towards death alone! There is always a human being whom you can make less unhappy, less lonely. This single person binds you to life, to life and to others. This single person is the single certainty you are sure of, you can depend on, this single human being, this single certainty is the umbilical cord that ties you to life, to this daily life here and now with its troubles and its trivia, its worries, sorrows, and joys. Yes, you can't choose death! You have no right to choose death! As long as there are two human beings,

Having a long talk with children in a school in China, where he was invited when his novel
The Flaw *was published, 1983*

one person and another, these two become a certainty. As long as there are two, there is a REFUSAL."

Allow me to mention that the *I Refuse* collection was awarded the State Short Story Award of 1962. I was, of course, overjoyed. But it was also the time of another unique happiness for me: my Elenitsa, my life's companion.

I met Elenitsa—that's what I call her, tenderly, instead of "Eleni"—during the reception that followed the award for *I Refuse*. It was December 20, 1962, and we were married on February 9, 1963. As if struck by lightning, we realized that our lives were fated to be joined, as they say in books. You see, at that moment I didn't greet my good luck with an "I Refuse" and ever since I have counted myself blessed. Forever since, Elenitsa has been my tender and energetic partner in all the good and hard times we've been through together. She is my companion and mentor whom I value beyond measure. It's not just her love and insight I cherish but also the unbiased, direct, and evenhanded criticism she makes of my ideas and actions. I am deeply grateful to her for all she has offered me. She has remained strong

through all the tough times we've had, especially during those bleak, nightmarish years of the junta (1967–74). I fully appreciate her feelings, thoughts, actions, but at the same time I owe her endless gratitude for something equally important: her whole perspective, her compassion and companionship which she offers not just because of convenience or overly sweet disposition, but spontaneously. She keeps me constantly alert and ready for anything. And so I not only live but thrive physically, mentally, and spiritually.

For example, there is more than the daily dialogue we maintain over the important and trivial matters. If I happen to be working on a text for days or even weeks and I give it to her to read—I always ask her to read everything I write and give me her opinion—she writes down her comments and argues her points with fervor. If I, as is often the case, "kick back" and refuse to make any changes, then the conversation becomes heated and the atmosphere charged. A miracle is then born out of this conflict: a feisty and sincere communication which is the most valuable kind of human contact that keeps our marriage from becoming a merely routine or bureaucratic relationship.

Right from the start, from the very first hours of meeting my Elenitsa, I could see that I was hooked for good. And I, a confirmed bachelor, detecting the future growth of my passion into marriage, became more and more confused. Besides the strong possibility of marriage, I was alarmed by the actual intensity of my passion. I suffered a mass of conflicting emotions: on the one hand, this burning passion was incredibly sweet and fascinating. But on the other hand, I wondered how I would disengage myself, keep my distance from blind submission to my heart's desires, to marriage, to permanent ties.

In the midst of such a dizzy state of mind, acting as if out of panic, I made an impulsive decision. I went to the office of the daily newspaper *I Kathimerini*, a prestigious and respected paper with a wide circulation which included a literary section every Thursday. It was mid-January 1963 and I paid for the following printed announcement:

ANTONIS SAMARAKIS

A DANGEROUS MAN

IN DANGER

circulates

Those who saw this must surely have thought it was an announcement for the "circulation" of a new book. The truth was that a different book was being written, and I could feel it being written every hour that passed, a work based on life and my companionship with Elenitsa. I felt caught up in a wonderful trap set for me by my own heart, but I felt also a certain hovering sense of danger, or so it seemed to me then. The notice was a message directed only to her. It was my confession to her and through it I revealed the deepest recesses of my soul and my subconscious.

I knew she would see my SOS and decipher its message immediately. She too was a writer having written an excellent novel, *The Revenge of the Idols,* at age eighteen which received a fantastic response from the public and warm praises from the critics. What a pity she did not pursue her outstanding talent!

So there I was, waiting for her to find my message, to receive and understand my cry. It was a cry of agony yet it also expressed a deep, secret desire for the fulfillment of what fate now clearly dictated to me. The funny thing is that on that particular Thursday, Elenitsa did not buy *Kathimerini* and so I had to tell her myself a few days later.

My novel *The Flaw* is dedicated to Elenitsa. And I dedicated a more recent story, "You, Shut Up!": "To my Elenitsa, to whom I owe this story *also.*" But what is the value of these two dedications when my whole life is dedicated to Elenitsa?

Even though there is a large age difference between us, she has made me feel as young as she is, and she continues to add new dimensions to my life.

My fourth book, *The Flaw,* came out in November 1965. The concept of totalitarianism had tortured me for a long time before I actually began writing the book in 1962. During the Second World War there was an uprising of hundreds of millions of people who came together and struggled to crush totalitarianism. Their main enemy was fascism, that Nazi monster, and totalitarianism generally under any disguise. But what came of the sacrifice of a whole generation that fought with a passion for freedom, with a vision of a postwar world free of oppressors, free of perpetrators and victims? Alas! What followed the holocaust was a glaring betrayal of these people's vision. Totalitarianism has always been around, and is still here today, in 1991.

The indifference shown by those untouched by the plague of totalitarianism towards the cruel fate of others has also preoccupied me. Freedom is a matter that may concern each person separately, but it also affects all people. You cannot rest easy when you know that your freedom may not have been deprived but that your neighbor's freedom has been taken away. You can't rest easy because you may lose your freedom tomorrow.

Freedom cannot be hidden away. Totalitarianism is like radioactivity: it spreads everywhere, into the most distant corner, the most secluded room. In the end nobody remains whole.

But even our democracies—to whatever extent they are truly democracies—are riddled with totalitarianism. Public and covert relentless reality, we ourselves, the victims of these terrorizing mechanisms of power, gradually retreat in our hearts and our consciences. Fear enters and corrodes our mental and ethical faculties, we compromise with tyranny, the "noble tissues" of human dignity and integrity rot, and we finally conform to these habits. We wind up betraying our natural freedom, that quintessence of the human condition, turning our face away from the very need for freedom which is innate in us. The instinct for freedom is deadened, the hunger and thirst for freedom are reduced to nothing. And the danger to whole generations which follow that have no notion of the significance of freedom, that will never know freedom, becomes very real. At this late date in human development, a biological distortion has appeared which is delivering us on the threshold of a new ice age. Unless we fight with every last breath for the protection of freedom, unless we go forward with relentless determination and militancy, a world will emerge in which freedom is utterly unknown.

In *The Flaw* I tried to convey the struggle of the individual, the man in the street, to free himself from the deadly embrace of any state power, but particularly that of totalitarianism. This novel contains, directly and indirectly, bitter experiences I had under both totalitarian systems before the 1967 junta: the dictatorship of August 4th and the German Occupation. These experiences infiltrated into *The Flaw* somehow while the story and narrative were born in my imagination. No name has been given to the country that is the location of the story, precisely because I wanted to underline the universal range of totalitarianism's danger. The power that governs this anonymous country is referred to as "The Establishment," the secret service is called "The Service," its headquarters is "The Central," while the officials of this arbitrary system are "the boss," "the examiner," "the manager," and the common man who falls into their clutches is "the man of the Cafe Sport." The spiderweb scheme that they contrived to break "the man of the Cafe Sport" and make him confess his participation in a resistance movement is simply referred to as "the Plan."

"You must pretend that you are also a man with feelings, you must appear human." This is the directive given to the examiner by the chief of The Service. The staff officials of The Establishment thought that they had created a perfect scheme for extracting the confession of the suspect. The examiner and the manager would pretend to take him for further questioning to the headquarters of The Service, hundreds of miles away from the place of arrest, on a long journey in a State car, a trip which included a ferryboat ride. They had prearranged various apparently chance adventures which would offer the examiner the opportunity to demonstrate his warmth and friendship gradually towards the man of the Cafe Sport, and they were thus sure that he would be gently brought around to confess.

But the chief and The Service were mistaken. Matters took a totally different course. It turns out that the "ideology" of the totalitarian mind does not apply to human relationships: "People are divided only into those who are with the State and those who aren't. To be an enemy of the State, you don't have to act against it. It's enough for you not to be for the State, that is, not to have demonstrated any definite action in its favor. Yes, for the State the law is: He who is not for me is against me."

At the end of the narrative, the examiner discovers that a secret human communication has grown and is at work between him and the man from the Cafe Sport. He discovers that though he started by simulating friendly feelings, he now feels a real friendship towards the prisoner. At this crucial moment, the examiner, the trusted man of the State, encourages the suspect to escape to freedom while he covers him. And the prisoner does so knowing that now only death awaits him since the manager, the faithful blind instrument of the State, suddenly enters the scene and becomes an eyewitness to the examiner's action.

With *The Flaw* I wanted to create a message of hope, that the human element, which is despised by totalitarian systems and which they therefore try to wipe out, nevertheless is always present and will finally triumph. Because life itself has taught me that no power—ideological, political, economic, technocratic, military, religious—will ever be able to reduce man to a pitiful automaton when by his very nature he is a free person. No power will ever be able to extinguish the holy flame of humanity and compassion in men's hearts.

In November 1973, *The Passport,* another collection of my stories, was published. The first three of the nine were "inspired" by the gloomy and terrifying years of the junta which lasted from April 21, 1967, to July 24, 1974. Once more I tried to express in these stories my hatred for any totalitarian system and at the same time my deep gratitude to the uncompromising struggle of our people for freedom and democracy. The youth were in the vanguard of this struggle in Greece as always in our country's most difficult periods.

I had a certain run-in with the junta—and it is a historical fact that it was aided and supported if not incited by the secret and overt agencies of the USA.

A few days before the coup made by the colonels, I discussed in interviews and articles in the press an imminent blow approaching Greece in the form of a dictatorship. And, unfortunately, my prophecies came true. Consequently, when the junta came, my passport was confiscated, and I was forbidden to leave the country "for reasons of public order and public interest." If I left the country, they said, I "would harm national interests to the maximum possible degree."

What throws light on the nature of any totalitarian system and the secret fears that consume it is, I think, the following incident. When I was summoned

*Antonis Samarakis, his wife, Eleni, Tania Ribakov, wife of the Russian author
Anatoli Ribakov, Moscow, 1990*

to the General Security office, I saw my "file," containing all the facts and information about me which the security police had been collecting for years. In fact, this happened not only under the dictatorships in Greece, which unfortunately have occurred frequently, but also during periods of democracy. To be exact, there was not just one "file," but many, four or five from what I was able to see, all tied together with dirty strings. On top was an official document that summed up all the "evidence" against me. This document was from the National Security General Management (GDEA) and was addressed to the General Security and presumably to other recipients. I mention in passing that GDEA was the highest security service during the junta years. The officer in front of me read the document. It talked at length and widely about my humble participation in democratic activities. But the last paragraph was striking:

> From a study of the literary works by the said person, his novels and short stories, it is clearly

deduced that he is against war and especially against nuclear war.

At the end, the document said that I ought to make a statement for the above . . . accusation! I had to do this in writing, and in duplicate.

In other words, no more no less, they were condemning me as an author to testify because I loved peace and was against war including nuclear war!

Naturally I categorically refused to make any "defense" or "statement" to the General Security.

I should have mentioned before that my brush with the junta is as nothing in face of the tortures and sufferings of thousands of fighters, often sacrificing their lives, during the ghastly years of the dictatorship. With profound and boundless respect for their sacrifice and suffering, I dare today to refer to my own small, insignificant story.

During the junta years, General Security was in a building at the corner of Bouboulinas and Tositsa Street. The Ministry of Labor, where I had been appointed a clerk on November 20, 1935, at age fifteen-and-a-half, used to be located in the same building. By coincidence, the room to which they took me for interrogation was the same one I had first entered in 1935. I mentioned this to my police interrogator with tears and anguish. "Do you know where you have brought me today? I came to work in this office as a young boy. I came then with dreams for Greece, with noble ambitions. How could I ever have imagined what would be happening today? That tyranny would rule and that I'd be standing accused before you!" The officer first made sure that he could not be heard, as far as was possible inside a security service room, then said to me, "D'you think I care about Papadopoulos and Patakos and the other men in power today? Today the junta is in power. Tomorrow or the day after it will fall. But we, the police, the security police, will always be indispensable no matter what regime comes along, even a democracy. Come on now, write down a couple of words for me so that we can finish. Look, write that the National Government (that was how the junta called itself) is beneficial to the country. That's all I want and then no more interrogations . . ."

On the first day of interrogations, I wrote a letter of protest when I left the building for what they had done to me there and especially for their outrageous demand that I offer an apology for loving peace and not war, and, in fact, nuclear war! I sent my letter to the daily paper *Vima* which was prestigious in Greece and abroad. My letter was published and then republished in many other newspapers and also in the foreign press.

On the same day that my letter of protest was published, I went to the Agence France-Presse to report what had happened to me and to ask to send out my account abroad with their telex which was not under junta censorship. My protest was very timely in France because at the same time my novel *The Flaw* had received the Grand Priz award for detective fiction. The statement from the French awards committee said, among other things, "In conjunction with its great literary and humane value, in addition to its message against totalitarianism, *The Flaw* is characterized by powerful suspense, and it reads like a detective novel."

The French publishers of the novel and the press had invited me to Paris to receive the award. But how could I go? I no longer had a passport and I was indicted by the security police.

The telex was published in the French press.

Late that night about 3 A.M., I was overcome with anger against the junta. I went out of the house leaving my wife, Eleni, and taking the tram even though I was badly unshaven and went to the main telegraph office on Patission Street. There was only one clerk there. I took a telegraph form and urgently wrote out a message in French, 300–400 words, for the awards committee in Paris and for the French press. An excerpt of this wire which criticised the junta harshly also appeared in the French papers the very next day and was read, together with the Agence France-Presse telex, in the small restaurant where by custom the award I was to receive is presented in the absence of the author. Representatives from all the press were there. Both these texts, accompanied by sarcastic comments against the junta, were reprinted in the press of many countries and particularly in the U.S. and England.

The Agence France-Presse's telex, of course, had no problem leaving the country, but I was certain that the omnipresent censorship—especially at a telegraph office—would stop my wire. However, the miracle happened. Unknown democrats must have been working at the telegraph office or other services. The tricks used to get that wire through to Paris are also unknown. And many are the unknown patriots who, with a free conscience, ran the risk involved in opposing tyranny, each in his or her own way.

A little later, while my interrogations continued constantly at General Security, something else happened that ridiculed the junta. By chance I turned on the TV one night and saw the "minister" of the press attacking the communist regimes for persecuting their authors. He spoke mainly of the Solzhenitsyn case with special emphasis on the withholding of his passport and the ban on his possibility of leaving the Soviet Union. I instantly got the idea of setting a trap for the "minister." It was known from the papers that on the next day he was going to host the foreign press correspondents at a "working luncheon." Such luncheons were given every week which was one of the junta's tricks in creating the image of a democratic government. Journalists were invited to ask questions which the "minister" would answer.

So I phoned my friend, Albert Coerant, a correspondent of the Dutch press and television, a strong enemy of the junta, and asked to see him. He had not seen the "minister" on television. I told him my plan: at the luncheon the next day he was going to pretend that he had seen the TV broadcast and had with great interest listened to what the "minister" had said. Then he was to ask him why their regime, which was strongly anti-communist, was persecuting writers and particularly Antonis Samarakis. I wanted to see what answer the "minister" would give.

I have kept the cassette with the whole discussion taped. When Albert posed the question, the sarcastic laughter of the other journalists at the "minister" can be heard. Nevertheless, the "minister" continued, "The Soviet Union is persecuting Solzhenitsyn only for his works whereas we are after Samarakis for purely political activities *as well."*

All these things were published immediately in the Greek and foreign press with new caustic comments against the junta.

Very early my life seemed to take on a pattern of successive hazardous adventures that left me with a feeling of lost youth as if there were a void, as if I had taken a leap in time. . . . This sensation is characteristic of my generation, the "kids" of the inter-war years, who were soon swept up into life's hurricanes: dictatorships, war, the Occupation, the heartbreak of civil strife.

Looking over what I have written, I see that I discuss matters that can hardly be regarded as strictly autobiographical, what we call the "events of one's life." I have expanded on thoughts, sentiments, and discussions brought up by my literary work. However, I am presuming that all of this contributed, step by step, to the overall portrait of somebody who joined the autobiographical game not as a businessman or the user of an impersonal computer, but as a writer, a man of letters. Isn't it true that small items that seem irrelevant can often be the keys to one's inner world, can control the threads that finally weave one's true character? And so, inevitably, they work towards the formation of external behavior, compelling one to those actions which become the events of one's life and thus the facts of an autobiography.

If you love with your heart and soul and want to speak of this love, you can, of course, spend a lot of time and energy analyzing and describing your feelings. It happens that from my youth I have mistrusted this approach. My feeling is that by innumerating your reasons for loving, you are providing a logical scheme but in the end, you have proved nothing. It is all in vain. It's impossible to penetrate the secret, the magic precincts of love, to discover and reveal the potion that has brought this upheaval into your body, your mind, your heart. It is enough and more than enough to say "I love you." That covers it all. So then, I would like to say right here, "Cyprus, I love you."

Fifteen years have passed since I was first introduced to Cyprus. All of these years this Greek island has been afloat within me, a raft of hope, struggle, and beauty for me, the castaway in the cruel seas of pettiness that have more or less enslaved us all. I have tasted Cyprus's charms many times. But I have felt her pain and her sorrow and her revolt against her unjust, infamous massacre by the Turkish invader.

Seventeen years have gone by since 1974 when the martyred island was knifed by Attila's invasion [Attila was the code name of the Turkish invasion—translators' note]. The first advance of the Turkish forces took place on July 20, 1974. They occupied 3.63 percent of Cyprus. The second advance followed on August 14, 1974, and the Turkish occupation spread to a total of 36.4 percent of Cypriot soil. Approximately 4,500 Greek-Cypriots were killed and innumerable were wounded. The International Red Cross confirms there were 2,526 POWs, and 1,619 missing, removed to concentration camps deep in Turkey, in Anatolia, and, according to cross-checked accounts, put to death. There were hundreds of thousands of people uprooted, turned into refugees in their own land. And the destruction was relentless, including the looting of Cyprus's cultural heritage, art treasures of inestimable value which for centuries had adorned the island.

What stand did the international community take in the face of Cyprus's tragedy? What was the reaction of the United Nations and of the superpowers to Turkey's crime? Turkey, a member country of NATO which proceeded to conduct a surprise attack and invasion of another member country of NATO, Cyprus? And this with guns from the U.S. and U.S.S.R. Their reaction was zero. Whereas in the case of the similar attack of Iraq on Kuwait, because of the existence of oil and the tremendous financial interests involved, the whole world was activated. If Cyprus had also had oil. . . . How dirty are international politics!

Every time I step on the sacred soil of Cyprus, full of joy but also pain, I feel the warm embrace of centuries of Greek culture. Orphaned from her mother Greece, Cyprus continues to suffer and to struggle.

I would like to mention that even before the Turkish invasion, in the preceding decades, Greek blood flowed freely, but then it was the English oppressors who mercilessly crushed the slightest protest and uprising of the Cypriot people with their young people leading the way. Many were the Greek patriots executed by the English and many were those hung by "Christian" hands.

Cyprus can trace nine thousand years of Hellenism. A Hellenism which even in today's difficult hours is creative and flourishes with an amazing youthful spirit.

My soul is Cyprus. I envisage her free and justified in her struggle. I think of her always with deep gratitude for the joy she has given me. I think of her with all my love, emotion, and tenderness. Instead of all these inadequate words that I say about Cyprus, I should perhaps write just three words on her soil, as a motto and sacred oath of endless resistance:

I DON'T FORGET!

How can I omit from this account of my life my experience in Ethiopia as a UNICEF volunteer? The word "experience" is, of course, a cold one when speaking about the scorched tragedy of Ethiopia as I knew it in my two journeys there in November and December of 1984.

The truth is that, dating back to the time I worked at the Ministry of Labor, I participated in many missions for social and labor causes, sponsored not only by the Greek government but mainly by the United Nations and particularly by the International Labor Organization. I already had firsthand contact with and knowledge of human suffering in many corners of the world. So, in almost every European country, I could see what pain and daily stress are often hidden behind the facade. And indeed I saw this beyond Europe as well: in the USA, Brazil, India, Pakistan, China, and even Australia, especially in the cruel extermination of the aborigines. I have left out Africa from this list because I wish to speak separately about this world that is Africa, to which I have given half of my heart.

I first knew black Africa in 1953. I returned many times before going to Ethiopia, my crowning trip being the two years I worked on the International Labor Organization mission to Zaire, Nigeria, Ghana, the Ivory Coast, Guinea, with a focal point on Guinea.

I loved Africa. I loved the people who were Africa. I wish I could be with them again, sharing their sufferings and their joys. But in our "civilized" world, our "Christian" world, we stand apathetic in the face of their plight.

When I parted from the living dead down there, I was overcome with conflicting emotions. I was leaving Ethiopia, that hell of death from hunger, need, and epidemics. But I was going to another hell, Europe.

I shared human understanding with the doomed Ethiopians, in other words, I shared what our world no longer knows as we drink soda to help our digestion while the dehydrated core of our being is devoured by a frightful inner loneliness. On the contrary, the warmth of the frozen, dying Ethiopians

was soul stirring. I was scorched by their thirst to communicate with me even though they knew I didn't understand their language. But they squeezed my hand. . . . Suddenly, surrounded by hundreds of children, hundreds of angels, I felt myself holding tightly to ten or eleven thin, tender little hands, so bony that they all fit in the palm of my hand.

But I am guilty now of trying to put the tragedy of Ethiopia into words, to give a certain picture of this multifaceted reality of death I experienced living in hunger-stricken Ethiopia. Terror struck me. I will continue to experience it forever and beyond time.

I plead guilty to having felt while living among the living dead of Ethiopia that I wanted to say, "Please don't die yet before I capture you in my camera, please have the courage to last, at least let me give you something to eat so that you don't die on us before we film you, before I've studied all the details of your agony and your imminent death, so that when we return to Athens, I'll be able to give dramatic interviews on TV and to the press, perhaps even write a prologue to an album of relevant photos of you."

In the face of Ethiopia's tragedy, as well as that of numerous other countries in the face of our own

In Ethiopia as a volunteer for UNICEF, 1984

apathy, how can one not reason that our so-called civilization is spiritually and morally bankrupt? With human values steadily degenerating in reality? Because our world and our civilization have triumphed in science and technology, have managed to survive two world holocausts and many other catastrophes, but they haven't escaped being put to the wall convicted and condemned by the purest of judges: children.

When even a single child dies of hunger and lack of care, when even a single child dies spiritually, on the fringe, in wretched living and work conditions, cut off from every possibility of participating in the community, then the skyscraper of our civilization is shattered in fragments, into dust and ashes. But unfortunately, today in 1991, death is not taking just a single child in one way or another, but hundreds of thousands of them who, of course, because of hunger are not rosy-cheeked.

We should consider how a child is coerced into becoming assimilated into a system that worships money, material gain, that worships political, social, and financial publicity of every kind. We should consider that the child is pressured from all sides to slaughter his inner being for a cold programming that will enable him not to exist in truth but just to vegetate as some listed item in the lists of males and females, as an ID number . . .

Today's world, so artfully dressed up in religions, philosophies, ideologies, sciences, technologies, and more, is in fact naked in regards to that humanity which if it existed would give it some justification for being. The gap between East and West, between this and that theory of existence, is not as critical for the spiritual and mental survival of mankind as is the gap between the world of adults and children. As it is today, mankind cannot enjoy the approval of any free and unbiased conscience. It is a world unanimously rejected, so artfully constructed that all of us adults hold the power. But what power does a child have? What power does the man in the street have? Their only power begins when each conscience ceases feeling irresponsible about the fate of the child in our paranoid world, about the fate of each fellow man.

"How beautiful our earth is! . . . How beautiful our world!" Neil Armstrong cried from the heavens.

Antonis Samarakis with Eleni, to whom he dedicated his novel The Flaw

As long as we fight wholeheartedly for a more humane mankind, hope is born in us that we shall one day be able to say the same without viewing the world from so high up, but rather in the joy of perceiving it close up and in depth, by touching, fingering a completely beautiful and tender picture of man's adventure.

Literature is, first and foremost, joy. It must faithfully portray the harsh and melancholy horizon of man's lunacy and jungle. Yet from inside the confusion and the conflicting currents of intimate life and social intercourse, literature indisputably leans towards joy, and has the strength to vaccinate our hearts with this wonderful joy. But more important: it builds a bridge of deeper understanding with others, the receivers. Literature starts communication.

For literature to be effective, we must not forget that it's not a monologue. It needs to tie in with the reader. Literature is a comrade's hand reaching out and should not be left without a response. The magic of literature and of art actually begins to exist the moment that another hand, the hand of the reader, reaches out and grasps yours with brotherly warmth. Literature is a voice in the night, a cry in the dark, and it has no meaning, is not complete if it does not bring forth a response.

The attempt at human communication that I make through my literary efforts was emphasized from my very first book, *Wanted: Hope,* and in another way too: I always printed my address inside my books. The same has been true of my foreign publications: my address appears there too. Precisely because I believe deeply in discussion with and criticism from the simple anonymous reader, I have made my heroes ordinary people, men of the street, not "intellectuals," not men of socio-political and financial power. My joy is tremendous, and I am greatly moved by the letters of readers who open their hearts to me and very often reveal themselves as being torn by pain, loneliness, and conflict.

Our world is tragically insane and insanely tragic. What does literature have to offer? Does it have any responsibility for what happens around us? Literature, of course, is concerned with the eternal, the acts and feelings that are everlastingly human: love, lust, friendship, daily joys, constant perpetual death. But at the same time our lives are filled with the tragedy of Hiroshima and the gloomy prospects that fatally threaten our world. Even love today, this great joy, this pure joy, is tinted by the nightmarish cold light of Hiroshima. Just as certain quality papers have watermarks, so our whole life bears the imprint of Hiroshima. It has affected our lives and the course

of mankind with the unleashing of terrible powers. We don't know if it's for the good or bad of the human race. It could lead to our annihilation. Hiroshima has become such a landmark that a new calendar for mankind began on August 6, 1945: A.D. has been superseded by A.H.—after Hiroshima, while B.C. should be replaced by B.H.—before Hiroshima.

We have, therefore, no right today to write about romantic sunsets as in other more serene times. No! In our times, the sunset too is stained with the anguished light of Hiroshima.

How is it possible for a writer to write for readers, his audience, if they are dead from some new world war? Or if they are the slaves of some totalitarian state? Or if they have been reduced to the status of the living dead because of hunger?

The writer must function as a galvanizing force of public opinion, must keep human concern from falling into oblivion. By the very nature of his calling, the writer is restless, unyielding before the powers of the world. Thus he or she should feel and behave, call people to arms, inciting them against all that is rotten, dirty, inhuman, anti-human.

But it's not enough for writers to describe honestly and correctly all that is unacceptable around them. It's not enough for writers only to protest and condemn. They must also use literature to offer some definite hope and to suggest solutions.

It is too much to expect miracles from literature. And to expect them constantly. Literature very gradually penetrates our conscience and heart with its slow-moving action. It generates a fertile uneasiness, not merely spiritual in the narrow sense. But it creates disturbances of the kind that spread to every aspect of life, both our inner and outer worlds. In this way we begin to see with a fresh eye what previously went unnoticed. Without realizing it, a small flame of protest lights up in our soul, revolting against whatever insults or lessens man's status. This flame steadily grows stronger. New emotions awaken the fighting spirit.

So let us writers today see if that small, tiny detail which we have ventured to give others has managed to touch them somehow, to warm their hearts, to offer comfort through a difficult hour, to whisper some sort of answer to the questions that torment them, to help them discern in the deep dark a small light, a streak of light, to keep them from abandoning themselves to the void at the last minute. This void is not just the abyss which waits under our feet and draws us when we are troubled with ourselves or others and calls us to jump into its cold embrace. This void includes also our apathy towards the terrible things that are happening around us, our indifference to the fate of others, which is also our fate or soon could be . . .

The responsibility of the writer today is specific to our times which are exceptionally crucial. We must leave aside our personal problems, our small egos, and fight. Let us not be disheartened if the situation doesn't change overnight. Let us always remember Chekhov's words in *The Three Sisters:*

> I think that everything on earth is going to change slowly, and in fact, has already started to change in front of our eyes. In two hundred, three hundred years, perhaps even in a thousand years—time is insignificant—a new, happy life will emerge. Naturally we won't be there, yet we live for that today. We work for that, yes, yes, we suffer for that. . . . We are creating it! . . . And in that alone is our reason for being and our happiness. . . . The time will come when we too shall depart forever. And we will be forgotten, our face and our voice will be forgotten.

This is exactly how a writer in our times and for all times should feel. He mustn't strive to make his work and his voice last for eternity. The only definite eternity is the eternity of our daily life here and now. But he must have the ambition, now while he or she still breathes, to become in his words and actions the voice of those who "have no voice," of the underdog, the tormented, the oppressed. To strive to have performed his duty towards others, to have spoken, to have fought for love, understanding, and compassion, to have approached simple people tenderly but also mercilessly and uncompromisingly in the face of the powers that be. The writer should also strive to honor his or her vocation before appearing as a date of birth and exit from this game of life in some likely autobiography.

BIBLIOGRAPHY

Fiction:

Zititai Elpis (stories; title means "Wanted: Hope"), I. D. Collaros (Athens), 1954.

Sēma Kindynou (novel; title means "Danger Signal"), I. D. Collaros, 1959.

Arnoumai (stories; title means "I Refuse"), I. D. Collaros, 1961.

To Lathos (novel), I. D. Collaros, 1965, translation by Peter Mansfield and Richard Burns published as *The Flaw,* Weybright & Talley, 1969.

I Zoungla (stories; title means "The Jungle"), Galaxias (Athens), 1966.

To Diavatērio, Eleutheroudakēs, 1973, published as *The Passport and Other Stories,* Longman Cheshire, 1980.

Translator into Greek and contributor to *Lincoln's Gettysburg Address in Translation,* 1972.

Contributor of poems to literary magazines. Contributor of stories to textbooks; short stories have been translated into English and published in the United States, Greece, and numerous other countries in anthologies, including *New Directions in Prose and Poetry,* edited by James Laughlin and others, New Directions, 1977; and magazines, including *Athenian, Charioteer, Literary Review,* and *Pilgrimage.* Contributor of fifty-one poems, under a pseudonym, to *To Tragoudi Tou Paidiou* (anthology of poems for children; title means "The Child's Song"), Damascos (Athens), 1947.

Nathaniel Tarn

1928-

Nathaniel Tarn beside his mother, with younger brother, Neville, mid-1930s

I notice, as I begin this, a strong reluctance to write in the first person. Recorded here, because a lifelong anthropologist's habit of objectifying and a care to write away from ego in contemporary poetry are both at work and both concern me closely. The unavoidable first person will be approached with circumspection.

Born, then, 50 rue François I in Paris, France, on June 30, 1928. Mother: Yvonne Cecile Leah, whose family, originally from Rumania, had been French for a time. Her father, a fine singer and sculptor (said to have made a statue for the Bucharest Opera), was wounded in the French Army during World War I: I scarcely knew him. His brother was a great ballistics expert for the same army but was irresponsibly killed off in ordinary service. Father: Mendel Myer, later (by Yvonne I guess) called Marcel, of Lithuanian stock, second-generation British. A cousin of his masterminded the National Health Service, became Professor of Medicine at Liverpool University, and a member of the House of Lords. Half the family landed up in the U.S. as the Shuberts of Broadway. I never knew them. It is unfortunate, given later circumstance, that I was not born a Shubert: I would have been provided with a sorely missed American childhood.

It has never been clear to me whether French or English was my first language. No one remembers. A first nurse was French. Apparently she stuck pins into me and got me to howl on the phone in order to bring my parents back from evening outings. She also made me walk too early. Fired, she was replaced by a Scotswoman, Eileen Gregory, who stayed with us over ten years, later to become a famous Hollywood figure, working with the children of Charles Chaplin, Fred Astaire, Charles Boyer, and the like. We are still in touch. So my guess is: first French, very soon after English.

I am told that a great deal of my life was taken up by being promenaded daily on the Champs-Elysées which I was nicknamed the "King of" by a concordance of governesses because of a certain haughtiness, reserved especially for little girls. One of these was allegedly in love with me for many years and sent me countless *billets doux* and presents. A great day came when my brother, Neville, and I were collected in a car by my mother's older brother Edmond, swept off to a cinema on the avenue, and introduced to Mickey Mouse. Another memory is of being fitted for clothes by a tailor who came from London once a year. There are various stories about a craze for flowers and "expert" critical pronouncements on any garden we chanced to visit.

At some point we moved to 1 avenue du Président Wilson, a stone's throw from the Seine, and, in 1936, to Antwerp, Belgium, where my father wished to join his father and brothers. A cozy town which has changed very little, as I witnessed fifty years later, recognizing all the old haunts with ease—

"Father leaving Bombay on SS Aquiligia,
May 1, 1927"

There was a third day but I cannot remember what we bought. Once, there was a great trip to the Dutch tulip fields in our black Packard. Those colors have haunted me ever since. There were other trips to coastal forests where I was into mushrooms and bugs. Only a dozen prized books or so survived the war (the Fénélon-Homer, *Tales of Shakespeare,* Andersen, Defoe, La Fontaine, Cooper, Michelet, Fabre, Balzac's *Napoléon,* Jules Verne among them) but these included my nature guidebooks.

Aged five, I had written a poem, "L'Ourson (The Bear Cub)," my mother still owns. At the lycée, which worked us extremely hard, temporary fame was conquered by writing another, "L'Hirondelle (The Swallow)," during an exam in which essays were expected. After the war, I went back and saw Monsieur Claude: a tall, red-haired teacher with a fiery mustache who had terrorized me into acceptable work, especially in maths. He had become very small but recognized me as "the boy who wrote the poem." I wore a black tie to school on the death of George V (later only for Roosevelt and Kennedy). "Nev" and I had a large toy chest in which I kept my substantial lead soldier army and my farm (missing these all my life, I recently bought a smaller army which I have on my study shelf).

I had a fantasy during those years: to own a room with closets from floor to ceiling, containing hundreds of drawers in which kits would be kept—animal parts of wood or metal which would constitute an ark of the whole world. Witness, no doubt, to my love of classification and my constant urge to totalize: *vide* an essay, "The Heraldic Vision," in the 1991 selected essays book, *View from the Weaving Mountain.* On a more pedestrian level, there was a famous tin policeman's helmet whose many crevasses bore witness to constant, fierce fratricidal strife. Nev would hide my possessions and taunt me; I would react and get punished. We were both in great fear of our father: a loving and generous man totally unable to manifest these qualities. He shouted a great deal. My daughter claims I shouted also when she was young. Sins of the fathers . . .

Sometimes, vacations were at the Home des Esserts, Leysin, Switzerland, run by a couple of old Nazis. An older Japanese student offered the alternative: "Heil Hitler!" or a broken arm. My parents never realized what went on. There were opportunities for making one's own lead soldiers and there were also marvelously pastoral trips into the mountains. Also skiing—a sport I would have made into a lifelong pursuit but for the war's hiatus.

though amused to find that our school building now housed an Institute of Buddhist Studies! We lived at 33 avenue Jan Van Rijwijck, where I kept a canary named Tino Rossi (it turned out to be a she and never sang) and a salamander. They both died in a mild earthquake. An excellent French school took us in: the Lycée d'Anvers, to which we would go every day on the Number 2 tram: French was spoken there and Flemish taught. A favorite haunt was the Nightingale Parc, which to me, then, was an extensive and miraculous wilderness. Another was the zoo, near the main train station and the Century Hotel; yet another: a movie theater where I used to disappear regularly under my seat, laughing myself into a helpless frenzy at Laurel and Hardy.

A great potlatch stands out in memory. My father's brother, David, came to see us once in a blue moon. On one occasion—I already had my library—he took me to a large bookstore and told me there was no limit. The next day, idem at a cactus store.

Other times, we were on the Belgian coast, mostly at Le Zoute. We rented a villa named Shere Khan, after Kipling's tiger; next door was Rikki-Tikki-Tavi, after his mongoose. People would drive us nuts as they passed repeating that last sonorous name. Nev and I, fierce cyclists, made maps of the hundreds of little cycling alleys serving as streets among the villas in the dunes area. I have always been nostalgic for that coast and took my own children there when they were very young.

We were there in the summer of 1939. Two close buddies (Steinfeld and Wiener) and I had spent all our spare time in the lycée playground discussing the coming war. Very suddenly, my bunch was on a ferry to England, ending up at Colwyn Bay, Wales, for the declaration of war. My paternal grandfather (said to have been a peddler in those parts in his youth) was crying copiously—I could not understand why. Nev and I expected the bombers immediately and saw spies everywhere. There were weeks at Torquay, Devon (where we were joined by Uncle Harry—later with the RAF at Hyderabad—and cousin Merton—later with the army in the Middle East, both with jaundice: they had stayed to pack up and had caught the last ship out). We also lived at Brighton, Sussex. This was a great period for Ping-Pong, friendships with waiters and a bandleader at our Brighton hotel.

After a while, Neville and I became boarders at the preparatory school for Clifton College near Bristol, next door to the great Clifton zoo. The lions roared all night. It was thought this place would not be bombed—or not early (it was). Life was full of savage small-boy cruelty. It was punctuated by the monthly candy rations I ate immediately on purchase, making myself sick so that I would not want candy until the next month. Little gangs of us would play "tracking" on the huge wild downs near the school and pay daily visits to the barrage balloon nearby.

At a certain point, boys began to disappear. America was the whispered destination. I longed to be told I would go but my father could not leave, my mother would not go without him, and neither would let us go alone.

Then there were weeks in the Cumberland Hotel at Marble Arch in London while the great blitz went on outside. Every night we were downstairs with all the guests in pyjamas—an extraordinary scene. I collected minisized toy soldiers and Frog model planes (all my toys had been given away in Belgium); read a life of Lincoln, forgot my Latin and my violin. I am still angry that I never *saw* anything since we were kept away from the danger of flying glass. We left a few days before a hit on the subway station next door caused great carnage.

There followed some years in Buxton, Derbyshire, first at a ghastly secondary school, next at a good prep school, Holm Leigh. My parents, much impoverished now, had begun the mean and skimpy boarding-house life that lasted most of the war, with some intervals in houses of their own. In one house I did my first paintings: irises and marigolds. I fell in love with a girl who passed on a bicycle every day, lying on a windowside couch by the hour waiting for her to come by. I also built a lot of plane models which rarely managed to fly. Nature-watching continued on the immense, fearsome, and wuthering moors. At thirteen, I went into Clifton College proper, now evacuated to Bude, Cornwall. Nev followed.

Clifton was raw. There was a terrorizing master, a Scotsman; though also some kind, guiding ones: Guy Lagarde (French), Michael Mounsey (Art), Donald Davie (Biology). The latter gave me the run of his library and introduced me to Thurber, Runyon, other Americans. The "terrorist" reported "this boy would amount to something if he could forget Virginia Woolf for a while and concentrate on Shakespeare." There were nightmarish rugby "games" on the freezing cliffs but also frequent expeditions to beautiful parts of Cornwall, many as an Officer's Training Corps cadet in uniform.

I painted a great deal, won many prizes, had some "mystical experiences"—one, especially, of superhuman freedom and virtual levitation after reading Woolf's *Jacob's Room*. Nev and I fenced with a ferocious sergeant-major for a while to improve our stamina. Frequent profound depression (manic in my remembrance) was a problem. One cure was reading about the first settlements of the U.S. I had the *Daily Telegraph* war map of the U.S. on my wall and learned the capitals of the forty-eight states. On many evenings, I went down to salute the Stars and Stripes as they were being lowered at a base nearby. Following on my *Life of Lincoln*, the dream of America continued.

One day, during Latin Prose, the terrorist teacher allowed us out on the downs: the immense D-day fleet was rounding Cornwall before moving into the Channel. Not long afterward, the school went back to Clifton. Vacations were spent at Gerrard's Cross in Buckinghamshire, where my parents had settled after Buxton. Intense and hopelessly timid first loves occurred there, usually at the tennis club and the Bull Inn dances: Miriam, Rosemary, Lynette, Ann—all friends of each other. On two occasions, deferred results of bombings brought down bedroom ceilings on Neville and me.

I strove to get my parents to allow visits to London bookstores despite the V-1 and V-2 bombs, envied RAF pilots whom I often saw drinking at the Bull, and saw many war movies alone, ardently believing in a better life for mankind after the war. I worked with the Women's Land Army once to get enough money for a book. Cash in hand, I chose *I Saw the Fall of the Philippines* by Carlos Romulo! Somewhere in the London suburbs, Hammersmith perhaps, I saw my first ballet company: the Ballet Rambert.

I detested public school life and courted expulsion by various means: going on strike at exam times; visiting movies and theaters(!)—the boldest move being a night escape with some fellows to get into Bristol, the town busy celebrating V-day. Poems were published in the school magazine and one (already back in Cornwall) had been given a prize in English! At seventeen, I demanded permission to sit for Cambridge scholarships. I remember dragging my parents around on my birthday to see every one of my teachers. They all thought me too young. I went up and slept in a room full of spiders over a fish-and-chips shop. Actually the first night I did not sleep for one moment. The old Provost of Kings told us myths and legends. Only a handful are chosen and I have never felt fate in the balance as I did that week. To the school's dismay, I won a history scholarship. Dire predictions about a profound fault in my intellectual make-up were my parting gift from my history teacher. They haunted me for years.

Cambridge was liberation: smoking, drinking, perhaps the opposite sex. "Digs" the first year. In my first week, I shut myself up and read all of Romain Rolland's *Jean-Christophe*. I found I had to study history for two years because of the scholarship—and did so, mainly with Butterfield and Postan. For the rest of my time I enjoyed a room in college overlooking the huge court by the river, Gibbs, the chapel, and Clare. Almost everyone was older than myself, returning from the war. A gang came together though: David Rowse, Christopher Moorsom, Richard Muir, Peter Dixon. In my third year, I "read" English, a devoted, nine-in-the-morning-by-any-weather fan of F. R. Leavis while being tutored by F. L. Lucas: no two pedagogues could have been more opposed. With only a year to play with, I decided to concentrate almost exclusively on the Elizabethans: only Wordsworth and Coleridge were exempted from this rule. A small book of poems posed as my "thesis."

There was much glamor (I was president and chief party-giver of the Cambridge Ballet Club) and

"scandalous" behavior. Women friends were few and far between in those days; this led to the most intense frustration. My first great love, Ruth, a Czech, eventually preferred another; a devoted and bounteous Wendy did not keep me. There was ardent intellectual passion; fascination with Gurdjieff and other manifestations of the esoteric; talk of getting away from the bomb, founding communes in distant places; growing dissatisfaction with England, weary of war, and unable to rest. Two (very rough) trips to Spain, one to Italy, occupied my three summers—usually alone, seeing hundreds of monuments and paintings a day, talking to no one. At the end of my time there were friendships with members of a U.S. Air Force burials group.

In 1949, tortured by bilingualism, I determined to return to Paris and my French "roots," to forget English and write in French. Disoriented, I continued to discipline myself as if at college: Dante, Gilson's great history of medieval philosophy, and so forth. My uncle Harry, living again in Belgium, tried me out in various jobs: tea-and-coffee busboy with a French film director, the United Nations, etc. He also, as a *bon viveur*, introduced me to some of the best tables in Paris. Eventually I read news for the French Radio and got a part-time reviewer and translator job with *Parisian Weekly Information,* a weekly tourist city-guide. The director liked me and allowed me to write anything, even philosophical manifestos. I reviewed nightclubs, sitting alone with a free bottle of champagne; later came theater, ballet, and art, in the course of which I met a great variety of actors, dancers, and artists: Villon, da Silva, Lurçat, Mathieu, Brauner, and, later, Giacometti.

I read *Combat* voraciously, a marvelous newspaper with which Camus was associated. It was perhaps from there that I got into French anthropology: the Africanist Marcel Griaule's *Dieu d'Eau* had recently been published and much other documentation was about. One day, I saw a movie about my generation in St. Germain des Prés: Jacques Becker's *Rendez Vous de Juillet.* The hero (Daniel Gelin) was an anthropologist of sorts and visited the Musée de l'Homme. I had never seen this museum and went immediately. It was overwhelming. There were posters advertising courses. I went back to my grandmother's where I lived with a bunch of French relatives—great-cousins Victor and Pauline Natanson and my maternal uncle Claude—and had the impression I was trembling for three days. On the third day, I enrolled, determined to get my degree in secret. The secret would have been kept had it not been for a visit by my parents two weeks before the finals: I found myself announcing that I had at last found a "respectable" job. They were dubiously happy.

I did my "B.A." equivalent with Marcel Griaule, Germaine Dieterlen, and their group; then the "M.A." apprenticeship with André Leroi-Gourhan, Pierre Métais, Jean Rouch, and others at the Centre de Formation aux Recherches Ethnologiques; also working with Claude Lévi-Strauss on mythology and Paul Lévy on Southeast Asia at the École des Hautes Etudes and the Collège de France. Close friends were Alexander MacDonald, Isaac Chiva, Claude Tardits, Igor de Garine, Bernard Laffont, Georges Condominas—all leading anthropologists in later life. First jobs included papers (after rudimentary fieldwork) on the barge people of the Seine and the Gypsies of Andalusia; also cataloguing the Assam Naga collection at the museum and writing "On Naga Tiger Mythology" for Paul Lévy.

I was taken to meet Lucien Biton, a bank clerk and one of the world's great scholars of Buddhism—though he had vowed never to publish. His private library in a small apartment, rue du Théâtre, was one of the great city secrets and he helped me devotedly

to build up my own collections. There I enjoyed the company of Rolf Stein, later professor of Tibetan and Chinese at the Collège de France, and many other scholars and artists. I saw Lucien at home this year: his whole body devoured by cancers, a leg amputated—yet he held forth for four hours with his customary ferocious panache as a grand adieu to an old friend.

These were heady days. I wrote an unsolicited essay on the poet Jules Supervielle, sent it to *Critique*, and was summoned by Georges Bataille, who handed me *Oublieuse Mémoire* to review. He offered a note at the back but it came out as the lead article. I was also summoned by the poet, recognized a girl I had fallen for in the street to be his daughter but also discovered she was married! I dreamed up my first book, an essay with Serge Jacques's photos and Marcel Jacno's typography (he designed the pack of Gauloises and the masterful Theatre National Populaire posters), which came out as *La Légende de Saint Germain des Prés*. Unfortunately, my text was totally rewritten for tourist consumption by the publisher who also absconded with all profits.

From left: typographer Marcel Jacno, Tarn, painter Henri Seigle, and painter No Seigle (far right), at Seigle opening, Paris, December 19, 1957

In a bookstore one day, I met Henri and No Seigle, painters, who convinced me that those I had thought of as long-dead gods in my schooldays—the Surrealists—could still be joined at Sunday café sessions in Montmartre. I attended these for about a year, enjoying André Breton's *superbia* and humor—until Jean Louis Bédouin accused me of committing the heinous crime of writing on the existentialists of St. Germain des Prés! The Seigles have been close friends ever since, a second family. Another friend at the time was Octavio Paz with whom I have kept up over the years.

I spent most of my evenings in St. Germain des Prés: at the Rose Rouge, where Juliette Greco and the Frères Jacques sang; the St. Thomas d'Aquin with Léo Ferré; the Abbaye run by two American singer-actors, Lee Payant and Gordon Heath, and the Club St. Yves, a 1900s place famous for its *cerises à l'eau de vie*. I would walk all the way back to my grandmother's, 17 rue de l'Arc de Triomphe, at the Étoile at 2 A.M., and the street ladies hailed me as *l'ouragan*—the whirlwind. During those walks I used to think that if I ever would be separated from this city I would die. Love and sex, however, continued, mainly unhappily "even in Paris." I made the mistake of falling head over heels in love with Lévi-Strauss's future wife, without knowing their secret. The fall was rough. There was a close friendship with the actress Varvara Pitoeff; others with Monique Fong, a member of the Surrealist group, and with Pilar de Betancourt, a Cuban socialite. Love for a young lesbian, Marie Hélène, was exceedingly bitter. I carved her initials into my hands one night, on a desolate train ride back to Paris from Antibes.

Poetry was not working: I felt I was always writing twenty-fifth rate Apollinaire. In cosmopolitan Paris, escaping English was out of the question. Most anthropology was written in English. A Smith-Mundt Fulbright grant led to the U.S. in 1951, on board the *De Grasse*. I have never forgotten my first night in New York: looking out and seeing the private lives of multitudes framed in a hundred windows. We were "oriented" at Yale, which depressed me as being imitation-Cambridge. I had fantasized a coed college like, say, Kansas. A young journalist, uncertain of himself as a Yale assistant, harassed us into having "problems." It was the first time the word "problem" became so problematic. I desperately wanted to avoid essays on Jefferson, Democracy, the Frontier, and such (all that had been "done" at Cambridge) and begged George Murdock, Ralph Linton, and other Yale anthropological greats in vain to get me out of them. We were taken to such places as New Canaan (the Phillips house and my first Jackson Pollock); to the United Nations, a baseball match, and other Americana in New York. Once on my own, I brashly went to see Abram Kardiner in New York, Matthew Stirling and James Fenton at the Smithsonian; D'Arcy McNickle at the Bureau of Indian Affairs who gave me an antiwar document of the Hopi I have kept ever since. At a Columbia lunch with Julian Stewart and Harry Shapiro, Alfred Kroeber only broke silence to advise me, "Take a scarf to Chicago, young man, against the terrible cold!"

Chicago was indeed "grey, windy, and Gothic." Fred Eggan extended a great welcome on registration. Claude Tardits and I shared digs, after a term at International House, and were invited everywhere as a "couple"—since just about everyone was married. We were worked infernally hard: the faculty feeling, erroneously, that, since we came from France, we must be most knowledgeable. I gave papers on Lévi-Strauss's kinship theory in Eggan's classes; on myth in Leenhardt and Griaule in Robert Redfield's, and sent back to Paris news of Sal Washburn's exciting advances in physical anthropology. One visitor, Paul Radin—who may have been a paternal relative and told me my family were bookbinders in a village of horse thieves—dined and breakfasted with us "as Europeans" far too often for the good of our homework but was a marvelous storyteller. There were girlfriends—but it was difficult to get beyond the "necking" stage without ritual declarations of passion which, as sophisticated young Frenchmen, we pretended to loathe and spurn as much as possible. Bogdanovich's movie *The Last Picture Show* has the sound track of that year exactly.

To enjoy a "real American campus with girls and ice cream" we would go to Melville Herskovits's seminars at Northwestern. There I met the Yoruba expert William Bascom and his Cuban wife—which led to a trip to Cuba during one vacation. After a hair-raising cross-country drive to Miami with a friend—we were nearly "Easy-Ridered" in the South—I got to Cuba on the day after Batista's last coup d'etat. There I worked on Santería cults with Argeliers León (later head of anthropology under Castro) and ate the painter Wilfredo Lam's cooking next door to Batista's main army camp, also meeting with Fernando Ortiz, Lydia Cabrera, and other Cuban anthropologists. Scary brushes with the army occurred during nights. A young lady who kept a book of her poems by her chamber pot became obsessed with the idea that I would take her to Paris and cause her to succeed Josephine Baker. Prompt escapes became a matter of survival.

The author (right) with anthropologist Paul Radin, University of Chicago, about 1952

These were heady days as a young pro. The great June 1952 Wenner Gren Foundation "Anthropology Today" meetings in New York, for instance, came with Lévi-Strauss introducing us to Roman Jakobson and impassioned talks on structural linguistics in a downtown bar. Graduate friends were on their way to becoming leaders in their fields in later life. Among them were Manning and June Nash (Guatemala, Burma); Charles and Zelda Leslie (Mexico, India); Victor Gourevitch (theory); Ed Bruner (Indonesia, North America); and Robert Fox (Philippines). There was no time for literature at all, though, on visits to New York, I would have coffee with Marcel Duchamp on Fourteenth Street. I only saw the city of Chicago itself on midnight rides to Black jazz clubs and churches and when shopping for fieldwork equipment to be used in Guatemala.

Robert Redfield and Milton Singer offered the hospitality of their legendary "Comparison of Total Cultures" seminar as well as doctoral fieldwork in Mesoamerica. I had always wanted to go to the Far East, but decided I was young enough to take a detour. A memorable train ride to St. Louis and on to Houston (walked right through, colossal, white, and deserted, on a Sunday morning); planes to the Mexico of Miguel Covarrubias at his dance school, Diego Rivera at the Colegio de México, Alfonso Caso, head of the Instituto Naçional de Antropologia e Historia (Mexico) and inordinately generous with their publications. And the great mass of Teotihuacán ascended without a single other tourist present (how often thus in those days and how different to go back twenty or thirty years later!); then Guatemala City and Panajachel from which I chose Santiago Atitlán as my place.

Work apart, these were desperately lonely days and nights, relieved by candlelit readings at night, Joyce's *Ulysses* for starters. Occasional flings with tourists (I remember getting a lift in a small plane to Antigua once, in pursuit of a U.S. general's daughter) and roistering in the city with Henri Lehmann from the Musée de l'Homme provided minivacations. Redfield was generous and financed walking forays all over the hills and mountains to acquire textiles. I was not to get as textile-happy again until the Shan and Kachin Hills in Burma.

Somewhere in there, a correspondence began with Sasha Moorsom, a brilliant young Cambridge graduate, sister to my friend Christopher. I had met her once aged sixteen or so: I believe she was holding hands under the table with both David Rowse and myself. The correspondence became more and more romantic and, in part, determined a return to England. Moreover, poetry in French had not worked out: I had kept diaries in French until Atitlán, then, for anthropological purposes, switched to English. Had the Fulbright rules not mandated return, however, I might well have stayed on at Chicago.

Enrollment as a postgraduate at the London School of Economics with Raymond Firth, Isaac Schapera, S. F. Nadel came with writing my thesis which was completed in 1957. Students and young professionals included Burton Benedict, Anthony Forge, Jim and Elizabeth Spillius, Philippe Garigue, Joseph Loudun, Colin Rosser, Lorraine Lancaster, Chris Carson, Chie Nakane, Michael Swift, and Julian Pitt-Rivers. Various British anthropologists, mainly Meyer Fortes, had told me to bury poetry as deep as possible: I never talked about it and, indeed, there was little time for it. At some point, though, I taught sociology at a U.S. Air Force base near Ely for the University of Maryland, discovered Ely cathedral on the last day, and wrote the first poem in my first book: "Ely Cathedral."

In mid-1958, after a period of studying Burmese and Pali at the School of Oriental and African Studies (SOAS) and extremely drawn out and arduous grant-getting procedures, I left for Burma by sea on a five-week Bibby Line trip with Patricia Renate Cramer, whom I had married in 1956. The Burma residence needs a book by itself. Virtually no poetry came of it. Sometimes, I felt as if I should heed Burmese astrologers who told me one and all that I should immediately drop everything, join an army, and enjoy a career as a field marshall! (It was also in my stars that my daughter would make her parents famous.)

Eighteen months later, after the most exhausting work of my life and much travel in Burma proper, Thailand, Cambodia, India, Nepal, and other countries, we arrived back in London to live, not in Manchester Street as we had at first, but at number 6 and later 21 Kidderpore Gardens, which became our permanent home. There Andrea was born in 1960 (she is now an architect-designer), and Marc (now a doctor) in 1963.

In the midst of great and ever-growing doubt about getting so far from a life devoted to poetry, I had accepted perhaps the best job of its kind in the world as lecturer in South East Asian anthropology at the SOAS. The work, with colleagues Christoph von

With Patricia, in London, about 1957

Fürer-Haimendorf, Adrian Mayer, Fred Bailey, Barbara Ward, David Snellgrove, Hla Pe, Anna Allott, and so many others brought many blessings. There were meetings with great scholars such as Georges Dumézil, Gershom Scholem, Edward Conze, Pierre Gourou, Giuseppe Tucci, Margaret Mead, and Arthur Waley at international conferences or at home; wonderfully enriching trips like a lengthy 1961 one to Hawaii, for the Tenth Pacific Science Congress where I had convened a seminar, and Japan, for work on Buddhism and the "New Religions." On the way to Hawaii, I had stopped in San Francisco and, hitting City Lights Bookstore, had bought up, by instinct, a lot of works (later precious first editions) by Charles Olson, Robert Duncan, Michael McClure, Jack Spicer, and the Beats.

In Mandalay, Burma, Patricia and I had befriended a young Canadian poet, David Wevill, and his wife Assia, later to be associated with the Plath-Hughes tragedy. After a time in London, the Wevills took me to "the Group," a small association of poets meeting weekly at the home of Edward Lucie-Smith to tear each other's poems to pieces. I felt no great kinship with the work of the poets but much appreciated the socializing. In 1960, after an agonizing wait, a first poem had been accepted by *A Review of English Literature;* other acceptances followed. By 1963, I had been chosen for a BBC "Group" broadcast and won the Guinness Prize for Poetry at Cheltenham. There, a friendship quickly developed with John and Elizabeth Fowles and John brought me to the attention of Tom Maschler at his publishers, Jonathan Cape.

In December 1963, I asked for a room at King's "to complete some anthropological papers" and worked feverishly for some fifteen days to polish what became *Old Savage/Young City*. At one point, I was hauled to our jewel of a chapel, dressed in a surplice, and asked to perform Christmas hymns (I did much lip work and little singing) for a BBC TV show! Close to the last night, I found E. M. Forster alone in the Fellows' Room and, feeling a burning need to record, or confess, what I had been doing to some authority figure, engaged him in conversation. He was quietly generous. Back in London, I became Maschler's poetry advisor and started refurbishing, then building, Cape's meager poetry list. My main thrust was American: I wanted Charles Olson, Duncan, and Louis Zukofsky (my "three pillars"), and whomever else I could get among the "New Americans." Some authors, of course (like Robert Creeley and Gary Snyder), already had U.K. publishers.

These were exciting years, reading and publishing all over the country. Friendships were formed—with Christopher Middleton, Ted Hughes, Jon Silkin, George MacBeth, George Steiner, Arnold Wesker, B. S. Johnson, Alan and Ruth Sillitoe. Maschler had sold *Old Savage* to Random House and other American contacts were forming. For a time, I enjoyed being on the "international circuit"—beginning with a keynote paper at Berlin in 1964 (Borges, Auden, Spender, Herbert Read, Wole Soyinka, Vasko Popa, Langston Hughes, Gunther Grass, Helmut Heissenbüttel, James Merrill were just a few of the luminaries present), continuing at the PEN Bled meeting in 1965 (where I handed Charles Olson his first Cape contract, encountered Gyula Illyes, Susan Sontag, Miroslav Holub, Jan Kott, and had epic meals with Neruda and Asturias), and witnessing the Dubceck "window" twice in Prague and Bratislava, continuing on to Russia once, all this as an executive member of the Société Européenne de Culture. A great sadness was returning to Prague a few months ago and finding that my dear friend Peter Pujman, onetime secretary of the Prague Poetry Club, had died of cancer at sixty the year before . . .

There were major events in London, also—such as the International Festival at the Festival Hall in

The author (center, back row) teaching English at the monastic university in Rangoon, Burma, 1958

July 1967, where I read for Pablo Neruda whose Cape translator I had become. Visits to Cape by Ginsberg, Burroughs, Duncan, and many other Americans enlarged the circle. I often read for the BBC and once interviewed Robert Duncan on that program. Or rather, I said a half dozen words and then Robert, a major talker as well as poet, captured the mike for good!

Nineteen sixty-eight was a vintage year, first at the huge *Congreso Cultural* in Havana, which I reached on an epic flight with Arnold Wesker and where I saw Argeliers León again. I was, however, immensely saddened by his inexplicably keeping me away from my old Santería priest friend to whom I had brought (he had asked me for "something African" ten years before) an Ashanti gold weight. The list of people there would fill a chapter: I recall meetings with Michel Leiris, Julio Cortázar (from whom I wanted the hilarious *Cronopios y Famas* stories for Cape), Blas de Otero, José Lezama Lima, whom I later translated, and an army of Cuban poets . . . Eschewing the arranged tours, Wesker and I held out for Santiago de Cuba with the banner *"Santiago o Muerte!"* until we were escorted there. Later in the year came the Knokke Poetry Biennale on my beloved Belgian coast.

In 1967, I had taken the giant step of leaving SOAS and working for Cape as general editor of Cape Editions: beginning with Charles Olson's *Call Me Ishmael*, Lévi-Strauss's *Scope of Anthropology,* and the two first Roland Barthes works in English—I commissioned their translation—*Writing Degree Zero* and *Essay in Semiology*. I also created the Cape-Goliard Press by marrying the creative power of Barry Hall and Tom Raworth's Goliard Press to Cape's distributional capacities. The change over was celebrated by a huge trip to the States and Canada with a good-bye to anthropology at the Asian studies meeting in Ann Arbor and a transamerican hello to poetry publishing just about everywhere. In New York, Zukofsky virtually sat me on his knee to explain his *Catullus* line by line while, in Aspen, I climbed to Conundrum Springs with Jonathan Williams, Toby Olson, and Paul Blackburn and thrived on Ronald Johnson's cooking. In Canada came the Montreal Expo Festival with Robert Creeley, Denise Levertov, Robert Lowell, George Barker, Czeslaw Milosz *inter alia* in attendance, and after the ride of a lifetime on the Canadian Pacific, Robin Blaser gave me my first reading on American soil at Simon Fraser in Vancouver. Moving south, I met Duncan, William Everson, and Kenneth Rexroth all in one go, reading together on Mt. Tamalpais, followed by an epic midnight visit

to Kenneth and Miriam Patchen in Palo Alto. At the time, I was editing a selected Patchen for Cape.

It was all over in two short years. For complex reasons Cape let me go: mainly, I believe, because I wanted to remain an editor and not become a complete, full-scale publisher. My own work, influenced more and more by the Black Mountain and Beat "schools" and other "New Americans" as well as by the great Scots poet Hugh MacDiarmid, had left the narrow confines of English poetry as then practiced and opened out considerably by the time of *The Beautiful Contradictions* (published in 1969 though written over the two previous years—a great deal of it at Maschler's Welsh house, Carney, where Ginsberg had composed his *Welsh Visitation Poem)*. Reentry into the academy on the literary side proved impossible in England (a mysterious episode at Essex University clinched the matter). More and more, every sign pointed West.

In the summer of 1969, I taught in the English department at State University of New York (SUNY) at Buffalo, with Anselm Hollo, James Wright, and John Knoepfle. Friendship with Jerome and Diane Rothenberg, working at the nearby Seneca reservation, began then. There was a visit to Ginsberg, Orlovsky, and Miles at Cherry Valley; one to Charles Olson in Gloucester, alas, did not materialize. Though I was expected back in London, a long and tortured stay of over six months back on Lake Atitlán followed this, motivated by a major life crisis. I was due to immigrate to the U.S.A. in January 1970 with the offer of a visiting professorship in Romance Languages at Princeton. At Christmas, I rejoined and gathered my family in Switzerland and London and we arrived in the U.S. on time. I did not know that, at that very moment, Charles Olson was dying in New York.

Before the end of the semester, it had become clear that the permanent position at Princeton I thought secure would not materialize and the search for jobs began, with McGill in Montreal, SUNY at Stony Brook, SUNY at Purchase, and Cal Arts as possibilities at one time or another. I was eventually picked up at Rutgers by Dean Ernest Linton, who believed that an anthropologist was just the person, as Chair, to solve the unending internecine conflicts in a small department of Comparative Literature. Miguel Algarin, now of the Newyorikan Cafe, and Marilyn Kallet, now at the University of Tennessee, were two graduates who helped in my election. In the event, the department neither forgave me for the color of my Ph.D. nor ever truly acknowledged my work as a writer and the conflicts continued most unpleasantly for the next fourteen years.

My marriage had finally unravelled by the end of the Princeton term: Patricia, Andrea, and Marc returned to London. Patricia was, and is, the kindest-hearted and most profoundly generous person I have ever known: this separation was a tragedy I have never recovered from and I do not believe I ever will. For the next three years, I lived alone, in rentals at Princeton, followed by an eighteenth-century cottage at 96 New Street in New Hope, Pennsylvania, with occasional visits from Martha Crewe, a longtime American close friend whom I had known through Tom Maschler when she lived in London. I owe her more than can be recorded here but the relationship ended in 1972 when Martha decided to remain in England.

Literary life continued in New York with Nan Talese offering an oasis at Random House: an old-fashioned publishing friendship with the occasional lunch and the offer of many free books. She took *The Beautiful Contradictions* from Cape-Goliard and, in 1971, was the initial publisher of *A Nowhere for Vallejo,* which she then sold back to Cape. The

Teaching at the University of Colorado Writers Conference, with Senator Eugene McCarthy, Boulder, Colorado, June 1971

Nowhere had been written under great stress in Guatemala and witnessed to a higher esteem for César Vallejo than I had ever held for any Latin American poet. Were it not for certain circumstances, I would have translated him as fully as possible.

Nan's departure to Simon and Schuster was a tragedy for me. She very kindly offered to take me with her but I felt that her new house was even less interested in poetry than Random House had been. Kenneth Rexroth had very kindly recommended me to New Directions in the wake of Jerome Rothenberg and David Antin and, after a great deal of palaver, they brought out my *Lyrics for the Bride of God* in 1975. I was given the impression that this was a permanent move: for reasons which were never made fully clear to me, this was not to be the case. While still under that impression, I had thought to take pressure off New Directions by offering *The House of Leaves* to Black Sparrow. John Martin had long been asking to do something of mine. This book came out in 1976.

Both these volumes, the *Lyrics* especially, cover the painful years of divorce, experiment, and search for a new life in new patterns—years which coincided, doubtless not by chance, with the socio-political ferment of the late Sixties. I believe that *Lyrics* has not yet had the attention it deserves—in part because it is too painful and too close to the bone for many readers.

The years from 1972 to 1974, still part of those Sixties it seemed to me, were crazy years during which I lived some of the "youth" I had never managed to experience to my satisfaction. Many new friendships were formed or continued: John Peck at Princeton; Eliot Weinberger and Nina Subin, George and Susan Quasha, Armand Schwerner in New York; Robert Kelly at Bard; John Matthias and Michael Anania in Indiana and Illinois; Gary Snyder both on Princeton and New Hope visits; Toby and Miriam Olson in New York, then Philadelphia; Ed and Jenny Dorn, Peter Michelson, and Jack Collom in Colorado: the list is very large and has been more fully recorded elsewhere. There were many summer trips during these times: to Santa Fe in 1970 where Jerome Rothenberg, Dennis and Barbara Tedlock, Larry Bird, and I put together the first issue of *Alcheringa* magazine (I had first seen New Mexico at Shiprock and Acoma in 1967); in 1971 to Boulder, Colorado, to teach summer writing school for the University of Colorado (I have, by and large, avoided teaching "creative writing" like the plague), and again to Santa Fe to see the last manifestations of Cape-Goliard at Barry Hall's ranch. I went fairly frequently to Califor-

Nathaniel Tarn with Janet Rodney, at home, New Hope, Pennsylvania, mid-1970s

nia for readings in various places, with visits to Robert Duncan, Kenneth Rexroth, and many others. Tokens of welcome and initial acceptance into the ranks of American poets were frequently extended in these years; only gradually did it become clearer how hard it was and is for immigrants poets—even if citizens— to be *fully* accepted in this land of immigrants.

The poet Janet Rodney had arrived as a graduate student at Rutgers after some fifteen years in Spain, anxious to reenter American life. When she had ceased being my student at the end of a year, we began seeing each other and she moved into New Hope after an initial trip to Alaska in 1975. Two more extensive trips to conferences and consultancies in Native Art matters followed in 1976 and 1977 (when I worked as lecturer in anthropology on the *Lindblad Explorer* as far as the Aleutians and Hokkaido), leading to a joint work, *Alashka*. John Martin, claiming absolute disbelief in joint works on principle, refused bluntly to have anything to do with it. He undertook to do the next "*echt* Tarn" work but, when the time came, never did. The *Alashka* was published together with my selected poems as *Atitlán/Alashka*

by a small Boulder press while Janet and I were in Atitlán in 1979. As a result, *Alashka* never received the attention it deserved—especially in Alaska—and Janet as well as I suffered from doing it.

Like a painter who keeps a dozen easels in his studio and returns to each in turn, I have often let go of a subject completely to go back to it after some years. Around 1977, Norman Hammond, a young Mayanist, came to the department of archaeology at Rutgers and his presence reawakened my interest in Mayan studies. I attended a class of his as a student in 1977. By 1978, Janet and I were down at Cuello, Belize, as dig assistants—cleaning pot shards with toothbrushes and occasionally lending a hand on the pyramid. We then went to Lake Atitlán to check out possibilities of working there in 1979. I began coteaching with Hammond. In 1979, we obtained support from the Wenner Grenn Foundation for Anthropological Research in New York to look for a new language for certain kinds of cultural anthropology, one which would not depart from scientific exactitude but would not abdicate one jot of its literary potential.

We drove down to Guatemala via the east coast of Mexico and the Peten jungle, photographing some fifteen sites on the way, and spent a year in Santiago Atitlán. In the course of complex adventures regarding the return to the Atitecos of a mask which I had saved from fire thirty years before, we teamed up with a young New Mexican, Martin Prechtel—painter, musician, married to an Atitecan, and risen to the high position of *Primer Mayor* in the Indian hierarchy. We went home via the west coast (after being taken back to Guatemala City once under armed guard for some small fault in the car papers), again studying sites all the way up to Casas Grandes. Our first hamburger in Texas tasted of heaven as did the food we were plied with at Keith and Heloise Wilson's house in Las Cruces. I had formed the plan of showing Janet the Santa Fe area with a view to making a home there.

Life continued at Rutgers, with over-frequent and arduous commutes between New Hope and both campus and major cities. On average, we only seemed to have spent two days a week at home! I tried to begin the Atitlán book but found the usual difficulties in getting writing time free from academic entanglements. New York continued to be a focus of literary life. A very fine anthropologist, Stanley Diamond, had made up his mind to be a poet and went about it very energetically with many readings and conferences. We also had friends in Princeton—the Germanist Stanley Corngold first and foremost—and in Philadelphia, where Toby and Miriam Olson had moved to work at Temple. Our closest companions at Rutgers were George and Cleo McNelly Kearns, both polymaths, superlative literary critics, and spiritual kin, as well as Renee Baigell and her husband Matthew, the art historian. There were visits up to Cobbleskill in New York State to stay with John and Katherine Ferguson: John had helped me save my Burma material when it had bogged down in the Sixties.

I had been interested in Buddhism since something very much akin to a nervous breakdown at the Seigle house in Penne in 1954. During this time, Janet and I committed ourselves to very serious Zen Buddhist training in New York. After a time, my daughter, Andrea's, arrival as a student at Parsons

With Martin Prechtel (center) and legendary Atiteco shaman Nicolas Chiviliu,
Santiago Atitlán, Guatemala, 1979

Son, Marc (center with white headband), mid-1970s

gave me a welcome opportunity to catch up with her and I used all the spare time I had in New York City to be in her company. Andrea also came out West during vacations, as did my son, Marc, now training to be a doctor. Marc and I did one long tour of major Western sites: I took care of the archaeology and he found us the best rooms and the best food available!

Janet and I took a few days off to get married in 1982 when we decided to do it "for the future" in Santa Fe. We also spent the summer of that year in Cerillos. In the same year, benefiting from a sister-university relationship, we went to Changchun in Manchuria to teach at Jilin University for two months. This led to a very long and adventurous tour of various parts of China, with emphasis on the Silk Road and the great Buddhist cave sites: Yunkang, Dunhuang, and Turfan (others were "opened" only a year later!). Getting back from Urumchi, we were bound, out of Xian, for Central China, the Longmen caves, and the canal area, when a great Yangtze flood drove us into Yunnan instead, then out via Kunming and Canton. In Kunming I was able to gape again at the gorgeously costumed tribal people I had admired

many years before from the Burma side of the border.

Nineteen eighty-three brought a sabbatical which we decided to spend in New Mexico: in El Rancho, some thirty miles north of Santa Fe. In great secret we began to look at land in all areas, finally fixing on the beautiful hilly country up the Buckman road in an area called Las Dos. A house was also put into the works. One significant event during that year was the Second Ethnopoetics Conference, organized by Jerome Rothenberg at the University of Southern California in Los Angeles—the occasion for a most enjoyable reunion with many West Coast writers.

Then we were back in New Hope for a final year. After worrying a good deal about selling the house, it was finally disposed of to our next-door neighbors. In the middle of February 1985, we drove off very early one morning in the old Dodge van (our mobile home in Alaska and Guatemala) and a newly acquired Jeep Cherokee. On arrival at the New Mexico border, we got out and performed a joyous little dance. After one night at the Posada Inn, we drove out to the new house on March 1. We had never seen it, except as a hole in the ground—during a conference organized by the Center for Contemporary Arts of Santa Fe in the middle of 1984. It seemed miraculous: the classic "adobe brown" outside; the brilliant white bare walls and spaces inside, the dizzying 360-degree view over the massive expanse of the desert roundabout, stretching out west to the Rio Grande and the Jemez mountains, south to the Sandias, north to the Colorado border, and east to the Sangre de Cristos.

Soon the house began to be filled. For the second time in my life (the first had been in London), I was able to see all my books together (both from London and New Hope) in a very large basement bunker. The desks were put down and the studios organized. Janet eventually had her own building in which to open her Weaselsleeves Letter Press: she had trained in New York with Leslie Miller of the Grenfell Press. We had met Leslie through Brad Morrow, the young editor of *Conjunctions* in New York. Through Rexroth's continuing kindness, Brad had picked me up as his first contributing editor: we had a loquacious first meeting at a breakfast on Cornelia Street which ended over twelve hours after it had begun!

Tarn and daughter, Andrea, Gallup, New Mexico, about 1983

And we live at Las Dos still at this date, a mile or so south of the Indian Pueblo of Tesuque (with a postbox—*only*—at the Hispanic village of Tesuque). Our relationship, while greatly loving and affectionate, is, in some senses, more like that of two co-workers than a "marriage" in the old-fashioned sense: in fact we have an ad we talk jokingly about putting in the papers: Two writers seek "wife." For nigh on seventeen years, we have had new things to say to each other every day and that, by all accounts, must be most rare.

I claim that the minute you put a desk down in a place, it ceases to be paradise. However, I continue to find the landscape enchanted (as the ads endlessly proclaim) and the view out of my window is a permanent miracle. Granted that one comes here to work and be alone, I do miss whatever sense of community I had on the East Coast: for some reason, this is an almost impossible place in which to sustain social relationships with fellow workers—who are probably also here to be alone. Which is not to say that we have no colleagues here: Charles and Danny Bell of St. John's College; Woody and Steina Vasulka in video; Linda Klosky in film; Eleanor Caponegro in book design; Morton Subotnik and Peter Garland, composers; Gene Youngblood, the critic; Phillip Foss, Arthur Sze, Christopher Merrill, Leo Romero, and other poets. My old Chicago professor, Fred Eggan, retired here but died suddenly last year.

Like so many other attractive places in the country, the town of Santa Fe has been ruthlessly boutiquized and, except for the architecture, has ceased to exist as the charming small town it was for so long. Ninety percent of the arts and cultural activities result in kitsch and there is such a glut of "New Age" practices and events that they seem to have almost shut out traditional intellectual activities altogether. From the time long ago when Santa Fe chose to have the state penitentiary rather than the state university, the library problem has been acute and, seemingly, insoluble.

The Center for Contemporary Arts in Santa Fe provides one haven: especially (as far as our tastes are concerned) for keeping up with international cinema. Albuquerque offers occasional doses of realism, with its somewhat rougher life and with the University of New Mexico and its library. One friend especially has made the literary life stimulating for me here: the brilliant young poet and critic Lee Bartlett, who now heads the English Department at the University of New Mexico. We have worked on many a project together, including my *Bibliography* (1987) and *Views from the Weaving Mountain: Selected Essays in Poetics and Anthropology* (1991). Henry Roth, the octogenarian author of the magisterial novel *Call It Sleep*, is another Albuquerque resident we see with joy. Further down, at Las Cruces, the poet Keith Wilson and his wife Heloise are treasured friends. Janet and I sometimes teach at the Naropa Institute in Boulder: its poetics school is particularly lively in the summer and most welcoming to artists of every stripe.

Many hold that Santa Fe is best when combined with frequent travel out. We get to both coasts as often as possible (though not to the Middle West, alas) and continue visits to Paris and London for family and work reasons both. A fellowship to the Rockefeller Foundation's country estate at Bellagio on Lake Como in November of 1988 was combined with an intensive study-trip to the small towns in the Po Valley. I was back to my passion for Renaissance painting. In the summer of 1990, I fulfilled a lifelong ambition by going to Tibet with the Buddhologists Jeffrey Hopkins and Elizabeth Napper, entering from the north via Labrang and Kumbum monasteries and the central plateau and going out via Chengdu, Canton, and my old "friend" Hong Kong. Shortly after, Janet and I toured Rajasthan and I then took her to such places as Agra, Benares, Sanchi, etc., in Central India, places I had seen as a very privileged young man with a dozen other tourists and now shared with something closer to two thousand. In May of 1991, there were readings in Berlin, Prague, and Budapest—seeing the last and Vienna for the first time.

I had formed many Asian travel plans as a young man, but jobs and family intervened. I am especially keen to study Ladakh and Central Java with Bali before I'm done. The truth is I have too many travel plans for the time I have left: for there is still a mass of things in Europe I have not seen. Over the years, I have discovered that my greatest joy comes from a great museum or a great monument. This seems to activate for me a fundamental philosophical debate between the Particular (the "ten thousand things" of the Chinese) and the General: one of two or three *koans* of my existence and a great trigger for the poetry. I also find that moving about facilitates writing more than staying still: in that sense, travel is part, indeed *sine qua non*, of method. A book like *At the Western Gates*, for instance, depends heavily on travel: part one is set in Baja California; part two in Chiapas, Mexico; part three in Alaskan and North Japan waters. I would not, however, call them "travel poems": the setting is one thing, the matter another.

I think it is Stendhal who enjoins us never to discuss our triggers. I strongly believe that the central mystery—the poet's marriage to language (as stuff and form) and the ways in which this marriage plays

itself out through time—should, or need, not be discussed by the poet and, further, that while poets depend for diffusion on biographers, reviewers, and critics, the mystery is as often weakened as strengthened by that apparently necessary and unavoidable intervention. I far prefer to talk about the matters and disciplines which engage me and leave it to readers to find out how, if at all, they influence, or enter into, the "content" aspect of the poetry.

I hope it is clear from this account that a lifelong interest in religions and symbolic systems—primarily, but not exclusively, Classical, Judaeo-Christian, Mayan and Buddhist—has been a very powerful motivating force. A strong sense of the interrelationships of man and *polis* and a dark view of man's inhumanity to man have also provided the "matter" of much poetry. In childhood and youth a passionate involvement with nature—especially ornithological and vegetal—occasioned many poems. Over the years, this has to some extent given way to an inextinguishable romance with culture in the form of great human works in any medium (the arts, architecture, technology) and a theoretical interest in the interplay between natural and civil ecology and conservation: that some can even discuss these apart from each other seems to me an impossible aberration. The urge to totalization is still strong: I constantly suffer the utopian dream of uninterruptible art/writing/poetry against which the discontinuity of creative energy is always pitting itself. *Ars longa, vita brevis* they say: in fact the two are interchangeable. Life is both far too long and far too short simultaneously: everything comes up every single moment against the intuition that, to be true and just, one should live (and write) forever.

The sense of the ending of an era, perhaps even of a whole concept of "civilization," has been strong throughout and occasioned much critical examination of "elegy," not as a *kind* of poem but as a formal *function* of poetry concerned with the whole act of *looking back* at previous poems/previous culture (and fully realizing and possessing that backward look) while in the very act of writing and therefore *looking forward*—a function for which I use the old term "lyric." In an essay which has been very important for me, "Archaeology, Elegy, Architecture: A Poet's Program for Lyric," I have manifested these processes through polymorphous interpretations of the Orphic myth—the various possibilities of Orpheus's interaction with his female manifestation Eurydice-Persephone. This myth I take to be the constitutive charter of, in Hugh MacDiarmid's words, "the kind of poetry I want."

This, combined with a more earthy sociological approach in my make-up, has led me to much concern

Nathaniel Tarn and Janet Rodney at the Soviet Aviation Monument, Changchun, Manchuria, People's Republic of China, while teaching at Jilin University, 1982

with the declining role of poetry and the poet in our increasingly illiterate culture. At a very banal level, almost all of us poets of my age sense some kind of great difference between the life we used to have and the one we lead now. I dare say I was more fortunate than many in my beginnings, but I treasured the sense of having a publishing house, an editor, the occasional lunch, the pretense that one's vocation was of use to the world, some moderate attention in reviews and notices, the gradual buildup of a modest reputation—all of which I was blessed with at the start. There was also the coincidence with the Sixties: a time of extraordinary interest in poetry; the possibility of substantial and extremely well-attended readings; the sense of a potential (probably illusory) for significant political action; the signs that the "redskins" in American Poetry might finally burst

through the containing walls erected for generations by the "palefaces."

All that began to give way—the very day, I believe, when the Vietnam War ended. Only the very smallest number of "known," "famed," "noted," "awarded" bards now enjoys such luxuries. The world of publishing, sold out to corporatism, is deliquescing beyond all recognition. The culture overproduces "poets" in the "creative writing" schools while at the same time underproducing readers throughout the educational system at all levels. For the first time in history perhaps, the material, sociological conditions exist for the drowning out of quality by quantity—cultural stereotypes like "there cannot be mute inglorious Miltons" notwithstanding. Virtually everyone—except other poets—has given up even the pretense of producing, reading, or enjoying poetry, so that incestuous schools and movements flourish, existing, because of their sheer complexity, way outside any "general readership" and doomed, one would think, to extinction by the resulting overspecialization. Competition for minute pieces of turf has virtually lost all meaning in that the turf itself is becoming meaningless. Continually injured and insulted by the kind of reception he or she suffers out there, the poet's life is now worth less than that of a liver fluke progressing through the guts of a sheep. Very few risk saying so.

Under these conditions, it is a matter for great wonder why so many young people continue to ache as much as they do toward gaining their poetic wings. Of course, it is in them, one is forced to believe, on pain of suicide ("*Eighteen* of the ranking U.S. poets of the Twentieth century committed suicide," Kenneth Rexroth to James Laughlin, October 26, 1950), and from that point of view—in the face of ever-deepening depression—poetry is the only "principle of hope" I can still enjoy. My own belief is that we have reached a point when only a major social revolution on a universal scale would be capable of changing the conditions I've described, and it is not at all certain that they would lead back toward the world of poetry.

What revolution can we be thinking of, in any case, when the triumph of capitalism seems as complete as possible and when only more and more and more consumerism seems to be the lot we can look forward to and the lot we can offer to "technologically underdeveloped" populations? This, incidentally, being to me the true moment of postmodernism, if such a thing can be meaningfully categorized.

We have to conjugate the words "young" and "technologically underdeveloped" or "evolving" (such terms always, of course, from *our* logocentric viewpoint and *no other*) and put our future hopes perhaps not so much in ourselves as in the poets of other areas in the world. The voices of the future, ancient in their own homes, may come onto our stages out of Africa, Asia, Latin America; many, and great ones at that, already have. The major conflicts looming on the internal empire's front in these United States—in the form of the question of multiculturalism—prefigure this. At this time, the entrance of "liberation poetries" onto the scene complicates the American White-Anglo statistical picture I've drawn above almost beyond measure. Even at the cost of the self-scuttling, or destruction, or radical reformulation of the White-Anglo literary world, however, these "liberation poetries" will become the poetries of the future and, we hope, resimplify the picture. I do not believe this to be a "Liberal" kowtow to the *burrocrassies* which are imposing

multiculturalism on this nation in a mostly crass and unimaginative way. I believe it to be the simple truth about the changes that have to occur if poetry is to survive as "marital" rather than "incestuous," that is: as meaningful to a substantial audience.

I will then hope that the new poetries will be more generous to us than we have ever been to them and that, after the initial alienations, we will once more be allowed onto the scene as part of a universal culture. For while we dispute among ourselves, the planet itself is in the process of becoming as endangered as those cold masses out there in space might at one time have been. And we all need a home, to whatever species we may belong. Given the time frame in question, this home may be all we have.

December 1991

BIBLIOGRAPHY

Poetry:

Old Savage/Young City, J. Cape (London), 1964, Random House, 1965.

(With Richard Murphy and Jon Silkin) *Penguin Modern Poets 7: Richard Murphy, Jon Silkin, Nathaniel Tarn,* Penguin, 1966.

Where Babylon Ends, Grossman, 1968.

The Beautiful Contradictions, J. Cape, 1969, Random House, 1970.

October: A Sequence of Ten Poems Followed by Requiem Pro Duabus Filiis Israel, Trigram Press (London), 1969.

The Silence, M'Arte (Milan), 1970.

A Nowhere for Vallejo, Random House, 1971.

Lyrics for the Bride of God: Section: The Artemision, Tree Books, 1973.

The Persephones, Christopher's Books, 1974.

Lyrics for the Bride of God, New Directions, 1975.

Narrative of This Fall, Black Sparrow Press, 1975.

The House of Leaves, Black Sparrow Press, 1976.

(With Janet Rodney) *From Alashka: The Ground of Our Great Admiration of Nature,* Permanent Press, 1977.

The Microcosm, Membrane Press, 1977.

Birdscapes, with Seaside, Black Sparrow Press, 1978.

(With Rodney) *The Forest,* Perishable Press, 1978.

(With Rodney) *Atitlán/Alashka: New and Selected Poems,* Brillig Works Press, 1979.

The Land Songs, Blue Guitar, 1981.

Weekends in Mexico, Oxus Press (London), 1982.

The Desert Mothers, Salt Works Press, 1984.

At the Western Gates, Tooth of Time Press, 1985.

Palenque: Selected Poems, Oasis Press (London), 1986.

Seeing America First, Coffee House Press, 1989.

Other:

(Translator) Pablo Neruda, *The Heights of Macchu Picchu* (bilingual edition), J. Cape, 1966, Farrar, Straus, 1967.

(Editor and co-translator) *Con Cuba: An Anthology of Cuban Poetry of the Last Sixty Years,* Grossman, 1969.

(Translator) Victor Segalen, *Stelae,* Unicorn Press, 1969.

(Editor and co-translator) Neruda, *Selected Poems,* (bilingual edition), J. Cape, 1970, Delacorte, 1972, Harper & Row, 1991.

Views from the Weaving Mountain: Selected Essays in Poetics and Anthropology, an "American Poetry" book, distributed by University of New Mexico Press, 1991.

Contributor to many anthologies in the United States, including *America: A Prophecy,* edited by Jerome Rothenberg and George Quasha; *For Neruda, For Chile,* edited by Walter Lowenfels; *Shaking the Pumpkin,* edited by Jerome Rothenberg, Doubleday, 1972; *Open Poetry,* edited by Ronald Gross, Simon & Schuster, 1973; *Perception,* edited by Don Wellman, O. ARS, 1982; *Random House Book of Twentieth Century French Poetry,* edited by Paul Auster, 1984; *Talking Poetry,* edited by Lee Bartlett, University of New Mexico Press, 1986; *Beneath a Single Moon,* Kent Johnson and Craig Paulenich, Shambhala, 1991; *The Forgotten Language,* edited by Christopher Merrill, Peregrine Smith, 1991.

Contributor to periodicals, including *Credences, New York Times, Observer, Sagetrieb, Sulfur, Temblor,* and *Times Literary Supplement.* Contributing editor, *Conjunctions, PO&SIE* (Paris), *Courrier du Centre International de Poésie* (Brussels), and *Modern Poetry in Translation* (London).

Contributor to anthologies in France, Italy, Mexico, and the Netherlands, including *Poeti Inglesi del 900,* edited by Roberto Sanesi; *Anthologie de la Poésie Américaine,* edited by Jacques Roubaud; *Levenstekens en Doodsinjalen,* edited by Hans Ten Berge; *Antología de la Poesía Norteamericana,* edited by Eliot Weinberger.

Edward O. Wilson

1929-

IN THE QUEENDOM OF THE ANTS:
A BRIEF AUTOBIOGRAPHY

Edward O. Wilson in his office, Harvard University, 1990

I have been often asked whether I arrived at a synthesis of sociobiology and the evolutionary study of human nature after a lifetime of planning. Did I start with the biology of ants (myrmecology) as a first step toward the distantly planned and ultimate coverage of all aspects of social behavior? The answer is no. My scientific career was far less grandly conceived. I began to work on ants in my teens because they fascinated me. I wanted only to be an entomologist, to ride around in one of those green pickup trucks used by the U.S. Department of Agriculture's extension service to visit rural areas.

Beyond that boyhood dream, I proceeded mostly one step at a time. In a sense, the ants gave me everything, and to them I will always return, like a shaman reconsecrating the tribal totem.

So what does it take to make a myrmecologist? The following ingredients were crucial in my case. My childhood was solitary—but not lonely. I was the only child of a couple who divorced when I was seven. Although I have remained in close and affectionate contact with my mother since then, financial conditions in the 1930s made it necessary for me to live with my father, and I was raised primarily by him and my stepmother, whom he married in 1937.

My father, Edward, Sr., was a typical federal employee of the Roosevelt era. He was also exceptionally peripatetic, working for one acronymic agency after another through the South, never remaining at the same address for more than two years. As a consequence I attended sixteen schools in the eleven years from first to twelfth grades, skipping the third grade because of rapid early progress. Because of the difficulty in social adjustment that resulted from being a perpetual newcomer, without siblings, and younger than most of my classmates, I took to the woods and fields. Natural history came like salvation at a very early age. It absorbed my energies and provided unlimited adventure. In time, it came to offer deeper emotional and aesthetic pleasure. I found a surrogate companionship in the organisms whose qualities I studied as intently as the faces and personalities of boyhood friends. I also had a real friend in each one- to two-year period, a close chum my own age I somehow acquired and turned into a part-time zoologist. But the full balance was attained, to a degree much greater than is ordinary even for professional naturalists, by the inexhaustible resources of the outdoors.

Add to that, a drive acquired early, and which frankly I do not understand to this day. I have always been a workaholic. When I became a Boy Scout, I kept on achieving until I had acquired the rank of Eagle Scout and beyond, accumulating a large percentage of the merit badges that could be earned.

To this not entirely flattering revelation can be added the disclosure of certain physical infirmities that predisposed me to work on insects. I had use of only my left eye; the right was mostly blinded by a traumatic cataract when I carelessly jerked a fish fin into it at the age of seven. As a result of monocular vision I found it very difficult to locate birds and mammals when I tried to familiarize myself with them in the field. At the same time, the vision in the good eye was (and is) exceptionally acute, allowing me to read considerably finer print than that on the bottom line of ophthalmologist's charts. I am the last to spot a hawk sitting in a tree, but I can examine the hairs and contours of an insect's body without the aid of a magnifying glass.

In four continuous months in the rain forests of New Guinea, I collected over four hundred species of ants and studied many of them in some detail, but I never once saw a bird of paradise. My hearing has also been slightly impaired since early childhood, and I experience particular difficulty at higher frequencies. So, gone are the opportunities to hear the songs of many kinds of birds, frogs, and cicadas.

And finally, I have a peculiar inability to memorize poems, the lyrics of songs, and more than one or two sentences of prose. I never held a part in a chorus or school play, and never even tried—the very idea panicked me. As a result I was and still am virtually compelled to reconstruct most of what I learn, often with new images and ways of phrasing. I have no doubt that this slight learning disability added something to whatever originality of thought I have managed and helped to nudge me into part-time theoretical work—attempts, as it were, to cope with the world by reconstructing it into a form that I could more easily recall.

I was born in Birmingham, Alabama, on June 10, 1929. For four generations previously, all of my forebears had lived in Alabama, the first arriving in that state during the 1830s and 1840s. Almost all were of English origin. On my father's side, all lived in Mobile, where the men were principally shipowners and river pilots; my father's father was a railroad engineer who ran the train from Mobile north to Thomasville. On my mother's side, almost all were farmers in northern Alabama. Several fought for the Confederacy during the Civil War. One paternal great-grandfather, William ("Black Bill") Wilson, used his ship and skills as a pilot to smuggle guns past the federal blockade at Mobile, until he was captured by Admiral Farragut and sent to a prison in New York for the duration of the war.

So I enjoyed a sense of family roots even as my father pulled me in tow through his complicated odyssey. Of great importance, I benefited from the general approval and even esteem of my relatives for my interests in natural history. "Sonny" Wilson was thought to be a little strange but smart, and he was expected to make something of himself; what, nobody could quite figure out, but *something*. In the later years of my adolescence, my mother (who was then living in Kentucky) added her strong spiritual as well as financial support to the unusual career I was pursuing. Let me tell the rest of the story with the aid of several vignettes.

Washington, D.C., 1939

During a two-year sojourn in Washington, D.C., I was enthralled by visits to the Smithsonian Institution and National Zoo. The collections of insects and living animals were testaments to a magic world to which I felt I was owed special entry. The grounds of the zoo and nearby Rock Creek Park became the wilderness where, at the age of ten, I fantasized "expeditions" to collect insects. About this time I met a boy my age, Ellis G. MacLeod, who lived a block away and soon came to share my enthusiasm. Together we netted our first red admirals and fritillaries and sought the elusive mourning cloak. Armed with Frank Lutz's *Field Guide to the Insects* and poring over R. E. Snodgrass's *Principles of Insect Morphology*—which we could hardly begin to understand—we decided that we would devote our lives to entomology. In fact, Ellis is now a professor of entomology at the University of Illinois.

At this time, 1939–40, I also became fascinated with ants. I discovered a large colony of *Acanthomyops* in Rock Creek Park that seemed miraculous in the abundance, glittering yellow bodies, and citronella smell of the workers. I read the article "Stalking Ants, Savage and Civilized," by William M. Mann, in the August 1934 issue of the *National Geographic*. In what was one of the more remarkable coincidences of my entire life, Mann was at that time director of the National Zoological Park. He became my hero from afar. In 1957, during the last year of his directorship, he gave me his large library on ants and escorted my wife and me on a special tour of the zoo—for me a truly fulfilling event.

Mobile, Alabama, 1940

My little family returned to the South to commence a complicated sequence of residences in Mobile and other small towns and cities: Evergreen, Brewton, Decatur, and Pensacola. The woods and streams were always a short bicycle ride away. In 1942 I undertook a serious study of ants in Mobile, collecting and studying the tropical hunting ponerine *Odontomachus insularis*, the Argentine ant *Iridiomyrmex humilis,* and a small species of *Pheidole*. At the age of thirteen, I made my first publishable observation, later to be used by William F. Buren and myself in scientific reports: that introduced fire ants were abundant in Mobile during 1942 and at that time included the reddish species, *Solenopsis invicta,* which has since spread throughout the southern United States.

My interests turned for a time to snakes. Little wonder—southern Alabama has one of the richest local faunas in the world. In 1942 I was appointed nature counselor at the Mobile area Boy Scout camp, primarily because the older, more competent young men had gone to war. I built a zoo with about ten species of snakes, which the other boys helped me to collect. Midway through the summer I was unfortunately bitten by one of my pygmy rattlesnakes and had to be rushed off for first aid. It was a bad day for

herpetology at Camp Pushmataha. When I returned a week later, the senior staff had wisely disposed of the poisonous snakes, and the summer was concluded without further incident.

In 1944 I built an even larger collection of living snakes and frogs in my backyard in Brewton. After capturing a specimen of the giant eel-like salamander *Amphiuma means,* I wrote a letter of inquiry, with sketches and notes, to *Natural History* magazine. The editors responded by stating their intention to publish an article on this remarkable animal, acknowledging the stimulus my letter had provided. I was thrilled! It was the first hint I had that the wondrous things in my private world might be valued outside Escambia County. Thus are Southern writers and artists born.

During the winter before entering college, at the now advanced age of sixteen, I decided that in order to realize my gathering ambitions I must specialize in a group of insects. Through competence in a specialty would come deep understanding of nature and a job in later years. After careful thought, I picked flies. These insects are abundant, extremely diverse, and with intriguing habits. Some are even beautiful! I was especially attracted to the metallescent blue and green dolichopodids. But this decision had to be quickly canceled. It was the last year of World War II and insect pins, manufactured mostly in Germany in that period, were unavailable. I turned to my old favorites, the ants: they could be collected in rubbing alcohol and stored in little medicine bottles purchased in pharmacies. With the generous help and encouragement of Marion R. Smith, the ant specialist of the U.S. National Museum, I set out to build a collection and prepare a monograph on the fauna of Alabama. The task was never completed, but in the course of pursuing it I learned a great deal about the classification and biology of this fascinating group of insects.

Tuscaloosa, Alabama, 1948

In my second year at the University of Alabama, I fell into the company of a remarkable group of young entomologists who had recently come from Cornell University: Ralph L. Chermock, with a new Ph.D., beginning an assistant professorship; and George E. Ball and Barry D. Valentine, who enrolled in order to join Chermock as undergraduate students.

These three brought a professionalism, national perspective, and almost religious excitement about entomology and evolutionary biology. They greatly expanded my horizons. We pored over Ernst Mayr's *Systematics and the Origin of Species* as holy scripture.

With Herbert Boschung, a fellow native of Alabama, we traveled all over the state, collecting and studying insects, reptiles, amphibians, and mammals. Our little band of zealots descended into caves to search for troglophilic crayfish and beetles, seined streams and ponds for fish, and drove along the highways on rainy nights looking for migrating tree frogs.

In 1948 I contacted William L. Brown, then a graduate student at Harvard University. Brown was (and is) a fanatic on ants, one of the warmest and most generous human beings I have ever known, and the single greatest influence on my scientific life. He fueled my already considerable enthusiasm with a stream of advice and urgings. What you must do, Wilson, he wrote, is to broaden the scope of your studies. Never mind a survey of the Alabama ants; start on a monograph of an important ant group. Look, you have the great advantage of living in the deep South, where there are a great many dacetine ants. No one has worked out the ecology and food habits of dacetine ants. There is an opportunity to do some really original research. See what you can come up with, and keep me posted.

I plunged into the project at once, tracking down one species after another, dissecting nests and culturing colonies in the laboratory. The dacetines are slender, ornately sculptured little ants with long, thin mandibles and bizarrely formed hairs covering most of their bodies. They also exhibit a striking form of behavior. The workers hunt collembolans and other soft-bodied arthropods with very slow, deliberate movements. They approach the prey with extended sensitive labral hairs and seize them with a convulsive snap when the hairs touch. Each dacetine species has a distinctive repertory directed toward the capture of a particular range of prey.

Several years before I heard of ethology, I prepared a detailed report on the comparative ethology of the Dacetini (Wilson, 1953). In 1959, Brown and I published a synthesis of dacetine biology (Brown and Wilson, 1959), in which we traced the evolution of food habits in correlation with social organization and biology. In brief, the anatomically most primitive species forage above ground for larger, more general insect prey; they form large colonies and often have well-differentiated worker castles and a marked division of labor. As specialization on collembolans increases across the spectrum of species, body size correspondingly decreases, along with colony size, the nests become more subterranean and hidden, and the workers lose their polymorphism and caste-based division of labor. This was the first such study in the evolution of socioecology of which I am aware. It preceded the work by J. H. Crook and

others in the 1960s on primate socioecology and in some respects was more definitive. But it remained known to only a few entomologists and had little effect on the subsequent development of behavioral ecology and sociobiology.

In 1949, while a senior at the University of Alabama, I was hired by the Alabama State Department of Conservation to conduct the first full-scale study of the imported fire ant. This formidable pest had been accidentally introduced into the port of Mobile by shipping from South America and had subsequently spread deep into Florida, Mississippi, and central Alabama. Much of my research that year was directed at the behavior of the ants (Wilson and Eads, 1949). At this time, for example, I discovered the phenomenon of queen execution by which colonies eliminate supernumerary queens (reported in Wilson, 1966).

In the fall of 1950, after completing a master's degree in biology, I moved to the University of Tennessee to begin work on the Ph.D. under the direction of the ant specialist Arthur C. Cole. But Brown intervened again like the good fairy. The dacetine and fire ant work was very promising, he said. You should come to Harvard, where the largest collection of ants in the world is kept. Get a global view; don't sell yourself short with entirely local studies. I also received encouragement from Frank M. Carpenter, the great authority on insect fossils and evolution, who was later to serve as my doctoral supervisor.

Cambridge, Massachusetts, 1953

I sat in the main lecture room of Harvard's Biological Laboratories listening to a lecture by Konrad Lorenz. At that moment things were going exceedingly well for an aspiring young entomologist. In the spring I had been elected to Harvard's Society of Fellows, which provided three years of completely unrestricted study anywhere in the world. In the summer I had traveled to Cuba and Mexico for two months of intensive study on tropical ants. A whole new world of ecology and behavior had been opened up, and I was primed for new ideas.

Now I heard Lorenz explain the basic principles of ethology in his unique, hortatory style. The importance of the central concept struck me like a thunderbolt. If birds and fish were guided to such a remarkable extent by auditory and visual releasers, ants and other social insects must be guided to an even greater degree by chemical releasers! Up to that time it was widely felt that ants were governed to a substantial degree by scent, such as nest odors, alarm substances, and trail secretions, but the sources of these substances and their chemical nature remained wholly unknown. Also, the notion that complex, stereotyped responses might be triggered by single chemical stimuli was quite new and strange.

The more theoretical work on ant behavior in 1953 was dominated by Theodore C. Schneirla, whose writings stressed the traditional ideas of comparative psychology, learning theory, and generalized concepts such as attraction/repulsion. Even while working out the life cycle of those ultimate instinct machines, the *Eciton* army ants, an accomplishment that may well stand as the major contribution of his life, Schneirla still sought ways to explain behavior on the basis of the simplest possible schemes of stimulus and response. This behaviorist viewpoint was not fundamentally wrong in the relatively few conclusions it was able to draw, but it turned attention away from the kind of heuristic theory and experimental approaches that characterized the new ethology.

So it was fated that I would go in search of the chemical releasers of ants. However, I postponed this pursuit in order to take advantage of an opportunity of a wholly different kind. In 1954 the Society of Fellows and Museum of Comparative Zoology awarded me grants to work in New Guinea and surrounding areas of the South Pacific. The ant fauna of this part of the world was still very imperfectly known. There were opportunities to discover many new species and to explore the ecology and behavior of major groups of ants rarely ever seen alive by entomologists.

For ten months, from November 1954 to September 1955, I worked on Fiji, New Caledonia, the New Hebrides, New Guinea, Australia, and Sri Lanka. On the way home I visited the leading ant collections of Europe to include taxonomic research. I had experienced the great expedition at last: New Guinea was Rock Creek Park writ large. Camus was quite right when he observed, "A man's work is nothing but this slow trek to rediscover, through the detours of art, those two or three great and simple images in whose presence his heart first opened."

Every young evolutionary biologist should have such a *Wanderjahr*. The impulse to explore the

Edward O. Wilson next to an ant nest in the Biological Laboratory, Harvard University, 1971

*Edward O. Wilson at the Museum of Comparative
Zoology, Harvard University, 1975*

physical world and discover hidden places, to see marvels and nameless creatures, and finally to return to the tribe with stories of the adventure is primitive and deep. It provides a source of information and ideas on which years of creative work can be built, and a lifetime of memories. "Something hidden," Kipling captured the thought for all. "Go and find it. Go and look behind the Ranges. Something lost behind the ranges. Lost and waiting for you. Go!"

In the fall of 1955 I married Irene Kelley, a Boston girl. We were fortunate to enjoy a relationship that was to last and grow in strength and pleasure for us both through the years ahead, and the raising of our daughter, Catherine. I accepted an assistant professorship at Harvard. It was time to take stock. At the age of twenty-six, I had successfully completed a diversity of studies on ants: the behavior of the dacetines; the history of the imported fire ant; the evolution of caste systems based on allometry and frequency distribution analysis; a monograph on *Lasius,* the most thorough revision of any genus of ants undertaken to that time; and a variety of special

studies of the ecology and behavior of hitherto little-known tropical forms.

With William L. Brown I had written an influential critique of the subspecies concept and explored the phenomenon of "character displacement" in species formation; we coined the term and popularized the study of the process. Now an embarrassment of opportunities lay before me. Modern biology was catching up with the social insects, yet only a handful of investigators worked on the group worldwide.

The result of this exceptional circumstance was that I commenced work in several fields simultaneously. I asked, what can the ants bring to modern biology? For the next twenty years my research comprised a thick tangle of studies spanning a large part of organismic and evolutionary biology. Immediately after my return from the Pacific, I began a series of taxonomic monographs on the ants of New Guinea and the surrounding Melanesian archipelagoes, describing new species, putting the classification of various groups in order, and incorporating my field notes of ecology and behavior. I published my way through about one-third of the fauna, which is one of the largest and most complex in the world. Later I completed a monograph of the ants of Polynesia with one of my students, Robert W. Taylor, now chief curator of the Australian national insect collection in Canberra, as well as special studies of other oceanic faunas.

In a second major effort at socioecology, I reconstructed the evolutionary history of the army ants. Relying in part on my own observations of the tropical Cerapachyini, which display the rudimentary elements of legionary behavior, I showed how mass raids and frequent nest change originated as adaptations to predation on other social insects and particularly large, formidable arthropods such as giant beetles and centipedes. Relying on the many species that comprise the mass raiders, I pieced together a reasonably full story of the steps leading to the origin of the advanced *Eciton* army ants of the New World tropics and *Anomma* driver ants of Africa. The procedure followed was similar to that used by previous workers to explain the origin of the balloon flies of the family Empididae. I was especially pleased with this accomplishment, because it added a much-needed evolutionary perspective to the splendid research of Schneirla on *Eciton* and Albert Raignier and others on *Anomma.*

Inspired by the theories of William D. Matthew and Philip J. Darlington on the origin of faunal dominance, I turned about the same time to the question of interspecific competition and the spread of groups of animals around the world. In his 1957 book *Zoogeography*, Darlington had identified the Old World tropics as the headquarters of major taxon evolution and the springboard for the evolution of dominant vertebrate groups.

As I sifted through the data from my taxonomic revisions and field notes, I detected patterns at the *species* level. I could see in finer detail the process of species multiplication as groups spread from tropical Asia into Australia and the Pacific islands. For the first time it was possible to correlate the passages of stages in geographic speciation with alterations in ecology and behavior. I invented the concept of the "taxon cycle," which has since been documented in modified form in some groups of birds, reptiles, beetles, and other organisms.

In essence, the cycle commences with the inter-island spread of species that live in ecologically more marginal habitats such as forest borders and savannas, and possess certain traits associated with this specialization, including larger colony size, soil-nesting, more frequent occurrence of caste systems and odor trails, and others. As the colonizing populations penetrate the more species-rich habitats of the inner rain forests, on islands such as New Guinea and Viti Levu, they tend to fission, while at the same time shifting toward wood-nesting and the associated social and behavioral traits.

The discovery of the taxon cycle in 1959 was an exercise not only in biogeography but also sociobiology, and it was to influence my thinking in the later attempt to synthesize that complicated subject. I also worked out area-species curves for the Pacific region, a prelude to later work with Robert MacArthur on the theory of island biogeography.

In the midst of these eclectic endeavors I returned to the idea of chemical releasers in ants. The story of how I hit on the first glandular origin of pheromones in ants may be of special interest. I was keeping imported fire ants *(Solenopsis invicta)* in culture. This species had always been a favorite of mine since my early work on it in Alabama. Fire ants have a dramatic odor trail system, and so I decided to try to find the source of the chemical scent. Could the key substance come from one of the organs in the posterior region of the abdomen? I painstakingly dissected out the rectal sac and two principal glands of the poison apparatus and washed them individually in insect Ringer's solution—not an easy procedure, since these organs are barely visible to the naked eye. I then crushed each in turn on the tip of an applicator stick and smeared it in an artificial trail across the glass plate being used by the fire ants as a foraging arena. At best I expected to find that some of the ants would follow the line when they were later stimulated

by the presentation of food. But when I tested Dufour's gland, an insignificant fingershaped organ located at the base of the sting, an astonishing thing happened. Worker ants poured out of the nest by the dozens, ran the length of the artificial trail, and milled around in confusion at its end. The same response occurred when I used an extract of the gland's contents in ether or ethanol. Dufour's gland, I saw at once, contains a chemical substance that not only guides the ants but also summons them out of the nest. The contents of one gland are enough to activate a large group of foragers. Stretched out in a line, the pheromone is not just the guidepost, but the entire message.

That night I couldn't sleep. I envisioned accounting for the entire social repertory of the ants with a small number of chemical releasers. Each of the substances might be produced by a different gland and stored in special reservoirs, to await release by the ant according to the message the insect wishes to transmit. I proceeded to discover alarm substances in the mandibular glands of fire ants and harvester ants. Independently in the same year Martin Lindauer and his coworkers demonstrated alarm substances in the mandibular glands of the major caste of leaf cutter ants. They also characterized the substances chemically, the first such identification made.

I went on to discover the "necrophoric substances" by which ants identify their own dead. When a corpse has decomposed for two or three days, it accumulates enough oleic acid and related esters to cause workers to remove it to the refuse pile. I was able to get workers to treat small ant-size wooden dummies as corpses by painting the objects with minute quantities of these substances. Even live nestmates were converted into "corpses" when contaminated with the necrophoric chemicals. They were carried off to the refuse, live and kicking. Only after they had cleaned themselves thoroughly were they allowed to return to the nest.

As this work proceeded, I felt confident enough to write the following:

> The complex social behavior of ants appears to be mediated in large part by chemoreceptors. If it can be assumed that "instinctive" behavior is organized in a fashion similar to that demonstrated for the better known invertebrates, a useful hypothesis would seem to be that there exists a series of behavioral "releasers," in this case chemical substances voided by individual ants that evoke specific responses in other members of the same species. It is further useful for purposes of investigation to suppose that the releasers are produced at least in part as glandu-

lar secretions and tend to be accumulated and stored in reservoirs. (Wilson, 1958)

Events have proved this prediction correct. In general, ants appear to communicate by approximately ten to twenty signals, most of which are chemical. In 1959 Peter Karlson and Adolf Butenandt first used the expression "pheromone" in a general review of chemotactic communication, and the word was quickly adopted by those of us working on the social insects.

The Sixties and Seventies

For several months in 1961 I suffered from a state of mild depression, and taking my first sabbatical leave, I headed, that spring, for a new round of fieldwork in Surinam and Trinidad-Tobago. The first several months went well, with the discovery of new forms of behavior and chemical communication in previously unstudied tropical ants. Then I transferred to Tobago to study and consolidate my work—still in a mood of deepening discontent. It just didn't seem enough to continue enlarging the natural history and biogeography of ants. The challenges were not commensurate to the forces then moving and shaking the biological sciences.

But doubts about my work were only a part of what was troubling me. A deeper cause of my malaise was the accumulated tensions stemming from nearly a decade of personal conflict and academic rivalries that had plagued Harvard's biology department.

Let me explain. In the 1950s the molecular revolution had begun, and vast sums of money and the best young talent were being committed to that end of biology. One major advance after another occurred at seemingly monthly intervals. I was in a particularly sensitive position at Harvard, because one of my colleagues was James D. Watson, one of the architects of molecular biology. In 1958 he and I were assistant professors in the Department of Biology. He openly expressed contempt for evolutionary biology, which he saw as a dying vestige that had hung on too long at Harvard. The Department of Biology was deeply split, and committee meetings were tense and often hostile. It pained me to see men of the stature of Ernst Mayr and George Wald at loggerheads. I was the only younger professor in evolutionary biology and seemingly the only heir to the imperiled tradition.

It must have come as a shock to Watson, therefore, when Stanford University offered me a tenured associate professorship in the spring of 1958,

and Harvard quickly countered with an equivalent offer. Although Watson was a year older, the avatar of the new order, and clearly only several years from a Nobel Prize (he received it in 1962), I was in the process of being promoted ahead of him. He soon received an offer of a tenured position at another university and obtained his own promotion.

Feelings were very mixed on the Harvard faculty concerning the ultimate relative value of the various endeavors within biology. No one seriously questioned the great future of molecular biology, but there were other prospects, and only a zealot could delude himself into thinking that all further advances would be at the chemical level. About this time Harlow Shapley, the great astronomer and a friend, stopped me in the faculty club and said, "I have just come from a meeting with Mr. Pusey [Harvard's president] in which I told him you are the most important assistant professor at Harvard." The Stanford episode did not improve my relationship with Watson and his close allies, and I was the object of even colder rudeness from then on.

Edward O. Wilson receiving the National Medal of Science from President Carter, the White House, November 1977

It was a double pity, because like most scientists of my generation I greatly admired Watson's achievement. I saw in its style and outrageous success the sword that might cut one Gordian knot in biology after another. As a graduate student in the early 1950s I had been taught that the gene was an immensely complicated tangle of protein and nucleic acids whose chemistry would not be worked out for generations. It was a thrill to learn that the underlying molecule was in fact quite simple and that straightforward, readily understood chemical principles could be translated upward into an all but limitless biological complexity. Could we look to the same form of mapping in the equally complex realms of population biology and behavior? The search for such a procedure was the logical task of the next generation of evolutionary biologists.

But in the late 1950s, there were exceedingly few such persons around; they seemed almost an endangered species. At Harvard lived some of the leaders of the earlier generation, including Philip J. Darlington, Ernst Mayr, Alfred S. Romer, and George G. Simpson. My respect for them bordered on awe. They also shared my distaste for the new molecular triumphalism that denied the value of a great deal of contemporary biological research at the organismic and population level. But these great men were not my allies. A full generation older, they were in the consolidation period of their careers. They were more concerned with pulling together the remaining loose ends into Modern Synthesis of evolutionary theory that they had engineered in the 1940s and 1950s. At Harvard I felt squeezed between the younger generation of molecular biologists and the older generation of evolutionary biologists. It was impossible to identify with either.

Evolutionary biologists of my own age group with a similar outlook and ambition were nevertheless to be found in other universities. I encountered Lawrence Slobodkin at the University of Michigan. He had just completed a brief textbook on population ecology that expounded the model-building approach evolutionary problems developed by his teacher, G. Evelyn Hutchinson at Yale. Slobodkin introduced me in turn to Robert H. MacArthur, a charismatic genius who was destined to have the greatest impact on theoretical ecology of any single person during the 1960s and 1970s. The three of us agreed to write a monograph covering all aspects of population biology including, in at least a nascent form, sociobiology. But Slobodkin soon developed an intense dislike for MacArthur, even though he had befriended and encouraged him during their graduate student days.

MacArthur in turn felt wounded by the sharpness of Slobodkin's criticisms, and the book project fell apart.

It was at this point that I went to South America and Trinidad-Tobago. The brief association with Slobodkin and MacArthur (and the looming presence of Hutchinson beyond) had persuaded me that much of the whole range of population biology was ripe for synthesis and rapid advance in experimental research; but this could only be accomplished with the aid of imaginative logical reasoning strengthened by mathematical models. I am at best a mediocre mathematician and in 1961 had no training beyond algebra and statistics.

So brooding in Tobago that summer, I realized that I would have to make a major effort in order to gain a minimal competence for the intellectual effort to come. I set a new goal: to lift myself to mathematical semiliteracy, to gain a sufficient competence to collaborate with those better gifted and trained. For the remaining months of the sabbatical I taught myself elementary calculus and probability theory. Returning to Harvard that fall, at the age of thirty-two, I began two years of undergraduate mathematics courses. As a result, I did acquire the level of competency I needed, and the collaborations I had envisioned were achieved.

The first joint effort was with MacArthur. Soon after we met in 1960 we had become fast friends. By comparing notes and establishing common interests, we realized that biogeography was an area in which rapid progress might be made in both the theoretical and empirical domains. From my studies on the Pacific ant fauna, we were aware that provocatively orderly patterns occurred in the diversity and distribution of faunas on islands. Still more data were available on birds, and we pieced those together. From all this, in 1962, emerged the first quantitative theory of species equilibrium, which was published in article form in *Evolution* in 1963. A full-scale monograph, *The Theory of Island Biogeography,* followed in 1967 (MacArthur and Wilson, 1967).

This work launched a whole array of similar studies, using various groups of plants and animals, and carried out in many parts of the world, and by the early 1970s became a substantial and generally successful part of both biogeography and ecology. From the time of our collaboration to his death from cancer in 1972, MacArthur referred to himself primarily as a biogeographer. He concentrated on patterns of distribution as well as the fundamental problems of demography and population interaction, and his last book, written while he was very ill, was entitled *Geographical Ecology.*

The author with Robert W. Taylor at Bobbin Head, Kuringai National Park, Australia, 1990

For my part, I collaborated with Daniel S. Simberloff, then a graduate student at Harvard, in conducting the first full-scale experiments on island colonization in the Florida Keys. This work, extending from 1966 through 1969, established the existence of species equilibria and tested some of the key assumptions of the MacArthur-Wilson models.

At the same time that the crucial work with MacArthur began, I collaborated with William H. Bossert in producing the first general theory of the chemical and physical design features of pheromones. Bossert was then a graduate student and is now Gordon McKay Professor of Applied Mathematics at Harvard, and a distinguished theoretical biologist. His skills in mathematics and physical theory were perfectly complementary to my own knowledge of the new but burgeoning field of pheromone research. Together we made the first distinction between primer and releaser pheromones, created the concept of the active space, measured the first Q/K ratios (that is, the ratios between emission rates of molecules and the response threshold), demonstrated the adaptive significance of the physical properties of phero-

mones, and devised techniques for the estimation of molecular response thresholds. This work had an important impact on later research on chemical communication, including the all-important role of pheromones in the organization of insect societies.

In July 1964 MacArthur and I met at his summer home at Marlboro, Vermont, with Egbert Leigh, Richard Levins, and Richard C. Lewontin, to discuss the future of population biology. To a certain extent we divided the subject up. We discussed what major problems lay ahead and how each of us, and others among the small number of colleagues interested at that time, might contribute to the push forward. The seeds of my own synthesis of sociobiology were now solidly planted. I saw that if MacArthur and I could make some sense out of biogeography, hitherto the most sprawling and disorganized of all biological disciplines, and Bossert and I were able to progress so quickly with the theory of pheromone evolution, the study of social organization should also be open to a rigorous theoretical and experimental approach.

That the Marlboro meeting should strengthen this conviction is ironic, for Levins and Lewontin were later to be among the bitterest opponents of sociobiology—not because of the failure of the dream we shared in 1964 but rather as a concession to their total commitment to Marxism, in a form incompatible with any notion of genetic determinism of human behavior.

The ideas of two other persons were decisive in leading me to a synthesis of sociobiology. The first was Stuart Altmann, who came to Harvard in the fall of 1955 just as I accepted an assistant professorship to begin the next fall. Altmann intended to work on the sociobiology (he used that name) of monkeys. At first he could not find a sponsor. Donald R. Griffin was a logical possibility but felt that Altmann's interests were too far from his own. And indeed, Altmann was an odd fish at that time. He was up to nothing less than the revival of primate field studies, which had lain fallow since C. Ray Carpenter's burst of research in the 1930s and early 1940s. Altmann had the courage, imagination, and vision to see the potentially great importance of the field. However, none of the senior Harvard faculty shared his view. They had difficulty seeing how the field study of primates could be made "scientific." It was suggested that because I at least worked on a *social* group (ants), I might serve as Altmann's thesis adviser. I realized that Altmann probably had more to teach me than I him, and I gladly accepted, even though my faculty appointment was not to begin for another eight months.

In January 1956 I joined Stuart at Cayo Santiago, Puerto Rico, and we spent several days on that hilly little island examining the free-ranging population of rhesus monkeys that was to be the object of his study. It was an illuminating experience, a firsthand look at an animal society radically different from those of the social insects. As we strolled among the chattering and gesturing monkeys, Altmann and I talked about the ways in which insect and primate societies might be critically compared, in effect how one might develop a unified sociobiology. There were few concepts on which to build such a framework in 1956. Altmann introduced me to the techniques of information analysis, which he was later to use with significant effect in his reports on rhesus behavior. I in turn employed similar methods in 1962 when I compared the accuracy of the fire ant odor trail to that of the honeybee waggle dance.

Other fundamental concepts for the construction of sociobiology were assembled during the 1960s. One of the most important was the application of kin selection theory to the social insects by William D. Hamilton in 1964. Others before Hamilton had conceived the idea, including Darwin, who used the notion to account for sterile castes in ants, and J. B. S.

Haldane, who had devised the elementary calculus by which the genetic impact of altruism is discounted according to the coefficient of relatedness.

What Hamilton achieved of great and unique importance was the recognition that the haplodiploid method of sex determination, found only in the Hymenoptera (bees, wasps, and ants) and a very few other groups of organisms, makes sisters more closely related to each other than mothers are to daughters. He pointed out that a great deal of what is peculiar about social insects seems to flow from this cardinal datum: the almost complete restriction of advanced social life to the Hymenoptera; the restriction of worker castes to females; the short, rather solitary lives of the drones within the colonies; and other, finer points. In one stroke Hamilton had made kin selection convincing, while providing a powerful unitary theory of the origin of higher social life in the Hymenoptera.

I first read Hamilton's article in the spring of 1965 while traveling from Boston to Miami to start work on the Florida Keys project. My first reaction was admiration blunted by incredulity. It was brilliant, but evolution just couldn't be that simple! Why, this fellow was proposing to change our whole way of thinking about the origin of the social insects with a numerical exercise that anyone could do in three minutes on the back of an envelope. I tried to put the whole thing out of my mind. I could not. I tried to find the fatal flaw in Hamilton's reasoning that would allow me to dismiss him and rest easy. I could find none. Within twenty-four hours, as the train pulled into Miami, I was a convert. I had to admit that Hamilton, who knew far less about social insects than I did, had made the single most important discovery about them in this century. He had done so with a mode of reasoning that probably would have otherwise escaped me all my life.

That September I journeyed to London to deliver a paper on the behavior of social insects at the annual symposium of the Royal Entomological Society. I looked up Hamilton, still a graduate student at the University of London, and we talked at length about the many subjects we held of common interest. I was shocked to discover that almost no one, including his advisers, appreciated the value of his work. When I gave my talk to the Royal Entomological Society, I devoted about a third of it to Hamilton's main argument. And sure enough, the sachems of British entomology present at my lecture—Vincent Wigglesworth, J. S. Kennedy, and O. W. Richards—experienced the same difficulty I had on the train to Miami. They each stood up to dismiss the Hamilton theory, using various of the counterarguments that I myself had tried out and finally reluctantly abandoned. Speaking in turn, Hamilton and I easily answered their objections and, to use an appropriately British expression, carried the day.

We are in the midst of a great disproportion in the allocation of scientific effort. The social insects are among the great wonders of the living world. Aside from their colonial structures, far more intricate than we have any reason to expect from the limitations of their minuscule brains, they are ecologically dominant elements of the land fauna. About one third of the animal biomass of the Amazon forest consists of ants and termites. In most climatic zones these insects also exceed the earthworms in the amount of earth and humus they excavate and turn over. The ants are the principal middle-level predators, while the termites rank among the foremost decomposers of wood. In South and Central America several species of leaf cutting ants *(Atta)* are the dominant consumers of fresh vegetation and the leading agricultural pests.

Yet, despite the great significance of the social insects for mankind on these and other grounds, less than a hundred specialists were active around the world in the 1960s, if we exclude the large force of apiculturists working on honey production and crop pollination. On mainland China there were just three such experts—approximately one per 300 million people! I perceived that one of the principal reasons for this underrepresentation was the extraordinarily diffuse nature of the technical literature, comprised of thousands of articles in many languages scattered through often highly specialized, sometimes obscure journals. There had been no general English-language review of the subject since William M. Wheeler's *The Social Insects* in 1928.

I decided to try to put the matter right by conducting a comprehensive review of all aspects of the biology of the social insects. In doing so I integrated as many of the available data as possible into a framework of modern population biology. After all, colonies of insects are populations. They can be better understood by reference to the principles of demography and the mass effects of caste determination and communication within large groups. The book, entitled *The Insect Societies,* was published in 1971 and received highly favorable reviews. I entitled the last chapter "The Prospect for a Unified Sociobiology." In it I argued that a single body of theory and vocabulary in the study of all kinds of social organisms is feasible:

When the same parameters and quantitative theory are used to analyze both termite colonies and troops of rhesus macaques, we will have a unified science of sociobiology. . . . In spite of the phylogenetic remoteness of vertebrates and insects and the basic distinction between their respective personal and impersonal systems of communication, these two groups of animals have evolved social behaviors that are similar in degree of complexity and convergent in many important details. This fact conveys a special promise that sociobiology can eventually be derived from the first principles of population and behavioral biology and developed into a single, mature science. The discipline can then be expected to increase our understanding of the unique qualities of social behavior in animals as opposed to those of men.

In 1968, as the writing of *The Insect Societies* was underway, I faced a major decision: whether to continue sociobiology as a central, perhaps wholly consuming activity, or whether to proceed more fully into biogeography and ecology. Both enterprises seemed extraordinarily interesting and promising. I chose sociobiology, because it was *more* interesting and promising. Sociobiology entailed large domains of behavior and population organization that had never been subjected to analysis in the mode of evolutionary biology. Sociobiology also offered the prospect of connecting biology to the social sciences, which is intellectual high adventure beyond the limits of the conventional biological sciences.

So in 1971 I began to study literature and films on the sociobiology of vertebrates and the colonial invertebrates. This work went with surprising quickness. The literature was less extensive and technical than that dealing with social insects, and it had been more frequently synthesized in the recent past. Also, I received the encouragement and active help of specialists, including Irven DeVore, John Eisenberg, Richard D. Estes, Sarah Hrdy, Peter Marler, Robert L. Trivers, and many others. I was able to lean on the exceptional skills of Kathleen M. Horton, who has played a key role in library research and manuscript preparation through all my research efforts since 1965. But an additional factor was that my devotion to the effort was total. For two years I averaged ninety hours of work a week in order to complete the book while meeting my duties at Harvard.

Sociobiology: The New Synthesis, containing 698 double-columned pages and over 2,000 references, appeared in the spring of 1975. The reviews, like those for *The Insect Societies,* were almost unanimously favorable, at first. Some were extremely generous in their praise, proclaiming the book a landmark and the start of a new discipline. There is no question that *Sociobiology* has had a major impact on the development of sociobiology, as well as on many domains of the social sciences and humanities, and that at this time of writing (1992) its influence continues to spread.

It also became the center of a major controversy, which proceeded at several levels. At issue was not general sociobiology, at least not the treatment of animal social organization and the integration of behavior with population biology, but rather the application of the basic ideas of the new discipline to human behavior. The bulk of *Sociobiology* was non-controversial, but in the first and final chapters (1 and 27) I recommended the importation of the sociobiological program into human behavior, using a deliberately provocative style:

> Let us now consider man in the free spirit of natural history, as though we were zoologists from another planet completing a catalog of social species on Earth. In this macroscopic view the humanities and social sciences shrink to specialized branches of biology; history, biography, and fiction are the research protocols of human ethology, and anthropology and sociology together constitute the sociobiology of a single primate species.

My intention in these two chapters was to call attention to the relevance of biology to human social behavior in a direct and forceful manner. What I anticipated was that some social scientists and humanists, their interest pricked, would then begin to absorb evolutionary theory and the techniques of population biology into their thinking. The ultimate result, I felt confident, would be a basic alteration in the foundations of social theory. It seemed inevitable that biology and the social sciences will eventually be united, and that many of the bridging ideas will be contributed by sociobiology.

The response, both positive and negative, was far greater than I had anticipated. The first level of criticism came from a wholly unexpected direction. A Marxist-oriented group called Science for the People, one of the last such organizations still active on American campuses in the post-Vietnam years, saw human sociobiology as a major ideological threat. To them it legitimizes "genetic determinism" of social behavior, and any form of genetic determinism can—and will—be used to justify the political status quo, IQ tests, racism, sexism, imperialism, and in fact the whole congerie of demons against which the far Left raged.

No concession was made to the possibility that a deeper knowledge of the biological basis of human nature might in fact be used to speed social progress in the direction desired by the radical Left. The reason, I suspect, lies in the precepts of traditional Marxist belief itself: that there is no human nature, that man's character is wholly the product of his political and economic practice, and that history is moving toward a dialectically achieved utopia in which human biology plays little or no part.

Sociobiology does seem to point in a direction wholly different from that perceived by the Marxist world view. To the extent that it can be made precise and subjected to verification, it appears to pit science against the dogmatic assumptions of Marxism and hence the main legitimation of revolutionary socialist change as it is being pressed worldwide.

In 1975–76 I took a crash course in political philosophy with the aid of Daniel Bell and a few other members of the Harvard faculty who could see I needed help. I succeeded in defending sociobiology on both scientific and philosophical grounds (e.g., Wilson, 1976). But the experience was made painful by the fact that the leaders of Science for the People were other members of the Harvard faculty, including Jonathan Beckwith, Stephen Jay Gould, Ruth Hubbard, and Richard Lewontin. Forming a special Sociobiology Study Group, they devoted large amounts of their time to the preparation of documents, including the famous letter to the *New York Review of Books* ("Against Sociobiology," November 3, 1975) and the organization of lectures and meetings. The attacks were often personal in nature. The critics implied that I and others working in this area were promoting racism, sexism, and other political evils, either deliberately or else as a side product of being enculturated by a capitalist-imperialist state.

A somewhat less cerebral radical group, the International Committee Against Racism, took up the campaign and picketed or actively disrupted some of my lectures—despite the fact that none of my talks dealt with any subject other than the unifying traits of the human species. At the American Association for the Advancement of Science meetings of February 1978, held in Washington, D.C., INCAR protesters seized the stage as I was about to commence speaking and dumped water on my head. In time I gave up open public lecturing, confining myself to talks and seminars to universities, colleges, and professional groups.

Fortunately, few people in the academic community believed the charges of Science for the People and INCAR, especially when it became more apparent that my colleagues in the radical Left were promoting a political philosophy and not just defending society from genetic determinism. As intellectuals and the American public at large shifted more toward conservatism in the late 1970s, the purely ideological opposition to human sociobiology diminished to near insignificance.

But more enduring critiques had developed at a deeper level. To put the matter in a nutshell, it was observed that while biological reasoning could illuminate the central tendencies of such human behaviors as altruism, aggression, and parent-offspring bonding, it had nothing to say about the mind, free will, and cultural diversity. Sociobiology might help to explain the psychobiological traits human beings hold in common with animals, but not the mental qualities that distinguish the species. Psychology had not been incorporated into evolutionary theory.

At a still deeper level, some authors argued that mental life and cultural diversity can *never* be given a conventional scientific explanation. This most basic disagreement was between what Loren Graham (1981) has called the expansionists, those who believe that the natural sciences can be extended to all forms of mental activity and social phenomena, and the restrictionists, who believe that scientific investigation is intrinsically powerless to go that far.

In *On Human Nature* (1978) I took a strongly expansionist view. While reviewing human sociobiology more fully than in my earlier writings, I argued that even religious dogma and moral reasoning are based upon biological processes. They and other mental processes can be fully understood only by means of population biology and evolutionary reconstruction.

But the question of the linkage of heredity, mental activity, and culture remained unresolved. In July 1978 Charles J. Lumsden, who was then a young lecturer at the University of Toronto, suggested that he come to Harvard to pursue a collaborative effort in sociobiological theory. The prospect was attractive. Lumsden was obviously a highly creative scientist, filled with new ideas, and he had a strong background in mathematics. At first I declined. I was battle fatigued from the controversy over human behavior and wanted to draw more completely back into research on social insects. But Lumsden was very persuasive. He pointed out that large domains of sociobiological theory were unexplored and, at that time in the early development of the field, relatively easily penetrated.

Soon after Lumsden's arrival at Harvard in January 1979, we gravitated toward the key problem of human sociobiology: the nature of the linkage between genetic and cultural evolution. During the next three years of hard work, we constructed as complete a picture as possible of gene-culture coevolution, incorporating the main findings of cognitive and developmental psychology into evolutionary theory and sociobiology. The result was a series of articles, culminating in the book *Genes, Mind, and Culture,* published in 1981—and a whole new controversy. Whether or not the theory and techniques we proposed constitute the dreamed-of breakthrough remains to be seen. The logic and evidence has so far held up under close and sometimes hostile scrutiny, but the critical tests needed to establish the ideas solidly within the corpus of the natural sciences remain to be devised. A shorter book by Lumsden and myself, *Promethean Fire,* explains gene-culture coevolution in less technical language and attempts to trace the evolution of human cognition.

While pursuing human sociobiology, I did not neglect the study of social insects, which I consider my beginning and ultimate life's pursuit. In 1968 I had constructed a general but still rudimentary theory of caste evolution based on the techniques of linear programming. Through the 1970s I studied caste systems of one ant species after another in considerable detail, adding to the natural history of this subject and my personal knowledge of it. In 1977 I was joined for a year by George F. Oster, one of the foremost theoretical population biologists in the world. Oster had a special interest in caste development and the mathematical abilities to advance the subject fundamentally. After a year's close collaboration, we produced the book *Caste and Ecology in the Social Insects* (1978). This monograph laid down the theory of optimization in the evolution of insect castes and identified a series of previously unrecognized research problems that have occupied me and other entomologists since.

The Eighties

By 1980 two nagging intellectual drives led me away from human behavior and into new paths of endeavor. One was the need I felt to write a comprehensive treatise on ants. Although these insects are highly diverse, comprising 9000 known species, among the dominant organisms of the land environment, and overall the most complexly social of all animals, their study was lagging and in substantial disarray. The most up-to-date complete treatise, by William Morton Wheeler, had been published in 1910. Taxonomic guides, essential to the identification of specimens, dated mostly to the 1920s and were largely obsolete. Furthermore, young scientists

Edward O. Wilson and Bert Hölldobler, authors of The Ants, *1990*

found it difficult to get hold of the literature, which was written in several languages and scattered through a huge array of journals, many rare and obscure. Thus myrmecology, the scientific study of ants, was in serious need of ventilation and synthesis.

The time was ripe to meet the challenge. Since 1972, I had been working closely with Bert Hölldobler, a fellow member of the Harvard faculty, on myrmecological projects. Hölldobler was and is a brilliant experimentalist and field biologist trained in Germany in the exacting "von Frisch school" of research. His knowledge of ants at the least matched mine, and his energies were endless. We decided to undertake a complete review of all knowledge about ants accumulated to that time. Our prospects for the herculean task were considerably brightened by the aid of Kathleen M. Horton, my research and bibliographic assistant since 1965, whose expertise in searching through literature and assembling big manuscripts was formidable. Moreover, we all had the superb Harvard zoological library to help us along the way. The result, a 7.5-pound tome entitled (what else?) *The Ants,* was published in 1990 by Harvard

University Press. *The Ants* met with universal critical success, popular fame, and surprisingly large sales; a successful computer game based on it, SimAnt, was created in 1991 by Maxis Company in California. The book was a true magnum opus by my criterion: big enough to kill a man when dropped from the roof of a three-story building. It was also approximately 100,000 times heavier than a typical ant. My lecture based on it, "Ants," given at the American Academy of Arts and Sciences in 1991, had the shortest title of any presentation at that organization during its 200-year history.

The other avenue of intellectual arena into which I was drawn was the biodiversity crisis. Other field biologists had known for decades that habitat destruction, pollution, and other forms of human disturbance of the natural environment were extinguishing species at an accelerating rate. By the late 1970s it had become possible to estimate roughly the rate of destruction in the major type of habitat: the rain forests, which are believed to contain more than half the species of organisms on earth. These "cathedrals of life" were being destroyed at the rate of one percent of their total cover per year, and that translates (by MacArthur's and my theory of island biogeography) to a quarter of a percent of the species lost annually. In my mind this hemorrhaging of a priceless resource was unacceptable. (By 1989 the situation had grown worse; annual deforestation rate had risen to 1.8 percent and the projected species loss to half a percent.) I therefore joined a small group of biologist activists, including Jared Diamond, Paul Ehrlich, Thomas Lovejoy, Norman Myers, and Peter Raven, in calling for a major increase in research and conservation action, especially in the tropics. One of my rhetorical successes was the observation in 1980 that allowing massive species loss is the "folly our descendants are least likely to forgive us" . . . which became one of the most quoted conservation maxims of the 1980s.

From the urge to articulate a culture of biodiversity, and from a need to express a sociobiological view of ethics and art especially in relation to this problem, I wrote *Biophilia,* published in 1984. Biophilia, the concept, means the innate affiliation human beings feel for other species. In the book I explored, for example, the intricate relation between human beings and snakes in generating myths of the serpent. I took a new look at dreams of monsters and totems and the archetypal qualities of the ideal living place. I tried to make art and science compatible as sibling products of a primal urge for discovery, and I wedded these several elements into an interpretation of environmental ethics as an innate product of the long biological evolution human beings experienced in the wild environment. John A. Murray said of *Biophilia* that it "synthesizes science writing, travel writing, and personal memoir into a new sort of nature writing that transcends and expands the genre." Two conferences, one national and the other international, have been held on biophilia, in order to consider it as a scientific construct and bridge between science and the humanities.

In 1988 I edited the volume *Biodiversity,* in which I and sixty other authors examined then current knowledge of diversity, the global extinction rate, conservation practice, and the economic and spiritual benefits of maintaining a biologically rich world. Published by the National Academy of Sciences, this book has been widely used as a textbook and vade mecum of the subject; it is said to be present in every Third World office of the U.S. Agency for International Development. Finally, as I write, Harvard University is preparing to release my new synthesis *The Diversity of Life,* a work ranging from basic evolutionary theory to economics and government policy in biodiversity management. It is both a

literary and scientific endeavor, combining stylistic elements used in *Biophilia* with a technically careful review of the substance of the new field. Written for a broad readership, *The Diversity of Life* is meant to arouse interest and help move the biodiversity crisis to center stage in the environment movement.

Cambridge, Massachusetts, 1992

I realize that the great majority of my principal scientific contributions have probably been made. Now in my sixties, I consider myself fortunate beyond any reasonable expectation to have been a young evolutionary biologist in a period of great opportunity, and I wish the same experience for younger generations of scientists as they each in turn cut more deeply into the phenomena of evolution and social behavior.

Although I and my family have suffered at times from the more unreasoning episodes of the sociobiology controversy, which was one of the most intense and divisive disputes in the recent history of ideas, we were sustained by the warmth and understanding of many friends and colleagues. I have also received more than my share of academic honors: the National Medal of Science from President Carter in 1977; the Crafoord Prize of the Royal Swedish Academy of Sciences, given in fields not covered by the Nobel prizes, from the hand of King Gustav; two Pulitzer Prizes, for *On Human Nature* and *The Ants,* membership in the National Academy of Science, American Philosophical Society, England's Royal Society, and other academies; honorary degrees; and many other prizes, awards, and endowed visiting lectureships. I cannot deny that this recognition has meant a great deal to me, especially because of the chancy and perilous nature of some of my investigations and the self-doubt and insecurity that such efforts inevitably engender.

I hope to continue research and writing in humanistic scholarship, pursuing the leads suggested by advances in sociobiology and ecology over the past twenty years. But every creative person carries an innermost image of the routes of imaginative pursuit to which he returns for a strength independent of praise and human influence, and mine lies elsewhere. My ultimate retreat is in the natural world through which we are privileged to travel an endless Magellanic voyage. Each species of organism can consume lifetimes of fulfilling endeavor, and out of the millions that exist and the immense tangled histories they culminate comes the sense that no matter how sophisticated and intense our efforts may be in the

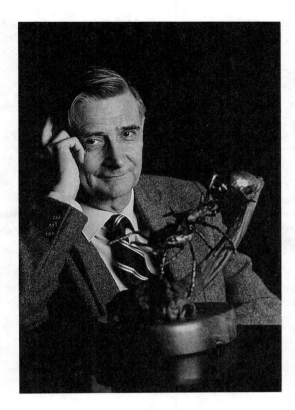

Edward O. Wilson with a sculpture of his favorite ant (Daceton armigerum), *Harvard University, 1990*

future, the voyage will still have only begun, and however wise we believe ourselves to be we will never lose the feeling that the world is infinite, unfathomable, and filled with wonders—only a bicycle ride away.

This essay is reprinted in entirety from "In the Queendom of the Ants: A Brief Autobiography" by Edward O. Wilson, in *Leaders in the Study of Animal Behavior: Autobiographical Perspectives*, edited by Donald A. Dewsbury, pp. 464–84. (Cranbury, NJ: Bucknell University Press, 1985). Updated for this series by the author.

REFERENCES

Brown, W. L., and Wilson, E. O. 1959. The evolution of the dacetine ants. *Q. Rev. Biol.* 34: 278–94.

Graham, L. 1981. *Between Science and Values.* New York: Columbia Univ. Press.

Hölldobler, B., and Wilson, E. O. 1990. *The Ants.* Cambridge, Mass.: Belknap Press of Harvard Univ. Press.

Lumsden, C. J., and Wilson, E. O. 1981. *Genes, Mind, and Culture: The Coevolutionary Process.* Cambridge, Mass.: Harvard Univ. Press.

———. 1983. *Promethean Fire.* Cambridge, Mass.: Harvard Univ. Press.

MacArthur, R. H., and Wilson, E. O. 1967. *The Theory of Island Biogeography.* Princeton: Princeton Univ. Press.

Murray, J. A. 1991. *The Islands and the Sea: Five Centuries of Nature Writing from the Caribbean.* New York: Oxford Univ. Press.

Oster, G. F., and Wilson, E. O. 1978. *Caste and Ecology in the Social Insects.* Princeton: Princeton Univ. Press.

Wilson, E. O. 1953. The ecology of some North American dacetine ants. *Ann. Ent. Soc. Am.* 46: 479–95.

———. 1958. A chemical releaser of alarm and digging behavior in the ant *Pogonomyrmex badius* (Latreille), *Psyche* 65: 41–51.

———. 1966. Behavior of social insects. In *Insect Behaviour*, ed. P. T. Haskell, pp. 81–96. (Symposium of the Royal Entomological Society, no. 3). London: Royal Entomological Society.

———. 1971. *The Insect Societies.* Cambridge, Mass.: Harvard Univ. Press.

———. 1975. *Sociobiology; The New Synthesis.* Cambridge, Mass.: Belknap Press of Harvard Univ. Press.

———. 1976. Academic vigilantism and the political significance of sociobiology. *BioScience* 26: 183, 187–90.

———. 1980. Resolutions for the eighties. *Harvard Magazine* 82: 21.

———. 1984. *Biophilia.* Cambridge, Mass.: Harvard Univ. Press.

———, ed. 1988. *Biodiversity.* Washington, D.C.: National Academy Press.

———. 1992. *The Diversity of Life.* Cambridge, Mass.: Harvard Univ. Press.

BIBLIOGRAPHY

Nonfiction:

(With R. H. MacArthur) *The Theory of Island Biogeography*, Princeton University Press, 1967.

The Insect Societies, Belknap Press, 1971.

(With W. H. Bossert) *A Primer of Population Biology*, Sinauer Associates, 1971.

(Co-author) *Life on Earth*, Sinauer Associates, 1973.

Animal Behavior: Readings from Scientific American, W. H. Freeman, 1975.

Sociobiology: The New Synthesis, Belknap Press, 1975, abridged edition, 1980.

(Author of introduction with Thomas Eisner) *The Insects: Readings from Scientific American,* Freeman, 1977.

(With George F. Oster) *Caste and Ecology in Social Insects,* Princeton University Press, 1978.

On Human Nature, Harvard University Press, 1978.

(With Charles J. Lumsden) *Genes, Mind, and Culture: The Coevolutionary Process,* Harvard University Press, 1981.

(With Lumsden) *Promethean Fire: Reflections on the Origin of Mind,* Harvard University Press, 1983.

Biophilia: The Human Bond to Other Species, Harvard University Press, 1984.

(Editor) *Biodiversity* (from the National Forum on BioDiversity, held in Washington, D.C., September 21–24, 1986, under the auspices of the National Academy of Sciences and Smithsonian Institution), National Academy Press, 1988.

(With Bert Hölldobler) *The Ants,* Belknap Press, 1990.

Edward O. Wilson: A Life in Science, videotape interview, Harvard University Press, 1990.

Contributor of about three hundred articles to scientific and popular journals. Co-editor, *Theoretical Population Biology,* 1971–74, *Behavioral Ecology and Sociobiology,* 1975–1988, and *Psyche,* 1958—.

Cumulative Index

CUMULATIVE INDEX

The names of essayists who appear in the series are in boldface type. Subject references are followed by volume and page number(s). When a subject reference appears in more than one essay, names of the essayists are also provided.